D1609553

EXPLORING COMMUNICATION

Richard D. Seymour, Ed.D.
Associate Professor
Department of Industry and Technology
Ball State University
Muncie, Indiana

John M. Ritz, Ed.D.
Professor and Chairman
Department of Occupational and Technical Studies
Old Dominion University
Norfolk, VA

Florence A. Cloghessy
Editorial Consultant
Dyer, IN

South Holland, Illinois
The Goodheart-Willcox Company, Inc.
Publishers

Library of Congress Catalog Card Number 93-47543
International Standard Book Number 1-56637-031-0

1 2 3 4 5 6 7 8 9 10 96 99 98 97 96 95

Library of Congress Cataloging-in-Publication Data

Seymour, Richard D.
Exploring communication / Richard D. Seymour, John M. Ritz, Florence A. Cloghessy.
p. cm.
Includes index.
ISBN 1-56637-031-0
1. Communication. [1. Communication.] I. Ritz, John M. II. Cloghessy, Florence A. III. Title.
P90.S44144 1996
302.2—dc20 93-47543
CIP
AC

Introduction

Exploring Communication will introduce you to the communication process. You will explore this process as it is used to exchange ideas and feelings. You will learn that the designing, coding, transmitting, and receiving steps are used in every message.

Exploring Communication also examines the technical devices that aid human communication. These devices range from simple to complex. You will learn how each device makes communication possible, for humans and machines. The telephone, printing press, satellite, and computer are some devices studied in this book.

The impact of communication on societies and cultures of the world will also be looked at in ***Exploring Communication.*** You will discover the purposes, influences, and uses of communication in our society. You will also gain knowledge about the variety of careers made possible by the communication industry.

Exploring Communication focuses on two areas of the communication industry. These areas are printed communication and electronic communication. Printed communication will cover both technical graphics and printed graphics. Each area has a chapter of introduction. In addition, there are chapters dealing with technical devices used in each of these areas.

Exploring Communication will help you gain a broad background in the study of communication. You will be able to use knowledge gained from this study in many other areas of your learning.

This text is divided into five sections. Each section ends with a section review and activities. These activities are designed to help you apply the information given in the section. Each activity will have several "icons," or small pictures, following the activity. These icons will help you identify the types of skills being applied by the activity.

CONTENTS

SECTION 1 INTRODUCTION TO COMMUNICATION

SECTION 2 TECHNICAL GRAPHICS

SECTION 3 PRINTED GRAPHICS

ColorArtist

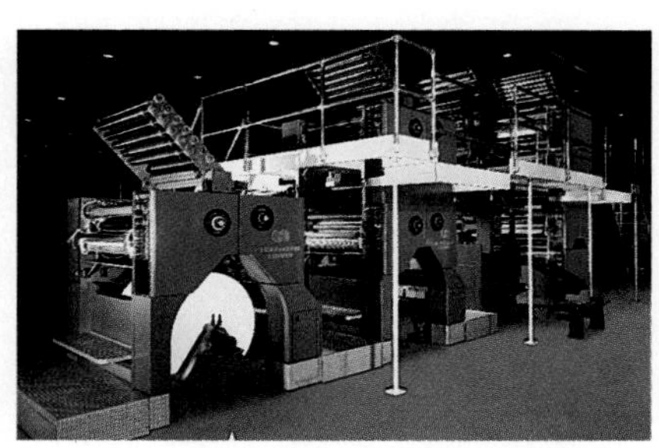

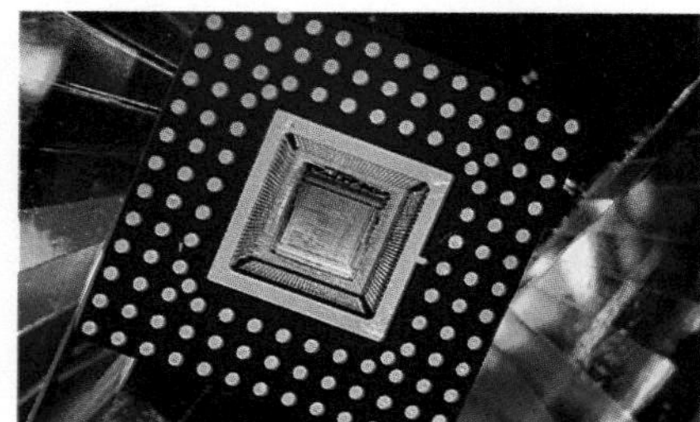

SIEMENS

SECTION 5 COMMUNICATION AND SOCIETY

ABOUT THE AUTHORS

Dr. John M. Ritz

Dr. John M. Ritz currently teaches technology education at Old Dominion University in Norfolk, Virginia. He has been recognized as a Distinguished Technology Educator by the International Technology Education Association and 1993 Technology Teacher of the Year by the Council on Technology Teacher Education. Dr. Ritz's current research and writings focus on technology standards and assisting teachers in implementing technology education.

Dr. Richard D. Seymour

Dr. Richard D. Seymour is an Associate Professor at Ball State University. He teaches a variety of communication, manufacturing, and transportation technology courses at BSU. In addition, he has served one term on the Board of Directors of the International Technology Education Association (ITEA). Previously, he was the International Adviser of the TECA (the collegiate student association). He is the current co-adviser of the Ball State Technology Education Club. Dr. Seymour has been very active in organizing and conducting in-service workshops for prospective technology teachers.

Florence A. Cloghessy

Florence A. Cloghessy is an independent editorial consultant. In addition to working with the staff at Goodheart-Willcox, Ms. Cloghessy has worked as a consultant with a variety of other publishing houses, including Loyola University Press, St. Meinrad Press, and Greenwood Publishing Group.

ACKNOWLEDGEMENTS

The authors and the publisher of this book wish to thank the following companies and individuals for their contributions to this book.

A.B. Dick
Advanced Promotion Technology
AFT-Davidson
AGFA Division of Miles Inc.
Alias Research Inc.
America Online®, Inc.
American Screen Printing Equipment Co.
Andy Johnston
Apple Computers, Inc.
Apple Computers, Inc./John Greenleigh
Applicon Research Inc.
Army Research Institute
ASCII Entertainment Software, Inc.
AT&T
AT&T/Michael Gaffney
Autodesk, Inc.
Ball State University
Bang & Olufson
Bausch & Lomb
Bell & Howell
Braille Institute
Chevron Corp.
Chicago Department of Aviation
Chrysler Corp.
Cincinnati Milacron
The Coleman Co.
Columbia College Chicago
Computer Support Corporation
Computervision Corp.
Comsat Corp.
Conoco
Corning Glass Works
Domino Amjet, Inc.
ENCAD, Inc.
Epson
ENCAD, Inc.
Fakespace
Federal Aviation Administration
Fibronics International
Ford
G.E. Plastics
Graphic Arts Technical Foundation
Graphic Products Corp.
Hammermill Paper Co.
Heidelberg Harris
Hewlett-Packard Co.
Honeywell Inc.
IBM
Identity
Indigo America, Inc.
Intel Corp.
InterBold
Intergraph Corp.
Kentucky Fried Chicken
Jack Klasey
Koh-I-Noor Rapidograph, Inc.
Kathy Kopf
Kreonite, Inc.
Kroy, Inc.
Letterguide, Inc.
The Lietz Company
Marsh Stencil Co.
John Metzger
Mustek
3M
Mitsubishi
NASA
National Braille Assoc.
National Pork Producers Council
NBC
NCR
nuArc Company, Inc.
Orbotech, Inc.
Panasonic Corp.
Precision Microlithics, Inc.
Radio Shack, A Division of the Tandy Corporation
Radisson Hotels
Ralston Purina
RCA
RCA—Thomson CE
Recording for the Blind
Reynolds Metals Co.
Rockwell International Corp.
San Angelo Standard Times
Santa Fe Railway
Siemens Solar Industries
Sof-Source
SOFTDESK, INC.
Sony Corp.
Sperry Corp.
Sprint
Square D Co.
Staedtler, Inc.
Technophone Corp.
Thomson Consumer Electronics
Toyota
UNISYS
United Airlines
U.S. Navy
Vemco Corp.
Viacom International, Inc.
Visual Edge
WBST, Muncie, Indiana
WGN Television, Chicago, Illinois
Westinghouse Corp.
Xerox Corp.
Xyvision Inc.
Zenith Electronics Corp.
Zenith Electronics Corp./Charlie Westerman

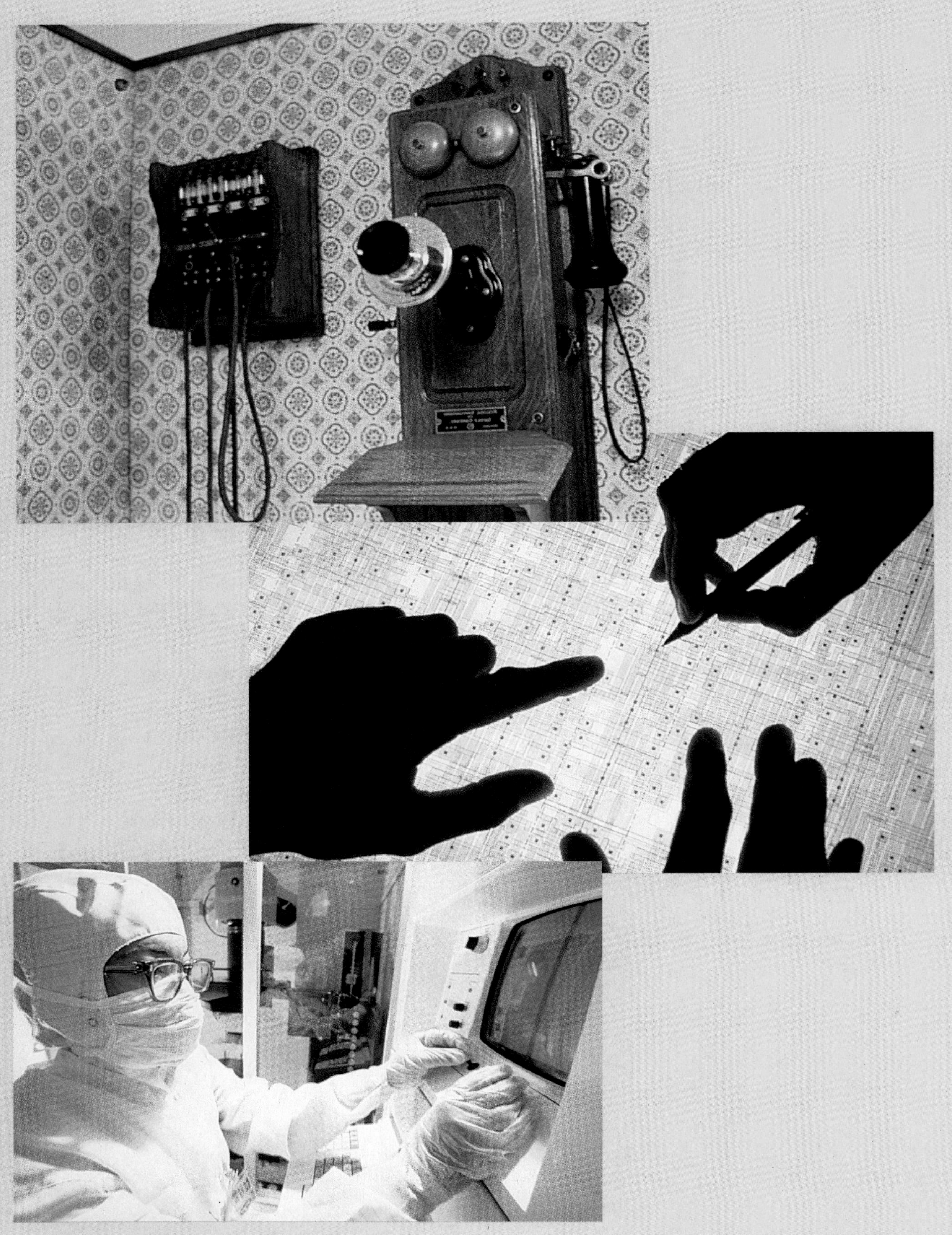

Section 1
Introduction to Communication

CHAPTER 1
INTRODUCTION TO COMMUNICATION

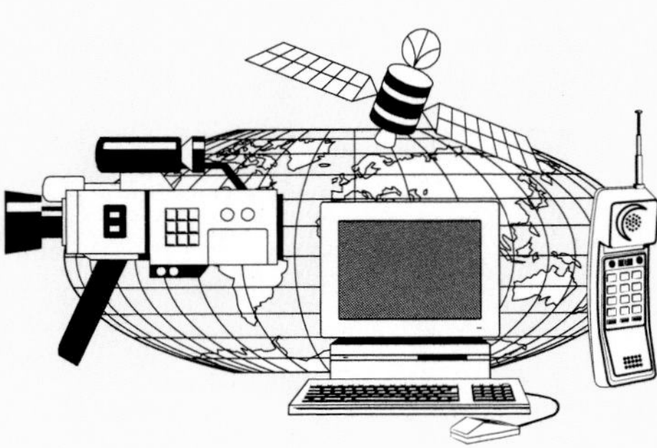

After studying this chapter, you will be able to:

- ❖ *Provide a definition for communication technology.*
- ❖ *Describe how communication devices extend our human senses.*
- ❖ *Explain how people and machines transfer information.*
- ❖ *List the four major types of communication systems.*

Forms of communication have been used since our world was first inhabited. Early civilizations expressed themselves using signs and symbols. Later, language systems came about so we could talk to each other. Language systems developed differently in various parts of the world. Today we have many languages. Some of these include English, German, Chinese, Polish, Hebrew, and Spanish, Figure 1-1. The use of languages is just one example of humans exchanging information.

Humans are not the only creatures on earth that exchange messages. Studies show that animals and plants communicate. For example, deer often raise their tails to indicate danger. Dolphins and whales are known for their ability to communicate with each other. Many forms of plant life react to natural signals, too. However, in this book we are interested in the technical side of communication. You will explore how people transmit important ideas and feelings. This book will focus on how information is transferred by technical means for human use.

Many technical systems exist to aid humans in communicating with each other. Some devices help to create books and newspapers. Others let you enjoy radio and TV programs. Computers often assist with processing important information. Many forms of communication technology improve our daily lives.

Figure 1-1. People around the world communicate in many languages. Languages use symbols to convey meaning. Here, the word "communication" is written in six languages.

COMMUNICATION TECHNOLOGY

Communication is the process of exchanging information. ***Information*** is knowledge that can be conveyed between two people. The word "communication" comes from a Latin word that means to transmit, pass along, or make known. Talking and listening are easy ways to pass along information. You use these methods every day to communicate. Sight is another simple form of exchanging messages. What you see gives meaning to what you know and hear. The saying "a picture is worth a thousand words" is very famous. You use your sight to read books and watch television. See Figure 1-2.

Figure 1-2. Many families enjoying watching television programs. What TV programs do you like to watch? (Zenith Electronics Corp./Charlie Westerman)

As mentioned earlier, many technical devices aid us in communicating. The telephone is a common example. People often talk to others around the world. Television is another important communication device. Traffic lights, door bells, and clocks are others. How would you communicate without these items?

Communication technology includes the application of technical processes to exchange information. Several steps make up this process, Figure 1-3. When people talk about communication technology, they are often only referring to one part of the process. For example, some people refer to the sending and receiving of messages. Many describe the use of symbols, signs, and words. Others explain how messages are transferred and stored for future use. Most people feel that feedback of transmitted signals is important to most systems. All of this can become confusing.

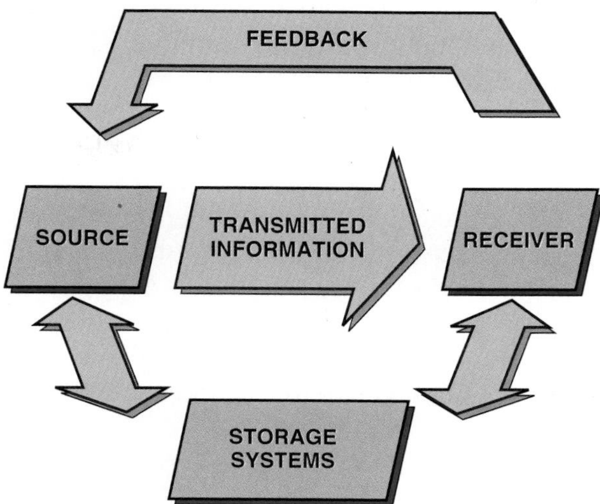

Figure 1-3. Technology has helped humans communicate more efficiently. Our systems of exchanging information include these elements.

To fully understand the meaning of communication technology a definition is needed. This definition must fully explain the process that takes place. It should include the act of communicating between humans and machines. ***Communication technology*** is the process of transmitting information from a source to a destination using codes and storage systems.

USING OUR SENSES

Most people have five senses. These senses include hearing, touching, seeing, smelling, and tasting, Figure 1-4. Hearing and seeing are the

Figue 1-4. You use five senses when communicating with others.

two senses most used by humans. Hearing is the sense that lets you receive messages by sound waves. Seeing is the sense associated with your eyes. You receive visual information in this manner. Touch is a third important sense. You feel pressure on the body by contact. With this sense you learn about temperature, shapes, and textures. Smelling is the ability to recognize various scents and odors. The fifth sense is taste. You enjoy many foods and beverages because of their pleasing taste.

You often use all five senses at once. If someone is cooking nearby, you can describe the event with all of your senses. Many times, however, only one sensory system is used. Talking on the telephone is an example. Reading a book is another. More often, a combination of senses are used when communicating. When you watch and listen to a movie or TV program, you use a combination of senses, Figure 1-5.

Figure 1-5. Most of us enjoy watching movies on TV or at the theater. When did you last watch a feature film with your friends or family? (RCA—Thomson CE)

These simple sensory exchanges of information are not available to all people. People with certain disabilities use other methods to communicate. For those not able to hear or speak, there is a language called signing, Figure 1-6. When ***signing,*** a person uses the hands and fingers to represent different signals. Each signal represents a letter or a number. In this way, words can be spelled out. Another system is used by people who are blind. It is known as ***braille.*** All letters of braille words are represented by a code that is printed as raised dots. By moving the fingers across a page, Figure 1-7, a blind person can "feel" the words. This technology provides communication for a person without sight.

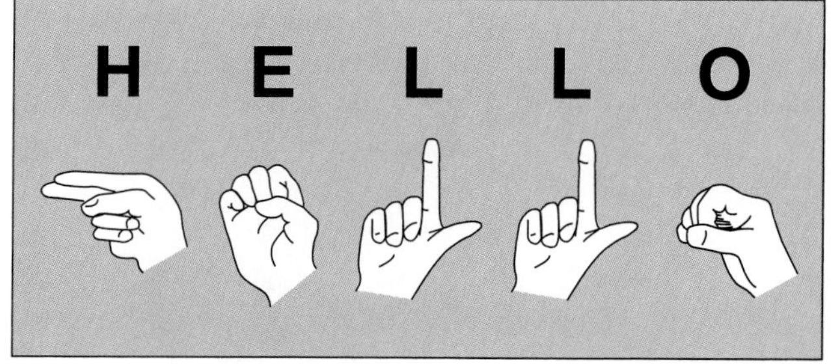

Figure 1-6. Individuals who are deaf use hand signals to communicate. This is called "signing."

Figure 1-7. People who are blind "read" using a code of raised dots on paper. The code is called *braille.* Each group of raised dots represents a letter or number. (American Printing House for the Blind)

People must use their senses to communicate. The five senses help you pick up and transfer messages. Many items are designed to aid these sensory abilities. Examples include radios and smoke alarms. The reason for communication technology is to allow your senses to receive small or faint messages. You will see how technology actually "extends" your senses.

EXTENDING HUMAN SENSES

You hear others speak to you with your sense of hearing. With radio or telephones, you can hear others over long distances. These two devices extend the human ability of hearing. This is an example of how technology assists you.

Inventors have developed many instruments to aid in communication, Figure 1-8. Look around any school building. Administrators use a public

Figure 1-8. Signs are communication devices. How many other communication devices can you think of? (Jack Klasey)

address (PA) system for general announcements. Telephones allow students and teachers to contact other people. Cheerleaders use megaphones at sporting events. Members of the school band play musical instruments. In your home, you may have televisions and stereos. Computerized bulletin boards and online services feature information and announcements, Figure 1-9.

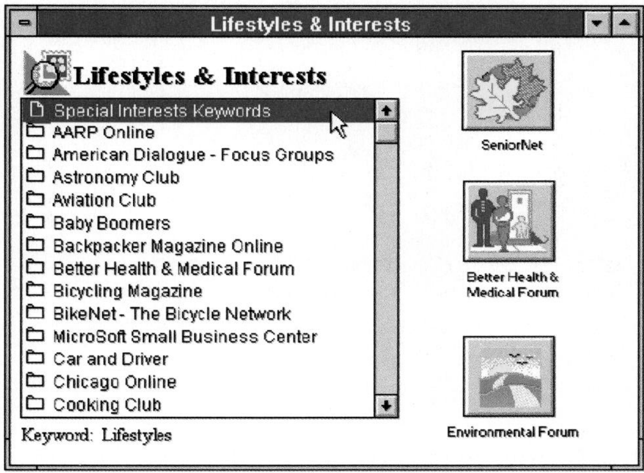

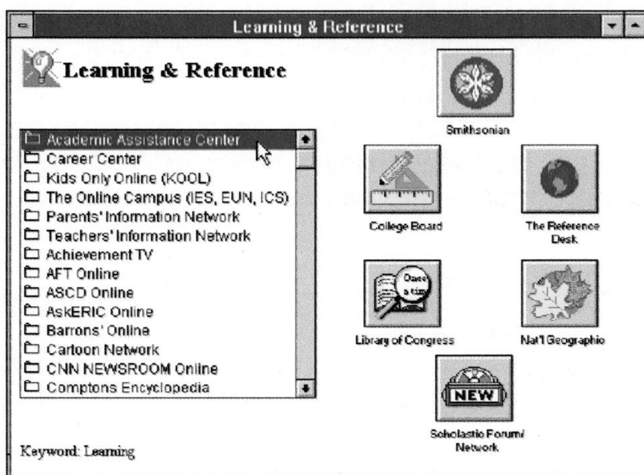

Figure 1-9. Online networks offer a large amount of information and services. All this information is available to anyone with a computer and a modem. (America Online®, Inc.)

These illustrations of communication are among the simplest found. Other forms are more complex. They involve entire systems of recording and transmitting messages. Using a computer to process data is an excellent example. A company will record vital information on computer disks and tapes, Figure 1-10. The computer might be connected to other machines across the country. Information is relayed by wires or radio signals. This advanced form of communication involves an entire system. You are now ready to further explore communication systems.

Figure 1-10. Modern computers store information on magnetic tape and disks. (NCR)

INFORMATION TRANSFER

There are four major types of communication systems. One is human-to-human communication. Others include human-to-machine, machine-to-human, and machine-to-machine. A fifth, minor system of communication is known as supplemental. These supplemental methods of communication are different than human and machine systems. Supplemental forms of communication will be discussed later. The five basic communication systems are shown in Figure 1-11.

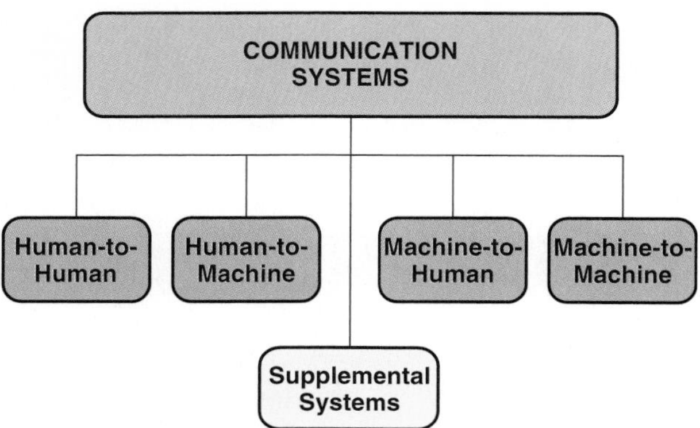

Figure 1-11. Information is transferred between machines and humans in several ways. Can you think of examples of each system?

Human-to-Human Systems

When you speak or write personal notes, you communicate with other people. This is the simplest method of exchanging information. It is called ***human-to-human communication.*** This type of exchange uses only basic forms of technology. Devices such as pens, pencils, paper, and signs are simple aids (simple machines) used in human-to-human communication. Languages and signals are others. In human-to-human communication, no complex machines assist the sensory system in receiving messages. Therefore, setting a combination lock, programming a computer, and setting an alarm clock, are not human-to-human communication. However, writing on the board does fit this description, Figure 1-12.

Figure 1-12. Instructors often use a board to provide a visual message for students. Visual images help you better understand facts and details.

Human-to-Machine Systems

Machines help humans produce many goods and services. However, people have to operate these devices, Figure 1-13. ***Human-to-machine communication*** involves information moving from a person to a machine. To complete a school assignment, you might use a computer. In doing so, you create and edit a message with your fingers. The final product can be a printed page. Communication between humans and machines is quite common. You "dial" telephones, turn on stereos, and operate hand-held calculators. The list is endless in our technological society. Human-to-machine communication extends our limited capabilities.

Figure 1-13. Some machines need human direction in order to operate. This is an example of human-to-machine communication. (Cincinnati Milacron)

Machine-to-Human Systems

Machine-to-human communication occurs when machines tell us how they are functioning, Figure 1-14. You also retrieve messages from machines. Answering machines and compact discs (CDs) are common examples. A voice or song can be recorded on a tape or disc. A machine can then reproduce the recorded signals so you may hear and enjoy it.

Machines in a factory will often make unusual noises when they need repair. This noise then alerts the person in charge that repairs are needed. Other machines that communicate with humans include automated teller machines and warning buzzers. Around the home you can find smoke detectors and alarm clocks. The fuel gauge in a car tells you how much fuel is in the tank, Figure 1-15.

Figure 1-14. Sensors on the pumps tell operators how much liquid is being moved. The sensors providing information are an example of machine-to-human communication. (Conoco)

Figure 1-15. The dashboard of an automobile includes many communication devices. How many can you identify in this photo? (Toyota)

The primary reason machines communicate with people is to provide information. These messages often save time and energy. At the same time, other machines entertain you. Machines have assisted humans in many areas of communication.

Machine-to-Machine Systems

When one machine provides information to another machine, it is called ***machine-to-machine communication.*** Machines communicating with other machines did not exist on a large scale until recent years. Computers are an example of machine-to-machine communication. They often direct the operation of other machines, taking the place of a human, Figure 1-16. A term related to this process is cybernetics. ***Cybernetics*** is the study of automatic control systems (that may be electro-mechanical), or one machine controlling another.

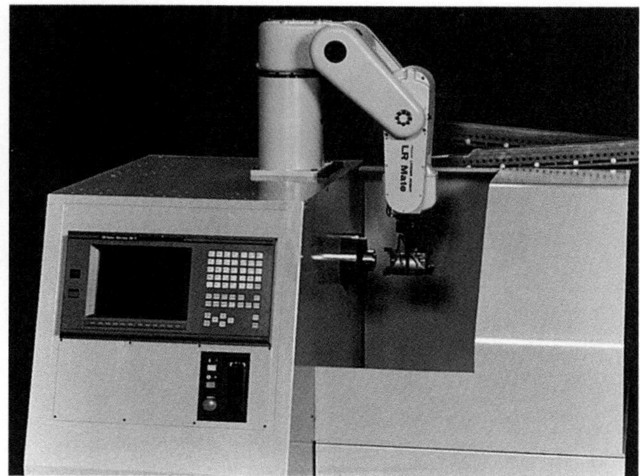

Figure 1-16. Many machines in factories are directed by other machines. A computer not only directs the operation of this CNC lathe, but it also controls a robot arm that loads the machine. This is called machine-to-machine communication. (GE Fanuc Automation)

Many forms of machine-to-machine communication are found in the home. Temperature controls (thermostats) on furnaces maintain warmth in rooms. They also control air conditioners during hot weather. These devices turn on the air conditioner or furnace when the temperature is too hot or too cold. Timers, sensors, and switches on a stove or microwave work the same way.

Communication between machines is important. It helps you get things done on time. Some controls turn machines on and off. Other controls change speed. Many devices stop machinery in times of danger. These systems prevent injury to people. Machine-to-machine communication can also be used to turn machines off when not needed. This saves energy. See Figure 1-17.

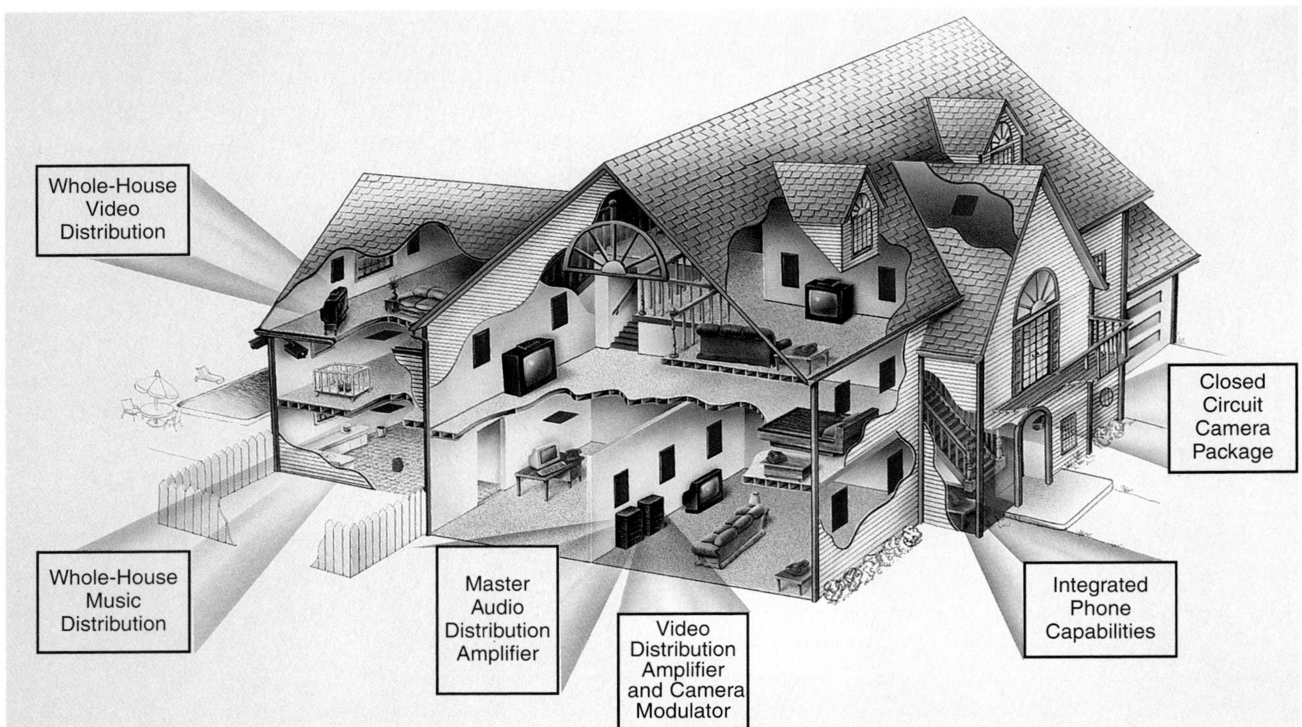

Figure 1-17. The ELAN system allows TV, VCR, phone, and stereo systems to work together. Other systems integrate security and climate control functions. In all of these systems, machines are communicating with other machines. (Square D Co.)

Supplemental Systems

Some methods of communication—"supplemental"—do not fit into the four general categories. Examples of ***supplemental systems*** include extrasensory perception (ESP), extraterrestrial, animal, plant, and mineral systems, Figure 1-18.

Extrasensory perception is thought to exist outside normal human senses. People with ESP claim to have mind-reading abilities. They attempt to predict events before they happen. Some scientists believe in this form of communication. Others doubt it can be proven. This method of communication is uncertain at best.

Supplemental Communication Systems
Extrasensory Perceptions (ESP) **Extraterrestrial** **Animal** **Plant** **Mineral**

Figure 1-18. There are five types of supplemental communication systems.

Information may also be exchanged between planets or spacecraft. Messages received from outside the Earth are called ***extraterrestrial.*** This system is often shown in science fiction movies. Many scientists are searching for extraterrestrial messages. They use large radio devices to scan the skies, Figure 1-19. Scientists hope to one day communicate with life on other planets if it exists.

Plants and ***animals*** communicate also. Research has revealed many interesting discoveries. For example, some animals can communicate by using common signals. Lightning bugs exchange information with their light signals. Honeybees fly in special formations to communicate. Even plant life reacts to natural signals. Some researchers believe plants grow better when exposed to music.

A final communication system involves different types of ***minerals.*** Rocks and other Earth substances communicate to humans when aided

Figure 1-19. Large radio telescopes continually scan the sky for signals from other stars. (National Radio Astronomy Observatory)

by instruments. Magnets attract iron ore and other metals. Radioactive materials send off dangerous waves. A compass (pointing towards the North Pole) is an example of mineral communication, Figure 1-20. Scientists often use complex devices to analyze minerals. This helps us learn about their qualities.

Figure 1-20. The transit used by surveyors typically has a compass. This allows the surveyors to take accurate measurements. (The Lietz Company)

CHAPTER 1 REVIEW

SUMMARY

This chapter has introduced the meaning of communication and communication technology. You rely on your senses to communicate with others. Technology has extended the capabilities of your human senses. You have learned what must occur in the communication process. Information (in the form of messages) is transmitted. These messages can also be stored for later usage. Finally, there are four major communication systems. These systems include human-to-human, human-to-machine, machine-to-human, and machine-to-machine.

KEY WORDS

All the following words have been used in this chapter. Do you know their meanings?

Animals
Braille
Communication
Communication technology
Cybernetics
Extrasensory perception
Extraterrestrial
Human-to-human communication
Human-to-machine communication
Information
Machine-to-human communication
Machine-to-machine communication
Minerals
Plants
Signing
Supplemental systems

TEST YOUR KNOWLEDGE

Write your answers on a separate sheet of paper. Please do not write in this book.

Matching questions 1-4: Match the definition on the left with the correct term on the right

1. A reading system for the blind.
2. The process of one machine running another machine.
3. A language that uses the hands and fingers to spell out words.
4. Messages received from outside the earth.

A Braille.
B. Extraterrestrial.
C. Cybernetics.
D. Signing.

5. Define communication technology.
6. The five senses include _____, _____, _____, _____, and _____.
7. Identify the five systems of information transfer. Give an example of each system.

ACTIVITIES

1. Collect five definitions of communication from other books. Write a short paper (two pages or less) describing the differences and similarities between these definitions and the one presented in this book.
2. Select three technical methods of communication (for example: a home computer, a telephone, and a newspaper). Illustrate them in diagram form. This diagram should be based upon the communication model found in Figure 1-3.
3. Invite an individual from a telephone company, local TV or radio station, or other communication business to speak to your class about the work done by the company.
4. Invite a teacher who works with deaf or blind individuals to visit your class. Ask the instructor to demonstrate the signing and braille systems of communication.
5. Make a collage illustrating the communication process, using either photographs or clippings from magazines.
6. Draw the symbols used for Olympic events or for international road signs. Make these into mobiles or bulletin boards.
7. Work with another student in class. Ask your partner to write down directions to their house. Then ask your partner to draw a map showing where they live. Which one is easier to communicate? Why? Which one is easier to follow? Why? Discuss your answers with the rest of the class.
8. Take a quick trip around the classroom or school. List all the communication devices you find and the type of information transfer system used.

CHAPTER 2

HISTORY OF COMMUNICATION TECHNOLOGY

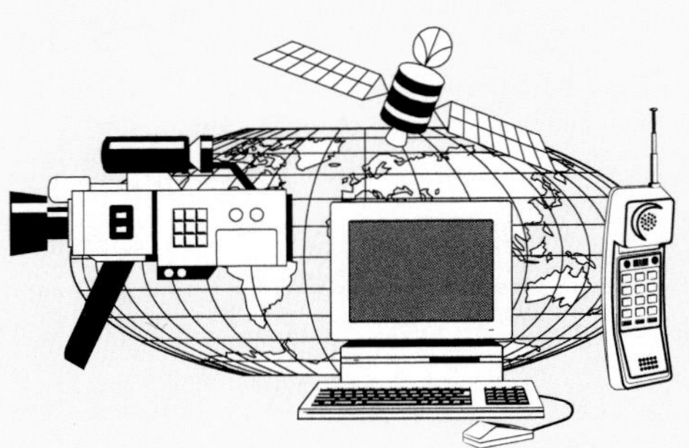

After studying this chapter, you will be able to:

- *Briefly describe the three major developments in early communication technology.*
- *Identify how science has assisted in the development of communication devices.*
- *List the most significant communication devices invented.*

Over the years, many technical developments have helped extend our senses. In particular, they aid our human senses of sight, sound, and touch. The progress in this area has been great. Thousands of years ago humans communicated through basic languages and drawings. Now we are able to make light, sound, and feelings more intense. This is called ***amplification.*** Amplification lets signals be sent faster and farther than ever possible. Amplification is done with the aid of electronic devices, Figure 2-1.

Most basic communication devices have changed only slightly. This chapter will focus on the important developments of communication technology.

Figure 2-1. Telephones let us communicate over long distances. Invented in 1876, they remain a popular communication device. (AT&T)

EARLY COMMUNICATION DEVELOPMENTS

Society uses communication devices for many reasons. The history of this technology is exciting. You will be surprised to learn how many early developments are still used today. You will see how humans have improved their ability to communicate using these developments.

Speech

The human species began "talking" thousands of years ago. At first only grunts and gestures were used. Then these simple sounds and actions developed into a system of spoken words. Today about 5,000 languages exist. One language probably began with each new society. Today, speech is the basis for most communication systems. Telephone, radio, and personal communication all depend on verbal communication (talking).

Drawing

Early humans also learned to communicate through drawings. The first signs of graphic communication were cave drawings. Drawings by cave dwellers developed into what is called

hieroglyphics, Figure 2-2. Hieroglyphics is a form of writing that used pictures to communicate ideas. Cave drawings were often pictures of animals or tools. Simple maps were often drawn. Early drawings were further improved with the use of instruments. The type of communication using drawings has developed into ***drafting.*** Drafting is the sketching and drawing of plans.

Figure 2-2. Early civilizations developed their own language systems. One society used symbols like these to communicate by visual means.

Communicating through graphics is very useful today. For example, new developments in computer graphics have set new standards of effective communication, Figure 2-3. The icons on a modern computer screen illustrate steps such as "trashing" or "printing" files.

Figure 2-3. A computer used to prepare an engineering drawing is an example of computer graphics. (Hewlett-Packard Co.)

Printing with Movable Type

Before the 1400s, the reproduction of drawings and writings was very slow. This work had to be done by hand. Therefore, printed materials like books were very expensive. Only the wealthy could afford them. Around the year 1450, Johannes Gutenberg was the first in the West to perfect ***movable type*** for printing, Figure 2-4. The type was a block of metal made to a uniform size with a raised letter on one end. The letter was cut reverse reading, or backward. The pieces of type could be assembled, used to print with, and then taken apart to be used again for other projects. Using movable type in a device called a ***press*** made printing cheaper. The press worked in the following manner. The paper to be printed was placed over the inked type. A smooth, flat plate, called a ***platen,*** was pressed down on the paper. This left an image of the type on the paper. The platen was lifted, and the printed paper removed. It was in this manner that the West's first book printed with the use of movable type, the Gutenberg Bible, was made.

Figure 2-4. Gutenberg perfected movable type in the 1400s. Letters could easily be assembled into words.

Gutenberg's press helped change the course of human history. Humans could now communicate more easily. Large quantities of books could now be printed much cheaper and with relative ease. Therefore, books also became available to people other than just the wealthy. The ability to print words and pictures caught on quickly. Many new ideas have changed printing technology since Gutenberg's day.

HOW SCIENCE AIDS COMMUNICATION

Gutenberg's invention of movable type came at an important time. A social revolution was beginning in Europe. This revolution was called the Renaissance. Between the 14th and 17th centuries, people gained new freedoms. They wanted to expand their knowledge. Beliefs from medieval times suddenly changed. During the Renaissance, sailors left Europe to discover new lands. People also began to study science and mathematics. This new research directly affected communication technology. New instruments were developed for research use. These devices helped measure and record experiments. The thermometer, microscope, and pendulum clock are common examples, Figure 2-5.

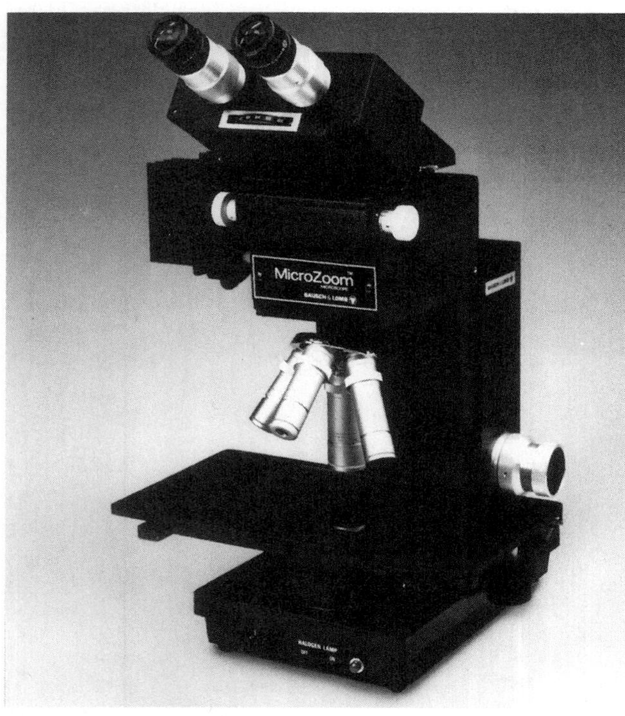

Figure 2-5. Have you ever used a microscope? With the aid of this instrument, it is possible to see very small details. (Bausch & Lomb)

By the 18th century, scientists began important experiments in chemistry. During the 19th century, several French scientists used their knowledge of chemicals to produce the first practical photograph. Reports of this work (printed on a Gutenberg press) circulated around Europe. New ideas spread among researchers quickly. Systems improved quickly. These new systems changed society.

Other scientists were experimenting with electrical principles. In 1831, Michael Faraday discovered induction. ***Induction*** is a process that produces an electrical current by moving a wire through a magnetic field. Further research by others led to a basic understanding of electricity. Understanding electricity led to the invention of many items that are now common, such as fluorescent lights and radios.

Industry grew quickly in the western world between 1750 and 1900. People moved from farms into cities to work in factories. Steam and electrical power came into common use. Research efforts increased in many areas. Scientific knowledge and technical growth combined to improve many communication devices. These items helped with the transfer of new information. People could be separated by great distances and yet communicate. This resulted in a continual desire for new media and information.

A number of early inventions are still in use today. Others have been replaced by more useful items, Figure 2-6. You will now look at these important communication developments.

Electric Telegraph

The electric telegraph was invented in the middle 1800s. This instrument simulated the practice of signaling others with flags. Communicating with flags is called semaphore. The ***telegraph*** uses electrical current in a coil to attract an iron lever called a ***sounder,*** Figure 2-7. This creates the familiar "clicking" sound.

With the telegraph, electrical pulses could be transmitted over long distances, but a system of understandable signals was required to make the telegraph more useful. The solution to this problem was introduced around the year 1837, shortly after the first telegraphs were patented. Samuel Morse devised a code using long and short sounds, or "dots and dashes," to represent each letter of the alphabet, Figure 2-8. Using Morse code, messages were sent along wires. Each word was spelled out as a series of "dots and dashes." This coding system was still slower than regular talking. However, it made the long-distance exchange of information more efficient.

Figure 2-6. The telephone, radio, and television are common communication devices. (Photos courtesy of Panasonic Corp.)

Figure 2-7. The telegraph was once an important communication device.

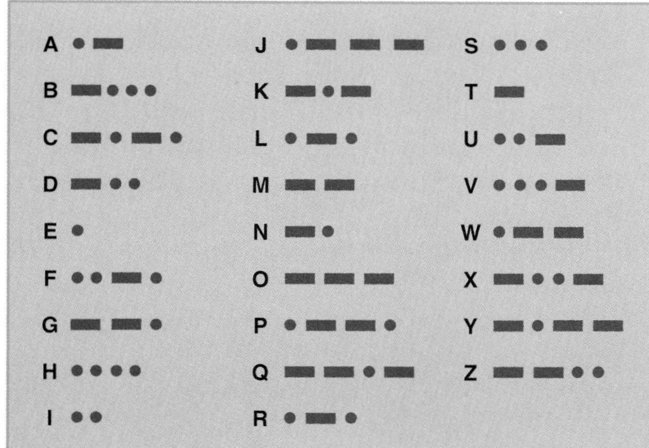

Figure 2-8. Morse code is a series of long and short sound transmitted by telegraph devices. This "language" represents a common type of coding system.

Telephone

The telegraph was a giant step in improving communication technology. The telegraph could not, however, transmit a human voice. Many people experimented with electricity to find a way around this problem. A solution finally appeared in the late 1800s. Alexander Graham Bell developed the first working telephone in 1876. A ***telephone*** is a device that can transmit sounds over a distance. Bell used a diaphragm (flexible disk) to vary the current in a circuit. The variations in the current were used to move another diaphragm. Thus, the sound is reproduced at the receiving end. The age of electronic media had arrived! Today's telephone systems allow us to talk to other people around the world. Automatic switchboards, microwave transmissions, satellites, and optic fibers send telephone signals around the globe, Figure 2-9. This communication system continues to play a major role in modern society.

Figure 2-9. Radio waves are transmitted across the country by a complex microwave network. (Rockwell International Corp.)

Recorder

The printing press allowed visual information to be stored. Both words and symbols (pictures) could be recorded for later use. However, the telegraph and telephone were different. They functioned by exchanging electrical impulses. There was no way to record and store these signals.

People often want to preserve voices and musical tunes. Therefore, an invention to record these messages was sought. In 1877, Thomas Edison developed the phonograph. It was the first ***recorder,*** a device that could store sounds for later reproduction. The phonograph could record sound and play the sound back at a later time. Other forms of recorders have since been developed. Among the first was the tape recorder. Tape recorders store the sound captured by a microphone on magnetic tape. People could easily "save" messages on tape at home or work. Cassette recorders have since become very common. Digital audio tape (DAT) recorders that use digital methods to record sound show great promise. Compact disc (CD) machines that also use this digital technology have become as common as cassette recorders.

Development of devices that could record video images began in the 1940s and by the 1950s such machines were in use. Radio and television programs are often recorded for later broadcast. Today, many firms produce commercial CDs and video tapes. These can be enjoyed at home on stereo equipment, Figure 2-10. Many homes have a video cassette recorder (VCR) that allows television programs to be recorded. Prerecorded tapes can also be viewed. The development of recording techniques was important in the history of communication technology.

Photography

The growth of sound communication was paralleled by the growth of photography. ***Photography*** produces images by capturing light on a film or by electronic means. The invention of photography occurred in the early 1800s. The first practical photograph was called a ***daguerreotype.*** This name came from the inventor of the process, Louis Daguerre of France. Producing daguerreotypes was costly and very complicated. However, the process remained popular until the 1870s.

Many improvements since then have made modern photography possible. Improvements have been made in camera design, film, lighting, lenses, and image processing. Today, people can take pictures at low cost. Color slides and prints are used by both business people and hobbyists. Developments in photography have led to motion pictures, video recording, and other reproduction processes. Cameras are using more electronic devices in their construction. Cameras that capture images using electronic methods instead of film are being used by newspapers and are now available for home use. These devices are generally referred to as ***video-still cameras.***

Radio

In 1895, Guglielmo Marconi devised the first "wireless" telegraph. This telegraph transmitted electrical impulses without wires. Wireless communication formed the basis for ***radio.*** His work combined the efforts of many other people. Along with several original ideas, Marconi paved the way for radio broadcasting. This was accomplished by using radio waves to carry signals. These signals were sent through the atmosphere to radio receivers, Figure 2-11.

Figure 2-10. Thomas A. Edison invented the first practical phonograph. This simple invention to play sound led to the creation of devices that can play and record tapes and can play compact discs and records. (Bang & Olufson)

Figure 2-11. Radio waves (signals) travel through the air to receiving units (radios). This is an effective means of communication. Most households in the United States have several radios. (Photo courtesy of Panasonic Corp.)

The most attractive characteristic of radio communication was its lack of wires. Radio waves could be sent to distant points easily. More importantly, news and other programs could be transmitted over large areas. Today, people around the world receive information by radio.

Motion Pictures

Many inventions led to the development of projected, moving images. In the late 1870s, Eadweard Maybridge was the first person to successfully record motion on film. These pictures were not "moving" pictures, but multiple pictures of a moving object. This accomplishment sparked the interest of several inventors around the world and soon the "moving" picture was developed. ***Moving pictures*** were images that actually reproduced the action recorded on film. In 1893, Thomas Edison's company introduced the first commercial "moving picture machine," called a kinetoscope. Edison's work with a ***kinetoscope*** was a key development in the area of motion pictures.

The kinetoscope was a machine used for viewing "moving" pictures. A group of photographs were put on a single roll of film. This roll was moved in a constant motion past a light source. When watched through a viewing hole, the image looked as if it were "moving," Figure 2-12.

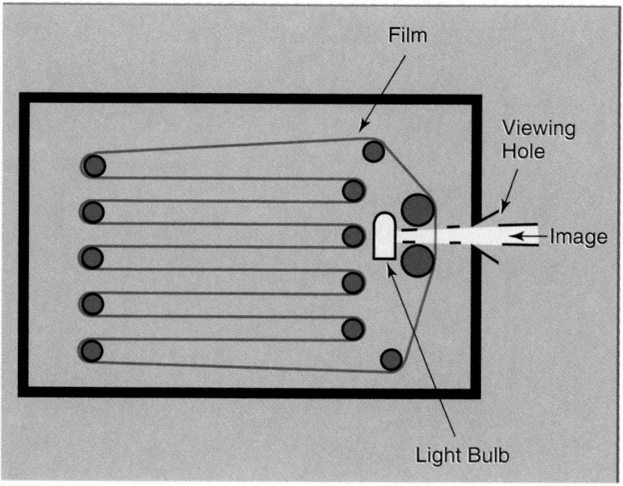

Figure 2-12. The first "motion" pictures were made possible with the kinetoscope. As single photographs passed the viewing window, action was created. Viewers had to look into the machine to watch the movie show.

As time passed, major improvements in motion pictures occurred. Projectors were developed and became more powerful, Figure 2-13. Sound and color added realism.

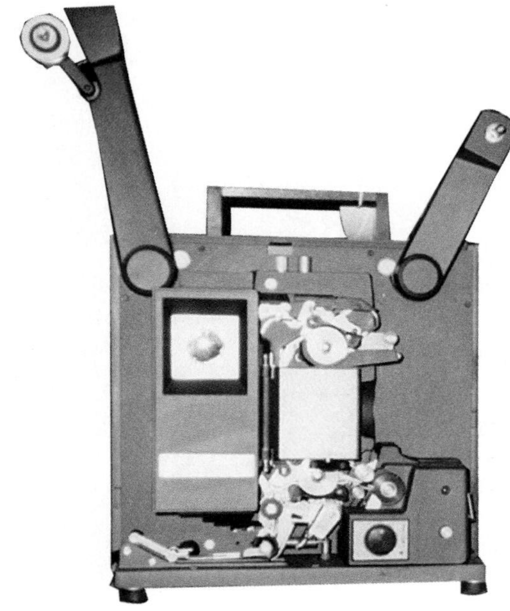

Figure 2-13. Most schools have movie projectors for showing instructional films. (Bell & Howell)

Visual processing techniques have produced new and interesting images. Production studios developed more realistic set designs. Animation and special effects make it possible to create images that could not be filmed on a set or on location. Today, computers are used to help create such images.

Television

Much of the theory that forms the basis for television (TV) broadcasting was known in the 1800s. It was not until the 1920s that the first working models were made. In 1923, Vladimir Zworykin invented the iconoscope and the kinescope *(not kinetoscope).* These devices were the basis for television. Television converts light and sound into electrical waves for transmission and then turns the waves back into light and sound for viewing.

After World War II, advancements in television came quickly. In just a few years television became a very popular communication device. TV could transfer information more quickly than any other form of communication (other than talking face to face), Figure 2-14.

Figure 2-14. Most households in the United States have at least one television set. Television viewing is a popular activity. Advancements in the quality of both the picture and the sound now allow the viewer to reproduce the movie theater experience at home. (G.E. Plastics)

Computers

Computers are devices that perform calculations and process data, Figure 2-15. Several early calculating machines were used before the automatic computer. The abacus was one. Adding machines and devices that used punch cards were others. The first practical computer was proposed by Charles Babbage as early as 1812.

Babbage's computing device could not be constructed at the time. The gear manufacturing techniques of the day were not up to the challenge. However, Babbage's theories formed the basis for modern computers. Researchers in Germany, England, and the United States began to use electronic components in the late 1930s. Early electronic computers were developed by:

- John Atanasoff at Iowa State University in 1939 (the first special-purpose digital computer).
- Howard Aiken at Harvard in 1944 (an early digital computer controlled by relays).
- Konrad Zuse in Germany (the first program-controlled computer).
- Alan Turing, Max Newman, and Tommy Flowers in England (the first computer to use vacuum tubes on a large scale).
- John Mauchly and J. Presper Eckert at the University of Pennsylvania in 1946 (the first computer to perform calculations at high speed).

Figure 2-15. Computers are used for many types of communication. Word and data processing machines are common in our modern information age. (Hewlett-Packard Co.)

These machines were the beginning of an industry. Early computers were large, expensive, and unreliable. It took the invention of the transistor to make computers really practical. Now computers can be found in almost every office and in many homes.

IMPROVING THE INVENTIONS

In 1947 scientists at Bell Laboratories invented the ***transistor.*** This item can amplify or control electronic signals. The transistor quickly replaced larger, more expensive vacuum tubes. As a result, transistors completely changed the electronic and communication industries.

Advancements in microelectronics continue to improve communication systems. ***Microelectronics*** is the reducing of circuits to miniature (very small) size. One advance in microelectronics was the integrating (combining into a whole) of many components and circuits that perform various functions. ***Integrated circuits (ICs)*** are fine examples, combining distinct functions into a single unit, Figure 2-16. ICs are complete systems manufactured on a single silicon chip. Electronic equipment continues to become smaller in size, to need less power, and to produce less heat. The integrated circuit was first patented in 1959.

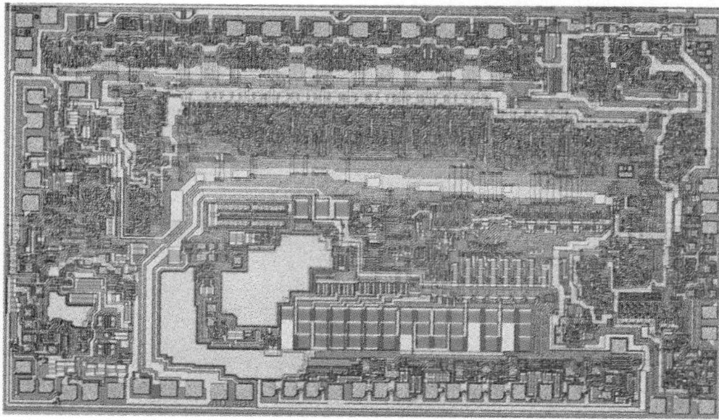

Figure 2-16. An electrical engineer designed this new integrated circuit. The circuit is shown many times larger than actual size. When produced, it will be smaller than a fingernail. (Precision Microlithics, Inc.)

Science also helped establish a communication network in space. A global communication system was proposed in the late 1940s. This plan became reality in 1960 when Echo I (a communication satellite) was launched. A ***satellite*** is a device that orbits the earth for communication or other purposes. To date, many satellites have been placed in orbit, Figure 2-17. Current satellites allow instant communication around the world. Telephone and TV signals are sent by satellites.

The future of communication technology looks bright. Many changes lie just ahead. Picture telephones may become common in our homes. Foreign languages will be translated by computer. Personal digital assistants will soon be common at school and in the home. You truly live in an "information age."

Figure 2-17. Communication satellites beam radio signals to all parts of the earth. Modern satellites orbit our planet far out in space. (Comsat Corp.)

CHAPTER 2 REVIEW

SUMMARY

As humans evolved, speech was developed. From verbal communication, forms of written communication were created. The earliest forms of written communication were simply pictures, called hieroglyphs, that represented actions or events. Eventually, alphabets came to be, but it is from these early "picture languages" that modern drafting came.

The period in history known as the Renaissance was when communication technology started to grow. During this time, movable type was perfected. This invention allowed books and other information to be printed in large quantities. Many new scientific discoveries were also made during the Renaissance, and this information could be spread quickly with the movable type press.

Since the Renaissance, many new devices have been invented. The telephone, the telegraph, TV, and the recorder are just a few of the many inventions. These devices paved the way for modern communication systems.

KEY WORDS

All of the following words have been used in this chapter. Do you know their meanings?

Amplification
Computer
Daguerreotype
Drafting
Hieroglyphics
Hieroglyphs
Induction
Integrated circuit (IC)
Kinetoscope
Microelectronics
Movable type
Moving pictures
Photography
Press
Platen
Radio
Recorder
Satellites
Sounder
Telegraph
Telephone
Transistor
Video still-camera

TEST YOUR KNOWLEDGE

Write your answers on a separate sheet of paper. Please do not write in this book.

1. The ability to make light, sound, and feeling more intense is called _____.
2. When people first communicated with their voices, they used a system of spoken words. True or false?
3. What is hieroglyphics? What are hieroplyphs?
4. Briefly describe what happened during the Renaissance.

Matching questions: Match the definition on the left with the correct term on the right.

5. A communication device that transfers information through audio and visual images.
6. Transmitted voices over wire.
7. System based on the practice of signaling others with flags.
8. Projection of moving images.
9. The "wireless" telegraph.
10. Used to preserve voices and other sounds.

A. Telegraph.
B. Telephone.
C. Radio.
D. Motion-pictures.
E. Recorder.
F. Television.

11. What were the first practical photographs called? How did they get this name?
12. List three improvements of early communication inventions.

ACTIVITIES

1. Visit a science and industry museum. Study displays that deal with early communication developments and inventions.
2. Make a list of communication devices found in your home. Decide what invention these devices came from. Bring your list to class and compare it with your classmates' lists.
3. Research an invention in communication technology that interests you. Prepare a short presentation. Your presentation should include such things as the evolution of this invention, how this invention came about, other devices that made this invention possible, and a brief biography of the inventor, however, do not limit your presentation to just these items.
4. Prepare a time line of the major developments of communication technology. Use drafting instruments or a computer to draw your time line.
5. View films or videos on the development of various technical devices in communication. Prepare a short paper of five pages or less on the development of these devices.
6. Have a representative of a telephone company speak to your class on the history of the telephone. What new functions can we expect to see in the future?
7. Use a microcomputer to make a database of major developments in communication technology.

CHAPTER 3
THE COMMUNICATION PROCESS

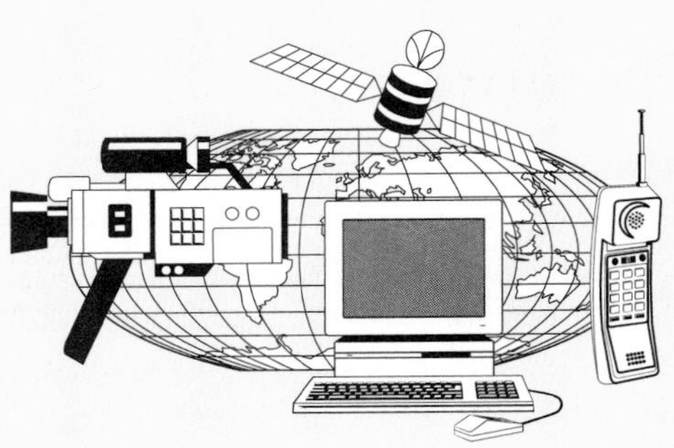

After studying this chapter, you will be able to:

- *Describe how messages are transmitted using a communication process model.*
- *Define the function of each part of the communication process model.*
- *Explain the importance of accuracy in the communication process.*

You learned earlier that communication is a process of exchanging information using our senses. Information is sent from a source to a destination with codes and signals. Designing, coding, transmitting, receiving, and storing systems are needed for the transfer of information. Feedback is also necessary, but often overlooked. Interference is unnecessary, but often present.

DESIGNING

The ***source*** is the starting point of messages to be sent. A source might be a machine, a person, or any supplemental system. A message is designed to be transmitted to others. The ***designing process*** includes ideation, purpose, and creation. ***Ideation*** means getting and working on ideas. Your skills, knowledge, and senses are then used to add purpose and create the message, Figure 3-1.

Figure 3-1. Many ideas and thoughts "pop" into our minds. We often remember happy thoughts or dream about future events.

Ideation

Suppose you were going to be late for dinner. What would be running through your mind? You might feel hungry. You could be thinking about a cold meal. The development of this message involves sensing (feeling). An idea is created from these feelings. These thoughts were developed by the ideation process.

After the need to communicate is established, a message must be constructed. Previous experience is important to this process. A past situation or problem might come to mind. You may remember eating a cold dinner the last time you were late. Reference to earlier experience helps form the message. This is a reflective (thinking back) process, Figure 3-2.

The message must now be further developed. Key questions still need to be answered. These include who, what, where, when, and why. For example, *who* will be given the information? *What* messages are to be exchanged? *Why* will one message be more effective than another message? Deciding *where* and *when* the communication process will occur is important. Like a good newspaper article, these questions are used to cover all the details when creating a message.

Figure 3-2. What does this photograph remind you of? Many images may come to mind: California, San Francisco, Golden Gate Bridge, earthquakes, energy, transportation. (Chevron Corp.)

The final phase of ideation is an evaluative process. This means you must rely on skill and prior experience to transmit the message. How might the information be exchanged? Was the procedure successful when used before? Was a verbal or written message used? Perhaps a telephone call might be best. All of this depends on your knowledge and experiences. The means of developing messages is an important stage in communication.

Purpose of the Message

When designing a message, you must have a purpose. A ***purpose*** is a reason for an action. Purposes can be classified in any of four groups. Messages can inform, instruct, persuade, or entertain, Figure 3-3.

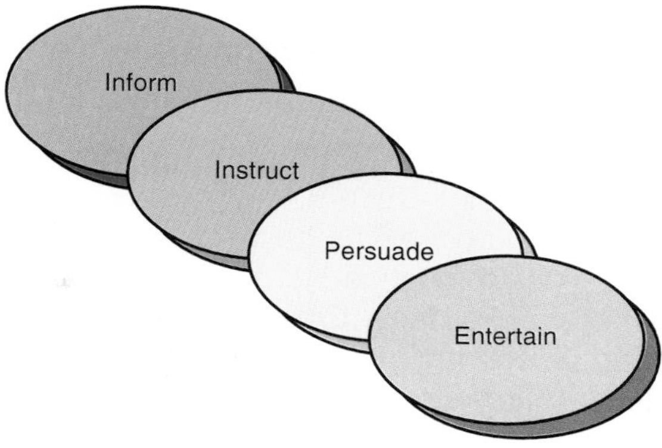

Figure 3-3. Purposes of messages.

A message that informs provides a receiver (a person or machine) with certain information. You read information in books and newspapers. The news programs on TV inform you of world events. Your parents also tell you important information.

A message that instructs provides direction or new knowledge. That is the purpose of this book. This book will instruct (or teach) you how to use communication technology. Machines can also instruct. For example, a computer often sends messages to other machines telling them what to do. Information is easily exchanged by machine.

A message that persuades helps convince others to take action. Advertising messages are designed to persuade the public. They tell you about new or improved products and their benefits, Figure 3-4. Often items are bought because of these persuasive advertisements.

Finally, a message that entertains attempts to amuse people. Most television shows entertain. Other common media are designed for the

Figure 3-4. Many posters and signs feature messages intended to persuade others. How does this sign try to influence your thinking?

purpose of entertainment. These include magazines, comic books, novels, and music.

Creation

All messages include a thought process, or ideation, and purpose. The next stage that every message goes through is the actual creation (or design) of the message. ***Creation*** is the assembling and recording of ideas. The ideas are then arranged to fit your purpose. In speaking, this process occurs automatically in our minds. You think of a topic and talk about it with ease. For example, what if you were asked about the weather? Your senses could create a description of current conditions.

However, this book is concerned with the technical means of transmitting messages (communication technology). These messages usually require much planning. The text of a newspaper must be written and edited. In the same way, radio and TV scripts are carefully prepared. Each scene of a television show is written before production starts. Drafters also organize their thoughts on paper or on a computer. They complete drawings of items to be produced, Figure 3-5. This is a form of prior planning.

Figure 3-5. This office layout was created for a business with the use of a computer. It will help them visualize the design of their building. Drafting and computer-aided design are major parts of technical communication. (UNISYS)

All messages are generated in this manner. Authors and designers start their work in the ideation phase. They begin with sketches or notes on paper or a computer. Technically, this may be called an outline or *draft.* Refinements will improve the message. Many rough sketches are necessary to select the best image. The early drafts of a television script will be refined many times. As writers prepare the story, various plots are considered. Good writers ask coworkers for advice, Figure 3-6. The final copy (text) is the result of these efforts.

Figure 3-6. Many people must work together in today's workplace. Good communication is very important. The creation of messages is just one example where working together is needed. Do you ever ask classmates for helpful suggestions? (Hewlett-Packard Co.)

CODING

After a message is designed, it must be coded. ***Codes*** are text, signals, and symbols used to transmit messages. This process can differ greatly from communication device to communication device. Depending on the method used, you receive different types of codes. Common categories include signs, electrical impulses, sound waves, and light signals. These are typical systems of coding messages.

Sign codes are often handwritten. Drawings, paintings, and symbols are all common examples, Figure 3-7.

Many forms of communication use electrical impulses. Computers, telephones, and radios all rely on these impulses. Radio waves traveling through air or space are electrical energy.

Figure 3-7. Various types of signs and symbols warn us of hazardous areas. Do you recognize any of these coded messages? (Jack Klasey)

Some devices change impulses into sound. Radios and CD players produce sound waves from electrical signals. On the other hand, bells and chimes operate by mechanical means. Sound is obviously an important communication channel.

Light signals represent another system of coding. Television, optics, and motion-pictures are perfect examples of visible codes. Fiber optics are another way of communicating with light.

Codes are vehicles for transmitting messages. A diagram of the coding techniques appears in Figure 3-8. The source or sender, must encode the message. This means the receiver must decode the information. Methods of decoding messages are covered later in this book.

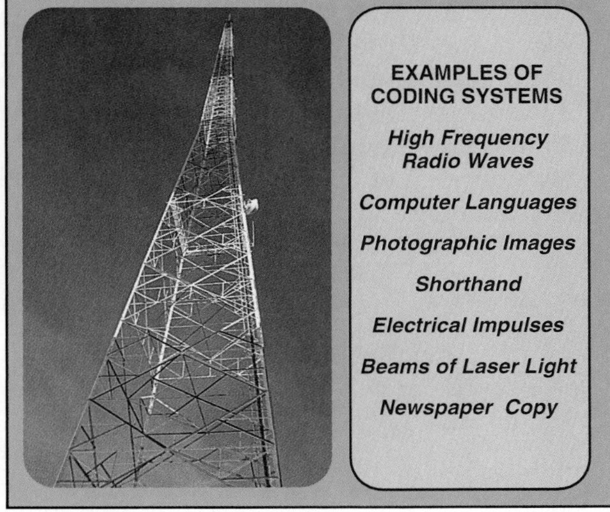

Figure 3-8. Many types of codes are common in communication systems.

TRANSMITTING

After a message has been designed and coded, the next step is ***transmitting,*** or sending, the message. If you write a note to a friend, how will it be transmitted? A piece of paper could be delivered in person. The note might be mailed in an envelope. A message may be transmitted by facsimile (FAX) machine. Each of these examples is a way of transmitting information to a destination. These ways of transmitting are called ***media.*** (*Media* is the plural of *medium.*) Different types of transmission media are available. Common channels include air, fluid, and solid materials such as wire or gears.

You learned in Chapter 2 that radio signals travel through the atmosphere (air). These waves of electrical energy carry radio programs, cellular transmissions, and TV broadcasts. The sounds created by whistles and bells are transmitted by the air. Other types of signals or electrical pulses travel along wires. Telephone conversations are transmitted through wires and fiber-optic cables.

Wires, signs, books, and gears are all examples of solids used in communication. Transmission of signals through fluids may not be familiar to you. One example includes locating underwater objects using sonar equipment.

Not all messages are sent through a single transmitting medium. Television broadcasting is an example of using different media for communication. A televised message changes form many times before the public can enjoy it. Various signals are designed and transmitted. Verbal, written, electrical, and visual signals are used in TV broadcasts. Different messages have been designed, coded, and transmitted. Thus, TV programs demand the use of various audio and visual technologies.

RECEIVING

The communication of any message involves a destination. ***Receiving*** is the process of acquiring and decoding a message. Someone or something must receive the information. The receiver also needs to decode (or interpret) the message. The exchanged information is then understood.

Decoding is important for success. It adds meaning to many communication efforts. For example, you are not able to see or hear radio waves. Fortunately, stereo receivers convert the radio waves into pleasant sounds that you can hear.

The same process takes place when you read this book. Your knowledge of letters and words is important. You are able to understand the printing and pictures. You, as the destination (or receiver), have your brain decode the visual signals. Prior knowledge helps you develop useful information from the letters, words, and pictures.

STORING

One of the final steps in the communication process is the storing of messages for later use. This procedure is known as ***storage.*** There are many reasons for storing messages. Keeping important knowledge in books and recording news events for historical purposes are just two reasons.

Information is stored in many ways. You often store information by memorizing details. You “teach” machines in much the same manner. Computers have an internal memory, Figure 3-9, that is used for storage. Information is also recorded as written symbols. Books, magazines, and newspapers all contain recorded messages. Electronic, mechanical, and film media are also common storage systems. Film storage include photographs, slides, and microfilm. Microfilm stores much information in a small place. Mechanical recording was once quite popular. Locks, analog clocks, and some industrial machines store information mechanically using gears and levers. Other industrial machines in the past were controlled with punched paper tapes. Some of these older machines are still used, however, electronically controlled machines have replaced almost all of them, Figure 3-10.

Figure 3-9. Large amounts of information can be stored even in small laptop computers. These computers offer portability and ease of use. When equipped with a cellular phone and a modem, these computers can be connected with millions of other computers anywhere in the world. (Technophone Corp.)

Storage of communicated ideas and information is important. The retrieval (recovery) of information for later use is also a necessary process. Some methods of storing information are shown in Figure 3-11.

FEEDBACK

After storage, the process of communication is not yet complete. An additional element is feedback. Successful communication is often the result of feedback provided to the sender.

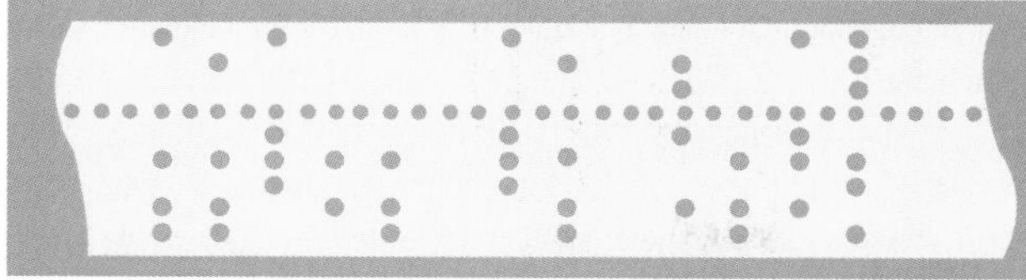

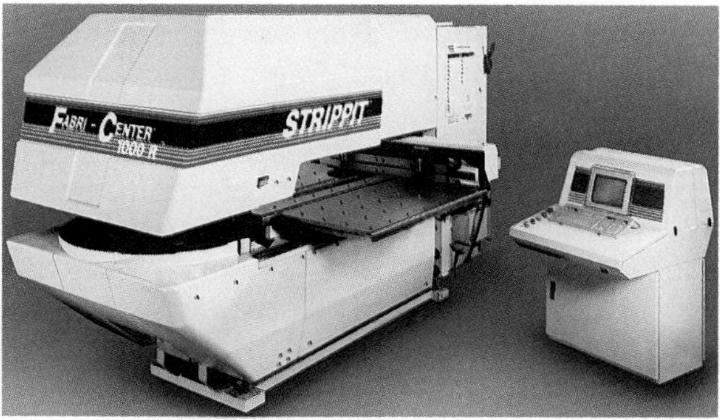

Figure 3-10. Paper tapes were once used to guide many manufacturing machines. Holes punched in the tape provided "directions" to the machine (above). Today, electronic networks now control most machines (below).

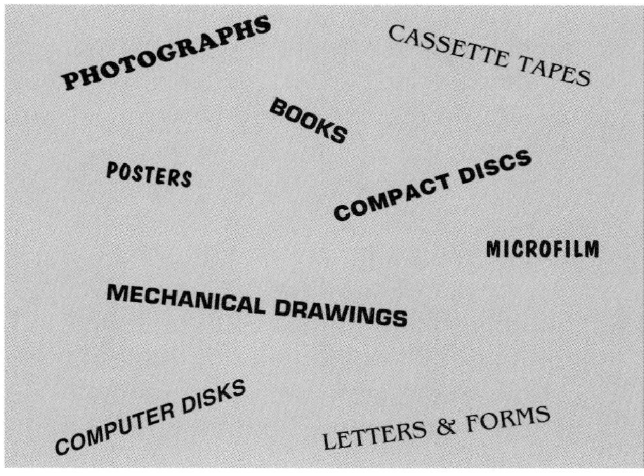

Figure 3-11. How many of these common types of "storage systems" do you recognize?

Feedback is information returned to the sender to show that a message has been received. This usually occurs by exchanging a signal. For example, suppose you send a message to a friend. You may want some type of feedback from that person. Did the message arrive? Was it understood? Many questions could arise after sending the message. The key is that some type of response is needed to complete the communication process.

Feedback may be direct or indirect. ***Direct feedback*** involves spoken or written words. It may also include gestures or body movements. When providing direct feedback, immediate contact is possible between the sender and receiver. ***Indirect feedback*** results from observing later actions. For example, you might tell a friend to lock your locker when he/she leaves. When you get there later, you find that the door is locked. Since the door is locked, you know that the message was received.

INTERFERENCE

Interference is a distortion of signals intended for the receiver. Interference is caused by the reception of undesired signals, Figure 3-12. It is often called *noise.* This noise or distraction interferes with the communication process. Mechanical interference is caused by failure in equipment. A broken television set is a good example. Electrical interference is very similar. The static your television picks up during a thunderstorm is a common form of electrical interference. Interruptions in radio signals are also considered noise.

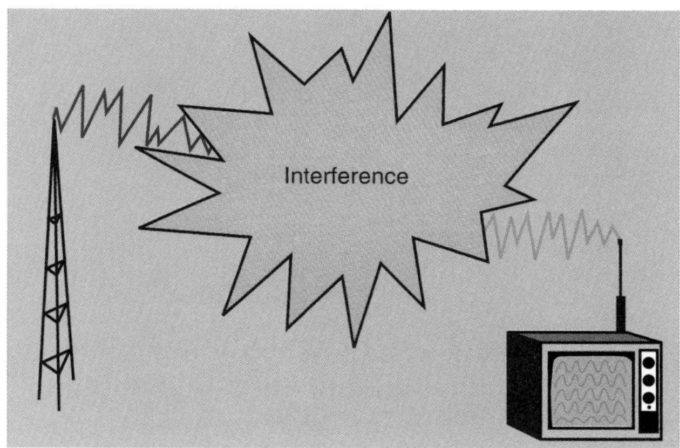

Figure 3-12. Interference causes problems in many types of communication. Static on the television is a common type of interference.

ACCURATE COMMUNICATION

You use communication methods today without giving much thought to how useful they are. This is because of the variety of means available to you. However, what value are these methods if they are not used correctly? How important is an accurate message? ***Accuracy*** is freedom from mistakes or errors.

What if you need to get a message to a friend? Will they receive something other than what you wanted communicated? If only verbal exchanges are used, the message could be misunderstood. What would happen then?

Careful planning may prevent inaccurate transmissions of information. For example, do you think it requires accurate communication to play football? The players must know what to do on each play, Figure 3-13. What is each individual's assignment during the play? When will the ball be snapped? Where will each player run? How does each player contribute to the success of the play? Also, coaches may ask why a previous play worked or failed. These are key questions if the team hopes to succeed. They also bring to light some essentials of accuracy. You learned earlier in this chapter that in communication you should always consider the who, what, when, where, how, and why of the message.

Figure 3-13. What happens if the quarterback gives his teammates the wrong play? Poor communication among the players might result in a lost game.

Today, you require an increasing amount of communication. Information is exchanged among people, machines, and governments. Business and industrial groups are included in this trend. Complex new laws and systems of ownership demand improved methods of communication. Errors and misunderstandings may occur if people do not communicate clearly. The questions – who, what, when, where, how, and why must be addressed. Only then will accurate communication be achieved.

Now look at a situation where exact communication is important. Suppose you have a job and it involves ordering materials for a factory in California. You receive a requisition (order) from your boss. The company needs 10,000 special plastic fasteners. These materials must be obtained from a company in Ohio within two weeks. What must you do to purchase the fasteners?

1. **Who.** First, a material order form should be completed accurately, Figure 3-14. The department that needs the fasteners will be identified.
2. **What.** A description of the exact type of fasteners needed is important.
3. **When.** The form will also include the date the items are needed.
4. **Where.** Fourth, the supplier in Ohio must be located. The address in your file tells you the location for placing the order.
5. **How**. The method for placing the order is dependent upon time constraints. The mail might be too slow. A telephone call or a FAX might be needed.
6. **Why.** This all brings up the questions, "Why?" The order is being placed to meet production demands. Failure to complete this communication process will lead to delays. The items may be delivered to the wrong place, delivered too late, or not delivered at all.

By now you see the effects of poor or inaccurate communication. It is the cause of numerous mistakes. Inaccurate communication leads to confusion, wasteful use of resources, and lost time. Accuracy in communication technology is important.

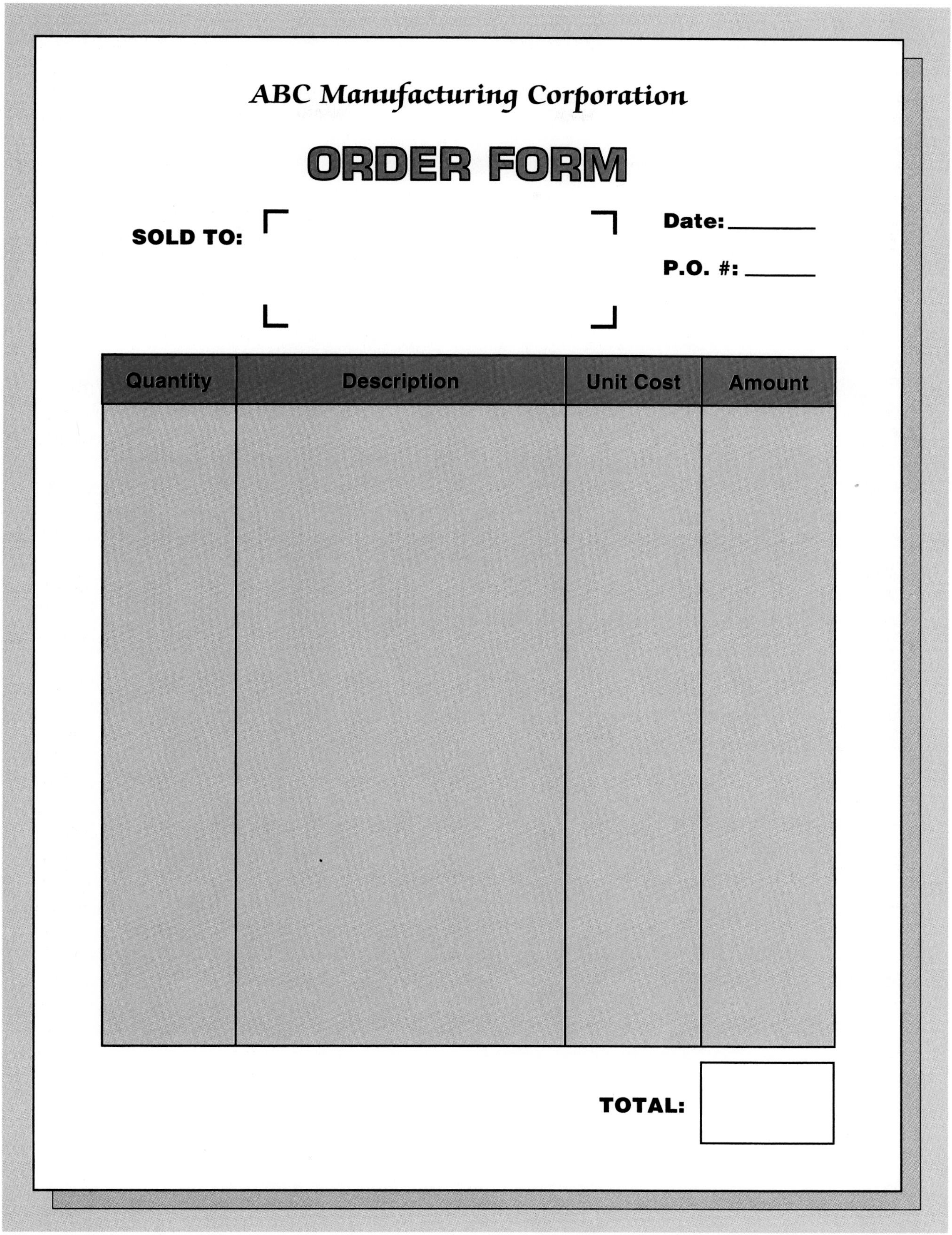

ABC Manufacturing Corporation

ORDER FORM

SOLD TO:

Date: ________

P.O. #: ______

Quantity	Description	Unit Cost	Amount

TOTAL:

Figure 3-14. Order forms represent a common type of communication. Businesses use many tons of paper each year in exchanging information.

CHAPTER 3 REVIEW

SUMMARY

The communication process consists of designing, coding, transmitting, receiving, and storing of messages. The designing process is quite complex. It includes thought, focusing, and creation. The acts of selection and revision follow. The final copy is now ready for use. However, early attempts may need refinement. Several drafts are often completed. Helpful suggestions from others are sought. The final design must be the best possible choice.

Coding can be done using electrical, sound, light, or mechanical means. When the message is received, it must also be decoded so that it may be understood. After the message is decoded and understood, it might be necessary to store the information for use at a later date. Electronic, film, and mechanical media are a few of the common storage media. Finally, feedback is important to inform the sender of the status of the message.

All communication involves one or more purposes. Four common purposes include informing, instructing, persuading, or entertaining.

Interference is a negative aspect of communication. Interference may be mechanical, electrical, or light interference. Static during a radio or TV broadcast is an example of interference.

Finally, accuracy is important in communication. Asking questions such as who, what, when, where, why, and how are useful in determining accuracy.

KEY WORDS

All of the following words have been used in this chapter. Do you know their meaning?

Accuracy
Codes
Creation
Designing process
Direct Feedback
Feedback
Ideation
Indirect feedback
Interference
Media
Purpose
Receiving
Source
Storage
Transmitting

TEST YOUR KNOWLEDGE

Write your answers on a separate sheet of paper. Please do not write in this book.

1. Information is transmitted from a sender to a _____ with _____ and storing.
2. The _____ is the starting point for a message.
3. The design process includes:
   A. Ideation, purpose, source.
   B. Coding, transmitting, receiving.
   C. Ideation, purpose, creation.
   D. Instruction, information, persuasion, entertainment.

Matching questions: Match the definition on the left with the correct term on the right.

4. The process of making up a message.
5. The process of putting the message into a certain form for transmitting.
6. The process of sending the message to a destination.
7. The process of saving information for later use.
8. The process of securing and decoding a message.
9. The sign that a message has been received.

A. Designing.
B. Coding.
C. Transmitting.
D. Receiving.
E. Storing.
F. Feedback.

10. What is interference?
11. Why is accurate communication so important?

ACTIVITIES

1. Make a drawing to show how the communication process works.
2. Invite a writer or illustrator to class. Ask your guest about the processes he/she goes through in designing a story or piece of artwork.
3. Make a list of transmitting media (air, wires, fiber optics) with examples of communication devices that use those media.
4. Invite a radio engineer or disc jockey to visit your class and explain how radio messages are transmitted and received.
5. List different ways messages have been stored throughout history.
6. Design a message. Whisper your message to a classmate. Then have each student whisper the message to the student next to him/her. Let the message go all the way around the classroom. How does this show accuracy and interference?
7. Act out different examples of "body language." Try to guess what each student is "saying." How do these actions show feedback in communication?
8. Invite a newspaper reporter to visit your class to discuss the importance of accuracy in writing news stories.

CHAPTER 4
SOCIAL AND CULTURAL INFLUENCES

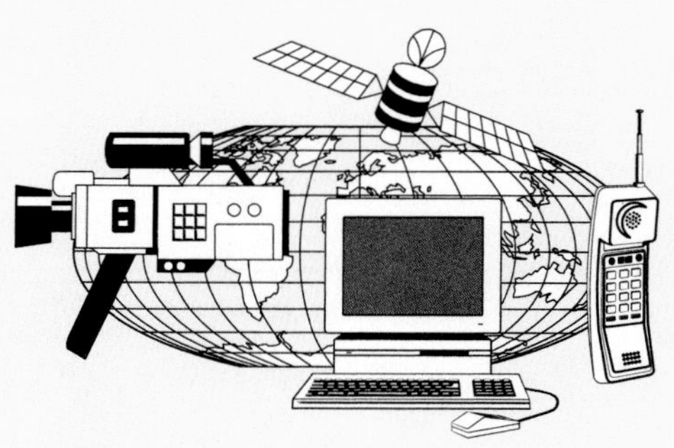

After studying this chapter, you will be able to:

- ❖ *Describe the purposes and impacts of communication.*
- ❖ *Cite uses of communication technology in modern society.*
- ❖ *Identify social issues associated with communication technology.*

Modern society relies heavily on communication systems. You use them in your personal life, at work, and at play. For this reason, the era of human progress that you live in is called the "information age." This chapter will focus on how you are affected by modern communication (information) technology.

Look around your home. Newspapers, television sets, telephones, facsimile (FAX) machines, smoke alarms, computers, video games, books, and magazines may be just a few of the communication devices present. Each influences your life in a different way. Each has an impact on your attitudes, feelings, and knowledge.

PURPOSES OF COMMUNICATION

No wonder this period in history is referred to as an information age. Your daily life depends on many communication devices. You awake to an alarm clock. Morning newspapers and TV shows entertain and inform you. Radio announcers tell you the weather forecast. Clocks tell you it's time for school or work.

A typical school could not exist without communication aids. Bells signal the start of classes. Announcements are delivered over the public address (PA) system. Teachers rely on chalkboards, movies, video tapes, and other instructional recordings such as computer software, Figure 4-1. Books contain the knowledge you need to complete assignments. Many interesting facts and details are stored on CD-ROM discs. Even computers and calculators help you with school work, Figure 4-2.

Figure 4-1. This teacher is preparing materials for a blind student in her class. (National Braille Assoc.)

A trip down any street reveals other communication devices, Figure 4-3. Road signs provide direction. Traffic signals control the flow of cars. Store fronts describe products or services. Billboards advertise consumer goods. Telephone booths line the highways and cellular phone antennas can be seen on many cars, Figure 4-4. Can you identify other useful communication devices or systems?

Figure 4-2. Calculators (top) and personal computers (bottom) are two popular examples of communication aids. (Hewlett-Packard Co.; Apple Computers, Inc./John Greenleigh)

When you arrive home, the impact of communication technology is reflected here as well. The mailbox contains personal letters or magazines. Inside your home are more devices for communication. A telephone answering machine might have recorded calls for you. Family members leave notes for you. Books are found next to a comfortable reading chair.

Figure 4-3. Signs along roads or streets provide valuable information. These visual displays tell us simple, yet important, details. (Jack Klasey)

Figure 4-4. Telephone booths are found along many streets. Cellular phones are quite common in cars. These devices allow quick and convenient communication. (Courtesy of Sprint)

Most homes have one or more television (TV) sets, a video cassette recorder (VCR), and a stereo sound system, Figure 4-5. You may also enjoy playing video games and using personal computers. Word processors, cassette tape recorders, and cordless phones are found in many homes, too.

The purposes of communication were briefly described in the last chapter. Most communication is meant to inform, entertain, persuade, or instruct. These purposes will be further explained now.

Information

To inform is to let people know what is happening. Many messages are intended to spread information. They relay interesting or important facts. For example, radio announcers inform you of special events. Newspapers carry news, weather, and sports stories. Have you ever read the graphics on a breakfast cereal box? The pictures and words on most packages are informative in nature, Figure 4-6. Countless methods are available to inform you of key messages.

In these instances, the media acts as a device for spreading information. Some information helps you plan your daily affairs. Other information aids in making decisions. People need and enjoy receiving information. This is a basic aspect of communication and information technologies.

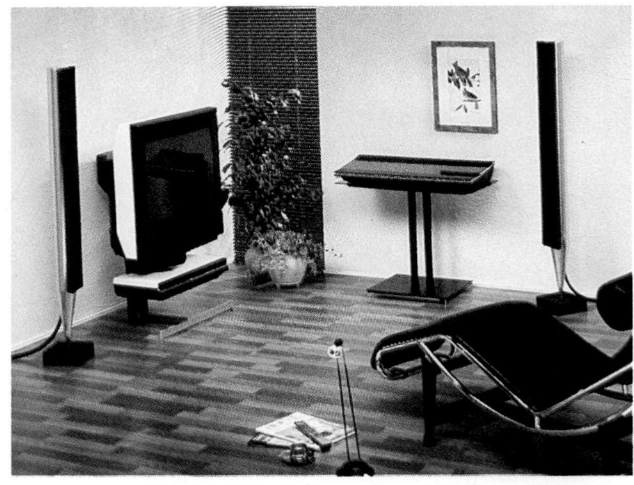

Figure 4-5. Almost every home in this country has at least one radio receiver. Many homes also have television sets. These communication devices keep us entertained and informed. (Bang & Olufson)

Entertainment

The mass media is used basically as entertainment. When you watch a television show you usually want to be entertained. If you listen to the

Figure 4-6. The labels on most packages give the size, weight, and ingredients. What information is shown on these packages? (Ralston Purina)

radio, you want to hear music you like. Many people also rely on mass media as a way to relax. You may know someone who likes to read newspapers, books, or magazines.

Television is the most popular form of entertainment. Today, many households have several television sets. VCRs and personal computers (PCs) are also common home entertainment devices, Figure 4-7. In addition, many households have stereo systems with CD players and tape decks.

Figure 4-7. Personal computers are very popular. They can be used to entertain as well as educate. (Sof-Source)

Instruction

Communication technology is also used in education. When you think of education, you usually think of schools. But, how do you learn in school? Teachers relate valuable information. Speech is one of the oldest methods of communication. You also learn by watching what others do. Action is communication. You may also learn by reading. These are all the result of communication technology. Instructional communication has become very popular today. Films, video tapes, and educational television are several examples.

Today there are thousands of magazines, newspapers, and books available, Figure 4-8. Thousands of new books and publications appear every year. Many are instructional in nature. Home fix-it books show you how to repair appliances or perform similar tasks. While these books explain fun and relaxing activities, their major purpose is to educate.

Figure 4-8. Magazines provide hours of enjoyment for their readers. Do you subscribe to any journals, magazines, or newspapers? (Jack Klasey)

Persuasion

Communication technology is used to influence your decisions.

This is called ***persuasion.*** Signs and banners urge you to make purchases, to vote, and to support certain causes, Figure 4-9. Many advertisements attempt to influence the way you act. Which soft drink do you buy? Which restaurants do you enjoy? Many times your decision to buy a certain product results from someone's persuasion.

Figure 4-9. Many communication materials are used to persuade. What reaction do you have to this visual display?

Forms of persuasion differ greatly. For example, news events are reported in different ways. A particular issue might be important in one city but another city may totally ignore it. What you are shown or told influences your outlook on life.

USES OF COMMUNICATION

You have examined the four purposes of communication—to inform, to instruct, to entertain, and to persuade. Now you will examine the uses of communication systems. Two broad classifications cover all communication. Humans generally communicate with other individuals ***(individual communication)*** or with large groups of people, Figure 4-10. When large numbers of people are involved, we call it ***mass communication.*** Much of modern communication is transmitted by mass media.

Figure 4-10. The exchange of information always involves receivers, or an "audience." An audience can be a single person (called individual communication) or large groups of people (called mass communication).

Individual Communication

You often use individual (one-to-one) communication systems. Personal notes and letters are simple examples. Using a calculator to check figures is another. A telephone conversation with a friend is also an example of individual communication. Most methods of individual communication are not suited to informing large numbers of people.

In business, individual communication is very important. Some of the most popular methods are the telephone, FAX machines, and the postal service. Much information is transmitted by these technical systems. This is how companies manage daily affairs and conduct routine business.

The computer is also an individual method of communication. Businesses, as well as private citizens, use computers, Figure 4-11. Most home systems are small. Business systems can be very large. Information is kept in electronic files for future use. These files are called a ***database.*** With a database, information is available for quick retrieval. This information may be brought up on a screen or printed on paper, Figure 4-12.

Mass Communication

Each day you receive messages aimed at reaching many people. Each of us is part of a large audience for advertisers, the government, and other groups. Mass communication systems are used to inform a large audience. Masses of people act as the receiver in this type of communication.

Communication to large audiences relies on modern technologies. Television, radio, newspapers, motion-pictures, and books are examples. Other mediums include billboards and road signs.

Figure 4-11. Many people use banking machines to make deposits or withdrawals. These machines send messages (information) to the person's bank. These machines are often used during hours when the bank is closed. (InterBold)

Figure 4-12. Great amounts of information can be stored in data banks. The information needed can be retrieved and reproduced in many ways. (IBM)

The impact of mass communication is important in modern society. None is more powerful than television. This medium provides a constant flow of messages. You see advertisements for toothpaste, autos, and food. News of local and world affairs is also shown.

Radio is another key mass communication system. You hear your favorite music on various stations. Weather and news reports are broadcast many times each hour. Advertisements promote products, services, and special events. Again, the focus is to communicate with the general public.

As you can see, mass communication technology is common in modern society. However, the trend is to make communication more personal. This alternative tries to focus various media on a particular segment of society. Messages are directed to particular groups. This is called ***targeting*** an audience, Figure 4-13. For example, sporting goods companies will advertise heavily during football game telecasts. These commercials are targeted at the sports-minded audience.

Figure 4-13. Advertisers create promotions for products that teenagers often purchase. Have you seen advertisements for any of these products? (Photos Courtesy of The Coleman Co., National Pork Producers Council, Xyvision Inc., Jack Klasey)

COMMUNICATION INFLUENCES

The influences of communication on society are meant to be positive. You are entertained, informed, and educated through the use of various media. News and weather reports are an example of useful information. There are many positive influences of communication. These influences can help you economically and socially. However, communication technology can have a negative influence on society. The distribution of false or misleading information is an example.

Education in Society

Citizens of the United States are very well educated. The U.S. guarantees a certain level of education for all its citizens. For example, you must remain in school until age 16. A large percentage of our population attends a community college or university. Education is available because of communication technology. Textbooks contribute to these instructional activities. Educators also use films, video tapes, television, and audiovisual equipment. In fact, our entire society benefits from educational efforts.

Freedom of Speech

The concept of freedom of speech means that you can express your views without experiencing a negative (or positive) impact from that action. You may express your views using newspapers, magazines, television, and radio. Freedom of speech allows each of us to express our opinion. This is a very important privilege. For example, a newspaper can endorse (recommend) a certain person for a political office, and the evening news can support another person for that same office. Citizens have the right to carry signs and banners in support of a third person for the same political office. All of this is done to *influence* those who have not made up their minds on which person is the best candidate. This is just one example of how freedom of speech allows us to communicate.

Economics

Many people are employed in various communication activities. Writers, printers, and broadcasters create messages. Countless technicians and engineers work in the communication field. All these people get paid for their work. They use their money to maintain a particular standard of life for themselves and their families. Food, clothing, and various services are bought with this money. This money goes back into the economy and helps other people.

Communication systems also help society in a less direct way. By using communication technologies, buyers can find available goods and services. Billboards, TV and radio commercials, telephone book yellow pages, and newspaper advertisements are examples of sellers describing their products and where to get those items. This helps businesses increase the sales of their products. Increased sales in turn allows them to sell more products or services. This keeps the economy of a country growing.

The Disabled in Society

Communication also helps in assisting people with disabilities. Tools continue to be developed to help disabled people communicate. Deaf persons can be informed and entertained by television shows with subtitles. These *close-captioned* broadcasts provide a written script on the screen, Figure 4-14. People who are deaf can also use a device called a **T**elecommunication **D**evice for the **D**eaf (TDD) to communicate by telephone. A TDD turns typed words into tones that can be sent over phone lines. Another TDD on the other end decodes and tones and shows the words on a screen. Conversations occur by words sent back and forth between the TDDs.

Figure 4-14. Closed-captioning symbols are used in many television program guides to identify shows using subtitles for the hearing impaired.

People who are visually impaired have many tools to help them communicate. "Talking books" are books recorded onto audio tapes. Books and magazines printed in large type or braille help the visually impaired to enjoy literature. Machines that can read a printed page and convert it to spoken text are helpful to the visually impaired. Spoken descriptions of television programs and movies allow people who are visually impaired to enjoy these programs.

Many other devices exist to help people with disabilities to communicate. New devices are constantly being developed. These devices allow people with disabilities to interact with others more effectively.

Figure 4-15. People often complain about too many signs along roadways. Is this an attractive sight? (Jack Klasey)

Information Overload

To this point, you have looked at the positive aspects of communication. However, there are some negative aspects of communication. Overexposure is a negative part of the mass media. You are often exposed to an excessive amount of information. A term for this overexposure is ***information overload.*** Your mind is just not accustomed to processing so many messages.

Sources of information overload are all too common, Figure 4-15. You see numerous billboards and signs along roadsides. Television commercials provide another familiar example. You often see too many advertisements to clearly remember a select few. In addition, many advertisements come in the mail or newspaper and are simply thrown away. This is a tremendous waste of both natural and human resources. Further, many people are annoyed by telephone solicitations (known as ***telemarketing***). These unwanted calls often come at awkward times. Some people see the calls as an invasion of their privacy. These are just a few examples of how communication can have a negative impact on your life.

Propaganda

Another harmful use of communication technology on society is propaganda. ***Propaganda*** is the use of false or misleading information to harm someone or something. It is used to force others to accept certain opinions. During election years, politicians may engage in "mudslinging," or making negative comments, against their opponent. Certain groups may provide what they call "facts," when what they present is really only one side of the story. Propaganda is a negative and dangerous use of communication methods.

LAWS AND REGULATIONS

With the growth of communication, federal laws and regulations were created to control various media so that those media are not used in a negative way. These rules limit many communication efforts. However, this regulation is designed to protect you. Various laws ensure that the public is being served fairly.

The ***Federal Communication Commission (FCC)*** regulates radio, TV, and telephone communication. Other governmental agencies control the publishing industry. The results of these regulations are quite evident. For example, tobacco advertisements cannot be broadcast on television and radio, obscene language is not allowed in most media, and advertisers may not show alcohol being consumed on TV commercials. Any violations of existing rules are handled by the FCC.

CHAPTER 4 REVIEW

SUMMARY

Your life relies heavily on communication systems. From the beginning to the end of the day, you use communication devices. In the morning you wake up to alarm clocks. In the evening you relax by watching television or by reading a book or magazine. These communication systems are used for instruction, entertainment, persuasion, or information. These systems can be used to communicate with individuals or with large groups. When large groups are involved in the communication, the process is called mass communication. However, no matter what way communication systems are used, they do have influences on society. These influences can be either positive or negative.

KEY WORDS

All of the following words have been used in this chapter. Do you know their meanings?

Database
Federal Communication Commission (FCC)
Individual communication
Information overload
Mass communication
Persuasion
Propaganda
Targeting
Telemarketing

TEST YOUR KNOWLEDGE

Write your answers on a separate sheet of paper. Please do not write in this book.

1. Why is this era called the information age?
2. Which of the following is NOT a purpose of communication technology?
   A Freedom of speech.
   B. Persuasion.
   C. Instruction.
   D. Information.
   E. Entertainment.
3. When large numbers of people are involved in the exchange of information it is called _____ communication.

Identify the use of each of the following devices as individual and/or mass communication.

4. Radio.
5. Letters.
6. Postal service.
7. Newspapers.
8. Calculators.
9. _____ is directing a message to a particular group.
10. Is information overload a positive or negative influence? Why?
11. The _____ _____ _____ is a federal organization that regulates radio, television, and telephone communication.

ACTIVITIES

1. Conduct a school-wide survey to learn the number of telephones, televisions, and radios found in each student's home. Report your results to the class.
2. Take the TV section of the newspaper and review the shows for different times of the day (8 a.m. - noon, noon - 4 p.m., 4 - 7 p.m., and 7 - 11 p.m.). Classify the programs as informational, entertainment, instructional, or persuasive. Does the most common type of program depend on what time of day it is?
3. Listen to the radio between 4 and 7 p.m. on a weekday. List the communication purposes, with examples heard during the broadcasts. Report the results to the class.
4. Analyze the sections in several magazines to identify the parts that inform, instruct, entertain, and persuade. Cut out examples of each and make a collage.
5. List the forms of communication technology you use in one day. Divide the list into individual and mass media communication uses. Write a one-page report comparing and contrasting the two types of uses.
6. Have a guest speaker from an organization for the deaf demonstrate sign language and other communication techniques used to assist the deaf.
7. Collect magazine and newspaper advertisements that inform, instruct, entertain, or persuade. Classify the ads by their purpose. Cut out examples and make a collage.

CHAPTER 5

INDUSTRIES AND CAREERS IN COMMUNICATION

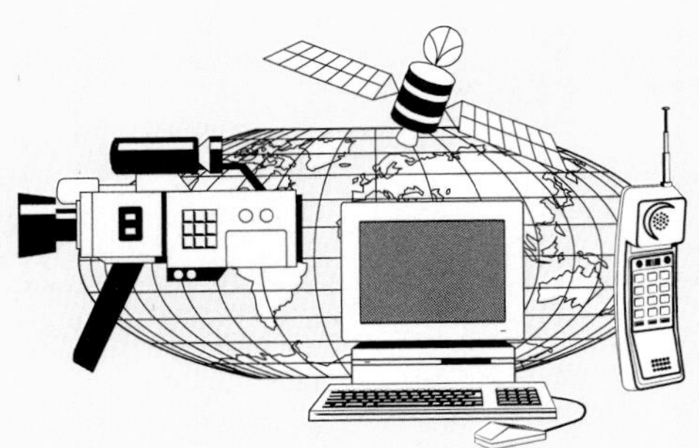

After studying this chapter, you will be able to:

- ❖ *Identify the major communication industries.*
- ❖ *Explain the importance of information industries in modern society.*
- ❖ *Describe the products and services offered by different communication industries.*
- ❖ *Recognize the variety of career opportunities in the field of communication.*

Creating and transferring information is one of the largest businesses in the world. These business activities are called the ***communication industry.*** Millions of people work in various jobs involving the transfer of messages. Some people produce and broadcast television shows. Other people write, illustrate, and publish newspapers, books, and magazines. Computer programmers and photographers are also involved in the communication of information. There are many examples of activities in this field. However, most activities in the communication industry have one thing in common: they are designed to make a profit (money) by spreading information to others. Religious and charitable groups are exceptions since they are considered "non-profit" or "not-for-profit" organizations. These groups are not driven by profit, but rather by something else (religious commitment, for example).

The size and complexity of the communication industry is astonishing. In the United States alone, 60 million (60,000,000) newspapers are circulated each day. Over 110 billion (110,000,000,000) pieces of mail are delivered yearly. Your home telephone is connected to over 360 million (360,000,000) phone lines around the world. Facsimile (FAX) machines and computer networks allow information to be sent quickly across town or across oceans. Some communication companies employ thousands of workers. Communication involves moving information. How information is moved can be simple or complex, Figure 5-1.

In this chapter, you will look at several business activities associated with communication industries. You will focus on those industries that rely on technical systems to transfer information. You will examine how typical industries are organized and operated. In addition, you will explore the many challenging professions available in the communication field, Figure 5-2.

COMMUNICATION INDUSTRIES

The economic activities in any country are mainly conducted by business enterprises. We call these organizations ***companies.*** The term ***industry*** describes a group of related businesses. For example, radio and television stations are classified as parts of the *broadcasting industry.* The printers of books, magazines, and other graphic materials are part of the *publishing industry,* Figure 5-3.

Very simply, industries add value to products and services. These products can be existing products or newly created products. Resources such as knowledge, raw materials, and money are used to create this value. Individuals and businesses then pay the industries for these products and services. Industries hope to generate a profit (money) in this manner, Figure 5-4.

Figure 5-1. Communication systems can be as simple as a storefront sign or as complex as a satellite dish.

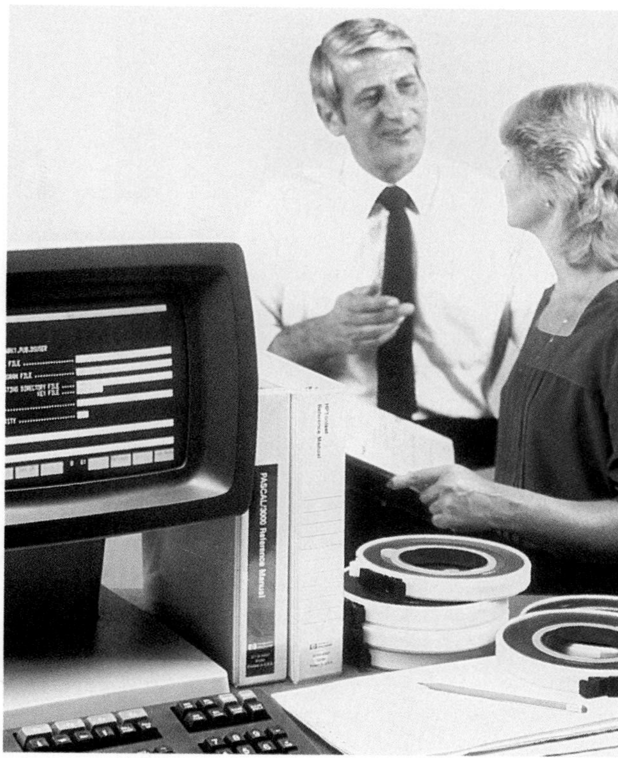

Figure 5-2. Information managers are an important link in the various fields of communication technology. They must process and update data so it is useful to business and industry. (Hewlett-Packard Co.)

Figure 5-3. Small printing shops turn out the majority of printed materials in this country. (A.B. Dick)

Figure 5-4. Companies charge others for the products and services that they offer.

Eleven types of communication industries have been identified in Figure 5-5. These types of communication are:

- Commercial art and design.
- Engineering drafting and design.
- Printing and publishing.

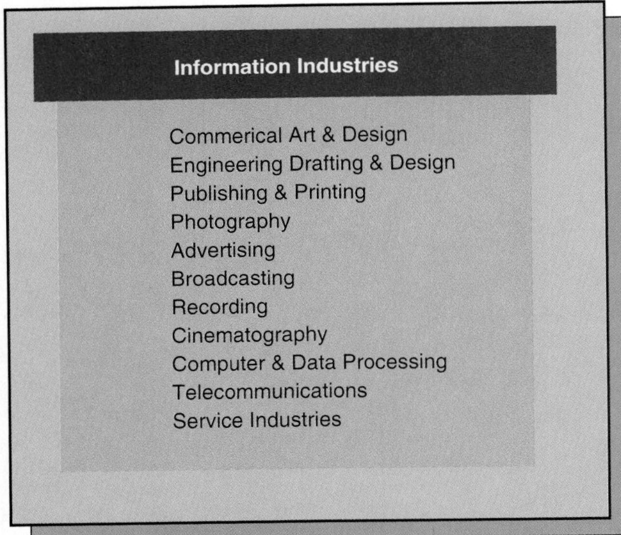

Figure 5-5. The eleven communication industries.

- Photography.
- Advertising.
- Broadcasting.
- Recording.
- Cinematography.
- Computers and data processing.
- Telecommunication.
- Service industries.

For discussion, you will examine each of these industries more closely.

Commercial Art and Design

Many companies specialize in the creative design of commercial items. These businesses are called ***design firms*** or ***design agencies.*** Design firms range in size from one person to hundreds of people. The work of design firms is visible in many products, Figure 5-6.

Commercial designers are very talented people. They have often times developed their skills through many years of education and work. Many designers have attended schools and colleges to study art and design. As a result, they are very good at sketching and drawing. This allows them to communicate their ideas on paper or through electronic means for others to evaluate and enjoy, Figure 5-7.

The work of designers is everywhere in your life, Figure 5-8. They design common items like posters, greeting cards, and candy wrappers. Other examples include postage stamps, book covers, and compact disc (CD) liners. Products

Figure 5-6. Designers create many of the labels, signs, and other visual displays we see everyday. (Photo of Union Station courtesy of Amtrak)

Figure 5-7. A designer has used a computer to visualize a new production model. (Hewlett-Packard Co.)

Figure 5-8. You use many materials produced by creative artists and writers. (Xyvision Inc.)

like these are carefully designed for your use and/or enjoyment.

Large agencies often employ hundreds of talented individuals. Each person specializes in a particular area. Layout artists develop plans based upon the desires of a client (customer). Staff artists are hired to produce the detailed sketches and drawings. Printers reproduce the designs on paper or other stock. During the entire design process, a project director supervises the job. This person coordinates the work of artists, photographers, printers, and many others. Everyone works together to create a completed product.

Engineering Drafting and Design

Sketches and drawings are excellent ways to communicate ideas. Presentation of ideas through line drawings is called ***drafting,*** Figure 5-9. Drafters use symbols and shapes to develop designs for many objects. Products and structures are carefully planned before being produced, Figure 5-10.

Figure 5-9. Drafters use computers to complete a drawing. Computers help speed up the design process in many industries. (Hewlett-Packard Co.)

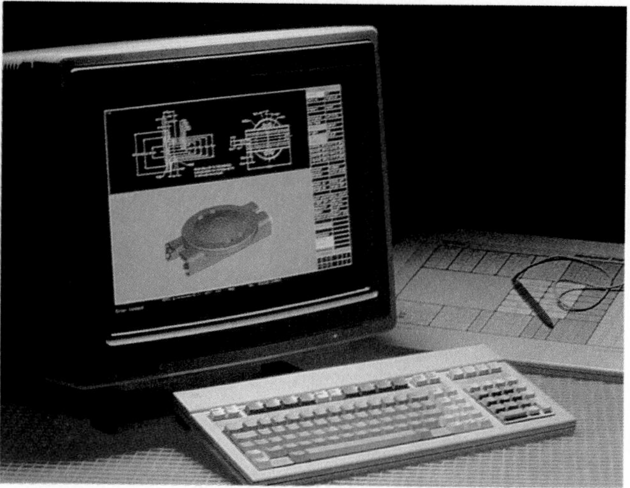

Figure 5-10. The design of this part is being carefully examined on the computer screen. (Hewlett-Packard Co.)

Drafters in industry develop plans for cars, toys, furniture, and other products. Their designs are called ***engineering drawings.*** Other drafters specialize in planning homes and buildings. The types of drawings created by these people (architectural drafters) are called ***architectural drawings.*** Your school building was designed by an architect, and the drawings completed by an architectural drafter. Many drawings were required to completely explain how the building would be built. When a large building is planned, hundreds of drawings are needed. A drawing is needed to show the arrangement of the rooms (floor plan). Another drawing is needed to show where electrical wires will be placed (electrical plan). Other drawings are needed for the heating and cooling systems, for the foundation, and for each of the many other systems.

Drafters must know how to produce many types of drawings. For example, plans for electrical devices are called ***schematic drawings,*** Figure 5-11. Other forms of drawing are ***technical illustrations*** and ***architectural illustrations.*** These are finely detailed drawings that represent what the final result will look like, Figure 5-12.

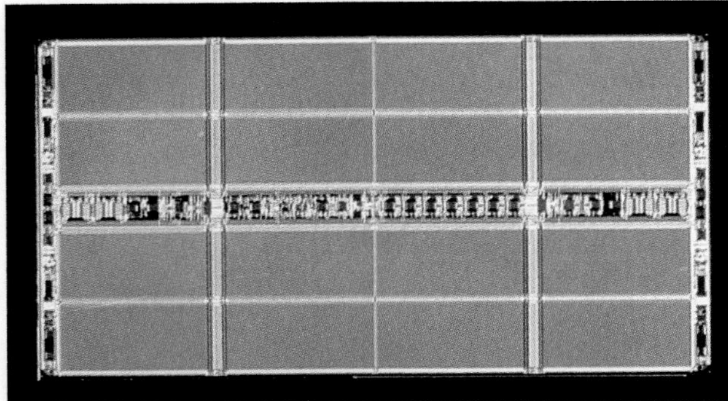

Figure 5-11. Drafters are able to complete many forms of drawings. This is a drawing of a memory chip, drawn on a Computer-Aided Drafting (CAD) system. (IBM)

Drafters are skilled workers. They attend special schools for training. Their education includes taking art, math, and technical courses (physics, drafting, etc.). Most will also work as apprentices or detail specialists for several years in design firms. Some areas of drafting require this experience before taking certification tests. Architectural drafters must pass these tests to become fully-licensed architects. Civil and product engineers must pass a similar exam.

Figure 5-12. This architectural drawing shows what the inside of a new luxury liner will look like when the ship is completed. Drawings of this type are important because they help executives visualize the final product and make decisions. (Radisson Hotels)

Modern drafting is often done with the aid of computer systems, Figure 5-13. Computers allow the drafter to develop prints and detail drawings much faster. If a certain shape or symbol is needed, the designer can "draw" the item by pushing a key or a button. Computers also make revisions of the drawings very simple when compared to the older method of using a pencil and T-square. Drawings stored on computer disk are easily changed.

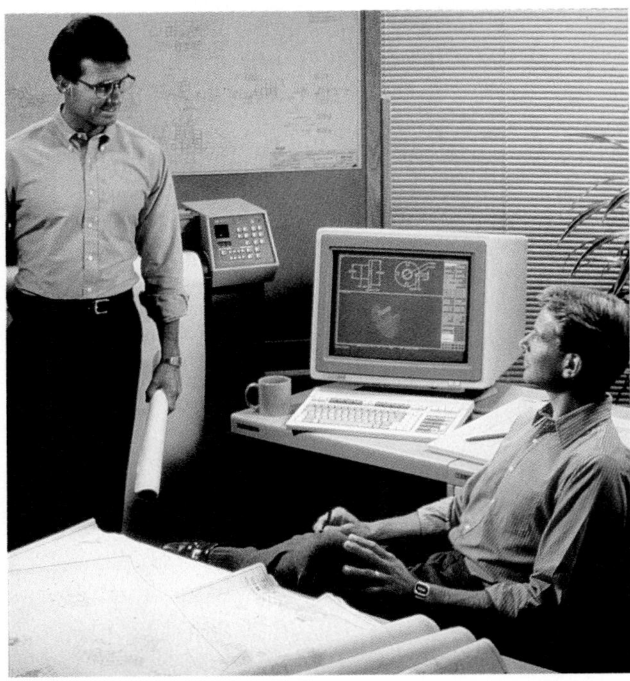

Figure 5-13. The drawing for this part is being completed on a computer. The drawing will then be printed using a plotter. The plotter can be seen to the left of the computer. (Hewlett-Packard Co.)

Printing and Publishing

Printing and publishing businesses are an important part of the graphic arts industry, Figure 5-14. Printing firms actually print books or magazines. Publishers, on the other hand, create and organize text and illustrations. A publisher will then send the final product to a printer. Publishing firms generally do not print the books and magazines that you read. This is left to the printing companies. Together, printers and publishers make money by creating and printing various materials to be used by others.

Figure 5-14. Newspaper inserts are a common product of the printing or publishing industry. Many companies use inserts to advertise specials or sales. (Heidelberg Harris)

Printing firms are classified by the type of service they offer. For example, commercial printers do small jobs involving limited numbers of copies. This would include business cards, stationery, and flyers. These ***quick printers*** can provide "while you wait" service for simple items. They make use of electrostatic copiers, or "Xerox™ machines," to offer fast service to customers, Figure 5-15. Another group of printing firms produce legal documents and related materials. These shops are called ***special-purpose printers.*** Finally, there are printing companies

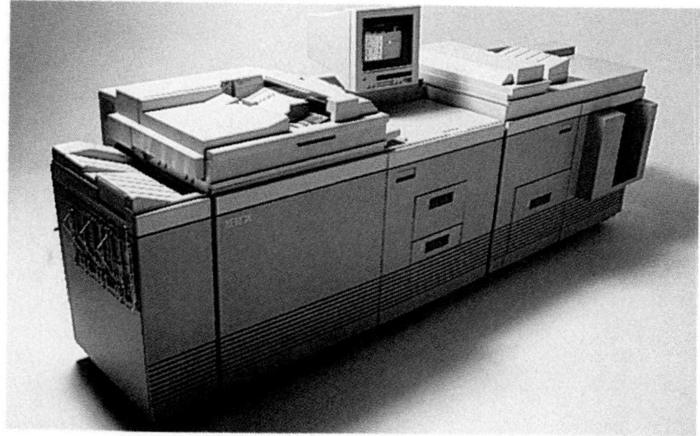

Figure 5-15. Quick print shops use copiers that are able to make large quantities of copies at a high speed. (Xerox Corp.)

called ***publishing houses.*** These are the companies that are most familiar to the majority of the people. Publishing houses produce newspapers, magazines, and many forms of books to be printed and sold.

Larger publishing houses often hire hundreds of workers. Employees help to write, edit, and illustrate articles or stories. Other workers are in charge of production tasks such as layout and printing. Desktop publishing specialists and typesetters transform all text and captions into the actual type to be used in the printed final product.

The training or education for each employee is different. Writers and editors must know how to prepare feature articles. They usually study journalism or English in college. Talented artists use their training in design to develop the required drawings and artwork, Figure 5-16. These skills may have been improved through practice, training, or on-the-job experience.

The production workers in a printing operation also require specialized training. Press operators are responsible for the actual printing of all materials, Figure 5-17. The printing presses these operators work with are very complex machines. Therefore, operators often have been to a technical school, in addition to receiving on-the-job training. Many of these workers have a college degree.

Other production tasks include platemaking, process camera work, bindery work, and paper cutting. Workers in these areas usually attend college or technical schools to learn their trade. Many times they are represented by a trade

Figure 5-16. Graphic artists use their talents to design the layouts for magazines and other publications.

Figure 5-17. Press operators check the quality of a reproduction during the printing of a job. (A.B. Dick)

(labor) union. As union employees, they will often spend several years learning techniques from people with many years of experience. These experienced people are called ***master printers.*** The time spent observing and working with a master printer is called an ***apprenticeship.***

Photography

Many people enjoy taking pictures simply for fun or relaxation. Professional photographers, however, earn money from the pictures they take. These photographers are employed by others for commercial purposes. For example, newspapers hire press photographers to "shoot" pictures of news and sporting events, Figure 5-18. Most television stations maintain a large photography staff for the same reason. In contrast, some individuals prefer to work for themselves. These people are called ***freelance photographers.*** They often take pictures for weddings, family reunions, or school yearbooks.

Figure 5-18. Press photographers crowd the sidelines to get the best pictures for their newspaper. (John Metzger)

A career in photography demands hard work and long hours. In addition, photographers must have training in many areas. Most photographers are knowledgeable about camera equipment, lighting, and visual composition (how the shapes and images in a picture "fit" or "work" together). Colleges and technical schools offer many courses in these areas. In addition, photographers improve their skills through many hours of instruction and practice.

Advertising

You see many forms of advertisements every day. Television commercials and magazine ads are common examples of advertising. Other media include billboards, banners, and signs, Figure 5-19. All advertising work involves communication between companies (or organizations) and the public.

Figure 5-19. Signs are an important medium for advertisers. How many different companies can you see advertised here? (Jack Klasey)

Most forms of marketing rely on communication technology to help "spread the word." The mass media (TV, newspapers, radio) is an effective way to inform and persuade large groups of people. After all, nearly everyone listens to radio and watches television. Using these two media for advertising purposes is very effective. Other systems are equally as effective for advertising. Some visual advertising media include:

- Packaging.
- Blimps.
- Posters.
- Coupons.
- Billboards.
- Neon Signs.
- Television.

These various media are shown in Figure 5-20.

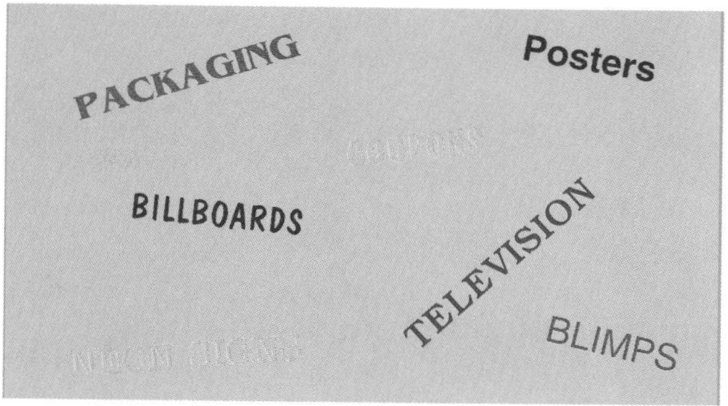

Figure 5-20. Here are examples of several advertising media.

Individuals in the advertising profession are highly trained. Their knowledge of design, marketing, and public relations is important. Therefore, advanced schooling is critical to becoming successful in this field. Courses in art, design, and graphic production are usually required. In addition, courses in business are important. Advertising professionals then improve their talents through on-the-job experience.

Many companies do not have the time or resources required to develop an advertising program. These companies often hire other companies to design their promotional materials. A large organization that specializes in the task of creating advertisements for other companies is called an ***advertising agency.*** Most advertising agencies employ dozens of artists, writers, and related personnel. Each person has a strong background in one area of advertising work. The agency offers the creative services of their employees to outside firms (for a fee). Major advertising campaigns require teamwork among the agency staff.

The work of advertisers can be fun and rewarding. Using creative talents to develop an advertisement is exciting and challenging. However, preparing a successful advertising program is hard work. Whether it's designing a billboard or recording a radio ad, much effort is expected of advertising personnel.

Broadcasting

The broadcasting industry includes work in the fields of radio and television. There are approximately 1400 TV stations and almost 10,000 radio stations in the United States. Almost 8500 cable systems provide programming to over

4.5 billion (4,500,000,000) households. Local TV stations can be representatives of major networks such as NBC, ABC, CBS, and Fox. Independent stations and stations that broadcast the Public Broadcasting Service (PBS) also play a key role in television. Radio has remained popular despite competition from television. Many people listen to radio programs while walking, running, riding buses, and driving cars.

Television stations are complex organizations. A large staff is required to prepare and produce a TV show, Figure 5-21. Programs must be developed by writers and reporters. Advertising time (commercials) must be sold by the marketing department. The production staff operates and maintains studio equipment, Figure 5-22. Business and personnel matters are handled by company officials.

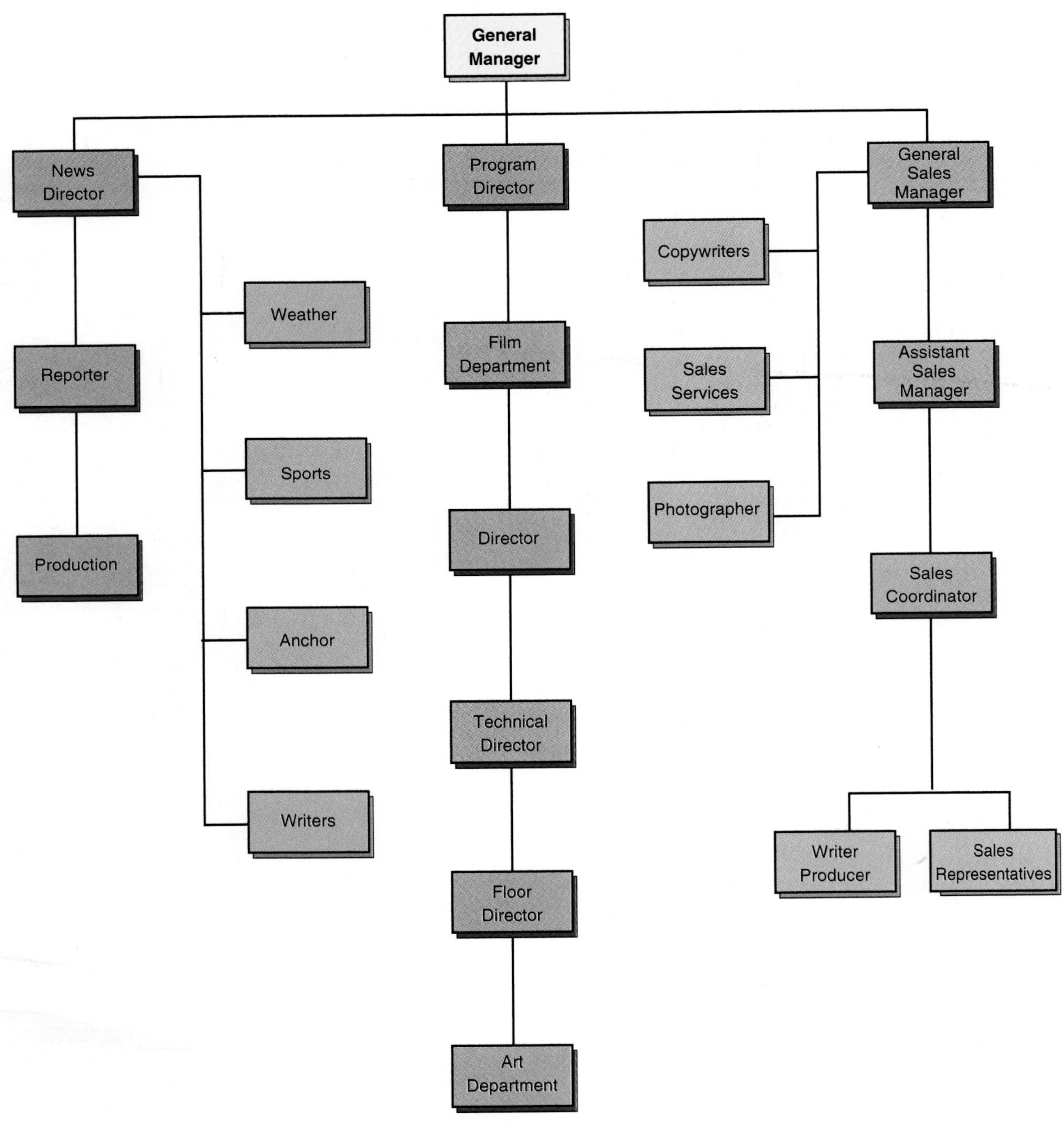

Figure 5-21. Many people are involved in the organization of a typical TV station.

Figure 5-22. The production staff operates the equipment for the newscast.

The structure of a radio station is much like a television station. Feature programs and news reports must be prepared for broadcast. Electrical engineers keep the transmitting equipment working. Radio announcers (also known as disc jockeys or DJs) read commercials and news items, conduct interviews, and introduce music, Figure 5-23. The success of a typical station depends upon the popularity of the announcers. The better announcers attract a larger share of the audience (more listeners). This leads to higher ratings and, generally, a more profitable station.

Figure 5-23. A radio disk jockey introduces songs and reads announcements on the air. (Westinghouse Corp.)

Radio and television broadcasting involves many talented, professional individuals. However, most of these individuals work "behind the scenes." Support personnel (like writers or directors) are rarely heard or seen "on the air." Their jobs are far less noticeable to you than the newscaster or reporter. However, their work is still very important and rewarding.

Most people in the broadcasting industry have some type of advanced training for the positions they hold. For example, talk show hosts often have college degrees in communication. Directors and producers often hold degrees in mass communication, telecommunication, or broadcasting. Studio technicians attend technical or trade schools to learn about electronic equipment and systems. Many people in the broadcasting industry start their career in a small, local station. The brightest and most talented individuals, however, discover new opportunities in larger stations throughout their careers.

Recording

The recording business is a $5 billion industry in the United States. Money is spent to see popular recording stars at concerts. Compact discs and cassettes of rock, jazz, alternative, and other music are purchased, Figure 5-24. Radio stations play your favorite hit songs. This describes just a part of the recording industry.

Figure 5-24. Compact discs (CDs) and cassettes are very popular. These are products of the recording industry.

Individuals in the recording industry have varied backgrounds and skills. Most studio and recording personnel are highly trained. These people must understand both acoustics (the science of sound) and electronic equipment. Microphones and instruments must be arranged correctly to obtain the best sound quality. Recording sessions for a demonstration (demo) or master tape often involve long hours in the studio, Figure 5-25.

Figure 5-25. Sound technicians check the audio level during production sessions. (Ball State University)

Cinematography

Cinematography is the science of motion-picture photography. This industry is more commonly known as the motion-picture industry. Like the recording industry, the motion-picture industry is a very popular and profitable form of communication. Every year, Americans spend over $4.25 billion ($4,250,000,000) on movie tickets. Across the United States, there are about 25,000 screens that show movies. The rental of movies that are on video tape and laser disc are a very important part of this industry, Figure 5-26.

Figure 5-26. The motion-picture industry entertains millions of people every year. Many movies make more money after they are released on home video than they did in the theaters.

Making a motion-picture is a complex task. Many talented people are needed to write, film, and edit the movie. Casting agents and directors select actors and actresses for each character. Set designers build the stage (or scene) and props. Rehearsal and production time is scheduled to complete the filming work. The camera crew and their support team film all action. After the camera work is completed (including the addition of any special effects), editors "cut" the film to final length and content. The sound track (voices and music) is then added by studio technicians. Various directors and managers supervise the entire production. After production is completed, the distribution process begins. Movie theaters compete to obtain the most popular movies available. Distribution companies contract and ship motion-pictures to theater owners. The film is then shown in your local theater. After the film has been in the theater for a while and ticket sales are decreasing, the film is transformed into video tapes and laser discs for home use. The home video market has become so big that some films never even go to the theater. These films are instead released directly on home video tape and laser disc.

Careers in the motion-picture industry require a great deal of hard work. Long hours are spent on the set or on location for the production staff, actresses, and actors. The camera crew may start filming early in the morning and continue past sunset. Production staff must be knowledgeable and willing to work hard. Members of the production team must be well trained and use their talents wisely. Editors and sound technicians may spend many weeks or months getting the film into its final form.

Computers and Data Processing

Computers are electronic devices that receive, change, communicate, and store information. Most modern forms of communication rely on computer systems. These systems have permitted the development of highly efficient methods of transferring information, Figure 5-27.

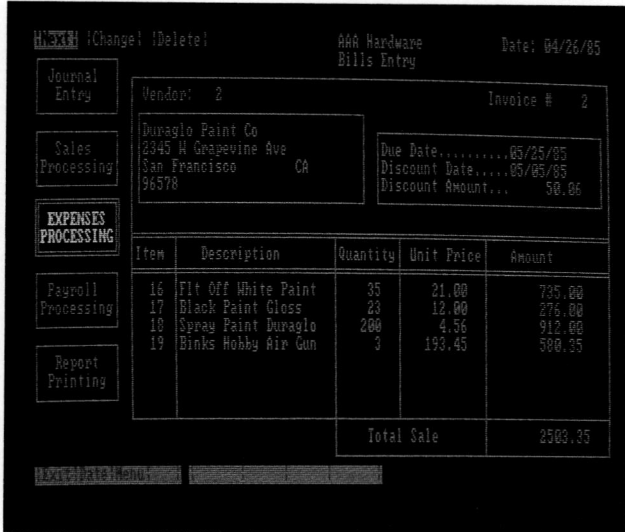

Figure 5-27. Computer programs can make it easy to keep track of customer orders and to charge them for their purchases. (UNISYS)

Since the computer industry is so complex, there are many career opportunities in this field. For example, designing and building the actual computer and related equipment (hardware) is a challenging career, Figure 5-28. Writing internal programs (instructions for the computer) or user programs (software) is an equally challenging career. The people that write software are called ***programmers.*** Most complicated software is developed by computer specialists. Simple programs, however, can easily be written by beginners.

Figure 5-28. The design and construction of electronic equipment is a very complex task. Electrical technicians assemble machines. A computer is used to track the machines through the manufacturing process. (UNISYS)

One of the largest uses of computers today is for ***data processing.*** In data processing, information, (reports, accounts receivable information, client addresses, etc.) is entered into a computer, instructions are entered, and results are received. This information can then be used for many different things, such as preparing a mailing for customers or balancing your checkbook.

Telecommunication

Telecommunication involves transmitting information (signals) between distant points. This industry includes a variety of systems for exchanging messages. The most common example is the telephone. The use of satellites to transmit radio signals around the globe is also an excellent example, Figure 5-29. Without communication satellites, you would be unable to receive many television and radio programs.

Figure 5-29. Satellites reflect various communication signals between distant points. This is how we receive TV and radio programs from other continents.

Few people realize how fast modern telecommunication systems are changing. New products and systems are developed almost daily. In fact, many of the systems in place today will be outdated in only a few years. This is true of telephone lines, microwave links, fiber-optic lines, and other communication devices. Obsolescence (something being out-of-date) is a problem in the telecommunication industry. Companies want the most up-to-date equipment installed, but in a few short years even that equipment is considered obsolete. Newer equipment is usually available that performs the same functions much better.

Workers in the telecommunication field must have many technical skills. To design radios, telephones, and other equipment demands special training. College degrees in math, science, engineering, and technology are common for telecommunication experts. There are many exciting opportunities for qualified individuals who enter the field, Figure 5-30.

Service Industries

Many firms indirectly provide communication services to consumers. Think about the person who delivers your mail. How does that individual help you communicate with others? The person in an airport control tower, known as an air traffic controller, provides a key communication service. That person helps aircraft communicate with

Figure 5-30. These engineers are assembling a communication satellite for launch. (Rockwell International Corp.)

each other, thereby avoiding disaster. Sometimes this process breaks down, or fails, and an accident occurs.

The largest segment of the service industry involves repair and maintenance work. Technicians are required to keep communication equipment in order, Figure 5-31. When complex electronic devices need repairing, the bill can exceed several thousand dollars. Although technicians are not directly involved with transferring information, they are an important part of the process that allows the information to be transferred. If the printing press breaks down and nobody fixes it, your local newspaper would never get to your doorstep in the morning.

The federal government is another service institution. Many of their tasks involve communication technology and systems. Various governmental agencies regulate the flow of information. The Federal Communication Commission (FCC) oversees the operations of communication companies. Their major task is to set policies and make certain the various companies in the industry follow these policies. The Federal Trade Commission (FTC) regulates trade and makes sure that no information is exchanged illegally. This illegal exchange of financial information in trade is called ***insider trading.*** Other governmental agencies monitor the frequencies of broadcasts, the content of TV programs, and claims made by advertisers.

Figure 5-31. Service and repair personnel are well-trained technicians. They must understand very complex machines. (UNISYS)

CHAPTER 5 REVIEW

SUMMARY

The world of communication includes a large, varied group of companies and organizations. However, all these companies are organized to create and transmit information. They are also, with the exception of non-profit organizations, setup to be profitable.

In the communication industry, you have identified eleven basic industries. Included are the following:

- Commercial art and design.
- Engineering drafting and design.
- Printing and publishing.
- Photography.
- Advertising.
- Broadcasting.
- Recording.
- Cinematography.
- Computers and data processing.
- Telecommunication.
- Service industries.

Each of these groups has a variety of career opportunities. The training or schooling required can vary by position. Many of the positions require a college degree. Other positions require technical training or apprenticeship.

KEY WORDS

All of the following words have all been used in this chapter. Do you know their meanings?

Advertising agency
Apprenticeship
Architectural drafters
Architectural drawings
Architectural illustrations
Communication industry
Companies
Data Processing
Design agencies
Design firms
Drafting
Engineering drawings
Freelance photographers
Industry
Insider trading
Master printers
Programmers
Publishing houses
Quick printers
Schematic drawings
Special-purpose printers
Technical illustrations

TEST YOUR KNOWLEDGE

Write your answers on a separate sheet of paper. Please do not write in this book.

1. _____ are business enterprises that conduct most economic activity. _____ are a group of related businesses.
2. Commercial design firms:
   A. Specialize in the creative design of commercial items.
   B. Employ layout artists, designers, and printers.
   C. Range in size from one person to hundreds of people.
   D. All of the above.

3. A finely detailed drawing that resembles a photograph is a(n):
   A. Engineering drawing.
   B. Schematic drawing.
   C. Technical illustration.
   D. None of the above.
4. What two media are closely associated with the broadcasting industry?
5. What is cinematography?

Matching questions: Match the definition on the left with the correct term on the right.

6. People who process information through a computer.	A. Programmers.
7. A computer and its related equipment.	B. Software.
8. People who write software.	C. Data processors.
9. Computer programs.	D. Hardware.

10. Name the three types of printing companies explained in the text.
11. A(n) _____ _____ specializes in designing the marketing campaigns of other companies.
12. The Federal Communication Commission belongs to what industry?
13. How is the Federal Trade Commission related to communication?

ACTIVITIES

1. Identify five companies in your community involved in the communication industry. Select one for an in-depth study. How many employees does the company have? What is the amount of their annual sales (dollar amount)? Obtain the name of the person in charge. Write this person a letter, requesting a tour of their facilities. Present a report of your findings to the class.
2. Select an occupation in the communication industry that interests you. It can be one of those mentioned in the chapter, or one that you know about personally. Compile a report on this occupation. What education/training is necessary? What is the future growth of the occupation? (Will it still be around in 15 years?) In what areas of the country are jobs in this occupation located? What is the beginning salary? What is the salary for an experienced professional? Write a short, two-page paper on this profession.
3. Along with your classmates, select one computer or broadcasting company from whom you will buy one share of stock. Follow the value of the stock in the business section of your daily paper for one month. Why does the value change? What factors affect the price of the stock? At the end of one month, report to the class how much money you "made" or "lost." How did the rest of the class do?
4. Make a list of the companies that print your textbooks. Include books from several different subjects and classes. Visit the library to research one or two of these companies. How large are these companies? Do they have only one office? Is all work completed in one location? Summarize your information in a short report.

CHAPTER 6

TECHNICAL COMMUNICATION SYSTEMS

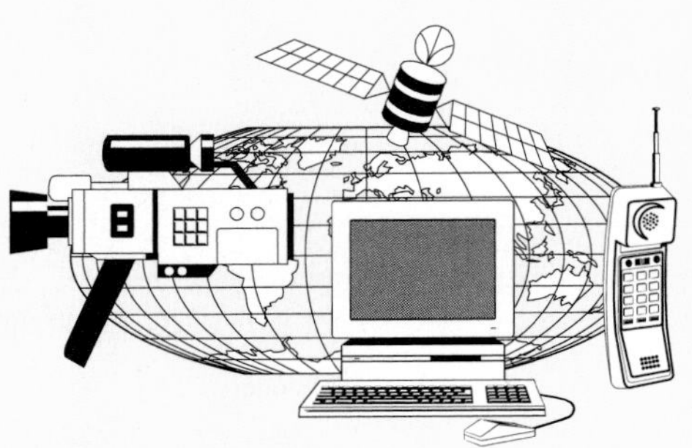

After studying this chapter, you will be able to:

- *Describe audio, visual, and audiovisual communication systems.*
- *Identify and define the two technical communication systems of graphic and electronic media.*
- *Cite examples and purposes for these technical communication systems.*

You will recall that communication is the process of exchanging information. The way that information is exchanged varies a great deal, Figure 6-1. The exchange may be as simple as talking with a friend, or the exchange may include two computers "talking" to each other over a network. No matter how communication takes place, it is a basic activity in daily life.

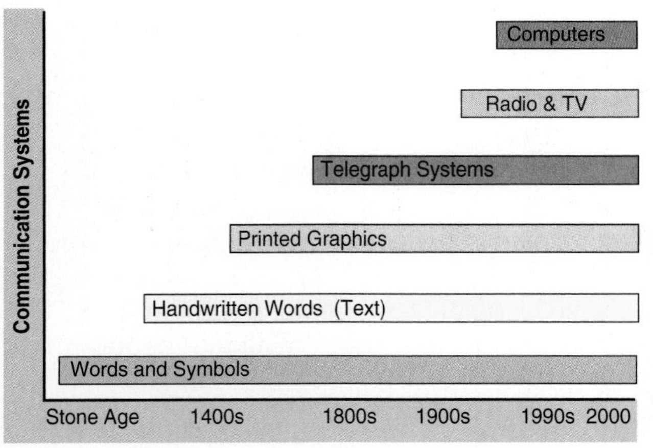

Figure 6-1. Our ability to communicate progressed slowly at first, but over the past 150 years it has grown very rapidly.

Communication can involve any of the five human senses. Your senses help you recognize and send information. For example, your senses of sight and hearing allow you to watch news on television. Many news stories would be difficult to understand without the help of pictures that accompany the verbal descriptions, Figure 6-2. In addition, your sense of smell can inform you of dangerous situations like a fire. Smoke from a fire can often be smelled before the flames are seen. In this case, your sense of smell gives you a very important message. Sometimes the sense of smell provides pleasant messages, such as "dinner is being prepared."

Over 90 percent of communication, however, is done using the senses of sight and hearing. Messages that involve your sense of sight are

Figure 6-2. Newspapers are filled with information on world and local news, sports, business, and the arts. Newspapers are a form of communication.

Figure 6-3. Millions of people stay informed every day by reading newspapers.

Figure 6-4. When you listen to a CD, you are receiving an audio message. Audio communication is a form of communication that most people use constantly everyday.

called ***visual*** (what can be seen) communication. Messages that involve your sense of hearing are called ***audio*** (what can be heard) communication. Often you use a combination of both sight and hearing. This is referred to as ***audiovisual*** communication.

Visual communication is used often in everyday life. Perhaps the most common example of visual communication is the daily newspaper, Figure 6-3. You see the print, you read the stories, and your mind translates the text into information.

A large number of your messages involve audio communication. When you listen to a radio, a tape, or a compact disc (CD), you use your sense of hearing to receive the message, Figure 6-4. Talking to your friend on the phone is another example of audio communication.

However, most attempts to communicate information are not simply audio or visual, but both. A high school marching band sends information that is seen and heard, Figure 6-5. Using only sight or hearing for this message would result in only a part of the message being received. Other examples of audio, visual, and audiovisual communication are shown in Figure 6-6.

Figure 6-5. Marching bands must be seen and heard to be enjoyed. (Andy Johnston)

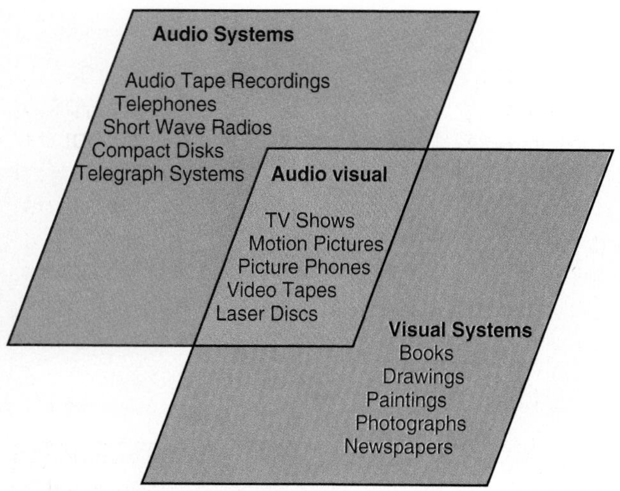

Figure 6-6. Examples of audio, visual, and audiovisual communication systems.

TECHNICAL COMMUNICATION SYSTEMS

In Chapter 1, communication technology was defined as *"the process of transmitting information from a source to a destination using codes and storage systems."* This definition includes all types of communication: letter writing, cybernetics, computer programming, and talking on the phone. Now you will look at those communication technologies that use technical devices or systems. You will leave behind topics that do not use technical devices, like public speaking and sign language.

Basic communication is improved with the help of technical devices. A telephone makes it possible for you to speak with your friend who lives across town. The label on a fruit drink informs you of the drink's nutritional value. For the remainder of your study, you will take an in-depth look at the areas of ***graphic communication*** and ***electronic communication,*** Figure 6-7.

GRAPHIC COMMUNICATION

Visual communication is often broken down into two subareas. These areas are technical graphics and printed graphics. Printed graphics is commonly called "graphic communication" and technical graphics is commonly called "drafting."

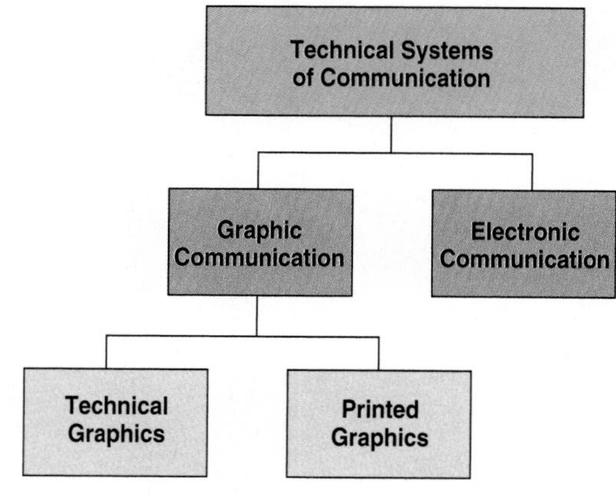

Figure 6-7. Systems of technical communication.

Technical Graphics

You depend on sketches and drawings to communicate. Have you ever given directions to others by means of a sketch? See Figure 6-8. Have you seen graphs or charts used to explain findings? How do simple pictures and directions help in putting a plastic model together?

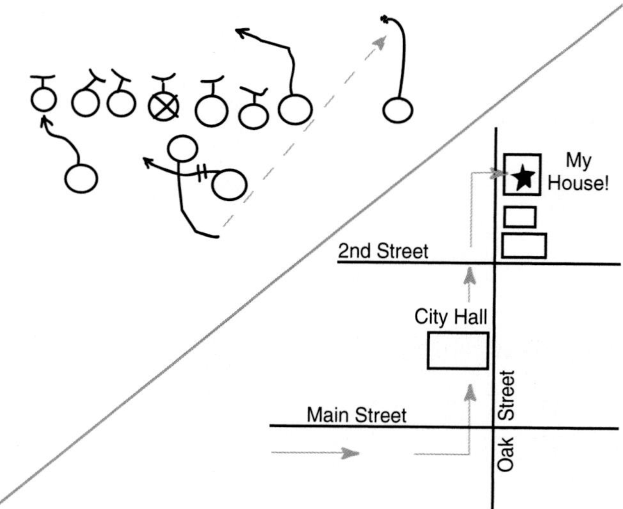

Figure 6-8. Simple sketches give meaning to many ideas and concepts.

For an architect or engineer, drawings are the basis for all communication. The design of buildings and machines are explained using technical drawings. Pictorial illustrations can help communicate ideas to the public, Figure 6-9. Simple sketches aid in the understanding of ideas and suggestions.

Figure 6-9. Pictorial views help to envision exactly what the final product will look like. Using computer-aided drafting software (CAD) it is possible to "remove" layers of the object to show how the item is built as well. (SOFTDESK, INC.)

The term ***technical graphics*** is often used to describe the work of drafters. Technical drawings are prepared with instruments and machines. The most common illustration is a standard engineering drawing or print. Other types of technical graphics are used to show assembly details or pictorial views. At times, engineering and architectural firms use computers to prepare drawings, Figure 6-10. These important systems will be covered fully in Chapter 7.

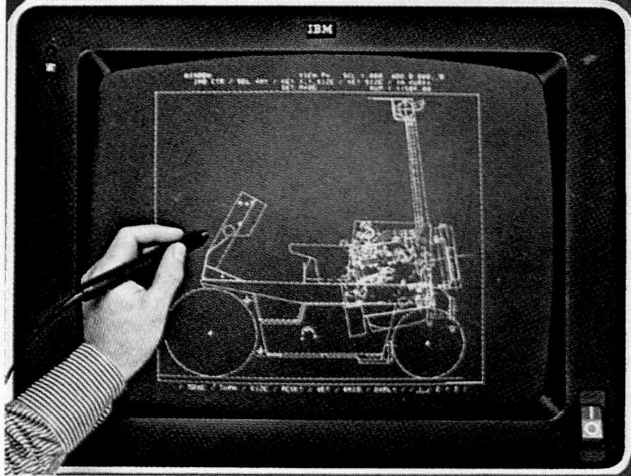

Figure 6-10. Modern computers help drafters save hours of time in completing drawings. (IBM)

Printed Graphics

Communicating with printed images ***(printed graphics)*** is the most common type of visual communication. Printed graphics appear everywhere, from T-shirts to soda cans, Figure 6-11. Words and pictures printed together transmit information very effectively. The text and pictures in this book are perfect examples. Posters, photographs, and large billboards include printed images. What other examples of printed graphics can you list?

Figure 6-11. Examples of printed graphics. (Graphic Arts Technical Foundation)

Most graphic messages require careful planning and design. The audience must be considered prior to developing the message. Creating the message involves several layout procedures, Figure 6-12. The actual printing of the messages is the final step. Printing work can be fun and rewarding, but the major purpose of graphic communication is transmitting messages to others with visual images.

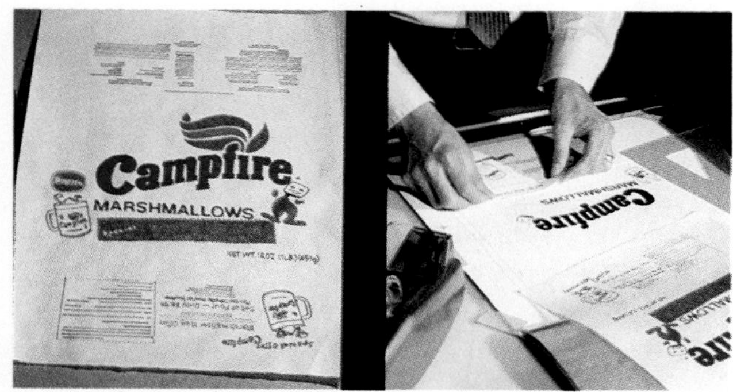

Figure 6-12. Layout artists prepare masters of printed materials. Masters are then photographed and reproduced by graphic means.

The graphic communication field also includes activities like photography and photocopying. Photography is an exciting hobby and business. Many people use pictures to record places they have been or things they have done, Figure 6-13. Other people earn incomes by taking wedding and anniversary pictures. Photocopying also represents a method of reproducing materials by graphic means, Figure 6-14.

Figure 6-13. Photography is a very popular hobby. Many people take pictures of vacations or memorable scenes. (Photo Courtesy of The Coleman Company)

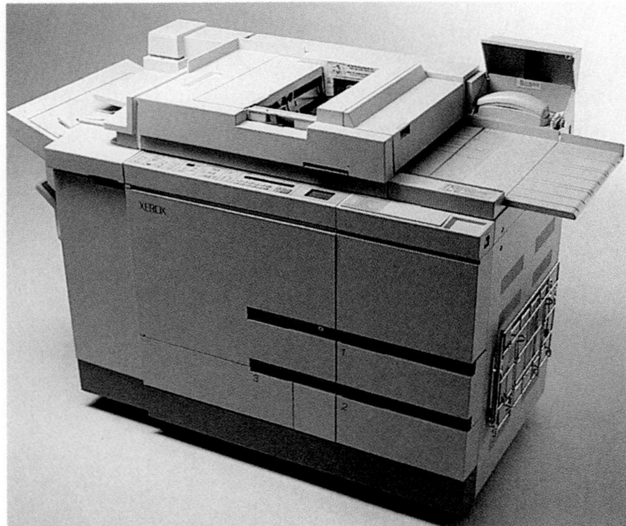

Figure 6-14. Photocopiers are useful to both schools and businesses. (Xerox Corp.)

There are seven major types of printing used today. Several of these techniques may be familiar to you. For instance, T-shirts and posters may be done by screen process printing. The handouts you receive at school may be run on ditto, mimeograph, or electrostatic copier (photocopier) machines. Books are usually printed on lithographic (or offset) presses. These and other graphic communication systems will be explained beginning with Chapter 12.

ELECTRONIC COMMUNICATION

Electronic communication represents all technical systems that involve audio and audiovisual messages. Typically, these systems are thought of as "electronic media." There are many forms of communication that rely on waves, current, or signals. You can probably think of radio and TV signals, but what about radar, computers, and stereo systems? Also consider satellites, telephones, and lasers.

Some electronic media rely on waves of acoustic (sound) energy as the communication medium. Your household stereo is a perfect example. Your receiver converts the radio waves into electrical impulses. These impulses are transmitted to the speakers. The "cones" inside the speakers then vibrate and create sound waves. These waves travel across the room to where you are and you hear the music (the music is the signal or information).

Beams (or waves) of light can also be used to exchange audio or audiovisual messages quickly and effectively. In fact, telephone calls are often transmitted by light signals. This is called fiber optics. Fiber optic systems use "pulses" of light in much the same way that electricity functions. The light is passed through flexible glass "wires," called fiber optic cables. A device at one end sends light pulses through the "cable." A similar device at the other end decodes the signals.

Most electronic media involves the use of electrical current and signals. Computers are electronic devices. They use current and pulses to store, retrieve, and process information. The information (signals) that computers produce may be audio, visual, or audiovisual. Video games are good examples of audiovisual communication. Often times computers use light pulses along with electrical current to make them run faster and capable of handling more data.

Modern computers are one of the biggest advances in electronic communication. When first used, computers were large, bulky objects that processed only the simplest information. Desktop

Figure 6-15. The sounds and images used in video games are made electronically. CD-ROM drives use lasers to transfer information. Much information can be stored on a single CD. (ASCII Entertainment Software, Inc.)

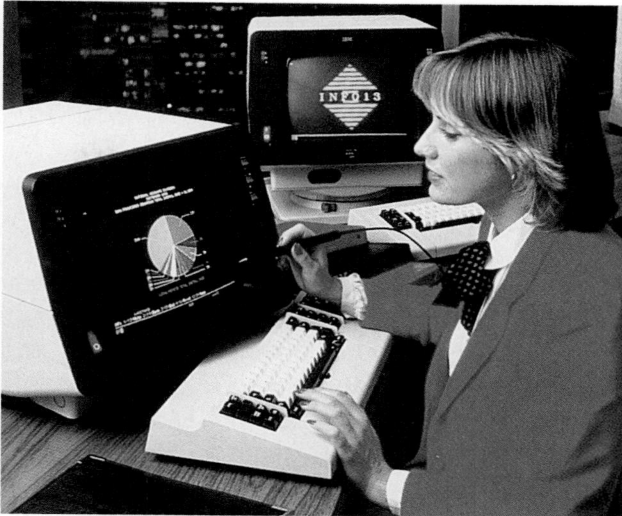

Figure 6-16. Desktop computers (top) and laptop computers (bottom) help people communicate by storing and transferring large amounts of information. (IBM, Identity)

and laptop models now available are powerful aids in communicating information, Figure 6-16. They can plan budgets, help write letters, or receive the latest information from Wall Street. More complex, business systems help complete drawings, track inventory, and make out paychecks. Electronic communication will be covered beginning in Chapter 18.

CHAPTER 6 REVIEW

SUMMARY

Communication takes place in many ways and can use all five of your senses. In most cases, however, your senses of sight and hearing are used. These senses may be used individually for audio or visual messages, or they may be used together as audiovisual communication. Audio, visual, or audiovisual communication is strengthened with the help of technical devices. Telephones, newspapers, movies, and computers are just some of the devices that aid in these types of communication.

For the remainder of this book you will study two primary technologies. Those technologies are the visual, or graphic, media and electronic media. Typically, graphic communication has two subareas—technical graphics and printed graphics. Electronic media covers many audio and audiovisual systems.

KEY WORDS

All of the following words have been used in this chapter. Do you know their meaning?

- Audio communication
- Audiovisual communication
- Electronic communication
- Fiber optics
- Fiber optic cables
- Graphic communication
- Printed graphics
- Technical graphics
- Visual communication

TEST YOUR KNOWLEDGE

Write your answers on a separate sheet of paper. Please do not write in this book.

1. Over 90% of communication is done with the senses of:

   A. Taste and smell.

   B. Touch and sight.

   C. Sight and hearing.

   D. None of the above.

2. List three examples each of audio communication, visual communication, and audiovisual communication.

Matching questions: Match the definition on the left with the correct term on the right.

3. Uses information sent by waves or currents.
4. Photography and photocopying are included in this technology.
5. Used to describe the work of drafters.
6. Includes printed graphics and technical graphics.

A. Printed graphics.

B. Technical graphics.

C. Electronic communication.

D. Graphic communication.

ACTIVITIES

1. Make a list of the electronic communication devices found in your school. Cut out pictures from magazines that represent these devices and make a collage.
2. Make a poster showing how the picture and sound gets from a television station to a home TV set. Include a brief explanation of the technical systems used.
3. Write a short report on the use of computers in your school. Include information on each type of computer and what it is used for.
4. Arrange for a demonstration of the printing and copying machines used in your school (laser, photocopier, offset). Which machines produce the best copies? Why? What is each machine used for?
5. Plan a demonstration of the tools used in technical graphics. What is each tool used for? How is each tool used? Show samples of work done with the various tools.
6. Compare your list from #2 in the "TEST YOUR KNOWLEDGE" section with the lists of your classmates. How are the lists different? How are they the same?

SECTION 1 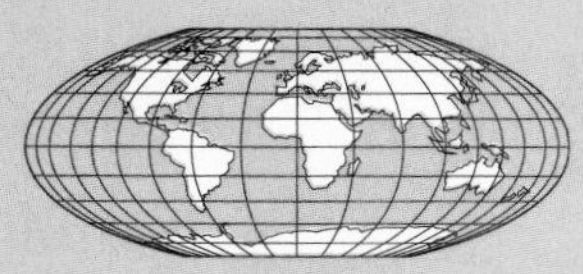 REVIEW

Section 1 Review

Communication technology is the process of transmitting information from a source to a destination using technical codes and storage systems. By using communication devices, the range of human senses is extended and communication options are increased.

The development of printed and electronic means of communication technology have extended the capabilities of humans to communicate around the globe. For communication to occur, messages must be created, coded, transmitted, and received. Messages can also be stored for later use. Communication influences individuals and societies. Communication influences can be positive, however, there are also negative aspects of communication.

Using communication techniques, businesses and industries can create many consumer products that are used to inform, entertain, educate, and persuade. As a result of the need for communication, many career possibilities have been created for members of our society. Technical communication consists of graphic or visual communication and electronic communication.

Section 1 Activities

1. Divide the class into three groups. One group will represent graphic communication, one group will represent electronic communication, and the remaining group will represent communication technology. Each group should research the area of communication that they are representing. Based on the research, each group should identify the twenty most significant technical developments for their area. The impact a development has made on society should determine the significance of the development. Each group should then make a visual illustration of a time line for the area of communication that they are representing. The time line should show the growth of communication technology as a graph.

2. Communication technology has significantly influenced your generation. Technical devices surround you in your home. These devices allow you to receive and transmit messages. How many televisions, telephones, and other communication devices does the average family own? Conduct a class discussion on the various communication devices found in your home. What types of devices are there? What

are these devices used for? How often is each device used? Also, how many people live in each house? As a class, develop a survey that will determine the answers to these questions, as well as the questions that you come up with. Pass the survey out among everybody at school.

Once all of the completed surveys have been returned, make a “master list” of the survey items. Determine the average number of people in a household, the average number of communication devices, and the average times per day that a person uses a communication device. Also, determine what other questions can be answered. Do research to determine how your school compares to national averages. Communicate with other communication technology classes across the country using a computer network. How does your school compare to their school? Write a report explaining all of your findings and submit it to your local newspaper for publication.

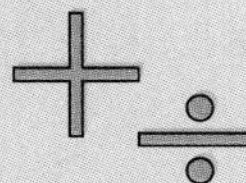  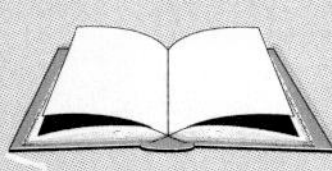

3. Establish a daily correspondence with another technology education class or with a local business involved with communication. The correspondence can be by letter, by FAX, or by computer network. Have a different student be responsible for the communication every day. The information exchange should be used to communicate the activities of your class. You should promote projects that your class is working on, local events that involve technology education or communication, and try to obtain information on similar activities elsewhere.

   Elect one student to act as an information manager. The information manager should make sure that the communication takes place every day. This person should also be responsible for writing a weekly progress report and distributing it to the rest of the class. Once a month the information manager should conduct a class discussion on the communication. After the discussion, the information manager should write a summary and submit it to the school or local paper. Also, at the end of the discussion elect another student as the information manager.

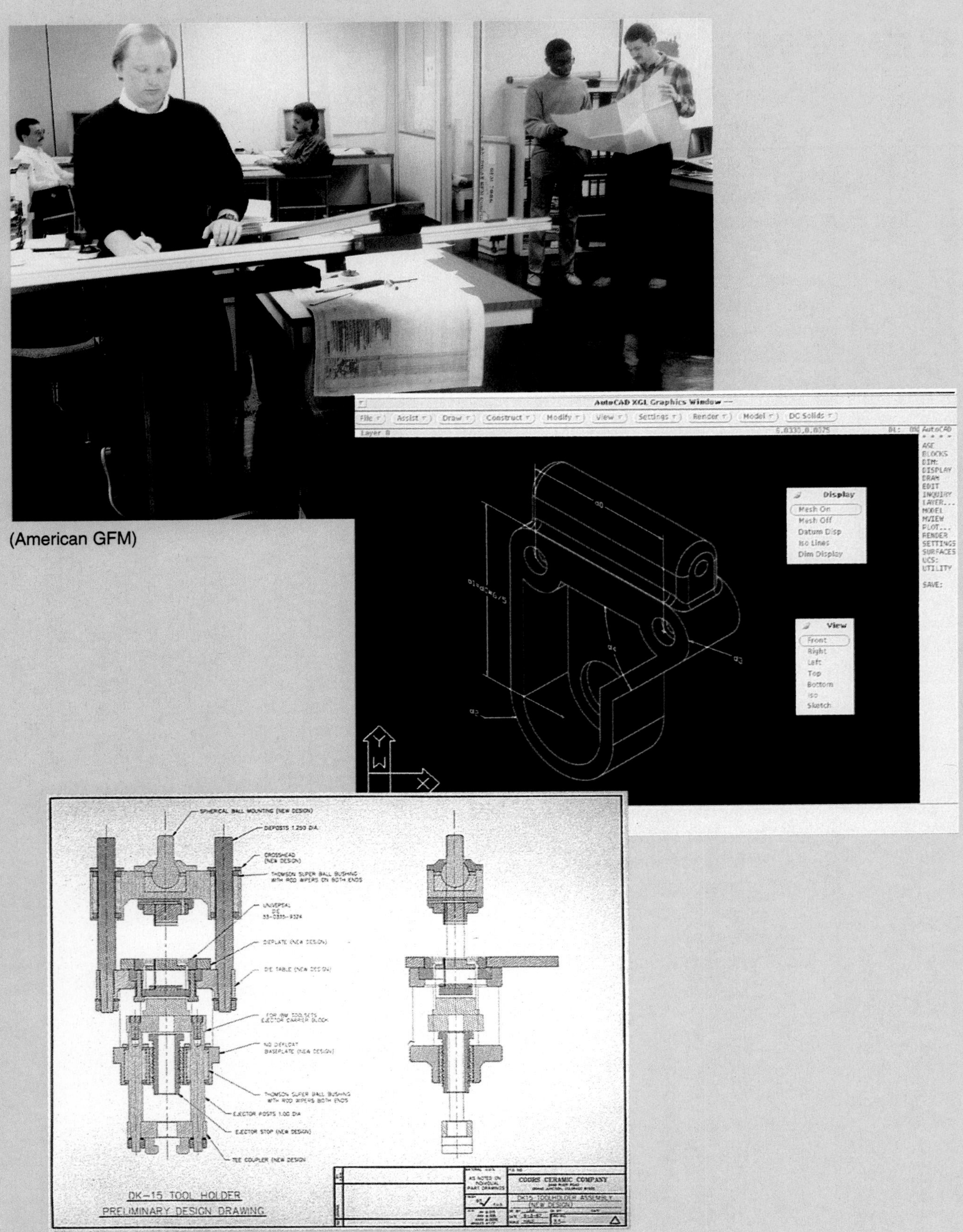

(American GFM)

SECTION 2
TECHNICAL GRAPHICS

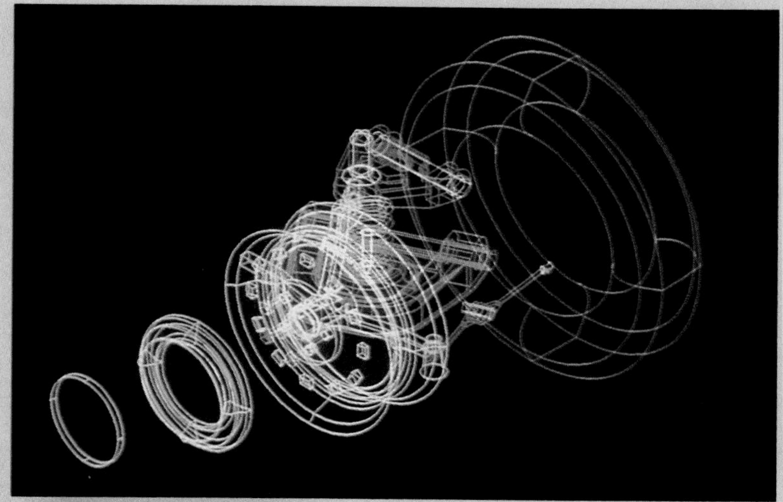

(Intergraph)

(Intel Corp)

CHAPTER 7

INTRODUCTION TO TECHNICAL GRAPHICS

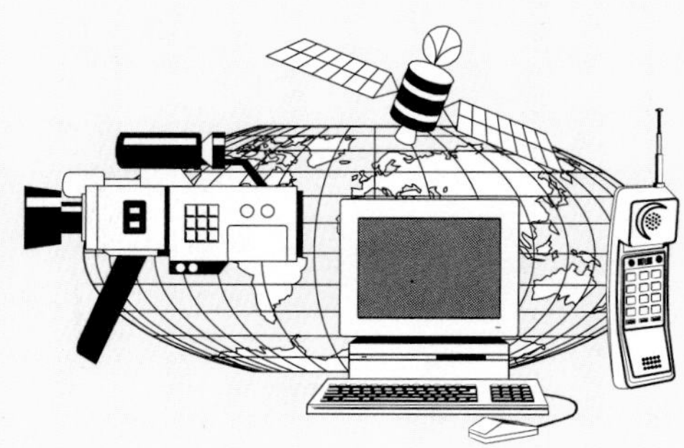

After studying this chapter, you will be able to:

- ❖ *Describe the purposes and uses of technical drawings.*
- ❖ *Identify the types of technical drawings used most often in business and industry.*
- ❖ *Discuss the development of technical graphics.*

Drawing is a common form of visual communication. It is one of the easiest and fastest ways to exchange ideas and information. Drawing is often a more effective means of communication than speaking. For example, how would you explain the shape and features of bones in the human body? A verbal description might not completely explain it. A simple drawing, however, can describe what words cannot clearly describe. With computer-aided drafting software, a person can even "remove" features of the human body to "see" inside, Figure 7-1.

Figure 7-1. Medical illustrations are useful in explaining parts of the human body. With CAD software, doctors and researchers can "remove" layers and "look" inside. (IBM)

Drafters, engineers, and architects use drawings to communicate ideas or messages. These drawings can be simple or very complex. They will include a line drawing and may also include symbols and letters to give additional information not explained by the line drawing, Figure 7-2.

Figure 7-2. Drafters can use computers to create many different types of drawings. (Hewlett-Packard Co.)

Details and concepts are also described with the help of technical drawings. ***Charts*** and ***graphs*** may provide a better view of statistics than a list of numbers. Structural features of buildings are explained on

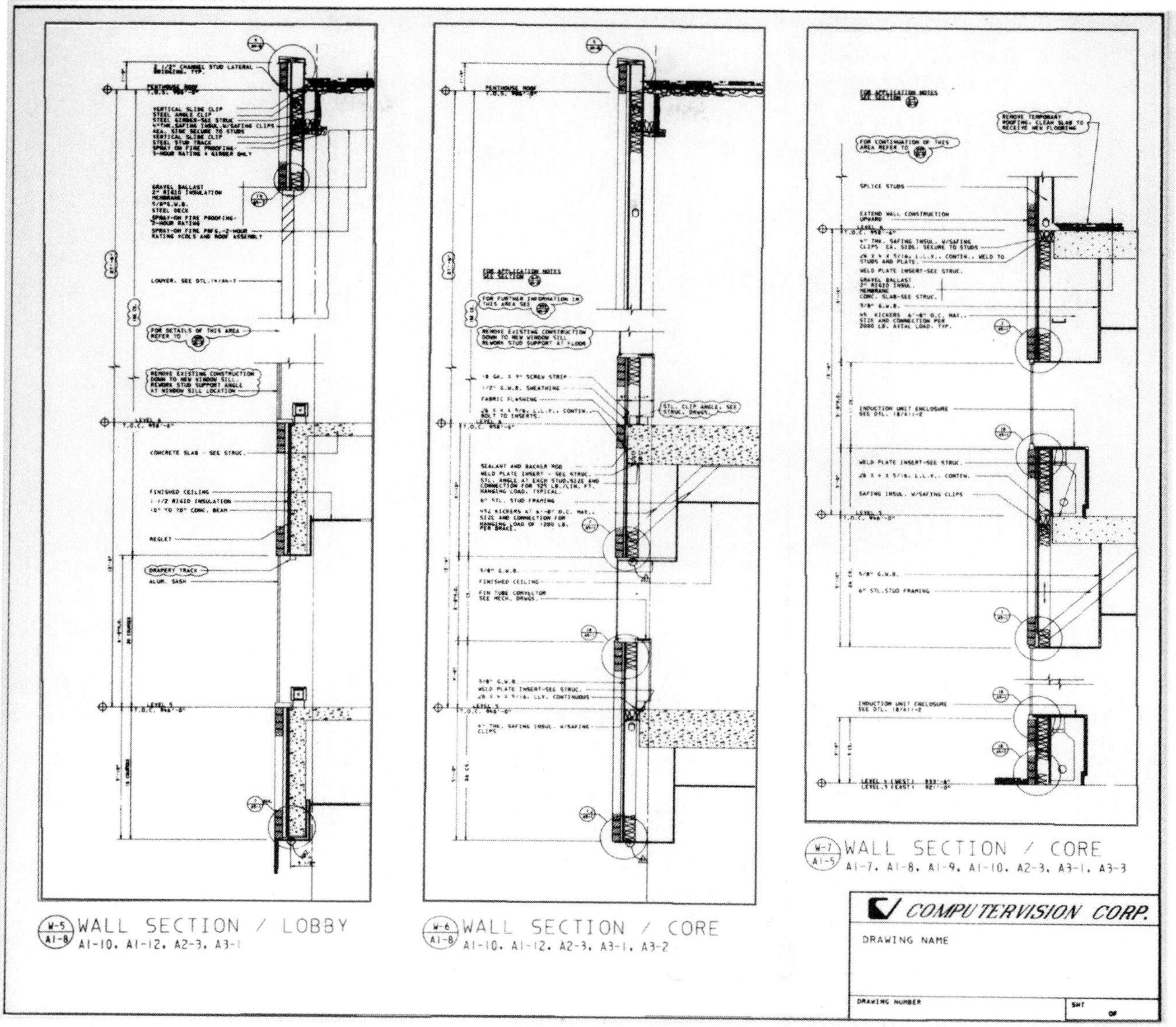

Figure 7-3. This drawing fully describes construction details for a large building. (Computervision Corp.)

architectural *drawings,* Figure 7-3. Products that are manufactured from several parts are described on ***working drawings.***

Technical drawings are completed by drafters. They produce a variety of drawings, Figure 7-4. You may have heard them called prints, blueprints, or mechanical drawings. Blueprints are technical drawings that have been copied using a process that turns the paper blue. As cheaper and more efficient ways of copying drawings have developed, the use of blueprints has declined. However, the term "blueprint" is sometimes still used when referring to copied drawings that are not really blueprints. The term that is being used now to describe a drawing that

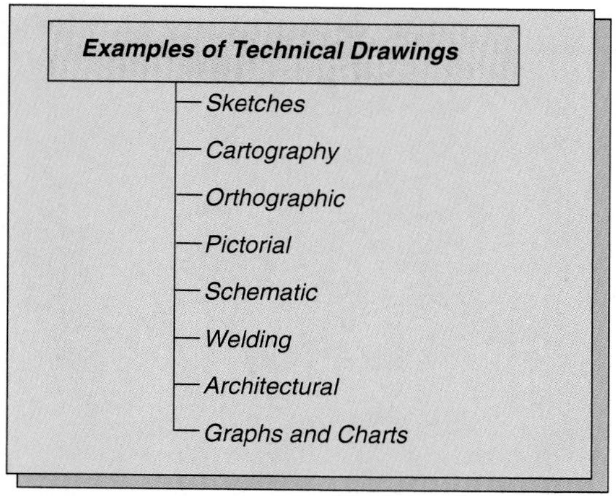

Figure 7-4. These types of technical drawings are the most commonly used.

has been copied is "print." Technical drawings are usually developed with computers or mechanical instruments, Figure 7-5. Computer systems that help drafters are called ***Computer-Aided Drafting*** systems, or ***CAD*** systems. These tools allow drafters to make finely detailed lines and symbols.

Figure 7-5. Drawings are often made by using computer equipment or drafting tools. (Hewlett-Packard Co.)

HISTORY OF TECHNICAL GRAPHICS

Long before the use of technical graphics, drawings were being used to communicate. The ancient Egyptians and other ancient cultures used drawings, called hieroglyphs, to communicate ideas, Figure 7-6.

During the Renaissance, as tools and machines advanced, people needed to know how they were built. Some people wanted to learn how to operate the new tools and machinery. Drawings of these devices became very important, Figure 7-7.

Figure 7-6. Hieroglyphics were an early way of recording information.

The Industrial Revolution during the 1800s brought new demand for drawings. Manufacturers were making machines and tools with many parts. They had to be put together and operated in a certain way. Detailed drawings of machines and tools were needed. This was the start of technical graphics. Drafters were trained to make the technical drawings that were needed.

Today, drafters are very important to many types of work, Figure 7-8. Construction workers need architectural drawings in order to do their jobs. Managers use charts and graphs to clearly understand trends. Even instructions for household appliances and new toys include illustrations of the products.

Drafters are highly trained. They must understand the subject they are working with. For instance, in order to make a roof detail the drafter must understand architecture. In addition, the drafter must know the best way to present the idea or concept. Will a north view be better than a south view? Finally, the drafter must be a creative and skillful artist. Therefore, a drafter's technical education is very important.

TYPES OF TECHNICAL SKETCHES AND DRAWINGS

There are several types of drawings in technical graphics. Some of these are described below.

Sketches

Sketches are often used to communicate ideas or details. The most basic drawing is called a ***thumbnail sketch.*** This sketch gives simple shapes with only a few lines, Figure 7-9. As more lines and details are added, the sketch begins to look more like the finished product. These improved thumbnail sketches are known as ***refined sketches.*** Professional drafters usually complete a refined sketch before completing the final drawing or artwork.

Graphs and Charts

How often have you seen information or numbers shown in chart form? A large amount of numbers are often organized into a graph or

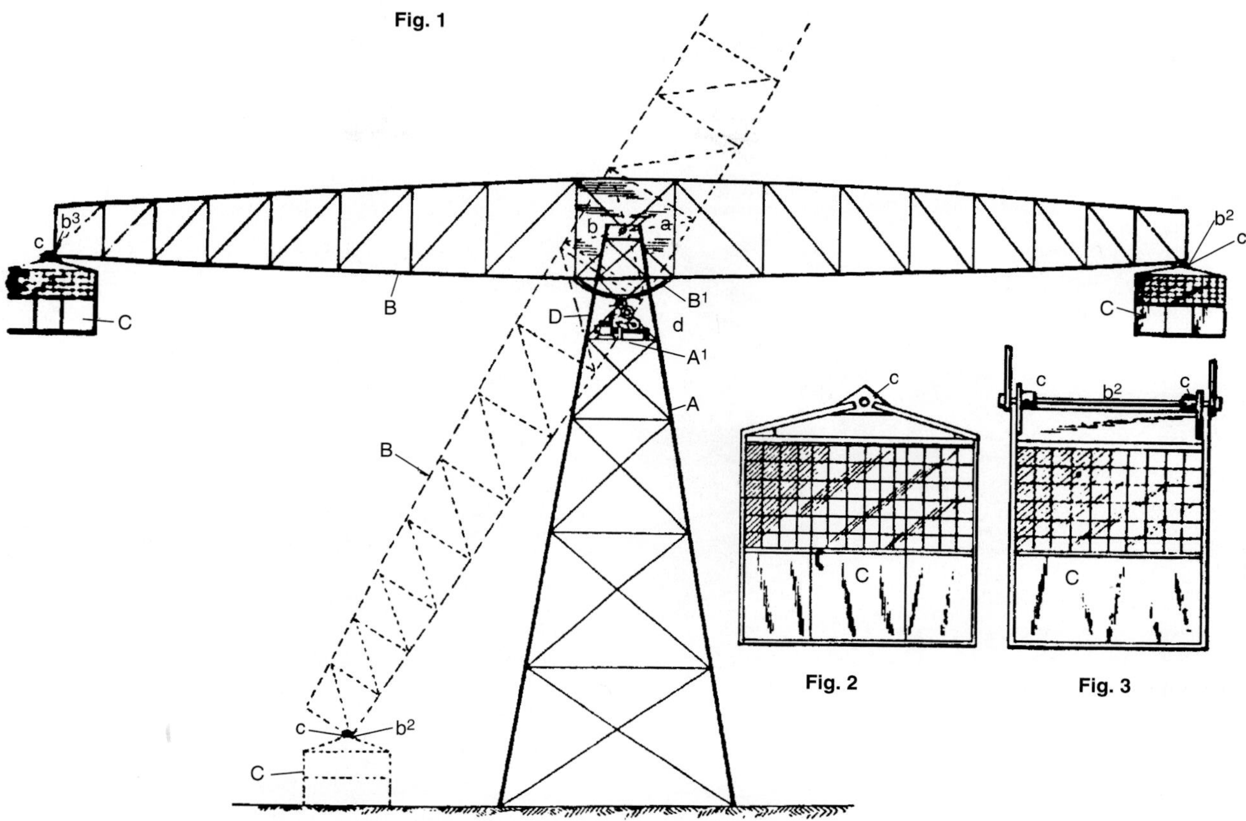

Figure 7-7. As machines became more complex and harder to operate, drawings were needed to tell people how to build and operate them. Drawings were also used to "define" a machine when a patent was granted.

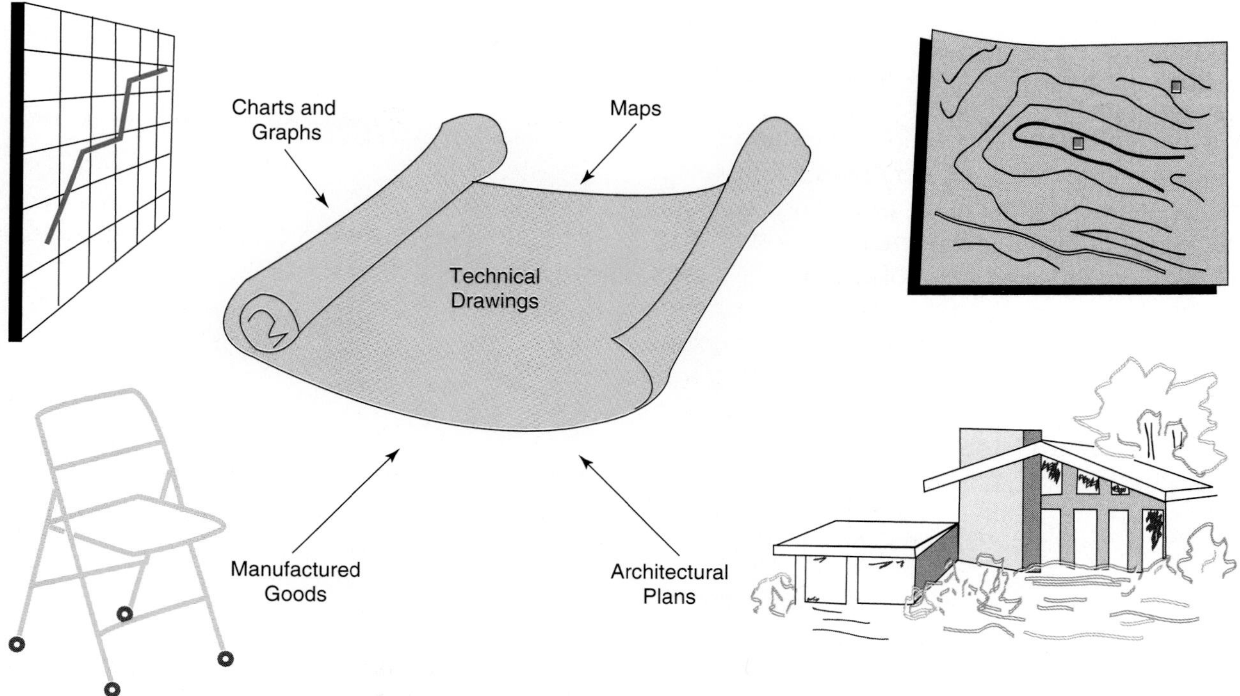

Figure 7-8. Many types of technical drawings are used in modern industries.

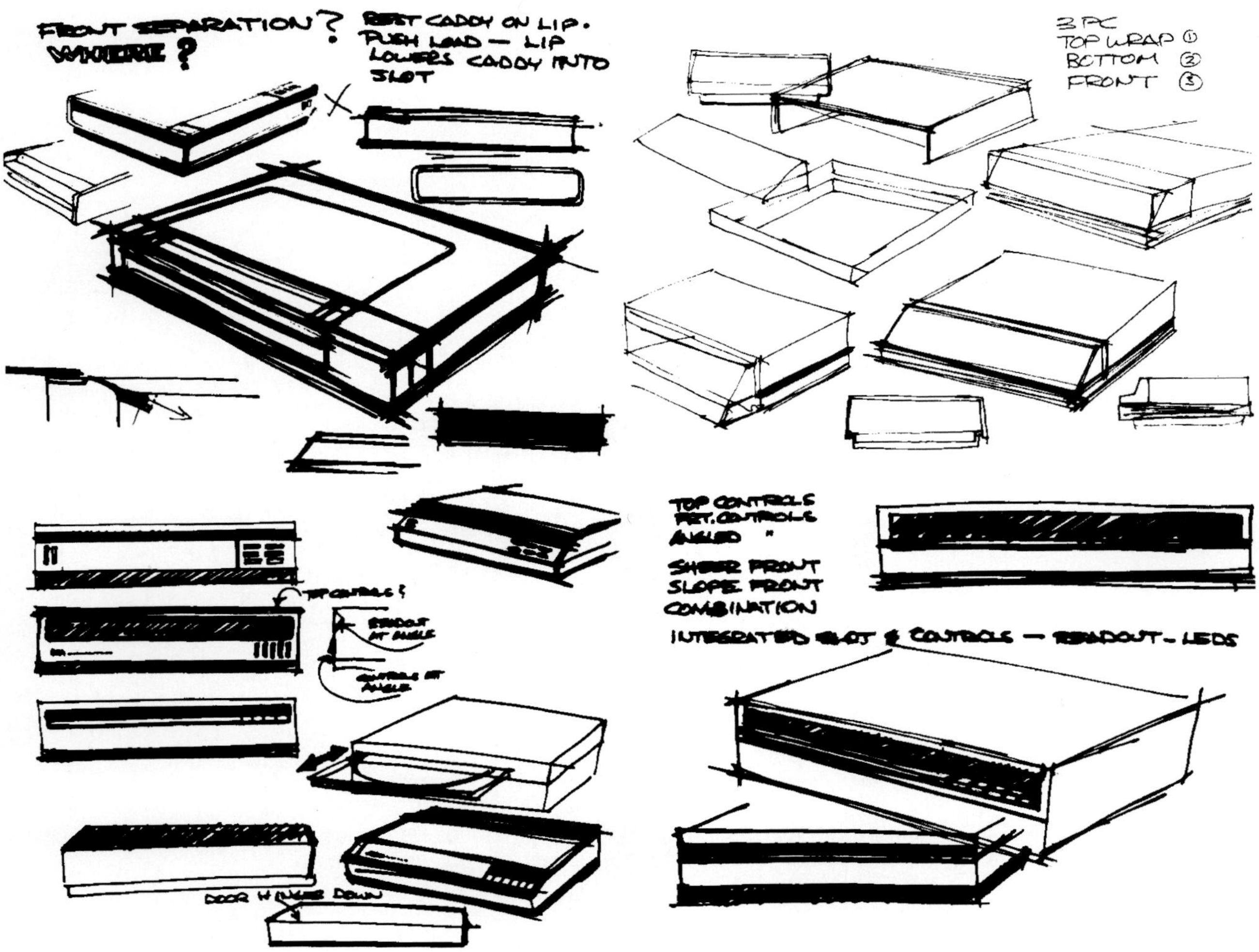

Figure 7-9. Thumbnail sketches show only the rough outline of an object. Additional ideas are often written next to the sketch. (RCA)

chart. This helps you see and understand important statistics. Graphs are very useful for explaining business trends and providing a visual representation of math formulas, Figure 7-10. There are three basic kinds of charts: bar charts, line charts, and pie charts. These three types are shown in Figure 7-11. Computers have become useful tools for generating charts and graphs since they can handle large amounts of information very quickly. Certain computer software will create charts automatically from selected data.

Figure 7-10. Bar charts, pie charts, and line charts are helpful when explaining statistics. These charts are often printed out on a computer for distribution. (Hewlett-Packard Co.)

Cartography

Many areas of land are measured for distance and elevation (height). Maps of the terrain (land) are then prepared from the measurements taken. This procedure is called ***cartography*** (map making). The people taking the measurements are called ***surveyors,*** Figure 7-12. Their sketches and measurements are given to technical drafters. The drafters who make the drawings

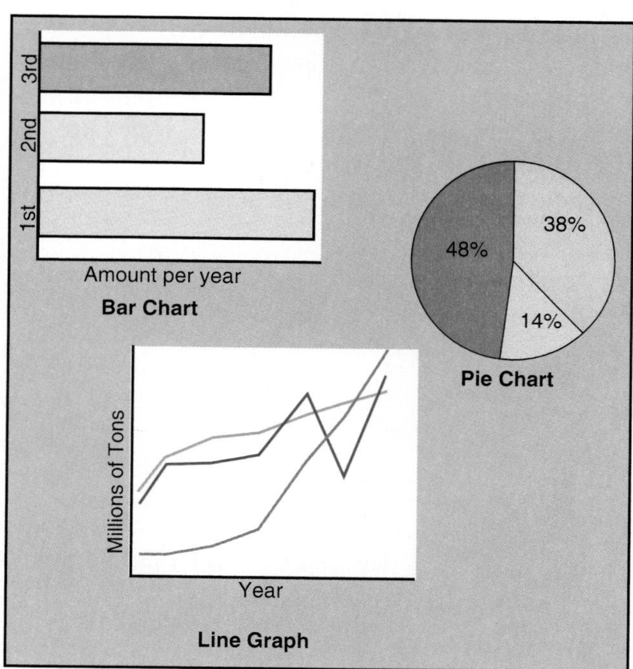

Figure 7-11. Business information is easier to understand when shown as a chart or graph.

Figure 7-12. Surveyors measure land areas for distance and elevation. Their measurements are given to drafters, who then prepare maps.

(maps) are called cartographers. The cartographers then draw a map of the land area using computers or drafting instruments, Figure 7-13.

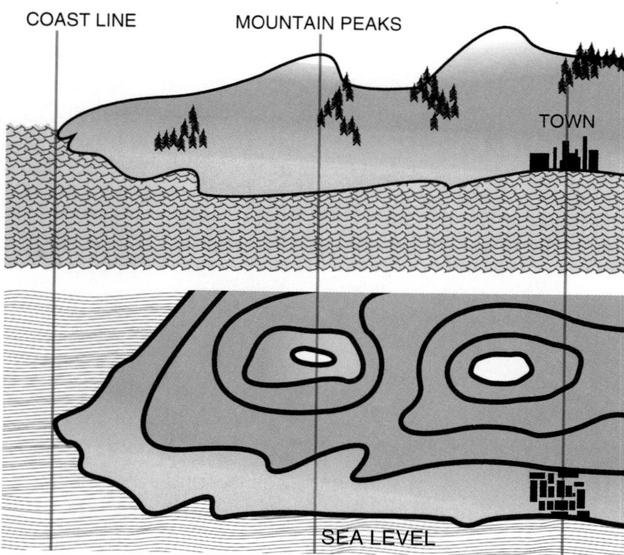

Figure 7-13. Contour maps provide a two-dimensional view of land areas.

Orthographic Drawings

The major purpose of technical drawings is to describe three-dimensional (3D) objects in two dimensions (2D). That means objects are shown on a flat surface such as a piece of paper or computer screen, Figure 7-14. In addition, most items

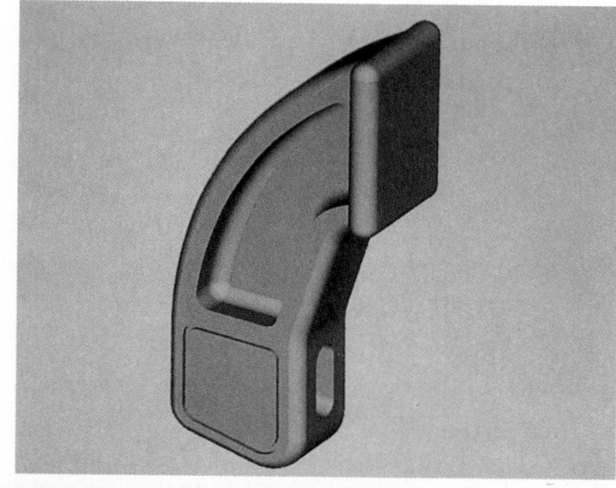

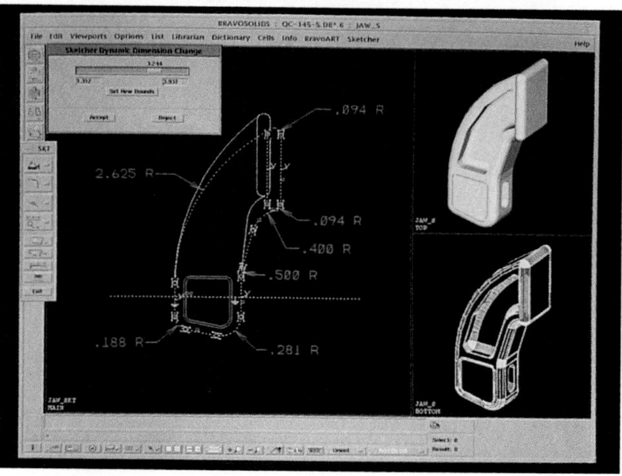

Figure 7-14. Computer monitors and paper are only two-dimensional. Therefore, a three-dimensional object (above) must be represented using more than one view (below). However, computers can create a realistic representation of the three-dimensional object in only two dimensions. (Applicon Research Inc.)

require more than one view to fully describe their features. The system of organizing these views is known as ***orthographic drawing,*** Figure 7-15.

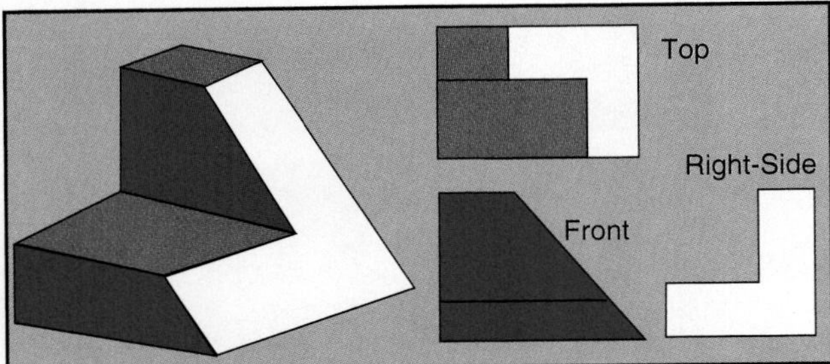

Figure 7-15. Orthographic drawings generally include a front, top, and right-side view in order to fully describe three-dimensional objects.

Normally, at least three views are needed to clearly describe any 3D object in a single plane. This allows the drafter to show the depth, width, and height of any object. A *front, top,* and *right-side* view are the primary views used in orthographic drawing, Figure 7-16.

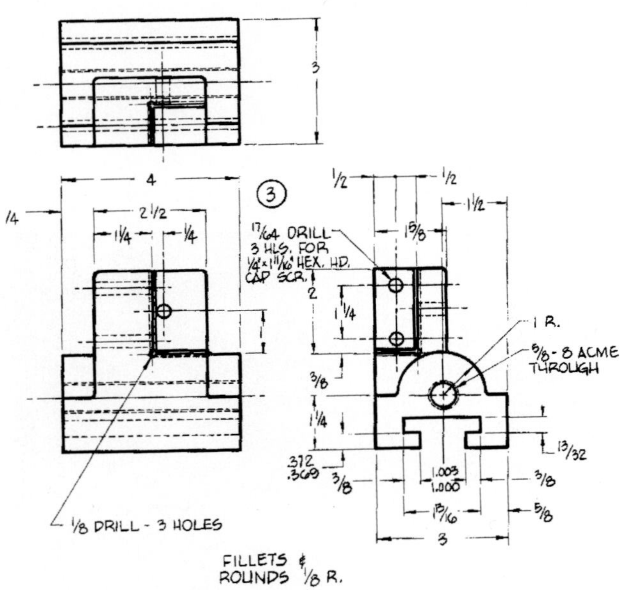

Figure 7-16. An actual orthographic drawing.

Orthographic drawings have several unique features. The most important is the ***viewing plane.*** Every orthographic drawing is developed as if you are looking at the object from a ***perpendicular viewing plane,*** Figure 7-17. In this way, all surfaces are seen as flat, even if the surface is actually curved. Viewing a drawing from a perpendicular viewing plane also means the drawing has the proper height and width but no depth. Another view (top or right-side) is required to show the depth or thickness.

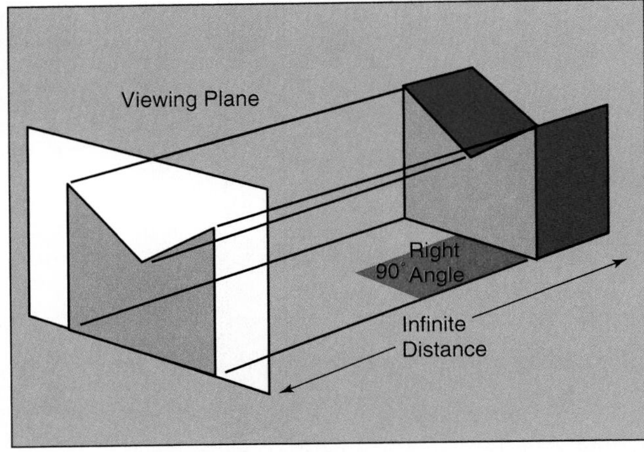

Figure 7-17. Orthographic viewing planes are perpendicular (at right angles) to each object.

Pictorial

Pictorial drawings can sometimes describe objects better than orthographic drawings. For instance, if you look at a coffee cup perpendicular to the side of the cup, you cannot see that the cup is hollow on the inside. However, a pictorial drawing can be used to describe internal features of an object, Figure 7-18.

Pictorial drawings are three-dimensional representations of an object. The term "pictorial" comes from the fact that the drawings resemble a "picture" (photograph).

Pictorial drawings have many uses in business and industry. Therefore, several types of views were developed, Figure 7-19. Some of these types are:

- Isometric.
- Oblique.
- Pictorial cutaway view.
- Rendering.
- Perspective.
- Technical illustration.

Isometric and ***oblique*** drawings are simple views. These show all of the object lines at the true proportions (same "size"), like orthographic drawings. (An exception is a type of oblique drawing called a *cabinet oblique* that has depth lines

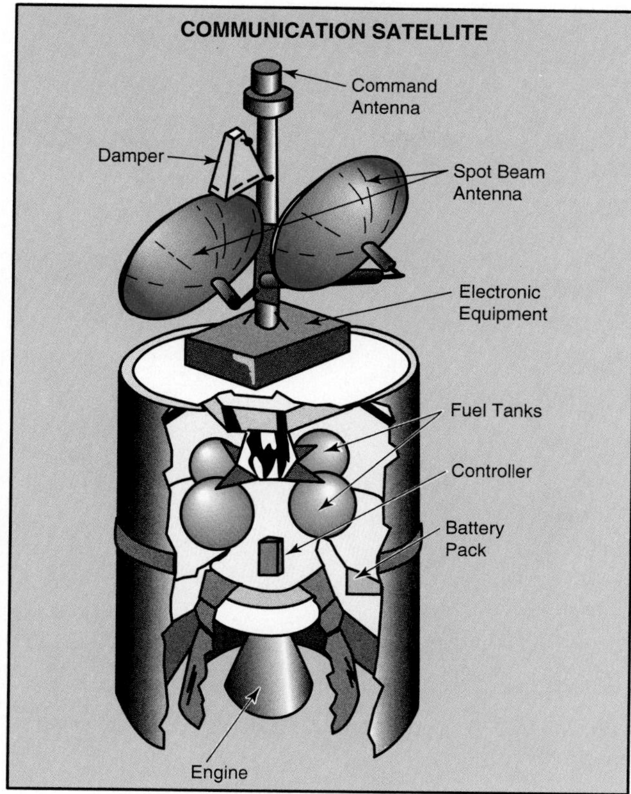

Figure 7-18. A cutaway view of a communication satellite. Drawings can be used in describing internal parts and details.

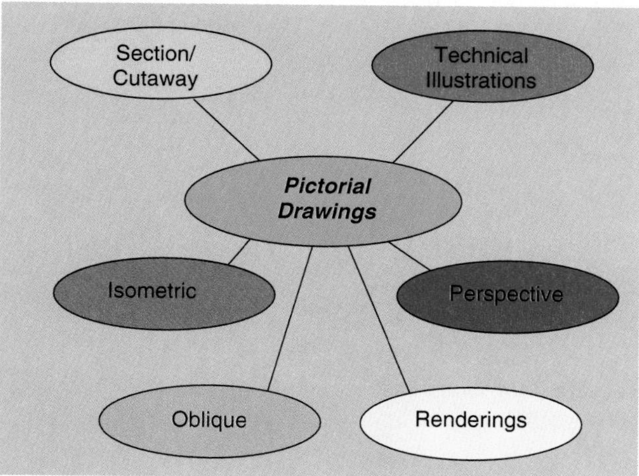

Figure 7-19. There are six types of pictorial drawings.

that are not true length.) However, all of the object lines can be seen in a single view, not in three views like orthographic drawings. In other words, they are 3D representations. Isometric and oblique drawings differ only in the viewing angle, Figure 7-20.

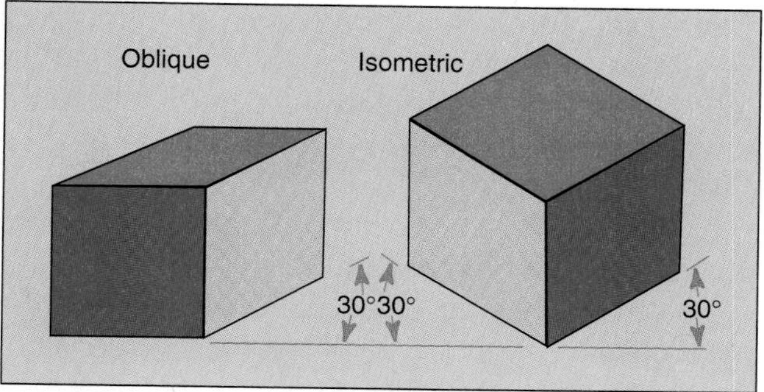

Figure 7-20. Isometric and oblique drawings differ in the viewing planes.

A pictorial ***cutaway view*** is often used in addition to an orthographic drawing. This view is a 3D representation that shows features you would not be able to see without "cutting away" the part. (Refer back to Figure 7-18 for an example of this.)

Rendering is the process of adding shading or color to a three-dimensional drawing to make it appear more realistic. Shading can also represent texture on a drawing. Methods for shading an object are shown in Figure 7-21. ***Renderings*** are drawings that have been

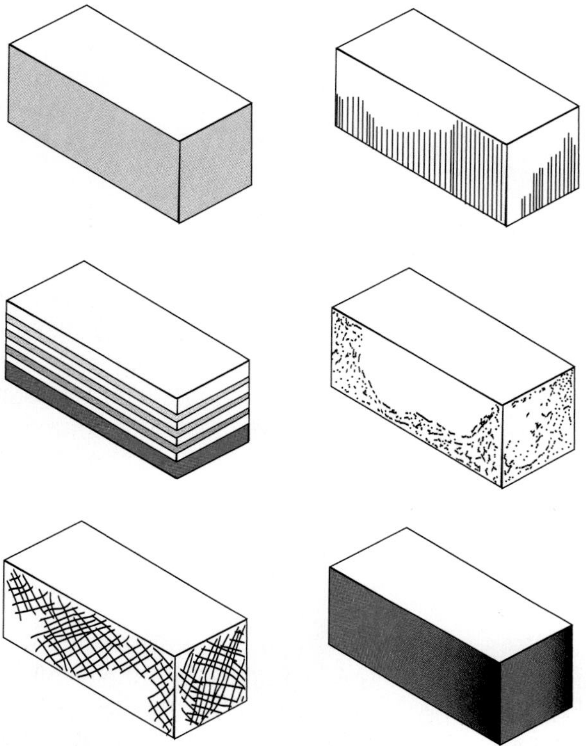

Figure 7-21. There are six methods for shading objects. Shading is especially useful in architectural renderings.

rendered. Some rendering done on computers is almost impossible to tell apart from actual photographs. (You should be careful not to be confused by *rendering* the action and *a rendering* the drawing.)

Perspective drawings show objects or scenes as they appear to the eye. For example, an architect may develop a perspective view of a new building, Figure 7-22. Perspectives may contain shading to make the drawing look more realistic or to indicate textures.

Figure 7-22. Perspective drawings provide a realistic view of large structures.

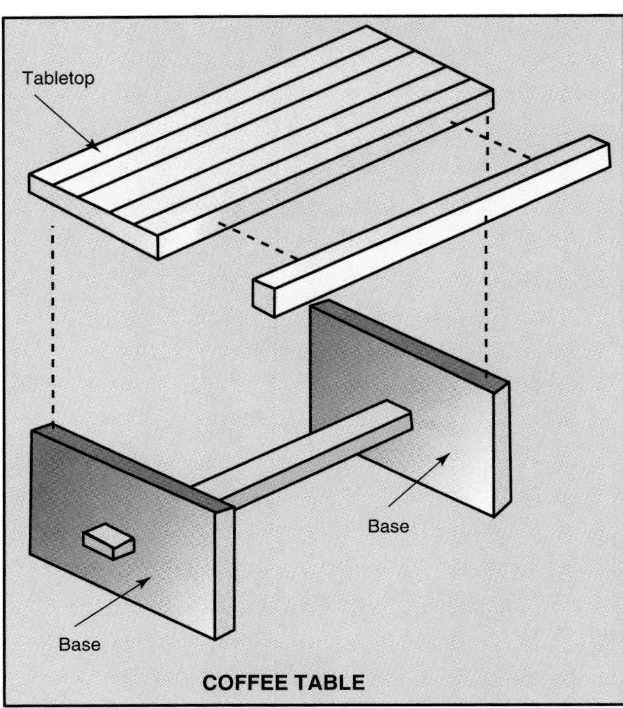

Figure 7-23. Exploded view illustrations show the way to assemble objects.

The final type of pictorial view is called a ***technical illustration.*** These drawings describe technical devices or systems. A familiar type of technical illustration is an ***exploded view,*** Figure 7-23. This type of drawing shows how all the parts of an object fit together.

Schematic Drawings

Technical drawings that show the parts of a system, how the parts are connected, and how the parts work together are called ***schematic drawings.*** Schematic drawings can be used to describe electrical, hydraulic, or pneumatic systems. The actual physical locations of the parts are not shown, only how the parts are connected together. Some electronic devices have thousands of parts, Figure 7-24. The schematic drawings of these devices may fill many pages.

Figure 7-24. Schematic views explain how the circuitry is put together but not the physical appearance. (Intel Corp.)

Welding Drawings

Welding is a popular assembly process in industry. Welding drawings serve as instructional plans for where welds are to be placed and what type of weld will be used, Figure 7-25. This form of drawing demands that the drafter understand welding procedures.

The symbols used in welding drawings are very important. Standard symbols have been developed by the American Welding Society (AWS). Drafters must be careful when using various welding symbols on drawings, Figure 7-26. Use of an improper symbol presents inaccurate instructions for the welder. This miscommunication can present a danger to the welder and others.

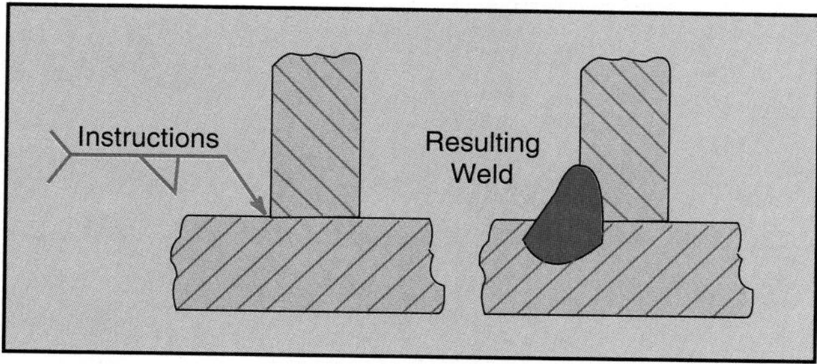

Figure 7-25. Welding drawings give instructions about where and how metal parts are to be welded.

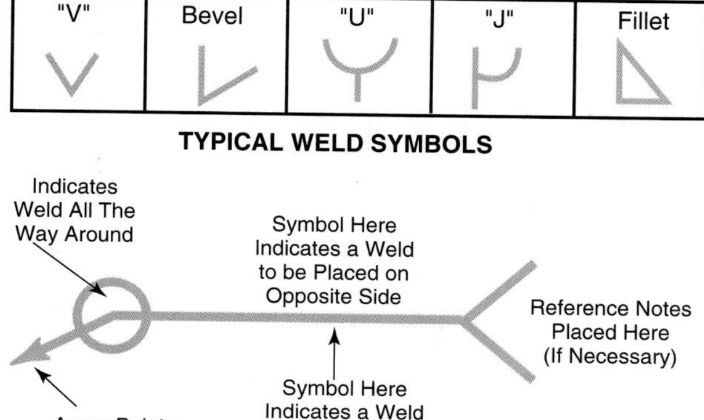

Figure 7-26. Common welding symbols

Architectural Drawings

The planning of buildings and homes is much like the planning of manufactured goods. Drafters develop detailed drawings of each part of the structure. Houses, stores, highrises, and other buildings are all designed on a computer screen or on paper before construction begins.

There are several different types of architectural drawings. The most familiar type of architectural drawing is called a floor plan, Figure 7-27. This type of drawing shows how the rooms of a house or building are arranged. Other drawings cover foundation, structural, roof, plumbing, and ventilation plans. All plans are important for showing key details and information. Complete and accurate drawings are necessary for proper construction, Figure 7-28. Technical drawings of each system are completed to describe different details. An entire set of these drawings is needed for a typical building, Figure 7-29.

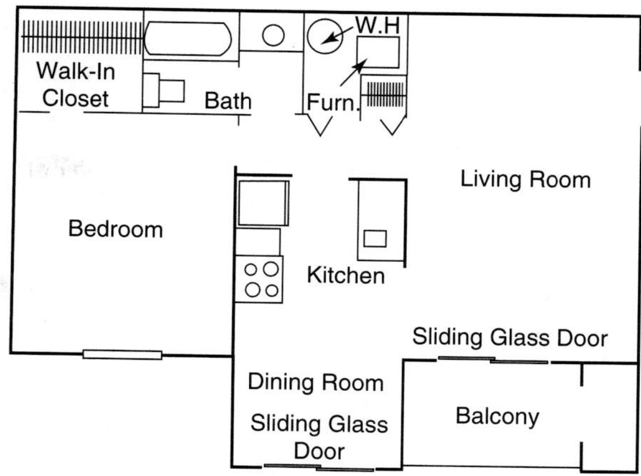

Figure 7-27. Floor plans show the layout of rooms in homes or offices.

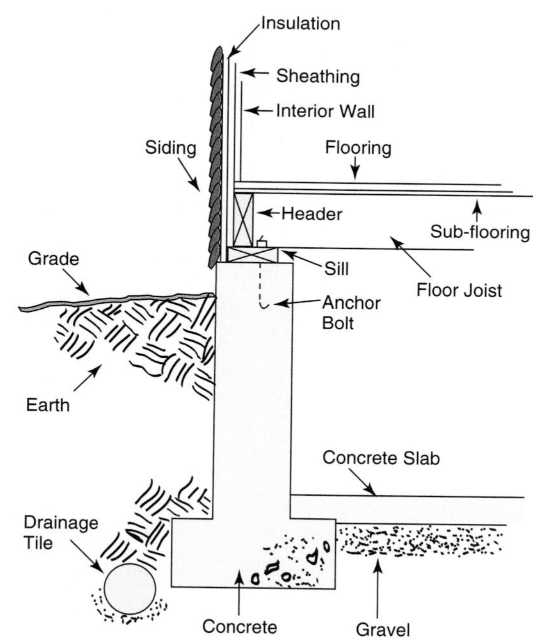

Figure 7-28. Foundation details of buildings are often shown as section views.

Figure 7-29. Every detail of a building is described in an architectural plan. (Photo Courtesy of Jack Klasey)

CHAPTER 7 REVIEW

SUMMARY

The purpose of technical graphics is to help the communication process in business and industry. Technical graphics include drawings, prints, charts, and graphs. In many cases, these graphics present ideas and objects better than a simple conversation could.

The growth of technology resulted in the need for technical graphics. Since the Industrial Revolution, technical graphics have become very important. Large, complicated machines require detailed drawings for production and use. Buildings require several drawings to explain how they will be built. Maps help you travel all around the world. The most common technical drawings are:

- Sketches.
- Graphs and charts.
- Cartography.
- Orthographic drawings.
- Pictorial drawings.
- Schematic drawings.
- Welding drawings.
- Architectural drawings.

KEY WORDS

All of the following words have been used in this chapter. Do you know their meanings?

Architectural drawing
Blueprints
Chart
Cartography
Computer-Aided Drafting (CAD)
Cutaway view
Exploded view
Isometric drawing
Mechanical Drawing
Oblique drawing
Orthographic drawing
Perpendicular viewing plane
Perspective drawing
Pictorial drawing
Refined sketch
Rendering
Renderings
Schematic drawing
Surveyors
Technical illustration
Thumbnail sketch
Viewing plane
Welding drawing

TEST YOUR KNOWLEDGE

Write your answers on a separate sheet of paper. Please do not write in this book.

1. Technical graphics use drawings to communicate:
   A. A message.
   B. Details.
   C. Concepts.
   D. All of the above.
   E. None of the above.
2. _____ are actually technical drawings that have been copied onto paper using a process that turns the paper blue.
3. Which of the following skills are needed by architectural drafters?
   A. Math skills.
   B. The ability to draw.
   C. Science skills.
   D. Understanding of technical topics.
   E. Understanding of computers.
   F. The ability to visualize a 3D object in 2D.

4. The people who take measurements for maps are called:
   A. Drafters.
   B. Architects.
   C. Surveyors.
   D. Cartographers.

Matching questions: Match the definition on the left with the correct term on the right.

5. A three-dimensional drawing that has color or shading added to make it look realistic.
6. Drawing of system components showing how they work together.
7. Mapmaking.
8. Drawing of houses or commercial buildings.
9. Sketches made with a few lines.
10. Drawing with multiple views.

A. Thumbnail.
B. Cartography.
C. Rendering.
D. Architectural.
E. Schematic.
F. Orthographic.

11. When a perpendicular viewing plane is used, drawings have the proper _____ and _____ but no depth.
12. Name three types of pictorial drawings.
13. What is the difference between rendering and a rendering?

ACTIVITIES

1. Secure the architectural drawings used for your school building. Identify each of the different drawings (plans). Report to the class how these drawings are different and how they are similar.
2. Practice shading sketches by using several of the methods presented in this chapter. Which method works the best?
3. Collect a sample of several of the drawings discussed in this chapter. What is each drawing used for? If possible, obtain a photograph of the finished product. Prepare a short report to be presented in class.
4. Develop a thumbnail sketch of a bicycle. Then refine the sketch. Finally, make a rendering of the bike.
5. Invite a surveyor to visit your class. Discuss the various maps that were made from measurements taken by the surveyor. What do the different shadings, lines, and symbols describe? Ask the surveyor about her/his job. What training or education is required?
6. Gather information from your local newspaper that would work well as a chart or graph. Use this information to design a bar chart, pie chart, line chart, or a graph. Explain your chart or graph to the class.

CHAPTER 8
TECHNICAL GRAPHICS PROCEDURES

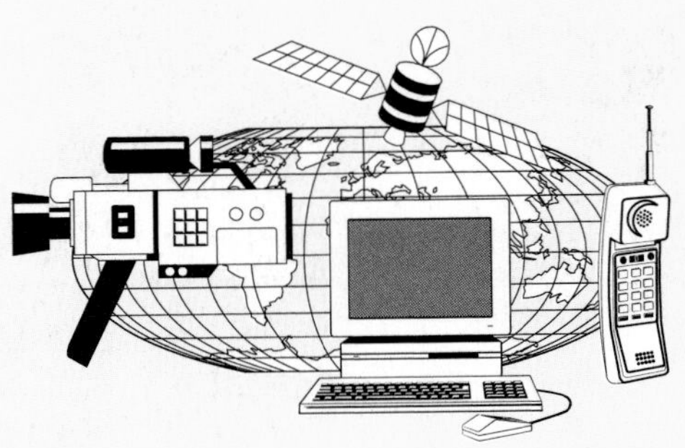

After studying this chapter, you will be able to:

- ❖ *List and explain freehand sketching techniques used in modern communication.*
- ❖ *Explain the uses of sketching in design and planning activities.*
- ❖ *Identify the tools and machines commonly used in technical graphics.*
- ❖ *Communicate with others by means of simple sketches and diagrams.*

As you learned in Chapter 7, there are many different types of technical drawings. Each type of drawing is used for a certain situation. For example, a pictorial drawing may not always be the best way to communicate an idea. A schematic drawing might better provide the information needed by a technician.

While technical drawings are different, the way they are made is basically the same. You will examine three of these procedures in this chapter. They are: freehand sketching, drawing with instruments, and computer-aided drafting, Figure 8-1.

FREEHAND SKETCHING

Technical communication starts with individuals attempting to solve problems or develop designs. While they "think through" different possibilities, many solutions come to mind. This practice is called ***visualization,*** Figure 8-2. As your plans or designs are developed, you like to communicate your thoughts. This leads to several options for exchanging information.

A simple method of exchanging ideas is talking. However, often a better method is by ***sketching*** the ideas, Figure 8-3. Simple pictures may fully explain your thoughts. If more exact details are needed, a formal drawing can be done.

Tools and Materials

Freehand sketching requires very few tools or supplies. That makes this form of communication useful in many instances. Sketches may be drawn anywhere a pencil and paper are handy. Chalk and a blackboard also work well for freehand sketching.

A.

B.

C.

Figure 8-1. Technical drawings are completed by three different means. A—Freehand. B—With instruments. C—By machine.

Figure 8-2. We try to tackle problems by visualizing possible solutions in our minds.

Figure 8-3. It is easier to describe objects with pictures than with words.

Graph paper is helpful in making simple sketches, Figure 8-4. The grid (lines) guides the drafter in keeping lines straight, parallel, or of equal length. Various types of graph paper are available in stores. One of the most popular types of graph paper for technical drafters is called ***isometric paper,*** Figure 8-5.

Sketching is done with a variety of pencils. Standard lead pencils work well for thumbnail sketches. When cleaner lines are required, a ***mechanical lead holder (pencil)*** is helpful. Lead holders are more convenient than standard pencils because the lead is replaceable and the pencil never needs sharpening. (The lead needs a "point" put on it. This is easily done with the use of a small, hand-held "lead pointer.") The lead for the pencil comes in standard widths and hardness, Figure 8-6.

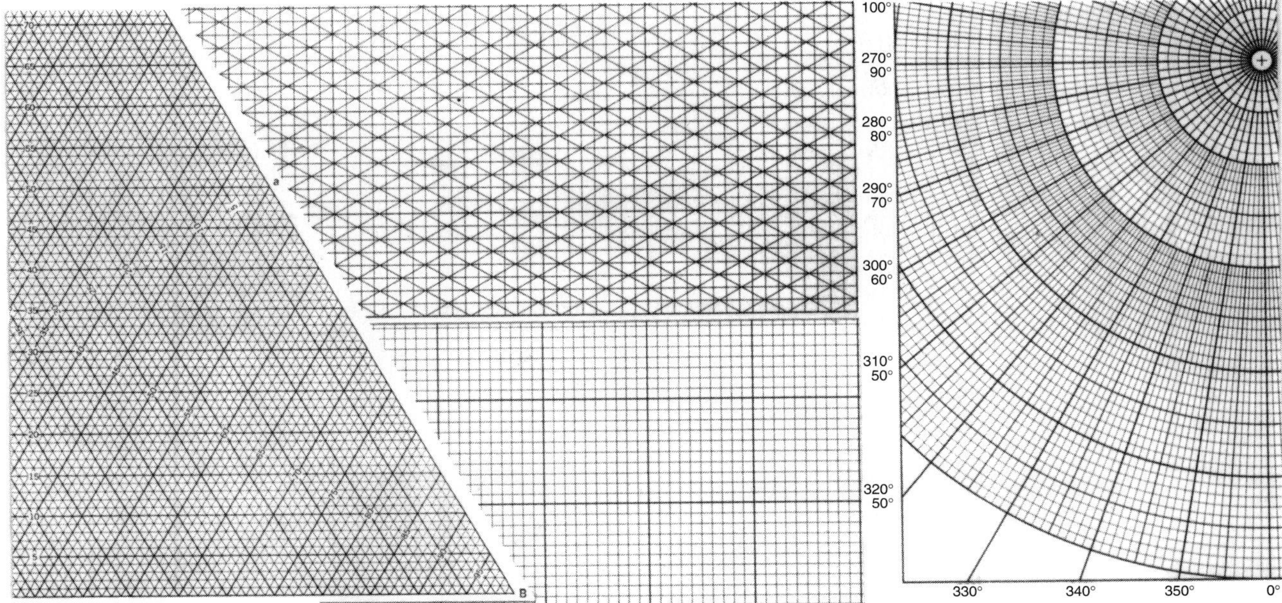

Figure 8-4. Graph paper is a valuable aid in producing freehand sketches.

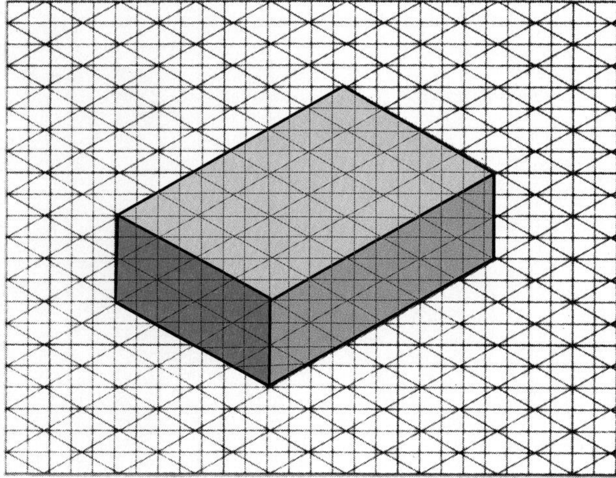

Figure 8-5. One of the many ways isometric (grid) graph paper is used.

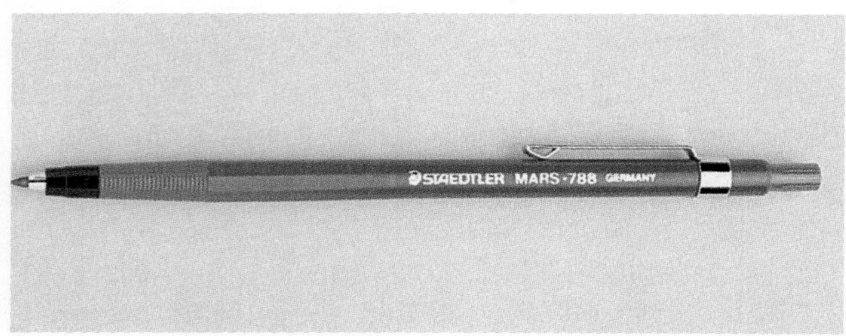

Figure 8-6. Mechanical lead holders are used to draw sharp, clean lines. (Staedtler, Inc.)

Figure 8-7. Sketching should be done in a comfortable position. (Intergraph Corp.)

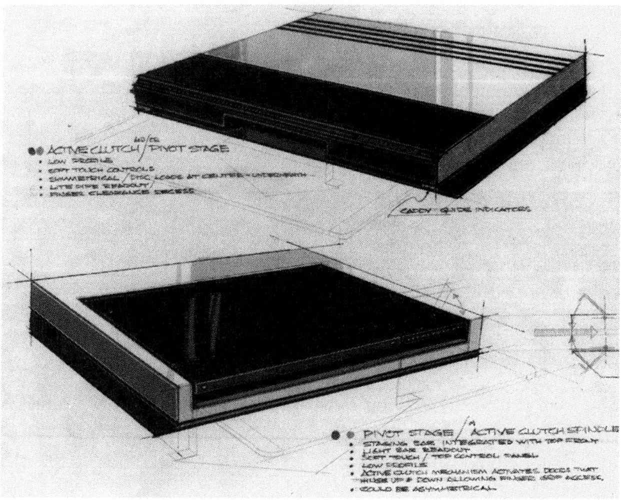

Figure 8-8. Very light lines often serve as construction lines in developing illustrations. (RCA)

Freehand Techniques

The best drawings are the result of careful and accurate sketching techniques. Placing your paper on a hard, flat, smooth surface is important. In addition, the writing surface should be at a comfortable height. All sketching work should be done in a relaxed position, Figure 8-7.

It is wise to sketch very light lines at first, Figure 8-8. Major lines are darkened as the drawing develops. With practice, simple drawings can be completed with ease.

Hand Lettering

Notes provide important information on technical sketches and drawings, Figure 8-9. Examples include labeling colors, materials, and critical dimensions. As sketches develop, the notes become more important. Thumbnail sketches may have only rough outlines and no labeling. Refined sketches are fully explained with the use of notes or other information when necessary, Figure 8-10.

DRAWING WITH INSTRUMENTS

Standard technical drawings can be made using a number of different instruments and machines, Figure 8-11. Drafting instruments allow people to create finely detailed drawings.

Drafting Instruments

Among the most commonly used instruments are the ***drafting board,*** the ***drafting machine,*** and the ***T-square,*** Figure 8-12. Other

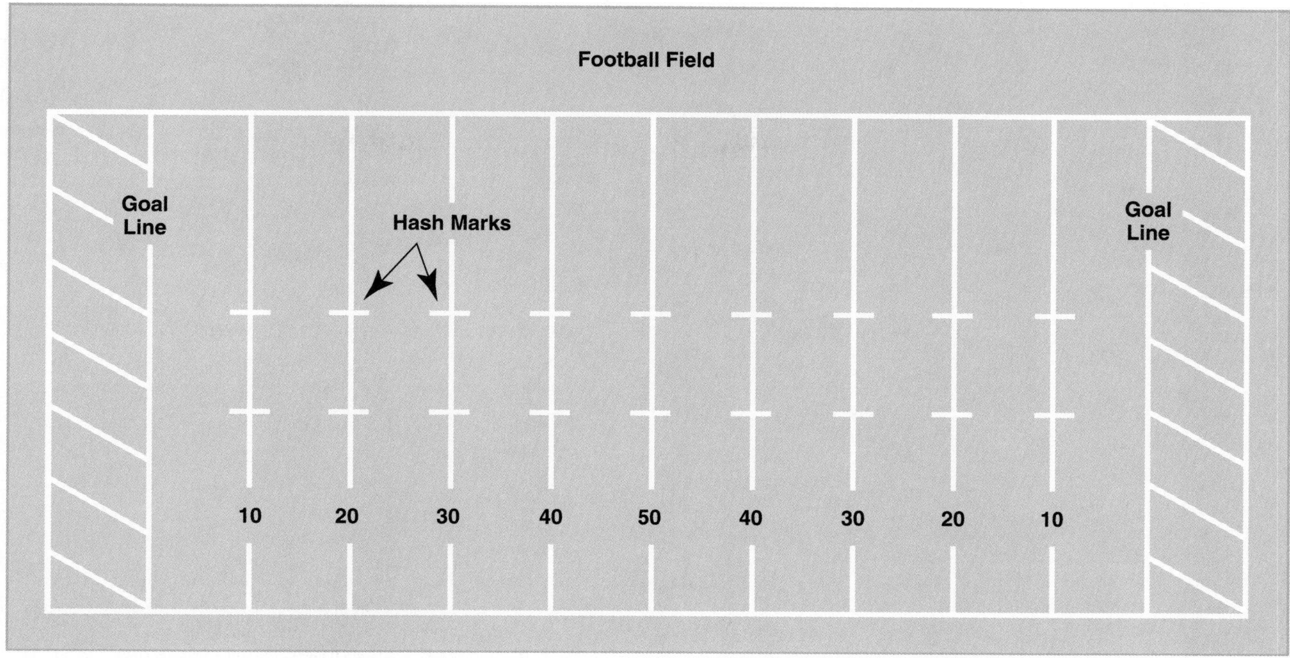

Figure 8-9. Notes and dimensions are required to fully explain most sketches.

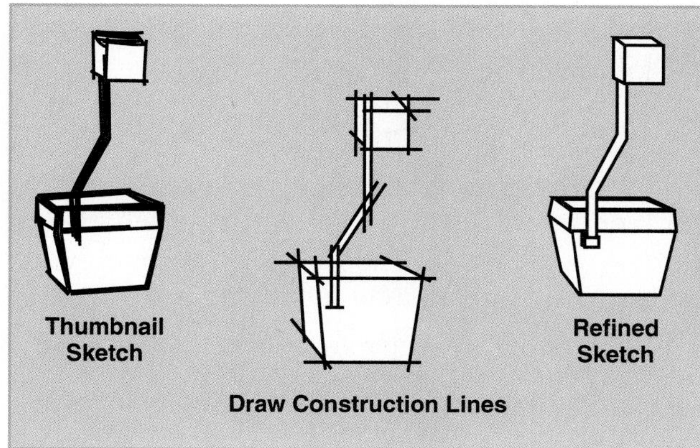

Figure 8-10. Refined sketches are usually developed from thumbnail views.

Figure 8-11. This drafter is using mechanical instruments to complete a certificate. (Letterguide, Inc.)

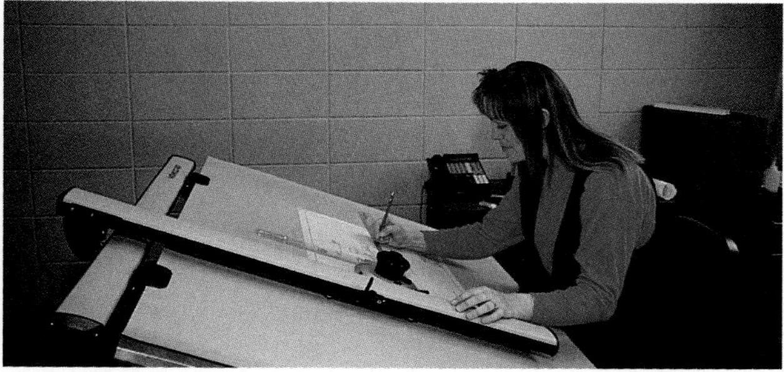

Figure 8-12. Mechanical drafters typically use a drafting table and a drafting machine.

common instruments include ***triangles*** and engineering scales ("rulers"). A list of important tools appears in Figure 8-13.

T-squares and triangles are used to draw straight lines—triangles for vertical lines and T-squares for horizontal lines. The lines may be parallel or perpendicular to each other. When circles or curved lines are required, different tools are available. ***French curves (irregular curves)*** are tools used for drawing curved lines. A compass is used to draw perfectly round circles. ***Templates*** are also used to create curves, circles, boxes, lines, and several other shapes. See Figure 8-14.

Remember that technical drawings must be prepared as neatly as possible. Therefore, typical

EQUIPMENT AND SUPPLIES FOR TECHNICAL DRAFTING

FURNITURE	INSTRUMENTS	SUPPLIES
Table	Triangles	Paper
Chair	Scale	Pencils
Drawing Board (with Machines)	T-Squares	Leads
	Lettering Guides	Eraser
	Protractor	Ink
	Pens	Tape
	Dusting Brush	Dusting Powder
	Compass	
	Eraser Shield	

Figure 8-13. Mechanical drafting equipment.

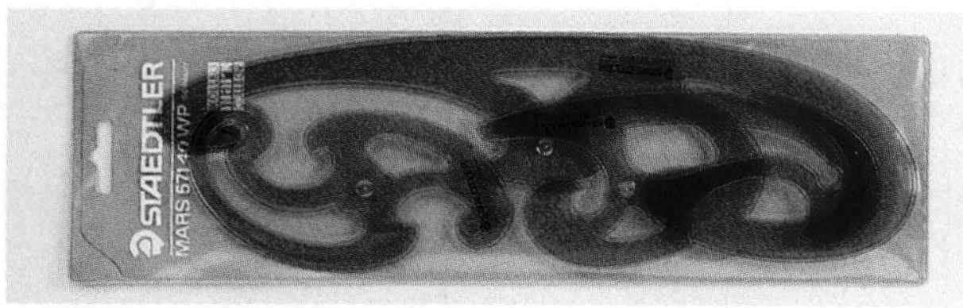

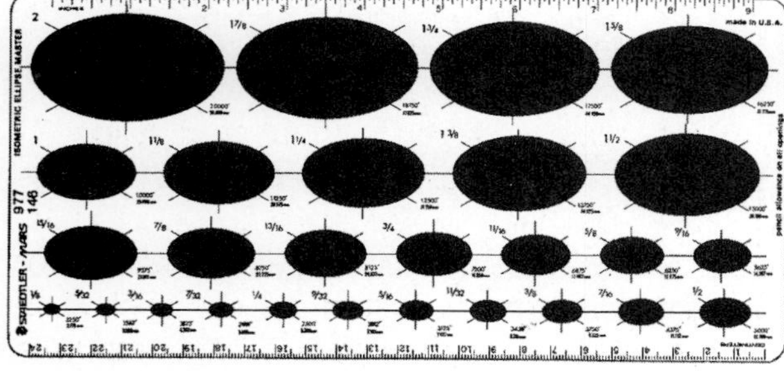

Figure 8-14. Two instruments that are useful for drawing circles or curved lines are a French or irregular curve (above) and a template (below). (Staedtler, Inc.)

equipment includes a pencil sharpener, erasers, and a dusting brush. Sharp pencils permit the drafter to draw and label each drawing in a professional manner, Figure 8-15. Erasers and dusting brushes help maintain a clean working surface.

Lettering guides are helpful in labeling technical drawings. When using a lead pencil, guidelines may be constructed with a T-square or Ames lettering guide. Special templates are useful when inking a drawing, Figure 8-16. Lettering guides help lessen the problem of smeared or smudged notes.

Figure 8-15. Electric sharpeners keep pencil leads sharp.

Figure 8-16. Neatly labeled drawings are made with the help of lettering guides. (Letterguide, Inc.)

A number of lettering styles are acceptable for technical drawings. Most lettering guides are flexible and allow drafters to produce several styles. Examples of lettering styles are shown in Figure 8-17.

Drafting Instrument Techniques

Using drafting instruments usually requires some instruction. While these instruments are not difficult to use, they do require practice. Also, it is important that the views and information on each drawing are accurate and follow industrial standards.

As with freehand sketching, it is important that the drawing surface be smooth and flat. The edges of the drafting board must be straight. This keeps the T-square aligned. A drafting machine can be used in place of a T-square, Figure 8-18.

COMPUTER-AIDED DRAFTING

Many businesses need drawings completed quickly and efficiently. Simple drawings can be completed easily by using drafting instruments.

Figure 8-17. Styles of technical lettering.

Figure 8-18. A drafting machine can be used to replace a T-square and triangles. A drafting machine attaches directly to the drafting table (VEMCO Corp.).

Figure 8-19. Computers are used in many industries to aid designers and drafters.

However, when a drawing is complex, changes are costly. Sometimes many versions of a particular design or feature are made. For each version, a new drawing must be completed. This is time consuming and costly. A tool that makes drawing complex items easier is the computer. See Figure 8-19.

The use of computers to develop drawings is known as ***computer graphics.*** A more familiar term is ***computer-aided drafting*** or ***CAD.*** (The letters CAD may also stand for computer-assisted drafting, computer-aided design, or computer-assisted design.)

There are many good reasons to use computers for drawing. They perform simple functions (like drawing) with great accuracy and speed. Information can be stored using several different means, including hard disks, floppy disks, and tapes. This means a complete drawing only needs to be done once. Changes can be made to a design quickly. Many variations of a design (similar, but slightly different designs) can be made without the need for a complete new drawing for each variation. After the drawing is complete it can be stored in the computer for future use and then printed out on paper.

The method used in computer-aided drafting are quite different from instrument drawing. T-squares and other tools are not required. No lines are drawn by hand or by drafting instruments. Instead, commands are entered on a keyboard or through the use of other input devices such as a mouse or digitizer tablet, Figure 8-20. Computers react to the instructions entered by the input device. How the computer reacts to the inputs is controlled by a ***program,*** or ***software.*** Even the simplest CAD system requires a complex program to control the computer. The program stores information about the drawing in a data file. A sample data file is shown in Figure 8-21.

Equipment

Sketching and drawing can be done on most computer systems. A common CAD system consists of the keyboard, the central processing unit (CPU), and the monitor (screen). A printer or plotter is often included. These two devices allow the drafter to transfer the drawings to paper. Also often included is a mouse and/or

Figure 8-20. Computer commands may be entered using a keyboard, mouse, or with a digitizer tablet.

a digitizer tablet to allow quicker input of information. The "equipment" of a computer is called ***hardware,*** Figure 8-22.

An important part of a CAD system is the set of instructions that the computer follows. These instructions are called a program or ***software.*** The CAD software instructs the computer to draw and keep track of objects. Many types of

Figure 8-22. Computer equipment is known as hardware. How many different examples of hardware can you see in this photo? (Intergraph Corp.)

software are available commercially. Some programs require special hardware, such as a math coprocessor or large amounts of memory, to operate correctly.

Computer programs and data files can be stored in a variety of ways. The most common storage media are magnetic disks and tapes, Figure 8-23. Media such as floptical disks (disks that use light instead of electronic means to store information) and compact disc-read only memory (CD-ROM) are now available. Completed drawings, current projects, and programs can be stored on a hard drive, floppy disks, tapes, or floptical disks.

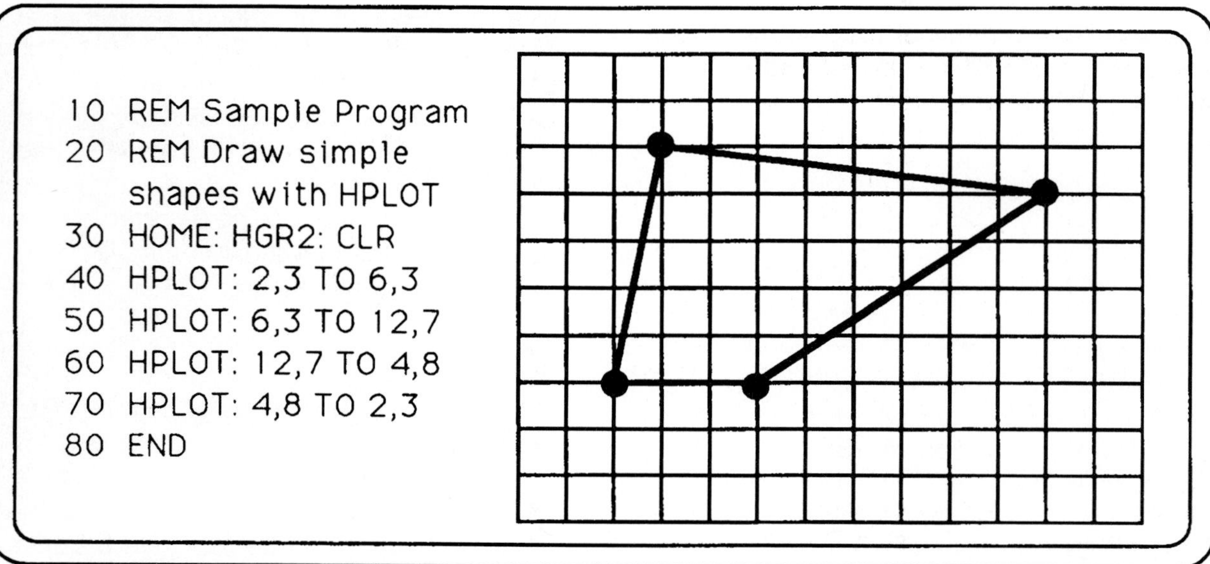

Figure 8-21. Computer programs "direct" the computer to draw lines.

Figure 8-23. Technical drawings may be stored on computer disks, optical disks, or magnetic types. (Hewlett-Packard Co.)

CAD Techniques

Computer-aided drafting hardware and software can vary from one computer system to another. Large industrial equipment allows drafters to complete very complex drawings. The computer systems found in typical schools are much smaller and easier to use. The techniques for creating drawings are different for each computer. You will now work through a typical example.

Turn the computer on. It tests itself and loads the ***operating system,*** a set of instructions that allows the computer to use other programs. The programs that complete certain tasks, such as a CAD program, are called ***applications software.*** Application software can be a word processor, a spreadsheet program, a CAD program, or a game. Each program tells the computer to work in a different way and allows the user to complete many different types of work.

When the operating system is ready, the CAD program can be started. This program instructs the computer how to draw the objects that you want to construct. A drafter will change the object (or objects) until the drawing is complete. The drawing is then saved as a data file. Each drawing has a unique filename. For example, the data file for a house may include separate filenames for each major drawing or view. Modern software offers many advantages for technical drafters. One bonus is color. Complex drawings may be developed with each part or system drawn in a different color. Another convenience is the ability to draw standard symbols easily. Some CAD software has routine symbols and figures already programmed. By pressing a single key, circles or labels are drawn automatically, Figure 8-24.

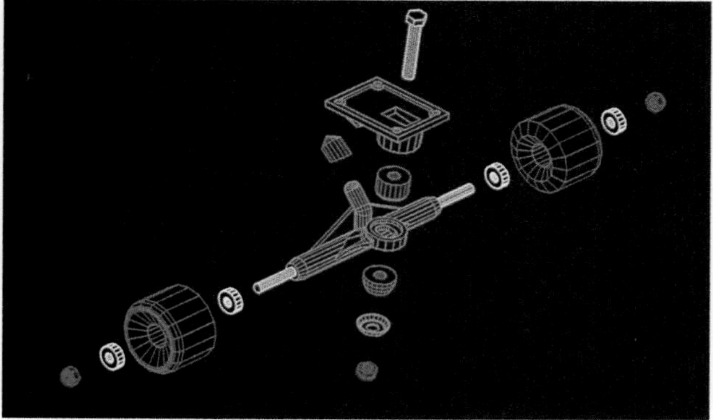

Figure 8-24. CAD software allows the drafter to call up commonly used items, like wheels, and place them directly into the drawing without having to redraw them every time.

Once the date file of the drawing is complete, the drawing can be transferred to paper immediately or stored for later use. Computer ***printers*** and ***plotters*** allow drafters to create a hard copy (copy on paper) of their drawings. These hard copies are called prints or plots, depending on the output device used to create them. Industrial printers can plot or print very complex drawings on paper in minutes, Figure 8-25.

Figure 8-25. Hard copies of technical drawings can be printed on plotters. (Hewlett-Packard Co.)

CHAPTER 8 REVIEW

SUMMARY

There are three ways to create technical drawings. They are: freehand sketching, drawing with instruments, and computer-aided drafting. Each procedure requires different levels of time and training, and different types of tools.

The first method for making technical drawings is freehand sketching. Details and notes are important in order to complete a good sketch. Very few tools are required for freehand sketching. In addition, training time is short.

The second method for producing technical drawings is drawing with instruments. Drafting boards, drafting machines, and T-squares are important tools for this method. A fair amount of instruction and practice are necessary in order to use this method.

The last method for making technical drawings is computer-aided drafting, or CAD. It has the longest training time of the three methods. Advanced schooling and technical training are necessary to be a drafter using CAD. However, CAD is by far the best and most practical way of completing technical drawings.

KEY WORDS

All the following words have been used in this chapter. Do you know their meanings?

- Applications software
- Computer-aided drafting (CAD)
- Computer graphics
- Drafting board
- Drafting machine
- French curve
- Graph paper
- Hardware
- Irregular curve
- Isometric paper
- Lettering Guides
- Mechanical lead holder
- Operating system
- Plotters
- Printers
- Sketch
- Software
- Templates
- Triangles
- T-square
- Visualization

TEST YOUR KNOWLEDGE

Write your answers on a separate sheet of paper. Please do not write in this book.

1. _____ is the practice of thinking through a problem.
2. Only _____ and _____ are needed to complete a simple sketch.
3. Which of the following is NOT a tool used in sketching?
   A. Grid paper.
   B. Mechanical lead holder (pencil).
   C. Standard pencil.
   D. Plotter.

4. CAD can stand for:
   A. Computer-aided drafting.
   B. Computer-aided design.
   C. Computer-assisted drafting.
   D. All of the above.
   E. None of the above.
5. _____ _____ prevent smudged or smeared letters from occurring.

Matching questions: Match the definition on the left with the correct term on the right.

6. Term for "equipment" used by a computer.	A. Program.
7. Used to enter commands into a computer.	B. Mouse.
8. Instructions for the computer to follow.	C. Plotter.
9. Machine used to transfer a drawing from screen to paper.	D. Hardware.

ACTIVITIES

1. Assemble a collection of mechanical drafting instruments. Display them on a table. On index cards, write a description of each tool and what the tool is used for. Display these cards next to the proper instrument.
2. Draw a picture of a cardboard box freehand and with drafting instruments. How do they differ? What might each particular drawing be used for? If possible, have the cardboard box drawn on a computer. How does this differ from the other two drawings?
3. Obtain samples of the various lettering styles. Using several of the styles, print your name and address.
4. Arrange to tour a local business that uses CAD. What does the business use it for? How many people are needed to operate this system? What is the quality of the graphics made by CAD?
5. Research the latest CAD equipment. Recent technical magazines are a good resource. Present a short report on your findings.
6. Draw a drafting board and T-square on isometric grid graph paper. Observe all the proper procedures for making a drawing with instruments.

Chapter 9
Technical Sketching and Drawing

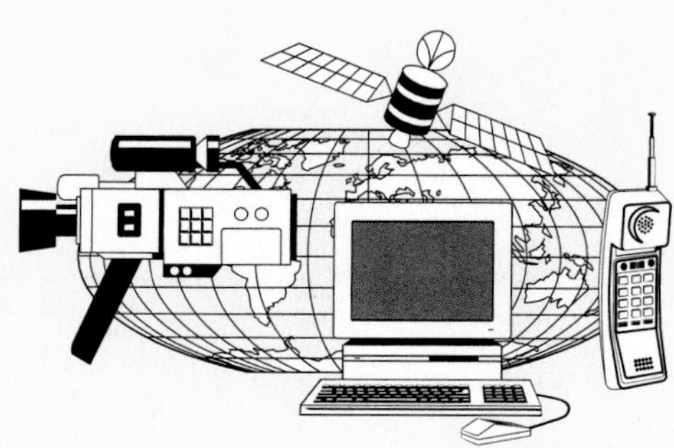

After studying this chapter, you will be able to:

- *List the purposes and uses of technical sketching in modern communication.*
- *Explain the skills necessary to prepare sketches and drawings.*
- *Produce simple illustrations and drawings using the various sketching techniques.*

Sketching is considered a common form of freehand drawing. Simple lines and figures are drawn without the aid of mechanical drafting instruments, Figure 9-1. Freehand sketches are often used as a guide for laying out technical drawings. Symbols and shapes can be drawn either by hand or computer. The processes you will look at in this chapter are basic and apply to other areas of graphic communication, not just to technical drafting.

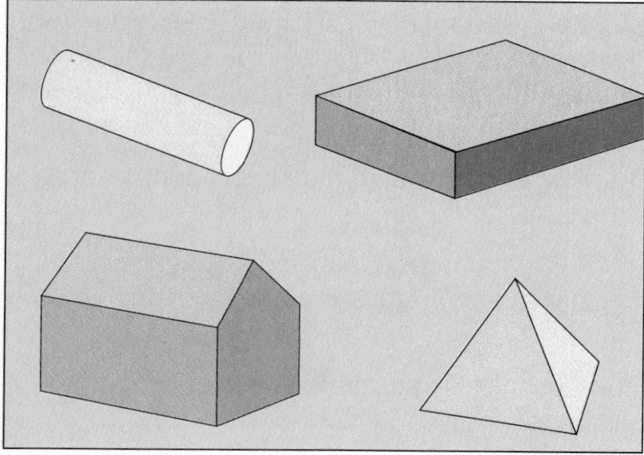

Figure 9-1. It would be very difficult to explain even basic figures without the use of sketches.

There are two basic types of sketches. These are ***two-dimensional (2D)*** and ***pictorial.*** Two-dimensional sketches only show *two* dimensions of an object, such as the height and width. Most engineering drawings are two-dimensional. A pictorial sketch includes the depth of the item, as well as the height and width. In other words, pictorial sketches are ***three-dimensional (3D).*** Examples of both types are shown in Figure 9-2.

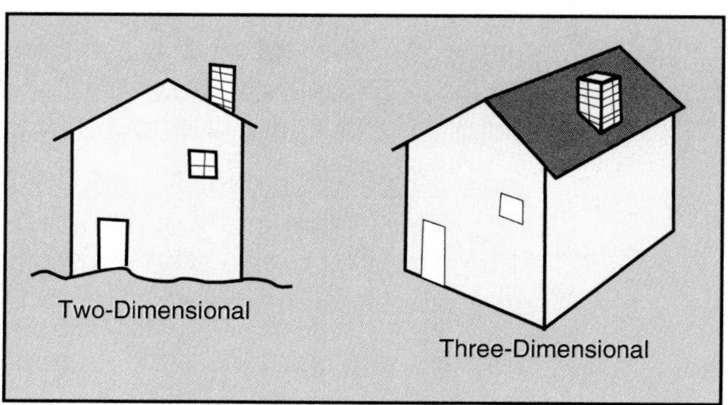

Figure 9-2. A two-dimensional view shows only *two* dimensions, like height and width. In a three-dimensional drawing, height, width and depth can all be seen.

PURPOSES AND USES

Sketches are used often as a part of daily work. How often do your teachers draw simple figures on the overhead projector or chalkboard? See Figure 9-3. These pictures communicate ideas or information. In much the same way, peo-

Figure 9-3. Math problems and hopscotch squares are types of sketches.

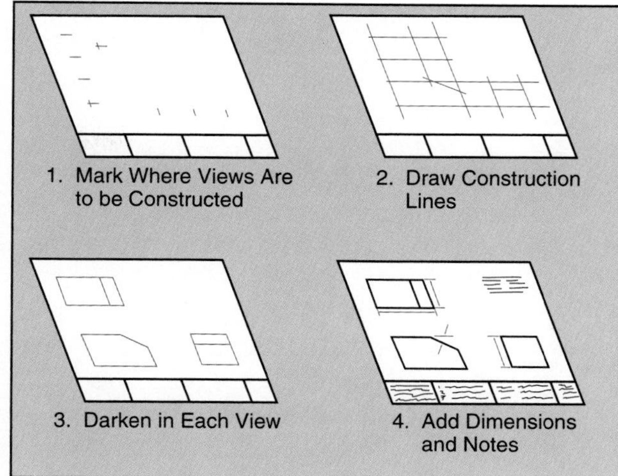

Figure 9-4. The stages of developing a mechanical drawing.

ple in industry explain details to others with sketches. They use simple drawings to explain the floor plan of a house or to show a plan for solving a problem.

Technical sketching and drawing are vital parts of many industries. Designers and drafters develop a variety of illustrations for every formal drawing they produce. Sketches are made of ideas. These sketches make it easy to evaluate possible designs. As an idea or design is improved, the sketches are refined. Careful review of these rough drawings allows many options to be considered. In addition, others may be asked to look at the preliminary sketches. Their suggestions might aid in improving or completing the design work.

Drawings of the final plans must be organized and prepared. A sketch of how the illustrations will be arranged is helpful, Figure 9-4. Light construction lines also aid in constructing the final drawings on paper.

SKETCHING TECHNIQUES

Sketching is the simplest form of visual communication. Whether you are sketching on a piece of paper, a chalkboard, or a computer screen, little equipment and supplies are required. Further, only basic skills are needed to produce simple sketches. They are outlined in the following sections.

Lines

You generally think of a line as being a fairly basic object, that there is only one kind of line and it is drawn with a ruler. This is not always the case with sketching. There are many types of lines used in graphic work, Figure 9-5. Each line has a purpose and must be used properly to avoid confusion.

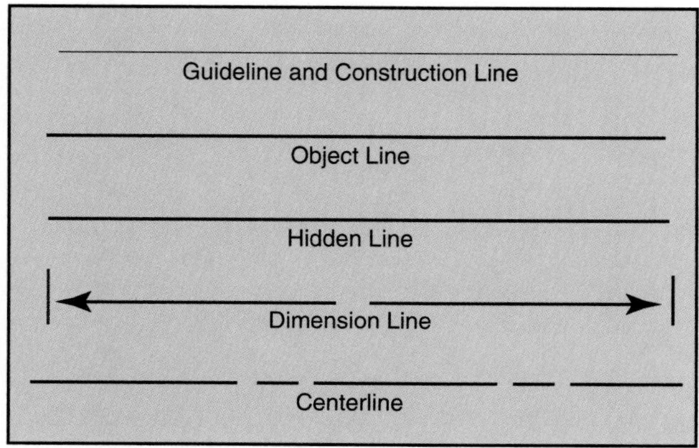

Figure 9-5. There are five types of lines used often in technical drafting.

- ***Construction lines*** are used to give a sketch its basic shape. These lines are drawn very lightly.
- ***Object lines*** are used to show the visible edges of an object. These lines are heavy and thick.

- ***Hidden lines*** are used to show edges or parts of an object that are not visible. They are drawn using a series of short dashes and spaces.
- ***Dimension lines*** are used to show the dimensions of an object. They usually have arrowheads at the ends of the lines. The distance between two points or features is indicated. Dimension lines are light and thin.
- ***Center lines*** are used to show the centers of objects. They are made up of a series of alternating long and short dashes with short spaces in between.

Sketching Lines

Generally, most of the lines used when sketching are drawn either horizontally or vertically. Sketching either of these types of lines is fairly simple, Figure 9-6.

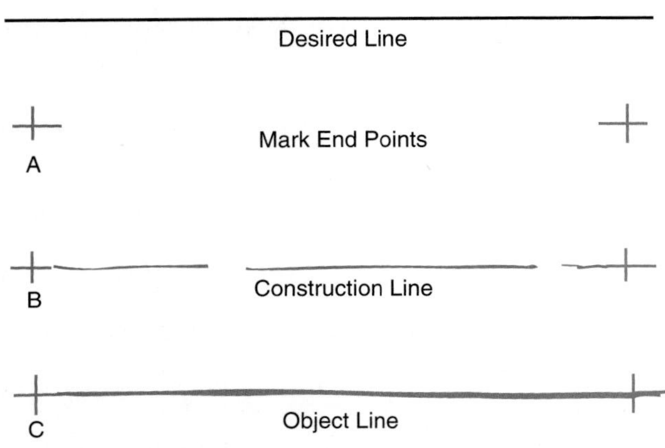

Figure 9-6. Use the following method when constructing a straight line. A—Mark off end points equal to the length of the desired line. B—Sketch construction lines. C—Sketch object line.

To sketch a ***horizontal line***, mark off two end points. The distance between these points should be equal to the length of the line you wish to draw, Figure 9-6A. In addition, the points should be located so that the line will be parallel to the top and bottom of your sheet of paper. Next, connect these points with a construction line, Figure 9-6B. Move your pencil back and forth lightly until the construction line is complete. Finally, sketch an object line over your construction line, Figure 9-6C. Move the pencil in *one* motion, from end point to end point.

Sketching a ***vertical line*** is very similar to sketching a horizontal line. Mark off two end points, making sure the distance between them is equal to the length of the line to be drawn. However, the two points should be chosen so that the line will be parallel to the right and left edges of your sheet of paper. Follow the same procedure used for horizontal lines when making the construction line and the object line.

Three-dimensional sketches also use horizontal and vertical lines. However, many times lines are drawn that are not parallel with the top and bottom or left and right sides of your paper. For example, depth lines do not run parallel to the edge of a sheet, Figure 9-7. These lines are called ***inclined lines***.

Figure 9-7. Three-dimensional sketches have many inclined lines. Can you find any others in this sketch?

Sketching inclined lines is similar to sketching horizontal or vertical lines. When marking off the two end points, place them so that the line will be at the desired angle. Connect the end points with a construction line, then sketch over the construction line with an object line.

Circles

Now that you have learned how to sketch horizontal, vertical, and inclined lines, you are ready to sketch circles and other curved surfaces. You will use horizontal and vertical lines to help you sketch a circle.

When sketching a circle, the first step is to select the spot on your paper where you want the center of the circle to be. Next, lightly sketch a horizontal line and a vertical line. These lines should cross one another at the spot you chose for the center of your circle. Next, on each line mark off a unit that is equal to the *radius* (half the distance across the circle through its center) of the circle you are drawing. When each line is marked, connect each point to the next point with curved construction lines. Finish by darkening the construction lines with object lines, Figure 9-8.

Many sketches contain details that appear circular, Figure 9-9. In most cases, it is better to draw the circular shapes first. These shapes can be used as a gauge for sketching the rest of the object.

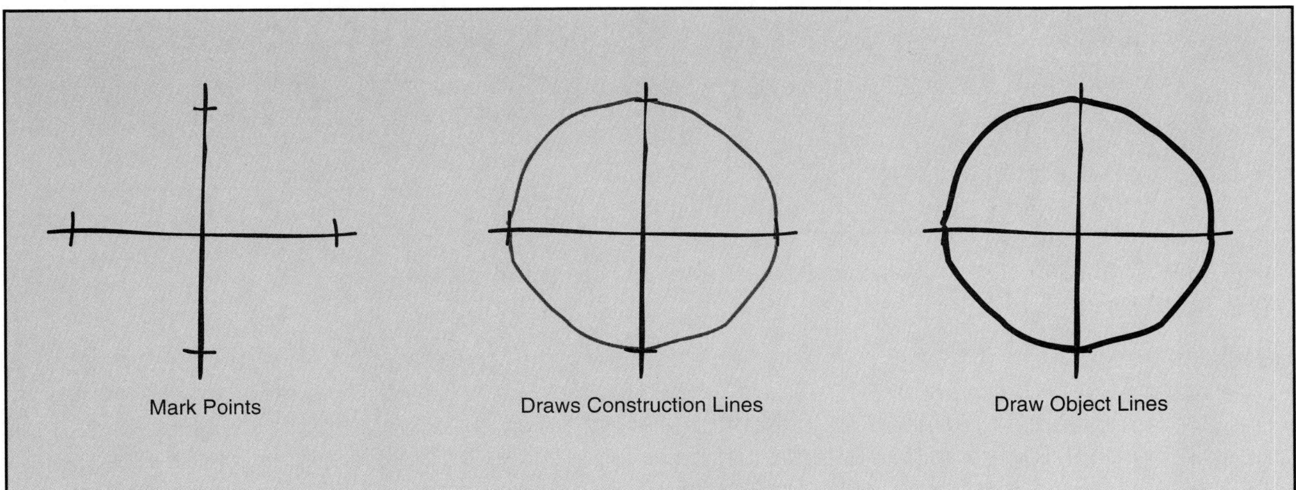

Figure 9-8. Sketching curved lines is easier with the use of construction lines.

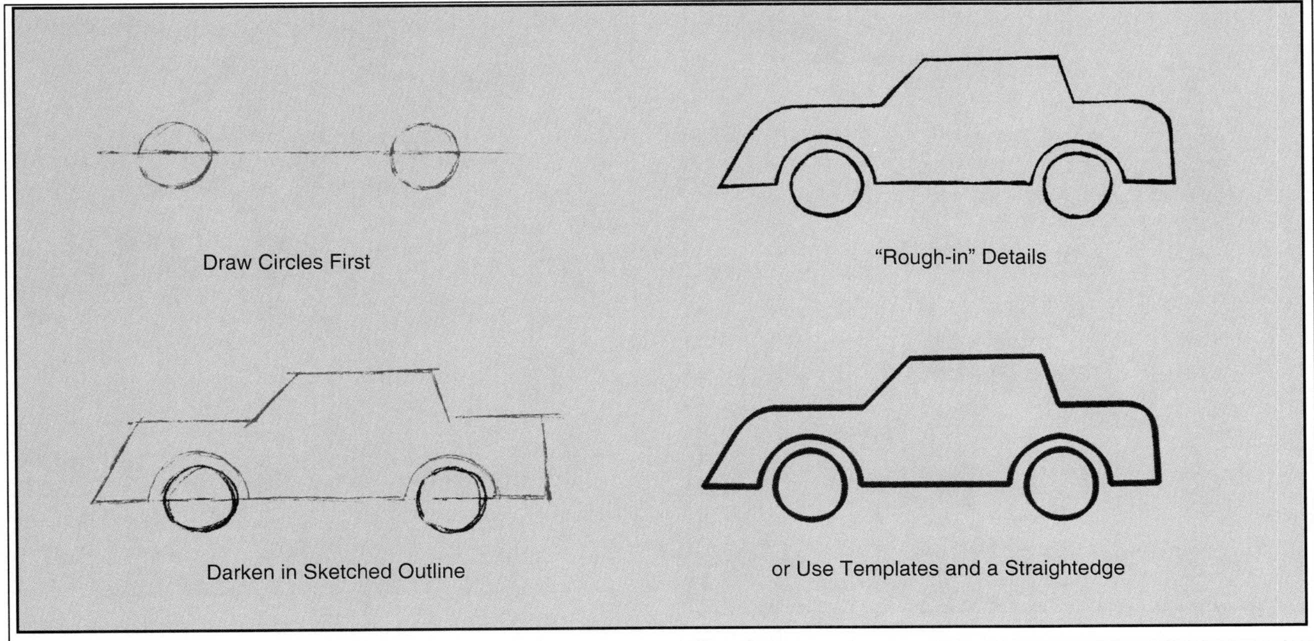

Figure 9-9. Make a sketch of a car. Sketching the tires first makes sketching the remainder of the car easier.

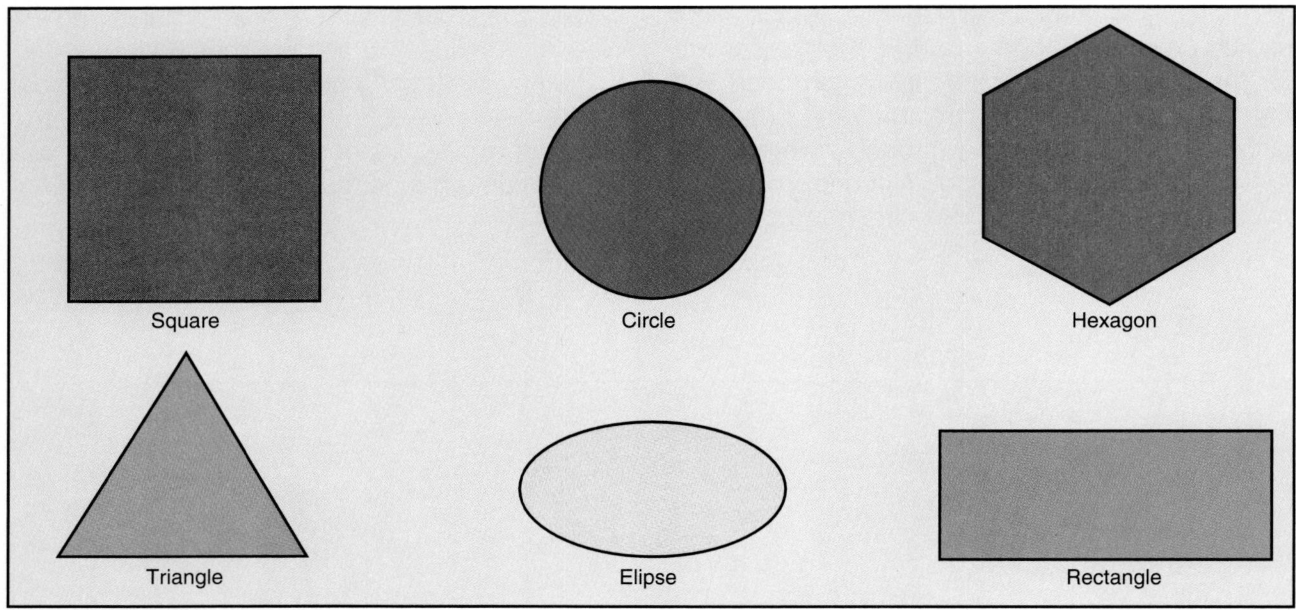

Figure 9-10. There are common geometric shapes that can be used to form detailed shapes.

Detailed Shapes

Geometric shapes are important in technical graphics, Figure 9-10. Technical drafters must be able to create these shapes quickly and easily. These basic figures are used for making more detailed shapes. Many figures are made up of standard shapes such as squares, triangles, or circles, Figure 9-11. This is important to remember when sketching detailed objects. If a basic shape can be determined, it can be used as a guide. For example, a traffic sign indicating that the road curves right is composed of several basic shapes, Figure 9-12. If you first sketch a large

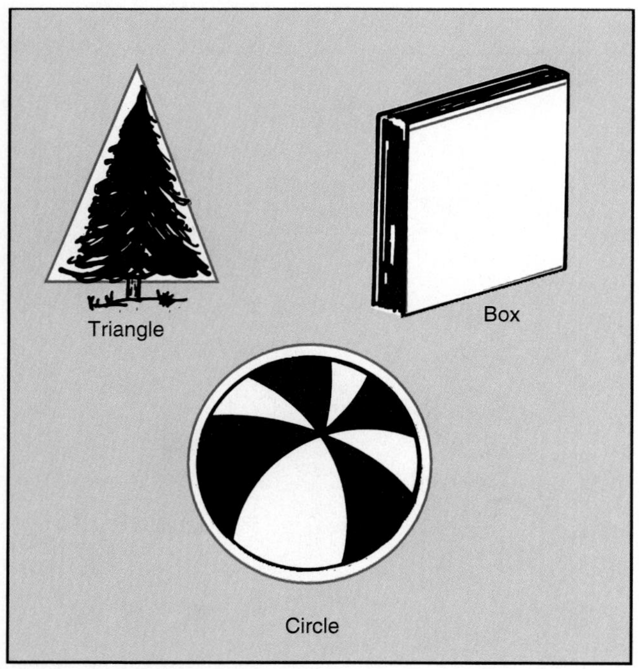

Figure 9-11. Most objects can be reduced to a few familiar shapes.

Figure 9-12. Breaking an object down into basic shapes and then sketching those shapes can make complex objects easy to draw.

square, you can then sketch the curved arrow. Sketching the arrow is easier if you can break it down into different geometric parts.

Architects often plan buildings by sketching how the structure will look upon completion. They use standard shapes to lay out the overall design, Figure 9-13. You may have noticed that the overall shape of most buildings is made up of several standard geometric shapes.

Proportion in Sketching

Drawings are often enlarged (made bigger) or reduced (made smaller) to fit the needs of the person using them. For instance, a particular detail might be easier to read if drawn on a larger scale (or proportion), Figure 9-14.

Changing the scale of a sketch requires an understanding of the term ***proportion.*** Objects

Figure 9-13. The design of a building is the result of combining simple shapes. How many simple shapes can you identify in the design of this house? (G.E. Plastics)

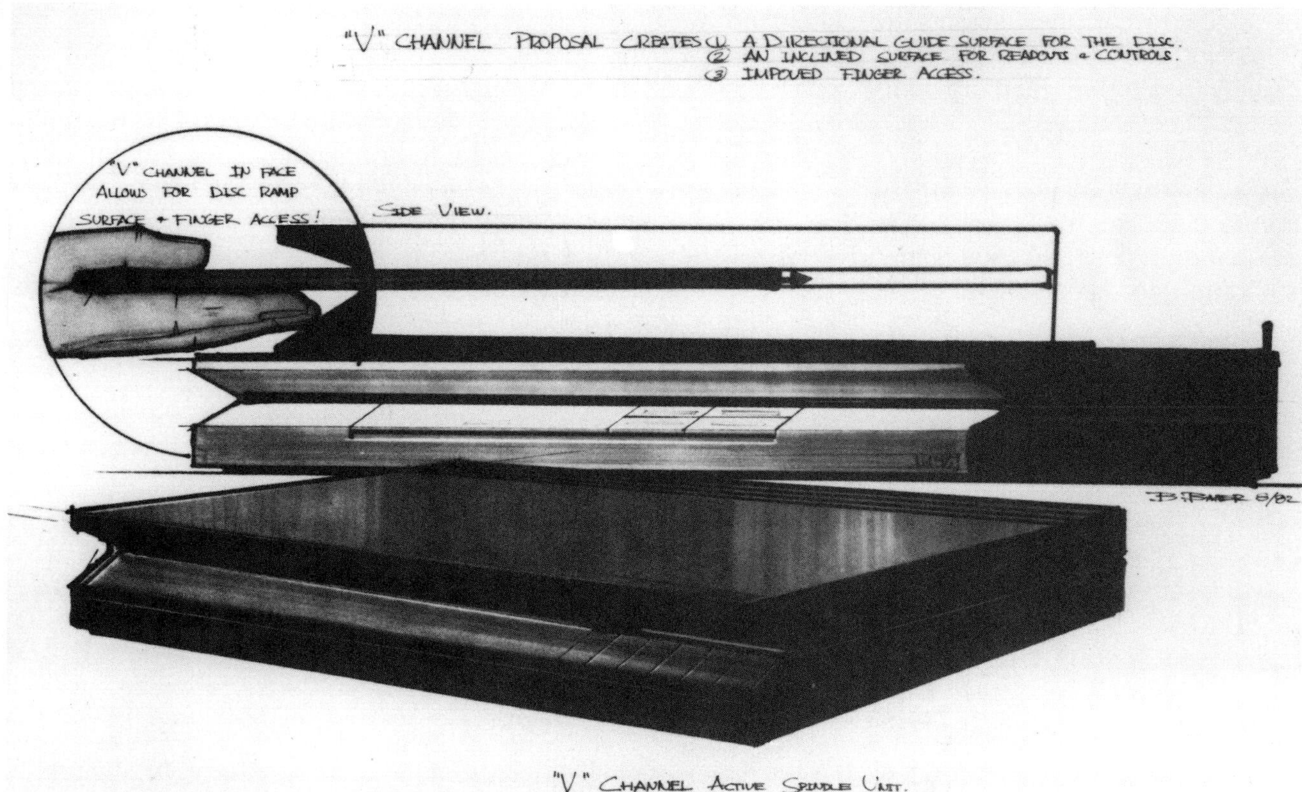

Figure 9-14. The enlarged view of a video disc being loaded into the recorder helps describe the technique. (RCA)

are often compared by physical size. Suppose there are two drawings of the same object. Each drawing is the same except one drawing is bigger than the other. If the bigger drawing has lines exactly twice the length of the same lines in the smaller drawing, the object in the bigger drawing is "proportionally" double-sized. You should note that while the lines are twice as long, the area is *more than* twice as much, Figure 9-15. When an object is called "half-scale" or "quarter-scale," the area is not being referred to, only the line length.

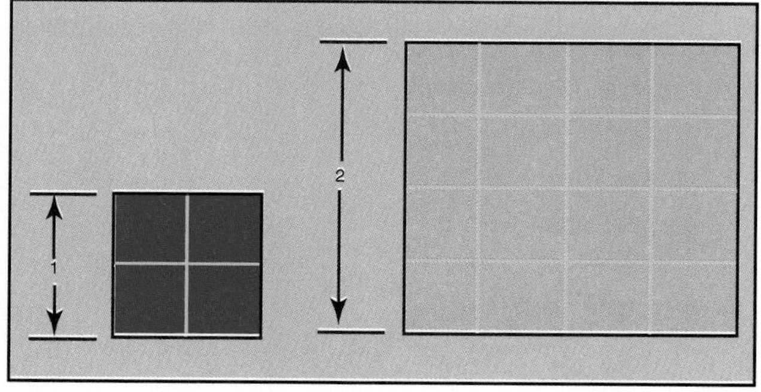

Figure 9-15. Proportion is the relationship of sizes among similar objects. The big box is twice the size of the small box. (However, the *area* of the big box is four times as great.)

Proportional sketches can be drawn very easily by using a ***grid system.*** The key is in developing a grid that is enlarged or reduced to the proper size or scale. This grid is a series of equally-sized boxes that may be similar to ones you have seen on graph paper.

The first step in changing the size of a drawing is to block off the original drawing into a grid. These squares should be drawn lightly and be of the *same size.* Lines are spaced every 1/4 inch to 2 inches, depending on the size of the original. Next, a second grid is drawn to the desired scale on a separate sheet of paper (or where you want the scaled drawing to be). For example, if the original drawing has 1/2 inch squares and the enlargement is to be twice the size of the original, the second grid will have 1 inch squares. See Figure 9-16. Carefully note where the object lines cross the grid markings in the original drawing. These points are transferred onto the larger grid, in the same place. Then, using the points as a guide, the shape is sketched onto the new grid. The outline is darkened with object lines to complete the sketch.

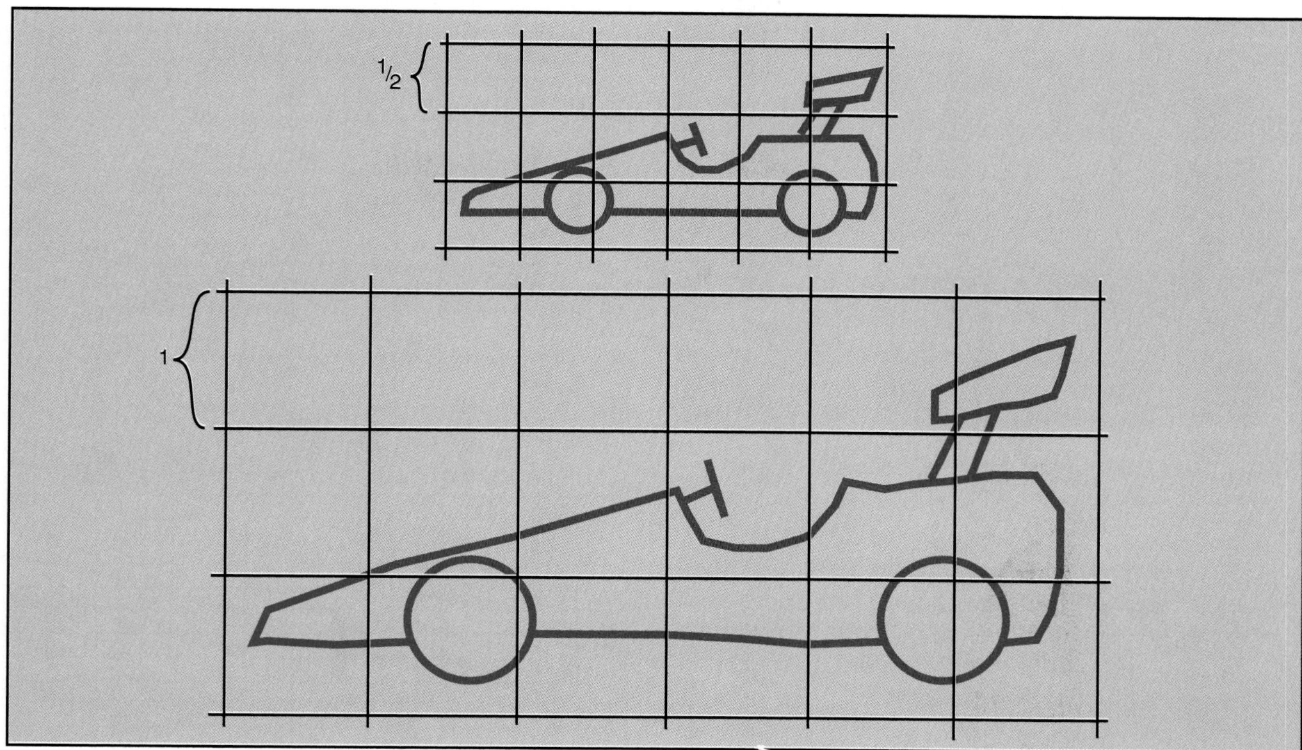

Figure 9-16. Example of a double-sized enlargement.

Just as drawings can be enlarged, they can also be reduced. The same procedure is followed. The difference is that the second grid is made smaller than the original grid.

Computer-Generated Sketching

In the last chapter, you discovered how computers help with sketching and drafting. Sketching may be done on computers as well as on paper, Figure 9-17. In fact, it may be easier "drawing" on a screen. Modern computer systems permit the development of very detailed three-dimensional views, Figure 9-18.

Most graphic programs reduce a drawing to a series of points. You may have followed this procedure when sketching the solution to a math problem on graph paper. When a line is created, the end points are determined and entered in the computer. Then the machine calculates all points between the end points of the line. A computer can then calculate what the surface of the object

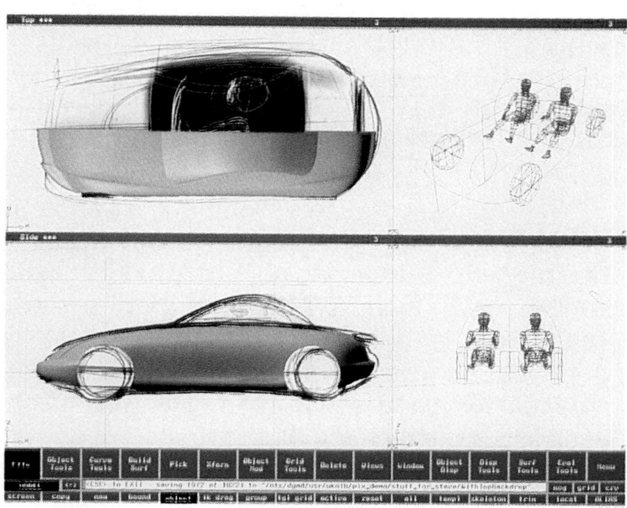

Figure 9-17. Computers can be used to sketch concepts for new objects. Various views and stages of the object can easily be shown. Modifications are also easy to make. (Alias Research, Inc.)

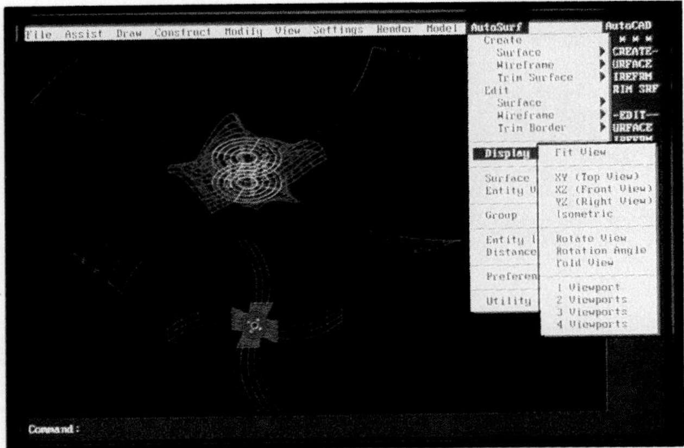

Figure 9-18. Complex parts can be reduced to simple points and lines. (Autodesk, Inc.)

will look like and represent that on screen as well, Figure 9-19. Therefore, to produce a drawing on a computer, you must understand how to describe the shape with numbers. This is an important process in technical design work.

Figure 9-19. A computer can generate lines that represent an object. The computer can then calculate what the surface of that object will look like and represent that on screen as well. This is very useful for designers when making design decisions. (Autodesk, Inc.)

The number of points along a line varies by the computer graphics program used. Systems with ***high-resolution*** capabilities produce more detailed lines than a ***low-resolution*** system. ***Resolution*** is determined by the number of "dots" that can be drawn per inch, Figure 9-20. More points along a line, or higher resolution, result in a smoother line or curve.

The newest computer systems allow drafters to produce drawings very efficiently. For example, a circle can be drawn by entering a center point and radius. The computer "draws" the image instantly on the screen. Triangles, rectangles, and other standard shapes are developed just as easily. A starting point is entered along with a height and width dimension. The computer system creates the shapes either on a screen or a print-out.

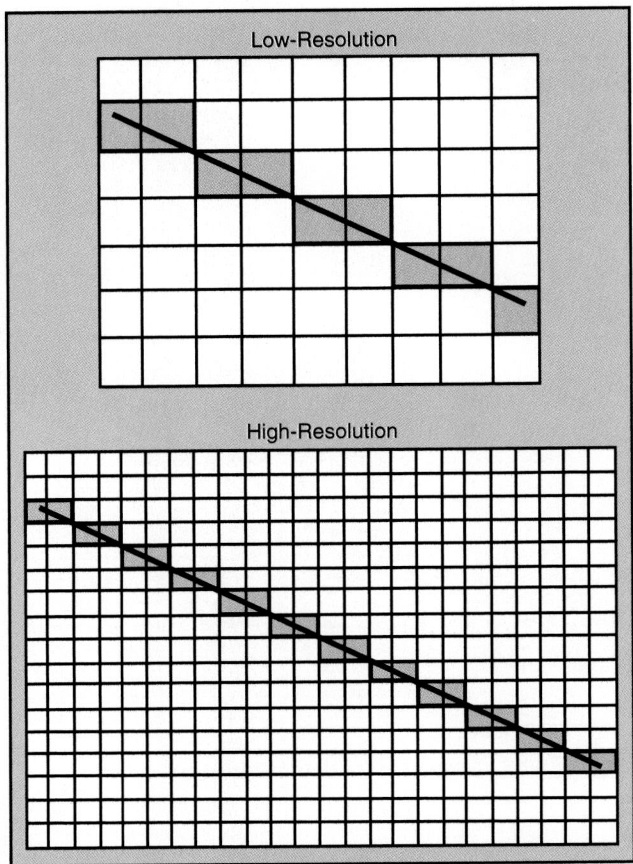

Figure 9-20. Resolution refers to the number of "dots" per inch. High-resolution lines are created by placing more, smaller "dots" along a line.

Computer graphics programs have other convenient features for developing drawings and sketches. One advantage is in labeling a sketch or drawing. Dimensions and notes can be added easily by keyboard. This replaces the need to hand-letter all text and numbers. Another useful feature is the ability to change the size (or scale) of various details. The sizes of a view can be enlarged or reduced. The drawing (or part of it) can also be moved to a different location or page.

Machines called ***digitizers*** allow you to change a drawing that was done by hand into a computer drawing, Figure 9-21. This is useful for drawings that have been around for many years. These machines save the time it would take to redraw the old drawings in the computer.

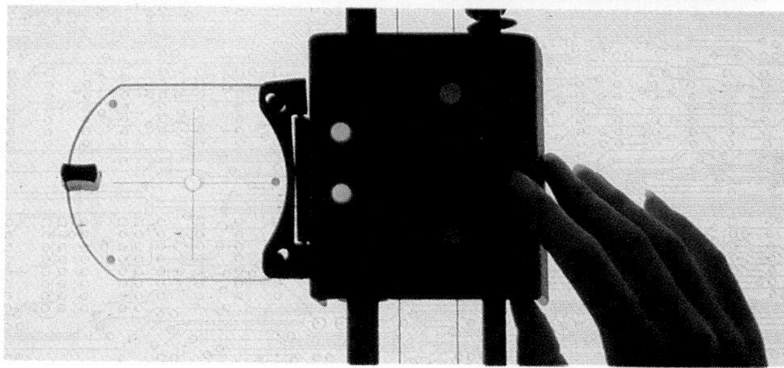

Figure 9-21. Digitizers are used to "copy" drawings into a computer. (Intel Corp.)

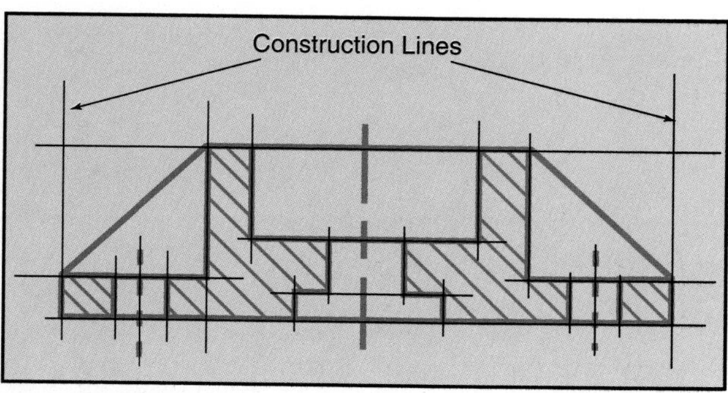

Figure 9-22. Internal features can be sketched before the final drawing is completed.

Pictorial views almost always start as sketches. Artists and drafters usually begin with a detailed sketch. When developing views, they look for familiar shapes, Figure 9-23. Light lines are then drawn to show the outline or shape. As more detail is included, the drawing looks more realistic.

DEVELOPING VIEWS

All of the sketching techniques you just looked at are involved in developing a view. Constructing lines, shapes, and figures in the proper way is important. If you use correct techniques, then the views that you develop will be accurate. When done properly, the result is a drawing that depicts technical details on a flat surface.

The procedure for developing 2D views often includes sketching guidelines. Generally, an entire drawing is sketched first. This includes sketching both an outline and any internal features. Then the major object lines are darkened as desired, Figure 9-22. This sketch will serve as a guide for developing the view.

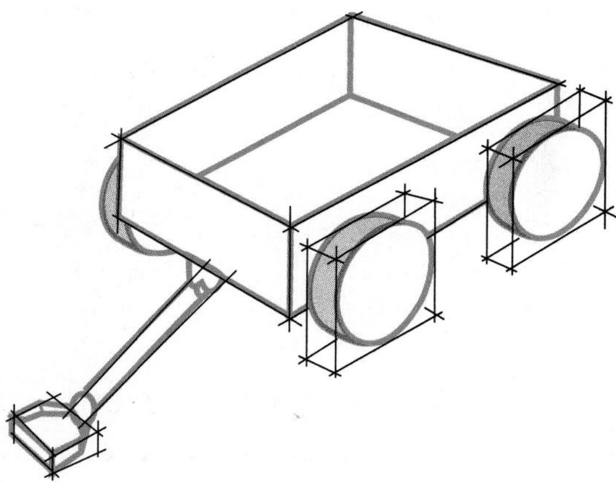

Figure 9-23. Pictorial sketches can be broken down into common shapes. What common shapes do you see in this pictorial sketch?

CHAPTER 9 REVIEW

SUMMARY

Everyone uses sketches at one time or another. These sketches help you communicate with others. They visually describe objects and scenes. Whether on paper or on a computer screen, sketching is an important procedure.

Sketches and drawings are produced in stages. Early ideas are generally nothing more than a rough sketch. Few pieces of equipment are required to complete these illustrations by hand. Detailed shapes can be sketched by following light construction lines. Sketches are complete when all major lines are darkened as needed.

Sketches developed by computer graphics systems are much the same. Lines and shapes must be organized on the screen. In most cases, a program will be used that "tells" the computer how to draw a line. A printout of the sketch or drawing can then be reproduced on paper.

KEY WORDS

All of the following words have been used in this chapter. Do you know their meanings?

- Center lines
- Construction lines
- Digitizers
- Dimension lines
- Grid system
- Hidden lines
- High-resolution
- Horizontal lines
- Inclined lines
- Low-resolution
- Object lines
- Pictorial sketch
- Proportion
- Resolution
- Three-dimensional (3D)
- Two-dimensional (2D)
- Vertical lines

TEST YOUR KNOWLEDGE

Write your answers on a separate sheet of paper. Please do not write in this book.

1. Two-dimensional sketches show only the _____ and _____ of an object. Three-dimensional sketches also show the _____.

REVIEW CHAPTER 9

Matching Questions: Match the definition on the left with the correct term on the right.

2.	Usually has arrowheads at the end of the line.	A.	Construction line.
3.	Shows the visible edges of an object.	B.	Hidden line.
4.	Used to give a sketch its basic shape.	C.	Dimension line.
5.	Shows the visible parts of an object.	D.	Object line.

6. What is the difference in sketching horizontal lines and vertical lines?
7. If a sketch has circles and lines, which should generally be drawn first?
8. Define proportion.

ACTIVITIES

1. Develop sketches of the following: a pyramid, a soda can, a textbook, and an overhead projector. Briefly explain to the class the techniques you used for each sketch.
2. Make two sketches of a sailboat; one should be exactly twice the size of the other. Use these to help you explain proportion to the class.
3. Invite a newspaper illustrator to visit your class. Ask for a demonstration of the different techniques discussed in this chapter. What kind of education is necessary to become an illustrator?
4. Collect a variety of freehand sketches. Separate them into two groups: two-dimensional and three-dimensional. Explain the purpose of each sketch.

CHAPTER 10

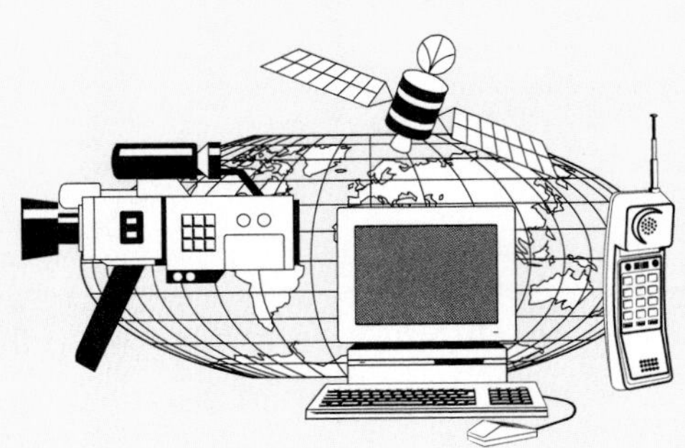

ORTHOGRAPHIC DRAWING

After studying this chapter, you will be able to:

- ❖ *State the uses of orthographic sketching and drawing.*
- ❖ *Identify typical systems of sketching and coding used in orthographic drawings.*
- ❖ *Explain techniques for developing orthographic projections.*

You already looked at the importance of communication in modern society. This is especially true in industry. Manufacturers and builders depend on accurate communication. Suppose a designer produced an incomplete drawing of your family car or an architect failed to include key details in your school's plans. These unsuccessful attempts to communicate vital information could be dangerous.

Modern industries rely on various forms of visual communication to exchange information and ideas. This may include computer-typed letters, photographs, computer images, or technical drawings. Sketching and drawing represents a major part of technical communication. Technical graphics has become both useful and necessary in industry, Figure 10-1.

In earlier chapters, you learned about different types of technical drawings, basic equipment, and supplies. This chapter will explore methods of preparing orthographic drawings. You will also look at the purposes behind orthographic drawings.

All technical drawings use a universal (worldwide) system for communicating ideas. That way the symbols and methods of layout are easily recognized around the world. We often refer to this as "following a ***convention***," Figure 10-2. The major groups that establish conventions for technical graphics are the American National Standards Institute (ANSI) and the International Standards Organization (ISO).

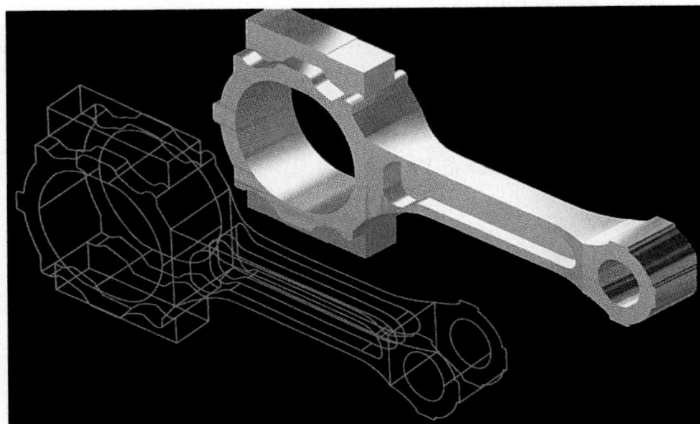

Figure 10-1. Designers use computer-aided drafting programs to design many different items. The design of engine components is just one example of how technical graphics is used in industry. (Autodesk, Inc.)

PURPOSES AND USES

As products and structures become more complex, designers face increased pressure. Drafters and designers are responsible for developing the plans for all details and parts, Figure 10-3. Much of their work goes into the technical drawings used during production.

Generally, design drawings illustrate the size and shape of objects. Information related to materials and function may also be included. These drawings serve as instructions for how the item is to be produced, Figure 10-4. Manufactured products may require many pages of drawings to fully

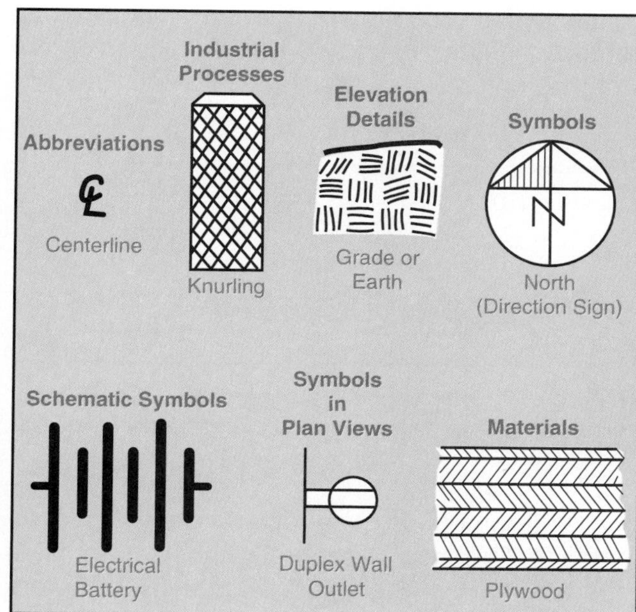

Figure 10-2. Drafting conventions are universal. They mean the same thing to all drafters and architects.

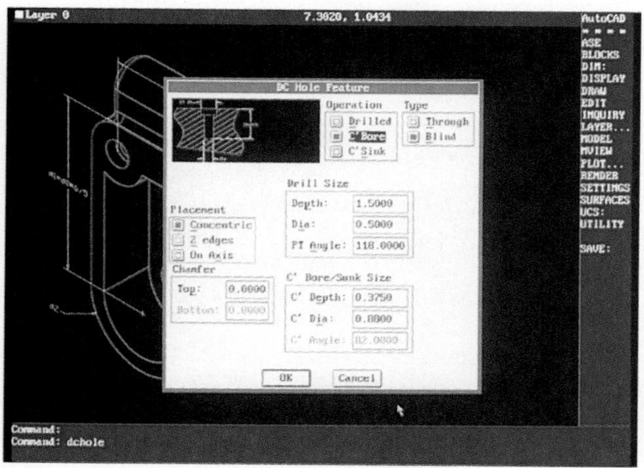

Figure 10-3. Technical drafters must specify every detail of a part, including details that may not be seen from standard views. (Autodesk, Inc.)

describe all parts. Prints for large buildings fill several books.

Technical drawings usually provide much more information than photographs. Sketches and drawings can describe shapes more accurately. Internal details may be illustrated in sectional views. Different features might be drawn on a larger scale to show fine details.

Plans and other design information are used by many people in a typical manufacturing firm. Technical drawings show shop personnel what is

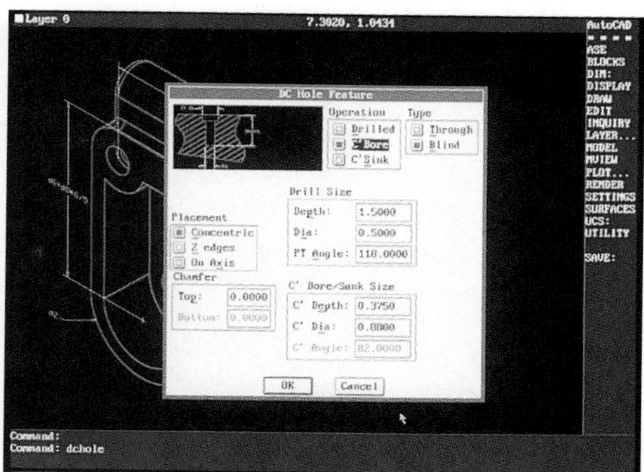

Figure 10-4. Production managers check design drawings that show how components are assembled. (Hewlett-Packard Co.)

to be produced and how it is to be produced. After review of the drawings, facilities and machines can be designed that will allow production to run smoothly. Materials can be ordered based on the plans and accompanying bill (list) of materials. During production, assembly drawings guide workers in assembling parts in the proper sequence.

Architectural drawings serve basically the same purpose. Materials and supplies are ordered after reading the architect's plans. The prints inform construction workers how to build the structure. Additional drawings describe details such as plumbing fixtures and heating ducts. Drawings for buildings often include plans for landscaping or other exterior work. A set of complete architectural plans fills many pages, Figure 10-5.

ORTHOGRAPHIC PROJECTION

The primary type of drawing used in industry is called an ***orthographic projection.*** The term ***multiview drawings*** is also used to describe these types of drawings. These types of drawings were briefly looked at in Chapter 7. Orthographic projection refers to the procedure of projecting images from an object. In order to project a view, a ***viewing plane*** is established. This plane will be perpendicular (at a right angle) to the object. Refer back to Figure 7-17. This ***perpendicular viewing plane*** provides the ***orthographic view.*** A drawing is then made from the view shown on the reference plane.

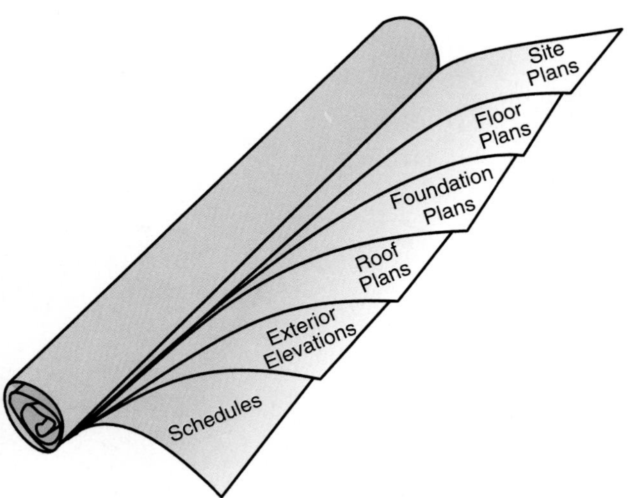

Figure 10-5. Architectural plans for buildings or structures can fill many pages.

In most cases, several views are necessary to describe an object. That is where the term "multiview" becomes important. Several drawings (or *multiple views*) are constructed to adequately illustrate important features. A standard set of orthographic drawings includes front, top, and right-side (or left-side) views. A typical multiview arrangement is shown in Figure 10-6.

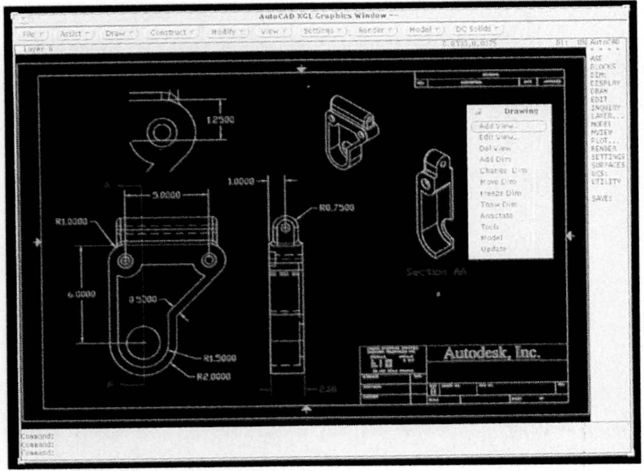

Figure 10-6. A typical orthographic, or multiview, drawing drawn on a CAD system. (Autodesk, Inc.)

Organization of Views

Orthographic drawings have many advantages. None is more important than the ability to completely describe an object on a single, two dimensional (2D) surface. Several views can be shown together, Figure 10-7. Even hidden details may be noted.

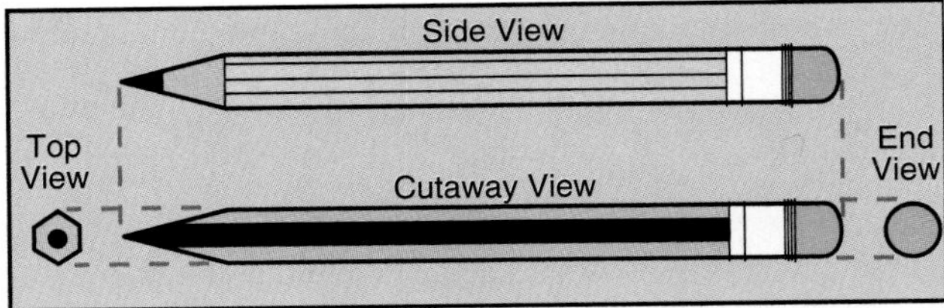

Figure 10-7. Orthographic drawings contain several views of the same object, as seen from different reference points.

A front view is constructed from the primary surface. This view is generally chosen to provide the best view of the object, Figure 10-8. To adequately describe the entire shape and size, other views are required. Both a top and right-side view are often used to complete the projection. Since these views sometimes describe the same details, one view may be unnecessary, Figure 10-9.

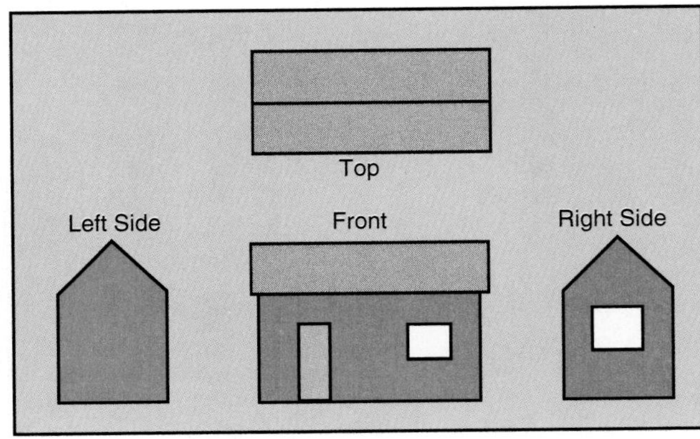

Figure 10-8. The view selected as the front view should show the most detail.

The placement of each view in orthographic projection is important. All drawings are located in relationship to the front (or primary) surface. This means a top view is drawn directly above the object, Figure 10-10. Left-side and right-side views are positioned beside the front view on the corresponding side. Auxiliary views are additional views that describe odd details. These views are drawn perpendicular to the surface being illustrated.

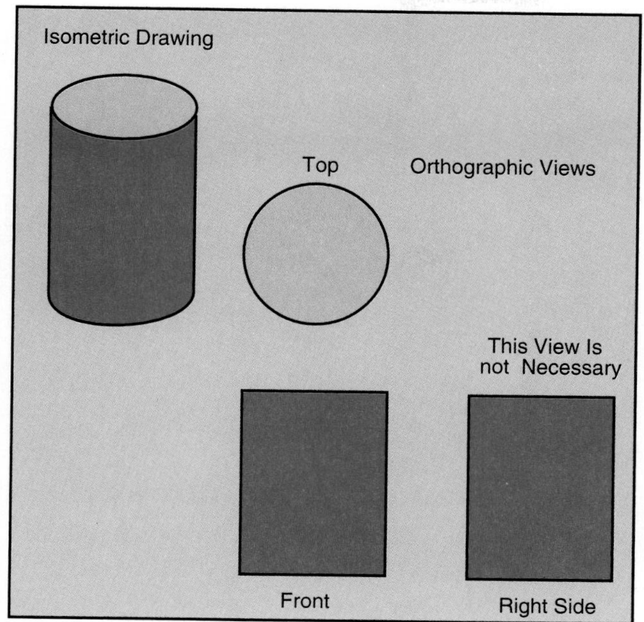

Figure 10-9. Many objects appear the same from different angles. In this case, there is no need to duplicate views.

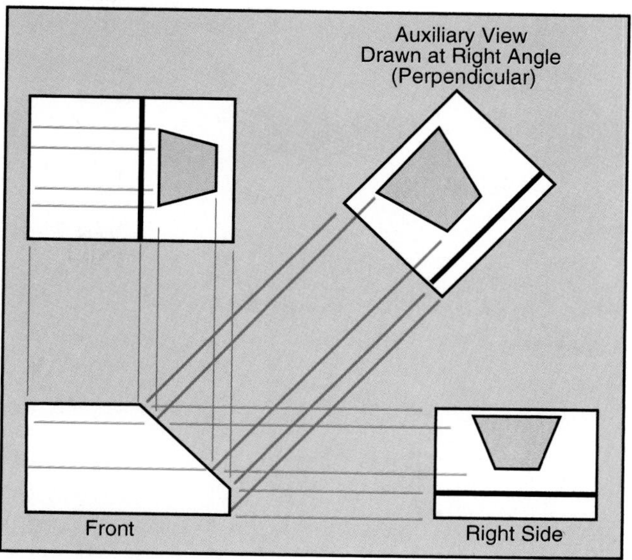

Figure 10-10. Orthographic views are developed in direct relationship to the front (primary) view.

Orthographic Lines and Symbols

A variety of lines are used in multiview drawings, Figure 10-11. Construction and placement of all lines is vital for accuracy. All object lines are drawn with bold (heavy) lines. Hidden features are shown with broken (dashed) lines. Center and dimension lines and symbols are generally drawn with thin, light lines.

Dimension lines and notes should be made carefully. Sizes and distances are labeled with dimension lines, Figure 10-12. Leader lines extend to the dimensioned object. Arrowheads show the endpoints of the distance being identified.

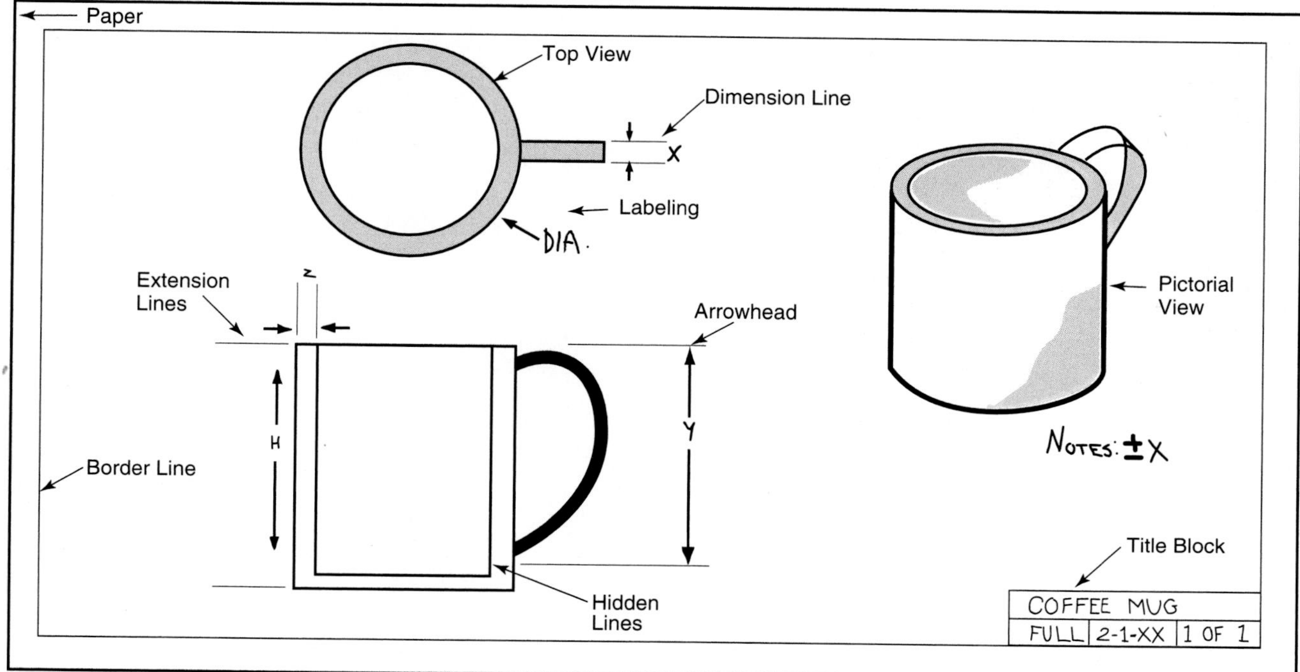

Figure 10-11. Multiview drawings use many different lines and symbols.

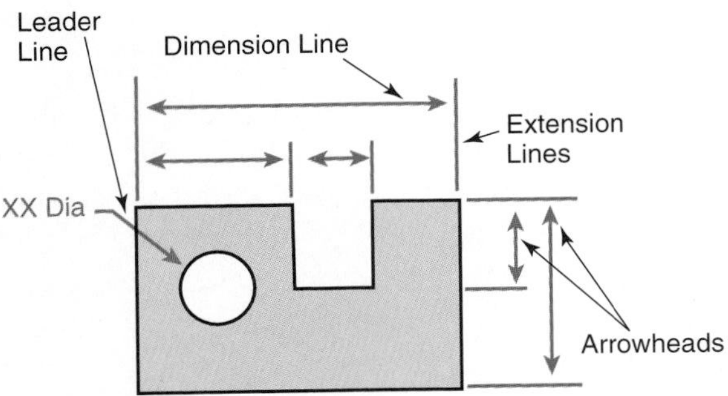

Figure 10-12. There are several parts to a dimension.

Internal features of many objects are important in overall function or design. A view may be drawn as if the object has been cut in two, Figure 10-13. This is called a sectioned, or cutaway, view. Section lines show where the cut is made. The adjoining view is crosshatched to illustrate solid areas. If several parts are identified, crosshatching is done at different angles for each part. In some cases, the crosshatching represents the material used, Figure 10-14.

Orthographic Conventions

Conventions are useful in developing orthographic views. One method of representation involves ***symmetry.*** Many objects appear identical on both sides or ends. That means one side of the drawing is the same as the other side (symmetry), Figure 10-15. Rather than drawing both sides, a centerline is developed to show the symmetry and only half of the drawing is completed. This saves time and space.

Another technique that reduces the total area needed for a drawing is ***break lines.*** Little is gained in drawing full lengths of pipes, I-beams, or other long objects. Instead, lines showing a

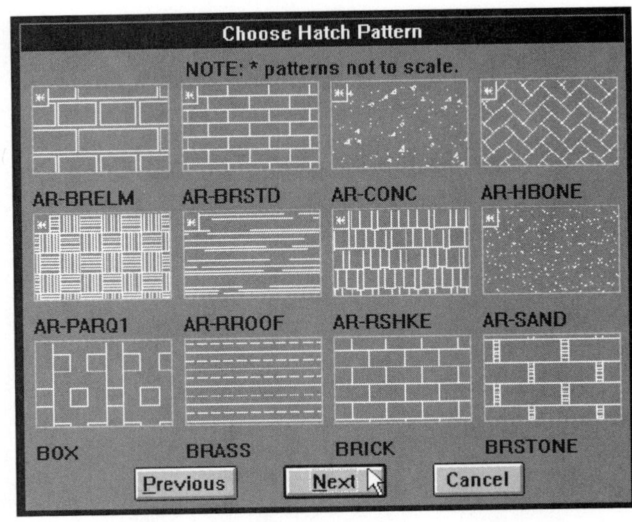

Figure 10-14. Many materials are represented by unique symbols. This is a sample of technical symbols used for sectional views.

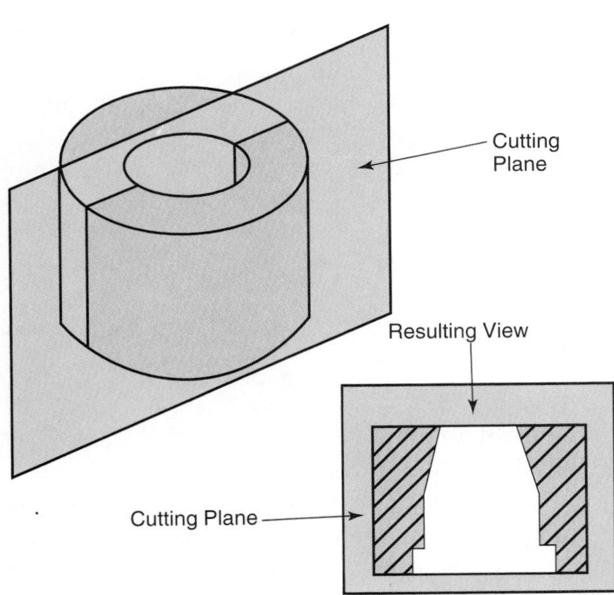

Figure 10-13. Sectional (cutaway) views show the internal features of objects. Drawings like this allow you to see important shapes in the center of an item.

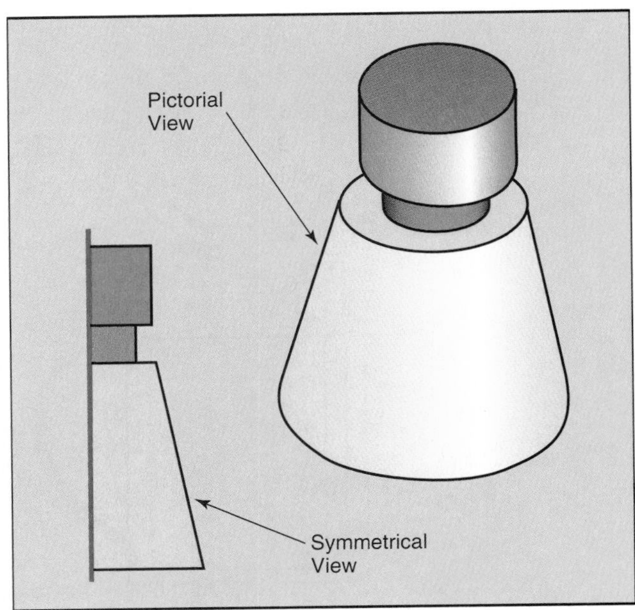

Figure 10-15. Technical drawings may be simplified when their shape is symmetric. A centerline shows the plane of symmetry in these objects.

break in the total distance are used, Figure 10-16. When doing this, a section of the object is "removed." The part removed will have no features on it that are not already explained and indicated. Very long distances can be shown without leaving out important features. Large details can be shown in a much smaller space. This will save room on the drawing.

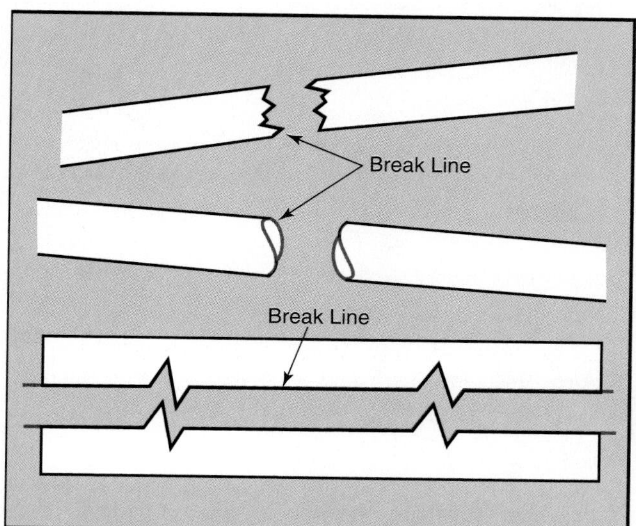

Figure 10-16. Break lines are used in views of long objects or distances. This saves room in the drawing, while maintaining all the necessary details.

Many objects are often difficult to draw. A perfect example is the threads on the end of a bolt. Rather than draw every thread, the bolt may be described with symbols and notes. This saves time without adding confusion, Figure 10-17. The sizes of threads are easily marked with simple notes.

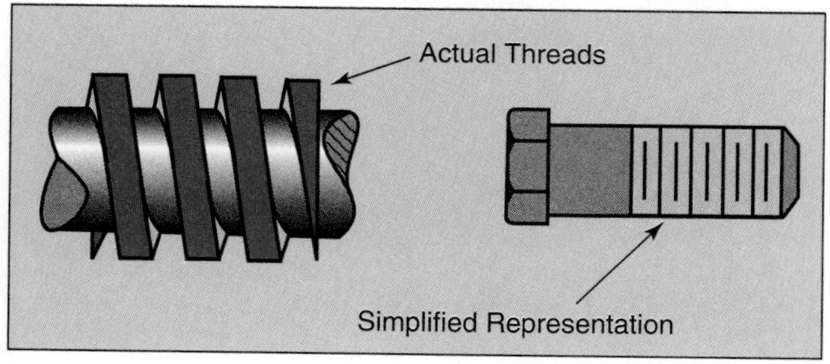

Figure 10-17. Drawing the threads of a typical bolt would take hours to do correctly. The method of representing threads with symbols is much quicker, easier, and understandable.

Notes and Dimensions

Dimensions and notes are often as important as the actual views in many technical drawings. Sizes, distances, and features must be identified to complete an accurate drawing. Labeling the drawing can be slow but is necessary, Figure 10-18. There are many rules for using dimensions and notes on orthographic drawings.

Figure 10-18. Adding notes and dimensions to drawings is usually a slow, demanding task. Lettering templates are helpful aids. When drawings are completed on computers, the task of lettering is simplified.

Generally, labeling is placed on the views that show the most features, Figure 10-19. Height and width dimensions are listed on the front view, depth dimensions are listed on the side or top view. Hidden lines are not dimensioned unless unavoidable.

Dimension lines and leaders must be constructed neatly on a drawing. Dimension lines should not be overlapped unless necessary. Dimensions are generally placed in the center of the dimension lines. However, staggering the dimensions (numbers) may "loosen up" a particular view, Figure 10-20. In certain cases, a few dimensions might be moved to another view. This helps reduce the clutter around a view that requires many dimensions.

There are different methods for placing dimensions on technical drawings. Standard figures, decimals, and fractions generally provide enough information to communicate sizes and distances, Figure 10-21. When sizes are allowed to vary slightly, several dimensions are listed. The range between these sizes is called

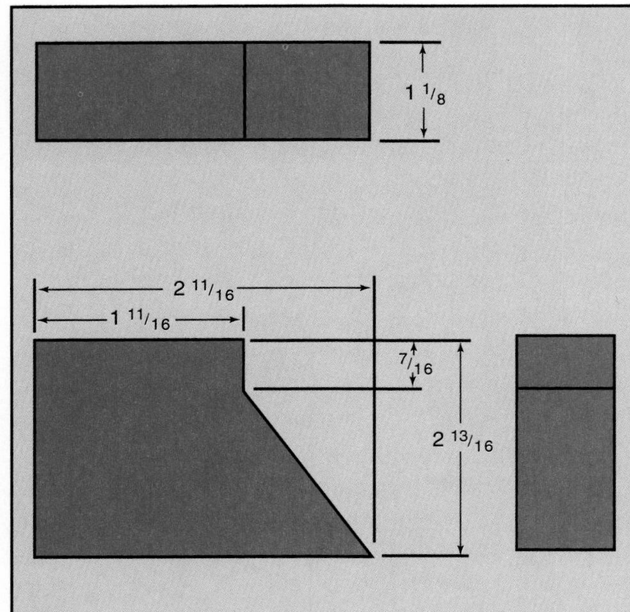

Figure 10-19. Dimensions and notes should be carefully placed on each view. Place labeling on the view that best describes the feature being described.

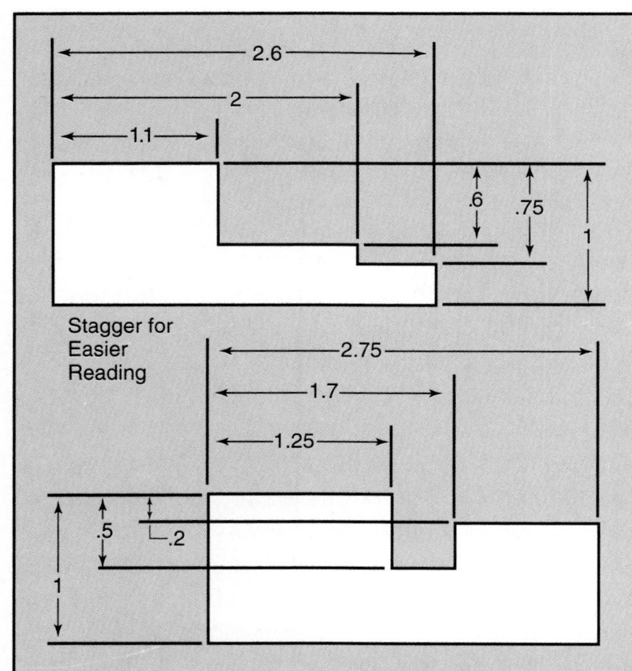

Figure 10-20. Dimensions are often crowded around a view. Staggering numbers allows for easier reading.

the ***tolerance.*** The tolerance range listed on drawings gives the maximum and/or minimum sizes permitted.

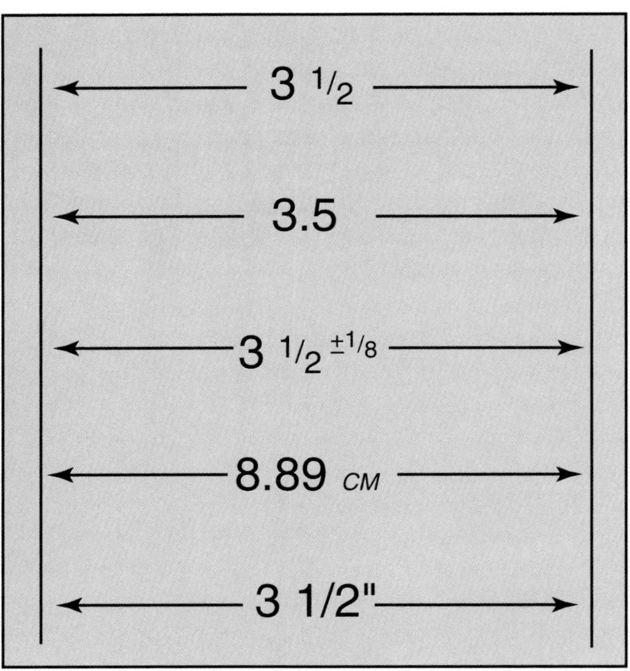

Figure 10-21. There are different methods of dimensioning a technical drawing.

Finally, lettering must be added to the drawing. Light guidelines are useful in lettering technical views. Templates or lettering guides also help when lettering a drawing. If a computer program is being used, all lettering is done by the computer. Most software can add dimension lines and values as well. Modern software allows drawings to be labeled easily, Figure 10-22.

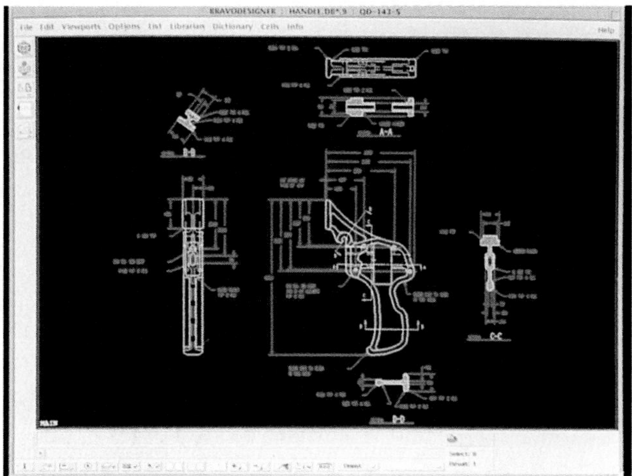

Figure 10-22. Computer-aided drafting (CAD) programs contain commands for dimensioning drawings according to current professional standards. (Applicon Research Inc.)

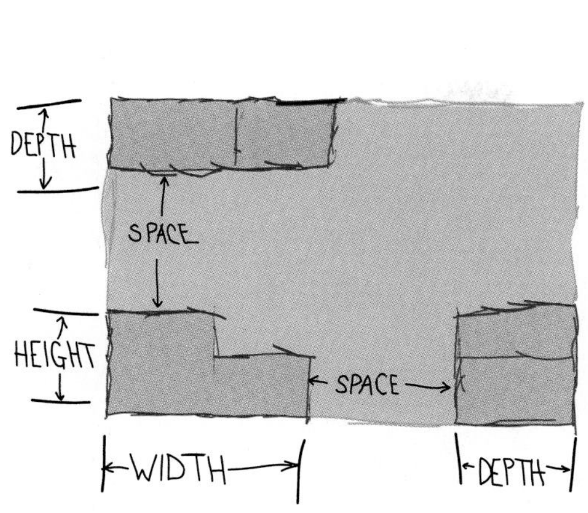

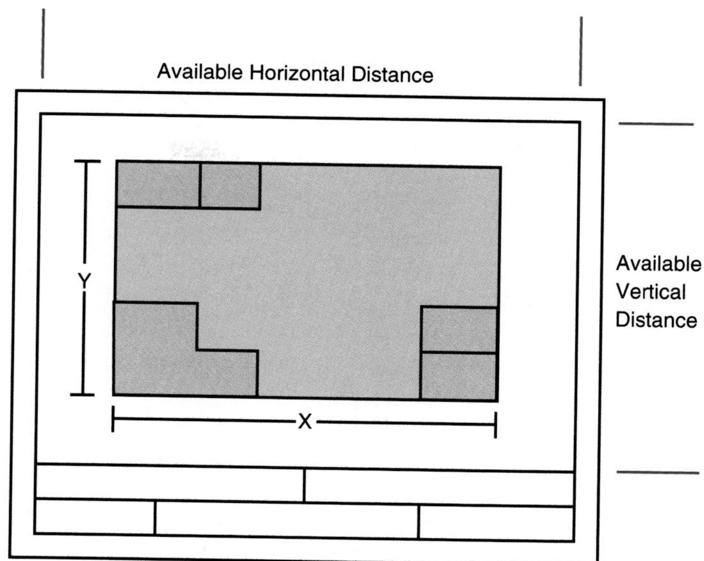

Figure 10-23. This shows how to calculate the starting point of an orthographic drawing. Left: "Y" = (the space between the top and front views + the height dimension + the depth dimension) and "X" = (the space between the front and side views + the width dimension + the depth dimension). Note: the two "spaces" should be equal. This calculation will give you the size of the "box." Right: the distance from the bottom of the "box" to the bottom border = (the available vertical space - "Y")/2 and the distance from the "box" to the side border = (the available horizontal distance - "X")/2. This will give you the starting corner of the "box."

DEVELOPING ORTHOGRAPHIC DRAWINGS

Technical or engineering drawings are often developed on large sheets of drafting paper. Many objects can be shown on the same page. However, a drafter must carefully select the best views to use on the drawing. Organization of the drawing is important. By properly laying out the views, dozens of orthographic views may be placed on one sheet.

The procedure for organizing orthographic views is quite simple. You should already know the exact sizes of the objects to be drawn. A smaller scale may be required to fit all views on the page. Once the desired scale is identified, the layout process can begin.

Centering Drawings

Technical drawings look best when centered on the page. Remember, the center of an orthographic drawing is based on the combination of three separate views. Space between the views must be considered. Therefore, the drafter must add many dimensions together to center the drawing. The method for calculating the center is given in Figure 10-23.

If more than one set of drawings is to appear on the same sheet, layout is more difficult. This happens with many engineering and architectural drawings, Figure 10-24. Generally, the largest (and most important) views are positioned first. Smaller, less important views are placed around the major details. Remember to maintain even spacing and borders for easier reading.

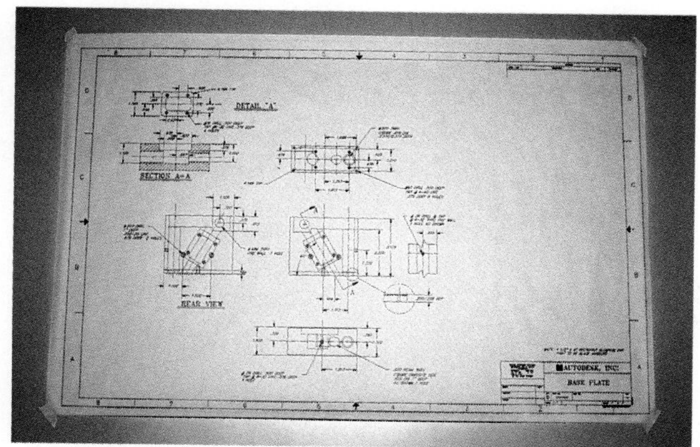

Figure 10-24. Large sheets of drafting paper can hold many drawings on the same page.

Developing Orthographic Views

After selecting the views to be drawn, layout of the drawing begins. Light construction lines are used to identify the location of each view, Figure 10-25. On a standard drafting board, use a drafting machine (or a T-square and triangles) to develop all lines. It is best to start with the front view. The width and height lines developed in this view will help in starting other views. The general outlines must be constructed for each view. The location of holes, arcs, slopes, and other features should be worked out.

All drawings must be developed in perfect alignment and follow the rules of orthographic projection. That means the height and width in each view are equal. In addition, details must be drawn to match each adjoining view, Figure 10-26. Hidden features are shown as dashed lines and are matched as well.

Once enough construction lines have been sketched, darken the object lines. Drafting by hand means using a lead holder or technical pen

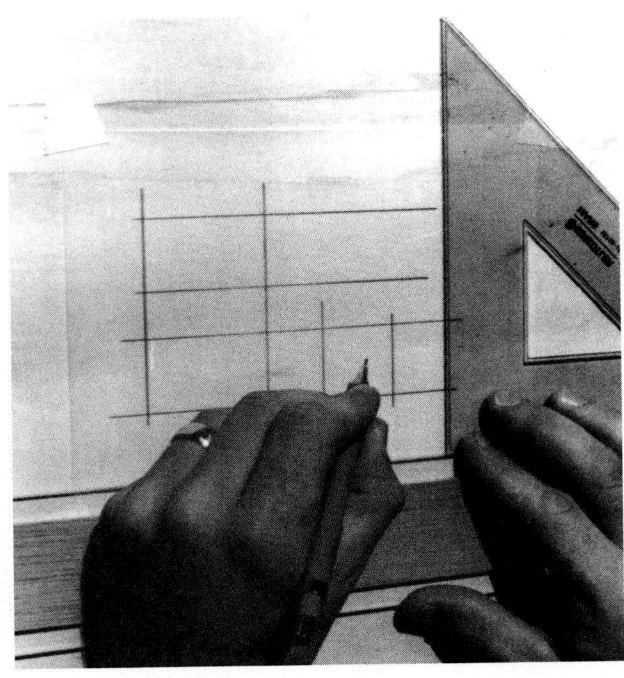

Figure 10-25. Construction lines (guidelines) are useful in identifying the location of each orthographic view.

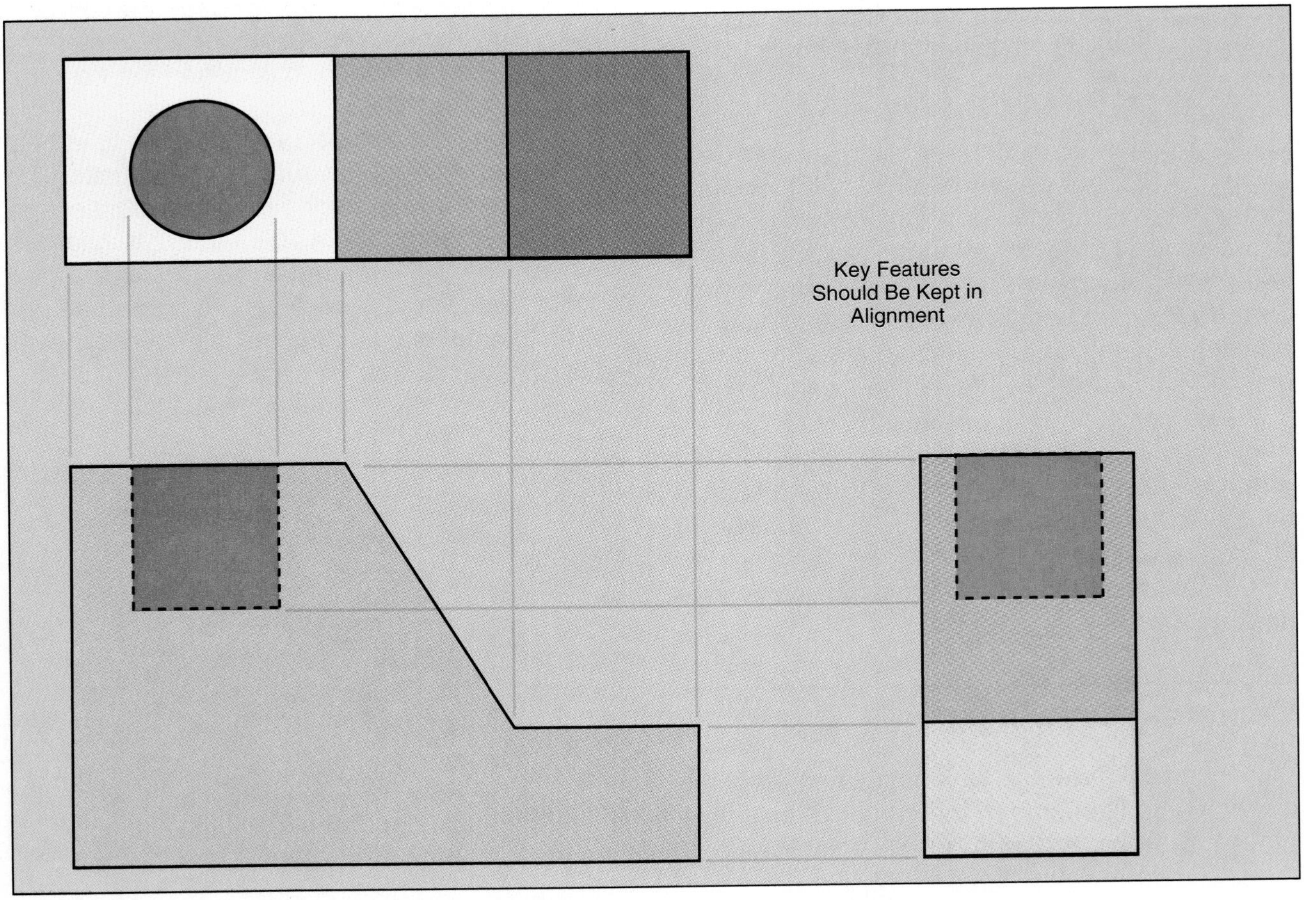

Figure 10-26. Alignment of features is critical in developing orthographic projections.

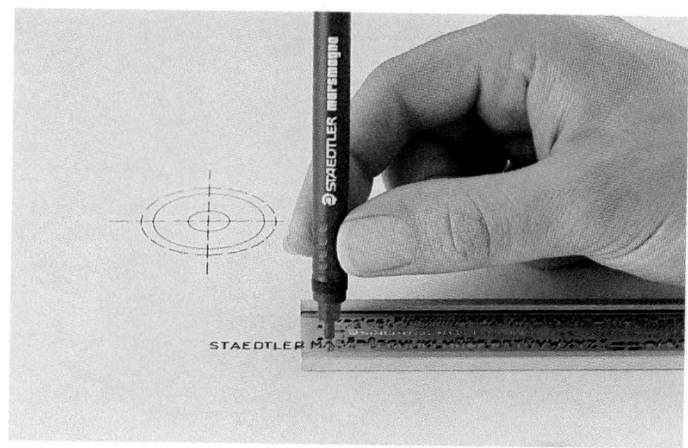

Figure 10-27. Ink is used for many drawings because it reproduces (copies) much better than pencil. (Staedtler, Inc.)

(ink pen), Figure 10-27. If the drawing is done by computer, a mouse or trackball may be required. Many printers and plotters are capable of making very detailed drawings, Figure 10-28.

Lines should be drawn in order of their weight (boldness). Object lines are the darkest, boldest lines. Draw these lines first. Hidden and section lines are drawn slightly thinner. Lettering and dimension lines are usually done last.

Finally, the drawing should be cleaned up to improve its appearance. Construction lines should be erased carefully from around the drawing. Eraser shields (or simply a piece of paper) protect other lines. Do not disturb any lines immediately near a view or labeling. This may leave smudge marks on the drawing.

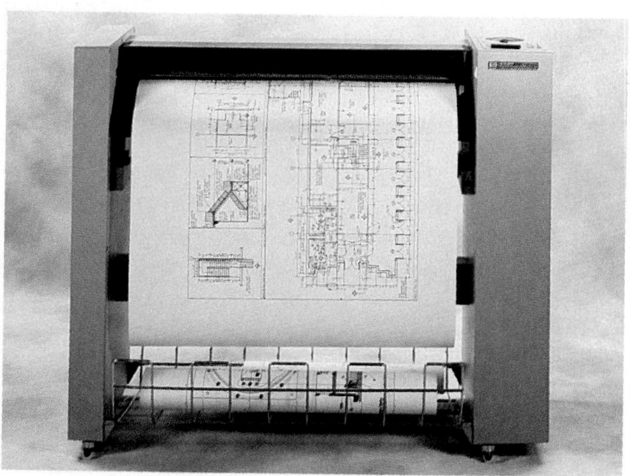

Figure 10-28. Technical drawings are transferred from computers to paper with the help of plotters. (Hewlett-Packard Co.)

CHAPTER 10 REVIEW

SUMMARY

Orthographic projection is also called multiview drawing. The term "orthographic" refers to the method of projecting image lines from an object. A reference point is established perpendicular to an object. Image lines projected through a reference plane show how the technical view is developed.

Most orthographic drawings include three views. The front, top, and right-side views are most often used. Lines and details in each view are drawn in relationship to each other. All features are shown by either object (solid) or hidden (dashed) lines. Labeling provides necessary information. Dimensions give lengths and tolerances. Notes provide other information, such as a description of thread size or the type of special surface finish.

KEY WORDS

All of the following words have been used in this chapter. Do you know their meanings?

Break lines
Convention
Multiview drawing
Orthographic projection
Orthographic view
Perpendicular viewing plane
Symmetry
Tolerance
Viewing plane

TEST YOUR KNOWLEDGE

Write your answers on a separate sheet of paper. Please do not write in this book.

1. ANSI and ISO are two examples of a _____.
2. _____ is the process of projecting images from an object.
3. What three views are most often used in orthographic projection?
4. What lines are drawn the boldest in multiview drawings?
   A. Hidden lines.
   B. Centerlines.
   C. Dimension lines.
   D. Object lines.
   E. None of the above.

5. What type of line is used to represent solid areas?
6. Name two orthographic conventions.
7. Which of the following is NOT a rule for using dimensions/notes on orthographic drawings?
   A. Place labeling on most descriptive features.
   B. Avoid dimensioning to hidden lines.
   C. Never stagger dimensions.
   D. All of the above.
8. What technique is used to draw very long distances in a smaller space?

ACTIVITIES

1. Develop an orthographic drawing of this book. Supply front, top, and right-side views. If possible, develop this drawing on a computer. Explain how you developed the drawing.
2. Obtain a set of architectural plans for your school building. Make a list of all the details you recognize. Include those details you learned in earlier chapters. Explain what details are shown on each plan.
3. Develop an orthographic view of all parts of a ball-point pen. Assemble these views onto a single sheet of drafting paper. Explain how you organized the drawings.
4. Do additional research on the process of orthographic drawing. Write a short report on what you learned. Include information on uses for orthographic drawing (other than those discussed in the chapter).

CHAPTER 11

PICTORIAL DRAWING

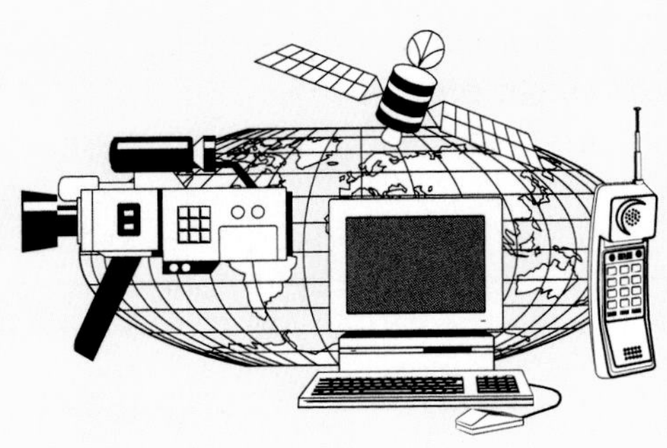

After studying this chapter, you will be able to:

- *Describe drawing techniques for developing pictorial drawings.*
- *Describe the four common forms of pictorial drawings.*
- *Prepare accurate oblique, isometric, technical, and perspective drawings.*

In Chapter 7, you learned that drawing is often divided into several classifications. Many drawings are developed using only two dimensions. Orthographic projections are examples of two-dimensional views. On the other hand, pictorial drawings are three-dimensional. These images have a third dimension (usually depth) added to the views, Figure 11-1. Texture and shading is sometimes added to make the drawing more realistic.

In most cases, pictorial drawings are designed to be as realistic as possible. This is especially true in the drawings produced by technical illustrators and architects. Illustrators in

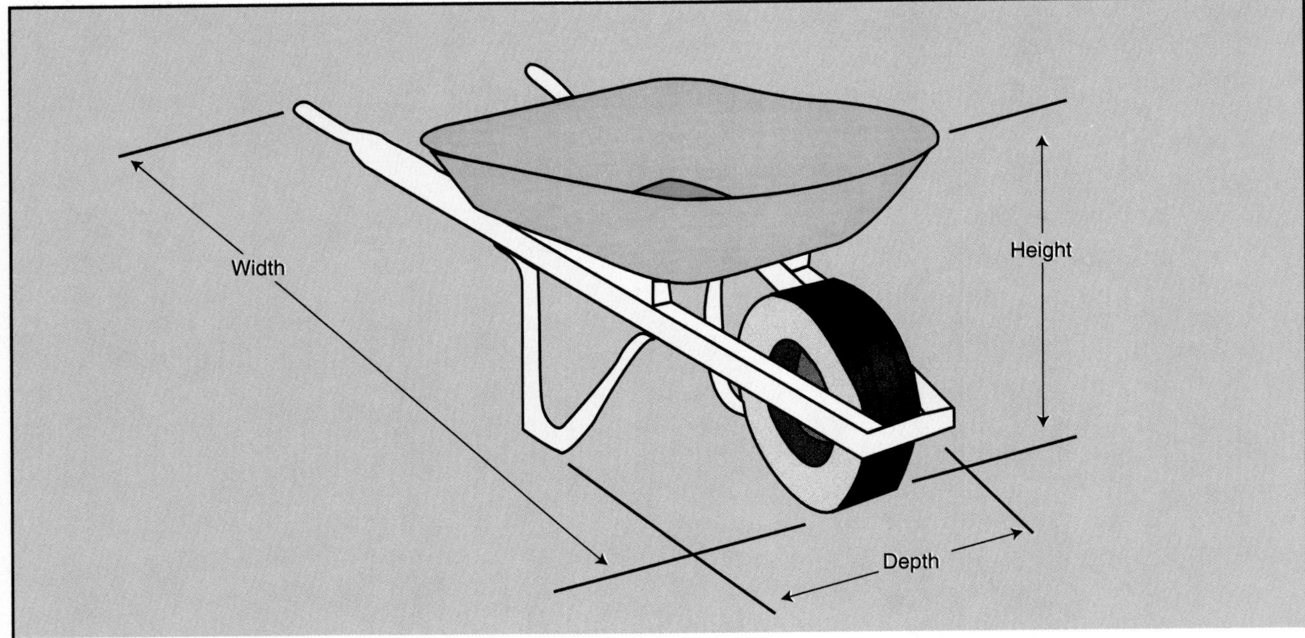

Figure 11-1. Pictorial drawings illustrate the three dimensions of height, width, and depth. The "width" view is chosen to show the most detail on the object. Therefore, the "width" of the object in a drawing might not be what you would normally consider to be how "wide" the object is.

industry make drawings that allow you to see products not yet made, Figure 11-2. Their drawings often look like photographs. Architectural drafters provide similar views of buildings in the design stage. Artistic renderings of new buildings permit others to see how the structures will appear when completed.

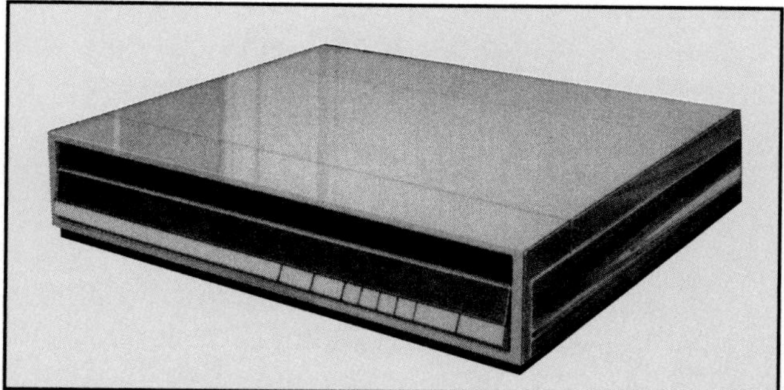

Figure 11-2. Pictorial drawings are sometimes used to illustrate how a final product will look. (RCA)

PICTORIAL DETAILING

What do you see when you look out a window? Perhaps your attention focuses on items like trees and clouds. Maybe your attention is drawn toward cars, streets, and buildings. You might notice colors and shapes first. Sizes and distance will often be obvious to you. When you are developing pictorial drawings, all of these details are important. These details make the drawing look realistic.

The person making a pictorial drawing must recognize many natural details. For example, size and detailing appear to decrease over distance. This is why train tracks seem to run together as they get farther away, Figure 11-3. This is also the reason that trees, cars, and buildings appear smaller when they are viewed from a distance. When photographs are taken, these differences are simply recorded on the film. A drafter, however, must learn to draw these differences. There are several techniques used for reproducing these details. You will look at five of these techniques. These are:

- Foreshortening.
- Overlapping.
- Horizontal viewing plane.
- Vanishing points.
- Shading and shadows.

Figure 11-3. When you look straight down railroad tracks, the tracks appear to get closer together and meet at the horizon.

Foreshortening

In nature, items appear smaller when observed from farther away. This is called ***foreshortening,*** Figure 11-4. It is the reason a mountain appears only inches high from a distance.

Figure 11-4. Foreshortening can be seen when looking at these solar panels. The panels farthest from your eye appear shorter than panels closer to your viewing point. In actuality, the panels are all the same height. (Siemens Solar Industries)

When drawing simple shapes, foreshortening is quite easy. Details developed towards the back of a view should be drawn slightly smaller, Figure 11-5. Almost any item in the back of a picture should appear shorter by comparison to details in the front of a picture.

Overlapping

The positioning of objects causes a condition called ***overlapping.*** Items near us are generally seen as whole, and close to actual size. As objects are observed from greater distances, certain things may get in the way or "block" the view of parts of the object, Figure 11-6.

This overlap is often ignored by mechanical drafters. They draw lines that cannot be seen from their point of reference. Architectural drafters, however, often use overlapping to their advantage. Depth is easily shown by overlapping cars, streets, and trees in a drawing. Hills in the background finish off a scene. Items that overlap help create a sense of distance or space.

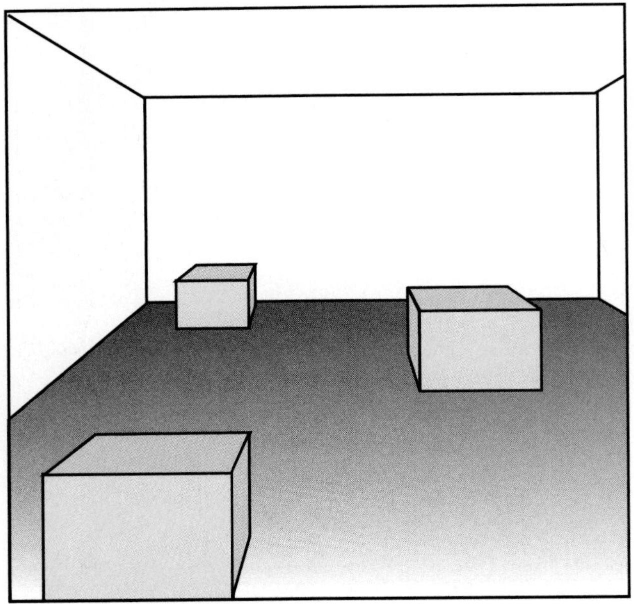

Figure 11-5. When foreshortening objects, the sizes of the objects are based on the distance between the viewer and the objects. Objects that are farther away will be drawn smaller.

Horizontal Viewing Plane

Everybody has a point of reference (or viewing plane) at some level. Items positioned horizontally, in front of your eyes, appear on the same plane. This plane is generally called ***eye level.*** Objects above or below are seen in a different viewing plane, Figure 11-7.

Most drawings developed by technical illustrators are done looking straight at an object or scene. This means the image is projected in a horizontal viewing plane. Lines indicating height appear vertical (as they always will). Lines representing width and depth, however, can be horizontal on the drawing or angle towards the rear of the scene.

Pictorial drawings can be developed from a number of viewing planes. This is a major advantage over photographs. Large, permanent objects can be drawn as they would appear from "odd" angles. Perhaps you have heard of a "bird's eye

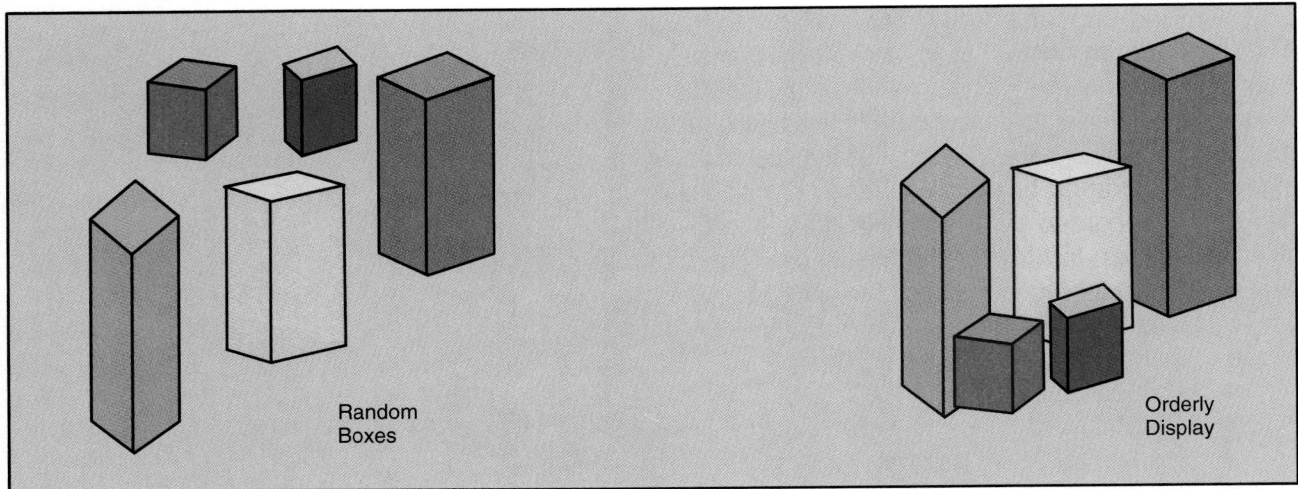

Figure 11-6. Overlapping creates organization of objects and adds depth to a view.

Figure 11-7. Objects will appear different from different viewing planes.

view?" This view is actually an overhead view. It is similar to what a bird might see when flying overhead, Figure 11-8.

Figure 11-8. Bird's eye views are developed from an overhead angle, looking down.

Vanishing Points

Humans can only see as far as the horizon, Fig 11-9. The horizon is a location in the distance where the Earth and the sky appear to meet. The result appears as a line. In technical drawings, the horizon is represented by a line chosen arbitrarily. (Arbitrarily means there are no set rules or guidelines to follow.) Along this line are points called ***vanishing points.*** Two vanishing points are selected along this "horizon." These two points are where all lines representing depth and width of an object will meet if extended, Fig 11-10.

Pictorial drawings are started by first identifying vanishing points. Then lines of sight are developed. The lines of sight are lines, arbitrarily chosen, that extend from the vanishing points

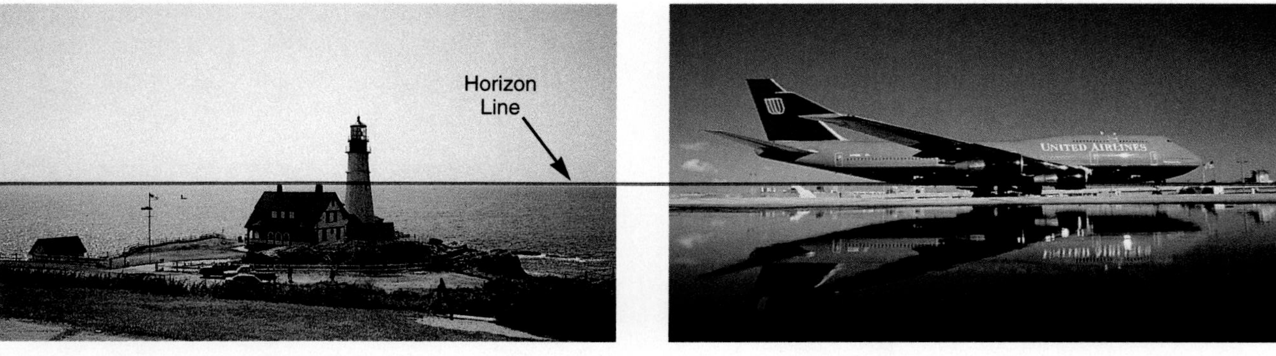

Figure 11-9. The horizon is where the sky and the Earth appear to meet. (Kathy Kopf, United Airlines)

and angle either up or down. The point where the two lines of sight meet will be the front corner of the object. Simple shapes are sketched from these projection lines. Finally, object lines are darkened. Shading and other details add to the realism of the drawing.

Shading and Shadowing

All objects reflect light differently. Light is often projected onto a scene causing a variety of light and dark spots. The object or parts of the object may block rays of light. The result is a darkened area either on or behind the object. This dark area is called a ***shadow***. The process of placing lines on a drawing to represent a shadow is called ***shading.***

There are several ways to shade a scene or object. One method starts by identifying the light source, Figure 11-11. Light construction lines are then drawn to show how light strikes the object. Areas that receive little or no light are darkened. This allows drafters to identify surfaces requiring shading.

DEVELOPING PICTORIAL DRAWINGS

Industry uses four types of pictorial views for describing products or scenes, Figure 11-12. These four types are: isometric, oblique, technical illustration, and perspective drawings. Each of these types uses methods of projection to make the drawings. These techniques

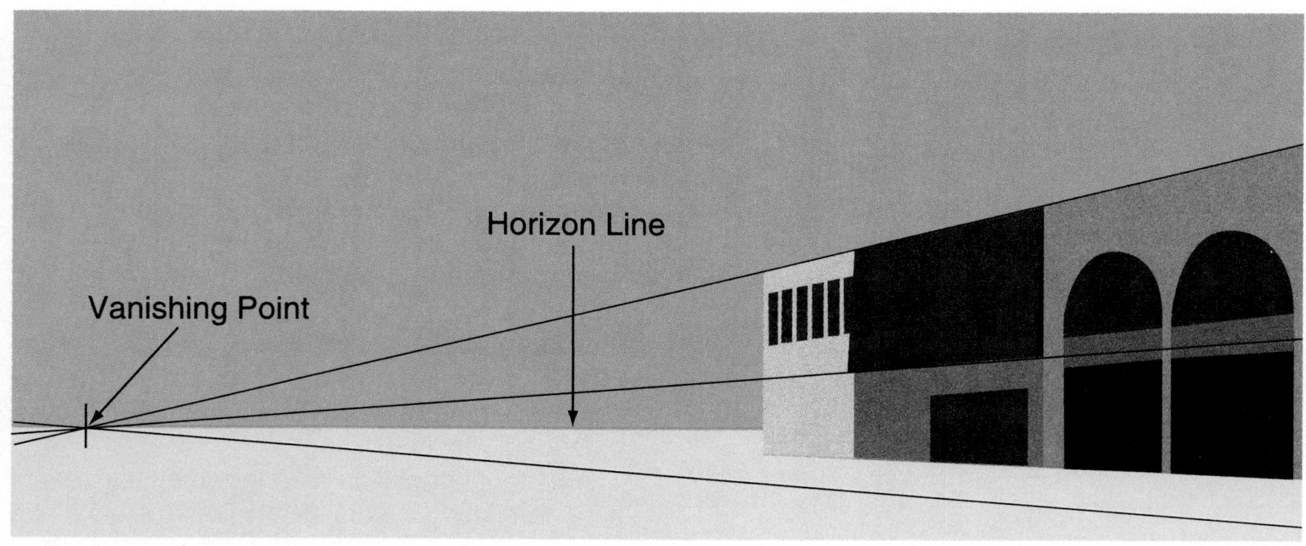

Figure 11-10. Vanishing points are fairly easy to locate in any scene.

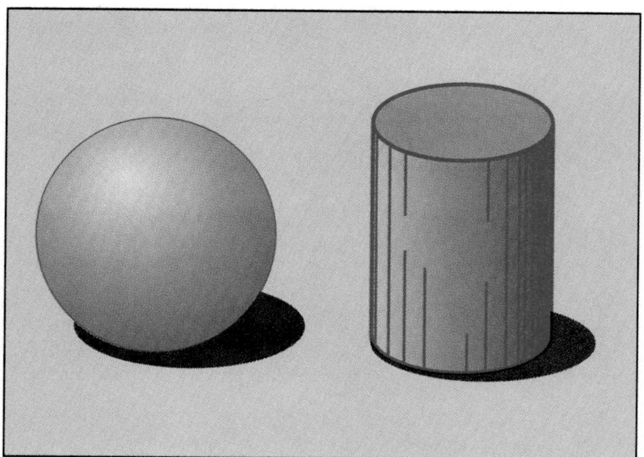

Figure 11-11. A light source creates shadows. Most pictorial views have a light source coming from the upper left corner of the drawing. Recreating this effect on a drawing is called shading.

are fairly simple to use. However, certain guidelines must be followed. These methods of projection are discussed in the following paragraphs.

Isometric and Oblique Drawings

Two of the simplest methods of creating pictorial views are ***isometric projection*** and ***oblique projection.*** Oblique drawings are the easiest to produce. However, they are not always accurate representations. Isometric drawings are more popular because the image is more realistic. Actual sizes and shapes can be displayed easily, Figure 11-13.

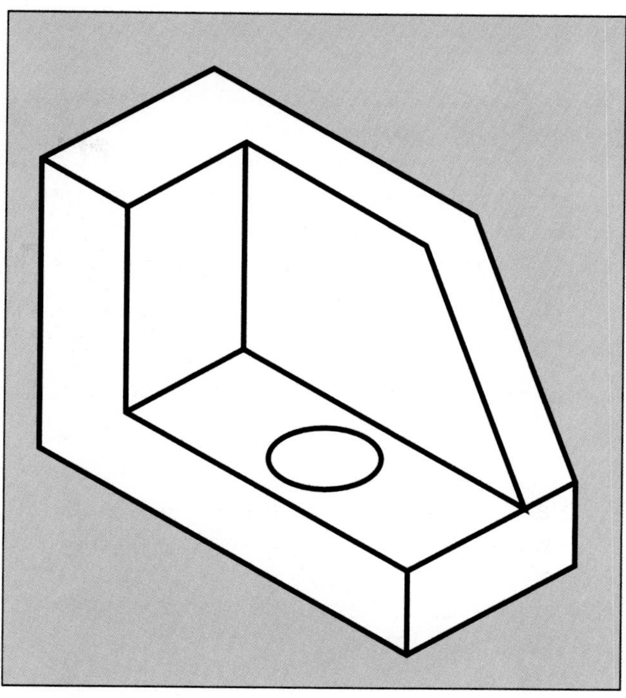

Figure 11-13. Isometric drawings are clear and easy to understand.

Oblique views contain a front view that is parallel to the picture plane. Depth is added by extending lines back at any angle. However, a 30 degree angle is used most often.

In contrast, isometric views are more difficult to develop. They are shown as they appear to the eye. Vertical edges are shown as vertical lines. Depth is usually shown with lines extend-

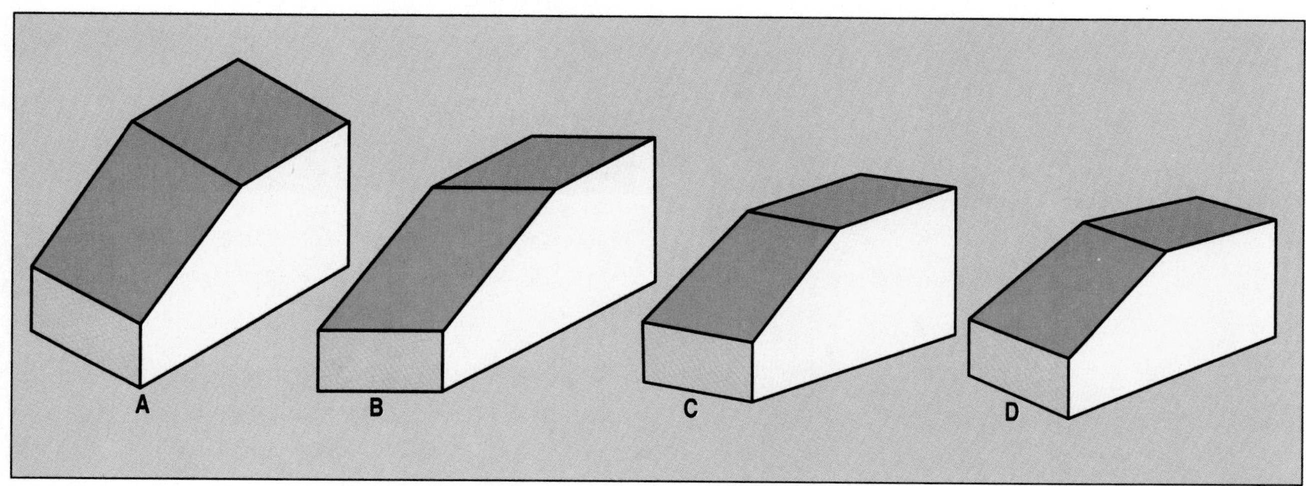

Figure 11-12. There are four types of pictorial views used most often in industry. A—Isometric drawing. B—Oblique drawing. C—Technical illustration. D—Perspective drawing.

ing back to the right at a 30 degree angle. Width is usually shown with lines extending back to the left at a 30 degree angle. Isometric views often become quite tall due to this method of layout. The view may need to be moved down the page in order for it to be centered. The total height cannot be larger than the available space on the sheet, Figure 11-14.

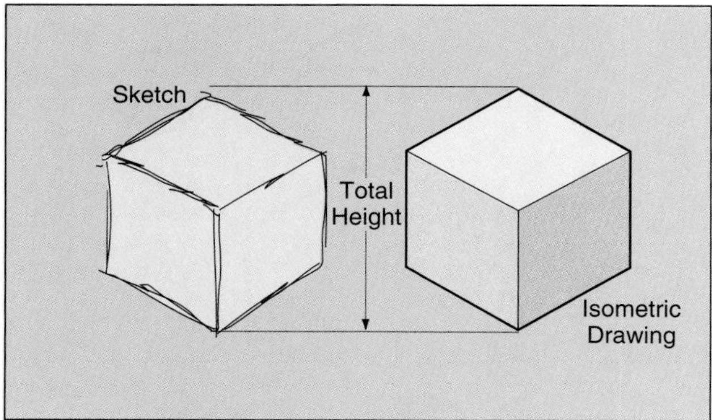

Figure 11-14. With isometric drawings, sketch the outline of the final drawing. This will make centering the drawing on the paper easier.

Isometric circles are often confusing to draw. Circles appear as ***ellipses*** in isometric drawings instead of true circles, Fig 11-15. Lines parallel to the object lines and that intersect the center of the circle should be sketched to help show the general shape. For the final drawing, an ***isometric template*** should be used, Figure 11-16. This permits the construction of clean, neat ellipses.

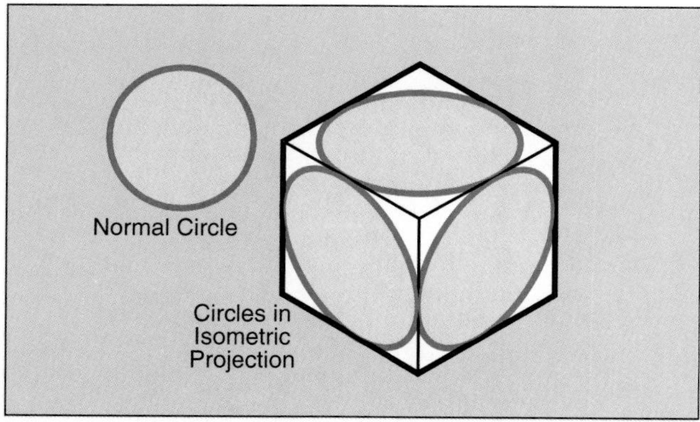

Figure 11-15. Circles in an isometric plane of projection appear as ellipses.

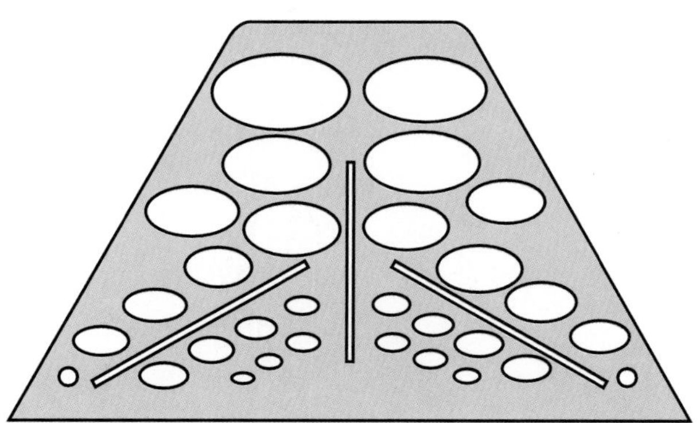

Figure 11-16. An isometric template is used to draw circles for a final isometric drawing.

Technical Illustrations

Many types of pictorial drawings are used in modern industry. A type where objects appear very realistic is called ***technical illustrations,*** Figure 11-17. These views often resemble photographs. Two types of technical illustrations are ***exploded views*** and ***cutaway views.*** Exploded views illustrate the assembly of a product. Cutaway views are designed to show internal details the eye is not able to see.

Figure 11-17. The illustration of a satellite in orbit is a scene that would be difficult to photograph. (AT&T)

Industrial drafters can describe many features of an object with a cutaway view. Cutaway views provide a "look" inside an object, Figure 11-18. Section lines are used to indicate where the object is "cut." Cutaway views will show the solid areas and the hollow areas.

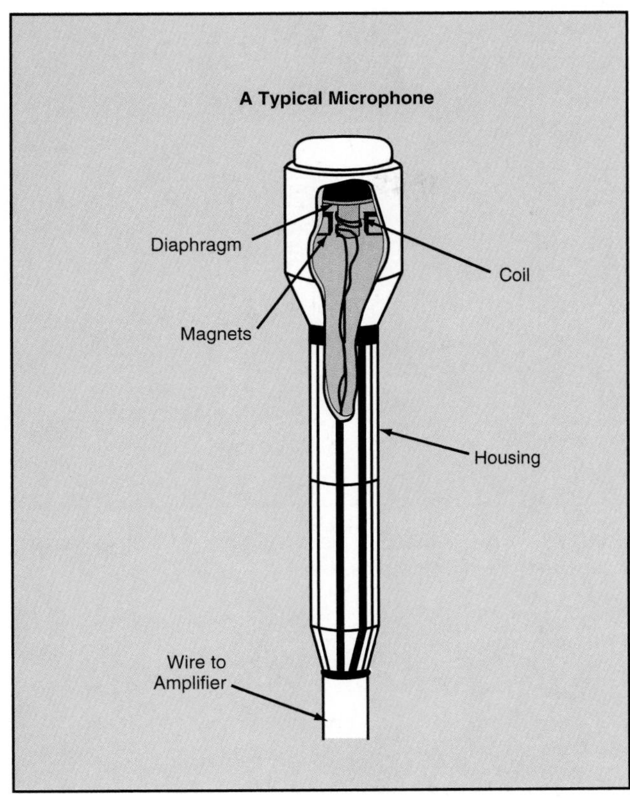

Figure 11-18. A typical cutaway view.

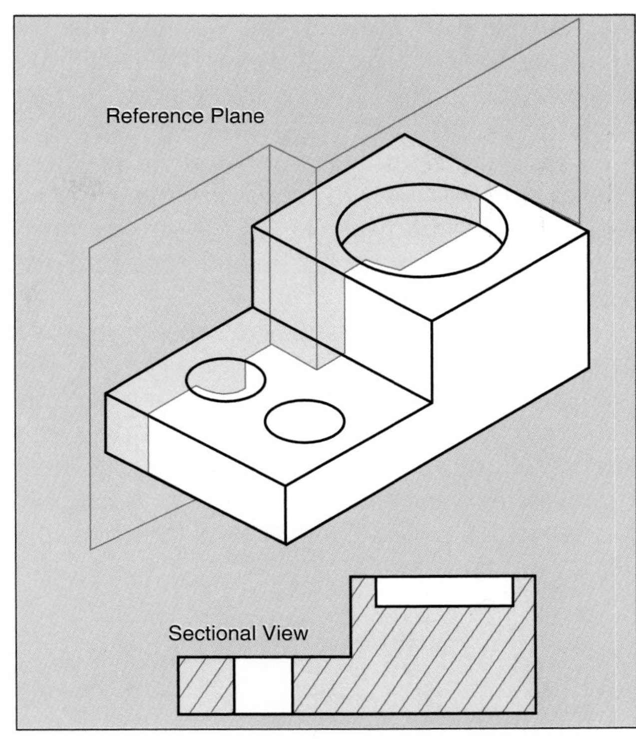

Figure 11-19. A reference plane is used to identify the line where the object will be "cut." The exposed area that results from the cut is called a section (or sectional) view.

Most cutaway views are made from an isometric drawing. The entire object is lightly drawn to begin the view. The desired plane of reference, or section line, is also shown on this view. The cutaway section view is then created from the section line. This view shows internal features not visible when the object is whole, Fig 11-19.

Exploded views are constructed in much the same manner. A rough isometric sketch is prepared to align and space each object. Spacing is sometimes difficult in exploded views. The total area required for the drawing is often very large. Individual parts are spread out around the page. To avoid confusion, the centerlines must be drawn through each object in the order of assembly, Figure 11-20. For this reason, these types of drawings are also referred to as ***assembly drawings.***

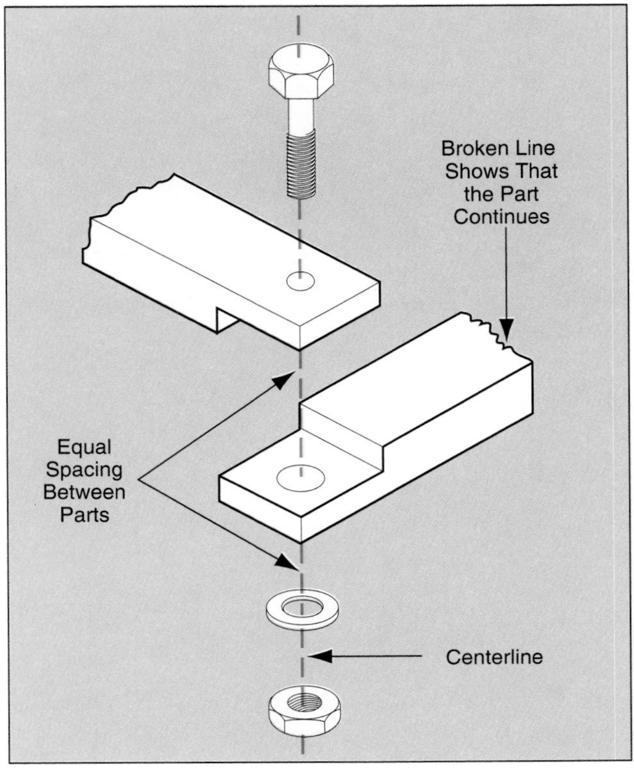

Figure 11-20. An exploded view shows the relationship of several parts and how they are assembled together.

Perspective Drawings

Perspective drawings are the most accurate and most realistic views for showing objects. This is due to the use of vanishing points. Items in these types of drawings are drawn as they appear to the eye. Lines extend to the horizon rather than at 30 degree angles. Refer to Figure 11-21.

To understand perspective views, start by examining several photographs, Figure 11-22. The image lines all seem to meet along points on the horizon. These are the vanishing points.

To develop a perspective view, a horizon line is made at normal eye level, Figure 11-23. Vanishing points are then placed on the horizon. All depth and width lines will run towards these points. Constructions lines should be constructed from the front surface of the object to the vanishing points. Try to spread the points out for a realistic image.

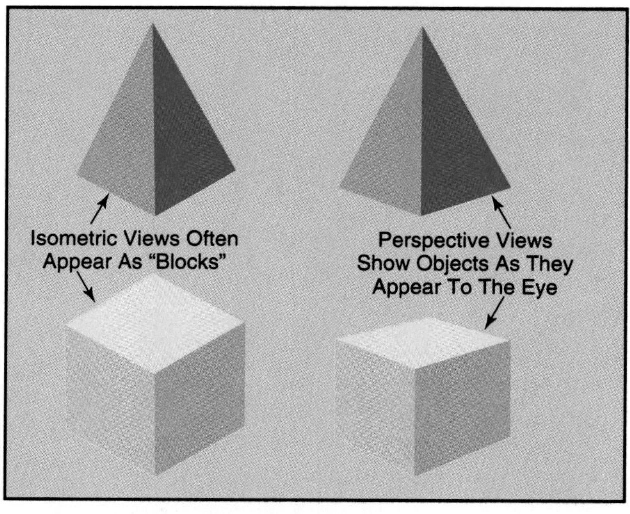

Figure 11-21. Perspective drawings provide a more realistic view than isometric drawings.

Figure 11-22. If image lines are traced onto a photograph, the vanishing points can be determined. (Kentucky Fried Chicken)

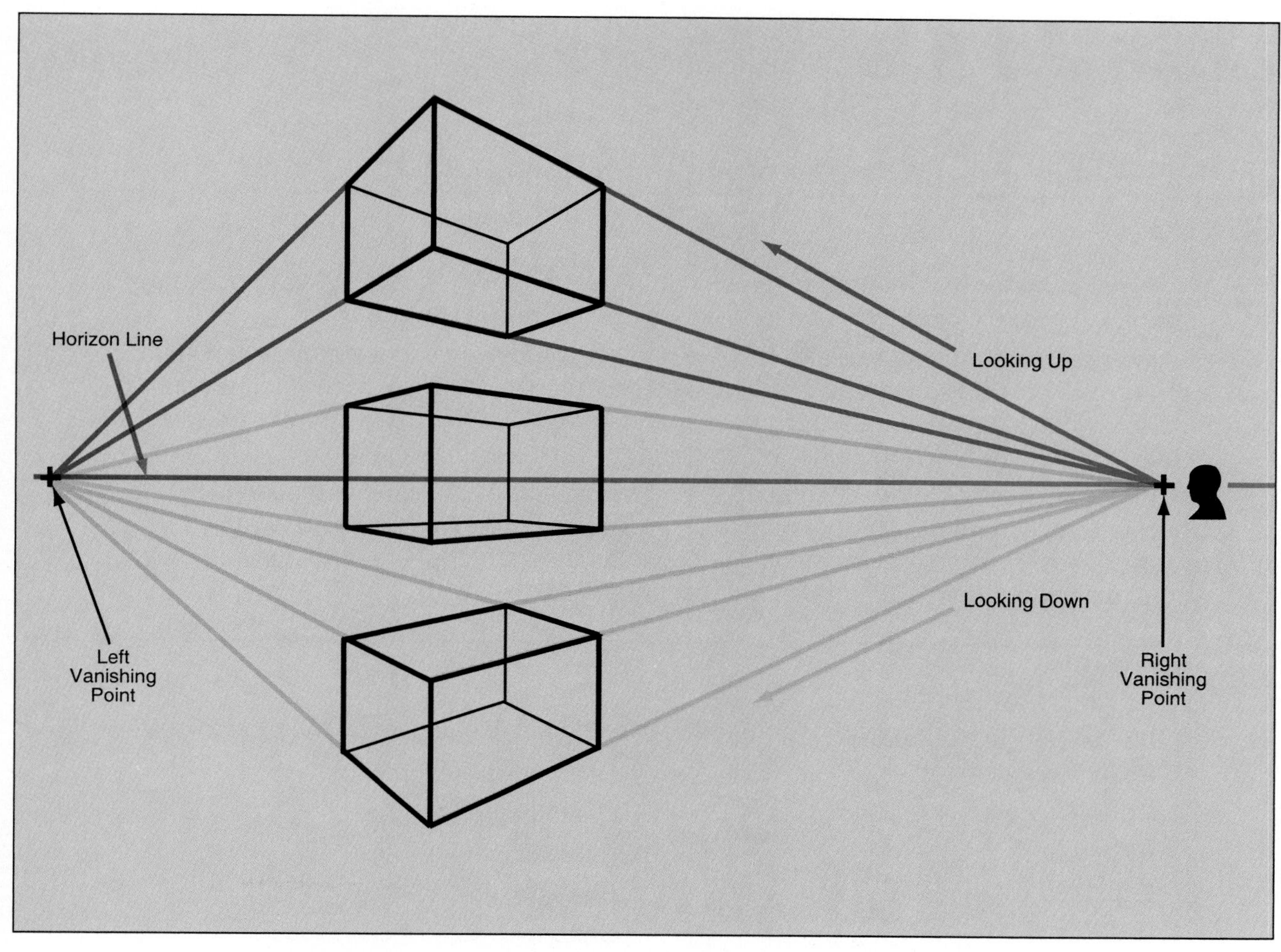

Figure 11-23. A perspective view of an object will look different when seen from different viewpoints.

CHAPTER 11 REVIEW

SUMMARY

Pictorial drawings are three-dimensional. They are more realistic than orthographic drawings. Often, pictorial drawings look very similar to photographs.

In order to get such a realistic drawing, the person developing a pictorial view must learn to use foreshortening and overlapping. The illustrator must also learn to recognize horizontal viewing planes, vanishing points, and shadows. Shading is important as well. All of these techniques help recreate the detailing of objects and scenes.

Pictorial drawings most often used in communicating technical information fall under four headings: isometric, oblique, technical, and perspective. Of these four areas, perspective is the most lifelike, since it is drawn as the item appears to the eye. In other words, objects appear to be natural and accurate.

KEY WORDS

All of the following words have been used in this chapter. Do you know their meanings?

- Assembly drawings
- Cutaway view
- Ellipse
- Exploded view
- Eye level
- Foreshortening
- Isometric projection
- Isometric template
- Oblique projection
- Overlapping
- Perspective drawings
- Shading
- Shadow
- Technical illustration
- Vanishing point

TEST YOUR KNOWLEDGE

Write your answers on a separate sheet of paper. Please do not write in this book.

1. A highrise building appears only a few inches tall when viewed from a great distance. This is an example of:

   A. Shortening.

   B. Overlapping.

   C. Foreshortening.

   D. None of the above.

2 Architects may use _____ to show the depth of a view.

3. Explain the difference between eye level and a bird's eye view.

4. _____ are points along the horizon used to develop perspective drawings.

5. A shadow is:

   A. The dark side of an object.

   B. A darkened area caused by blocked light.

   C. A bright spot.

   D. None of the above.

   E. Both A and B.

6. _____ drawings are more realistic than oblique drawings.

7. In perspective views items are drawn as they appear:

   A. From the top.

   B. From the bottom.

   C. To the eye.

   D. None of the above.

ACTIVITIES

1. Sketch a perspective view of the front of your classroom while seated on the left side of the room. Then develop another view of the front of the classroom while seated on the right side of the room. How are the two drawings different? Why are they different?

2. Develop an exploded view of a cabinet, with the top, sides, back, and doors removed. How would this type of drawing help you?

3. Using a cereal box, develop isometric, oblique, and perspective drawings. Use the same view for each drawing. How are the drawings alike? How are they different? Which one looks the most real?

4. Invite several architects to visit your class. Ask them to discuss the four types of pictorial drawings that were explained in the chapter. Ask them to include pictorial renderings of buildings they have designed.

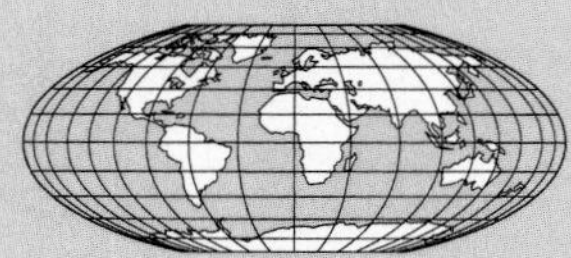

Section 2 Review

The ability to convert ideas and concepts into visual pictures is key to understanding technology. Everyone should be able to prepare technical images of products and systems. This section explained ways to develop sketches, pictorial views, schematics, and formal drawings. This area is called technical graphics.

Technical graphics is the language of the industry. Products, buildings, and systems all start as ideas. These ideas are often communicated with rough sketches. Further planning involves detailed renderings, graphs, charts, and multiview drawings. As products and systems gain approval, more formal technical communication is needed. This leads to complex drawings and computer images. Have you ever seen a realistic view of a skyscraper on a computer screen?

Today, most technical illustrations are produced with advanced software and computers. Computer-aided design (CAD) programs help in the making of sketches and drawings. Freehand sketches become pictorial views with simple computer commands. More detailed drawings can be produced with the stroke of several keys. Some of these drawings include section views, assembly drawings, and exploded views. Other CAD functions include the ability to produce solid models and multiple colors to illustrate different parts.

Success using modern CAD systems starts with an understanding of technical graphics fundamentals. The sketching tools and techniques outlined in this section have changed little over the past decades. The types of lines and views described are still important. Knowledge of orthographic views is also useful. Even large drawings are made up of simple three-view drawings and pictorial views.

Section 2 Activities

1. Create a simple three-view sketch of the outside of your home or apartment building. Estimate the overall size of the structure including the depth, width, and height. Multiply these dimensions to determine the volume of the building.

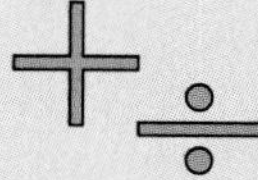

2. If you have two drawings to center on a sheet of paper, what formula would you use? Remember, you want to center the view horizontally and vertically. Make a sketch of two simple drawings and center them on the same sheet of paper. List the formula(s) you used on the sketch. Prepare a short speech explaining the process.

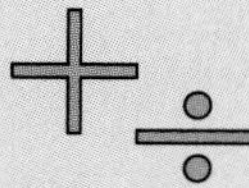  

3. Since technical drawing is the language of a technological world, you should understand the key terms related to technical drawings. Define the following terms. Prepare a short report on how each of these things affect everyday life.

Proportion	Rendering
Symmetry	Schematic
Orthographic	Solids modeling

4. Drawing has been important throughout history. Obtain pictures or copies of drawings from past centuries. These products may be scientific instruments or industrial machines. How did the engineers and inventors produce the drawings? Also, explain how the products shown in the drawings affected society. Explain your findings in a short report. Prepare the report on a word processor.

5. Create a chart illustrating the scores of one of your school's sports teams. Include the opponent's scores. If possible, use a computer. Develop a graph of the individual player statistics. Include their averages. Display the chart on a bulletin board in the classroom. Explain to the class the different parts of your chart.

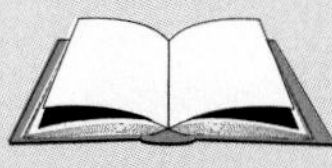 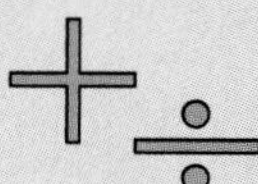 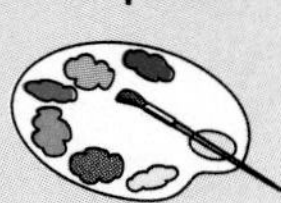

Mitsubishi

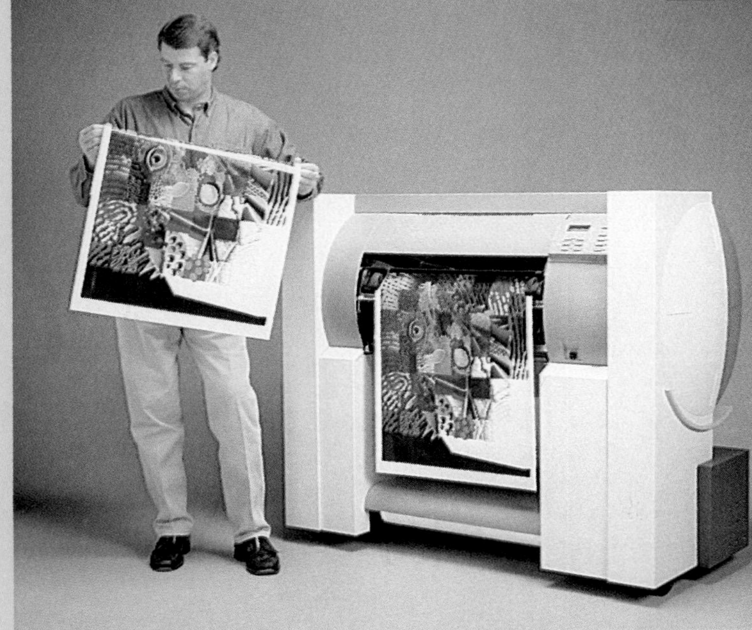

Summagraphics Corp.

Autodesk, Inc.

SECTION 3
PRINTED GRAPHICS

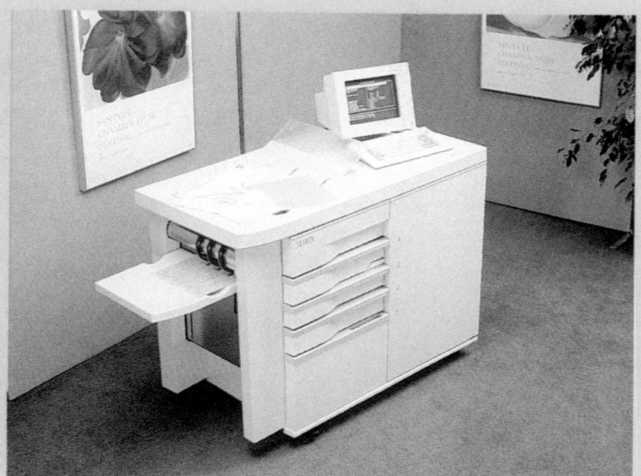

Xerox

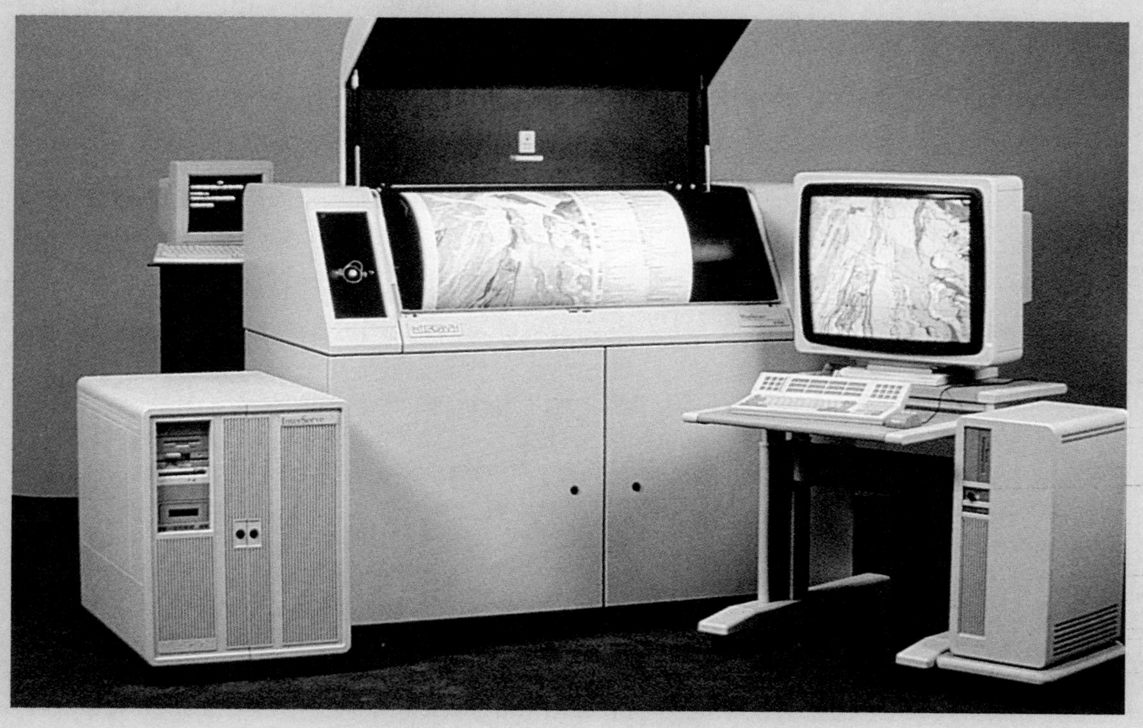

Integraph

CHAPTER 12

INTRODUCTION TO PRINTED GRAPHICS

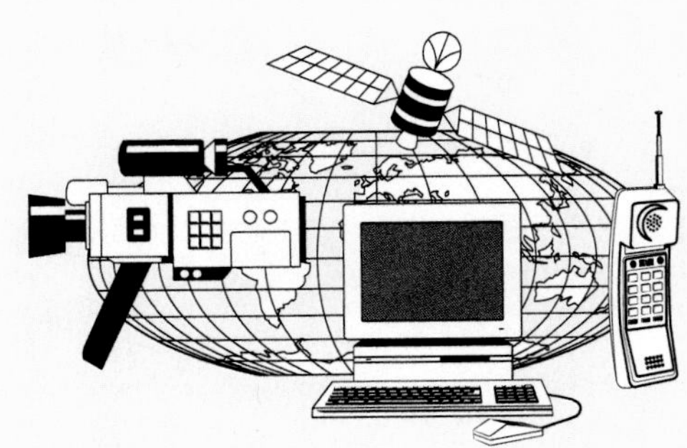

After studying this chapter, you will be able to:

- *Explain the development of printed graphics.*
- *Identify and describe the major types of printing techniques used in printed graphics.*
- *Cite the uses of printing procedures in consumer and industrial products.*

Graphic communication is one of the two technology-based communication systems (graphic communication and electronic communication). As you will recall from Chapter 6, graphic communication is made up of "printed graphics" and "technical graphics." In the last five chapters you have looked at different aspects of technical graphics, commonly called "drafting." Now you will look at printed graphics, commonly called "graphic communication." (This is not to be confused with graphic communication that refers to the industrial communication system as a whole.) In printed graphics, all messages are transmitted (sent) using images that are reproduced on printers or copiers. Individuals and businesses both use this technology. You see and use examples of printed materials daily. Items like books, magazines, and posters are produced by graphic means. So are beverage containers, brochures, and T-shirts, Figure 12-1. Many forms of printing exist today. Communicating with visual messages is an important practice in modern society. In this chapter you will look at the various types and uses of graphic techniques.

Figure 12-1. Printing of graphic images is commonly used in packaging most products. Can you think of other items that use printing? (Graphic Arts Technical Foundation)

HISTORY OF GRAPHIC COMMUNICATION

Printed images were first made on cave walls by our earliest ancestors. As time passed, people found new ways to communicate with graphics. You looked at several of these practices in Chapter 2 and in Chapter 7. This chapter will focus on the reproduction (copying) of graphic images. Reproduction processes include everything from duplicating a single photograph to printing thousands of newspapers.

Early reproductions were done by hand. This method obviously took a great deal of time. Just think how long it would take you to recopy this entire book by hand. Handwriting is not an efficient method of reproduction. A faster method of copying materials was developed in China around the year 700 AD. The Europeans began using the same method around the year 1200

AD. With this improved method, an image (picture) or text was cut into a wooden block, Figure 12-2. These blocks were used to print images on plaster, textiles, and parchment (paper). This process is known as ***block printing.*** This was a big improvement over handwriting. However, the process was still very slow since each page had to be carved and the wooden block had to be placed on each page by hand.

Figure 12-2. Relief printing is done from a raised surface. Image areas (letters or symbols) are above the plate or printing block.

The introduction of the printing press greatly improved this process. Simple presses that were used in making wine and paper were easily modified to make printing presses. An early printing press is shown in Figure 12-3. Several improvements came from the introduction of the printing press. The biggest improvement was the quality of ***impressions*** (transferred images). By locking the blocks of text in place, smudges and alignment problems were reduced.

Additional advances helped make printing more efficient. For example, it took hours to carve pages of text into printing blocks. However, around the year 1450, Johannes Gutenberg invented the ***type mold.*** This mold allowed several identical pieces of type to be made. This uniformity (all the same) made movable type practical. (Movable type had been invented by the Chinese about four hundred years earlier, but because of their complex language, it was never used.) Movable type allowed pages of text to be easily assembled

Figure 12-3. Early printing presses were operated by hand. Paper was forced against inked blocks of type.

into large racks. This development led to an increase in the amount of printed material. Books became available to many people, both for education and entertainment.

While movable type and the printing press vastly improved printed graphics, these methods remained quite slow. It would often take an entire day to set a page of type. Inventions such as the typewriter and typecasting machine helped make printing more efficient. Steam-powered platen presses improved speed. Rotary presses were developed to print on both sides of the paper at once. Rolled paper made the printing of newspapers much faster.

At the same time, changes in other areas of visual media progressed. Photographic techniques developed steadily. New types of films improved the quality of photographs. Cameras with advanced features simplified the photography process.

Eventually, new types of printing evolved. A good example is ***lithography,*** or ***offset printing.*** This procedure is based on the scientific principle that grease (oil) and water do not mix. ***Screen process printing*** works by forcing ink through prepared screens. ***Electrostatic copiers*** use powdered inks for copying, Figure 12-4. Modern ***ink jet printers*** reproduce detailed images quickly and efficiently.

Today, desktop publishing has allowed everyone to become efficient printers. Personal computers with word-processing software are used in most offices, Figure 12-5. School

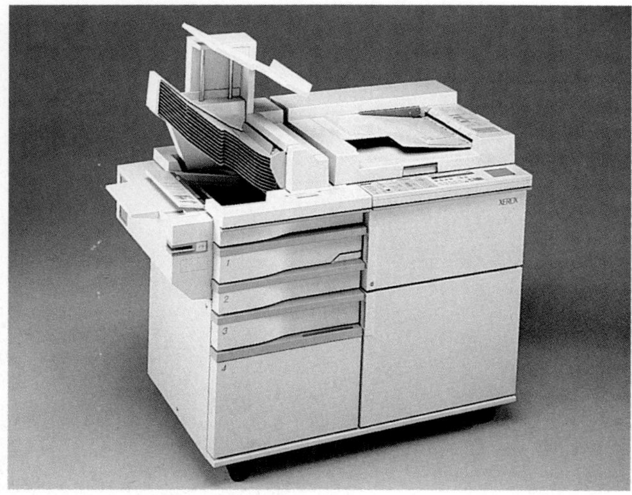

Figure 12-4. Modern photocopiers can produce transparencies, automatic two-sided copies, and automatic reductions along with the features of traditional copiers. (Xerox Corp.)

Figure 12-5. Word-processing is easy with computers. When text and graphics are combined on a personal computer to produce a document, it is called "desktop publishing."

homework is also easier using computers. Software helps in the layout and printing of complex documents.

PRINTED GRAPHICS USES

Look around where you are reading this book. What forms of printed graphics do you see? The items you notice are produced by one of several different printing techniques. These techniques can be divided into categories. These categories include documents, packages, textiles, labels, products, and the arts, Figure 12-6.

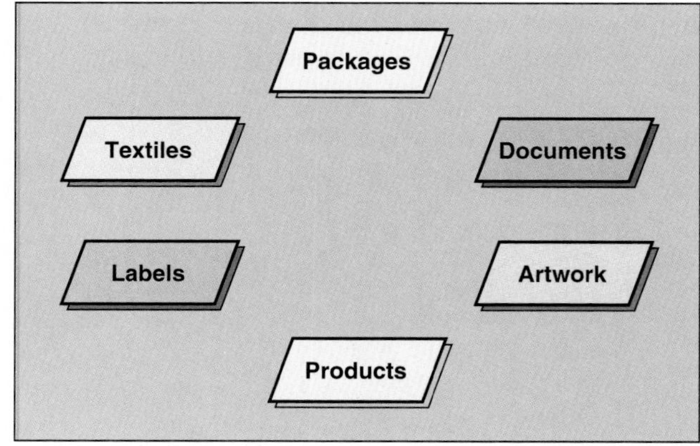

Figure 12-6. The six groups of printed products.

This book is an example of a document. Printed documents usually require reading. They contain information for use at a later date. Newspapers, menus, maps, and brochures are documents. So are catalogs, greeting cards, and stationery. These materials contain printed images (text and/or pictures) that have meaning.

Most packages have printed graphics. Designs and information are printed on cans, boxes, and plastic bags, Figure 12-7. You read many packages for information and enjoyment. Have you ever read a cereal box at the breakfast table? Important details are given about the food inside.

Figure 12-7. Most packages have some form of printing on them. Printing describes the products inside and printing is also used for various product codes. Bags, boxes, balloons, and special event cups or mugs often have printing on them.

Textiles are another major category of printed graphics. Many articles of clothing have printed messages on them. Messages on shirts show your favorite school, activity, or athletic team. Shirts may show a place you have been or simply have an attractive design, Figure 12-8. Designer labels make fashion items popular. Graphic messages on caps and uniforms display name brands.

Figure 12-8. T-shirts and sweatshirts may feature many types of messages, school names, products, pictures, and advertisements.

Figure 12-9. These boxes of paper are ready for shipping. Notice the information on each label. (Hammermill Paper Company)

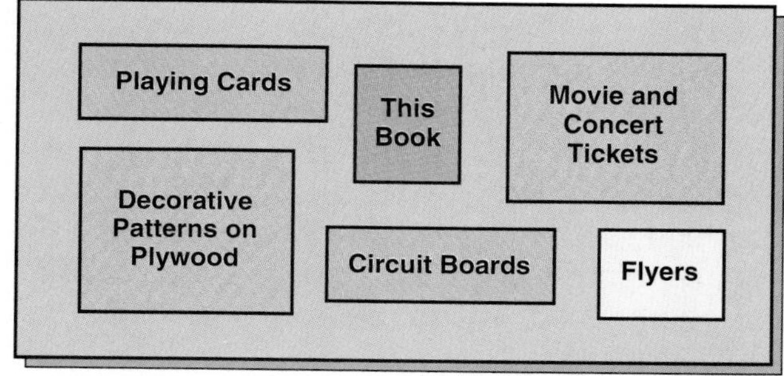

Figure 12-10. How many of these printed products do you recognize?

Labels are found everywhere in our society. People collect bumper stickers and decals. Address stickers are commonly used on envelopes. Many purchased products are marked by labels. These describe their contents, Figure 12-9. Most labels are prepared by screen process printing.

Many consumer products include graphic images in their design, Figure 12-10. Board games and playing cards are good examples. The printed designs create a message or symbol. The appearance of other items is produced entirely by graphic means. For instance, plywood paneling is a printed product. Large presses are used to print a wood grain pattern on each panel. Circuit boards are produced in a similar way.

Printing practices are often used in the display of art. Painting is a form of artwork. To reproduce the work of artists, the original paintings are copied. Then posters and prints are produced. Photographs are also a form of artwork. Printing techniques are used to turn a negative into a usable photograph. Other times printing techniques are used to create the art itself. Lithography and intaglio are popular processes among artists.

As you can see, printing techniques are used daily. Industry also relies on these techniques for routine operations. Activities such as recordkeeping and correspondence are examples. From company reports to employee paychecks, printed materials are vital in today's business world.

PRINTING TECHNIQUES

Today's technology has produced six major types of printed graphics processes. These include relief process, continuous tone photography, electrostatic, intaglio, screen process, and lithography, Figure 12-11. You will examine these techniques, along with several specialty processes.

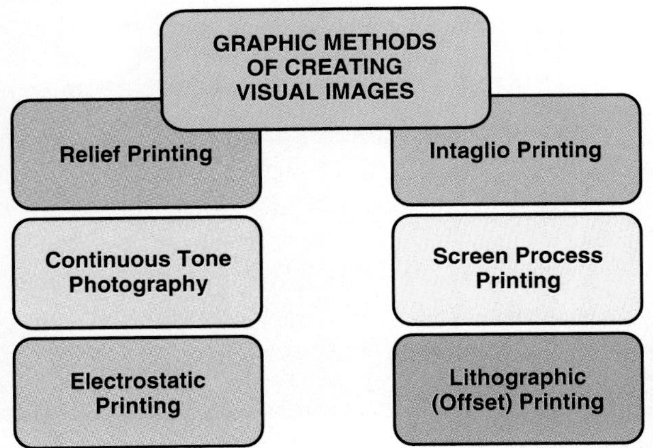

Figure 12-11. The six methods of creating graphic images.

Relief Printing

Relief printing is the transfer of images from a raised surface. Typically, this surface is type (letters and numbers) contained on engraved blocks. The text can be hand or machine set. All relief work is prepared in reverse, Figure 12-12. When pressed into paper, the reproduced image becomes readable, or ***right-reading.***

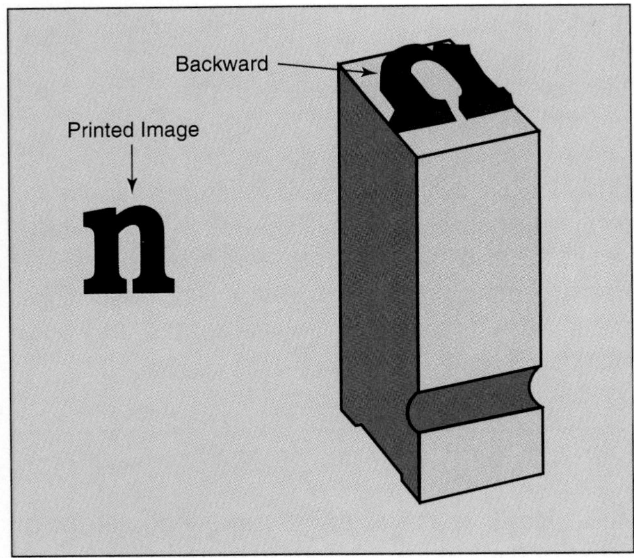

Figure 12-12. Text for relief printing is created backwards or "wrong-reading."

In relief printing, the ink is applied on the type with a roller. The paper is then brought in contact with the image area. A printing press is often used for this. Simple platen presses use the principles of relief printing, Figure 12-13.

Figure 12-13. The platen press is an early example of printing machinery. Have you seen a press like this before?

Relief printing is rarely used in modern industry. Relief work now mostly involves printing small orders. Wedding invitations are usually completed in this manner. Rubber stamps are often prepared using a special type of relief printing.

Although standard relief printing practices are on the decline, a process called ***flexography*** has become more common. Flexography is similar to relief printing in that printing is done from a raised surface. However, the raised surface is a flexible rubber or plastic plate, not raised metal type.

Flexography is used on items such as paper and plastic bags, and cardboard cartons. It is also growing in popularity for printing books, newspapers, and catalogs.

Screen Process Printing

Screen printing starts with an original design. A stencil of the image is produced. Stencils are cut in a film either by hand, or by photographic or thermal means. The stencil is attached to a screen. Most screens are plastic or metal. At one time, all screens were silk. Consequently this procedure is often called ***silk screening.*** Today silk is seldom used because of the high cost.

Images are created by forcing ink through a screen with a rubber squeegee. The ink appears on the transfer medium. Separate screens are prepared for each color desired.

Forms of screen printing have been around since the middle ages. However, screen printing did not become widely used until recently. Modern industries rely heavily on screen process printing. Many common products are completed with screen images. Examples include T-shirts, signs, CDs, and glass containers, Figure 12-14.

Figure 12-14. Screen process printing is common. Many different everyday items are screen printed during production.

Continuous Tone Photography

Continuous tone photography has two uses in graphic communication. Photographs may serve as a final product, or they can help create pictures (or masters) to be used with other printing processes. However, making masters requires additional steps. For example, stencils used in screen printing are often prepared by photographic means.

To produce continuous tone photographs, a camera and film are needed. Light entering the camera strikes the light-sensitive film. The film is later developed in a chemical bath. Resulting pictures may be black and white or in full color. Slides, prints, and movie film are produced this way. You will look more closely at this procedure in Chapter 17.

Intaglio

Intaglio (in-'tal-yo) printing transfers ink from an image engraved into (below) a surface. In industry, this engraving is done on a metal plate or cylinder. Ink is applied to the engraved surface. A blade is used to wipe off excess ink from the surface of the plate. The ink will stay below the surface in the engraved areas. When paper is pressed on to the surface, ink lifts out of the engraved image area and is transferred to the paper.

In industry this method is better known as ***gravure printing.*** This printing method is frequently used to publish newspaper supplements and to make the designs on wooden wall panelling. The gravure, or intaglio, process is illustrated in Figure 12-15.

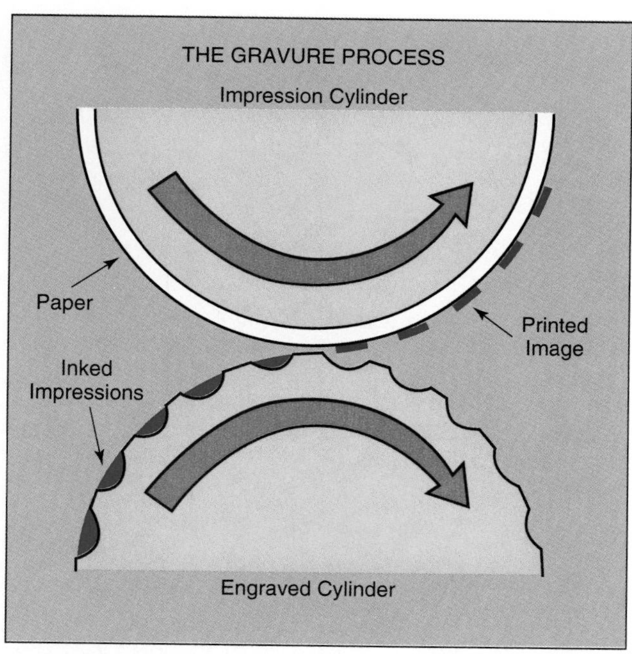

Figure 12-15. Intaglio means "below the surface." Gravure (or intaglio) images are printed from inked areas below a smooth surface.

Electrostatic Copying

Much of modern office communication is reproduced using electrostatic copying. This is better known as ***photocopying.*** Some copiers produce black and white images while others are capable of producing full-color copies.

The electrostatic process relies on the principles of physics. Science has demonstrated that unlike electrical charges (negative and positive) attract each other. In photocopying machines, a picture is taken on a metal plate. The image on this plate has a positive charge (+) and attracts the toner (a powder) that has a negative charge (-). As paper passes by the plate, toner is transferred to the paper. After heating, the toner burns into the paper. This leaves a permanent image on the page. Electrostatic copying is shown in Figure 12-16.

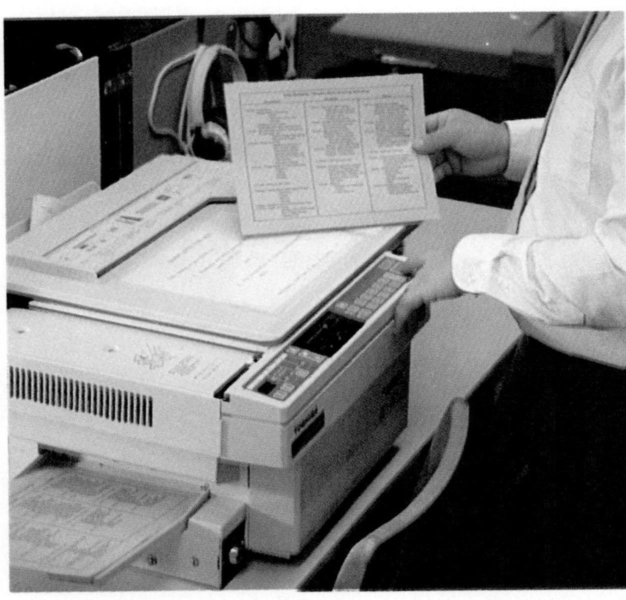

Figure 12-16. An electrostatic printer creates graphic images using electricity. Electrical charges direct the flow of powdered or liquid inks.

Laser printers use the same basic process as electrostatic copiers. A plate, or drum, is negatively charged. A laser beam is used to positively charge an image onto the plate. (A laser beam is a concentrated, single wave-length light.) The negatively charged toner will stick to the positively charged image, but not to the rest of the negatively charged plate. The toner is then fused to the paper in the same way as in photocopiers.

Lithography

Lithography is also known as ***offset printing,*** Figure 12-17. In offset work, an original is prepared on a metal, paper, or plastic plate. Normally, the plate is prepared both chemically and mechanically to hold moisture.

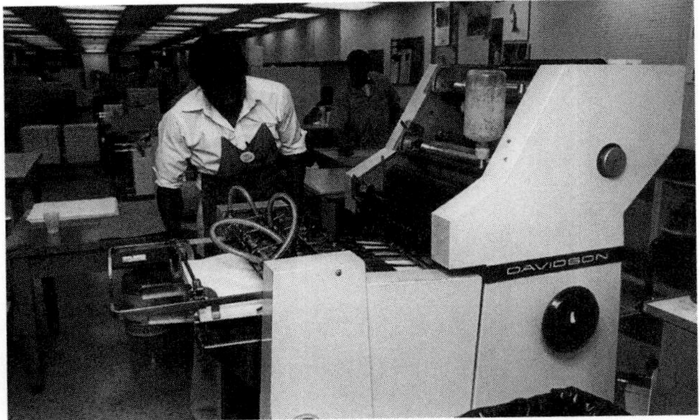

Figure 12-17. Offset presses are found in many industries and schools. Flyers, pamphlets, and other handouts are often offset printed. (AFT-Davidson)

The offset technique works on the principle that grease and water do not mix. The image to be printed is made with a greasy ink on the printing plate. The plate is coated with a film of moisture (water). The water sticks only to the clear areas (those without ink). Ink that will make the image is rolled over the plate. This ink sticks only to the "greasy" image area. The inked image is transferred to a rubber blanket in reverse (offset). As the paper passes under the roller, the image is transferred from the rubber blanket. The impression leaves a deposit of ink on the page that is right-reading.

Lithography is the most common industrial printing process in use today. Quick printing establishments use this method. Larger firms also rely on offset procedures. Most books and magazines are printed by lithographic means. We will explore lithographic printing more in Chapter 15.

Specialty Processes

Technical growth permitted the development of different methods of printing. Some of these methods are used in schools, offices, and homes. Others are used in industry.

The ***ditto printing process*** works by typing or drawing onto a special master. This leaves a carbon deposit on the carrier sheet. A spirit fluid (similar to paint thinner) softens the carbon during the printing process. This allows the images to be deposited on paper. The color of the print is determined by the master. A purple image is most common. Green, red, black, and blue are also available.

The ***mimeograph printing process*** is another specialty process, Figure 12-18. This type of master can also be prepared by typing or drawing. This procedure is similar to screen process printing. The master acts like a stencil. This stencil is attached to a cylinder on a mimeograph machine. Ink is forced through the openings of the master. As paper passes the master, a deposit of ink is transferred. Black ink is most commonly used.

Figure 12-18. The mimeograph process resembles screen process printing. Can you describe how the two are alike?

Diazo printing is also a specialty printing process. It has many uses in business and industry. The most common use is reproducing engineering drawings. The resulting copies are called ***whiteprints.*** Unlike blueprints, the background is white and all lines are blue, although these drawings are sometimes referred to as "blueprints." Making a whiteprint is relatively easy. The process is similar to making a blueprint. The original is passed through a diazo machine along with a copy paper. The image is copied by exposing the paper to light. The copied image is developed by exposing it to ammonia gases.

Heat is also used to produce special text or images. It is especially popular in T-shirt printing. Designs are first created using offset or screen process printing. The designs are printed on thin tissue paper. These images are then bonded to the textile (cloth) surface using heat. This process is called ***heat transfer printing.***

Another thermal technique is used in small electronic calculators and **facsimile (FAX) machines.** The paper on these instruments is heat sensitive. Hot wires (or a stylus) contact the rolled paper. The dye in the sheets creates the imagery when it comes in contact with the heat.

Another specialty process is ***ink jet printing.*** In this method, droplets of ink are shot onto paper. A rectangular pattern of dots form the characters. This procedure is controlled by a computer. In fact, the most common use of this practice is as a computer output device. Many home computer systems use this type of printer. Mailing labels and name tags are often produced by ink jet. These printers produce high-quality reproductions and are affordable. Some ink jet printers even produce color printouts, Figure 12-19.

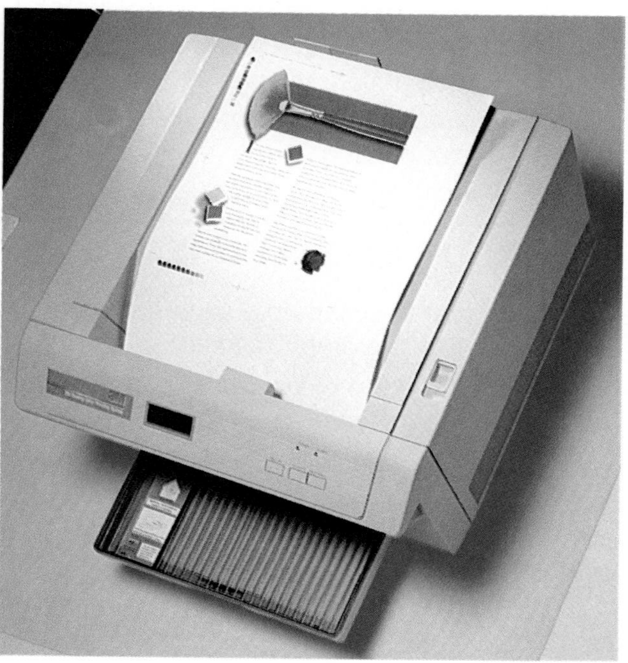

Figure 12-19. Color proof printers use four different ink jets to print the four basic colors cyan, magenta, yellow, and black. (3M)

CHAPTER 12 REVIEW

SUMMARY

Graphic communication is one of the technology-based communication systems. This system is broken down into "technical graphics" and "printed graphics."

In printed graphics, all messages transmitted are printed images. Documents, packages, textiles, labels, products, and artistic work are all types of printed graphics. They are reproduced using a printing technique.

Printed graphics has grown and improved steadily throughout history. Inventions like the printing press and movable type helped this growth. Today there are six major types of graphic printing processes. These processes are relief, screen process, continuous tone photography, intaglio, electrostatic, and lithography. In addition to these major types, there are other specialty types of processes. These processes have improved the quality of visual communication.

KEY WORDS

All of the following words have been used in this chapter. Do you know their meanings?

- Block printing
- Continuous tone photography
- Diazo printing
- Ditto printing process
- Electrostatic copying
- Facsimile (FAX) machines
- Flexography
- Gravure printing
- Heat transfer printing
- Impression
- Ink jet printing
- Intaglio printing
- Lithography
- Mimeograph printing process
- Offset printing
- Photocopying
- Relief printing
- Right-reading
- Screen process printing
- Screen printing
- Silk screening
- Type molds
- Whiteprints

TEST YOUR KNOWLEDGE

Write your answers on a separate sheet of paper. Please do not write in this book.

1. Printed graphics sends all its messages using _____.
2. Give five examples of how industry uses printed graphics to carry out daily operations.
3. Which printing method would be used to reproduce a small number of office copies?
   A. Relief.
   B. Screen process.
   C. Offset.
   D. Electrostatic.
4. Which method of printing would be used to print wall paneling?
   A. Relief.
   B. Screen process.
   C. Intaglio.
   D. Offset.

5. Photocopying newspapers and magazines for future use is an example of what part of the communication process?
   - A. Designing.
   - B. Coding.
   - C. Transmitting.
   - D. Storing.

Matching questions: Match the definition in the left-hand column with the correct term in the right-hand column.

6. Projecting images through film onto light sensitive paper.
7. A popular office reproduction method.
8. Based on the scientific principle that oil and water do not mix.
9. Thermal method used to print images on textiles.
10. Printing from a raised surface.
11. Printing from an engraved surface.
12. Computer directs droplets of ink into the transfer medium.
13. Forcing ink through a stencil.

- A. Relief printing.
- B. Screen process printing.
- C. Continuous tone photography.
- D. Intaglio printing.
- E. Electrostatic printing.
- F. Lithographic printing.
- G. Ink jet printing.
- H. Heat transfer printing.

ACTIVITIES

1. Collect samples of products that use graphic techniques in their manufacture. Identify the type of printing practice used in producing these items. Which items look the best? Why?
2. Research the development of printed graphics. Construct a time line to illustrate this development. Prepare a short report and present it to the class.
3. View videos on various methods of graphic reproduction. Write a short report on the similarities and differences of the various types.
4. Invite a professional photographer to visit your class to explain the techniques used to develop and print photographic film.
5. Use an electrostatic copier to create a class newsletter. Include short articles, photographs, and artwork done by you and your classmates. Write a short report explaining how you did this.
6. Research the career of Johannes Gutenberg. Present the information to your class as an oral report.
7. Arrange a visit to a quick-print shop. Observe the printing methods used. Prepare a short report on what you observed. Discuss with the rest of the class what you observed.
8. Create a display board featuring the six major types of graphic techniques. Present this to the class.

CHAPTER 13

PRINTED GRAPHICS DESIGN AND PRODUCTION

After studying this chapter, you will be able to:

- ❖ *Identify the stages used to create and transmit the graphic message.*
- ❖ *Explain common production techniques in developing visual messages.*
- ❖ *Compose a visual message using graphic production techniques and the elements and principles of design.*

The purpose of a printed graphics design is to transmit visual information. The message may instruct, persuade, inform, or entertain the audience. It should look pleasing and be easy to understand. If the design is not good, the message may be lost.

In order to communicate effectively, certain design elements and principles must be understood. In this chapter, you will look at the elements and principles used in the production and design of printed graphics, Figure 13-1.

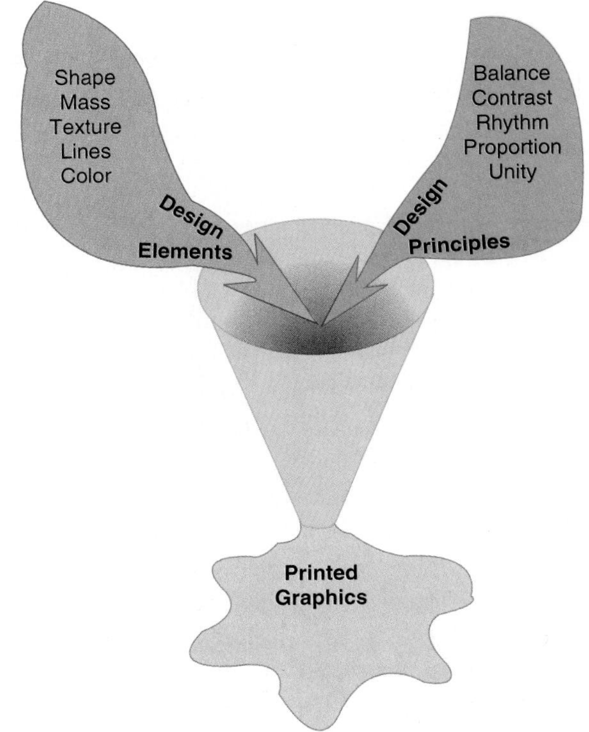

Figure 13-1. A graphic designer uses both design principles and design elements to create printed graphics.

DESIGNING

Design is the first step in transmitting a visual message. A design is decided upon before illustrations are picked or text is printed. ***Design elements*** and ***design principles*** are used in the creation of a printed graphics message. Every graphic message has a purpose and an audience. These factors are combined with creative ideas to design the message.

Design Elements

Creating a visual message requires the following *elements of design:*

- Shape.
- Mass.
- Texture.
- Lines.
- Color.

These elements are considered when constructing artwork and copy. The design phase begins with development of basic lines.

Shape is the result of the combination of lines and mass. Examples include rectangles, circles, and other geometric designs. You may recognize the familiar shapes of the signs in Figure 13-2. Many shapes add form or structure to a message. The shape of lettering also creates different impressions.

Figure 13-2. Signs and symbols are common graphic designs. The shape of the sign has a certain meaning. An orange traffic sign always transmits the message "contruction."

Mass refers to the amount of space taken up on the page. Larger objects, those with more mass, are noticed before smaller objects. Dark (or bold) objects give the appearance of mass (appear larger). That is why bold print is used in many books. **Bold type appears larger and more important** than normal type. This is a key design element.

Texture describes the surface of an object. In other words, texture tells whether the surface of an object is smooth or rough. The texture of a surface affects what you see or feel. Shading on drawings creates a feeling of texture. It provides realism, Figure 13-3. Graphic designers realize the effect of texture and use this element.

Lines are strokes made with pens or pencils, or they can be formed using tape or computers. The tape can be clear adhesive tape with pre-printed solid, dashed, and/or colored lines. Lines vary in width and length, Figure 13-4. Lines can be straight, wavy, or curved to help create the desired visual effect. Words and handwriting are simply images made up of lines.

Color is the final element of design. Color adds emphasis to graphic work. Red and yellow attract attention. Blue and green are calming (or mild) colors. Changing the color of text draws attention to the printed material.

Figure 13-3. Sketches can be shaded to closely resemble actual scenes.

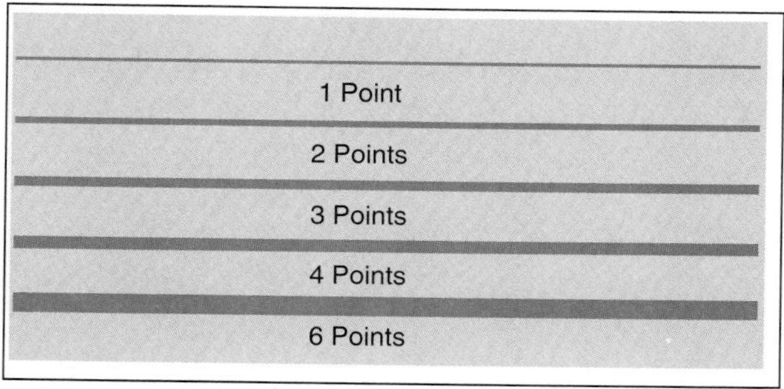

Figure 13-4. The width (thickness) of a line is indicated by "points." Point values are shown here.

Design Principles

Design principles describe the nature of the layout. *Principles of design* include:

- Balance.
- Contrast.
- Rhythm.
- Proportion.
- Unity.

Three examples are shown in Figure 13-5.

Balance deals with the location of parts or objects within a layout. If the parts are centered, the layout is referred to as having ***formal balance.*** In this case, each item is orderly and evenly weighted. If the arrangement of objects is random, the layout has ***informal balance.*** Figure 13-6 shows two examples of informal balance.

Contrast is important in providing a point of emphasis in a layout. Contrast can be achieved with colors, text, or lines. Bold styles of lettering often provide contrast. Color or

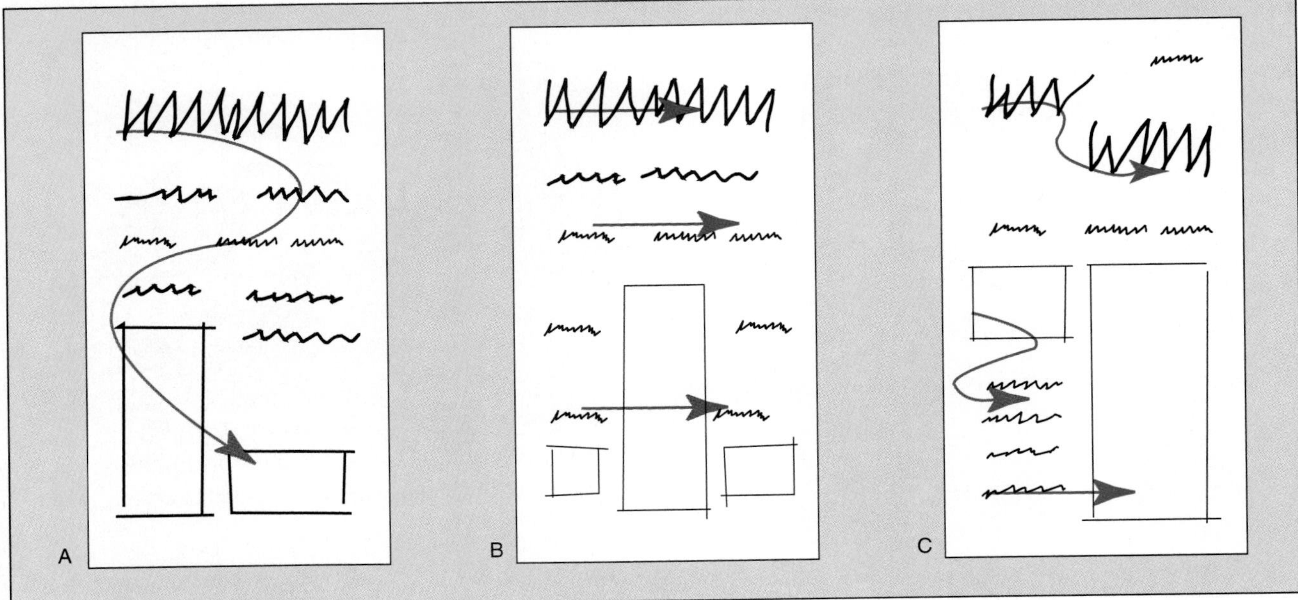

Figure 13-5. Different design principles affect the way you see a design. A—Rhythm: the eye "flows" over the design. B—Formal balance: the eye follows the design from left to right. C—Contrast: the eye wanders across the design.

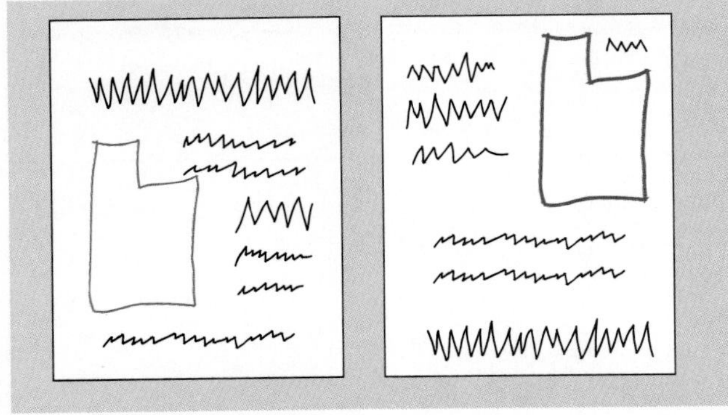

Figure 13-6. Balance can change the "feel" of a layout.

Figure 13-7. The design of this poster is improved with the addition of lines that create rhythm. Your eye tends to focus on the artwork and titles.

shading of artwork can also provide contrast. Attempts to "catch" your eye usually are examples of contrast.

Rhythm deals with the way a message is constructed. Certain designs seem to guide your eye through the message. The peaks in Figure 13-7 have rhythm.

Proportion is the relationship of sizes in a design. Object size should be uniform throughout the whole message. Titles should not be much larger or smaller than the rest of the text. Large pictures often detract from the design. Sometimes it can be difficult to complete a pleasing, uniform design, Figure 13-8.

Unity is the final design principle. The function of unity is to "pull" the total design together. Designs that lack unity rarely communicate a message well. The exchange of ideas or feelings becomes confusing. This is shown in Figure 13-9.

CODING

In communication, after the message has been designed it must be coded. In the case of a printed visual message, coding is known as layout. ***Layout*** is the assembly of copy (text) and artwork (illustrations), Figure 13-10.

Figure 13-8. Many illustrations contain titles or artwork that appear "out of place." What is wrong with this design?

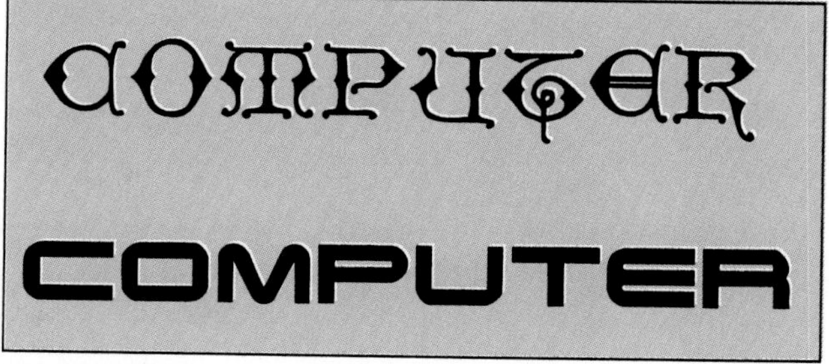

Figure 13-9. Computers are examples of modern technology. The term, "computer" looks odd in certain old-fashioned typefaces (above). The use of an old-style typeface when talking about a modern item like a computer does not lead to unity in the message. However, if a modern typeface is used, unity is achieved in the message.

This book is a good example of layout. After the text was written and the illustrations selected, a layout was designed. The copy includes the words, sentences, and paragraphs of the book. Copy also includes the captions that go along with the artwork. The artwork includes drawings

Figure 13-10. Graphic designers often create a rough layout of a job. They are then able to compare designs and select the best format.

and photographs. They add meaning to the copy. There are five steps involved in layout. They are:

- Thumbnail sketches.
- Rough layout.
- Comprehensive layout.
- Pasteup.
- Mechanical layout.

Thumbnail Sketches

Layout starts with ***thumbnail sketches.*** These are small, crude drawings similar to the thumbnail sketches discussed in Chapter 2 when you looked at technical illustrations, Figure 13-11. Thumbnail sketches are initial ideas for layout of the message. Thumbnail sketches are used as a reference when discussing and developing initial designs. When one idea is decided upon, the layout then moves to the next stage.

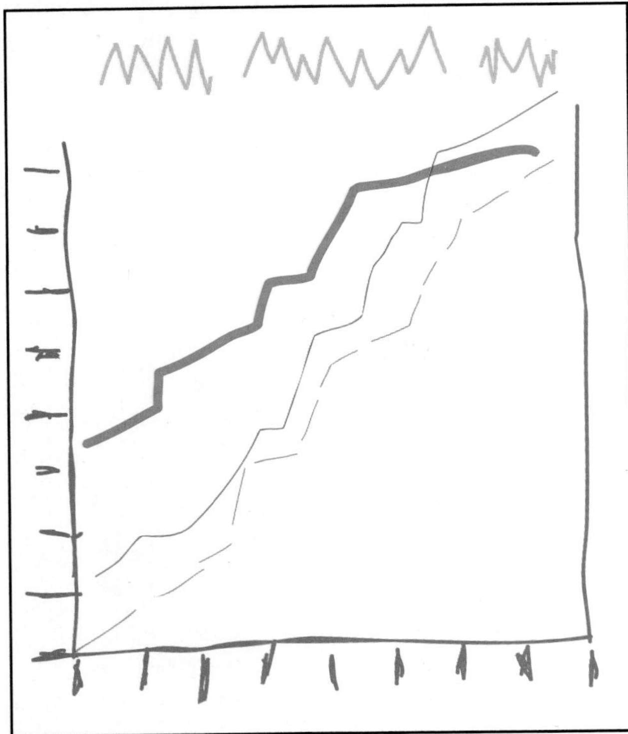

Figure 13-11. Thumbnail sketches give the basic idea of a message.

Rough Layout

In a rough layout, the idea is developed further. A ***rough layout*** is more accurate and detailed than a thumbnail sketch. A rough layout is produced to scale. This means text and artwork will be shown in their proper proportions, Figure 13-12. A rough layout is used to show how the text and art will fit together. In other words, a rough layout will appear very similar to the final product, only less refined.

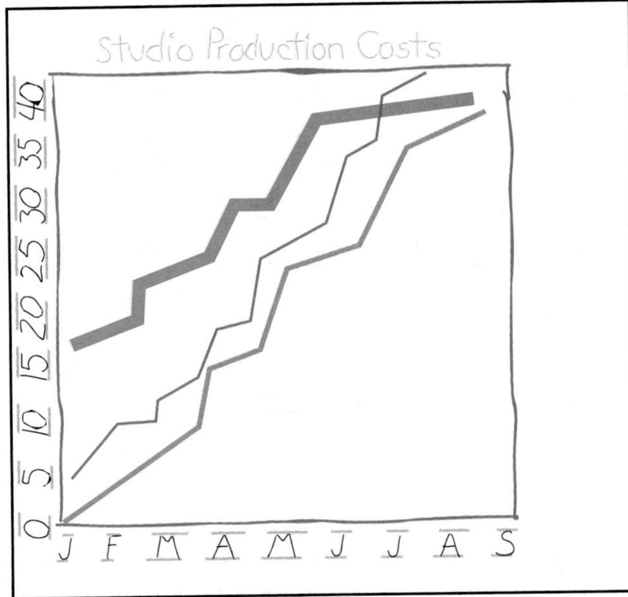

Figure 13-12. Rough layouts are prepared to check the appearance of the final design.

Comprehensive Layout

The rough layout provides a guide for a ***comprehensive layout.*** A comprehensive layout is used by the layout person as a guide during the reproduction work. However, the actual type (typeset text) and illustrations are still not used at this point. Therefore, final corrections of the layout can still be made. An example of a comprehensive layout is shown in Figure 13-13.

Pasteup

Next, the designer must create an assembly of the complete message, called a ***pasteup.*** In this process, the copy (text) is typeset and the necessary artwork is located, or "pasted," on the page. Using computers and software, this step is greatly simplified, Figure 13-14.

Mechanical Layout

The final step is a neatly prepared ***mechanical layout.*** After the pasteup is finished, it is then placed on a clean, white sheet of paper or card-

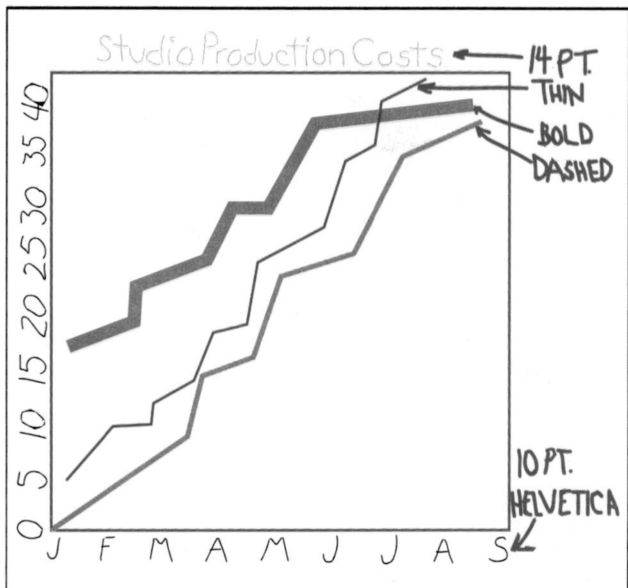

Figure 13-13. A comprehensive layout is designed as a guide for the layout artist. The color blue will not copy during the reproduction process.

stock. Tracing paper or special layout sheets can also be used. Artwork and type must be located and positioned. Blue pencils are used in marking the pasteup sheets. The color blue will not reproduce during processing. Artwork can be secured with rubber cement, glue sticks, tape, or wax. This layout is ***camera ready*** and will serve as the master for production work. It is an exact copy of the finished product.

Copy and Artwork

Copy can be set in type in several ways. Hand lettering and stencils are two procedures. If a more precise look is needed, a computer and word processing software can be used to create the copy. Transfer lettering is also used in creating copy. Kroy™ machines can also be used. These are machines that produce printed text on adhesive-backed tape. Computers and typesetting machines prepare most type set by commercial firms. Type can be made photographically on light-sensitive film. This is called ***phototypesetting,*** Figure 13-15.

The artwork (photographs and illustrations) usually comes from four major sources. Artwork can come from hand drawings, computer generated or printed clip art, photographs, or mechanical drawings (drafting).

Clip art is drawn by professional artists. It usually is sold in book form with several drawings on each page. The drawings are arranged and sized in several ways. This makes it possible to

Figure 13-14. Each page of a book is carefully "pasted-up" by layout artists. Here an editor (standing) is checking for possible layout problems.

Figure 13-15. Most phototypesetting is done on a computer.

use them in different displays. This art can be "clipped" from the book and pasted into the layout where needed. Desktop publishing programs for computers often contain clip art files that can be used in the same way. Many additional clip art files can be purchased and used with the layout program. With CD-ROM technology, tens of thousands of pieces of clip art can be stored on one CD, Figure 13-16. These pieces of clip art can be easily called up and "pasted" into a layout.

TRANSMITTING

While designing a visual message it is important to think about ways to reproduce (transmit) the message. You looked at the six major methods of transmitting a printed graphics image in Chapter 12. These are:

- Relief printing process.
- Screen printing process.
- Continuous tone photography.
- Intaglio process.
- Electrostatic printing process.
- Lithography.

In addition to these six, you looked at several specialty processes. Selecting the best method of transmission is often determined by purpose, the medium used, time, and cost.

Purpose

The ***purpose*** of the message sometimes determines the printing process used. If the purpose of the message is to create a strong, lasting impression, a display using just illustrations may be used. An offset process would reproduce this type message best. However, if the purpose of the message is to store a large amount of information in text only, electrostatic copying or offset lithography might be the best option. Can you identify other ways an item might be printed?

Media

The transmitting ***medium*** often determines the printing procedure. The medium is what is used to "carry" the message. This book has paper as its transmitting medium. ("Medium" is the singular form of "media.") You know that T-shirts are best printed by screen process methods. Transfer

Figure 13-16. Commercially prepared clip art is useful for design work. This artwork saves time in completing graphic layouts. Clip art is still available in books, however, much is now used in electronic publishing. CD-ROM discs can contain many thousands of images.

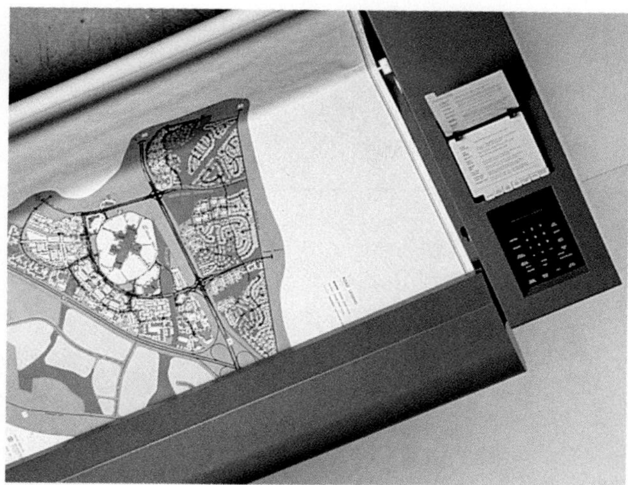

Figure 13-17. A plotter (computerized printer) can quickly complete a drawing that was created on a CAD system. Plotters can usually print many different colors. (Intergraph Corp.)

images (applied with heat) might also be selected. This is because the transmitting medium, cloth, is hard to print on with other printing processes. In industry, other restrictions limit the options. When printing on a flat surface, offset printing is used. Round objects (cans and glasses) require screen process printing. In addition, different inks are needed for these special jobs.

Time and Cost

Other factors determine why one process may be better than another. ***Time*** and ***cost*** are critical. Companies always want to do things as inexpensively as possible. However, sometimes a deadline is involved and time becomes more important than cost. In that case, a more expensive process might be used because it is faster.

RECEIVING AND STORING

When selecting the best process for a product, you also identify the receiving medium. Magazines, clothing, and beverage cans are all printed by various methods. They are all examples of receiving systems. The visual message remains on the product. In the case of computer-generated charts, the receiving medium is paper. Other receiving media include wood, textile, plastic, and metal.

Many types of storage media are available. Each has a different use. Photographic paper (from developed film) is a storage medium. The information used to make the illustraion in Figure 13-17 is probably stored on a disk in a computer file. Many libraries store reference materials (newspapers and magazines) on microfilm. These are all examples of different types of storage media.

The receiving and storing of printed graphics messages is important in communication systems. Many new methods of printing will be refined in the years ahead. This will add new work challenges for graphic designers.

CHAPTER 13 REVIEW

SUMMARY

There are five stages a printed graphics message goes through in order to become a finished product. During the design stage, design elements and design principles are used. These help shape ideas into a message to be transmitted. This leads to the coding stage. This stage, also called "layout," starts with thumbnail sketches of the ideas from the design stage. The thumbnail sketches are then developed into a rough layout, then a comprehensive layout, and finally a pasteup. The third stage is transmitting. In this stage, the message is reproduced to the final form. Receiving and storing are the two final stages in transmitting a printed graphics message.

KEY WORDS

All of the following words have been used in this chapter. Do you know their meanings?

- Balance
- Camera ready
- Clip art
- Color
- Cost
- Comprehensive layout
- Contrast
- Design elements
- Design principles
- Formal balance
- Formal layout
- Informal balance
- Informal layout
- Layout
- Lines
- Mass
- Mechanical layout
- Medium
- Pasteup
- Phototypesetting
- Proportion
- Purpose
- Rhythm
- Rough layout
- Shape
- Texture
- Thumbnail sketches
- Time
- Unity

TEST YOUR KNOWLEDGE

Write your answers on a separate sheet of paper. Please do not write in this book.

1. List the five stages in developing a printed graphics message.
2. Identify each of the following as either a design element or a design principle.
   A. Contrast.
   B. Shape.
   C. Mass.
   D. Lines.
   E. Unity.
   F. Balance.

3. _____ are used to create a printed graphics message. _____ describe the nature of the layout.
4. Explain the difference between formal balance and informal balance.
5. Explain what layout is.
6. Which of the following is (are) not part of the layout process?
   A. Mechanical layout.
   B. Computer layout.
   C. Thumbnail sketch.
   D. Rough layout.
   E. None of the above.
7. Define pasteup.
8. When selecting a method for transmitting a printed graphics message, what can determine the best method?
9. Give five examples of storing a printed graphics message.

ACTIVITIES

1. Collect several posters advertising different events. Identify the use of design elements and principles. Present what you find to the class.
2. Create designs for school stationery. Develop the idea from thumbnail sketches through a mechanical layout. Use these drawings to explain to the class how you completed this process.
3. Use clip art and transfer lettering to design a schedule of school activities. Present the final product to the class and explain how you created it.
4. Use sketching techniques to develop a class logo or symbol. Present this to the class and explain the processes that you used.
5. Collect a variety of printed materials. Conduct a discussion with the class about the different styles of lettering used for titles, caption, and text.
6. Examine different types of paper and card stock used in graphic communication. Write a short report explaining what you found out.

CHAPTER 14

DESKTOP PUBLISHING

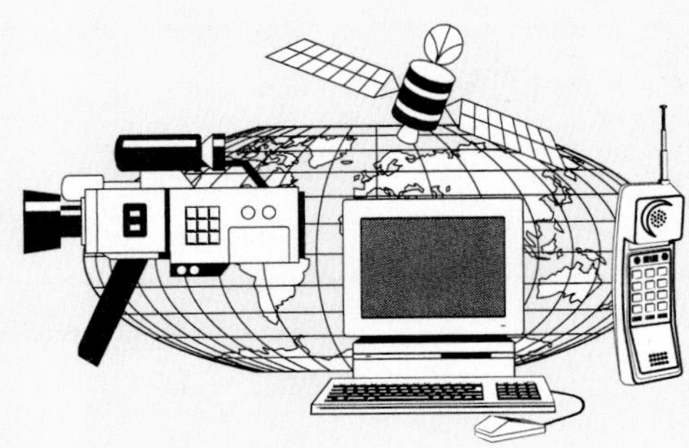

After studying this chapter, you will be able to:

- *Discuss the application of computers to visual communication.*
- *Describe the functions of desktop publishing software.*
- *Identify important considerations for purchasing desktop publishing software.*
- *Explain the operation of desktop publishing programs.*

COMPUTER APPLICATIONS IN GRAPHIC COMMUNICATION

Prior to the mid-1980s, most graphic layout and paste-up work involved hand composition. ***Hand composition*** means assembling text and graphic images manually. Text was produced on phototypesetting machines. Graphic images were hand drawn, cut from clip art booklets, or composed from photographs. With the quick pace of development in computer technology, this process has changed. A graphic composition technique known as desktop publishing has emerged.

Desktop publishing (DTP) involves using a ***personal computer***, or "desktop" computer, to perform what was previously done by hand. Today a variety of word processing and graphic programs can be combined using a personal computer, publishing software, and a high-resolution printer, Figure 14-1. (***Resolution*** refers to the quality of the printed image. A high-resolution image will appear more realistic than a low-resolution image.)

To set up a desktop publishing center, two components are needed: a personal computer and publishing software, Figure 14-2. If immediate printouts are required, a quality printer is also needed, Figure 14-3. ("Dot matrix," or "pin," printers are not acceptable for most DTP applications.) This equipment, combined with graphic

Figure 14-1. Desktop publishing is a very flexible means of creating visual messages. Modern computers and software have allowed advances that seemed impossible a few years ago. (Visual Edge)

Figure 14-2. A desktop computer and desktop publishing software can be used to produce professional documents. However, you still need to know about design elements and principles, and to apply these to the document. (Hewlett-Packard Co.)

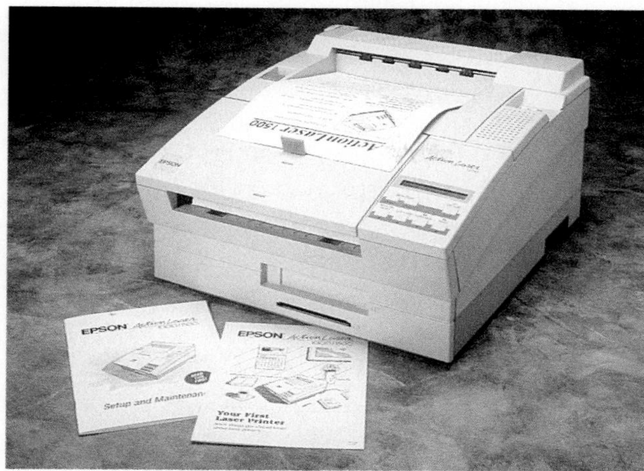

Figure 14-3. A high quality printer is required for immediate printouts of documents produced with desktop publishing software. Many companies perform this service, but it requires more time. (Photo courtesy of Epson)

layout skills and practice, allows office workers and home computer enthusiasts to produce professional documents. These documents are ready for printing, Figure 14-4.

Figure 14-4. Desktop publishing allows graphic designers to create and edit both text and art. The text and art can then be merged and the page composed. The final document is ready to be output directly to a high-quality printer, or taken to a company that performs this service. (Xyvision, Inc.)

If the DTP setup includes a high-resolution printer, the documents can be directly printed. However, many companies exist that take the output from a personal computer and print out the final documents.

FUNCTIONS OF DESKTOP PUBLISHING SOFTWARE

Computers can combine the three major publishing tasks into one computer program. These components include word processing, page composition, and ***graphic illustration*** capabilities. Before desktop publishing, these were three separate stages in preparing documents for publication. Each one of these stages was done by a different group of people in a printing enterprise. Today a desktop publishing program allows a single user to manipulate text and graphic materials into a finished document. This saves much time over the manual method. Desktop publishing is also much more flexible than manual layout.

Word Processing

Word processing is creating the text (body) of a document using computer software. Most desktop publishing software programs have limited capabilities to produce text. They can be used to process words for flyers, titles and subheadings, and text for charts and graphs. However, word processing is not the major function of a desktop publishing program. Most desktop publishing programs can, however, import text from other word processing software. ***Importing*** is taking text (or an image) from a different computer application (program) and moving it into the program that you are using (a DTP program). This is a major advantage of desktop publishing software.

Most word processing software, and the word processing function of most DTP programs, allow the appearance of the type to be changed. Various lettering styles and fonts of type are built into the programs. A ***style*** may be normal, **bold,** *italics,* ~~strikethru~~, or reverse. A ***font*** is the way a particular typeface "looks." For example, type can be generated as Courier, Helvetica, Schoolbook, Times Roman, or other fonts. The size of the type can also be changed. Sizes usually range from 6 points to 72 points. ***Point size*** refers to the size of the type. The size of the type is measured in ***points.*** Remember when changing the appearance of the type to make sure the point size is not too small. Type that is smaller than 8 points is very hard to read. Also be sure that the font is appropriate to the material (text). An Old English font for an article about a modern scientific development would be totally inappropriate. In addition, many aftermarket font "bundles" are available. ***Aftermarket fonts*** are ones that did not originally come with the word processing or DTP software. These fonts can be contained on magnetic disks or on CD-ROMs, Fig 14-5.

Figure 14-5. Additional fonts and clip art can be purchased for use with desktop publishing software. These fonts and clip art can be contained on floppy disks, but often professional graphic artists purchase these on CD-ROM to take advantage of the additional storage space. (AGFA Division of Miles, Inc.)

Text material is easy to type with word processing software. This text can then be easily "composed" in desktop publishing software. Some office workers may then specialize in text entry. Other workers may specialize in the design and layout of the document using desktop publishing software.

Page Composition

Page composition is the major function of a desktop publishing program. ***Page composition*** refers to assembling text and graphic images in an appropriate order, or layout. Text and graphics can be imported, and then moved around on the page. A graphic designer uses a personal computer and desktop publishing software to create page layouts. In the past, designers had to use blue pencils, straight edges, rulers, and various sizes of line tape to do the same thing, Figure 14-6. Using a computer and DTP software bar, the designer can now easily custom design a page. The designer can specify the page to be one, two, or more columns. In many programs, the text and graphics can then be inserted into text frames and graphic frames. ***Text frames*** and ***graphic frames*** are temporary guidelines, Figure 14-7. These guidelines "define" where the text or graphics will be placed on the page. These "frames" can be moved around on the page until everything is in the precise location that the graphic designer wants.

Figure 14-6. In the past, visual messages had to be created using manual layout. Desktop publishing is quickly replacing manual layout.

Through special commands, the graphic designer can "cut and paste" similar images or lines of text. The text or graphic image that was "cut" can then be moved to any location on the page and "pasted," Figure 14-8. The size of the displayed page can also be changed. The document can be made to fit on the monitor, be the actual size of the document (100%), be increased to a percentage of its size, or be reduced to a percentage of its size, Figure 14-9. This allows the designer to see their layout in many different ways. The designer can even see how the layout will look from a distance by

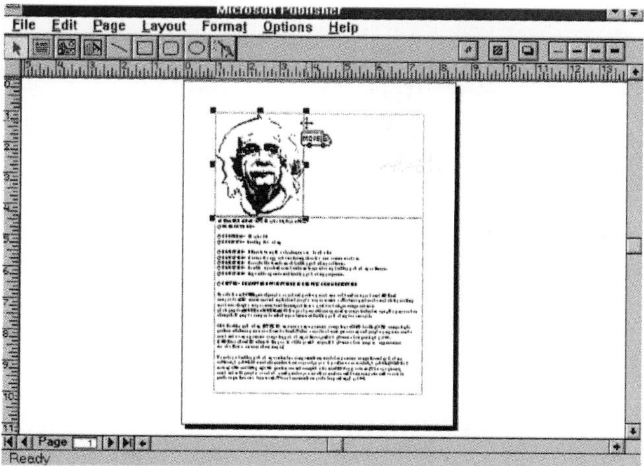

Figure 14-7. Text frames and graphic frames are guidelines that "define" where the text or art will be placed. These frames can be moved around the page to modify the design. Frames can also be "cut" and "pasted" to different pages or documents.

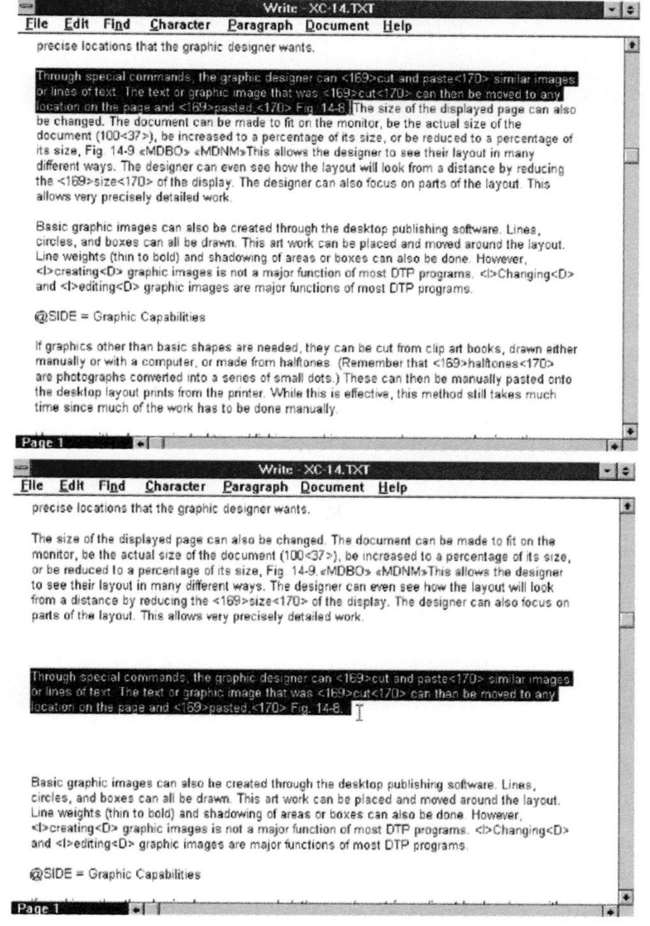

Figure 14-8. A big advantage of desktop publishing programs is the ability to "cut and paste." This allows the designer to easily move large blocks of text or artwork. This type of change in manual layout takes a lot of time. Saving time saves money.

Figure 14-9. Most desktop publishing programs allow the designer to "zoom in" and "zoom out" on an image. Here, the photo the designer is working with is larger than the computer screen. To see the entire photo, the image must be viewed at 50% (or 1:2). When viewed at 100% (or 1:1), the designer can see a more detailed view of part of the photo. The image appears much clearer, however the designer cannot see the whole image.

reducing the "size" of the display. The designer can also focus on parts of the layout. This allows very precisely detailed work.

Basic graphic images can also be created through the desktop publishing software. Lines, circles, and boxes can all be drawn. This art work can be placed and moved around the layout. Line weights (thin to bold) and shadowing of areas or boxes can also be done. However, *creating* graphic images is not a major function of most DTP programs. *Changing* and *editing* graphic images are major functions of most DTP programs.

Graphic Capabilities

If graphics other than basic shapes are needed, they can be cut from clip art books, drawn either manually or with a computer, or made from halftones. (Remember that "halftones" are photographs converted into a series of small dots.) These can then be manually pasted onto the desktop layout prints from the printer. While this is effective, this method still takes much time since much of the work has to be done manually.

However, with advances in desktop publishing, graphics can now be composed using other software and imported into the desktop publishing software. ***Paint programs*** and ***draw programs*** allow talented people to create graphic images that will enhance the design of a publication, Figure 14-10.

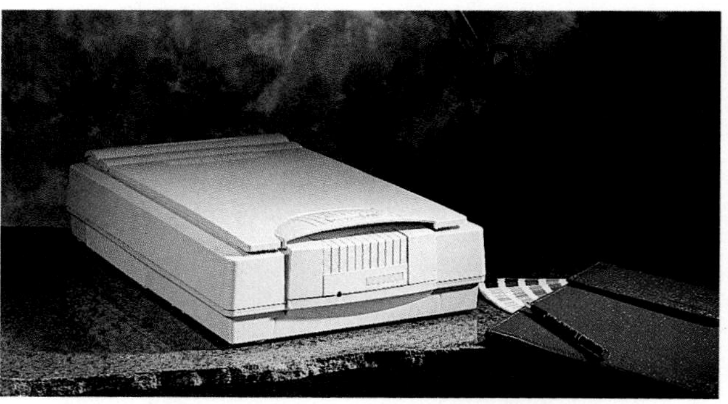

Figure 14-11. Scanners can be used to digitize images. These digitized images can then be imported into a desktop publishing program. The images can be edited or altered to fit the document that is being worked on. "Flatbed" scanners are good for scanning large images or large documents. (Mustek)

Figure 14-10. "Paint" and "draw" programs allow a variety of interesting visual effects to be easily created. (Computer Support Corporation)

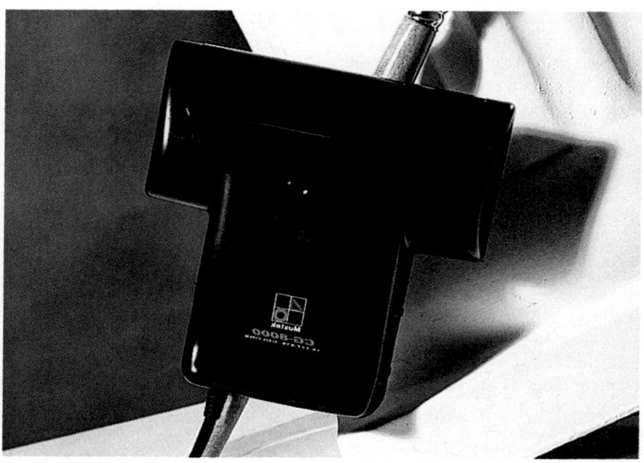

Figure 14-12. Hand-held scanners are inexpensive and easy to use. These devices allow images to be quickly "scanned" and imported into desktop publishing software. (Mustek)

Electronic scanners allow the graphic designer to take line art work and photographs and digitize them, Figure 14-11. ***Digitizing*** is converting drawings, text, photographs, or other "hard copy" images into computer images by electronically tracing over them. A high intensity light passes over the image and the image is reflected. This image is then recorded electronically. Scanners function much like a photostatic copier. Many also physically look like copiers. Other scanners are small, hand-held units, Figure 14-12. Digitized images can then be placed into documents.

Electronic clip art is a very inexpensive and flexible way to put graphic images into a document. Clip art files are collections of art work on various topics, Figure 14-13. They function in the same way that conventional clip art does, except that everything is done electronically. After the clip art is imported, it can be moved, cropped to size, or touched-up electronically just like any other graphic image.

DESKTOP PUBLISHING SOFTWARE

As with any purchase, decisions must be made, and all options looked at, before purchasing a desktop publishing program. Considerations must be based on the size of memory

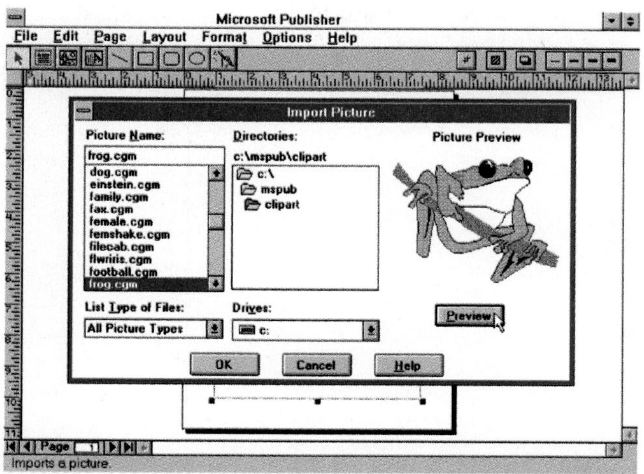

Figure 14-13. Electronic clip art functions the same as traditional clip art. An image is selected and placed in the document. Many desktop publishing programs allow the clip art to be previewed before placing it in the document. Some even come with a book that has all of the images printed out.

your personal computer has available, the cost of the program, and the complexity or "user friendliness" of the program.

Many inexpensive DTP programs have many of the same functions as the more expensive programs. If the work is going to be just small home projects such as greeting cards, an inexpensive program might be the most cost effective. These programs typically require a small amount of computer memory. Many home and school systems do not have the memory to run the more expensive programs. The inexpensive programs typically have limited capabilities. Texts fonts are limited, as are the graphics found in the programs. However, these programs are easy to use and can be found in many schools and small businesses.

Mid-priced desktop publishing packages are also available. Mid-priced software will typically have more features than the inexpensive software. More fonts are typically available, as well as more graphics. These programs may be able to import text and graphics from many more programs than the inexpensive programs. Some schools, community colleges, and universities use these programs, as well as some mid-sized businesses.

The more expensive programs, called "high-end" programs, are much more sophisticated than either the mid-priced or inexpensive programs. They typically require a large amount of computer memory to run. These programs may also require a computer set-up that is very expensive. High-end programs typically cost from five hundred to several thousand dollars. However, these programs do offer many more features and capabilities. Typically these programs are able to handle very large documents, perform color separations, and interface with commercial typesetting equipment. These programs also typically support many more colors, up to 16.7 million in some cases. High-end programs may have several thousand pieces of clip art preloaded, along with over a thousand different fonts. The graphic images can usually be altered and edited in many more ways than the mid-priced or inexpensive programs. Photographs can be imported from scanners or from photo CDs. These images can then be edited in many different ways and inserted into a document, Figure 14-14. All of these features are required for businesses that work with large documents or a large number of documents.

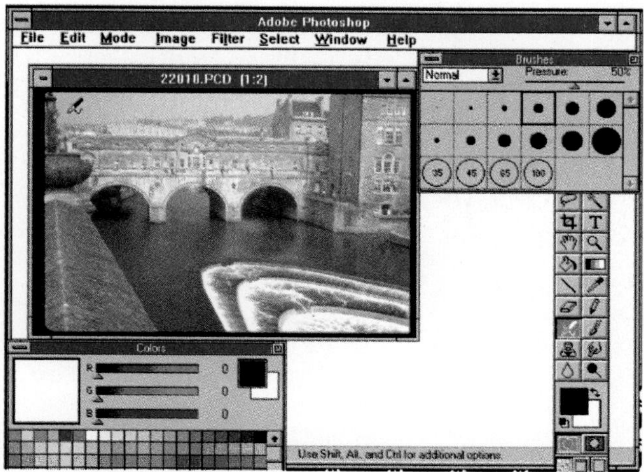

Figure 14-14. Several desktop publishing programs allow the designer to change photos. These photos are "scanned" or taken from a photo CD. Many companies make CDs with hundreds of photos already scanned and ready to "import" into a desktop publishing program.

OPERATION OF DESKTOP PUBLISHING PROGRAMS

To operate desktop publishing software, you need to understand the basic design and layout principles covered in Chapter 13. These principles will be combined with functions available to you through the desktop publishing software. Through practice, desktop publishing software will allow you to compose documents that will communicate your ideas more effectively.

If you are unfamiliar with using a microcomputer with a mouse, you should probably use a learning program called a "tutorial." These individual learning programs will aid you in becoming familiar with the use, commands, and functions of a personal computer.

The initial step in desktop publishing is to select a project to present graphically through a printed medium. This might be a flyer for an activity that the Technology Student Association (TSA) is presenting. A thumbnail sketch of your idea will help by serving as a guideline, Figure 14-15.

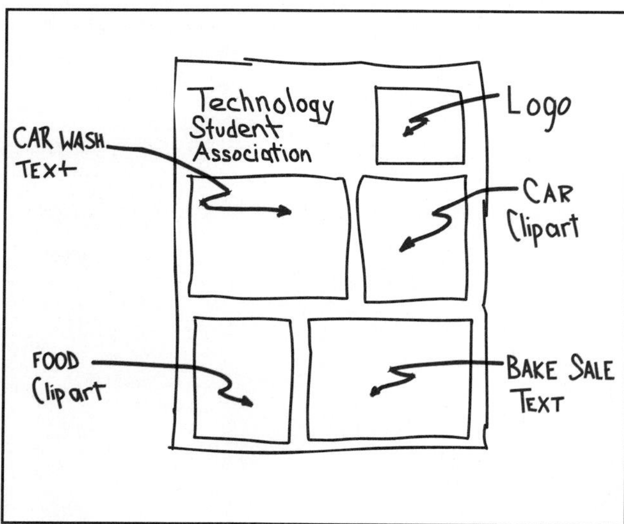

Figure 14-15. A thumbnail sketch of your idea may help you to "work out" your ideas. Thumbnail sketches can be done with pencil and paper, or they can be done on a computer.

With a project in mind, you need to think about how you wish to present your ideas. This is done through ideation (visual designing). Think over "who, what, when, and where." This will help you to think of all the information that needs to go into your document. You may even wish to sketch some of these ideas into "thumbnail layouts" of potential options for creating your layout. At this time you will begin to think about page orientation (tall or wide), page size, the use of columns, type font, type style, type size, and graphics, Figure 14-16.

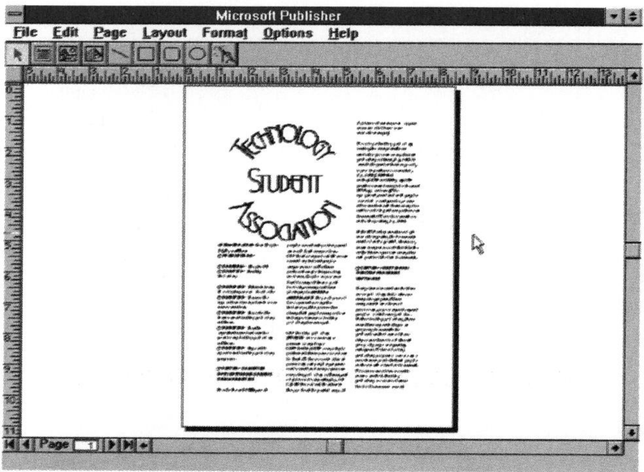

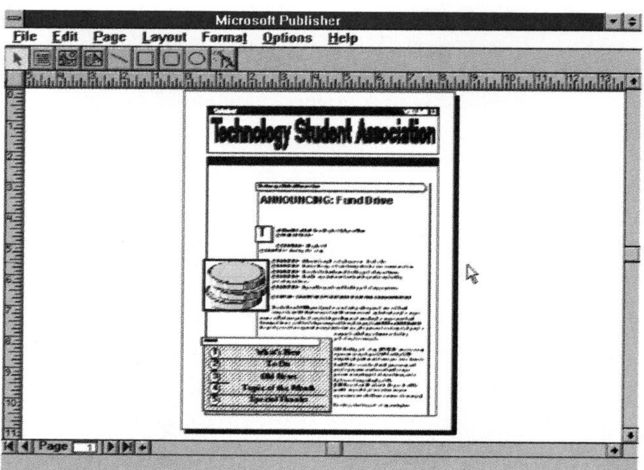

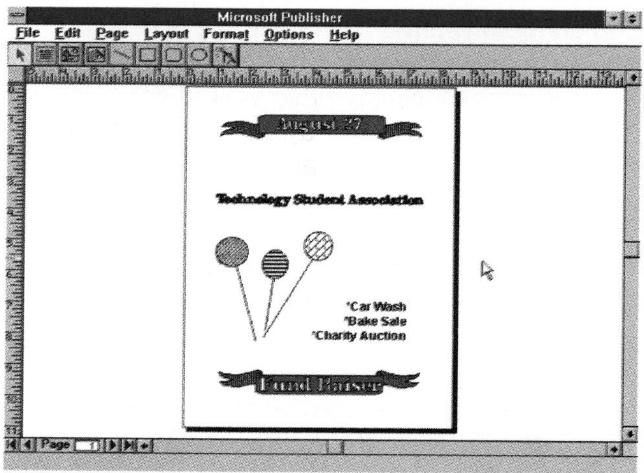

Figure 14-16. When designing a layout, it helps to have several different ideas. You can sketch your ideas for layouts on paper. However, since changes in desktop publishing are so quick and easy to make, several ideas can be done on the computer. At this point, do not worry about the actual words. Instead, concentrate on the way the layout looks.

With your ideas in mind, it is time to begin the word processing. If your project has a lot of writing or text, you may first want to compose this information on a word processing program. However, if your document is going to be a poster or flyer (with limited text), it might be easiest to use the desktop publishing program directly, Figure 14-17.

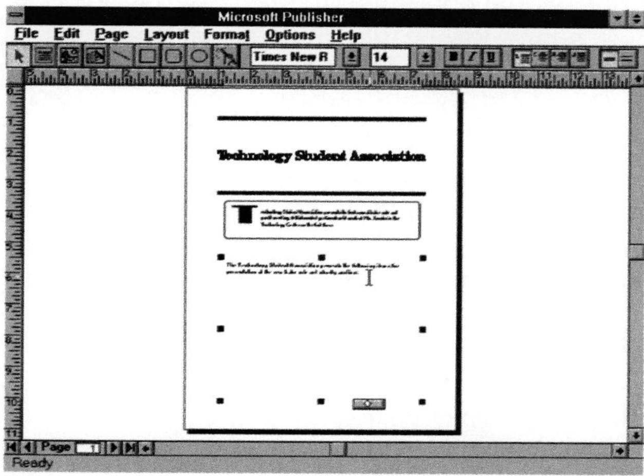

Figure 14-17. Small amounts of text can be entered in desktop publishing programs. If a large amount of text is to be entered, it is best to use a word processing program. Once the text is created, it can then be imported into the desktop publishing program.

To use a desktop publishing program, it must first be executed (started). Most DTP opening screens will appear with a menu scroll, tool box, and a page outline, Figure 14-18. The procedure outlined here is general. The specific program that you are using may vary slightly. Refer to your instructor and the manuals that came with the software you are using.

The outline of the page may be changed and guidelines added for custom layouts. If you want a 5 inch by 7 inch layout you can set these margins from the page setup dialog box. For an 8 1/2 inch by 11 inch page, most layouts will probably have a working area of 7 1/2 inch by 10 inch, Figure 14-19. The layout can be either tall (***portrait***) or wide (***landscape***), Figure 14-20.

After you established your layout size and orientation, text frames and graphic frames

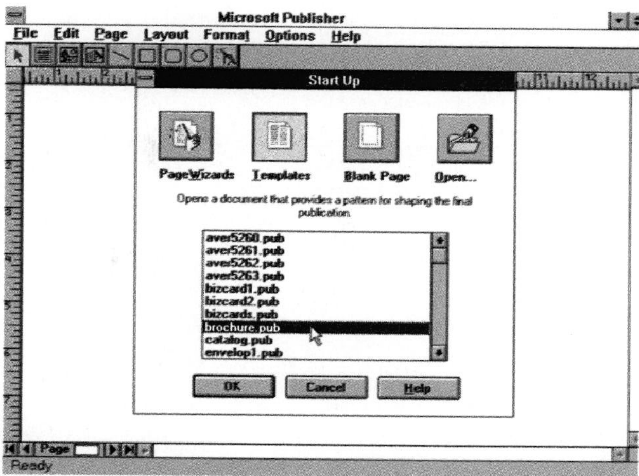

Figure 14-18. When a desktop publishing program is started, most give the user several options. These options vary from program to program. Most programs have a standard layout that will appear every time the program is started. This standard layout can then be changed for different layouts.

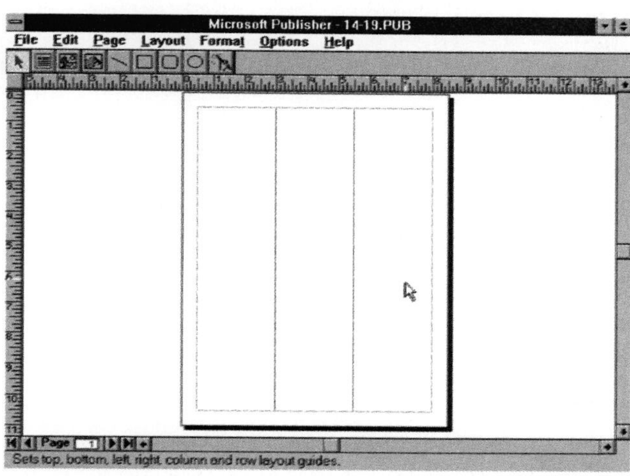

Figure 14-19. Layout guidelines can be used to help the designer. Here, the red lines define the "edges" of the layout. Notice that these lines are 1/2" from the edge of the paper. The blue lines define the columns of the page. In this layout, there will be three columns.

can be placed, Figure 14-21. These guidelines can typically be moved or changed by using the mouse or a pull-down menu.

Next, compose the page using the layout principles you learned in Chapter 13. Text can be created using the DTP program, or it can be imported from a separate word processing program. Graphics can be created in some DTP programs, but typically clip art or other

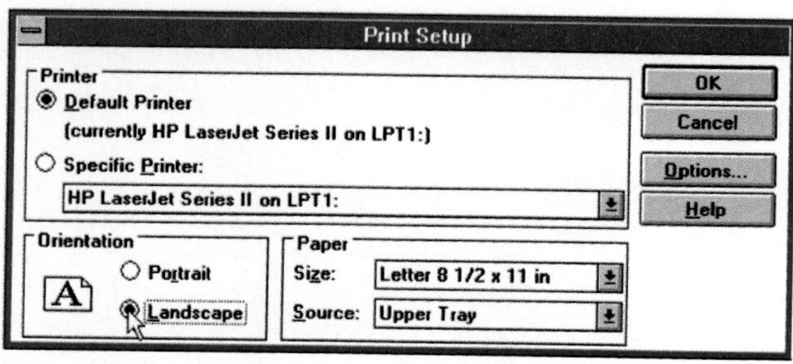

Figure 14-20. A landscape layout can be thought of as a "wide" layout. A portrait layout is a "tall" layout. Here, the designer has selected landscape.

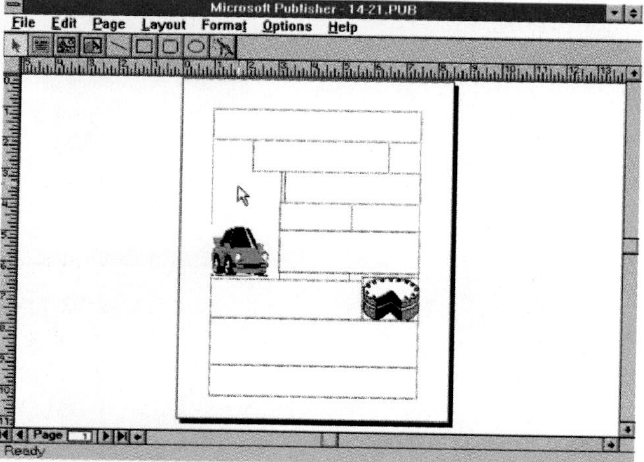

Figure 14-21. Once the layout style is decided on, text and graphic frames are placed on the page. With the frames in place, the art and text can then be imported. For small amounts of text, it is often easiest to use the desktop publishing program to create the text.

graphics are imported. You can ***zoom in*** or ***zoom out*** on the screen, Figure 14-22. This will allow you to move the text and graphics into precise locations.

When your work begins to look like the layout you were trying to achieve, ***save*** the document. The document can be saved on the hard drive or a floppy disk. Floppy disks will hold enough information for most home and school desktop publishing applications. However, many professional publishers require much more storage space for the documents that they create. Special storage devices are used by these industries, Figure 14-23. After saving your document, ***print*** a copy. This rough copy is called a ***proof.*** Many times with desktop publishing programs, what appears on the screen is not exactly what is produced. This is especially true when working in color. Examine the proof to see if any changes need to be made, Figure 14-24. Be particularly careful in proofreading your text material. After you make changes, have another student or your instructor look at your work to make suggestions. If changes are needed, edit your work electronically. Then save and reprint your design. Repeat this process as many times as needed in order to produce a final product that looks like you want it to. Remember, your work can be modified quickly and easily with electronic desktop publishing programs.

After everybody working on the project is satisfied, it is time for reproducing the number of copies needed. Limited numbers can be pro-

Figure 14-22. Use the zoom in and zoom out commands as you layout the document. This will allow you to see the entire document and to see detailed views.

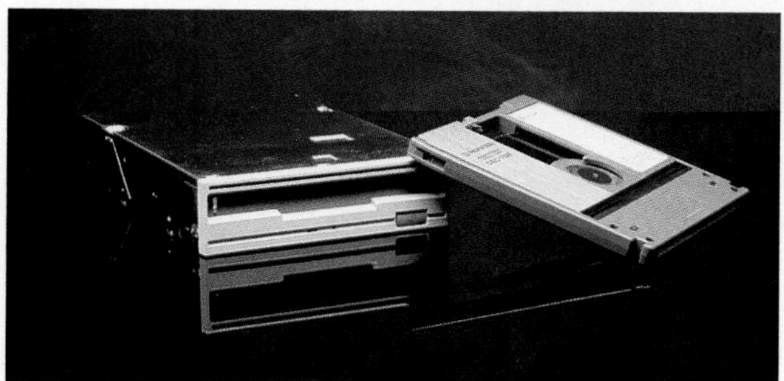

Figure 14-23. Standard floppy disks have enough storage space for most home and school desktop publishing applications. Professional publishers require special storage devices to hold the documents that they produce. (IBM; Pioneer New Media Technologies, Inc./Laser Optical Systems Group)

Figure 14-24. Examining a proof is an important part of the desktop publishing process. It is important to look at proofs closely because many times what appears on the computer screen is not what is output from the printer.

duced using the printer in the desktop publishing system, if it has one. Larger numbers can be duplicated on photocopiers or through offset lithographic means. If the desktop system does not have a printer, an outside source must be contacted to print the final product.

CHAPTER 14 REVIEW

SUMMARY

Graphic designers can use the many advantages of desktop publishing. Text can be created through word processing software. This text can then be imported into a desktop publishing program. Graphics can also be created in other software and imported into DTP software. Desktop publishing greatly decreases the amount of time needed for layout work. Desktop publishing also makes corrections and changes much easier. When selecting desktop publishing software, cost, applications, and system requirements all need to be considered. Desktop publishing is rapidly replacing conventional layout methods. However, the principles of good layout for a manual layout must also be applied to a desktop publishing layout.

KEY WORDS

All of the following terms have been used in this chapter. Do you know their meanings?

Aftermarket fonts
Desktop publishing (DTP)
Digitizing
Draw programs
Electronic clip art
Electronic scanners
Font
Graphic frames
Graphic illustration
Hand composition
Importing
Landscape
Page composition
Paint programs
Personal computer
Point size
Points
Portrait
Print
Proof
Resolution
Save
Style
Text frames
Word processing
Zoom in
Zoom out

TEST YOUR KNOWLEDGE

Write your answers on a separate sheet of paper. Please do not write in this book.

1. What are the necessary components of a desktop publishing system?

2. What are the three publishing tasks combined through desktop publishing?
3. What is the minimum size of type that should be used in a printed document?
4. What type of computer software program should be used to develop text information?
5. What does the term resolution mean?
6. The major attribute to a desktop publishing program is:

   A. Word processing.

   B. Page composition.

   C. Creating graphic.

   D. Color separation.
7. Identify the three price ranges for desktop publishing software. List a typical user for each of the three price ranges.
8. What are three considerations to be evaluated in selecting a desktop publishing software program?

ACTIVITIES

1. Collect sample documents that have been generated through desktop publishing. Have a class discussion on the text and graphic compositions, and on graphic layouts of the documents.
2. Use a software tutorial to become familiar with the operations and functions of a desktop publishing program.
3. Create text material for a school project using word processing software.
4. View electronic clip art to see what artwork you have available for composing a document. Select an appropriate image for the text that you created in Activity 3.
5. Prepare a flyer on a school or organization function using a desktop publishing system.

CHAPTER 15

SCREEN PROCESS PRINTING

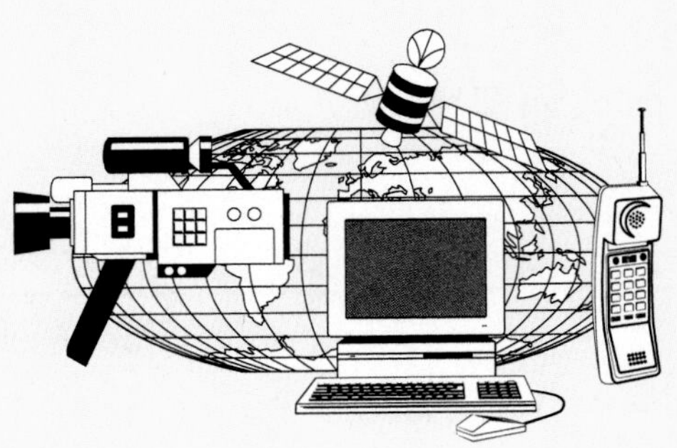

After studying this chapter, you will be able to:

- ❖ *Describe the purposes and uses of screen process printing.*
- ❖ *Prepare screen process stencils using a variety of methods.*
- ❖ *Use screen process printing techniques to produce several products.*

Screen process printing is a popular method of graphic communication. This method of printing involves forcing ink or paint through a ***stencil*** that is on a screen. The screen is made of a fine mesh that allows ink to pass through. The stencil prevents ink from going through certain areas. This is how the image is formed. You will remember from Chapter 12 that early screens were made from silk. That is why the process is often called ***silk screening.***

Screen process printing is a versatile printing process. It is useful for many industrial and classroom purposes. Images can be reproduced on a variety of materials, or transfer media.

PURPOSES AND USES

Screen process printing is used when a heavy deposit of ink is required. This thick layer of ink may be needed because of extreme conditions. For example, washing a T-shirt or a sign that is left out in the weather requires a thick layer of ink to maintain the image. The ink is usually applied to flat surfaces. The final image may feel "raised" above the surface because of the thick coat of ink. Special machines permit printing messages on rounded surfaces such as jars, bottles, and cans.

Screen process printing is a specialty process. Most screen process work is done on materials other than paper. Very few screen printed products use paper as a medium to transmit a message. Some exceptions include decals, stickers, and heat transfers. These items are produced on thin sheets of tissue paper.

Street signs and posters are examples of typical products printed using a screen process, Figure 15-1. Dials and labels on machines are also screen printed (or "screened"). These all have been printed using special machines. Other examples include ceramics, bags and backpacks, and many types of clothing, Figure 15-2.

There are several disadvantages with screen process printing. This method is slow as a reproduction process. One reason for this is the long drying time required. In addition, it is difficult to transfer images having fine detail. Therefore, bold text would reproduce well, but photographs would not. Still, screen process printing is a popular technique for many visual messages.

STENCIL PREPARATION

Many methods for preparing stencils have been developed. These include hand-cut paper stencils, hand-cut film stencils, photo direct stencils, photo indirect stencils, and thermal stencils, Figure 15-3. Hand-cut and photo indirect methods will be explained in detail in this book. These are the primary methods used in schools.

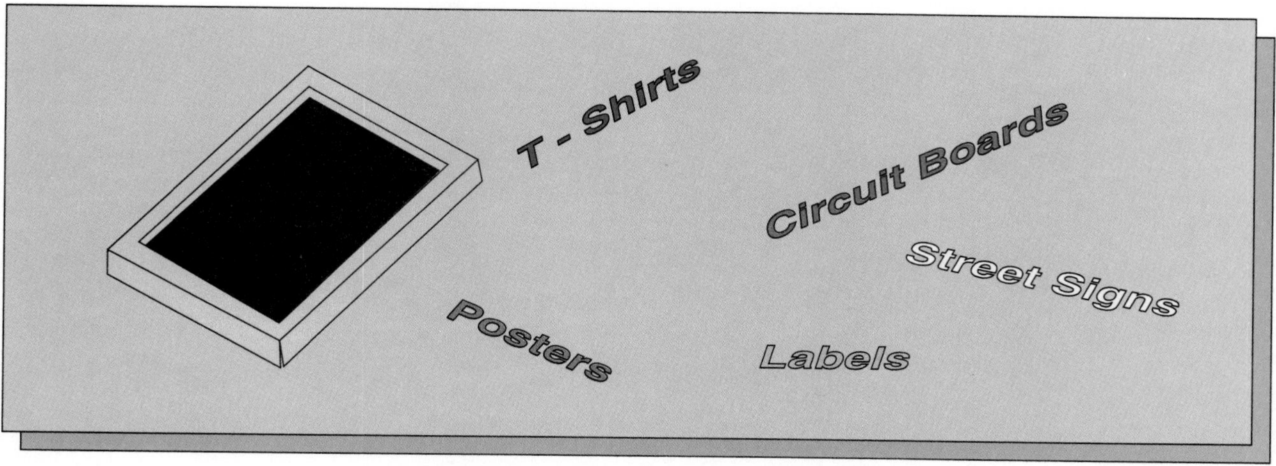

Figure 15-1. Many visual displays are completed by screen process printing. How many examples can you think of?

Figure 15-2. How many printed shirts, cups, or mugs do you own?

Hand-cut Paper
Hand-cut Film
Photo Direct
Photo Indirect
Thermal

Figure 15-3. There are several methods of preparing stencils.

WARNING

WHEN PREPARING STENCILS AND USING INKS, OBSERVE PROPER SAFETY PRECAUTIONS. Sharp items like knifes will be used in stencil preparation. Use care when working with glass as it may break. Broken glass can be very dangerous. When using inks, observe the safety precautions of the ink manufacturer. Some inks may be harmful to humans if not used correctly. Listen to your instructor and follow classroom safety procedures. Ink can be permanent. If you get it on your clothes, it may never come off!

Hand-cut Paper Stencils

Paper stencils for screen process printing are easy and inexpensive to prepare. For these reasons, many schools use hand-cut paper stencils. They can also be used at home as a hobby since they are easy to make and don't require expensive equipment.

However, three major drawbacks limit the use of hand-cut paper stencils. First, objects with centers cannot be printed. The outside lines of the image area will print, but the center part will fall out. The use of lettering is thus limited. The letter "A," for example, cannot be printed since the "inside triangle" of the letter will appear as one large spot of ink, Figure 15-4. All parts of the image must remain attached to the outside of the stencil.

The second disadvantage is that the design must remain simple. Fine detailing is not possible with paper stencils. To "screen" a photograph, you

Figure 15-4. Hand-cut stencil designs must be simple. Centers of complex figures are difficult to prepare. Avoid designs with internal features.

Figure 15-5. Simple designs can be drawn directly on paper stencils. The design can then be easily cut out.

would not be able to use a hand-cut stencil. That type of image requires very fine detail not possible with a hand-cut stencil. Images with sharp, well-defined lines are best. Basic geometric shapes work well.

The final drawback is the limited number of copies that may be reproduced. Paper stencils do not last very long. Printing inks and pressure break these stencils down quickly. Think about how long a brown paper grocery bag lasts once it gets wet. The paper used in hand-cut stencils is much like a brown paper grocery bag.

Kraft (brown wrapping) paper or paper grocery bags are often used for hand-cut stencils. Waxed paper is also good for use with oil-based ink. The paper should be about the size of the screen frame. It should not be creased or torn.

The preparation of paper stencils starts with an original design. The design is drawn on paper. After the original design is completed, it is traced or drawn on the stencil paper. A light table may be used to help in tracing the design. When tracing, lines should be only dark enough to be seen (not bold or heavy). Pencils are preferred for tracing.

After the design is transferred onto the stencil paper, the stencil is then cut, Figure 15-5. A sharp stencil knife should be used for cutting the stencil. Place the paper on a hard surface when cutting. A piece of pressboard or glass makes an excellent surface for cutting on. **Do not use tabletops!** Carefully cut out the stencil with smooth strokes, Figure 15-6. Edges should be clean and

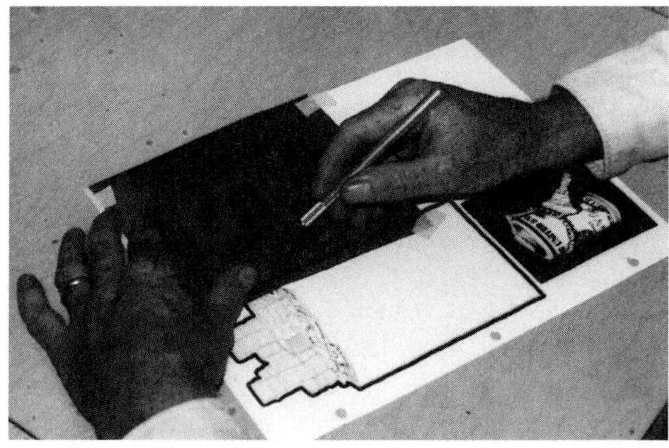

Figure 15-6. A stencil knife is used to cut paper stencil. Follow the pattern carefully with the blade.

not be jagged or torn. If a dull knife is used, the edges may be jagged and the resulting image will not have a sharp outline.

Location of the stencil is very important. When making several prints, you want each image to be in the same place as the print made before it. In order to make sure that the transfer medium is always in the same place, ***registration marks*** are used. Registration marks are indicators, usually "X's," on the stencil that can be used to place the screen on the transfer medium in the same place every time, Figure 15-7. Locate registration marks once the image is cut out.

Tape the original design on the ***printing base.*** The printing base is the surface that the transfer medium will rest on during the screening process. Make certain the stencil is in the position where you want the image to appear on the final product. The stencil and its position should look exactly like

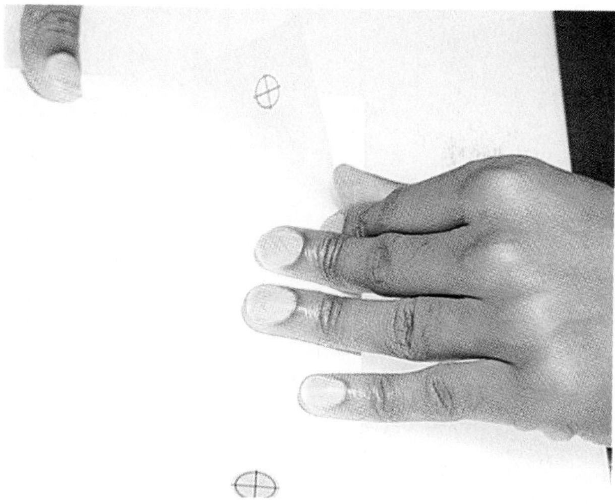

Figure 15-7. Registration marks help in positioning stencils and overlays for proper alignment.

you want the completed product to look. Next, set the guides. ***Guides*** mark the base in order to position each transfer medium in the same place. (Guides position the transfer medium on the base while registration marks position the screen on the transfer medium.) Masking tape is often used as a guide for thin material. Short dowels may be used for thicker material such as metal.

The stencil is now ready for adhering (sticking) to the screen. Use several drops of white glue to secure the stencil. Spread the drops around the stencil design. Place the screen on top of the base so that the stencil comes in contact with the screen. **Be sure no glue gets on the open image area of the stencil!** If this happens, ink will not pass through the image area during printing. Allow several minutes for the glue to dry. The screen will then be ready to use.

Hand-cut Film Stencils

There are two types of film used for hand-cut film stencils. They are aqua (water) film and lacquer film, Figure 15-8. The preparation of these films is similar to that used for paper stencils. The major difference is adhering the film to the screen. Paper stencils are positioned and glued. Films are attached with water or special fluids. Aqua film is adhered to the screen with water. Lacquer or oil-based inks are used during printing. Lacquer-based film is attached with an adhering fluid. This special fluid does not dissolve the stencil as quickly as some other thinners. Water or oil-based inks are used to print with these stencils.

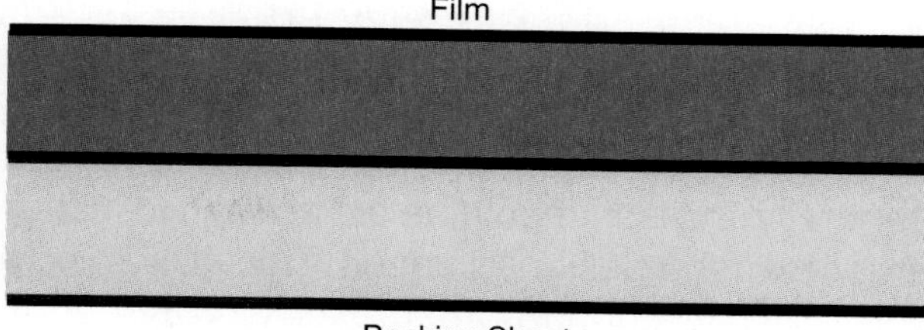

Figure 15-8. Hand-cut film has two layers. The film layer is cut when making the design. The backing sheet remains in place until the stencil is adhered to the screen.

To prepare a hand-cut film stencil, a design is first needed. One master is used for each color to be printed. For example, to print a bull's-eye, three stencils are needed, Figure 15-9. There are three colors (red, white, and blue) and each color requires a separate stencil and screen.

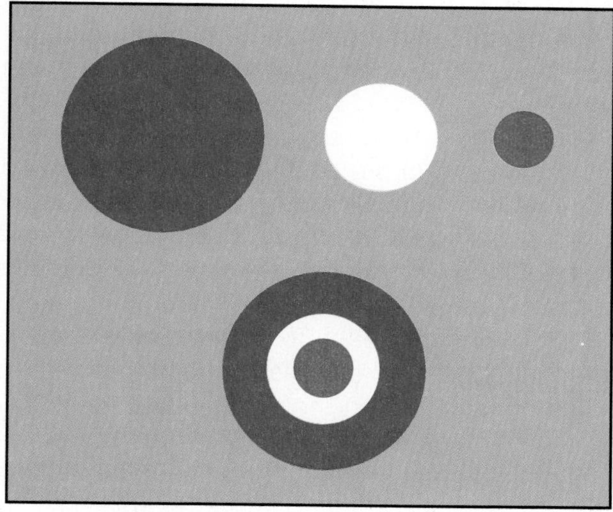

Figure 15-9. When this bull's-eye is printed, the white layer is printed first, the blue layer typically second, and the red layer typically last. Do you know why?

WARNING

Knifes are sharp! Be careful when using a knife.

Glass can break easily. Broken glass is sharp and very dangerous! Be careful when you are working around glass.

Some chemicals can be harmful if not used properly. Be sure to follow the manufacturer's precautions. Listen to your instructor and follow classroom safety procedures.

Next, obtain the film to be used. Most films come in large rolls or sheets. However, a small piece of material is all that is needed for the stencil. Remember, each color requires a stencil. Generally, the film should be cut about two inches larger than the designed image. This allows extra working space during preparation and the printing process. Tape the design on a hard surface. Again, a pressboard or a light table are best. Lay the stencil film on top of the design. The shiny (or gelatin) side **must be facing up**. The design should be in the middle of the film. Use tape to secure the film in the proper place.

With a stencil knife, carefully cut the film. Trace the lines of the image area. Light, even strokes with a sharp blade work best. Do not press too hard. **Only the gelatin coating is to be cut. The clear backing sheet of the film should remain intact.** Cutting entirely through the backing will cause problems later. Lines forming corners may be over-cut (cut beyond the edge of the corner). These over-cuts will fuse (combine) together when adhering the film to the screen.

Once the lines are cut, slowly peel back the gelatin coating in the design area. The sharp tip of the knife is helpful in lifting the edges. Slowly remove the **gelatin coating only** inside the scribed lines. The area to be printed will become noticeable.

You are now ready to adhere the stencil to a screen. Use a screen that is clean and free of holes or ink. Position the screen over the stencil. Registration marks may be needed to properly position the stencil. Aqua film requires tap water to dissolve the film. Adhering fluid is used with lacquer film. Moisten a rag or cotton pad with the water or the proper adhering fluid. A second dry rag should be ready for cleanup purposes.

The proper adhering fluid will soften the gelatin layer on the film. The film will dissolve and move into the small holes in the screen. With the dampened rag, press the screen into the film. Then blot up the moisture with the dry rag. Repeat this process over the entire stencil, Figure 15-10. Always rub lightly. Too much pressure will remove (or ***burn out***) areas of the stencil. Take your time for this step. Rushing the procedure will probably ruin your stencil.

As the film dries, it will darken. If there are light spots on the film, an incorrect amount of fluid was used. These areas may not print properly. A new screened master may be needed. After the stencil is adhered, let the screen dry totally. Propping the screen in front of a fan will speed the process. Your hand-cut film stencil will then be ready for printing.

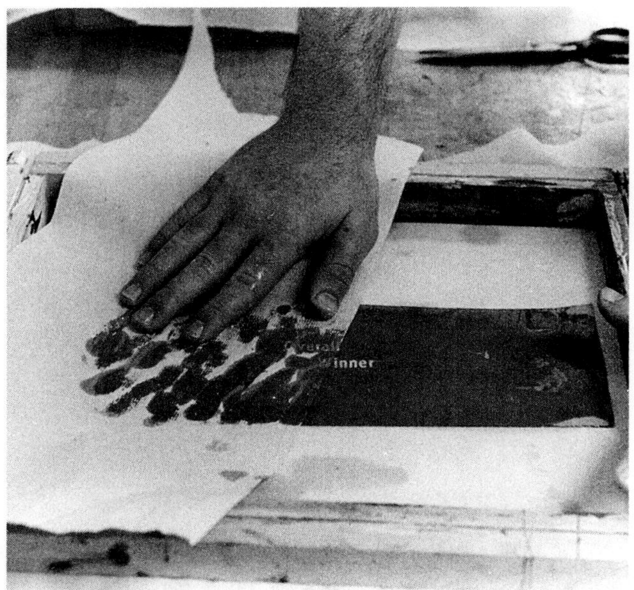

Figure 15-10. Moisture is best removed with a clean rag or paper towels. The stencil must then air dry before further preparation and printing. Be sure to wear safety glasses. If the fluid is harmful to the skin, wear protective gloves as well.

Photo Indirect Stencils

Paper and film stencils are prepared by hand cutting. ***Photo indirect stencils*** use light and chemicals to produce the stencil. As with hand-cut film stencils, separate originals are prepared for each color to be printed. The original design must be created in an opaque (solid) color. This is usually black. Opaque films used in industry also come in red and orange.

After the original is created, a ***positive*** must be made. The positive appears as a black image on clear background. There are three ways to accomplish this. A good, sharp photocopy is best for simple designs. A Thermofax® transparency is made from the photocopy. A second way to produce the positive is by photographic means. A process camera helps create very detailed positives. The third method for preparing positives is to apply opaque films and inks to clear plastic sheets.

Once the positive is made, the stencil is produced. This process is called ***burning.*** The positive is placed on the emulsion (dull) side of the film. The emulsion side of the film is then exposed to light. A ***platemaker*** is often used for this process, Figure 15-11. A platemaker is a machine that photographically burns images in film. A high-intensity light source (like an overhead projector) may also work for school use. Exposure time will vary depending upon film and light source. The positive shields part of the film from light, leaving an image area on the film. This image area will wash away during developing.

Figure 15-11. A commercial platemaker. (Photo courtesy of nuArc Co.)

WARNING

The chemicals used in developing film can be dangerous! Use caution when handling these chemicals. Observe all safety precautions of the manufacturer and follow classroom safety procedures. If a platemaker is being used to burn a stencil, ***do not*** look at the light through the sides of the machine. The light will damage your eyes.

The exposed film must be developed with chemicals. A special commercially available developer will process the film. Place the developer in a tray, Figure 15-12. Agitate (slowly move) the exposed film by rocking the tray back and forth. Recommended developing times will differ with the type of film used. Follow the manufacturer's directions.

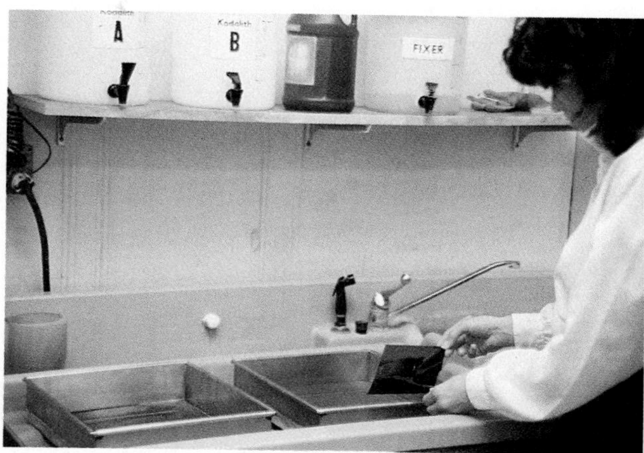

Figure 15-12. Film is developed by dipping it in trays filled with the developing chemicals.

Next, hold the film by the corners while lightly spraying the film with water. Warm water (about 100° F) will dissolve the unexposed image area. The nonprinting area (the area exposed to light) will remain solid.

Adhering film to a framed screen is done much the same way as a hand-cut film stencil. Water on the film acts as the adhering fluid. Blot excess water up through the film. Dry paper towels or rags work best. A layer of newspaper placed under the film and frame also helps remove water. Pressing on the newspaper also creates pressure, helping to adhere the film. Use a small roller (called a ***brayer***) to help adhere the film, Figure 15-13. Let the screen dry. Remove the clear backing sheet when dry. Peel the sheet off carefully. The screen is then ready to use for printing.

Thermal Stencils

Another method of preparing screen process stencils is by using ***thermal stencils.*** Thermal stencils are quickly prepared. However, fine detail cannot be reproduced. In addition, the image must be reproduced with a carbon based material. Therefore, all images must first be photocopied. Line drawings work well with this method.

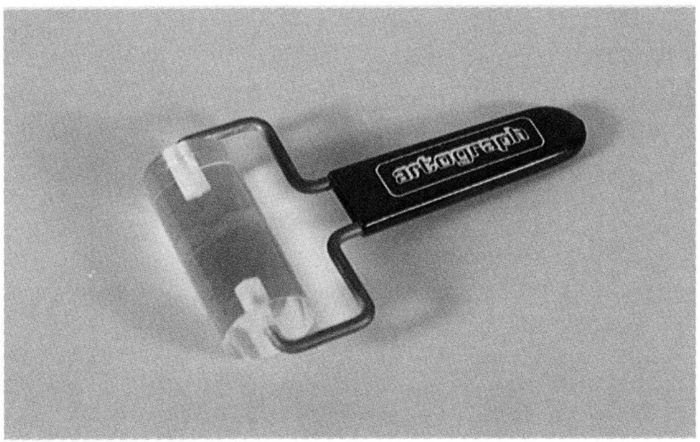

Figure 15-13. A brayer (roller) is useful in adhering the film and forcing water out of the screen. Can you think of other ways to help dry the stencil?

A thermal stencil comes in a two part set. This set includes the thermal screen and a backing sheet. The heat transfers the image directly from the carbon-based artwork onto a screening material. This is then attached to the printing frame after it is processed.

To make a thermal stencil, the photocopied image is placed between the thermal screen and the backing material. These are then processed in a thermal copier. After the stencil is prepared, it is taped to a thin plastic frame for printing.

PRINTING PROCEDURES

With the stencil material now placed on a screen, the printing process can be completed. There are four more steps. The screen must be framed, the screen prepared, the print completed, and the screen cleaned up.

Frame Preparation

Common sizes of frames can be purchased. These will be placed on a hinged backing board for printing, Figure 15-14. The screen is usually wedged in place on the frame by ropes. Strong tape or staples are also used. The screen must be stretched tightly across the frame. If it is not, a different frame must be selected. If the screen is not tight, the resulting image transfer may be blurred. The screen may need washing before the stencil or film is attached to the frame. This will also make the screen tighter on the frame as it dries.

Figure 15-14. Screen frames are attached to hinged backing boards. The frame is lowered into place for printing.

Screen Preparation

After adhering the stencil or film, the region outside the image area will still be open. Ink will pass through this area if it is not blocked. Use masking tape or heavy paper to block this area, Figure 15-15. This procedure is called ***masking off.*** Newsprint or cardstock also works well as a mask. For a small number of prints, only the top side of the screen needs masking.

Figure 15-15. Nonprinting areas should be blocked off. This saves ink, speeds cleanup, and prevents unwanted printed areas.

Next, carefully check the image area of your stencil. Small openings may have developed in the film or paper. These must be blocked before printing. A liquid masking fluid is available for this work. Tape will also block the opening, but it should only be used as a "quick-fix." The masking agent must be applied between the screen and the stencil backing.

The backing sheet of film stencils may be removed at any time. It is wise to leave the sheet in place until you are ready to print. The stencil is protected by leaving this sheet in place.

Printing

Printing requires several pieces of equipment. The screen should be prepared. The transfer medium needs to be in place. A spatula, squeegee, and ink are also needed. The ink selected depends on the stencil material. Water-based inks are preferred for paper stencils. Hand-cut lacquer films permit the use of oil-based or water-based inks. Stencils from aqua or photo indirect film require lacquer or oil-based inks. The proper solvent (water or thinner) should be present also. This is necessary for cleanup.

WARNING

When using inks, observe the safety precautions of the ink manufacturer. Some inks may be harmful to humans if not used correctly. Listen to your instructor and follow classroom safety procedures. Ink can be permanent and if you get it on your clothes, it may never come off!

The transfer medium (paper, textiles, glass, etc.) should be prepared and in place. The transfer medium must be aligned with the guides on the printing base. The frame assembly is closed over the aligned transfer medium. The registration marks on the stencil must line up with the marks on the transfer medium.

The ink or paint needs to be stirred, usually with a spatula. The color must be well mixed. Some ink is applied to the top portion of the screen. The deposit of ink should be placed just above the image area. Do not use too much ink. More ink can always be added.

A ***squeegee*** is used to spread the ink, Figure 15-16. Squeegees come in various shapes and sizes. The shape of the blade is important. A square edge is used for printing on paper or other flat surfaces. A rounded squeegee blade is recommended for textile (cloth) work. A beveled squeegee is used for glass and ceramic surfaces. The squeegee should also be the proper length. It must be just wide enough to cover the image area. If it is too wide, it will ride on the masking material. If the squeegee is too narrow, more than one pass will have to be made. The incorrect squeegee will result in a poor print.

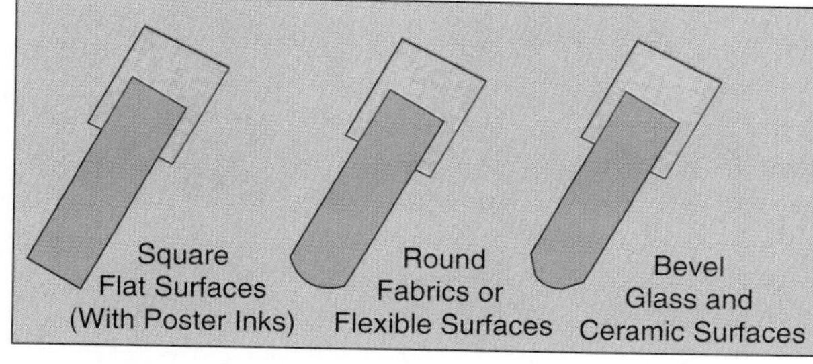

Figure 15-16. A squeegee is used to force ink through the stencil. Different shapes aid the printer in screening a variety of materials.

Next, the squeegee is pulled firmly across the stencil to force ink through the screen. Too much pressure may tear the screen. A single pass is preferred. However, thick ink or a large image area may need additional passes. The screen assembly must be raised carefully and the print removed. **Do not touch the image!** The print must be allowed to completely dry before touching the image or adding another color.

Industrial screen process printing is usually done by machine. Mechanical arms pull the squeegee across the stencil. Special machines allow the printing of round objects such as bottles or cans. Screen process printing is used in many areas, Figure 15-17.

Cleanup

After printing, the screen and supplies must be cleaned. A piece of cardstock can clear excess ink from the screen. Also, extra ink must be removed from the spatula and squeegee. Next, the mask is peeled away and discarded. A rag with the proper ink solvent is used to clean the screen, Figure 15-18. The printing area must be completely clear of ink. Most screens are reusable with adequate cleaning. Clean the squeegee and spatula as well.

Figure 15-17. This large, industrial screening machine is used in printing two-color jobs. (American Screen Printing Equipment Co.)

Finally, if the image will never be used again, the stencil or film must be removed from the screen. That way the screen can be used later for another job. Old newspapers can be placed under the screen. Stencil solvent is poured over the stencil area on the screen. The dissolved stencil material will come off the screen onto the newsprint. The solvent is lightly rubbed over the screen until the screen is clean. The screen can be checked to see if it is clear by holding the screen up to the light. This clean-up procedure can be repeated if necessary.

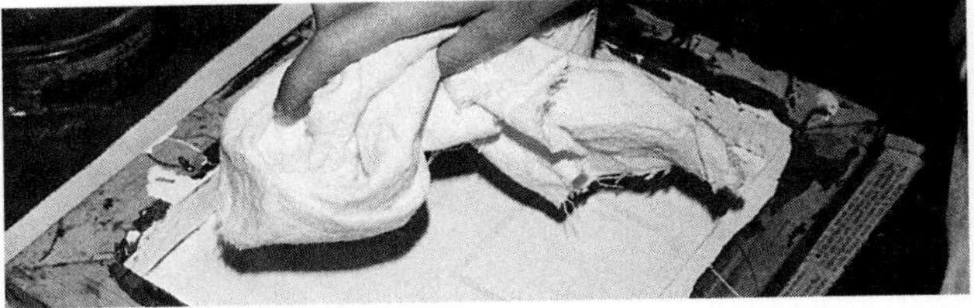

Figure 15-18. Clean off the screening equipment with the correct ink solvent.

CHAPTER 15 REVIEW

SUMMARY

Screen process printing involves forcing ink through a stencil on a screen. Screen stencils can be prepared by either hand or photographic means. The best method to use depends on available equipment and print quality desired.

After it has been determined which type of stencil to use, the stencil must be prepared. When the stencil is completed, it must be transferred to a screen. The screen must be secured in a frame. Once that is done, the transfer medium is placed on the printing base and the screen is placed on top of it. Ink is then forced through the screen and the transfer medium is carefully removed. The final image can be seen at this point, however, the ink must dry before it can be touched.

After all of the printing is done, everything must be cleaned up. This includes the tools and the screen. The stencil must be removed from the screen if that particular image will not be used again.

KEY WORDS

All of the following words have been used in this chapter. Do you know their meanings?

Brayer
Burn out
Burning
Guides
Masking off
Photo indirect stencil
Platemaker
Positive
Printing base
Registration marks
Screen process printing
Silk screening
Stencil
Squeegee
Thermal stencil

TEST YOUR KNOWLEDGE

Write your answers on a separate sheet of paper. Please do not write in this book.

1. Screen process printing involves forcing _____ or paint through a _____.
2. List several disadvantages of screen process printing.
3. Stencil preparation methods include:
   A. Photo indirect.
   B. Hand-cut paper.
   C. Hand-cut film.
   D. Thermal transfer.
   E. All of the above.

4. What is the difference between a registration mark and a guide?
5. Name the two types of film used in hand-cut film stencils. How is each type adhered to the screen?
6. When preparing a hand-cut film stencil, which layer is cut through and removed?
7. What machine can be used to produce photo indirect stencils?
8. Define burning. When is it used?
9. The printing procedure includes:
   A. Cleaning the screen.
   B. Assembling the frame.
   C. Preparing the screen.
   D. Making the print.
   E. All of the above.
10. A _____ is used to stir ink or paint and a _____ is used to spread it.

ACTIVITIES

1. Make your own screen process printing frames. They may be mass-produced by the entire class. Use several different methods to attach the screen fabrics to the frames. Write a short report explaining the similarities and differences in the processes that you used.
2. Design and print a three-color greeting or holiday card using the hand-cut stencil method. Explain to the class how you did this.
3. Collect samples of different products that use screen process printing in their manufacture. Present a short oral report to the class explaining how the products use the screen printing process.
4. Visit a local screen process printing shop. Write a report on what you saw.
5. Bring in your own T-shirts that were made by screen printing. Use them as a basis for discussion on the types of screen printing techniques.
6. Design and print one-color posters for a school spirit activity.
7. Design and print decals using the photo indirect screen process printing method.

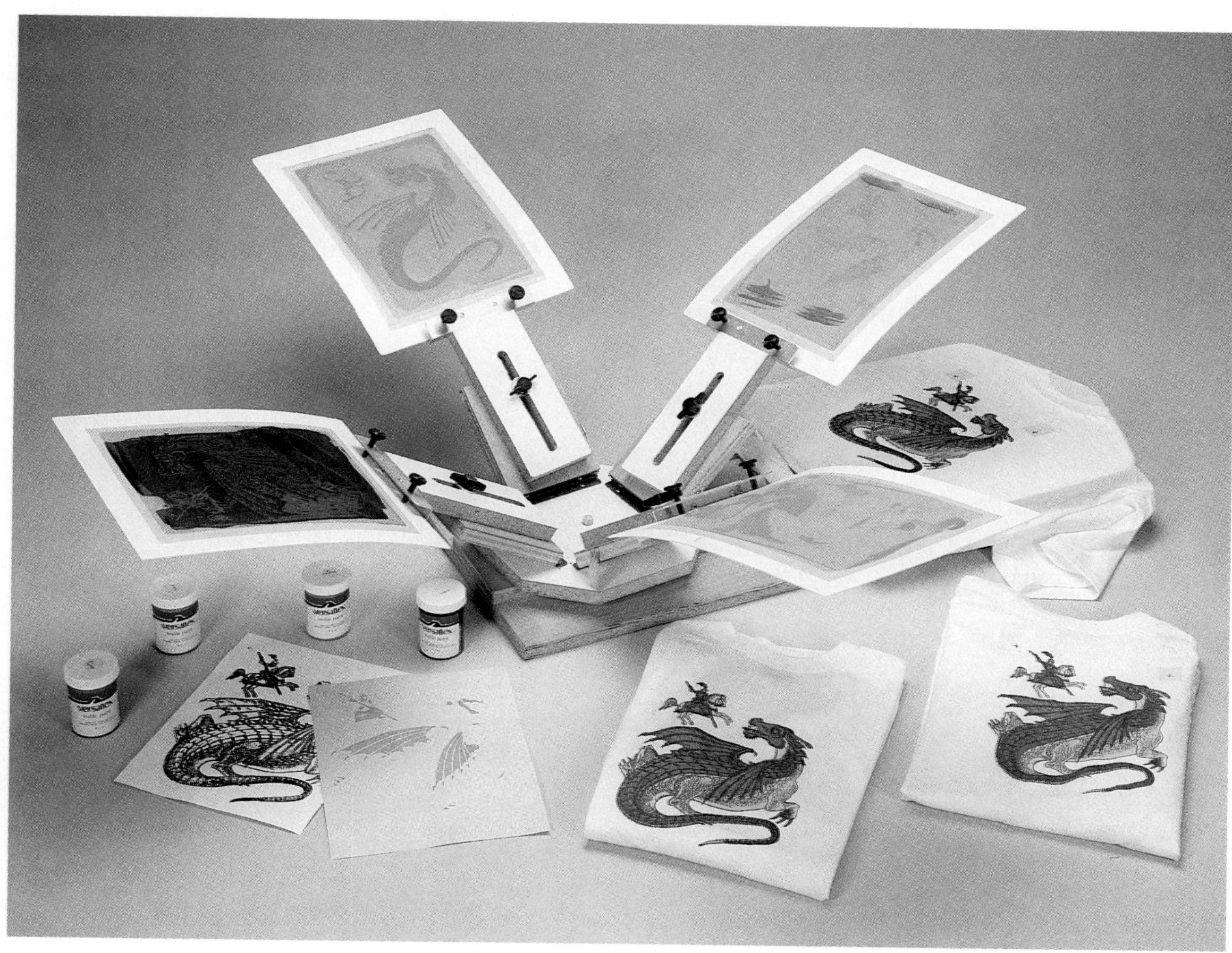

Screen process printing has many uses. New ways of creating the screens are making it easier for students to use the screen printing process. (Welsh Products, Inc.)

CHAPTER 16

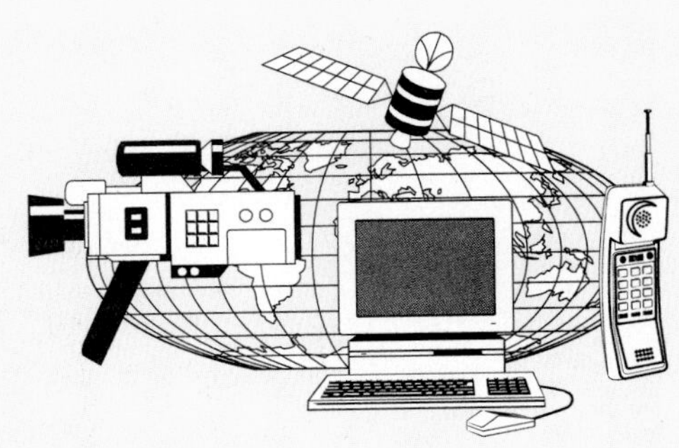

LITHOGRAPHIC PRINTING

After studying this chapter, you will be able to:

- *Describe the purposes and uses of lithographic printing.*
- *Prepare masters for lithographic printing.*
- *Produce a variety of products using the lithographic process.*

Lithographic printing is the most widely used reproduction technique in the printing industry. It is commonly known as ***offset printing*** or ***offset lithography.*** This method reproduces (prints) images from a flat printing surface. The image area is not recessed below, or raised above, the printing surface. This is why the printing surface is referred to as "flat." The printing surface can be, and often is, a round cylinder. Lithographic printing is based on the scientific principle that grease (oil) and water do not mix.

In the lithographic process, an original design is first prepared. A ***master plate*** is produced from this design for the printing process. A greasy ink is used to make the image area. The nonimage area is kept clean. This nonimage area will attract water. The greasy image area will attract an oil-based ink. The ink, which only adheres to the image area, produces an image when brought into contact with paper.

Early lithographic printers had trouble with the procedure. Their masters (usually made on limestone) had to be made backwards, or ***wrong-reading,*** Figure 16-1. However, a system of printing the image twice was developed. This is called "offset printing" because the final printed image is not taken directly from the original master. An offset press transfers the image from the master, which is made right-reading, to a second surface, Figure 16-2. The image appears wrong-reading on this second surface. From the second surface, the image is then transferred to the paper (transfer medium). The final image appears right-reading. Offset printing allows masters to be made right-reading.

Figure 16-1. Early stone masters had to be created "wrong-reading" or backwards.

PURPOSES AND USES

Lithographic printing is used primarily when a large quantity of copies are needed. This method of reproduction is fast and fairly inexpensive. Also, detailed photographs can be printed with excellent results. Jobs requiring multiple colors are also easily printed.

Offset lithography is used widely in industry. Most lithographic printing is done on paper or cardstock. Examples include textbooks, flyers, and newspapers, and packages, Figure 16-3.

Figure 16-2. An offset press transfers the image onto a blanket roller before printing on the actual sheets of paper. (Photo courtesy of Swaneck Graphic Equipment)

Figure 16-3. You probably see many examples of offset printed products every day.

Newspapers are produced using large offset presses. Rolls of paper are fed into the presses. As the paper flows through the presses, it is printed, folded, cut, and assembled. Modern printing techniques allow color photographs to be reproduced as well. These huge machines are very expensive.

The lithographic process is also used in printing posters, magazines, catalogs, and packages. Many of these contain colorful graphics. Only one color can be printed at a time. However, some presses can print the four basic colors one after another. The four basic colors are magenta (red), yellow, cyan (blue), and black. Magenta is really a red/blue shade and cyan is a blue/green shade. These four colors can be blended to produce any other color.

Packaging is designed to attract attention. This is done by using bold, colorful graphics. Large presses often lay down the four basic colors, one immediately after another, Figure 16-4. This speeds up the production process.

Figure 16-4. Some larger offset machines fill an entire room. They permit the printing of thousands of images each hour. Many of these presses are also able to print several colors at the same time. (Mitsubishi)

Besides printing on paper and cardstock, lithography is used for printing on metal, such as beverage cans. Sheets of metal are fed through the press. Designs and lettering are transferred onto these flat sheets. Later the metal can be cut, rolled, and assembled, Figure 16-5.

Figure 16-5. Many containers are printed with the aid of offset presses. This large roll of aluminum will eventually become cans used for the packaging of food items. (Reynolds Metals Co.)

MASTER PLATE PREPARATION

Early lithographic printers used large stones as the surface for printing. Modern offset lithography relies on flexible plates, Figure 16-6. Two types of plates are generally used in schools and small industries. These are ***photo-direct*** and ***presensitized*** plates. Photo-direct plates are made of paper. Presensitized plates are made of metal. The quality and number of copies required helps determine the best plate to use for a particular job.

Figure 16-6. A lithographic plate.

Photo-direct Plates

Photo-direct plates are produced quickly but have several limitations. The major drawback is the limited number of copies that can be produced. These plates are designed for runs of under 100 copies.

To prepare photo-direct plates, an original piece of artwork or text is required. The original must be clear and dark (black is preferred). A paper platemaker is also required. The platemaker projects an image of the original design onto a light-sensitive paper. This paper becomes the printing plate. Paper used for plates comes in rolls or sheets. Some machines will develop the paper internally. Others require that a separate processor be used.

After the paper is exposed and developed, it is ready for printing. The paper plate may be loaded on the press by hand. Some commercial offset presses with attached platemakers are available. These machines automatically feed the original into the platemaker and then the developed plate onto the press.

Presensitized Plates

The presensitized plate process is more complex than the photo-direct methods. In addition, it requires some expensive equipment. However, a very high-quality reproduction is possible with these plates. A platemaker required for this process is shown in Figure 16-7.

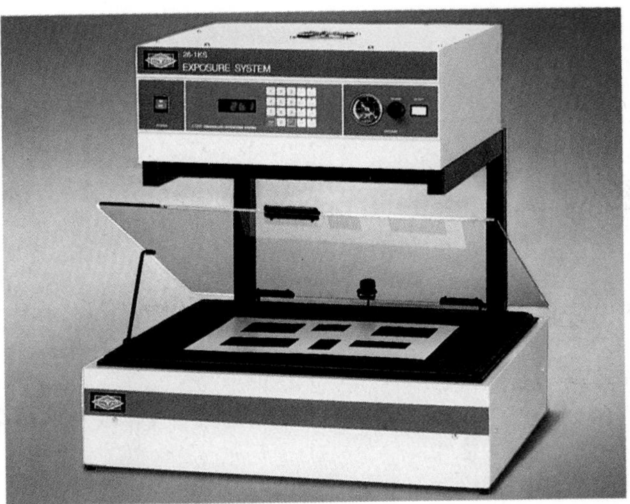

Figure 16-7. Platemakers use a high intensity light to expose the photo-sensitive plate. (Photo courtesy of nuArc Company, Inc.)

Presensitized plates are usually made of aluminum. Many have both sides prepared for printing purposes. This permits images to be developed on either side, Figure 16-8.

All copy and artwork for presensitized plates must be created with opaque (black) markings on a white background. A line and/or halftone negative is produced from this original. A ***halftone negative*** is actually a photograph that is converted into a series of dots, Figure 16-9.

WARNING

CHEMICALS CAN BE DANGEROUS! When using chemicals, be sure to follow the safety instructions given by the chemical manufacturer. Also, listen to your instructor and follow classroom safety procedures.

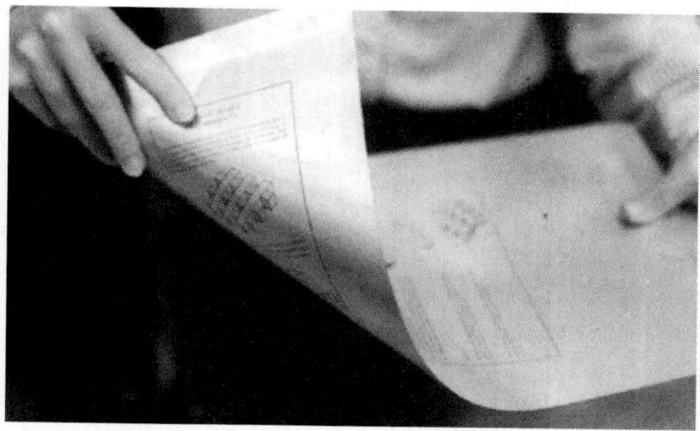

Figure 16-8. Aluminum plates like this are commercially available for lithographic work. Both sides are presensitized for easy usage.

Figure 16-9. A black and white half-tone is actually a series of "dots" that create the image. (Photo courtesy of The Coleman Company)

Making line or halftone negatives requires a process camera, a darkroom, and developing chemicals. These are shown in Figure 16-10. Orthochromatic film is also needed. This film provides a high contrast reproduction. Chemicals required in developing must be mixed and arranged in the order of their use, Figure 16-11. Process photography uses a developer, a stop bath, a fixer, and rinse water. Refer to the manufacturer's or your instructor's directions for preparing the chemicals **and follow the correct safety procedures.**

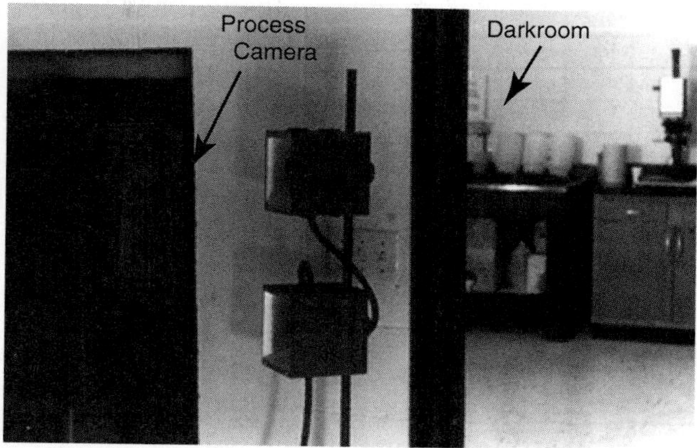

Figure 16-10. Most photographic work for offset printing requires a darkroom facility. The area shown here has the process camera and darkroom together. This equipment is used to produce the halftone negatives needed for making offset plates.

Figure 16-11. The chemicals needed to develop film must be prepared before work begins. These containers are arranged in order of developing.

A ***process camera*** is used to produce the negative, Figure 16-12. Artwork is placed on a ***copy board***. A copy board holds the original artwork in place for photographing. Film is placed in the process camera. This type of camera allows many adjustments, or fine tuning, to be made, Figure 16-13. You can adjust the ***exposure time*** (the amount of time that the film receives light), the ***f-stop*** (lens opening size), and the ***image focus.*** The percentage of enlargement or reduction can also be changed. A proportion scale and exposure table are helpful in establishing the proper settings.

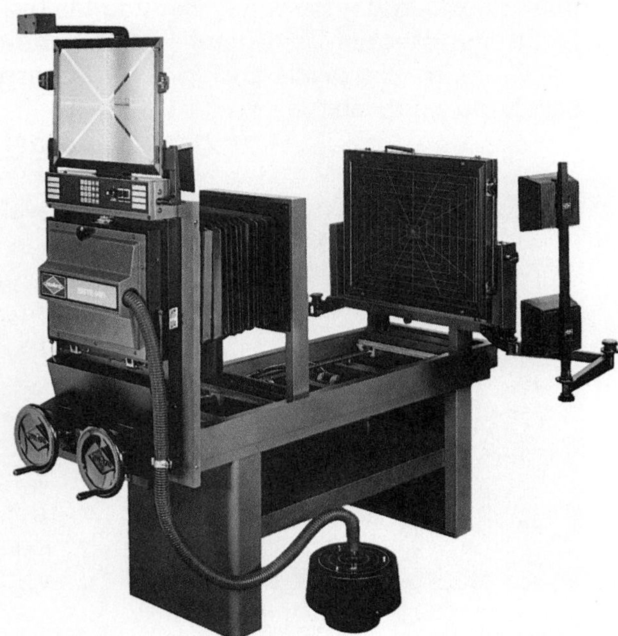

Figure 16-12. A horizontal process camera has many features. Can you identify the copy board, lights, and main body of the camera? (Photo courtesy of nuArc Company, Inc.)

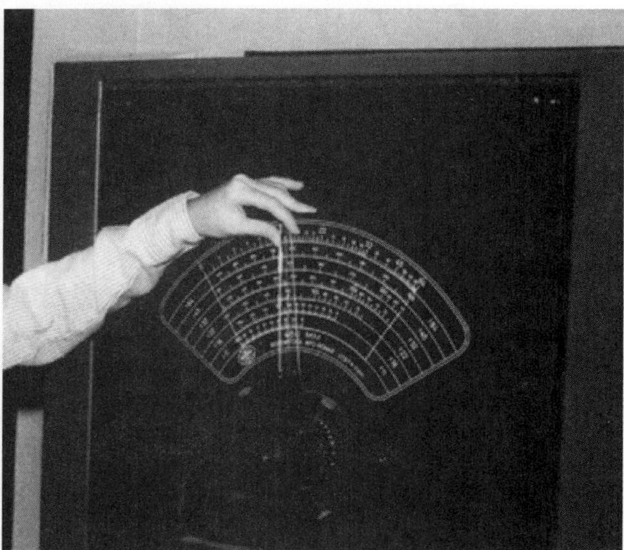

Figure 16-13. Process cameras have many controls to adjust for different films and light conditions.

When ready to photograph the original artwork, certain procedures should be followed. The glass on the copy board should first be cleaned. Both sides of the glass should be dust free. Any dirt or foreign material on the glass will lower the quality of the final print. The original is then centered under the glass with a ***gray scale*** placed near the copy. A gray scale is a strip of film with a range of grays from clear to totally black, Figure 16-14. It aids in exposing the film the proper amount of time. The f-stop and exposure time must also be set.

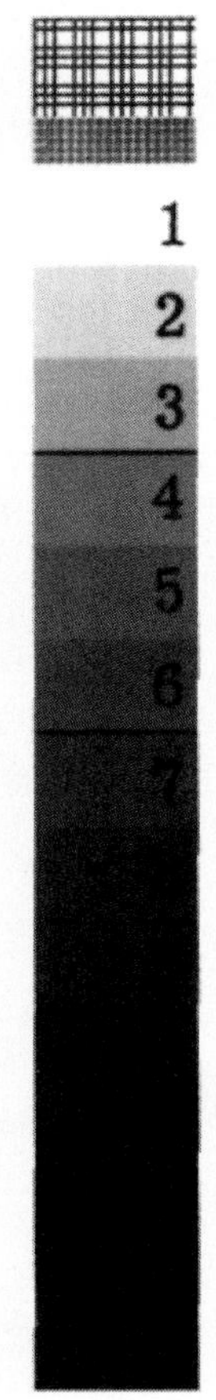

Figure 16-14. A photographic gray scale.

The next step is to load the camera with orthochromatic film. ***Orthochromatic film*** reproduces images in black and white. Remember that photographic film is light sensitive. This means that the film must be handled in a darkroom under safety lighting. Safe lights are normally red because orthochromatic film cannot detect red light. Only open the film box under these lights. Also, the film should only be handled by the edges. The film is placed on the camera's vacuum board with the light (emulsion) side up. After the film is loaded and centered, it is ready to be exposed.

If the final print will be in color, a separate piece of film must be printed for each of the four basic colors. A filter is used to screen out all but one color. For example, when making the film for the cyan layer, a filter is used that only allows cyan (and different shades of cyan) to appear on the film. This film will then be used to make a plate for printing the cyan color on the final product. A different filter must be used for each of the four basic colors. By printing the four basic colors on top of each other, color photographs and illustrations can be reproduced, Figure 16-15.

A method that is used more often is ***scanning*** the film. A scanner is connected to a computer. The original film is scanned one "line" at a time. The computer transfers the image into electronic signals. At this point, changes can be made to the image. If the original was too dark or too light, or if the colors appear odd, these things can be corrected. The different colors can be separated into layers at this point as well. Once the image appears in the desired final form and any colors are separated, then the image is printed onto orthographic film. In the case of color images, the four color layers are printed onto four separate pieces of film.

Once the film is exposed, it is removed from the camera or scanner. **Remember that until the film is developed, it must be handled under a safe light!** The film is placed in the developer tray with the emulsion side up. The tray is then agitated (moved slowly in a back and forth motion) so the developer covers the entire sheet. An image will slowly appear. ***Developer*** is the chemical that produces the image on the film. Film is usually developed for 2 3/4 minutes, or to a solid step 4 on the gray scale. (This is how the gray scale is used to help in developing.)

Next, the film is placed in the stop bath for about 10 seconds. The ***stop bath*** is the chemical solution that "stops" the developer from developing the film any farther. The film is next put in the fixer for 2 to 4 minutes. The ***fixer*** is a chemical that makes the developed image on the film permanent. From the fixer, the print is washed in the rinse water tray. This will clear away all of the developing chemicals. Usually, the film is left in this tray for at least 10 minutes.

Following the rinse cycle, the film must be dried. This can be done by hanging it up in a dust-free area, or placing it in a vacuum film dryer. Water spots on the negative should be avoided. The film is then ready to prepare in a flat.

There are machines used that are called ***imagesetters.*** These machines take the artwork and layout from a computer and electronically print those images on film. The machine will then develop the film. The resulting image (usually a negative) can then be used to "burn" the plate, Figure 16-16.

Lithographic plates are produced using the sheet of developed film assembled in a flat. A ***flat*** is a ruled (lined) goldenrod sheet, Figure 16-17. The film is taped to the backside of the goldenrod sheet. A small window (hole) is cut in the sheet. Opaque red tape is used to secure the film. (Light

Figure 16-15. Four separate layers (cyan, magenta, yellow, and black) are combined to make color photographs. (Photo courtesy of The Coleman Company)

will not go through the colored tape.) Guidelines, or ***registration lines,*** on the sheet help register the print. The term ***register*** refers to the alignment of the printing. You have seen color photos in the newspaper that appear "blurry." This is because they are "out of registration." The assembly of a flat is shown in Figure 16-18.

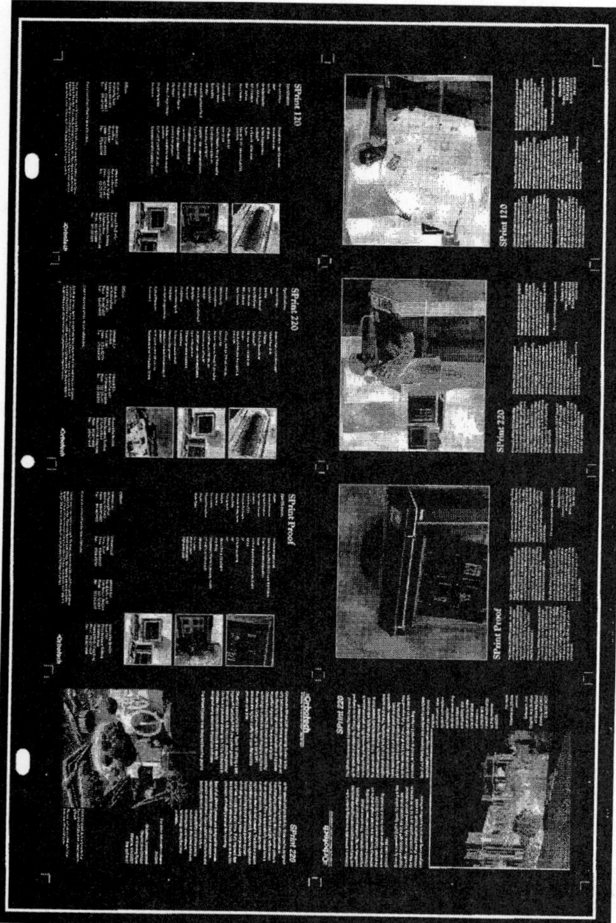

Figure 16-16. Imagesetters can take electronic art and layouts from a computer and print the images on film. The output of these machines is typically a negative that can then be used to "burn" the plate. (Orbotech, Inc.)

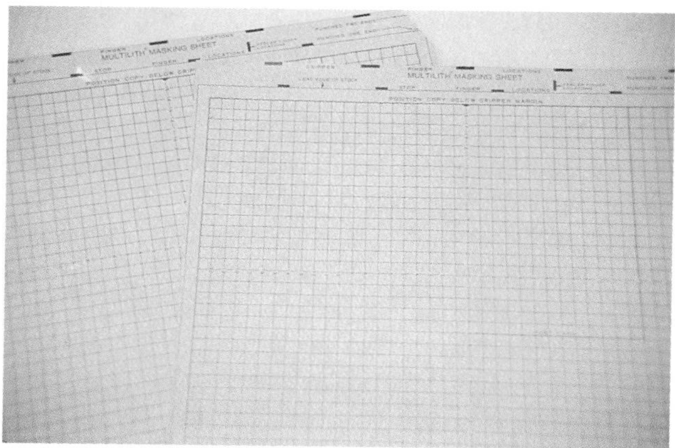

Figure 16-17. The goldenrod sheet used for producing a plate is called a "flat."

Figure 16-18. This film is being taped into place on the flat. The goldenrod flat will next be attached to the plate.

The presensitized plate may now be exposed. A platemaker is needed along with several developing supplies. These include a desensitizer solution, a developer solution, cotton pads, and gum arabic (a chemical that helps preserve the image on the plate). Running water is also required.

The assembled flat is placed on top of the plate (right-reading). The flat and the plate are then placed together on the vacuum table of the platemaker. The glass is closed and the vacuum turned on. On some platemakers, the frame is rotated closed. The timer is set. Exposure times vary due to light source and type of plate. The platemaker burns the image from the film into the plate. This procedure is repeated if the other side of the presensitized plate needs to be exposed as well.

Developing the plate is fairly simple. A small amount of desensitizer is poured on the surface of the plate. This is gently wiped over the plate. A clean cotton pad is useful. While the plate is still damp with the desensitizer, the developer is applied. As the developer covers the plate, an image will appear, Figure 16-19. The image will be either red, blue, or black depending on the type of plate used. Once a bold image appears, the plate is washed off. A gentle spray of water is best. The plate is then allowed to dry for several minutes.

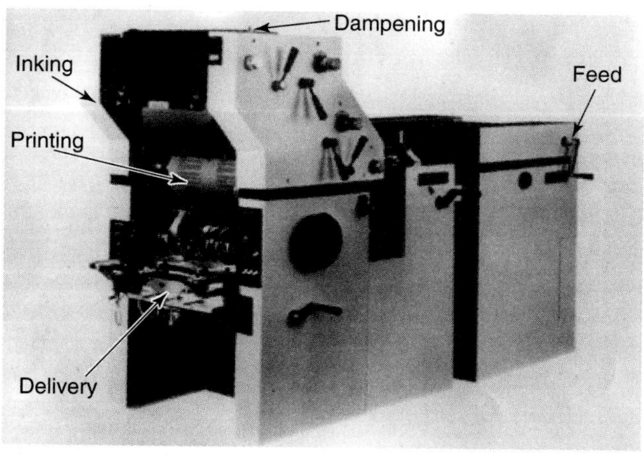

Figure 16-20. Standard systems of an offset press. (AFT-Davidson)

Figure 16-19. Chemicals are used to develop the plate after it is exposed to a bright light. An image will appear as these chemicals are rubbed across the plate.

The plate is then ready for printing. If the plate is to be stored, the surface is coated with gum arabic. This protects the image areas. A cotton pad is useful in spreading the gum arabic fluid over the plate.

PRINTING PROCEDURES

Offset presses all operate using the same basic systems. Each press has a dampening, inking, printing, feeding, and delivery system, Figure 16-20. The dampening system provides the water solution needed for the lithographic process. Ink is applied to various rollers and cylinders inside the press through the inking system. The printing system actually transfers the image to the paper (or other transfer medium). The feed and delivery systems move the paper through the press in registration (alignment).

Press Make-ready

Prior to printing, the five systems of a press must be prepared. This is known as ***press make-ready.*** The fountain solution (water) is mixed and placed in the reservoir. Adjustment of the inking system may take some time. Several control knobs help adjust the inking rollers, Figure 16-21.

Figure 16-21. Control knobs on the press help adjust the flow of ink and water to the rollers.

WARNING

MACHINERY CAN BE DANGEROUS! When operating machinery, be sure to follow classroom safety procedures. Listen to your instructor and follow the directions given to you.

Before printing, review the key safety suggestions shown in Figure 16-22. Printing presses are industrial machines. Caution must be observed in using this equipment.

RULES FOR OPERATING PRINTING EQUIPMENT

- Read instruction manual carefully before using any equipment.
- Be sure machine is in good working order.
- Safety guards should be in their proper place.
- Proper clothing is important; loose clothing, jewelry, and long hair are hazardous around machinery.
- Keep hands, arms, and fingers away from moving parts.
- Do not make adjustments while the press is running.
- Run the press at a safe speed.
- Follow the directions of your instructor in using the equipment.
- Store inks, solvents, and cleaning fluids in safe containers.
- Discard rags in safety cans with tight lids.
- Ask permission before using any equipment or supplies.

Figure 16-22. Safety rules to follow when using a printing press.

The press is first turned on at its slowest speed. At this point, it is checked to see that the inking rollers have an even flow of ink. Also, the dampening system is set. The dampening system provides the water to the plate. Once all adjustments have been made, the press is then turned off.

Next, the paper is loaded in the feed end of the press. The press is usually adjusted to register (align) standard stock pages. ***Standard stock*** is paper that is made to a standard size set by the printing industry. This means that the paper will always be the same size. There are several standard sizes available. Handles (or electric switches) raise and lower the pile of paper, Figure 16-23. The specific procedure will vary from one press to another. Consult your instructor for specific details.

To prepare for printing, the plate must be etched with a special solution. This solution also removes any gum arabic that may have been applied. The etching solution is rubbed over the plate with a cotton pad.

Figure 16-23. This employee is loading paper onto the feed system of the press. (AFT-Davidson)

Printing

The developed plate is then loaded onto the press. The plate is attached to the master cylinder, Figure 16-24. Some machines use pins to hold the master cylinder in place. Other machines use clamps to hold the master cylinder in place. You should refer to the manufacturer's manual for the specific machine that you will be using.

Next, the motor that drives the cylinders is turned on. Some presses specify that the moistening controls be engaged next. Other presses

Figure 16-24. The master plate is clamped onto the cylinder of the press as shown.

simply require the inking controls be started. Follow the instructions for the machine that you will be working on. Then the image must be transferred (offset) from the ink plate to the printing blanket. The ink should be allowed to transfer to the printing blanket for several revolutions before the paper is engaged. This allows an even layer of ink to develop on the blanket. Once a sufficient layer of ink has been transferred to the printing blanket, the paper feed is engaged, Figure 16-25.

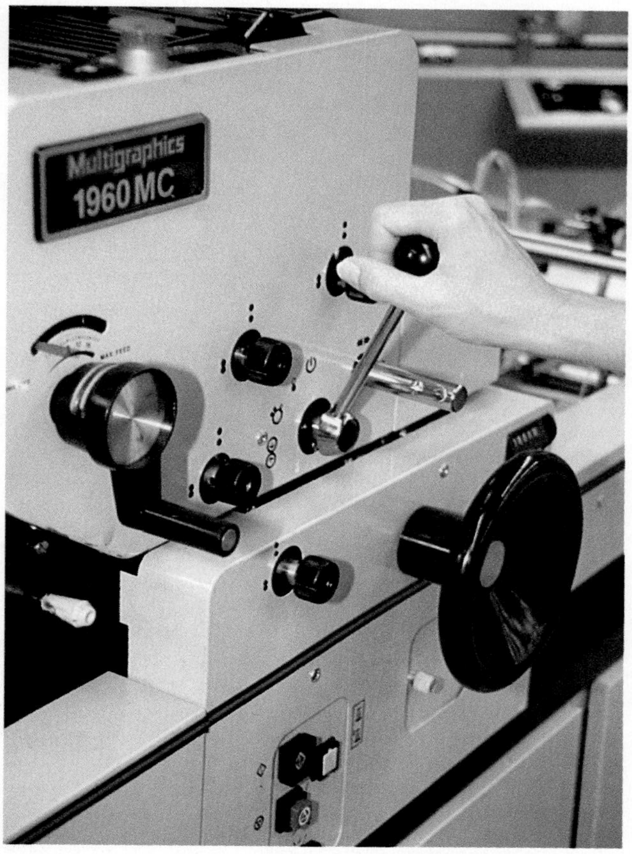

Figure 16-25. Turn the paper feed control to start the feeding of paper into the press.

As paper moves through the press, the image is offset from the blanket to each page. The printed sheets are inspected as they exit from the delivery system. If the image is clear and in its proper place (registered), the press is allowed to run. However, small adjustments may be required before continuing the run. During the run, a counter will total the pages sent through the press, Figure 16-26.

When the job is finished, the inking and water systems are turned off. The control switch is usually turned to "neutral." A solvent is used to clean the impression and blanket cylinders. This is all of the cleanup necessary if the press will be used again soon.

Figure 16-26. The counter on the press will keep track of the total number of pages printed.

Press Cleanup

If a different color is going to be run, or if the press will not be used for a long period of time, additional cleaning is necessary. Care should be used during cleanup. Do not let fingers or rags get caught in a moving press.

WARNING

MACHINERY CAN BE DANGEROUS! When near operating machinery, be sure to follow classroom safety procedures. Moving parts can quickly grab fingers, loose clothing, and rags. Listen to your instructor and follow the directions given to you.

The water fountain is first drained and removed. The ink fountain is then removed and cleaned. A rag with the proper solvent is best for cleaning purposes. **Carefully** apply solvent directly to the press rollers as they rotate **slowly**. Cleaning sheets should also be used. Some rollers are removable for easy cleaning. The blanket and impression cylinders are cleaned with solvent and a clean rag. Then all components are reassembled.

Finally, your hands should be cleaned and all soiled rags properly disposed of. Greasy rags **must** be kept in safety containers. Cloth rags can later be laundered and recycled. Unwanted paper is stored for later use or recycling. All supplies need to be stored as well.

CHAPTER 16 REVIEW

SUMMARY

Lithography is commonly called offset printing. This process is based on the scientific principle that grease (oil) and water do not mix. Offset printing is used in a variety of products, from posters to beverage cans.

Two types of plates are frequently used in offset work: photo-direct plates and presensitized plates. Each is prepared in a specific way. The presensitized process is the most complex way to produce a plate. The quality of the image produced with this plate is very high and a large number of items can be printed.

There are several types of printing presses. However, the basic printing procedure is the same for all presses. The plate must be loaded in the press. The press must be adjusted. Then the paper must be fed through the press. Cleanup is the final step in lithographic printing.

KEY WORDS

All of the following words have been used in this chapter. Do you know their meanings?

Copy board
Developer
Exposure time
f-stop
Fixer
Flat
Gray scale
Halftone negative
Image focus
Imagesetters
Master plate
Offset lithography
Offset printing
Orthochromatic film
Photo-direct plates
Presensitized plates
Press make-ready
Process camera
Register
Registration lines
Scanning
Standard stock
Stop bath
Wrong-reading

TEST YOUR KNOWLEDGE

Place your answers on a separate sheet of paper. Please do not write in this book.

MATCHING QUESTIONS: Match the definition in the left-hand column with the correct term in the right-hand column.

1. A photograph that is converted to a series of dots.
2. Lines used to align film onto a flat.
3. A strip of film used to help determine the proper exposure time.
4. Plates made of aluminum.
5. A ruled goldenrod sheet.
6. Plates designed for runs of under 100 copies.

A. Gray scale.
B. Photo-direct plates.
C. Flat.
D. Presensitized plates.
E. Halftone photograph.
F. Registration lines.

REVIEW CHAPTER 16

7. Two other names for lithographic printing are _____ and _____.
8. Lithographic printing:
   A. Is used when a small number of copies are needed.
   B. Is fast and fairly inexpensive.
   C. Cannot print detailed photographs.
   D. Can use only one color.
9. _____ is a red/blue shade and _____ is a blue/green shade.
10. What is the proper order of chemicals for film development?
    A. Rinse water, developer, stop bath, and fixer.
    B. Fixer, developer, stop bath, and rinse water.
    C. Developer, stop bath, fixer, and rinse water.
    D. Stop bath, developer, fixer, and rinse water.
11. Name the five operating systems found in all offset presses.
12. What is the proper order of chemicals for developing presensitized plates?
    A. Developer, water, and desensitizer.
    B. Water, developer, and desensitizer.
    C. Gum arabic, developer, and water.
    D. Desensitizer, developer, and water.

ACTIVITIES

1. Visit a newspaper printing room to observe lithographic printing in progress. How does this process differ from the screen process that you looked at in Chapter 12? Write a short paper explaining the differences.
2. Design a notepad. Divide the class into two groups. Have one group reproduce the notepad with photo-direct plates. Have the other group reproduce the notepad using presensitized plates. Conduct a class discussion on the differences and similarities of the two processes.
3. Design an advertisement for a school event. Make a plate using the photo-direct printing method and then print the advertisement. Write a short paper explaining the difference between making this plate and the one that you used in Activity 3.
4. Design your own personal stationary. Make a plate using a presensitized metal plate. Display a copy of each student's design on a bulletin board. Discuss with the class how the two different methods for making printing plates are similar and different.
5. Make a worksheet of steps to follow for operating your school's offset press. Include safety precautions!
6. Compose and print a two-color newsletter using the offset method. Write a short report explaining how you did this.
7. Research occupations associated with lithographic printing. Prepare a short oral report on the occupation that sounds most interesting to you.

Chapter 17

Continuous Tone Photography

After studying this chapter, you will be able to:

- *Describe the purposes and uses of continuous tone photography.*
- *Take photographs using proper composition techniques.*
- *Develop film using photographic chemicals and darkroom equipment.*

Photography is an exciting and interesting area of graphic communication technology. Photographers of all ages can produce pictures and slides, Figure 17-1. Many people take pictures for fun. Other people earn money for taking pictures.

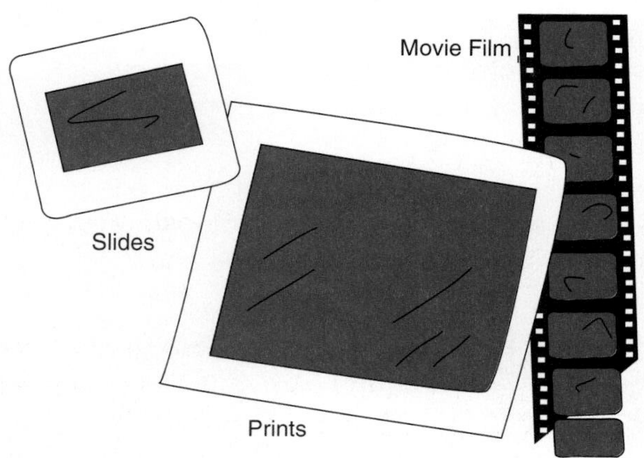

Figure 17-1. There are several examples of continuous tone photography.

Very simply defined, photography uses light to form images on light-sensitive film. A camera focuses rays of light on the film. A ***latent*** (invisible) image is created on the film upon exposure. Developing the film with chemicals produces a ***negative.*** On a negative, the image appears the exact opposite of the original. For example, white appears as black and black appears as white (actually clear since the negative is transparent).

To make prints (pictures), light is passed through the negative onto light-sensitive paper. This print is called a ***continuous tone photograph.*** A latent image is created on the paper. The light-sensitive paper is later developed to produce the picture. The process of developing pictures is illustrated in Figure 17-2.

PURPOSES AND USES

Photographs record visual images of persons, places, or things. Pictures are "worth a thousand words." Pictures can transfer information better than either written or spoken words. Pictures also provide a better understanding of magazine articles, newspaper articles, and books. Watching the news on television is much different than listening to it on the radio. Pictures bring the news to life. Events seem to unfold before your eyes. This form of communication shapes your emotions and attitudes.

Continuous tone photography has four major uses, Figure 17-3. These uses include aiding comprehension (understanding), recording events, decorating, and advertising.

First, photographs help you understand information. For example, this book has photographs to illustrate the topics being

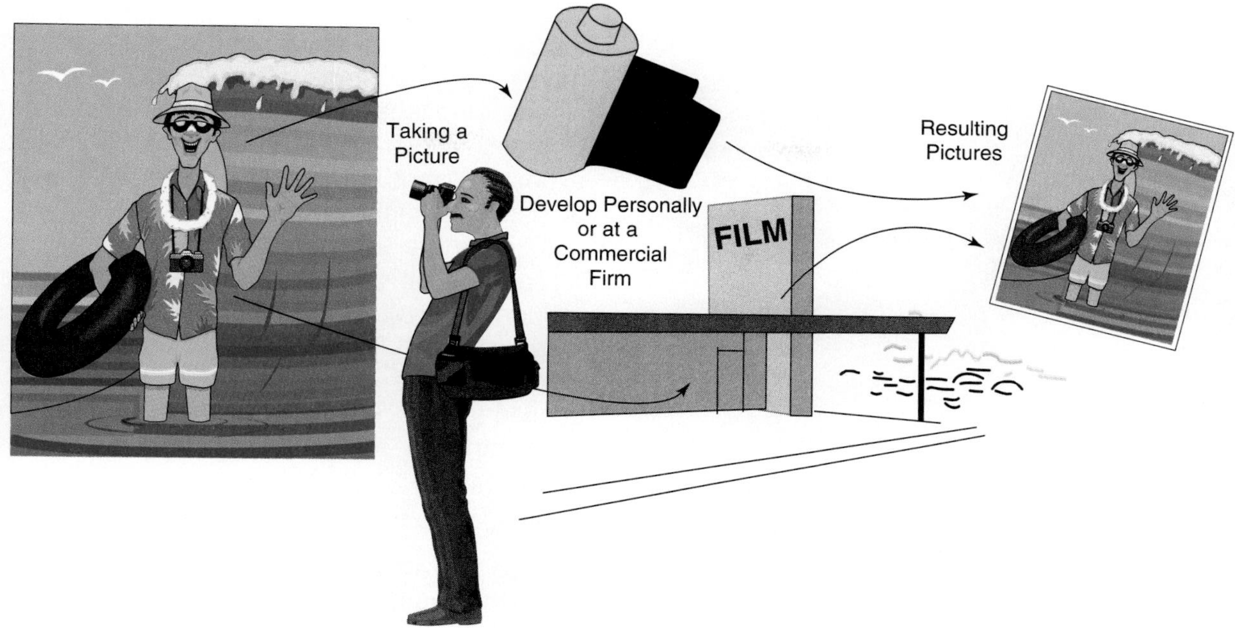

Figure 17-2. Photographs are taken with photographic equipment, developed with chemicals, and then printed on paper.

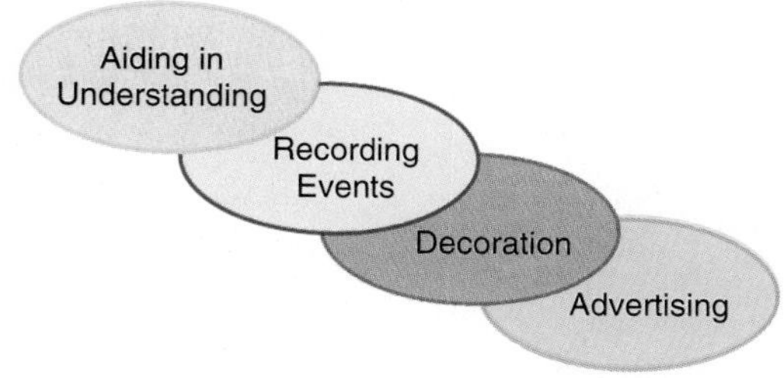

Figure 17-3. There are four uses of continuous tone photography.

Figure 17-4. The pictures in a school yearbook help you remember school events.

presented. Instructional books can show "how-to" assemble things through the use of photographs.

Photographs are also used to store or record events. Pictures of weddings, vacations, parties, and family gatherings are typical examples. At school, a yearbook is produced to help you remember friends and events, Figure 17-4.

Photographs are often used to decorate. Pictures of family members can be displayed on walls at home. Friends or special places are photographed, framed, and hung as a reminder. Artistic photographs are placed in art museums and art galleries.

Finally, photography is used in advertising. A company can use photographs to show their products and services. Photos of different items often appear in newspaper or catalog advertisements, Figure 17-5. These pictures create interest and help inform you enough to buy the product or service. Companies project a certain "image" through attractive photographs. Their advertisements remind the public of their service to the community. Interesting photographs also help attract readers to magazine articles, Figure 17-6. This is also a form of advertising.

CAMERA USE

A ***camera*** is a "box" that controls the transfer of light to film. Most cameras consist of two major parts: the box and the lens, Figure 17-7. The sim-

Figure 17-5. Newspaper advertisements announce sales to attract more customers.

Figure 17-6. Many corporate brochures have photos to illustrate important points. These booklets usually contain several pictures along with text.

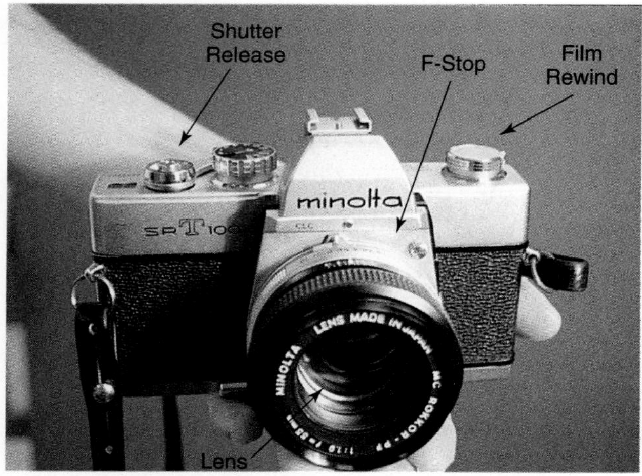

Figure 17-7. Most cameras have several different parts that the user must know how to operate properly.

plest cameras have no adjustable parts on either the box or the lens. Complex units, however, often have many controls. These controls permit clearer and sharper photographs to be taken. Complex cameras can be adjusted for different exposure times. The image focus can also be adjusted for improved photographs.

There are several cameras commonly used in commercial and private photography. These include the 110mm (pocket camera), disc, single lens reflex (SLR), twin lens reflex, press, and instant picture cameras. The processes discussed in this book will be related to the 35mm SLR camera.

Using the Camera

Before taking pictures, you must know how to use the camera. The instruction manual describes specific procedures. It gives instructions for focusing and loading the camera. In addition, unique features will be pointed out for that particular model. It is important that this manual be reviewed before operating the camera.

Film

Using the proper type of photographic film is important. Film comes in many forms, Figure 17-8. Common formats include 35mm rolls, 110mm cartridges, and disc cartridges. These may be in either black and white or color, and come in slide or print format. The number of exposures (pictures) on the roll of film is specified. The "speed" of the film is also indicated on each package.

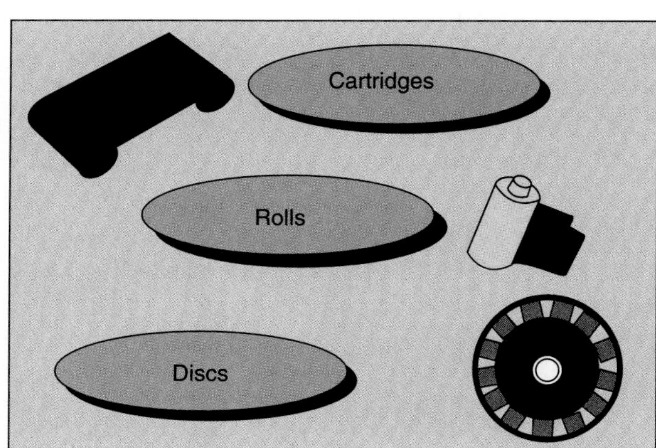

Figure 17-8. Several formats of film are commercially available.

Film speed is measured in ISO units. ISO stands for the International Standards Organization. The ***ISO rating*** indicates the amount of light needed to expose the film. Low ISO ratings (such as ISO 100) are slow films and will produce sharp images. Faster film (such as ISO 400) are useful for photographing in limited lighting and for photographing moving objects. A "slow" film requires more light to reproduce exactly the same image as a "fast" film.

Once the correct film has been selected, the camera can be loaded. Disc and cartridge films are simply inserted into the camera unit. Rolled film demands a slightly different procedure. This film must be threaded onto a take-up reel, Figure 17-9. The leader (film extending out of the canister) is attached to a slot in the take-up reel. The film is advanced several times to be certain of proper loading. This may require pushing the shutter release. The camera is then closed and locked before taking any pictures. Many new cameras have automatic take-up reels. This makes loading film easy.

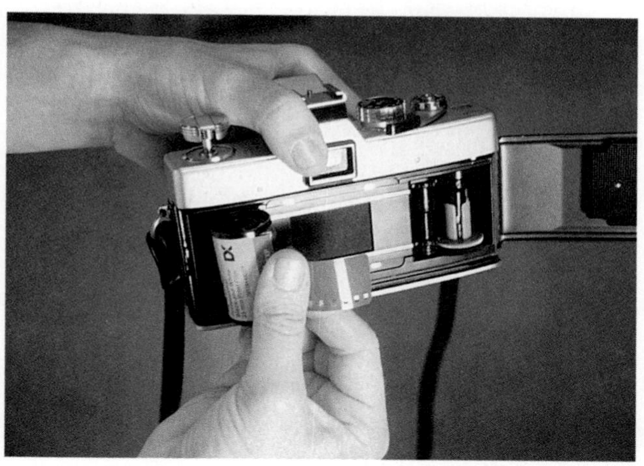

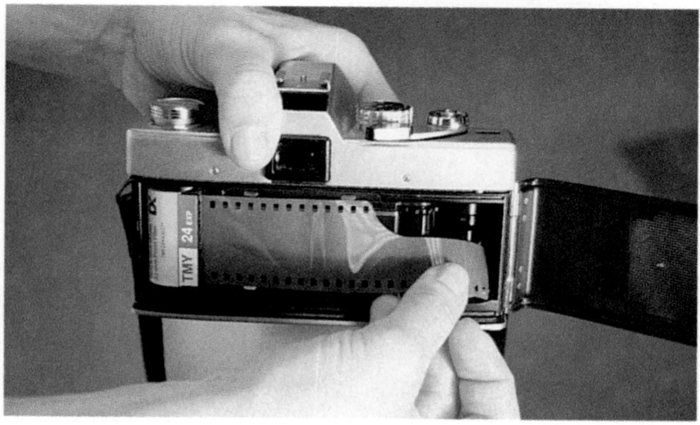

Figure 17-9. Loading film into a 35mm camera is more difficult than loading film into a disc camera. First, the film canister is loaded into the camera body (top). The film is then threaded onto the take-up reel (bottom).

Exposing the Film

With the film loaded, it is now time to frame and shoot the photograph. A ***viewfinder*** is used in selecting scenes. Look through the viewfinder to determine what you are going to photograph. Frame it carefully and make sure it is in focus. When the shutter release button is pushed, light will enter the camera box. The image is made when the light travels through the lens and strikes the film. Before pressing the shutter release button, remember to hold the camera steady. Any movement may result in a fuzzy or blurred picture.

The setting of other camera controls depends on film and available light. Film speed is set to the ISO rating listed on the container. The size of the shutter opening will determine the amount of light that will strike the film. This opening is called the ***aperture.*** The aperture size is indicated by a number called the ***f-stop.*** The higher the f-stop number, the smaller the aperture. A smaller aperture (or opening) means less light will strike the film.

Film Removal

After taking pictures, the film must be developed. Removal of the film from the camera is fairly simple. Rolled film must be rewound before removing. Turn the film rewind knob until the film is completely in the canister. Then open the camera box. Raise the film rewind knob or tilt the film to free it. Your instructor will have specific instructions for the type of camera you will be using.

PHOTO COMPOSITION

Good photographers know a great deal about photo composition. They take their time when composing pictures, Figure 17-10. ***Photographic composition*** means arranging or selecting scenes so that the final picture has a nice appearance. Photographic composition is the design stage in the communication process when the transmission medium is a photograph.

Photographs are composed by looking through the viewfinder. Study the scene for the best camera angle and range. Obstructions (distractions in the photograph) should be avoided. Obstructions are a form of "interference," Figure 17-11. They can usually be avoided by simply

Figure 17-10. Photographers attempt to get the best angle to "capture the action" on film.

Figure 17-11. Photographs must be carefully planned to eliminate clutter. This photo was taken too far from the action, making it hard to see important details.

moving the camera to another location. Turning the camera to a vertical position may also help in the composition process, Figure 17-12.

The principle of balance is critical for composition. Smaller objects or persons should be placed near the front of the view. Avoid exact centering of landscapes or people. This tends to make the photo look posed or unnatural. Proper centering is achieved by using the "thirds principle," Figure 17-13. The principle of thirds uses imaginary lines to divide a scene (picture) into thirds. These imaginary lines will intersect each other at four places. The center of the scene should be at one of the intersections, Figure 17-14.

Remember, good photographs require planning. Visualize what you want to photograph. Compose the scene so that the final photograph will have a nice appearance. Remember that what you see in the viewfinder is what the final picture will look like. The negative produced by "shooting" a picture represents the coding phase of communication.

Figure 17-12. Turning the camera often results in a better picture. Notice how these two photographs appear significantly different.

FILM DEVELOPMENT

After the roll of film is exposed, the next step is ***developing.*** This procedure is also called ***processing.*** The simplest film to process is black and white negative film. In this book, you will look at black and white film processing.

Preparation

To start film processing, the following is needed: an exposed roll of film, a developing

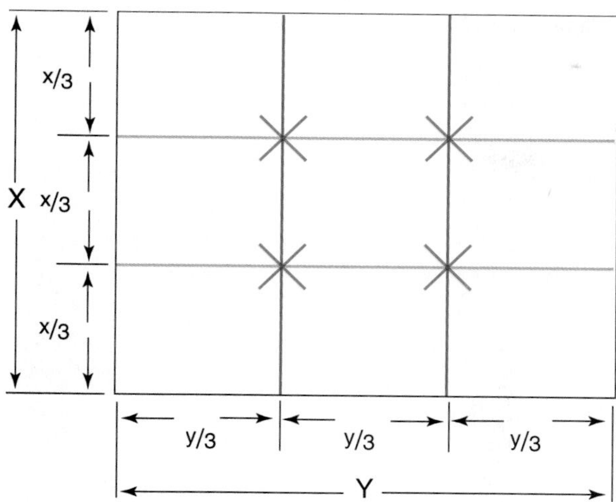

Figure 17-13. Photographs should be composed with the "thirds principle" in mind. Draw imaginary lines dividing the scene into thirds. There will be four spots where these lines intersect. The center of the scene should be at one of these spots.

Figure 17-14. Any scene can be divide into "thirds" to identify where the major details should appear.

tank, a film reel, a darkroom or film change bag, and developing chemicals. These materials are shown in Figure 17-15.

Perhaps the most difficult part of film development is loading the film reel. This is because exposed film must be loaded in total darkness. A darkroom or a film change bag is normally used for this procedure. Naturally, loading the film under these conditions will require practice.

When ready to load the film onto the reel, the following items are needed: exposed film, film reel, and developing tank. These should all be placed either in the darkroom or the film change bag. Once in total darkness, the canister is opened. The film is loaded onto the reel carefully, Figure 17-16. It is sometimes easier to thread the film if the edges of the film leader are cut in a rounded shape. Then the loaded reel is placed into the developing tank. The lid of the tank must be on tight!

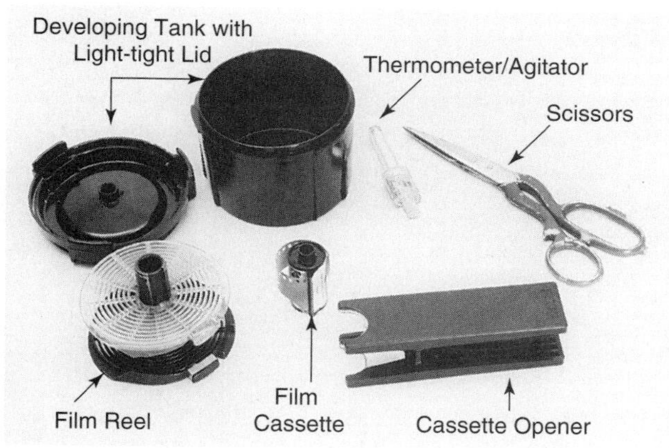

Figure 17-15. There are several different supplies needed for developing film.

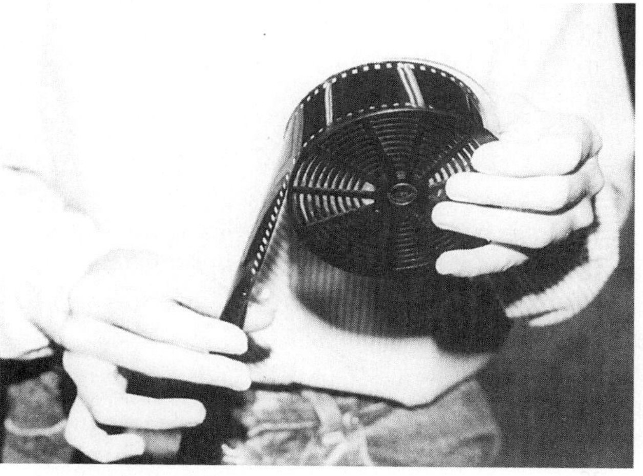

Figure 17-16. To develop exposed film, it must first be loaded onto a reel. Be sure this is done in total darkness!

WARNING

CHEMICALS CAN BE DANGEROUS! Use care when handling chemicals. Be sure to follow all safety precautions that are given by the chemicals' manufacturer. Be sure to listen to your instructor and follow classroom safety procedures.

Developing

Three chemicals are needed to develop the film: the ***developer*** solution, the stop bath solution, and the fixer solution. Handle all photographic chemicals with caution. They can irritate your skin and eyes, and can ruin your clothes on contact.

It is very important to have the chemicals at 68°F (20°C) when processing. By placing the chemical containers in running water of the proper temperature, the chemical temperature can be controlled. Water temperature is easily measured with a thermometer, Figure 17-17.

Figure 17-17. Keep developing chemicals in marked containers and at the proper temperature.

Working near a sink, the developer is poured into the tank. Keep track of the time the developer is in the tank. Proper development time varies for each processing session. After the chemicals are added to the tank, the container is agitated slowly. This assures that developer covers the entire film surface.

At the end of the processing time, the developer is poured out. Immediately, the ***stop bath*** solution is added to the tank. This is left in the tank for about 1-2 minutes. Then the stop bath is poured back into its container for reuse. The stop bath keeps any remaining developer solution from developing the film any farther.

Next, the ***fixer*** solution is poured into the developing tank. The container is agitated for 7-10 minutes. This solution will "fix" the developed image onto the film. After the image is "fixed," light will not affect the film. When finished with the fixer solution, it is poured back into its container for reuse. The film can now be handled under a "non-safe" light.

At this point, water must be poured into the tank for at least 20 minutes. This washes the chemicals off the processed film, Figure 17-18. A wetting agent should be added to the water for the last few minutes. This prevents water spots from forming on the film.

Figure 17-18. After developing, film is washed while still in the developing tank.

The film is removed from the developing tank and reel. It should be hung up to dry, Figure 17-19. A clip is used to hang the film while drying. Attaching another clip to the bottom will keep tension on the film and prevent it from curling. When the film has dried, it is cut into sections. Avoid cutting each negative apart. Cut them into groups of two or more for easier handling.

PRINT MAKING

Making a photographic print is a two-step process. First, the negative must be enlarged. Next it must be developed into a photograph. The entire procedure is referred to as ***printing.***

Figure 17-19. Hang up film to dry. Be sure clips are attached to both ends to keep the film from curling up and sticking together.

Making prints requires an enlarger, developing chemicals, and photographic paper for printing. A ***contact printing frame*** is helpful for inspecting your negatives. This frame allows you to make a one-sheet print of all the negatives from a single roll of film, Figure 17-20. It is likely that you will only want to make full-size prints of your best shots. Contact sheets allow the opportunity to select the best shots.

WARNING

CHEMICALS CAN BE DANGEROUS! Use care when handling chemicals. Be sure to follow all safety precautions that are given by the chemicals' manufacturer. Be sure to listen to your instructor and follow classroom safety procedures.

The developing chemicals are assembled before producing the contact print. The developing and fixing of paper prints requires different chemicals than those used for film negatives. Be sure to prepare the correct chemicals. About one inch of each chemical is placed in trays arranged in order (developer, stop bath, and fixer). A bath of circulating water should follow the fixer tray.

Figure 17-20. Test sheets are useful to help determine which shot is the best.

Contact Sheets

In safe light (red or yellow), a sheet of print paper is removed from the box. Remember to close the film box to avoid exposing the remaining sheets. The paper is placed, shiny side up, on the enlarger stand. The negatives are positioned on top of the print paper. The emulsion side of the negatives should contact the paper. A piece of glass is placed over the negatives. This holds the paper and negatives in position.

The light in the enlarger is turned on. A timer on the light switch controls the exposure time. Most prints are exposed for about 10 seconds on an f/11 setting (this is a specific f-stop setting). Recommended exposure times and f-stop settings will vary. Consult your instructor for what is best for your negatives.

When the light goes off, the negatives and the paper are removed. The paper is then placed into the developer tray. Remember to handle only the corners of the paper. After the proper amount of time in the developer (usually about one minute), the paper is removed with tongs. Allow the developer to drain off the sheet before it is placed in the stop bath. Next, the sheet is placed in the stop bath for five seconds. The paper should be drained before putting it in the fixer for two minutes. Finally, the print is put in the wash water for a minimum of five minutes.

After washing, the sheet is examined and the best photographs are selected. You may want to cut the contact sheet into strips. Tape these strips to your negative cover for print identification.

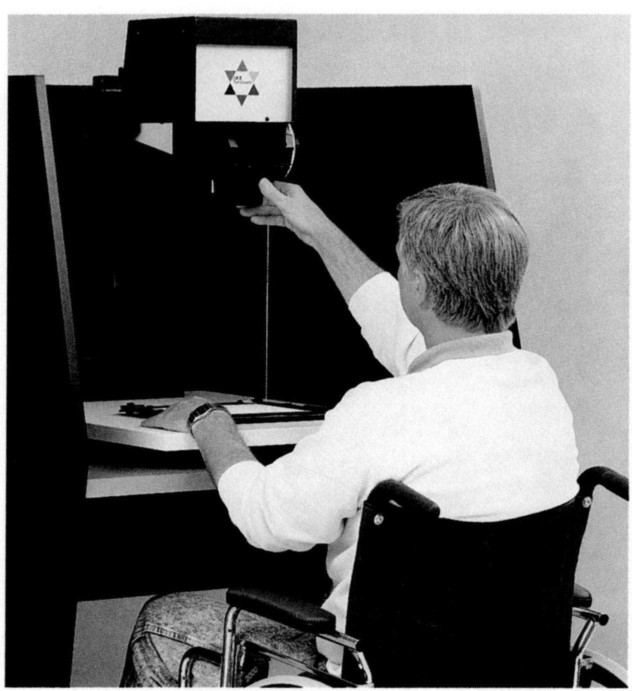

Figure 17-21. Photographic enlargers allow print size to be increased. (Kreonite, Inc.)

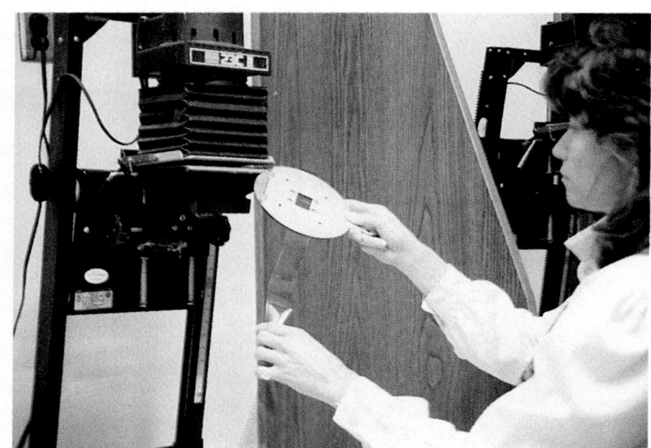

Figure 17-22. The photographic negative is loaded into a carrier, and then placed in the enlarger.

Enlargements

The process for making enlargements (actual photographs) is similar to producing contact prints. However, the enlarger is used to control the size as well as provide a light source. It is possible to produce prints of various sizes with an enlarger, Figure 17-21. The lens and assembly (head) will need to be adjusted for each shot.

The negative is loaded into the carrier, which is then placed in the enlarger head. Remember to place the negative emulsion side down in the carrier, Figure 17-22. Next, the enlarger easel is positioned on the stand. The light is turned on to check alignment. The entire surface of the easel should be illuminated. The lens is focused so the photograph appears clear and sharp.

After these adjustments, a ***test sheet*** is usually produced to determine exposure time, Figure 17-23. A sheet of cardboard is needed for this process. Under safe lights, a sheet of print paper is removed from its package. The paper is placed on the easel, shiny side up. All but one-

Figure 17-23. This test sheet has been exposed from 5 seconds (far left) to 25 seconds (far right).

fifth of the paper is covered with the cardboard. The timer is set for five seconds and the enlarger is turned on. The light will shut off after five seconds. The cardboard is moved so that another fifth of the sheet is showing (two-fifths total). The paper is exposed for another five seconds. This process is repeated for a total of five times, until all of the paper is exposed. The last section will have been exposed for only five seconds, while the first section will have been exposed for a total of 25 seconds.

The developing process is the same as in making a contact sheet. That developing process is repeated for this print. Remember to handle the sheet by the corners only.

The test sheet is inspected. The time that provided the best contrast (ranges of blacks, whites, and grays) is selected. The timer is set for that value. A new sheet of paper is placed on the easel. The whole sheet of paper is exposed for the proper time. Finally, the paper is developed in the same way as the test sheet.

The completed print should then be dried. Excess water is best removed with a squeegee, Figure 17-24. Prints can be air dried, or placed in a drying machine.

Figure 17-24. Drying a print with a squeegee.

Figure 17-25. This photograph will be cropped to leave out clutter and interference.

As your skill in developing increases, you will become familiar with other advanced techniques. One technique is called ***cropping,*** Figure 17-25. Cropping is a common way of removing unwanted sections of a negative from the print. It is done by changing the alignment of the paper and easel. Burning-in is a technique used to darken certain areas of the print. Dodging is used to lighten certain areas of the print.

CHAPTER 17 REVIEW

SUMMARY

Photographs transfer information better than either written or spoken words. The four major uses of photography are to aid understanding, record events, decorate, and advertise.

A "picture" is taken on film in a camera. That film is developed into a negative. The negative is then used to make a print, or final photograph.

Using a camera, processing film, and printing film takes practice. As you practice, following the guidelines in the chapter, you will gain new skills. Your understanding of the principles of photography will grow steadily.

KEY WORDS

All of the following words have been used in this chapter. Do you know their meanings?

Aperture
Camera
Contact printing frame
Continuous tone photograph
Cropping
Developer
Developing
f-stop
Fixer
ISO rating
Latent
Negative
Photographic composition
Printing
Processing
Stop bath
Test sheet
Viewfinder

TEST YOUR KNOWLEDGE

Place your answers on a separate sheet of paper. Please do not write in this book.

1. Photography uses _____ to form _____ on light-sensitive paper.
2. What is an invisible image called?
3. List the four major uses of photography. Give an example of each.
4. Film speed is measured in:
   A. SLR units.
   B. ASE units.
   C. ISO units.
   D. None of the above.

5. Photographic composition does NOT include:
   A. The fifths principle.
   B. Balance.
   C. Planning.
   D. Avoiding obstructions.
6. Film development is also known as _____.
7. Outline the steps in the development of film negatives.

Matching Questions: Match the definition in the left-hand column with the correct term in the right-hand column.

8. Used to determine correct exposure time.
9. A two-step process for making photographs.
10. Process of removing unwanted sections from a photograph.
11. Used to make different size prints.
12. A one sheet print of all the negatives from a single roll of film.

A. Enlarger.
B. Contact sheet.
C. Cropping.
D. Printing.
E. Test sheet.

ACTIVITIES

1. Visit a camera/photography shop. Ask a salesperson to show and explain the various pieces of equipment and supplies available to the beginning photographer. Take notes and ask for brochures. Write a short paper on the camera and equipment you would prefer to use, and why you would prefer to use it.
2. Bring photographs from home. Use these to discuss with the class composition techniques. Find examples of both good and bad techniques.
3. Invite a professional photographer to speak to your class about their experiences. Ask your guest to bring sample photographs, as well as the equipment and supplies used.
4. Choose two or three of your best prints to present to the class. Explain the composition techniques you used. Why do you like these photographs? What makes them good photographs?
5. Give a brief oral report on a famous photographer. Present your report to class, along with several examples of their photography.

CHAPTER 18

SPECIALTY PRINTING METHODS

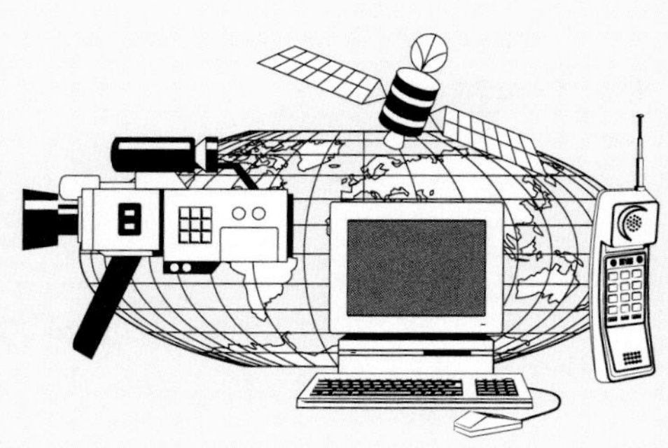

After studying this chapter, you will be able to:

- *List several specialty printing processes.*
- *Describe the purposes and uses of specialty printing processes.*
- *Use various specialty printing methods.*

Specialty printing methods help produce and communicate an endless flow of information. Several of these techniques are very familiar. For example, computer printers are a useful printing process, Figure 18-1. Ditto and mimeograph methods have been common for school work. Typewriters have been around for many years, Figure 18-2.

Figure 18-1. Color ink jet printers can produce high quality, four-color output. These printers are much more inexpensive to purchase and operate than color laser printers. (ENCAD, Inc.)

Figure 18-2. The typewriter was invented in the 1800s. Today, much office work is completed on computers, but typewriters are still the best process for very small jobs like labels and forms.

PURPOSES AND USES

There are several specialty printing processes. Some of these processes were looked at in Chapter 12. Some of the processes that you have looked at are ditto printing, mimeograph printing, diazo printing, heat transfer printing, and ink jet printing. These processes are utilized for several reasons. One reason is because of the limited number of copies required. Low cost and ease of use are other important reasons.

Some processes are used mostly in schools and in offices. Other specialty processes are used mostly in industry. Some specialty processes can be found in homes, schools, offices, and industry.

SPECIALTY PRINTING IN SCHOOLS AND OFFICES

Computers are very common in schools and offices. Two types of computer printers that use specialty printing processes are ink jet printers and dot matrix printers. Laser printers can be considered a specialty process, however, they form images using electrostatic means. Other types of specialty printing processes that can be found mostly in schools and offices are ditto and mimeograph machines. Typewriters and Kroy machines are also specialty printing processes found in schools and offices.

Computer Printers/Plotters in Schools and Businesses

The use of computers has led to many types of specialty printing. Computers can be found in schools, offices, and industry (as well as many homes). Computer printers and plotters provide outstanding graphic displays, Figure 18-3.

Figure 18-3. Plotters can print images (drawings) and text in several colors. (Hewlett-Packard Co.)

Ink jet and dot matrix printers use a system, or "matrix," of dots to print images. Any letter or number can be formed from a "matrix" of dots. Normal arrangements include patterns that are 5 dots x 7 dots, 7 dots x 9 dots, or 9 dots x 9 dots, Figure 18-4. Different sizes and styles of lettering can be produced by this method of printing. Text can be printed in different sizes (point size), in different styles (fonts), or a combination of normal text and modified text. A variety of graphic images can also be printed.

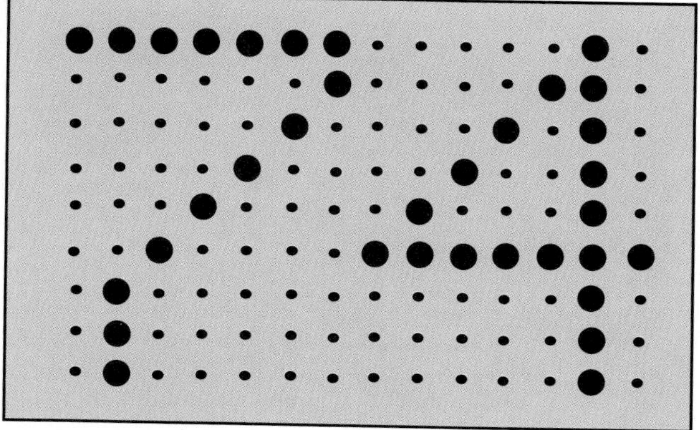

Figure 18-4. Any number or letter can be created with an arrangement of dots. A 7 x 9 pattern of dots is common.

Dot matrix printers (also known as ***pin printers***) form text and images with tiny "dots" transferred from a ribbon, Figure 18-5. A set of "pins" mechanically drives the ribbon into the paper. These printers are referred to by the number of "pins" they have (9 pin, 24 pin). The image quality of pin printers varies by the application. Cash register receipts have a low-quality image. Pin printers that are used for printing text can produce a higher quality of image. Some pin printers can produce text with almost the same high quality as typewriters. Dot matrix printers (pin printers) are very popular in school settings since they are very inexpensive. Some businesses use dot matrix printers when printing invoices, order forms, and paychecks.

Computers also direct ***ink jet printers.*** These are similar to dot matrix printers, but use droplets of ink instead of a ribbon, Figure 18-6. These machines are capable of producing very high-quality text and graphics. These printers are very popular in small businesses and schools because they are relatively inexpensive and still

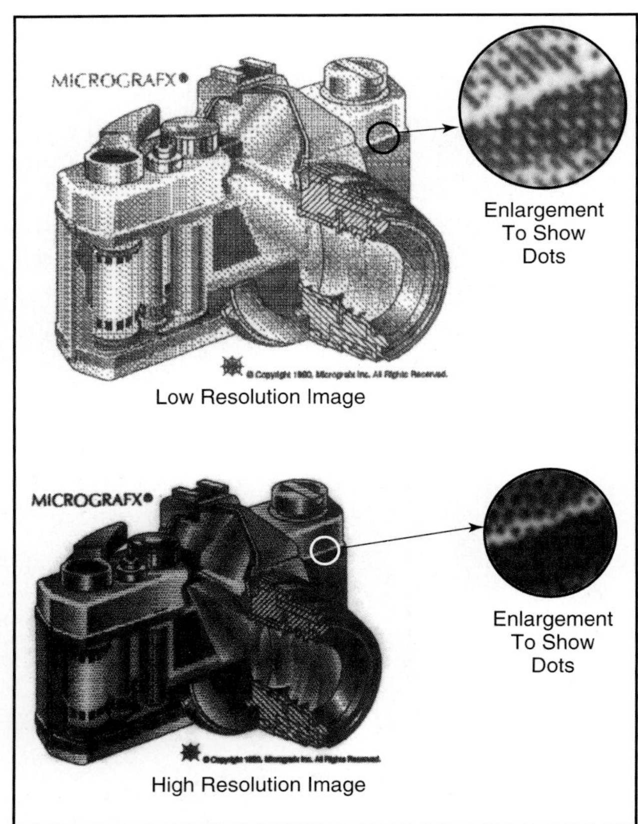

Figure 18-5. Dot matrix, or pin, printers use tiny "dots" to form images. The quality of these printers can be changed to meet the needs of a particular application. As you can see from these actual dot matrix printouts, the resolution can range from low to high. (Courtesy of Epson)

produce a high-quality image. These printers are called "non-impact printers" because no mechanical part of the printer strikes the paper. Instead, the ink is "shot" onto the paper through tiny "jets." Businesses use these printers to produce reports and letters. Some schools produce student materials with ink jet printers. Some schools have these printers available for the students to use for reports and other projects.

Other types of computer printers operate like a typewriter. They create text by forcing a ribbon against the paper with preformed letters and numbers. These printers are called ***daisy wheel printers.*** The name comes from the odd-shaped wheel that rotates into position for printing. Letter-quality printing is achieved with these printers. ("Letter-quality" means the printout appears as if it was typed on a typewriter.) However, these printers, like typewriters, are primarily capable of producing text only. These printers are used in schools and businesses where only text is printed. Examples include printing invoices, letters, and package labels.

While laser printers use the electrostatic process, they have become very popular as a specialty process. Many desktop publishers use laser printers because they are very reliable and produce high-quality images. Many laser printers in business applications can print multiple colors. Laser printers can also be used as an output device for CAD programs.

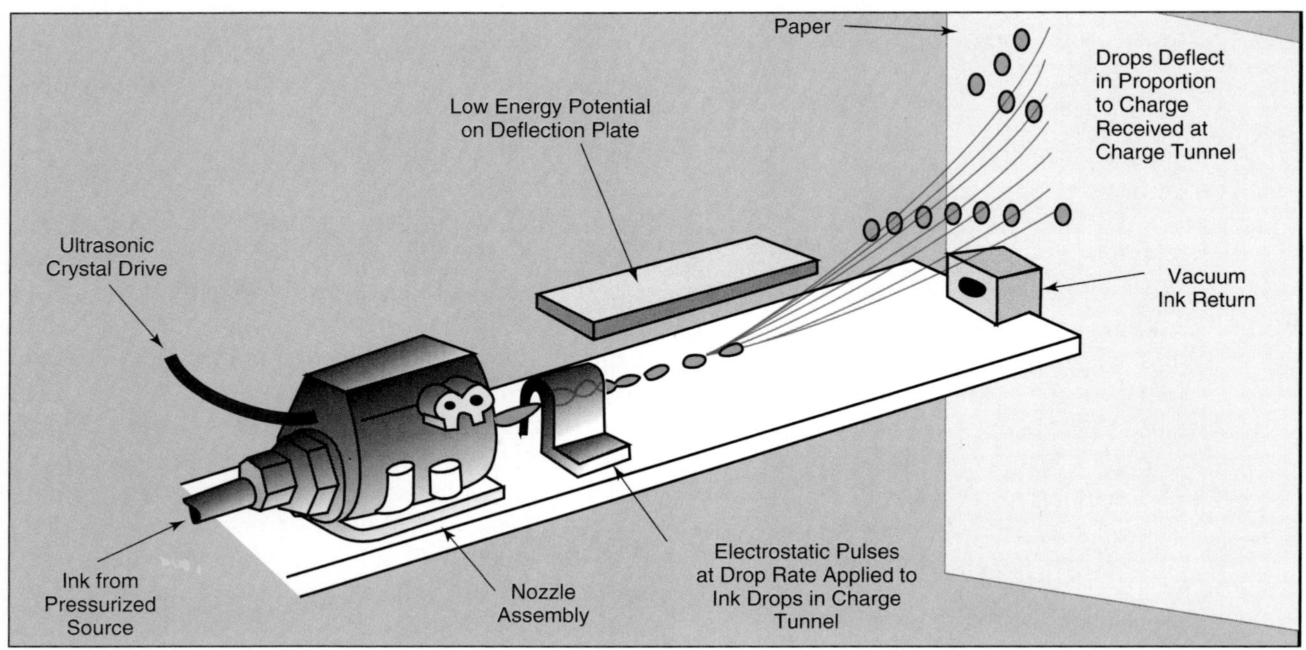

Figure 18-6. Ink jet printers "shoot" droplets of ink onto the paper. A computer controls where the ink goes. (Marsh Stencil Co.)

Plotters are connected to computers and are used to print out Computer-aided Drafting (CAD) drawings, Figure 18-7. These types of printers can be found in many schools and offices that use CAD applications. Some plotters can handle very large sheets of paper and, therefore, can print very large drawings. Engineering and architectural firms may use many plotters. Schools have plotters in their CAD laboratories. Plotters are good for producing drawings and labeling on those drawings, but they are not suited for producing large amounts of text.

Figure 18-7. Plotters are the most common way to print CAD drawings. Many plotters are capable of printing in several colors. (Hewlett-Packard Co.)

Ditto

The ditto process has been used in schools because it is very inexpensive and easy to use. The ***ditto process*** requires the use of a ditto machine and a master. The masters are purchased commercially and are available in a variety of colors. Purple is the most common. Ditto masters may be direct image or heat-transfer. With direct image masters, the original design is typed or drawn directly on the master sheet. For example, if the design includes a sketch, you could draw your sketch on the master sheet itself.

Heat-transfer masters are often used for ditto projects. These two-part masters are prepared differently. The original design is created on regular paper and then photocopied (a printout from a laser printer will also work). The photocopy is sandwiched with the master and processed with a ***Thermofax®*** machine. Heat from the light in this machine burns (transfers) the image onto the master. This process can be used for originals which contain artwork, text, or a combination of the two.

After preparing the ditto master, it is ready for printing. The master is attached to the cylinder of the machine upside down (wrong-reading). As the master is rotated, ditto fluid is wiped on it. This softens the image. The wet image is transferred to paper as it contacts the master. The image is partly removed with each copy produced. Student handouts, tests, quizzes, and homework all can be quickly and effectively created with the ditto process.

Mimeograph

The ***mimeograph*** process is another specialty printing process found in schools and offices. This process utilizes a stencil, much like the screen process printing method. Mimeograph stencils are prepared by direct contact or electrostatic means.

The direct contact method is the simplest of the two methods. An image is typed or drawn directly on the master. This will cut right into the stencil material. In the electrostatic method, a scanner reproduces the original onto a black stencil. Artwork is easily copied by this procedure.

After the stencil is completed, it is positioned for printing. The master is fastened to the mimeograph cylinder. Ink is forced through the stencil onto the paper. A uniform layer of ink is applied to each page.

Both the ditto and mimeograph processes are being quickly replaced by the use of electrostatic copiers.

Other Specialty Printing Processes in Schools and Offices

Other specialty printing methods have important applications in offices and schools. Typewriters and Kroy machines help create text for various communication materials.

Modern typewriters are computerized. Data is generated and sent directly to a printing head. Copies are produced on paper that is inserted directly in the machine. This technique is useful in completing forms and other office material. Ease of use and speed are two attractive features of this process. However, typewriters are still primarily capable of producing only text. Modern typewriters do, however, permit printing of various lettering styles. This is a large improvement over earlier typewriters, which could print in only one style.

The use of Kroy machines has decreased steadily with the popularity of electronic publishing. These machines print letters and symbols on adhesive-backed tape. Cartridges or wheels containing various styles of type and color of tape produce many variations. Graphic designers sometimes use Kroy lettering for titles and headings of printed materials. They are also useful in making name badges.

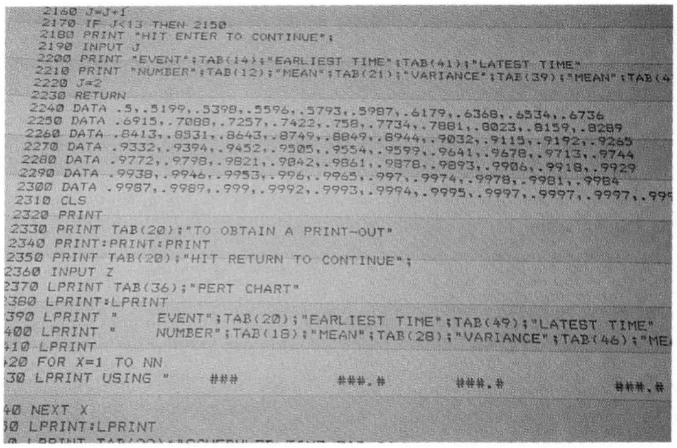

SPECIALTY PRINTING IN INDUSTRY

Many graphic procedures aid in the production of common industrial goods. You looked at the most common types of printing in the previous chapters. However, there are specialty printing processes that are used in industry. Computers are used very often in industry. Many firms use plotters to print out CAD drawings. Whiteprints, rubber stamps, and clothing are typical industrial products printed with specialty printing. Some of the specialty printing processes found in industry are computer printing, diazo, foundry type, and heat transfer.

Computer Printers/Plotters in Industry

Dot matrix printers are used in industry. These printers operate exactly like those found in schools and businesses. The difference is that they are larger, and they are used for different purposes. The dot matrix printers that can be found in an industrial setting print on "green bar" paper. This paper is typically 14 7/8 inches wide and has alternating 1/2 inch light and dark green "bars" across the page, Figure 18-8. This type of paper makes it easy to trace numbers and figures across the page. This type of paper is frequently useful for printouts of computer programs.

Plotters are also frequently used in industry. CAD drawings are printed out on plotters. These drawings can be quite large. Plotters found in industry can be much larger than those found in schools or businesses. The prints that are generated by plotters can be used in the field or on the shop floor, or they can be reproduced. As the cost of plotters and creating drawings on plotters decreases, drawings are more frequently being taken directly to the shop floor or out in the field. Fewer prints are being reproduced.

Figure 18-8. Dot matrix printers in industry typically print on "green bar" paper. This paper makes it very easy to trace numbers across the page. Computer programs are usually printed out on green bar paper.

Diazo

Diazo printing is also a specialty printing process. It has many uses in industry. The most common use is reproducing engineering drawings. The resulting copies are called ***whiteprints.*** Unlike blueprints, the background is white and all lines are blue, although these drawings are sometimes referred to as "blueprints." Making a whiteprint is relatively easy. The process is similar to making a blueprint. The original is passed through a diazo machine along with a copy paper. The image is copied by exposing the paper to light. The copied image is then developed by exposing it to ammonia gases.

Foundry Type

Foundry type (actually a form of relief printing) was developed by Johannes Gutenberg. (Gutenberg invented the "type mold" which made certain that each piece of type was exactly the same size. This made movable type practical.) This system of movable type is still useful in the production of certain items, such as rubber stamps.

Hand composition of type is generally used for making rubber stamps. The foundry type is brass because heat is required in the process.

Figure 18-9. The California job case holds foundry type. The layout of this case is in the order of most-used letters and not alphabetical.

Type is stored in ***California job cases,*** Figure 18-9. Letters in this case are not arranged in alphabetical order. Their location is determined by frequency of use. Commonly used letters occupy larger boxes in the center of the case.

The type is put together, and heated at approximately 300°F (150°C) for several minutes. The hot type is then forced into a plastic material called ***Bakelite.®*** The heat from the type will set the Bakelite® into a permanent solid shape. This shape becomes the mold used to form the rubber stamp.

Next, the rubber is heated and pressed into the mold. The material vulcanizes (hardens), resulting in the surface portion of a rubber stamp. The piece of rubber is cemented to a handle, Figure 18-10.

Figure 18-10. The mold for making rubber stamps is made using a specialty printing process.

Heat Transfer

Heat transfer is a popular printing method in the textile industry. Many T-shirts are printed using heat transfer, Figure 18-11. Masters are usually prepared by lithographic or screen process printing. An image is printed onto a backing material. The image is then transferred by heating in a dry mount press or with an iron. There is one important disadvantage to heat transfer printing. The image generally does not wear as long as designs screened directly onto the cloth or other transfer medium.

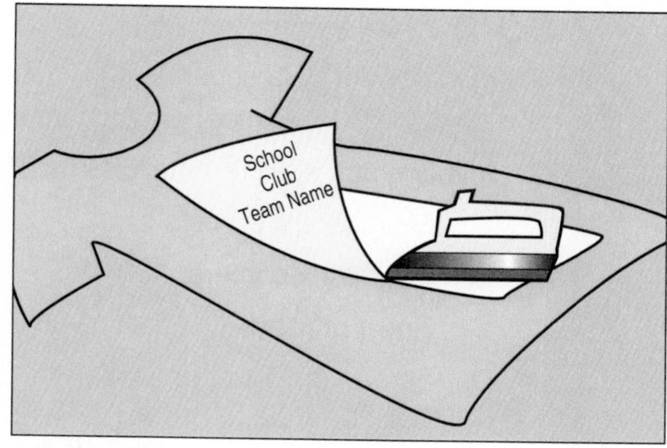

Figure 18-11. The designs on T-shirts are often produced with the heat transfer method of printing.

CHAPTER 18 REVIEW

SUMMARY

There are many types of specialty printing processes. These processes can be divided into two categories: those used primarily in schools and offices, and those used mostly in industry. Some processes, like ink-jet printing, are used in schools, offices, and industry.

Specialty printing processes are used for several reasons. The number of copies needed is usually limited. The cost of using these processes is relatively low. These processes are quick and easy to use. Computer printers and plotters are used frequently in schools, offices, and industry. Now that much work is completed on a computer, and the cost of using computer printers and plotters has decreased, this form of specialty printing has become very popular. Ditto and mimeograph machines are also printing processes that are sometimes used in schools and offices. Typewriters and Kroy machines also have important application in schools and offices.

Specialty process printing in industry include foundry type and heat transfer. These are used to make items such as rubber stamps and T-shirt designs. Computer printers are also very common in industry. Diazo machines are used to copy drawings for use on the factory floor or at construction sites.

KEY WORDS

All of the following words have been used in this chapter. Do you know their meanings?

Bakelite®
California job case
Daisy wheel printer
Diazo printing
Ditto process
Dot matrix printer
Foundry type
Heat transfer
Ink jet printer
Mimeograph
Pin printer
Thermofax®
Whiteprint

TEST YOUR KNOWLEDGE

Place your answers on a separate sheet of paper. Please do not write in this book.

1 How do ink jet printers produce an image on paper?

2. Mimeograph stencils function similar to:

   A. Electrostatic printers.

   B. Dot matrix printers.

   C. Relief printing.

   D. Screen process printing.

   E. None of the above.

3. _____ printers are classified as non-impact printers because machine parts never strike the paper.

MATCHING QUESTIONS: Match the definition in the left-hand column with the correct term in the right-hand column.

4. Used to duplicate prints for use on the factory floor or in the field.
5. Perfected by Johannes Gutenberg.
6. Very quick and easy to use, but primarily only capable of producing text.
7. Place where foundry type is stored.
8. Devices used to output computer images.

A. California job case.
B. Typewriters.
C. Printers and plotters.
D. Movable type.
E. Diazo machine.

9. Identify the major disadvantage of heat transfer printing.

ACTIVITIES

1. Choose a specialty printing process to research. Write a paper about the process based on your research. Include information on the invention, inventor, and history of the process. List several items for which it is currently used. Present the report to the class. Get examples of items made by this process.
2. Visit a shop that uses heat transfer printing to make designs on clothing. Arrange to tour the entire business, from the production of the stencils to the heat transfer of the design. Write a report on what you saw.
3. Collect samples of computer-generated printing from several different printing devices. Identify where each sample came from and what device was used to print it. Which has the best quality? Which is the least expensive to use?
4. Make a rubber stamp with your name and address as the design. Give a short oral report to the class explaining how you completed this project.
5. Design a two-color flyer for an upcoming school event. Print it using ditto masters and a ditto machine. (You will need two masters that print in different colors.)
6. Compose a one-page class newspaper. Use a Kroy machine to make the masthead (top of the paper, or "heading"). Use typewriters to compose the stories. Use different letter styles to make the headlines. Then do the same project using a computer and desktop publishing software. Which project looks better? Which project was easier to use? Write a report explaining the differences between the two processes. Come up with a conclusion stating which method is better.

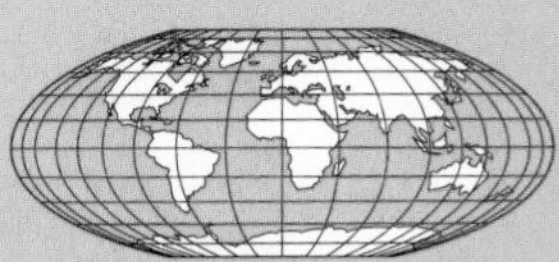

Section 3 Review

Graphic communication, or printed graphics, describes the various processes and methods that are used to reproduce printed images. Graphic communication has developed from symbols, called hieroglyphs, through handwritten books, to the methods that are used today. Movable type was one of the most important developments. It was perfected by Johannes Gutenberg around the year 1450. Types of printing used today include offset lithography, screen process, electrostatic, and other specialty processes.

However, to produce printed materials, the visual message must be designed and produced through a layout. When designing a visual message, certain design principles and design elements should be followed. Various sketches should be made to help determine the best design and layout for the message. As the sketches are refined, graphic tools and supplies are used to improve the layout. These refinements include using different forms of lettering (fonts), line drawings, clip art, and photographs to improve the visual quality. Computers have become very important when making graphic layouts. Desktop publishing software allows text and graphics to be merged. This allows layouts to be produced (and redesigned if necessary) very easily.

Section 3 Activities

1. Produce a newsletter covering positive activities and functions around your school and community. As a class, determine what functions and activities are to be covered. Assign groups to cover and write about each function or activity. After the "stories" are written, design the layout of the newsletter. The design should be discussed and decided upon with the class as a whole. After a design is decided on, determine how the newsletter will be reproduced. Then determine groups to perform the various tasks. Once the newsletter is reproduced, determine where to send it to gain support for your school and technology program.

  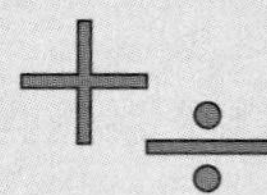 

2. Design a T-shirt with the names of your class or Technology Student Association. Include the TSA emblem or design an emblem to represent your class. Pay attention to the design principles and elements that have been discussed in this section. Reproduce the design on T-shirts using the screen printing process. Write a report explaining what process. After the T-shirts are reproduced, wear them to activities and functions so that your class or TSA can be recognized.

   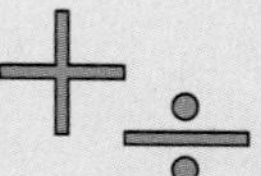 

3. Use the visual communication skills that you have learned in this section to design and reproduce illustrations, lettering, and images to improve the appearance of your room. You can select an area of your technology laboratory or another area of your school. You can use desktop publishing and other graphic communication processes for the design and reproduction. Be sure to follow the design elements and principles that you have learned. Write a report on your activities and submit it to the school newspaper.

Kathy Kopf

Westinghouse Electric Corp

Sprint

Section 4

Electronic Communication

AT&T

NASA

CHAPTER 19
INTRODUCTION TO ELECTRONIC COMMUNICATION

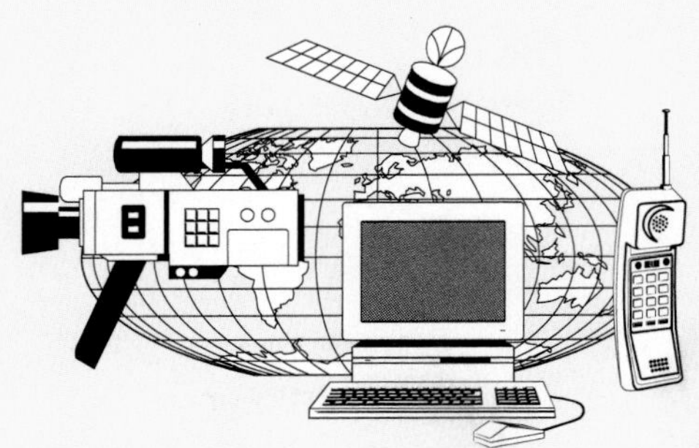

After studying this chapter, you will be able to:

- ❖ *Identify the major areas of electronic communication.*
- ❖ *Explain the historical developments of electronic communication.*
- ❖ *Discuss current developments in electronic communication.*

Electronic communication involves the use of electrical energy to transmit information between individuals or technical systems. Electronic communication has not always been available. In the past, much communication was done through graphic communication methods such as letters, newspapers, and books. However, as scientific knowledge increased, electronic communication began to develop. This development was, and continues to be, full of exciting discoveries.

HISTORY OF ELECTRONIC COMMUNICATION

You learned briefly about several of the more important communication devices in Chapter 2. Some of these devices include the electric telegraph, telephone, radio, television, computers, and transistor. In this chapter you will explore more fully the history and current developments of electronic communication.

Early Transmission Techniques

Among the most important developments in history were early experiments with the telegraph and telephone. These inventions allowed humans to send messages between remote locations. Of course, simple methods of communicating over long distances existed before the invention of the telephone and telegraph. The Native Americans of the Great Plains used smoke signals, Figure 19-1. Church bells and flags were common in most towns. At sea, cannons, reflections, and lights were used to signal to other ships. Postal systems allowed the exchange of letters and packages. The famous Pony Express system carried messages across the North American continent for several years.

Figure 19-1. Native Americans used smoke signals to communicate over long distances before the invention of electronic communication systems.

However, experiments with electricity in the 1800s provided new potential for communication. No longer were humans limited by how far they could see or by how far they could shout, Figure 19-2. Messages could be sent along wires in the form of electrical current. This is still the basis for modern telephone technology, Figure 19-3. Spoken words are changed to electrical or light pulses for transmission (message is coded). These transmissions are received at the opposite end and changed back into a recognizable tone (message is decoded).

Figure 19-2. Without technical assistance, the human voice can only be heard over short distances. With the aid of a telephone, you may talk to others anywhere on earth.

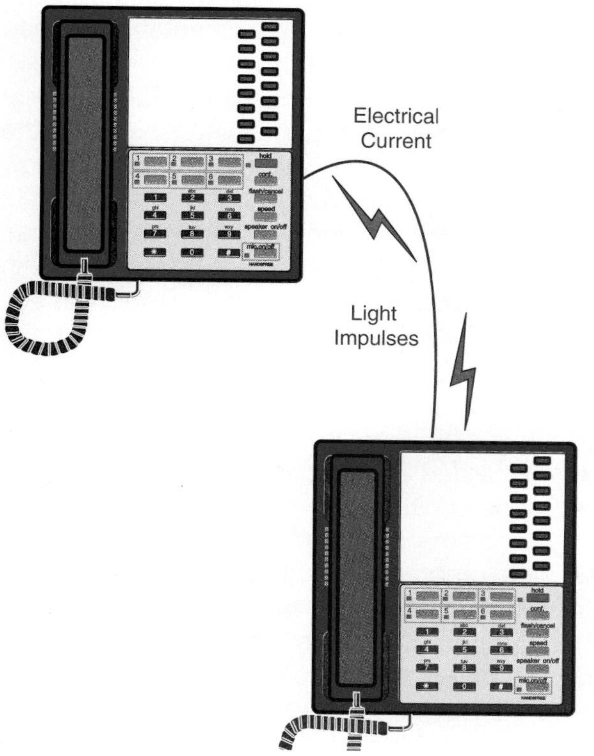

Figure 19-3. Sounds travel along telephone lines in the form of electrical current or light impulses.

Experiments with Radio Waves

From 1886 to 1889, Heinrich Hertz conducted many laboratory experiments with electrical sparks. His work led to the discovery of ***electromagnetic energy***, including ***radio waves.*** Guglielmo Marconi used Hertz's ideas to develop a simple radio signal generator. This invention became known as the "wireless." It was given this name because sounds were transmitted without the use of wires. The wireless was tested successfully in 1895. Marconi's first broadcast across the Atlantic Ocean took place in December of 1901. The world suddenly had a new means of long distance communication.

Naturally, many problems plagued these early transmissions. The signals were still in Morse code. This meant that only a trained operator could send and translate messages. Eventually, methods for changing voices to electromagnetic energy and then back to voices enabled all people to communicate by radio. Another challenge included designing an antenna that could pick up the faint signals.

Radio station broadcasts have been operating in the United States since 1920. These broadcasts have four distinctive features that identify them as radio broadcasts. They are wireless, transmit to the public, and are licensed by the government. In addition, the signal is said to be transmitted by ***telephony.*** This means that the transmitted sounds (for example, music or talking) are easily understood by the listener. These radio broadcasts used ***amplitude modulation*** to encode the broadcasts. This form of radio communication is referred to as ***AM*** radio.

The ***frequency modulation (FM)*** system of radio transmission was perfected in the 1930s. This provided listeners with a signal that remained relatively unaffected by weather and related static. Stereo signals also became possible with the invention of FM radio. However, the most important development to affect radio was the invention of the transistor.

Transistor Technology

In the early years of wireless transmissions, the vacuum tube was used. Vacuum tubes act like electronic switches and amplifiers. They produce the electronic frequencies necessary to carry the human voice. However, vacuum tubes have many disadvantages. They are often large and noisy. They operate at high temperatures. It takes time and power to heat them to this temperature.

In 1948, researchers at Bell Laboratories developed a new device that soon replaced the vacuum tube. Experiments by John Bardeen and William Shockley led to the invention of the ***transistor,*** Figure 19-4. Transistors are powerful amplifiers. They also perform the same switching function as vacuum tubes. Modern transistors are made of germanium or silicon. Most are very small and inexpensive.

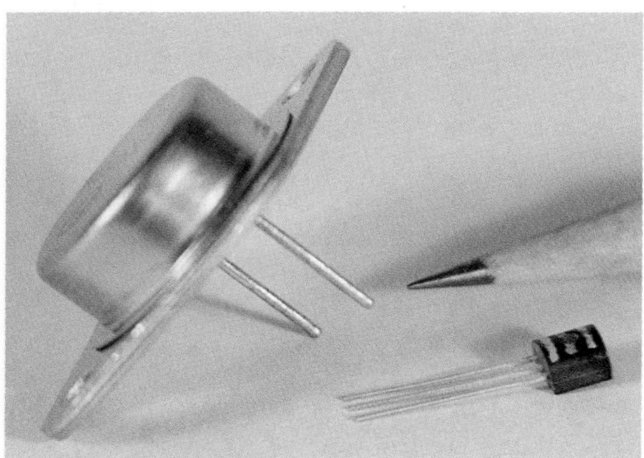

Figure 19-4. Transistors are the basis for many electronic circuits in current communication devices.

Modern electronics was made possible by the invention of the transistor. This electronic device can switch current on and off (as in a computer). It can amplify a signal (for radio or TV reception). Electronic devices often contain thousands of transistors. They are arranged in ***integrated circuits*** or on ***printed circuit boards,*** Figure 19-5. In fact, some printed boards are so small, they are made on silicon or germanium crystals. These are referred to as ***silicon chips.*** Integrated circuitry and silicon chips have replaced many full-sized transistors in modern electrical devices.

Early Computer Technology

Electronic computing started in the 1940s. Early computers required hand assembly and were quite large. The Electronic Numerical Integrator and Computer (ENIAC) of 1946 contained 18,000 vacuum tubes! The machine filled a entire room. It was fairly slow and needed an internal cooling system. Still, the ENIAC caused a great deal of excitement in the electronics industry.

Figure 19-5. Printed circuit boards are designed on a larger than normal scale. They are then reduced to required size during the manufacturing process. (Intel Corp.)

Computer technology is said to have progressed through five "generations," Figure 19-6. The earliest models typically depended on vacuum tubes for electronic switching. This marked the first generation of computers. Vacuum tubes gave way to transistor technology. This became the second generation of computers. These machines of the early 1960s relied on the smaller, more powerful transistors. The reduced size greatly increased the calculating speed of the machine. However, the computer was still slow and complex by today's standards.

The third generation of computers contained several distinct improvements. Machines built in the late 1960s included small silicon wafers, known a ***microprocessors.*** This allowed the entire "brain" of the computer to be reduced to a small chip. These printed chips replaced the wires and tubes of earlier devices. Fully electronic circuitry provided new possibilities for computer users. The most useful was the ability to load many programs into the machine. Up to that time, only one program at a time could be used or stored in the computer's memory.

Personal computers are examples of the fourth generation of computers, Figure 19-7. These very powerful machines are small and fit easily on a desk or table top. They operate much more efficiently and at a fraction of the cost of earlier models.

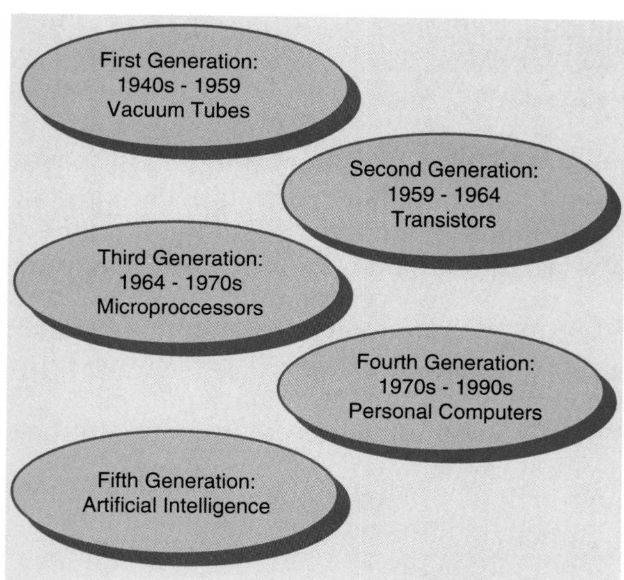

Figure 19-6. There are five generations of computers.

Figure 19-7. Desktop computers take up very little space yet are very powerful. (IBM)

The term ***artificial intelligence*** is closely associated with the fifth generation of computers. These computers are capable of making decisions and ethical judgments. However, there is some controversy about the need or value of these computers. As this technology advances, the controversy continues.

Early Hard-wired Systems

By definition, a ***hard-wired system*** includes systems or equipment permanently connected by wire. The telephone is a good example. Most household telephones are linked to millions of other telephones by wires. This same concept is also true of telegraph and teletext devices.

Original development of the telephone was made famous by Alexander Graham Bell. Bell became fascinated by the study of electricity while a speech student in the 1860s. His experiments with tuning forks "sparked" several ideas. Most notably, he wondered if two tuning forks connected with a wire could transfer audible sounds between two remote points. Eventually Bell started work on a device to send and receive the vibrations (or tones). By 1876, he publicly demonstrated the first telephone to the world, Figure 19-8.

Figure 19-8. The invention of the telephone changed the history of communication. Modern telephones are very different from the early telephones. Notice that this early telephone has no "dialer." Can you think of any other differences between modern phones and early phones? (Courtesy of Sprint)

The telephone industry has improved dramatically over the years. Modern switching machines help route thousands of telephone conversations at one time, Figure 19-9. In addition, the term "wire" does apply to many calls placed along communication lines. Instead, a typical telephone call today may travel through an

Figure 19-9. Modern telephone switching machines route conversations quickly and efficiently. (Courtesy of Sprint)

orbiting satellite instead of across land wires. Also, the communication may be transmitted along fiber optic cables.

Many changes can be seen in modern home telephones, Figure 19-10. Features like multiple lines and portable units are significant improvements. Many models have a memory for frequently-called numbers. Pushing one button automatically "dials" a friend or an emergency number. Phones can even transmit a video image as well as voices or sounds. These phones are called videophones.

Figure 19-10. A modern telephone unit can include a variety of options: second lines, call waiting, automatic redial, hold, and "hands-free" speakers.

Advances in Light Communication

Light has long been a medium of human communication. From the earliest camp fires, humans have utilized visible light for signaling others. Lighthouses were originally built to warn ships of dangerous areas along shorelines or to guide them to port. An entire system of railroad signals that use light has directed railroads since their early days. Light has been used to communicate throughout history. Perhaps you remember reading about Paul Revere and the signals from the Old North Church?

Modern transportation would be impossible without light communication. When riding in a car, count the number of traffic lights you pass. Sea and air travel require light signals, too, Figure 19-11. Can you think of several examples of each signaling system?

Figure 19-11. Visual communication is especially important around airports. Can you identify how light signals are used in this scene? (Federal Aviation Administration)

Recently, light has been used in a slightly different form. Many telephone conversations now travel as a series of light signals, instead of as electrical pulses. This is called ***fiber optics,*** Figure 19-12. Instead of using copper wires, signals are sent through materials such as glass or quartz fibers. These are called ***fiber optic cables.*** Rather than an electrical current, small pulses of light are flashed along the wires. The light signals are then converted to electrical pulses and sent to the telephone (which uses electrical signals). Light signals can be transmitted much faster along fiber optic cables than can electrical current along a copper wire. In addition, glass fiber lines are capable of carrying thousands of messages at once, instead of a single electrical pulse typical in other systems.

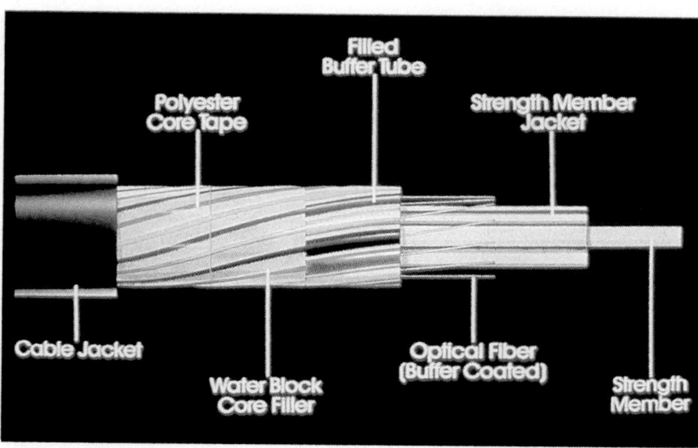

Figure 19-12. Fiber-optic cables are made of optic fibers. Optic fibers are glass or quartz fibers. (Courtesy of Sprint)

Advances in Acoustical Communication

During your life, you will receive a great deal of information through sound. Conversations with friends depend on the exchange of sound waves, Figure 19-13. Listening to music is also dependent upon sound waves. In both of these examples, the sound waves are types of acoustical communication.

Figure 19-13. Human conversation is the most common form of acoustical communication.

Undoubtedly, the earliest form of acoustical communication started with the grunts of cave dwellers. Languages and musical instruments soon added to the sounds created by humans. Technical systems of acoustical communication started with the clicking sound of the telegraph.

Sonar (***So***und ***N***avigation and ***R***anging) systems are used in water. Sonar was developed by British scientists shortly after World War I. It was designed to keep track of submarines under the surface of the water. With sonar, sound waves are used instead of radio waves. This is because radio waves would be absorbed by the water. However, the operation is basically the same. The time is monitored from the point the sound leaves the transmitter until it returns. Sound moves at a constant rate through water as well, though that rate is different from air. A simple mathematical equation will determine how far away an object is. Many pleasure and commercial boats are equipped with "fish-finders." These devices are sonar systems used to locate schools of fish.

MODERN ELECTRONIC COMMUNICATION

The next six chapters of this book explore electronic communication, and its various systems, in detail. Each of these chapters will explore a specific use of electricity for communication. You will discover how electrical energy is used during the communication process. You will also discover how electrical energy is changed to usable forms. The next few pages will give you a brief introduction to the content in these chapters.

Hard-wired Systems

A vast majority of modern electronic communication systems are still connected by wires. Transmission lines for telephones and telegraphs are typical examples. The internal circuitry of stereos and computers are also hard-wired. Your school public address (P.A.) system is connected by wires to the main office.

The first method of electronic communication sent pulses along wires. Even today, wires (and larger cables) are important transfer media, Figure 19-14. Most wiring used in electronics is made of copper. Silver, tungsten, brass, and other conductors are also used in wires and cables. Large underground cables often include a combination of metals, called alloys.

Telecommunications

Have you ever noticed all the antennas and satellite dishes in your community? Large radio towers dot the countryside and rooftops of our nation. These are examples of the latest technology in telecommunications, Figure 19-15.

Figure 19-14. Large electronic devices often include miles of wires. Inspectors must carefully check each wire before installing the equipment. (UNISYS)

Figure 19-15. Microwave antennas and satellite dishes are familiar sights in many communities.

Telecommunications generally refers to any exchange of messages over long distances. It is much more than a local telephone call to a neighbor. Modern telecommunication systems operate around the globe.

Today, the field of telecommunications typically includes the broadcast and information technologies. This includes radio, television (TV), computers, and cable TV. Citizen's band (CB) radios are a form of personal telecommunication.

The most important advantage of telecommunications is its ability to transmit messages to another location easily and quickly. Permanent wires or cables are not required between stations and receivers. Portable radios and TVs can pick up stations almost everywhere. Newscasters can go directly to the scene for remote location reports. With a satellite system, anyone can be in touch with others around the globe, Figure 19-16.

Light Communication

Lasers and fiber optics highlight current systems of light communication. However, traditional methods of communicating with visible light should not be ignored. Common examples of communicating with visible light that can be seen every day include traffic signals and railroad crossings, Figure 19-17. These techniques are far from outdated. Do you enjoy watching movies? This is a form of light communication.

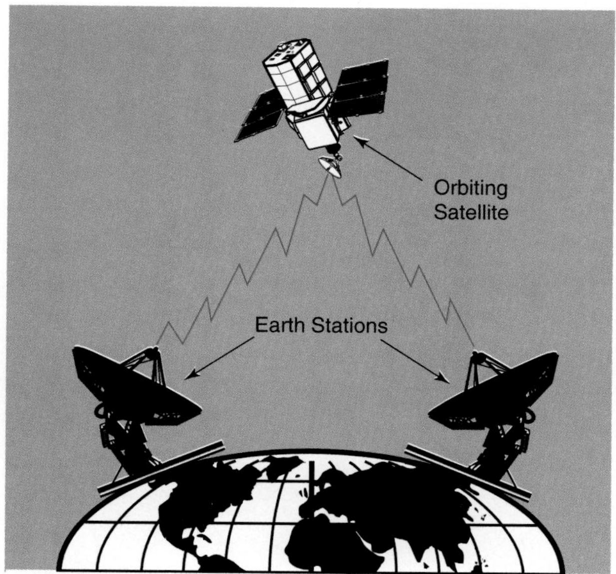

Figure 19-16. Information is easily beamed around the globe by bouncing signals off orbiting satellites.

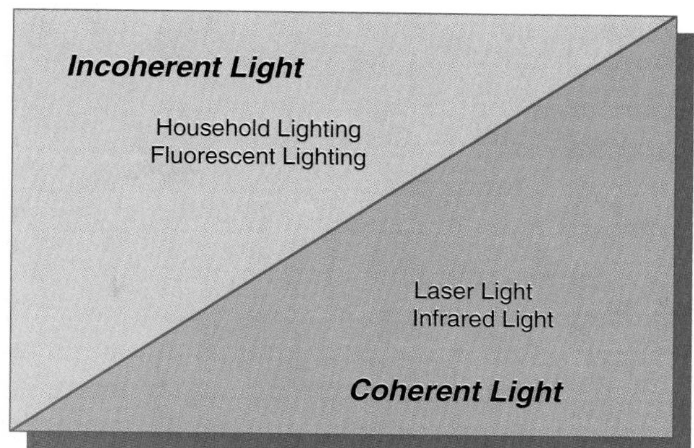

Figure 19-18. There are two types of light waves: coherent and incoherent.

Light waves are a form of energy. Producing light that is visible to the naked eye is fairly simple. This type of light is called ***incoherent.*** It includes a variety of frequencies (wavelengths). Different "colors" of light are caused by these varying wavelengths. Other types of light waves, for instance laser light, are all the same wavelength. The entire beam is created by waves of a single frequency. This type of light is called ***coherent*** light, Figure 19-18.

The majority of light communication systems used today are formed by incoherent light. Good examples include control devices for transportation, traffic lights, and emergency lights on cars. The fluorescent bulbs in lighted store displays are also incoherent light.

Acoustical Communication

The most unique characteristic of acoustical communication is the use of sound as the medium of transmission. These signals may or may not be detectable to the human ear.

Figure 19-17. Both traffic signals and railroad crossing lights represent an important type of light communication. Next time you are traveling through your town or city, count the number of traffic signals and railroad crossing lights you see.

The major systems of acoustical communication will be described in Chapter 23. Most of these will deal with audible signals (signals that humans can hear). Sonar and radar will also be explored. These forms of communication are used very frequently in a highly technological world.

Computers and Data Processing

Computer technology allows humans to exchange large amounts of information in many forms. Large or small, computers have tremendous potential in handling vast amounts of data, Figure 19-19. They can add daily sales to a yearly total, or compute a difficult engineering equation.

Figure 19-19. Business computer systems can manage and process large amounts of data. (IBM)

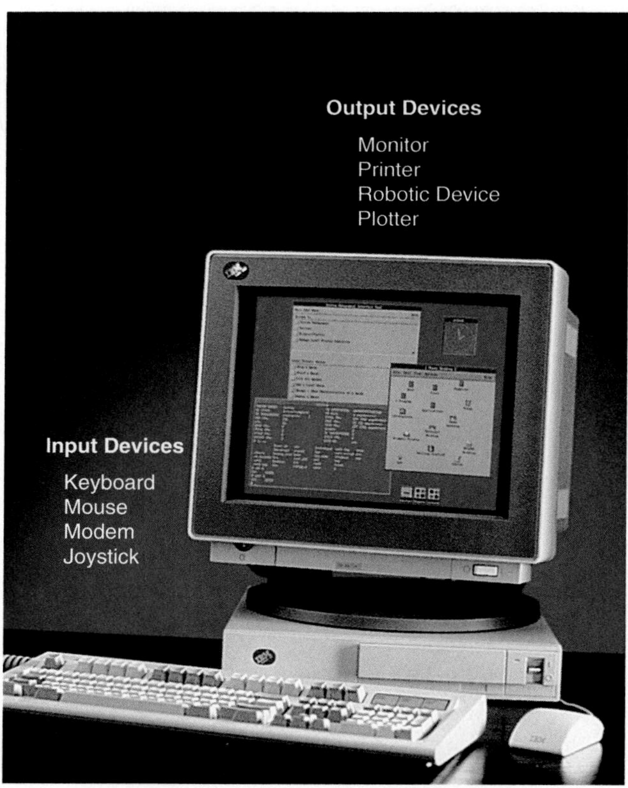

Figure 19-20. There are several input and output devices that may be on a computer system. (IBM)

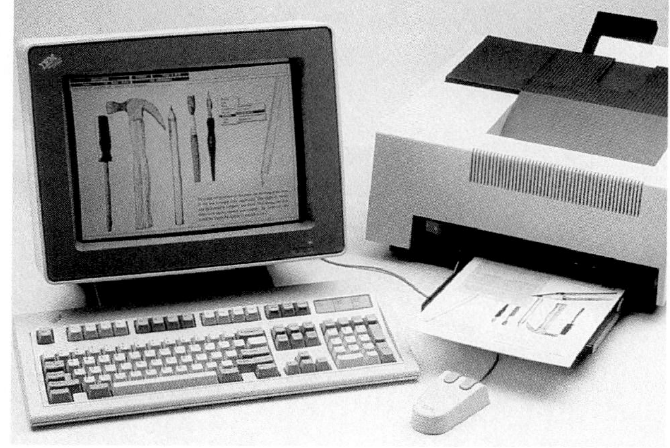

Figure 19-21. Computer monitors and printers are two familiar types of output devices. Can you think of others? (IBM)

Computer equipment can be divided into very simple systems. These systems are input devices, output devices, central processing unit, and software, Figure 19-20. ***Input devices*** are a means for putting data into the computer. The keyboard on a personal computer is a common input device. ***Universal Product Code (UPC)*** readers at grocery stores are another type of input device. They "read" coded strips from packages with beams of light. These strips are the black lines that you see on packages. The numbers are then fed into the computer memory of the cash register for recording.

Output devices provide the needed information in a usable form, Figure 19-21. A computer monitor (screen) is the most common type of output device. Words, numbers, and pictures appear on the screen for quick reference. Information may be output to other pieces of hardware, too. For example, data is easily "dumped" (stored) onto computer disks or magnetic tape. The information might be sent directly to a printer. The printer will produce the data in printed form. Other messages may travel along phone lines to other computers.

The internal memory of a computer is called a ***central processing unit (CPU).*** This electronic device can calculate and manipulate information at great speeds. Early CPUs often filled entire rooms and required large amounts of energy. With the invention of the silicon chip, computers have become smaller. Microprocessing CPUs are small enough to fit into wristwatches and small toys.

Computers operate by following a series of instructions called ***programs.*** Another familiar term for programs is ***software.*** Word processing software is useful when typing letters or reports. Mathematical software can perform calculations quickly. Graphics software helps in creating charts or pictures. Operation software is necessary just to "tell" the computer how to use other programmed instructions.

CHAPTER 19 REVIEW

SUMMARY

Most modern communication systems are familiar to you. Several of these systems rely on electricity in order to function. These include telecommunication, hard-wired, light, and acoustical systems. Computers and data processing systems are also important communication tools in our society. Each type of system was introduced in this chapter.

These electronic systems evolved over the course of many years. Probably one of the earliest electronic communication devices was the telegraph. In the years since the development of the telegraph, electronic communication has progressed quickly. It is now even possible to send telephone messages with light waves.

KEY WORDS

All the following words have been used in this chapter. Do you know their meanings?

Amplitude modulation (AM)
Artificial intelligence
Central processing unit (CPU)
Coherent light
Electromagnetic energy
Electronic communication
Fiber optics
Fiber optic cables
Frequency modulation (FM)
Hard-wired system
Incoherent light
Input devices
Integrated circuits
Microprocessors
Output devices
Printed circuit boards
Programs
Radio waves
Silicon chips
Software
Sonar
Telecommunications
Telephony
Transistor
Universal Product Code (UPC)

TEST YOUR KNOWLEDGE

Place your answers on a separate sheet of paper. Please do not write in this book.

1. What is electronic communication?
2. List the four features of radio broadcasts.

3. Which of the following is NOT a characteristic of transistors?
   A. They are powerful amplifiers.
   B. They are very large.
   C. They are inexpensive.
   D. All of the above.
4. _____ are printed circuit boards made on silicon or germanium crystals.
5. Briefly explain each of the five generations of computers.
6. Define "hard-wired system."
7. What are inaudible sounds?
8. What is telecommunication?
9. How do incoherent light and coherent light differ?
10. What does the term CPU stand for?

ACTIVITIES

1. Take apart an old radio. Identify the major components. It may be necessary to obtain books from the library in order to help you with your research. Make note of any "unusual" parts.
2. Using a frequency generator, create different radio and sound waves. Discuss in class the various waves made and how each of them may be used.
3. Build your own telegraph system. Keep a list of the materials that were necessary in order to build the system. When your telegraph is complete, use it to send messages to your classmates.
4. Research how satellite dishes operate. Write a report on your research. Include photos of some of the different models, along with prices and the primary users of the different models.
5. Arrange to tour a local telephone switching station. After your tour, write a short paper explaining the route a typical phone call takes into and out of the switching station.

CHAPTER 20
BASICS OF ELECTRONIC COMMUNICATION SYSTEMS

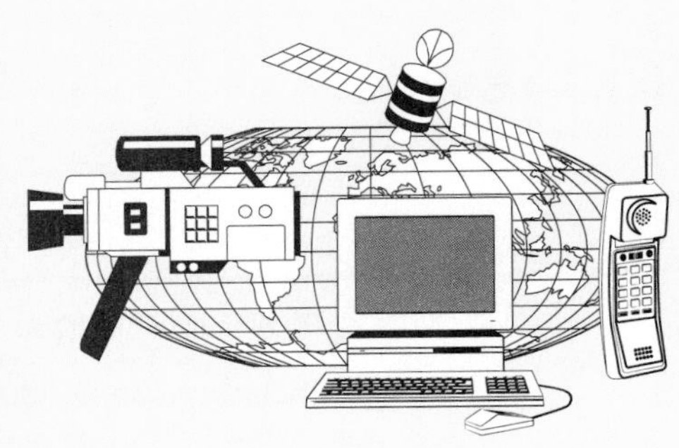

After studying this chapter, you will be able to:

- *Discuss the basic concepts of electrical energy.*
- *List the types of signals used in electronic communication.*
- *Explain how to create, code, transmit, and receive messages using electronic devices.*
- *Identify the technical equipment that aids many electronic communication systems.*

Electricity has been available to humans for a long time. Your world could not exist without electricity. When the first telegraph systems were made, electricity provided the power to transmit the messages over great distances. Now, computers, televisions, disc players, and radios all rely on electrical energy.

In order to understand electronic communication systems, you must first understand the terms used in this complex technology. The basics of electronic systems are covered in this chapter. You will review basic concepts of electricity. You will also study the ways electricity is used in communications. This knowledge will help you better understand electronic communication systems.

Neutron
Proton
Electron

Figure 20-1. Study this model of an atom. Can you name what electrical charge is associated with each part?

CONCEPTS OF ELECTRICAL ENERGY

The ***atom*** is the building block of all substances. Land, water, and people are all made up of atoms. A model of an atom is shown in Figure 20-1.

The center of an atom is called the ***nucleus.*** Inside the nucleus are ***protons*** and ***neutrons.*** Protons and neutrons are the same size. Protons have a positive (+) electrical charge. Neutrons have neither a positive nor negative charge. Neutrons are "neutral." ***Electrons*** revolve around the nucleus in "rings," much like planets revolve around the Sun. Electrons are smaller than protons and neutrons. Electrons have a negative (-) electrical charge.

Generally, each atom has an equal number of protons and electrons. The positive charge from the proton cancels the negative charge from the electron. When the number of protons equals the number of electrons, the atom is ***balanced,*** Figure 20-2.

An atom will usually stay in a balanced state, unless some type of energy is added. When energy is added, the atom becomes "excited." Any electrons loosely "bound" to the atom (those

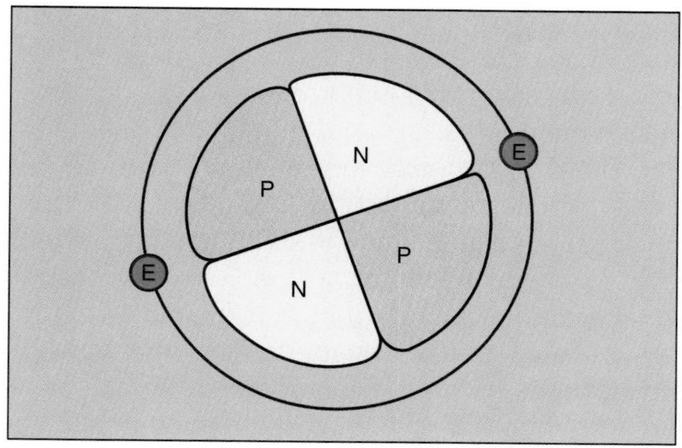

Figure 20-2. A helium atom has an equal number of protons and electrons.

Conductors	Insulators
Silver Iron Brass Copper	Glass Rubber Dry Air

Figure 20-4. Some materials "help" electricity to flow. Other materials "hinder" the flow of electricity.

in outer rings) may break free. If this happens, the atom is no longer balanced. The unbalanced atom attracts electrons from other atoms. When these electrons are pulled away, a different, "new" atom is then unbalanced. This "new" unbalanced atom then attracts electrons from yet other atoms, creating another set of "new" unbalanced atoms. The process then continues and the electrons "flow" over a distance (through a wire, for example). This movement of electrons is known as ***electricity,*** Figure 20-3.

Some materials, such as copper and silver, allow easy movement of free electrons. These materials are called ***conductors.*** Other materials, such as plastic and glass, do not allow easy movement. They are called ***insulators.*** Several conductors and insulators are listed in Figure 20-4.

A force must be applied to produce electricity. The force can be produced by chemical means, such as a battery. The force can also be produced by physical means, such as compressing a crystal. The potential, or "amount," of this force is called ***voltage***. The actual "flow" of electrons is known as ***electric current,*** or ***amperage.*** If there is no "flow," there is no current. However, there still may be the potential for electrons to "flow," or voltage. A battery that is not connected to anything is an example of voltage without current.

Electricity can be compared to water. Wires can be compared to pipes. When you walk up to the sink in your house, there is the "potential" for water to flow. This is similar to voltage. Water is stored in your town's water tower. The water tower is like a battery. However, there is no water flowing until you turn on the faucet. Once you turn on the faucet, the water flows. The water "flowing" through the pipes is like electric current "flowing" through a wire.

Electric current produces a field of magnetic energy. This field is called an ***electromagnetic field.*** If this field is made to

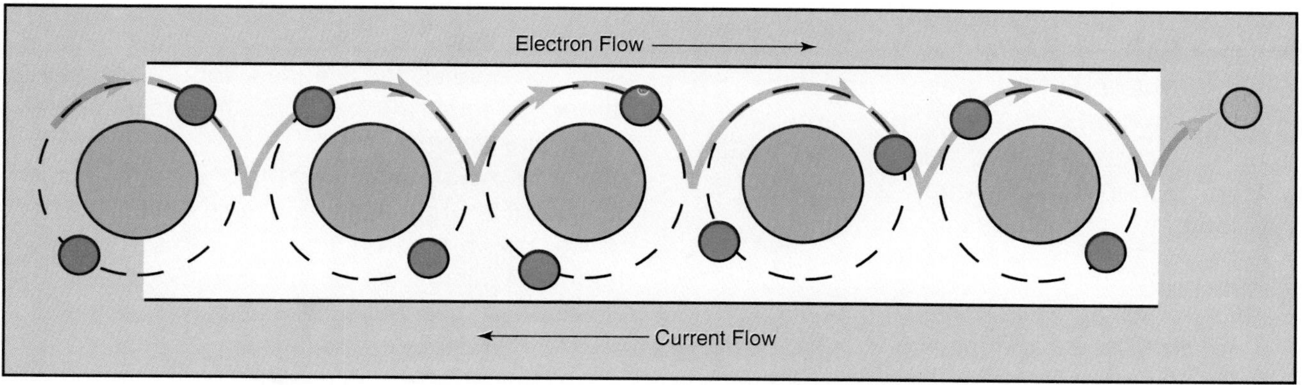

Figure 20-3. Electrons "bounce" from atom to atom to create electric current. Electrons move from positive to negative, however current flow is from negative to positive.

oscillate (rapidly change direction back and forth), ***electromagnetic waves*** are created. These waves allow messages to be transmitted electronically.

Electromagnetic waves can take any number of forms. The signals sent out by your favorite radio station are electromagnetic waves. So is a dental X-ray. Lightning is another form of electromagnetic waves.

Typical electromagnetic waves are measured in three ways: amplitude, wavelength, and frequency. As the wave passes a point (or object), the energy level changes, or "fluctuates." This fluctuation is the result of high and low points formed in the wave, Figure 20-5. The highest point is called a ***crest.*** The lowest point is called the ***trough.*** One half of the distance (height) between the crest and trough is referred to as the ***amplitude.*** The distance (length) between two sequential (in order) waves is called the ***wavelength.*** Wavelength is a physical measurement. Finally, the number of waves passing a given point in one second is the ***frequency*** of the wave. Frequency is a timed measurement. Frequency and wavelength are inversely proportional. This means that the higher the frequency, the shorter the wavelength.

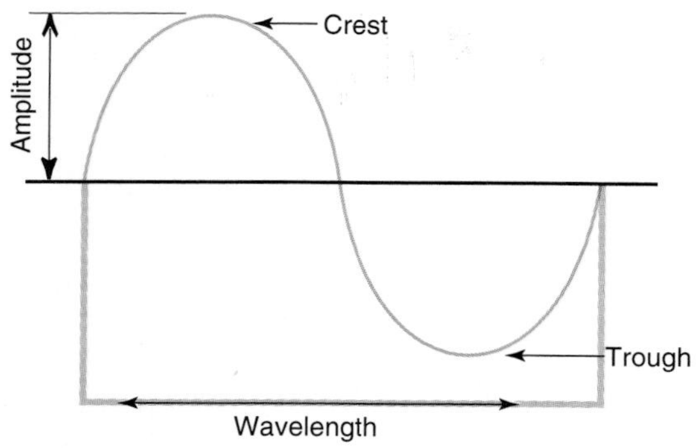

Figure 20-5. The parts of an electromagnetic wave.

Resistance

Resistance is the opposition to electric current. Resistance can be caused by a material, substance, component, or device. Resistance is found in every part of an electric circuit. Even the wires in a circuit provide resistance. This type of resistance cannot be avoided. It is caused by the actual makeup of the electrons in wires and electrical components.

There are times when the strength of the current must be varied. In this case, a device can be placed in a circuit to get a specific result. This device is called a ***resistor.*** Resistors divide voltage and/or limit current. For example, many cars have a variable resistor to dim the lights on the instrument panel. The variable resistor limits the amount of current that reaches the lights.

Electromagnetic Spectrum

All electromagnetic energy can be found in the ***electromagnetic spectrum,*** Figure 20-6. The human eye can see only a small portion of this spectrum. This is known as ***visible light*** or the ***visible spectrum.*** You cannot see above violet or below red in the spectrum. Other visible colors in the spectrum include orange, yellow, green, blue, and indigo.

There are many more waves in the electromagnetic spectrum than just visible light. ***Gamma rays*** are the shortest waves in the spectrum. Gamma rays also have the highest frequency. Next to gamma rays are ***X-rays.*** These wavelengths are slightly longer than gamma ray wavelengths. After X-rays, there are ***ultraviolet light*** waves. These waves are slightly shorter than visible light waves.

Visible light ranges from violet to red. Violet light has the shortest wavelength of visible light. Red light has the longest wavelength of visible light.

After visible red light, the next longest waves are infrared light waves. This light is not visible to the human eye. Infrared light is used for many functions. For example, infrared light is used to determine distance for self-focusing cameras, Figure 20-7. Infrared light is also used for burglar alarms.

Microwaves and radio waves are longer wavelengths than infrared light waves. Microwaves follow infrared light waves and include radar and microwave emitters. Radio waves are longer than microwaves. Radio waves include radio, TV, and integrated circuits.

All of these waves are electromagnetic energy. They are voltages or currents that change with time. To communicate using electromagnetic

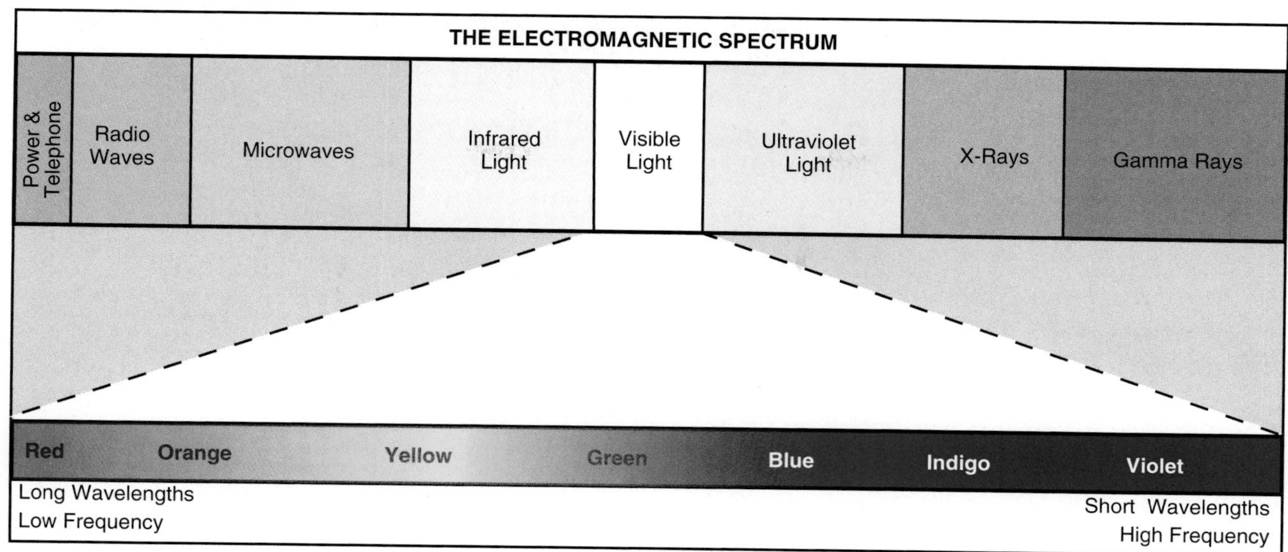

Figure 20-6. The electromagnetic spectrum contains all waves. Are you surprised to learn how little of the spectrum you can actually see?

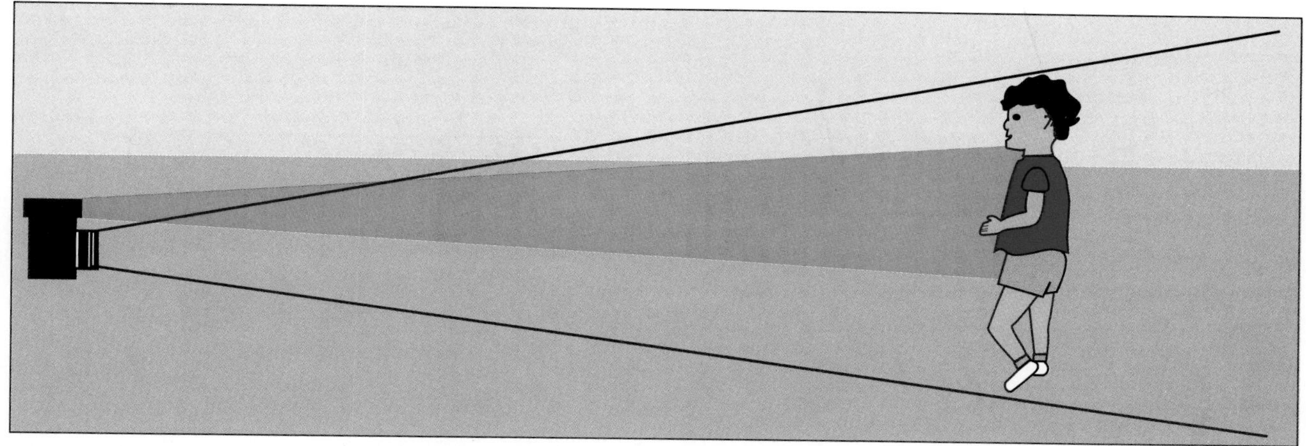

Figure 20-7. Self-focusing cameras use infrared light to detect distances.

waves, the waves must be sent, received, amplified, and modified. The waves must be able to be used as signals.

SIGNALS

A ***signal*** is a sound or image that is transmitted. A signal has a noticeable voltage or current that can be used to transmit information. Two signals used quite often in communications are analog signals and digital signals. These signals are used for recordings, telephone conversations, and computers.

Analog Signals

Analog signals tend to vary constantly. They are smooth and continuous. Voices are analog signals. Voices change constantly over a wide range. A voice can be soft. Other times a voice can be very loud. Analog signals can vary a great deal in amplitude and frequency.

Analog signals can be troublesome when being transmitted. Since a message varies in strength, weak signals, high points, and low points can be distorted by noise or other interference.

Despite this drawback, analog signals are useful. These signals allow you to hear voice inflection (change). They allow you to see shades of color. Analog devices that transmit these varying signals add to the complete reception of a message.

Digital Signals

Digital signals can represent only discrete numbers. The most common example is 0 or 1, Figure 20-8. There is nothing that represents 1.5 or .25, only a 1 or a 0. The resulting "code" is known as a ***binary code.*** Digital signals are used in computers, compact disc (CD) players, laser disc players, and digital audio tape (DAT) players. The number of "1's" or "0's" in a specific place on a computer disk, CD, laser disc, or DAT represents a number, letter, sound, or visual image, Figure 20-9.

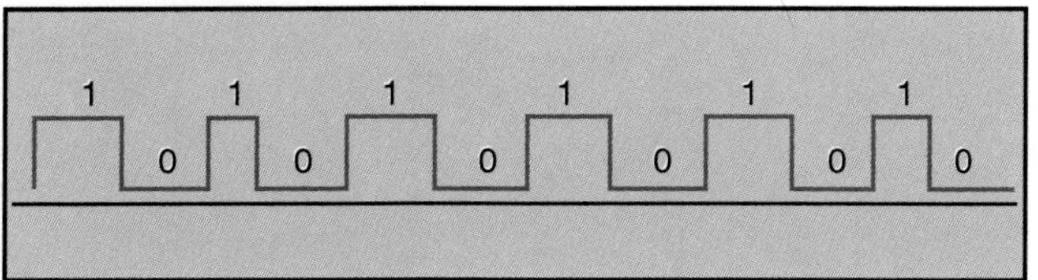

Figure 20-8. Digital signals represent discrete numbers. "Discrete" means that the change is abrupt. There is no gradual change.

Binary Codes	Decimal Equivalent	Alphabetic Equivalent
1000	8	S
1001	9	T
0100	4	O
0101	5	P

Figure 20-9. Combinations of 0's and 1's represent numbers. This is called a binary code.

Digital signals are also used in telephone transmissions. However, the signals are converted from an analog signal (voice) to a digital signal before transmission. This change takes place in the following manner.

The sound wave from a voice is first converted into an electronic analog signal. The analog signal is tested and sampled at certain intervals. Each of the points that was tested and sampled is given a value. This value is a combination of on/off pulses, or a digital signal. Refer to Figure 20-10. The digital signal is then transmitted through the telephone cable (metal wire or fiber-optic cable).

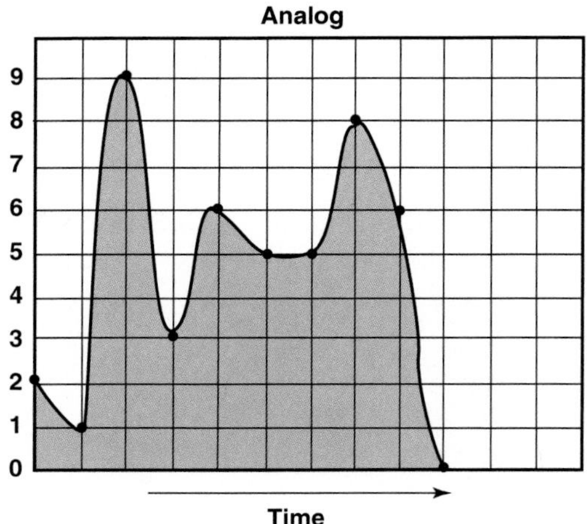

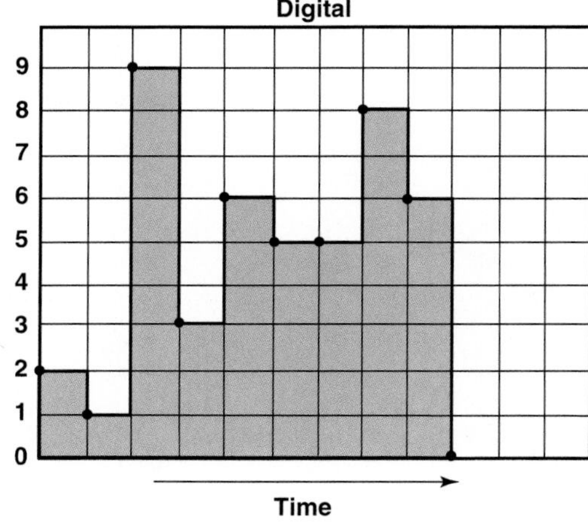

Figure 20-10. An analog signal is sampled thousands of times each second to create an equal digital signal.

BASIC ELECTRONIC COMMUNICATION SYSTEMS

Waves and signals would be useless without the technology to transmit them. The systems that are used to transmit and receive messages are the basis of modern electronic communication.

Three pieces of equipment are needed to send and receive electronic messages. They are a transmitter, a transmission link, and a receiver.

Transmitters

A ***transmitter*** is used to start a message on its journey. The transmitter changes the message into electrical signals. The signals may be analog or digital. The signals are then sent to an ***amplifier.*** The amplifier increases the signal strength for transmission.

There are instances in which electrical signals need help in being transmitted. These signals are modulated. ***Modulation*** is the process of controlling a carrier wave. A ***carrier wave*** is the wave that "carries" the information (message). The signal is fed into a modulator. The modulator causes the carrier wave to change. It changes either in amplitude (AM) or frequency (FM).

Amplitude Modulation

Amplitude modulation (AM) is used most often in AM radio broadcasts. The audio signal in an AM broadcast is voice or music. Audio signals in this case are changed into electrical signals by a microphone, tape player, CD player, or turntable.

The electronic signals created by these devices are often low in voltage. Therefore, the signal must be amplified before it goes to the modulator. In addition, a carrier wave must be created. Both the information wave and the carrier wave are sent through the modulator. The resulting wave "carries" the "information" to the receiver, Figure 20-11.

At the destination of the message (your radio), a ***demodulator*** is used. It sends out only the original audio signal. The amplifier in the demodulator boosts the signal to the power levels needed by the speakers. The speakers then deliver the original sound.

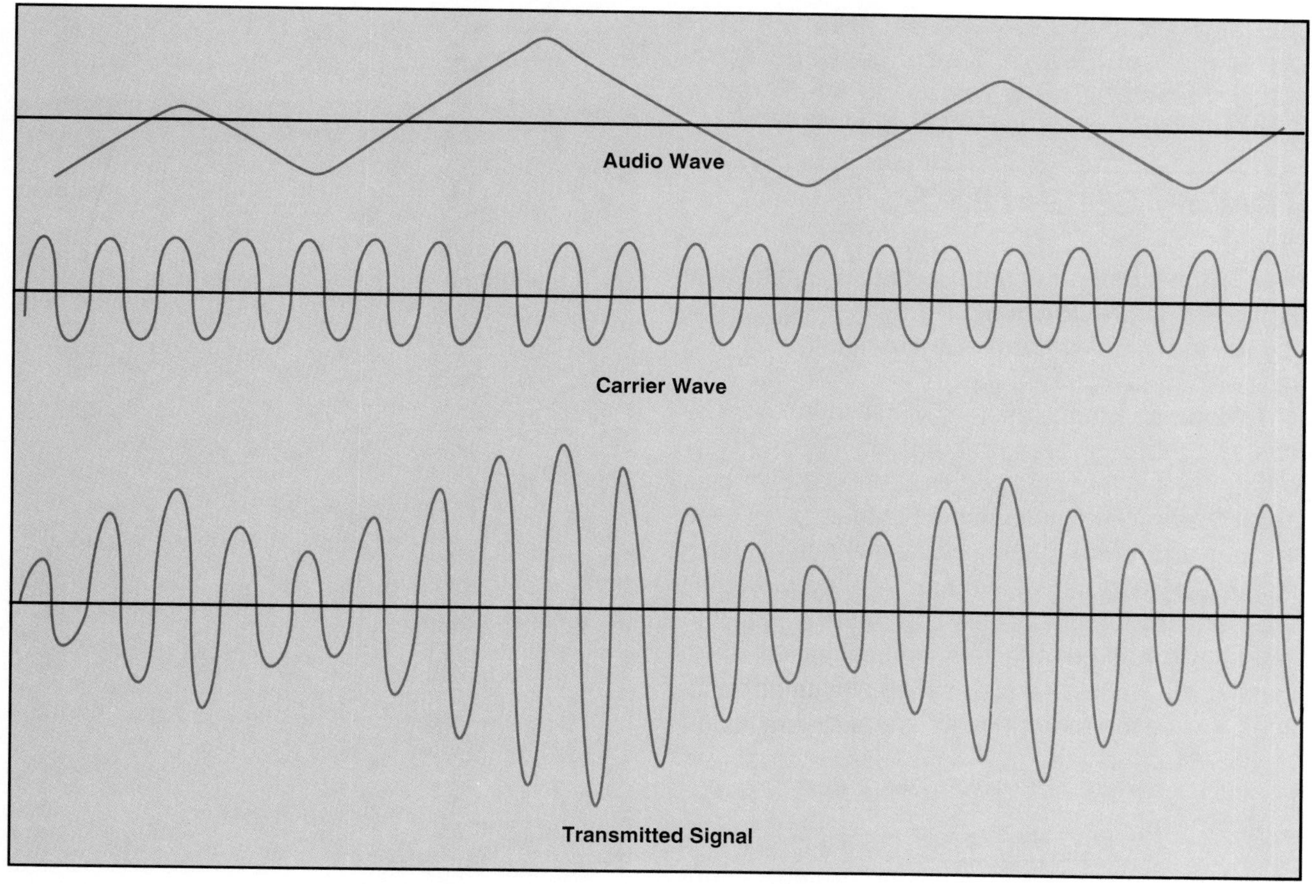

Figure 20-11. An AM radio broadcast signal consists of an audio wave and a carrier wave that are joined to make the transmitted signal.

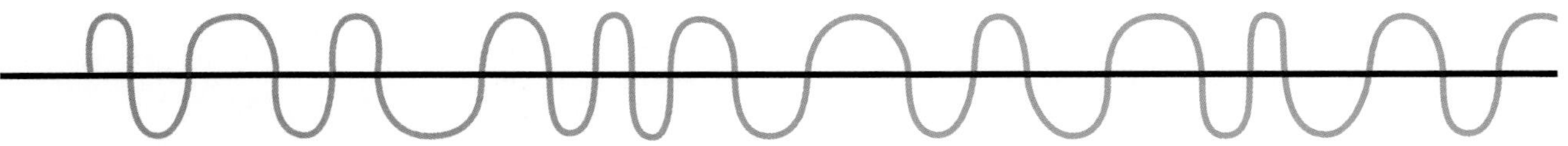

Figure 20-12. The frequency varies in an FM signal, but the amplitude remains the same.

Frequency Modulation

Frequency modulation (FM) is similar to AM. However, in FM the modulator varies the frequency of the wave, not the amplitude, Figure 20-12.

FM has a few advantages over AM. FM uses power more efficiently than AM. Noise has little effect on FM. This improves sound quality of the transmission. FM radio signals are generally clearer because all the information is in the frequency of the signal. Noise usually appears in the amplitude of a signal. Also, when two separate signals reach an antenna at the same time, only the stronger signal will be heard. This means that when you listen to the radio in a car, you will hear the signal sent from the strongest and nearest transmitter. There will be no interference from another, more distant, transmitter.

TRANSMISSION LINKS

The next step in communicating a message is the ***transmission link.*** The transmission link relays the signals from the transmitter to the receiver (destination).

Most communication signals are sent by cables or through the atmosphere. These methods allow for the best transmission of a signal. Most radio and television signals are sent through the atmosphere. However, cable television is very popular. With cable TV, the TV signals are sent through a cable. This means that the signal will not be affected by storms or wind. Radio broadcasts are also sent through cable TV lines. These radio broadcasts are also unaffected by the weather.

Antennas

Antennas aid in receiving signals sent through the atmosphere. Though antennas vary greatly in size and shape, they all function in the same way. First, an oscillating wave is sent from a transmitter. The wave is then picked up by an antenna attached to a receiver. Inside the receiver, special electronic devices receive and boost the signal back to a usable level.

Antennas are made in a variety of shapes and sizes. This is because each type of antenna is made to receive a certain type of signal. For example, a microwave antenna is used to receive signals from distant satellites or other microwave antennas. The dish portion is usually quite large. This size helps pick up distant signals, Figure 20-13. Other types of antennas include whip antennas (radio) and yagi antennas (television), Figure 20-14.

Figure 20-13. Microwave relay towers have very large "dishes" that receive the microwave signals.

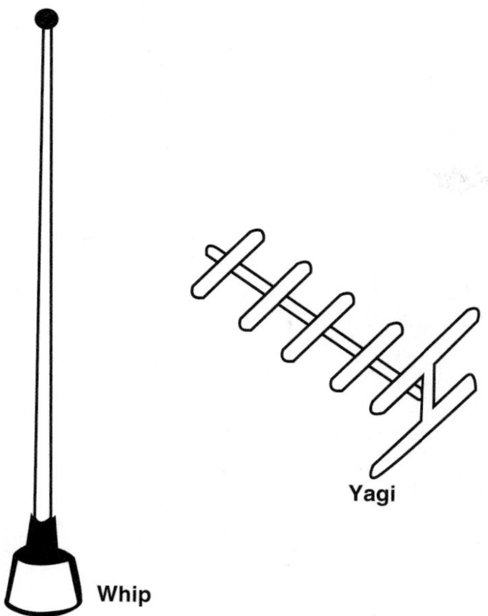

Figure 20-14. The yagi antenna works in only one direction. Whip antennas operate in many directions.

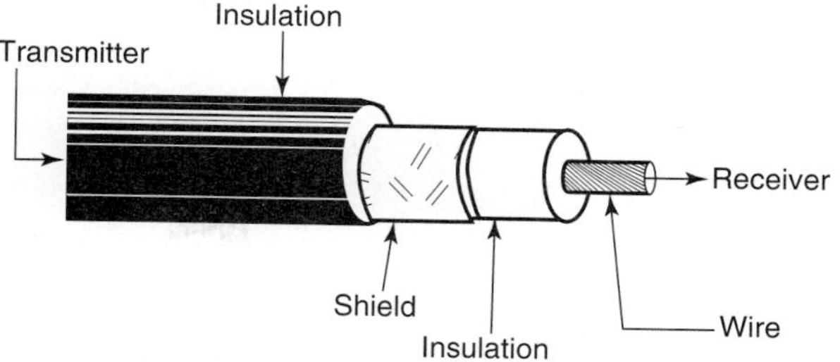

Figure 20-15. Coaxial cables are used in the transmission of cable TV.

The diameter of the optical fiber is very small. This reduces the chance for interference. Figure 20-16 illustrates the construction of a fiber-optic cable. The transmitting fiber is surrounded by an energy-absorbing glass. This glass will absorb any rays that escape the optical fiber. The transmitter and receiver are designed to work at very high speeds. This allows signals to be exchanged quickly.

Cables

Another method for linking signals is cables. ***Cables*** allow the transmission to be controlled. This is because the signals are sent along wires enclosed in a protective covering. These cables can be buried underground, run above ground between poles, or laid underwater. The signals inside of cable are almost totally free from weather interference. Also, the signal will reach only the intended receiver. Transmitting through the atmosphere allows anybody with an antenna to receive the transmission.

For signals in very-high frequency (VHF) and lower ranges, coaxial cables are the best transmitters, Figure 20-15. The cable is a wire that is surrounded by insulating material. This material holds the wire in place and shields the wire from external interference. The wire and insulation are then enclosed in the protective coating.

When sending signals in the infrared, ultraviolet, and visible light ranges, another type of cable is used. This cable is called a ***fiber-optic cable.*** Fiber-optic cables are made up of small glass "wires" called ***optical fibers.*** Using these cables to transmit signals is known as ***fiber optics.*** Fiber-optic cables are effective for linking very-high frequency messages over a long distance.

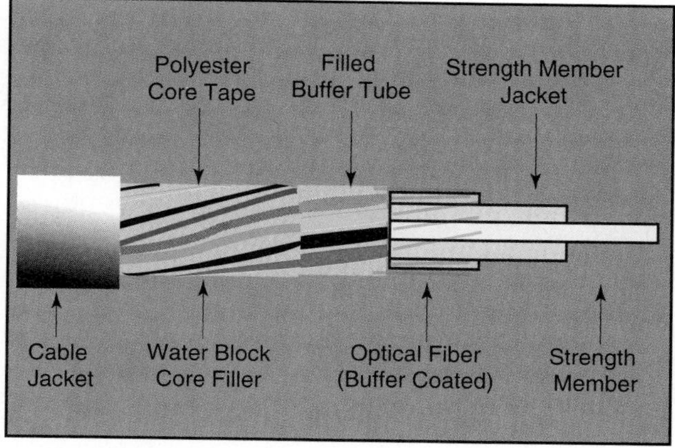

Figure 20-16. Fiber-optic cables are a high-speed link between a source and a destination. Information is transmitted using light.

Noise

Noise is any signal not present in the source message. Noise is usually picked up in the "linking stage." In the "linking stage," the signal often goes through the atmosphere. For example, an AM broadcast is likely to attract noise. The noise is picked up when the message leaves the transmitter on its way to the receiver. At that point, the signal is moving

Figure 20-17. During thunderstorms, you may have noticed interference, or noise, while watching TV.

through the atmosphere. Rain, lightning, thunder, and even the sun can cause noise, Figure 20-17. (Sun "noise" is caused by "sun spots." ***Sun spots*** are explosions on the sun's surface.) Devices such as cables reduce the noise in transmission.

Noise must be accounted for when sending a message. While a message may be sent in several ways, the method with the least noise will usually be chosen. A clear message is very important in the communication process.

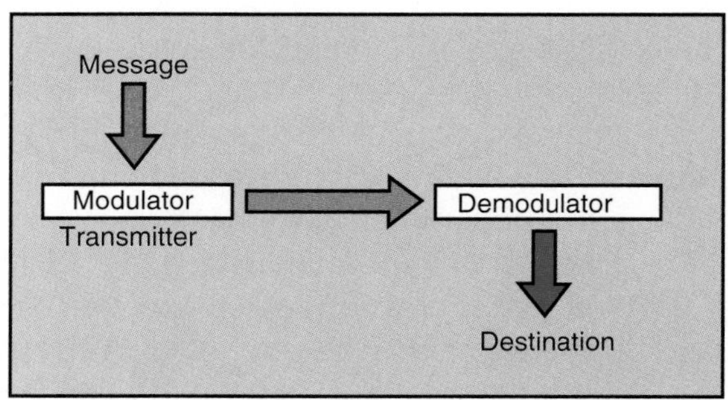

Figure 20-18. A message travels through three basic devices in electronic communication.

RECEIVERS

The ***receiver*** is the final electrical stop for a message. Here, the signal is detected and converted back to the source message. The complete journey of a message is shown in Figure 20-18.

There are many electronic devices that receive signals. The receiver in a stereo system "receives" signals. It changes an electronic wave to voice or music. Similar receiving units can be found in a television set, a radar system, and a computer terminal.

Several functions and conversions occur during the trip taken by a message. These processes happen in devices such as amplifiers, converters, switches, and oscillators. With these components, electronic communication is possible.

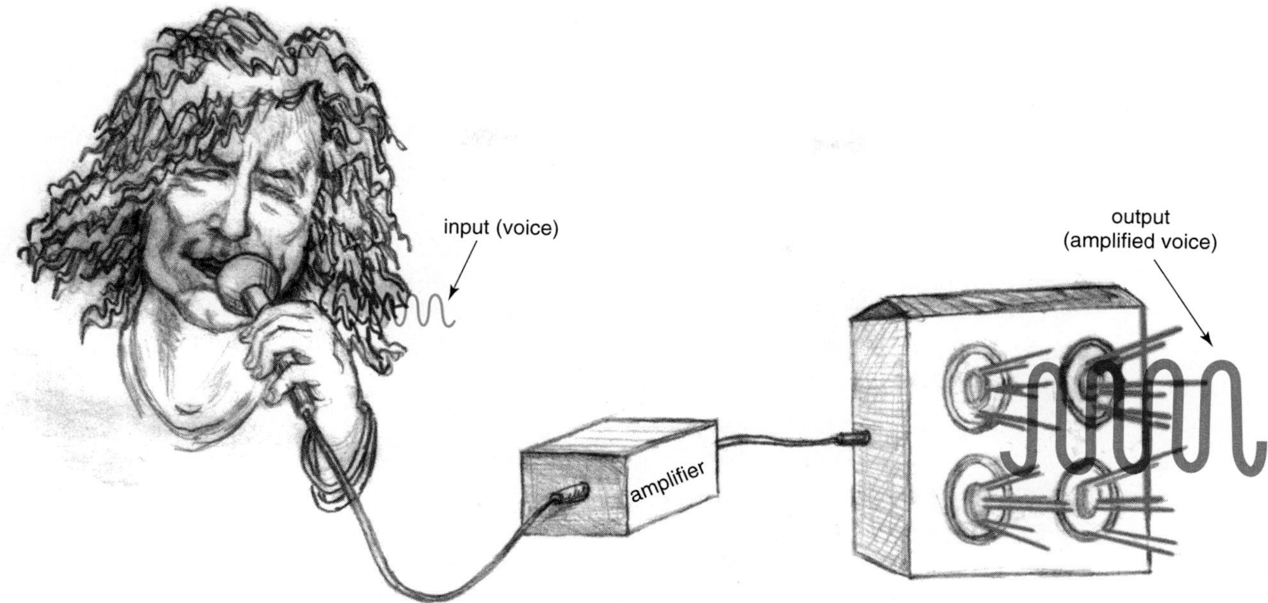

Figure 20-19. The signal that a microphone picks up (such as your voice) is sent to an amplifier and then to the speakers.

Amplifiers

One device that aids in the electronic communication process is the amplifier. An ***amplifier*** increases the power, or amplitude, of the signal. An amplifier is used on weak signals. By amplifying the signal, the signal becomes powerful enough to be used, Figure 20-19. For example, the amplifier in a stereo system boosts signals from a CD, tape, or radio. The signal is then at a level that can activate the speakers.

Converter

Another device that aids the transmission of a message is a ***converter.*** A converter in an AM radio changes the incoming signal frequencies to a single, specific frequency. The signal can then be amplified and converted back to audio.

Oscillator

A third device that aids the electronic communication process is the ***oscillator.*** This device produces repeating signals. These signals are of a certain frequency and amplitude. An oscillator is a special type of amplifier. An oscillator makes a constant signal in analog and digital systems. This signal is added to the original signal in radio broadcasts to create modulation. (Refer back to Figure 20-11.)

Switches

Switches direct the flow of electricity, Figure 20-20. They are very basic to electronic communication. Switches allow electricity to flow along the correct path. This allows the signal to reach the correct destination. If the electronic signal reaches the correct destination, the message will reach the correct destination as well.

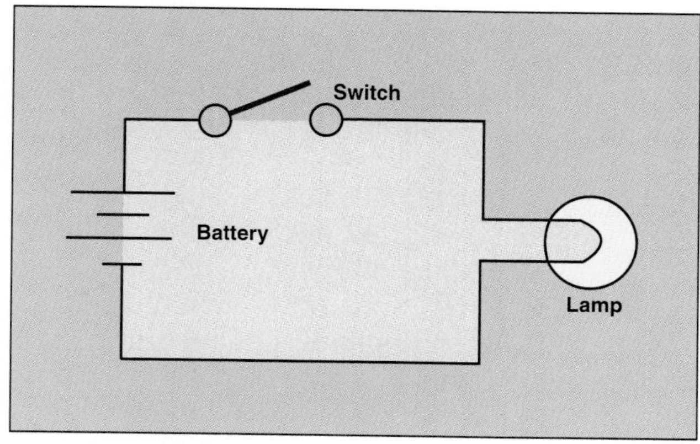

Figure 20-20. Switches direct the flow of electricity in an electronic circuit.

CHAPTER 20 REVIEW

SUMMARY

Many modern communication systems rely on electricity in order to function. To learn about these systems, you must first understand the theory of electricity. Electricity is the movement of electrons. The electron movement is caused by a force. Heat, friction, or even light are common forces. The potential to create electricity is called voltage. The flow of electricity is known as amperage, or electric current. Resistance is the opposition to electric current.

Electricity can be used to create electromagnetic waves. Electromagnetic waves can be used as signals. Signals are used to communicate.

Basic electronic communication systems use signals to communicate. To send a complete message, a transmitter, a transmission link, and a receiver are needed. A transmitter starts the message on its way to the destination. A transmission link relays the message to its destination. Finally, a receiver (the destination) accepts and decodes the message.

KEY WORDS

All of the following words have been used in this chapter. Do you know their meanings?

Amperage
Amplifier
Amplitude
Amplitude modulation (AM)
Analog signals
Antennas
Atom
Balanced
Binary code
Cables
Carrier waves
Conductor
Convertor
Crest
Demodulator
Digital signals
Electric current
Electricity
Electromagnetic field
Electromagnetic spectrum
Electromagnetic waves
Electron
Fiber-optic cable
Fiber optics
Frequency
Frequency modulation (FM)
Gamma rays
Insulators
Modulation
Neutron
Noise
Nucleus
Optical fibers
Oscillate
Oscillator
Proton
Receivers
Resistance
Resistors
Signals
Sun spots
Switches
Transmission links
Transmitter
Trough
Ultraviolet light
Visible light
Visible spectrum
Voltage
Wavelength
X-rays

TEST YOUR KNOWLEDGE

Place your answers on a separate sheet of paper. Please do not write in this book.

MATCHING QUESTIONS: Match the definition in the left-hand column with the correct term in the right-hand column.

1.	Movement of an electron from one atom to another.	A.	Nucleus.
2.	Positively-charged particle.	B.	Conductors.
3.	Materials that allow the easy movement of free electrons.	C.	Electric current.
4.	The building block of all substances.	D.	Atom.
5.	The center of the atom.	E.	Electricity.
6.	The "flow" of electrons.	F.	Proton.

7. X-rays, lightning, and radar are examples of _____ waves.
8. Explain the concept of resistance.
9. Name two types of signals used often in electronic communication.
10. Define modulation.
11. Cables and the atmosphere are examples of:
    - A. Receivers.
    - B. Transmission links.
    - C. Transmitters.
    - D. None of the above.

ACTIVITIES

1. Make a model of an atom using styrofoam balls and wire. Label and explain each part. If available, use a computer and 3-D modeling software to create the model of the atom.
2. Consult the Periodic Table to learn the structure of well-known elements such as gold, silver, and sodium. Choose one element and explain its structure. Write a report explaining your research.
3. Invite a radio engineer to visit your class to discuss their job. Ask your guest to explain the duties of a radio engineer. Find out what type of schooling or training is needed. Write a short report explaining what you learned.

CHAPTER 21
TELECOMMUNICATION

After studying this chapter, you will be able to:

- *List and explain each of the Federal Communications Commission categories.*
- *Discuss the frequency bands used in telecommunications.*
- *Identify the types of telecommunication systems.*
- *Explain the workings of a data communications system.*

In Chapter 5, you learned that ***telecommunication*** means transmitting information between distant points. Telephone networks are a good example of telecommunication. Many other systems are part of this industry. Satellites are used to send radio messages around the world, Figure 21-1. Cable television allows students in Seattle to watch a session of Congress in Washington, D.C., while it is actually happening. Microwave networks provide a link between banks, stores, and other businesses.

Telecommunication is still an area of rapid change. A "state-of-the-art" product is often outdated in only a few months. This is due to the constant increase in understanding of this technology. As technologists, scientists, computer engineers, electrical engineers, and others involved in this industry learn more, telecommunications improves and changes. New and better ways for communicating between distant points are constantly being found.

Figure 21-1. Satellites make quick worldwide communication possible. (NASA)

USES AND PURPOSES OF TELECOMMUNICATION

You probably use a telecommunication system every day. When you call a friend on the telephone, you are using telecommunication. Your call is sent through a series of switches until it is connected with the telephone at your friend's house. When you listen to the radio or watch television, you are also using telecommunication systems.

If you did not have these methods of communicating, how would you react? You might feel out-of-touch and alone. You have come to depend on the convenience of communicating quickly and easily, over any distance.

In this way, telecommunication serves two purposes. First, it makes possible the quick exchange of messages over long and short distances. Second, telecommunication can be used in a number of ways. Almost any information can be coded, transmitted, and received in electronic form. If you need to send a photograph to a business associate in Germany, it can be sent through a telecommunication system as a photograph.

MODERN COMMUNICATION SYSTEM

There are many types of telecommunication systems. There are also many users of these systems. Each of these users requires a frequency on which to broadcast. Because of the large number of users involved, some regulation (control) is required. In the United States, regulation is the responsibility of the ***Federal Communications Commission (FCC).***

FCC CATEGORIES	
Broadcasting	AM FM Television Links Common Carriers
Citizen Communication	Amateur Citizen Band
Government and Industrial Communication	Armed Services Government Departments Public Safety Industrial Communication Meteorological Services Telemetry Industrial, Scientific, and Medical Equipment
Commercial Transportation Communication	Paging Services and Car Telephones Mobile Land Vehicles Aeronautical Control Aviation Maritime Navigational Beacons

Figure 21-2. There are several different Federal Communications Commission categories.

FCC CATEGORIES

The FCC uses four major categories to classify telecommunication. These categories are: broadcasting, citizen communication, industrial and governmental communication, and commercial transportation communication. Each of these categories can be used as shown in Figure 21-2. In most cases, the user must get a license to operate a telecommunication system.

Broadcasting

Broadcasting includes AM radio, FM radio, and television transmissions. Television and radio broadcast services are used widely every day. These should be familiar to you. The frequency ranges of broadcast stations are shown in Figure 21-3. There are also broadcast frequencies assigned for the actual operation of broadcast stations. These frequencies are normally only used by engineers in the broadcasting industry.

Broadcasting is perhaps the most common of the FCC categories. It uses many smaller, basic telecommunication systems, like the radio and television, to make up a completely new industry. The broadcasting industry will be discussed more fully in Chapter 23.

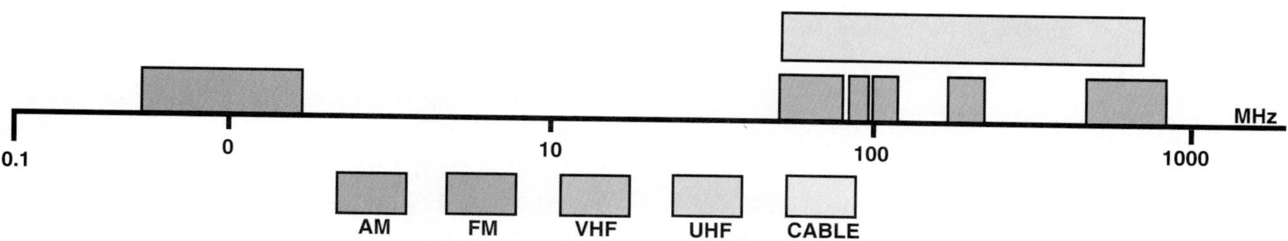

Figure 21-3. There are several different broadcast bands in the United States.

Citizen Communication

Citizen communication consists of two areas: citizen band and amateur band transmissions. These bands are used by citizens for personal communication. ***Citizen band*** frequencies are used for short distance communication and remote control products. For example, Citizen Band (CB) radios, garage door openers, and television remote controls all use frequencies that are citizen bands.

The ***amateur bands*** are used for long-distance personal communication. These frequencies allow more options than CB bands. For example, amateur bands allow the user to send transmissions around the world. This can be helpful during emergency situations. During these times, radios are set up as an emergency communications network. They are staffed by civilian citizens. Other people use these frequencies to communicate as a hobby. These people are called "ham" radio operators.

Industrial and Government Communication

Industrial and government communication frequencies are for use only in industrial or governmental applications. These frequencies are used in local and global communication of the government, armed services, and weather services. Local businesses and factories also use these frequencies during a regular business day. Using radios that operate on these frequencies links the company and its business cars and trucks.

Commercial Transportation Communication

These frequencies are used by taxi, ambulance, ship radios, and are also used by paging services. Frequencies are also set aside in this category for coded electromagnetic waves. These coded waves are used to guide the direction of aircraft and ships. One system is known as the ***Instrument Landing System (ILS).*** All major airports are equipped with this system.

FREQUENCY BANDS

Each of the FCC categories operates within a certain group of frequencies. The names used for each of these groups of frequencies are shown in Figure 21-4. You will review several of the frequency bands briefly.

Terminology of Frequency Bands

Band Number	Frequency Range	Frequency Subdivison
2	30-300H	ELF Extremely low frequency
3	300-3,000H	VF Voice frequency
4	3-30kH	VLF Very low frequency
5	30-300kH	LF Low frequency
6	300-3,000kH	MF Medium frequency
7	3,000-30,000kH	HF High frequency
8	30-300MH	VHF Very high frequency
9	300-3,000MH	UHF Ultra high frequency
10	3,000-30.000MH	SHF Super high frequency
11	30,000-300,000MH	EHF Extremely high frequency
12	300,000-3,000,000MH	

Figure 21-4. Study this chart of frequency terminology. Where do AM and FM broadcasts fit in the chart?

The extremely low frequency (ELF) and voice frequency (VF) bands cover frequencies from musical instruments to voices. Very low frequency (VLF) and low frequency (LF) have very long wavelengths. (Remember from Chapter 19 that wavelength and frequency are inversely proportional.) Huge antennas must be used for transmission. This is not very practical, so they are used only in special communication systems.

Medium frequency (MF) and high frequency (HF) are used for commercial AM broadcasting and also for short wave and amateur broadcasts.

When a transmission from any of these frequencies is sent out, the waves hit a layer of the Earth's atmosphere called the ***ionosphere.*** The ionosphere reflects the waves back down to the Earth. These waves may reflect back and forth any number of times. This can be compared to a ball that is bounced in a room with a low ceiling. The ball bounces off the floor and ceiling several times before it stops bouncing. Given enough time, the ball will most likely strike a chair that is placed in the middle of the room. A wave that is bounced off the ionosphere is very similar. Sooner or later the signal will contact a receiver, Figure 21-5. These reflections off the ionosphere make transmissions over great distances possible.

Very high frequency (VHF) and ultra high frequency (UHF) are two terms with which you may be familiar. These bands are used for TV transmissions. VHF and UHF bands are used in short distance, line-of-sight communications. In other words, receivers and transmitters must be directly in sight of one another. This limits the broadcast range of most TV stations.

Microwaves include all frequencies above the UHF range, but below infrared light. The term microwave comes from the short ("micro") nature of these wavelengths. Radar communication is a common use of microwaves.

Microwaves have several advantages because their wavelength is so small. One advantage is that the signals can be projected into a very small area. This means the energy is used efficiently. This intense beam of energy allows antennas to be very small in microwave use.

However, there are also disadvantages with microwave signals. Perhaps the biggest drawback is the effect of poor weather on microwaves. Since the wavelengths are so small, rain, snow, hail, or even a high wind can absorb the energy in the signal.

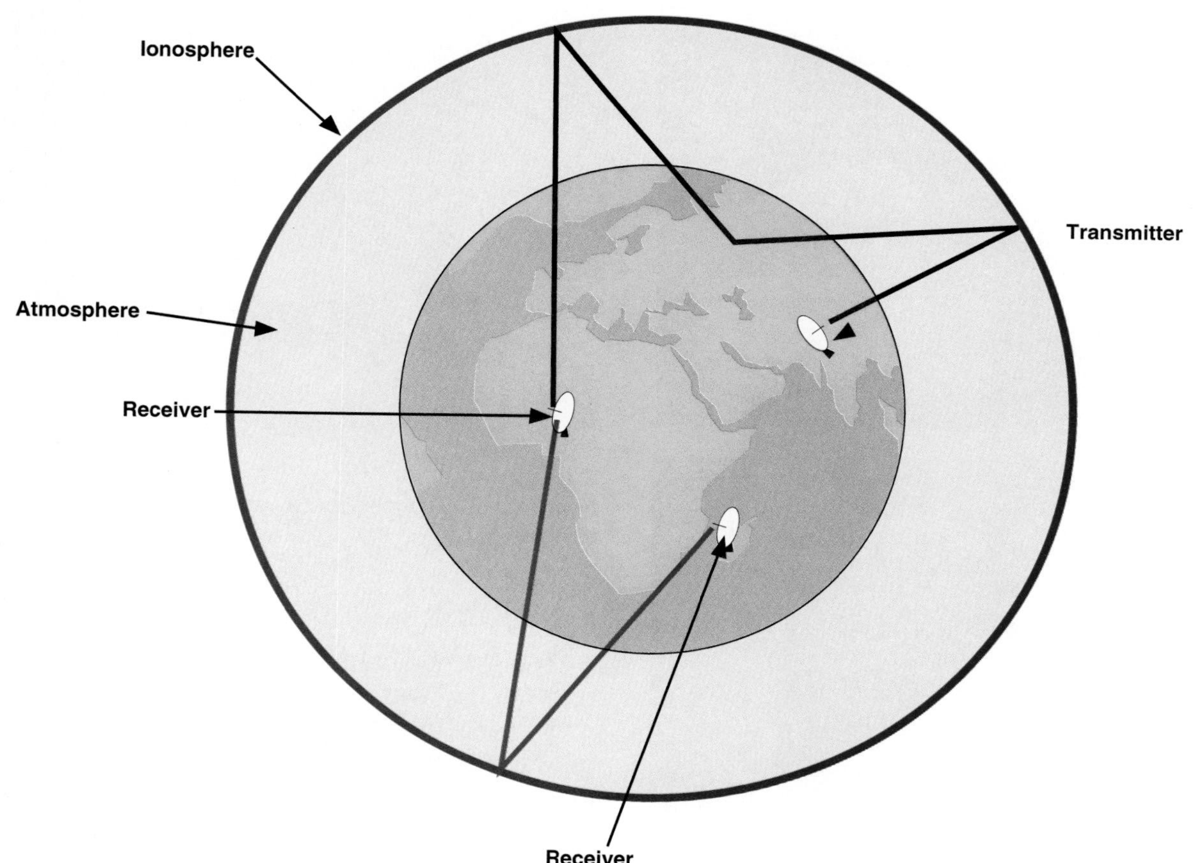

Figure 21-5. MF and HF signals are sent out and hit the ionosphere. These signals are then reflected back down to a receiver.

TYPES OF TELECOMMUNICATION SYSTEMS

The categories and frequencies you have looked at so far are only part of the area of telecommunication. In order for telecommunication to be useful, it is necessary to have devices to receive and transmit signals. These devices make a complete communication system.

You are very likely familiar with several of the systems you will look at, Figure 21-6. Perhaps a few are new to you. In the following sections you will look at how and where each of these systems is used in modern telecommunication.

Figure 21-6. Many types of telecommunication devices are available. (Xerox Corp., Zenith Electronics Corp.)

Radio

Radio is one of the most widely used telecommunication systems. It is used every day. Common uses include AM and FM broadcasts. There are many other uses for radio. Some of these uses might not seem like radio to you at first. One example is a cellular telephone. This works using radio waves, Figure 21-7. Another example is a remote controlled model airplane. It also uses a certain radio frequency.

Figure 21-7. Car telephones use radio waves to transmit signals.

Radio messages can be transmitted using one-way or two-way radios. ***One-way radios*** only send messages or receive messages between a source and a destination. There is no feedback involved. AM and FM broadcasts are one-way. Other one-way radio messages include some pager systems or "beepers," weather band radio broadcasts, and garage door openers. The frequencies of these devices vary. They are all along the electromagnetic spectrum. Most, however, can be found along the MF, HF, and UHF bands. Refer back to Figure 21-3.

Radio messages can also be sent and received using ***two-way radios.*** With two-way radios, it is possible to have feedback. You can respond directly to messages on two-way devices. Taxi radios and CB radios are examples of two-way radios. When a taxi driver receives a message from a dispatcher (operator), the driver can respond to the dispatcher directly.

The telephone is also an example of a two-way radio. It has one major difference, however, from most other two-way radios. With a telephone, two signals can be sent at the same time. For example, suppose you and a friend are talking to each other on the telephone. If you both speak at the same time, both voices will be heard. However with a taxi radio, only one person can talk at a time. This is because when speaking on a taxi radio, walkie-talkie, or a police radio, a "talk" button must be pressed. When the button is pressed, the radio cannot receive a message, only send a message, Figure 21-8. The telephone is such a major part of telecommunications that it is given a classification of its own.

Figure 21-8. There are two types of radio communication.

Telephone

The telephone is an excellent example of telecommunication. It allows you to communicate over long distances quickly. Quick and efficient service is very important in telecommunication.

Quick service is supplied by telephone ***switching systems,*** Figure 21-9. Telephone switching systems route calls from the source to the destination.

Figure 21-9. Telephone switching systems direct calls for fast and efficient service. (Courtesy of Sprint)

In the early years of telephone use, switching was done by hand. Operators connected the wire from the telephone line making the call to the telephone line of the person being called. But as telephone use grew, automatic systems came into use. Until recently, the major portion of switching was electromechanical. That is, an electronic impulse (number "dialed") caused the switching to occur.

While electromechanical switching is still used, most switching is now done through electronic switching systems (ESS). In these systems, computer programs are used to do routine operations like switching. These programs are stored in computer memory. When a friend "dials" your number at home, the electronic pulses from dialing are collected. After all the digits have been dialed, the computer reviews them. It then maps out the quickest switching route to complete the call.

Electronic switching systems are far more efficient than electromechanical switching systems. ESS are quicker, less costly, smaller, more reliable, and use less power. The computers not only complete calls, they also control the overall function of the system.

Switching systems belong to a ***network.*** A network is a system of interconnected subsystems that work together. Telephones are one example. Computers can also be "networked." The telephone network is worldwide and provides a common "link." Phone service in Italy is able to work with the system used in the United States. If you wish to call a relative in Italy, there will be no problem with the two phone systems working together.

The telephone network is made up of transmission links, terminals (telephones), switching operations, and more. All these pieces work together and are necessary for completing a call. For example, transmission links transmit the call, Figure 21-10. Network switching systems complete the circuit. Telephones allow you to hear and be heard, Figure 21-11.

Television

All television broadcasts, including cable, can be found in the frequency bands ranging from VHF through UHF. VHF and UHF signals can be sent through the atmosphere or through coaxial cables, Figure 21-12.

The FCC has assigned specific channels for each television broadcast. Broadcasts in the

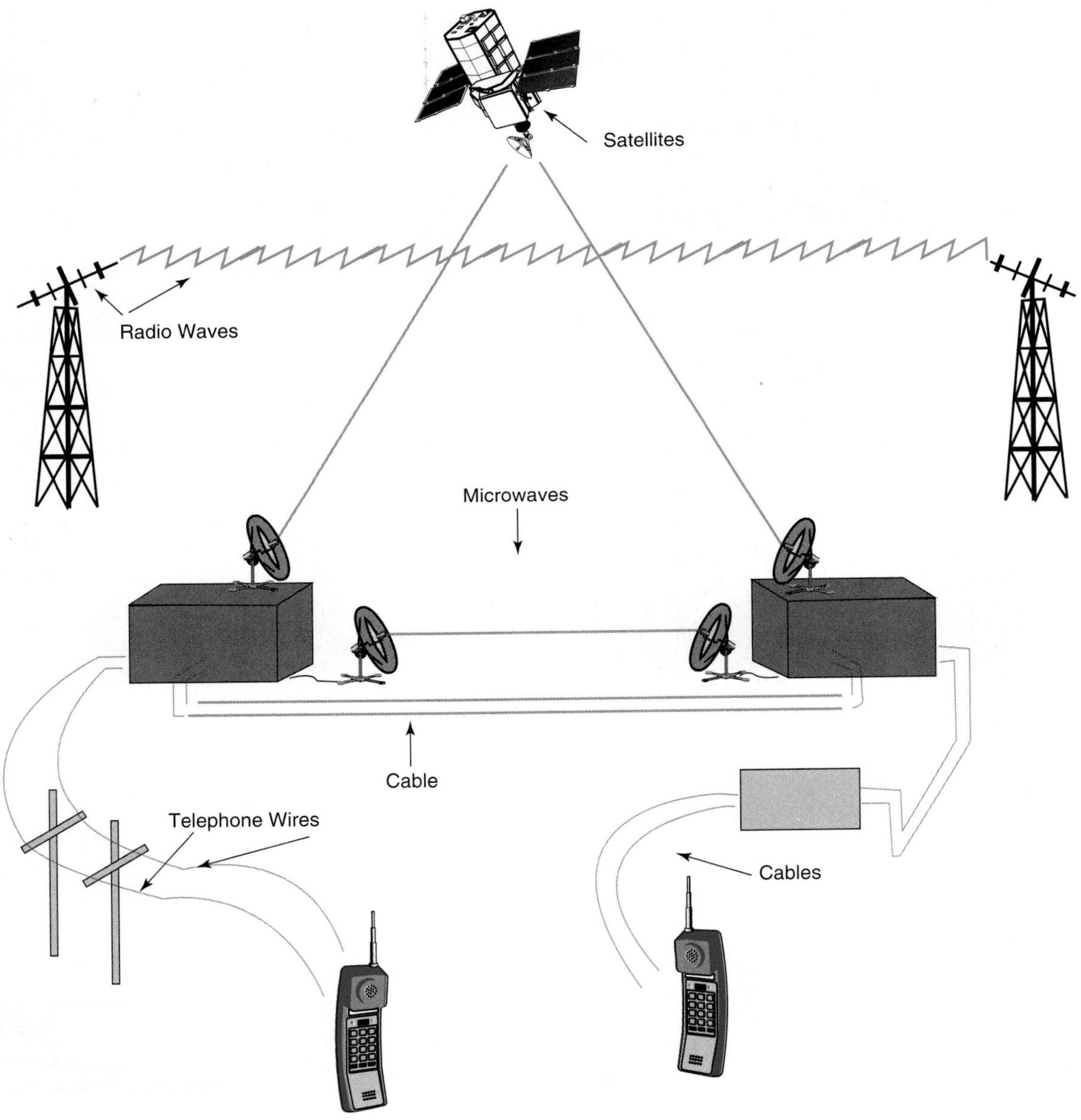

Figure 21-10. There are several transmission options.

Figure 21-11. Telephones allow messages to reach their destination. (AT&T)

Figure 21-12. Television signals can be sent through the atmosphere or through cables.

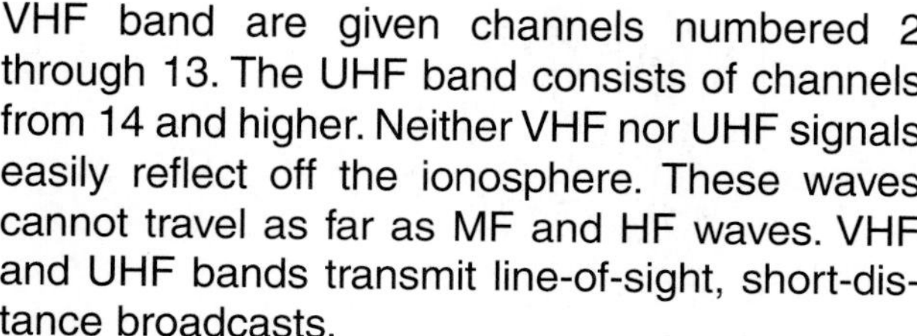

VHF band are given channels numbered 2 through 13. The UHF band consists of channels from 14 and higher. Neither VHF nor UHF signals easily reflect off the ionosphere. These waves cannot travel as far as MF and HF waves. VHF and UHF bands transmit line-of-sight, short-distance broadcasts.

Transmitting broadcasts through cables solves the problem of short-distance broadcasts. The transmissions are made in the same way as telephone transmissions, Figure 21-13. The studio sends out television broadcasts to each ***subscriber*** (household that rents the service). These broadcasts are sent down a main

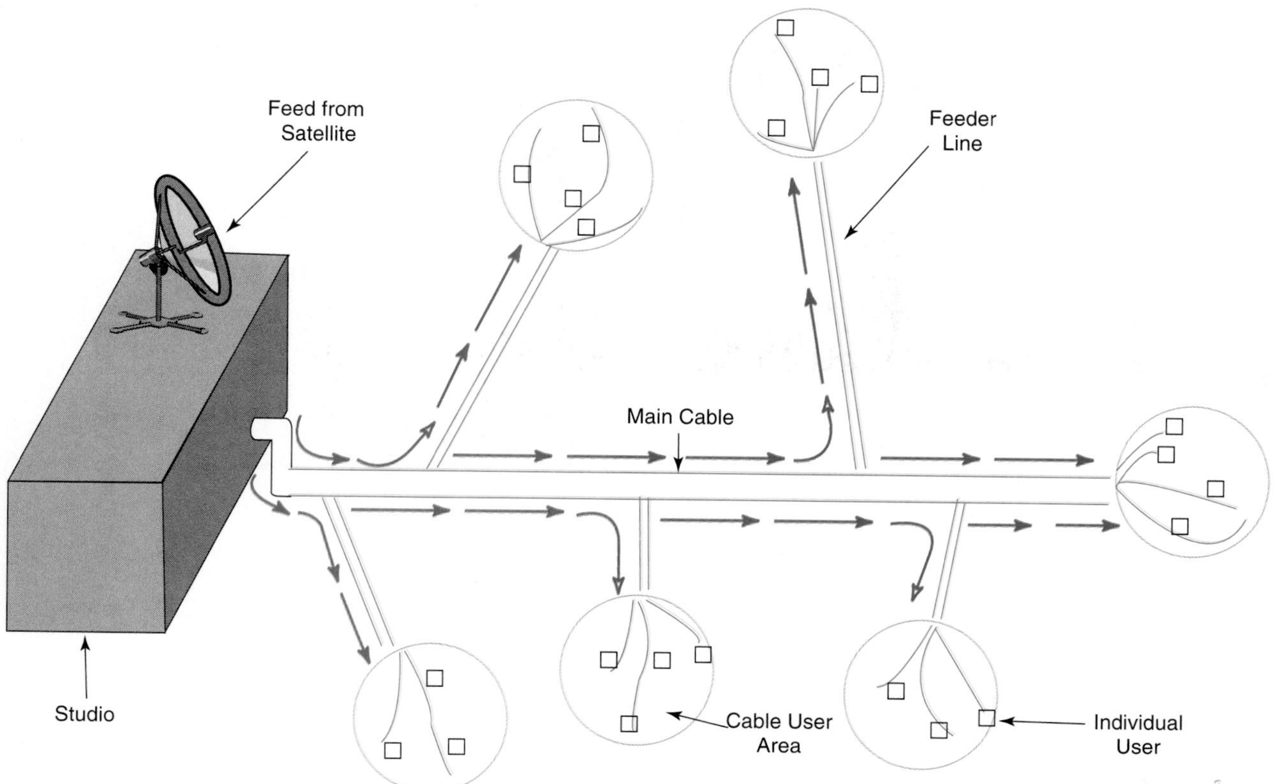

Figure 21-13. A cable broadcast has several steps to go through before it reaches your house.

line which has feeder lines tied into it. Each feeder line is connected to the lines that go to each subscriber.

As you learned in Chapter 19, interference does not affect a cable transmission much. Also, cables offer a more focused signal. With the protective covering surrounding the cable, signals are directed without losing much power. This means a cable-transmitted broadcast will be clearer and will travel farther than a broadcast sent through the atmosphere.

Once these transmissions are sent, however, how are the images reproduced (made) on the television screen? The picture is made by light that constantly moves and changes in levels of brilliance (lightness, darkness, color). These changes occur so rapidly the human eye cannot detect them.

A television contains a ***cathode ray tube (CRT),*** Figure 21-14. The CRT contains an electron gun that shoots electrons out onto the television screen. The screen is divided into 525 (or more) lines. Each of these lines is scanned every time the flow of electrons changes. The screen is coated with phosphors that light up when the electrons hit them. Depending on the image being sent from the television studio, the electron beam will change according to the strength of the signal. Now imagine this process taking place 30 times a second over the lines on the screen! Now it is clear why the human eye cannot detect the movement.

Whether or not the picture is black and white or color depends on the picture tube. The process just explained is typical of a black and white picture. In the screen of a color television, there are three electron guns; one each for green, blue, and red. The screen is coated with three kinds of phosphors. When the electron beam contacts the phosphors, some glow red, some glow blue, and some glow green, Figure 21-15.

Television has grown a great deal since its beginning. With the constant improvements and innovations (new ideas), television plays a very important part in the telecommunication industry.

Online Computer Services

Online computer services contain a wealth of information stored in computers all over the world. These services can be accessed through a computer with a modem. A ***modem*** is a device that allows a computer to communicate with other computers over telephone lines. Online service can be accessed from any computer that has a modem. You can use your home computer or a business can use their computers. Some of these services are free and others charge fees for the service.

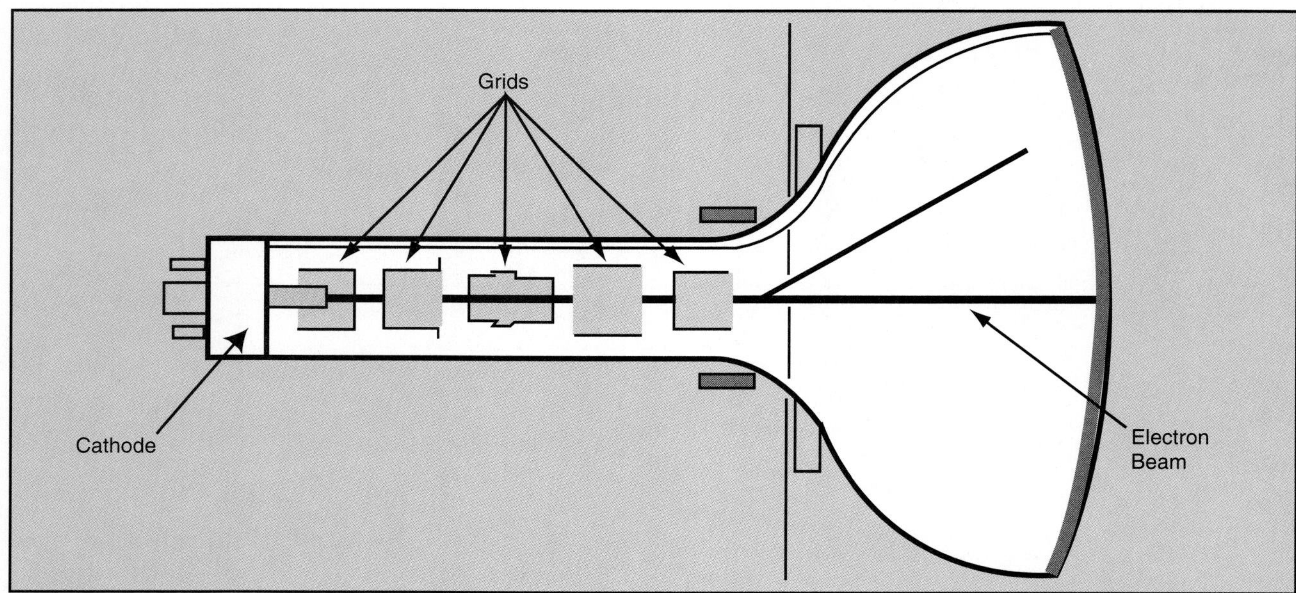

Figure 21-14. The operation of a basic black and white television picture tube and screen is simple. The cathode shoots an electron beam through a series of grids. These grids speed up and focus the electrons.

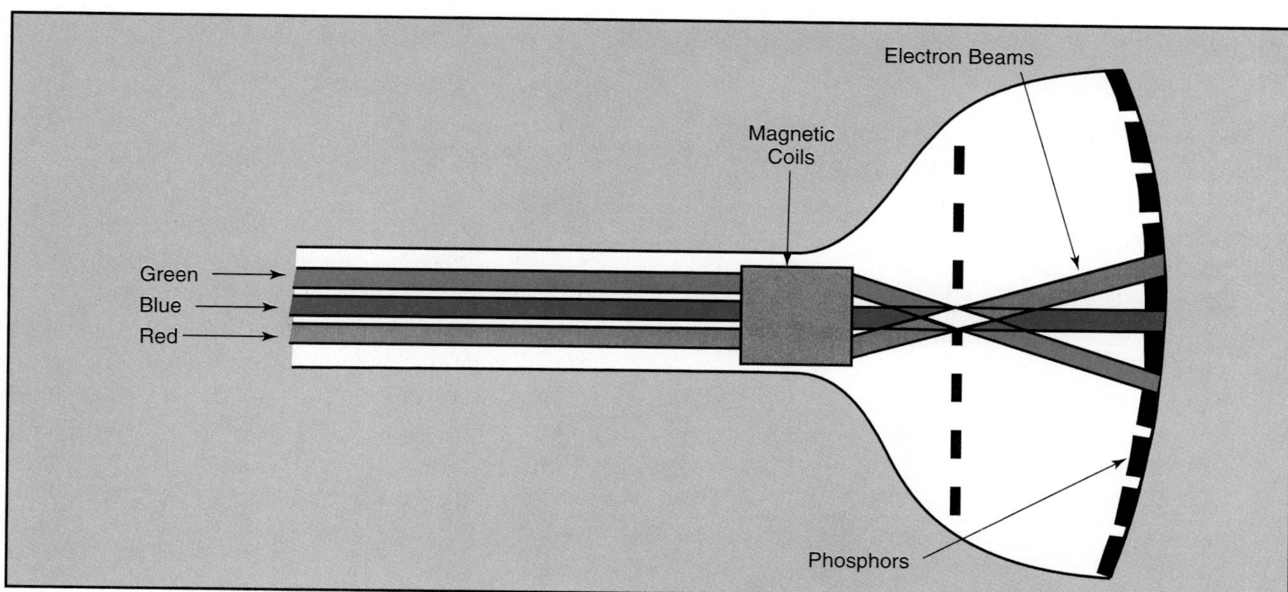

Figure 21-15. A color TV picture tube and screen operate much like a black and white picture tube and screen.

Online services provide access to information stored in other computers, Figure 21-16. Libraries have the ability to search other libraries for books and materials through the use of on-line computer networks. Law enforcement agencies are connected to on-line networks to make arrest record information available.

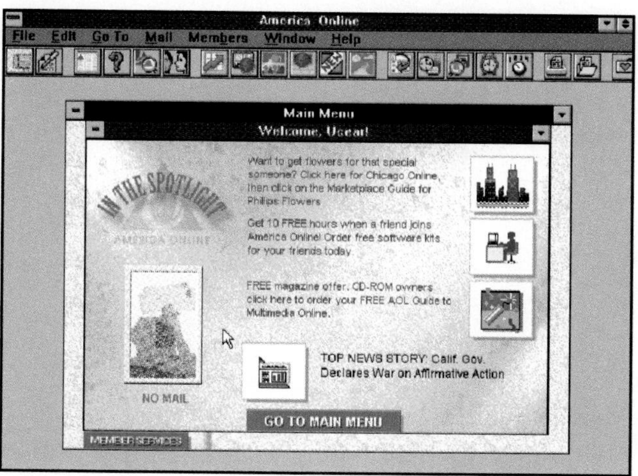

Figure 21-16. Online services allow a person access to much information. This information is stored on remote computers and is accessed through a modem. (America Online©, Inc.)

Another example of an online service is a visitor information center. These systems can be used to find restaurants and points of interest in a particular area. All the information is stored in a remote computer that can be accessed by all of the visitor centers in that area. Some stores also use on-line systems as a store directory. By answering a series of questions at a computer, you are directed to the area of the store you seek.

Online services also include shopping and banking using a home computer. Many newspapers are also available "online," Figure 21-17. Online networks are also a source for software, games, stock quotes, and electronic mail (e-mail) pen pals, Figure 21-18. Online services contribute a great deal to the Information Age.

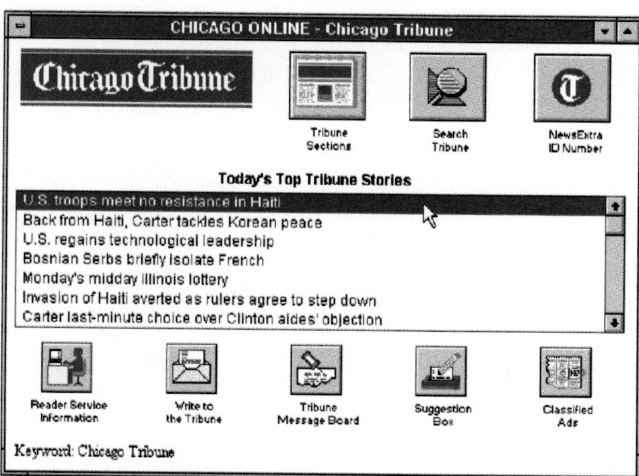

Figure 21-17. Some newspapers are available "online." This means that you can read the newspaper from your home computer using a modem to access the information. (America Online©, Inc.)

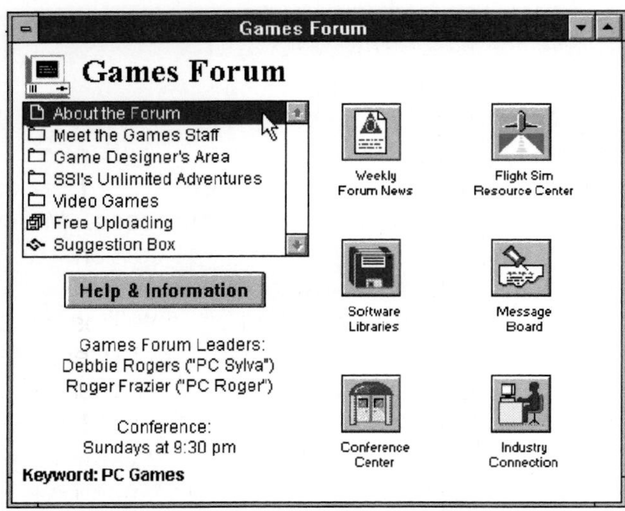

Portfolio

Total portfolio value: 3,438.75 (+728.75)

Symbol	Qty.	Curr. Price	Change	Purch. Price	Gain/ Loss	Value
AAPL	10	35 1/2	-7/8	31.50	+40.00	355.00
AMER	10	74 3/4	+1	56	+187.50	747.50
BMY	10	58 1/8	-3/8	57.50	+6.25	581.25
IBM	10	70 3/8	-5/8	46	+243.75	703.75
XRX	10	105 1/8	----	80	+251.25	1,051.25

Details Remove Save Portfolio

Figure 21-18. Online networks can provide a wide variety of information, from help with computer games to the latest stock quotes. (America Online©, Inc.)

Figure 21-19. Satellites orbit the Earth constantly. (NASA)

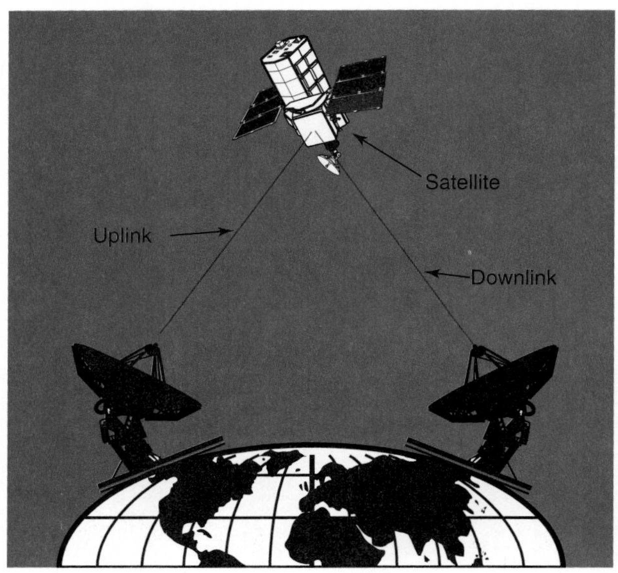

Figure 21-20. There are several steps in a satellite transmission.

Satellites

Satellites are truly a space-age device, Figure 21-19. The development and improvement of satellites is due to advances made in such areas as space research, electronics, and robotics. Satellites are used as tools, as broadcasting devices, and as military communication systems. In order to understand satellites fully, you must understand basically how they work.

A communication satellite is designed to receive and send signals, Figure 21-20. These signals must travel a great distance from ground stations on the Earth's surface to the satellite ***(uplink)*** and back to the earth ***(downlink)*** again. Microwave beams are used for these transmissions. Microwaves are able to cut through the Earth's atmosphere easily. The beams must be carefully aimed toward the proper ground station or satellite. The signals are sent and received using special antennas. The ground antenna and the satellite must be able to stay in constant contact with each other in order to transmit. If the satellite moves faster than the earth revolves, the contact would be broken.

Satellites must circle the Earth at the same speed the earth revolves on its axis: once every 24 hours. They will move at this rate when placed into orbit at 22,300 miles above Earth. This is known as ***geosynchronous orbit.*** At this point, a satellite downlink covers 40 percent of the Earth's surface. That means that signals transmitted from one Earth station can be received by another earth station 8000 miles away! Therefore, a message sent from Boston, Massachusetts, could reach a ground station in Munich, Germany, using the same satellite.

A variety of telecommunication is done using satellites. You might be most familiar with television and radio broadcasts via (by) satellite. Perhaps your family, or a friend's family, has a satellite "dish." The dish is actually a ground station that receives signals transmitted from another point. The large number of satellite "feeds" available in North America is shown in Figure 21-21.

Satellites are also used to obtain weather information. These weather satellites send photographs of weather patterns such as air currents and cloud formations. Weather satellites also carry equipment to record temperature and humidity information. All this data helps meteorologists (weather scientists) to forecast weather patterns, Figure 21-22.

Other users of satellites include the armed services, the government, and independent businesses. The military operates an entire fleet of satellites for communication purposes. Many large companies rely on satellites to send and receive up-to-date information.

Telecommunication through satellites is a booming industry. However, individual users are often unable to afford the cost of using satellite systems. By launching ***direct broadcast satellites (DBS)*** satellite use has opened up to the individual. These particular satellites can broadcast directly to the home. Current satellite broadcasts are supplied by communication companies who own the satellites. DBS systems have enough power to transmit signals to a smaller (and less costly) antenna than is currently

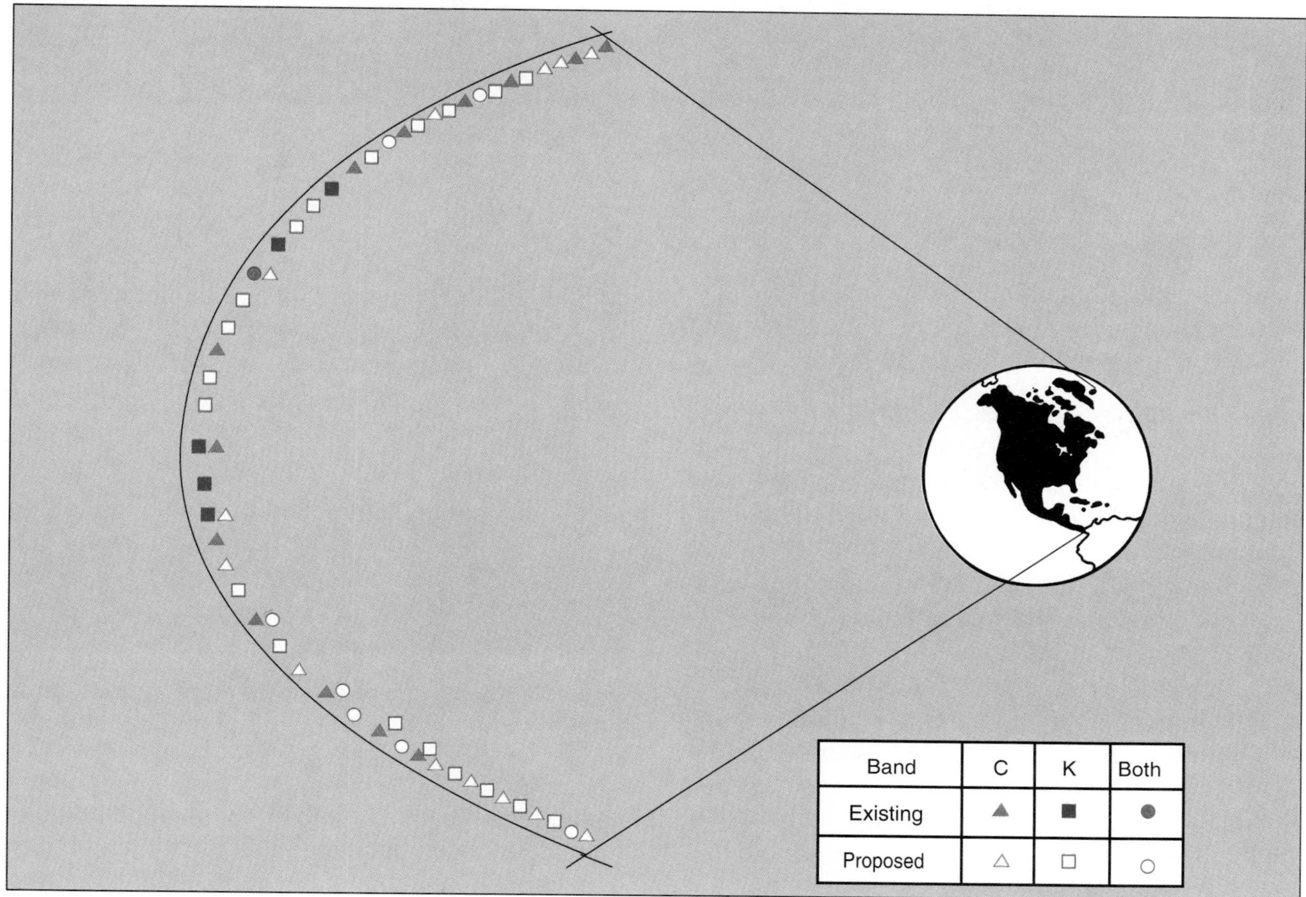

Figure 21-21. There are several satellite broadcasts available in North America for the C and K bands. The C and K bands can be compared to the UHF and VHF bands on "free" television.

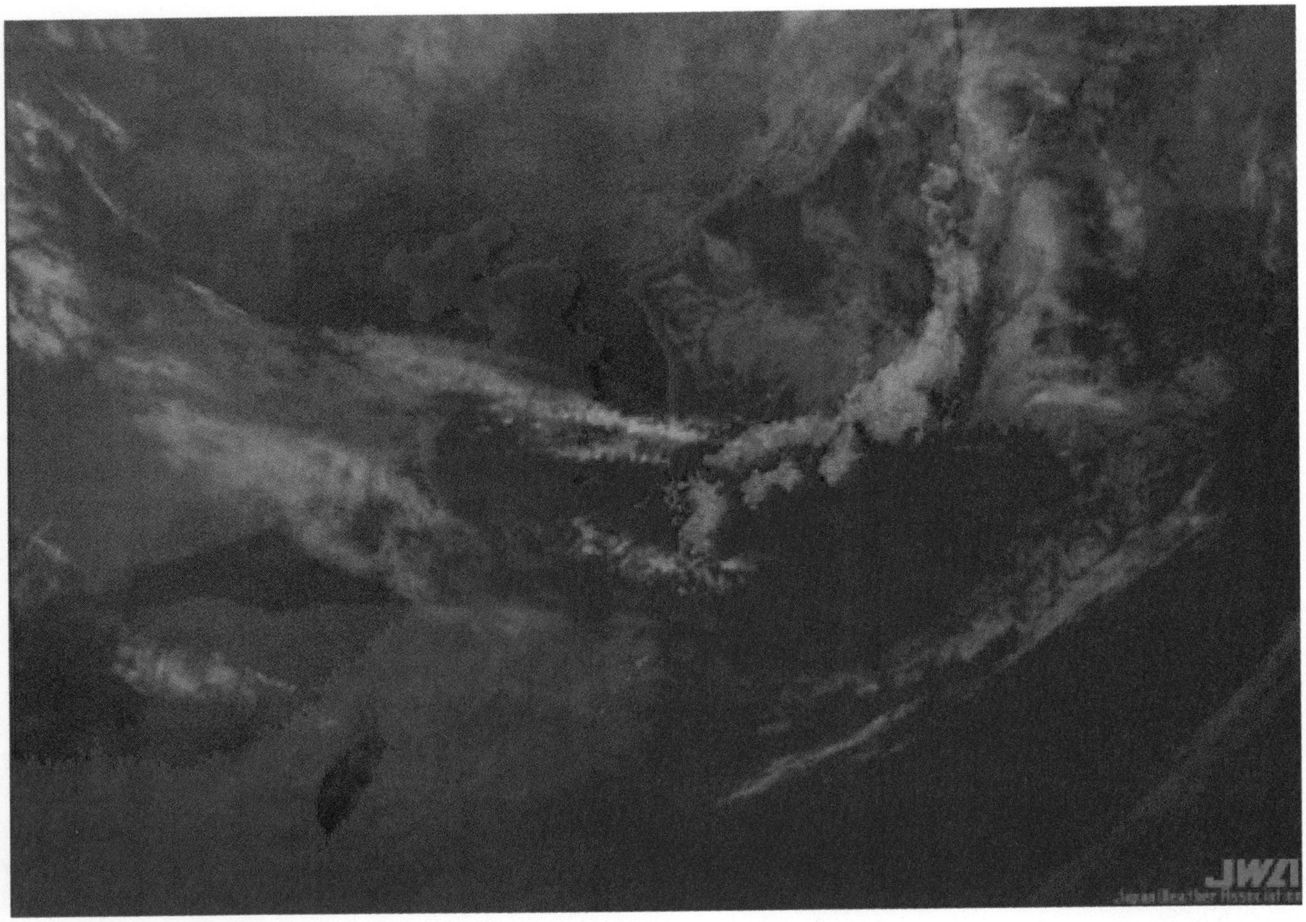

Figure 21-22. Weather patterns are detected using satellites. (JWA)

needed. As DBS systems continue to grow, satellite communication might become as common to individual users as letter writing.

Microwave Links

Many of the telecommunication systems discussed so far use microwaves as a link when transmitting messages, Figure 21-23. For example, many television broadcasts travel through a network of microwave relay stations. Many telephone conversations travel through microwave relay stations as well.

There are several reasons for the large use of microwave links. First, with increased use, the VHF and UHF bands have become too crowded. As fewer frequencies were available on these bands, the FCC began using microwave bands.

Another reason for the large use of microwaves is the vast amount of information that can be transmitted. This is because microwaves are extremely short. Therefore, microwaves can be concentrated (focused) into a very small, narrow beam. This allows powerful, efficient transmissions. For example, a very large and powerful transmitter can send about 100 billion bits of

Figure 21-23. Microwave towers aid in the transmission of many messages. (AT&T)

information per second. That is equal to about 12 television broadcasts and thousands of telephone calls every second!

DATA COMMUNICATION

Data communication is the process of transmitting information in binary form between two points. (Remember from Chapter 20 that a binary code is a series of 1's and 0's that represent a number, letter, sound, or visual image.) Simply stated, data communication is a process that allows computers to "talk" with each other. Data communication systems are used a great deal in our society. Automatic teller machines (ATMs) are good examples of data communications, Figure 21-24.

Figure 21-24. An ATM is a smaller computer hooked up to a larger computer at a bank. (IBM)

In the following sections you will look at how data communication works as a large-scale communications model.

Coding

In Chapter 3, "code" was defined as a vehicle for transmitting messages. In data communication, codes are the languages computers use to communicate with one another. Most often, the languages are built into the hardware of the machine. Therefore, users of the computer seldom need to understand the coding process. If, however, two machines manufactured by different companies need to talk to each other, the user may need to write some code. Writing code is commonly known as ***programming,*** Figure 21-25. This code is different from the codes that the computer uses internally to operate (operating software such as MS-DOS).

```
NO, FAIL = NO, FAIL + 1
IF NO,FAIL= 1000 THEN RETURN
IF NO,FAIL = NO,PAGE*55 THEN__
   NO,PAGE = NO,PAGE + 1 :__
   LPRINT CHR$(12)

NO,GOOD$(NO,FAIL) + CHANGED, ID$
```

Figure 21-25. Computers can understand instructions that may seem like gibberish.

The most common standard code is the American Standard Code for Information Interchange. This is commonly known as ***ASCII*** (pronounced as-ski). ASCII consists of several different characters, Figure 21-26. It includes all the letters of the English alphabet, the numbers 0 through 9, and punctuation. Also included are symbols and some foreign letters. These ASCII symbols do not represent a printed character, like a letter, comma, or number. Instead they tell the computer what to do. For example, EOT means end of transmission.

CHANNELS

After a message has been coded, it must be transmitted. Channels, or ***media,*** are the physical equipment used to send the message. Basically, there are two types of channels: bounded and unbounded.

Bounded transmission channels in data communication contain the transmission in a controlled medium. Examples include wire pairs, coaxial cables, waveguides, and fiber-optic cables.

Bounded transmission channels lessen noise and increase the distance signals can travel. If you study a large, mainframe computer, you will see cables running from the terminals into the mainframe. These cables are an example of bounded transmission channels.

In ***unbounded transmission channels,*** the transmission is not contained in a controlled

80 Ç 128	90 É 144	A0 á 160	B0 ░ 176	C0 └ 192	D0 ╨ 208	E0 α 224	F0 ≡ 240
81 ü 129	91 æ 145	A1 í 161	B1 ▒ 177	C1 ┴ 193	D1 ╤ 209	E1 ß 225	F1 ± 241
82 é 130	92 Æ 146	A2 ó 162	B2 ▓ 178	C2 ┬ 194	D2 ╥ 210	E2 Γ 228	F2 ≥ 242
83 â 131	93 ô 147	A3 ú 163	B3 │ 179	C3 ├ 195	D3 ╙ 211	E3 π 227	F3 ≤ 243
84 ä 132	94 ö 148	A4 ñ 164	B4 ┤ 180	C4 ─ 196	D4 ╘ 212	E4 Σ 228	F4 ⌠ 244
85 à 133	95 ò 149	A5 Ñ 165	B5 ╡ 181	C5 ┼ 197	D5 ╒ 213	E5 σ 229	F5 ⌡ 245
86 å 134	96 û 150	A6 ª 166	B6 ╢ 182	C6 ╞ 198	D6 ╓ 214	E6 µ 230	F6 ÷ 246
87 ç 135	97 ú 151	A7 º 167	B7 ╖ 183	C7 ╟ 199	D7 ╫ 215	E7 τ 231	F7 ≈ 247
88 ê 136	98 ÿ 152	A8 ¿ 168	B8 ╕ 184	C8 ╚ 200	D8 ╪ 216	E8 Φ 232	F8 ○ 248
89 ë 137	99 Ö 153	A9 ⌐ 169	B9 ╣ 185	C9 ╔ 201	D9 ┘ 217	E9 Θ 233	F9 ● 249
8A è 138	9A Ü 154	AA ¬ 170	BA ║ 186	CA ╩ 202	DA ┌ 218	EA Ω 234	FA • 250
8B ï 139	9B ¢ 155	AB ½ 171	BB ╗ 187	CB ╦ 203	DB █ 219	EB δ 235	FB √ 251
8C î 140	9C £ 156	AC ¼ 172	BC ╝ 188	CC ╠ 204	DC ▄ 220	EC ∞ 236	FC n 252
8D ì 141	9D ¥ 157	AD ¡ 173	BD ╜ 189	CD ═ 205	DD ▌ 221	ED ∅ 237	FD ² 253
8E Ä 142	9E ₧ 158	AE « 174	BE ╛ 190	CE ╬ 206	DE ▐ 222	EE ∈ 238	FE ■ 254
8F Å 143	9F ƒ 159	AF » 175	BF ┐ 191	CF ╧ 207	DF ▀ 223	EF ∩ 239	FF Blank "FF" 255

LEGEND

HEX	FF ♪ CR	ASCII Name
	←	Display Character
Key	CTRL M 13	Decimal

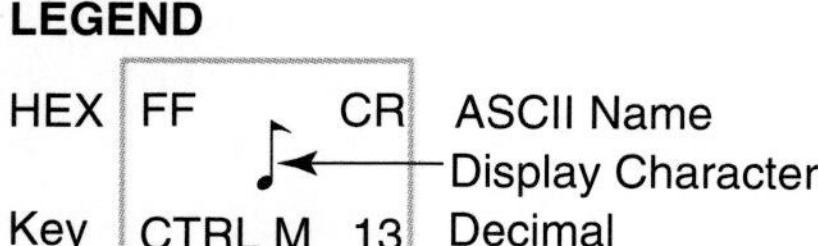

Figure 21-26. ASCII characters represent different values.

0	1	2	3	4	5	6	7
00 NUL CTRL @ 0	10 ◄ DLE CTRL P 16	20 SP 32	30 0 48	40 @ 64	50 P 80	60 ` 96	70 p 112
01 ☺ SOH CTRL A 1	11 ► DC1 CTRL Q 17	21 ! 33	31 1 49	41 A 65	51 Q 81	61 a 97	71 q 113
02 ☻ STX CTRL B 2	12 ↕ DC2 CTRL R 18	22 ” 34	32 2 50	42 B 66	52 R 82	62 b 98	72 r 114
03 ♥ EXT CTRL C 3	13 ‼ DC3 CTRL S 19	23 # 35	33 3 51	43 C 67	53 S 83	63 c 99	73 s 115
04 ♦ EOT CTRL D 4	14 ¶ DC4 CTRL T 20	24 $ 36	34 4 52	44 D 68	54 T 84	64 d 100	74 t 116
05 ♣ ENQ CTRL E 5	15 § NAK CTRL U 21	25 % 37	35 5 53	45 E 69	55 U 85	65 e 101	75 u 117
06 ♠ ACK CTRL F 6	16 ▬ SYN CTRL V 22	26 & 38	36 6 54	46 F 70	56 V 86	66 f 102	76 v 118
07 ● BEL CTRL G 7	17 ↨ ETB CTRL W 23	27 '	37 7	47 G	57 W	67 g	77 w
08 ◘ BS CTRL H 8	18 ↑ CAN CTRL X 24	28 (40	38 8 56	48 H 72	58 X 88	68 h 104	78 x 120
09 ○ HT CTRL I 9	19 ↓ EM CTRL Y 25	29) 41	39 9 57	49 I 73	59 Y 89	69 i 105	79 y 121
OA ◙ LF TRL J 10	1A → SUB CTRL Z 26	2A * 41	3A : 57	4A J 73	5A Z 89	6A j 105	7A z 121
OB ♂ VT CTRL K 11	1B ← ESC CTRL [27	2B + 43	3B ; 59	4B K 75	5B [91	6B k 107	7B { 123
OC ♀ FF CTRL L 12	1C ∟ FS CTRL \ 28	2C , 44	3C < 60	4C L 76	5C / 92	6C l 108	7C ¦ 124
OD ♪ CR CTRL M 13	1D ↔ GS CTRL] 29	2D - 45	3D = 61	4D M 77	5D] 93	6D m 109	7D } 125
OE ♫ SO CTRL N 14	1E ▲ RS CTRL ∧ 30	2E . 46	3E > 62	4E N 78	5E 94	6E n 110	7E ~ 126
OF ☼ S1 CTRL O 15	1F ▼ US CTRL _ 31	2F / 47	3F ? 63	4F O 79	5F — 95	6F o 111	7F Δ DEL 127

LEGEND

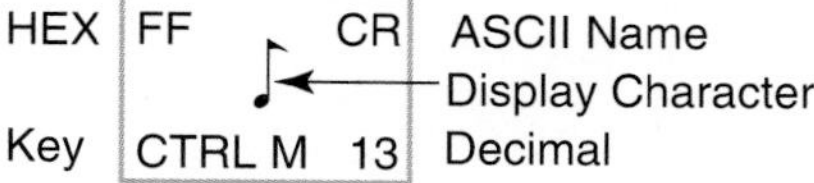

Figure 21-26. (Continued)

medium such as wires. The atmosphere and outer space are two examples of unbounded transmission channels used in data communications. These channels are affected by noise.

The atmosphere is used as a channel in satellite television broadcasts. The satellite codes the message and sends it down to the antenna. The antenna "understands" the message, then decodes it into a form your TV will recognize. This is an example of using an unbounded transmission channel.

Transmission

Data is normally sent between computers and terminals by varying the current or voltage of a channel. Computer transmissions are normally parallel or serial.

In ***parallel transmissions,*** several pieces (bits) of information are sent on several wires at the same time, Figure 21-27. Parallel transmission is usually used with systems located near each other. For example, a system located within one office building will usually use parallel transmission, Figure 21-28. Printers and plotters are usually connected to a computer's parallel port.

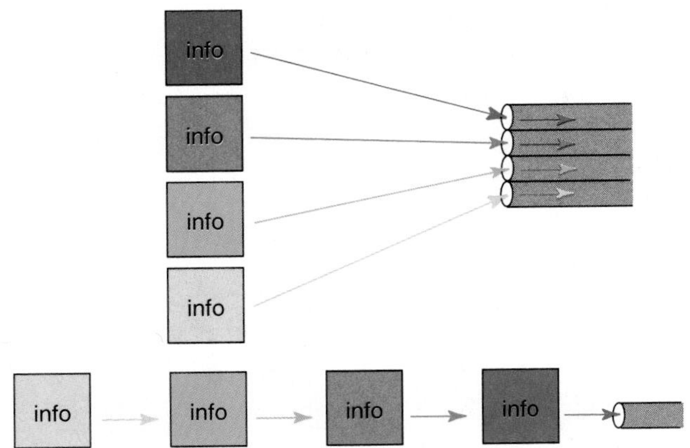

Figure 21-27. Parallel communication (top) sends information through several wires at the same time. Serial communication (bottom) sends information in sequence through a single wire.

Wire is costly, however, so as the distance between equipment increases, so does cost.

Serial transmissions are used for long distance messages. The bits of information are sent one at a time over a single wire. Computer modems are usually connected to a computer's serial port. External hard drives and floppy drives

Figure 21-28. Companies can locate all of their computer needs in one location. (IBM)

are also usually connected to a serial port. Serial transmissions can be synchronous or asynchronous. An ***asynchronous transmission*** sends each bit by itself. In ***synchronous transmission*** bits are sent in groups, or "blocks."

Interfaces

An interface is a group of rules that control the way in which two machines or processes interact. These rules are usually part of the computer itself.

A modem is an interface. By changing signals over telephone wires, the modem allows one computer to talk to another computer. A modem can allow a terminal in one location to "talk" to a central processing unit (CPU) in another location.

Networks

Data communication systems are sometimes very large. In order to make them work to their best ability, they are organized into ***networks.*** A network is a system of interconnected sub-systems that work together. Generally, there are three types of computer networks: local area networks (LANs), time-sharing networks, and distributed networks.

In a ***time-sharing network*** any number of terminals are connected to one large central computer. Users rent part of the computer for as long as they need it. Therefore, the cost of the computer ends up being divided between all the users. This is a good method for businesses that need computers for their resources, but cannot afford to own a big system.

The data in a time-sharing network travels through telephone wires or space using radio waves. The central computer may never be seen by the user. It may be located in another city, another state, or another country.

Distributed networks contain a central computer attached to other computers. Resources in this network are spread among all the computers. One computer does not contain all the information.

Sometimes in a distributed network, each computer is responsible for a certain task. These computers gather the information for their areas. This information can be stored in memory or sent on to the main computer.

CHAPTER 21 REVIEW

SUMMARY

There are many uses for telecommunication. A use can be a simple telephone call or a complex satellite transmission. Telecommunication systems allow you to stay in close contact with friends, relatives, and others around the globe.

Telecommunication is regulated by the Federal Communications Commission (FCC). The FCC has divided telecommunication systems into categories. These categories determine what area and frequencies a certain system can use. This helps keep the telecommunication industry organized.

There are many devices used to receive and transmit messages in telecommunication systems. Some devices include radio, telephone, television, teletext, videotext, satellites, and microwave links.

Data communication allow different computers to "talk" to each other. Communication can be over a very short distance, such as a computer "talking" to a printer. The communication can also be over a very long distance, such as using a modem to communicate with another computer that is on the other side of the country. Parallel transmissions are used primarily for short distances and serial transmissions are used primarily for long distances.

KEY WORDS

All of the following words have been used in this chapter. Do you know their meanings?

- Amateur bands
- ASCII
- Asynchronous transmission
- Bounded transmission channel
- Cathode ray tube (CRT)
- Citizen band
- Data communication
- Direct broadcast satellite (DBS)
- Distributed network
- Downlink
- Federal Communications Commission (FCC)
- Geosynchronous orbit
- Instrument Landing System (ILS)
- Ionosphere
- Local area network (LAN)
- Media
- Modem
- Network
- Online services
- One-way radio
- Parallel transmission
- Programming
- Serial transmission
- Subscriber
- Switching systems
- Synchronous transmission
- Telecommunication
- Time-sharing network
- Two-way radio
- Unbounded transmission channels
- Uplink

TEST YOUR KNOWLEDGE

Place your answer on a separate sheet of paper. Please do not write in this book.

1. What governmental agency regulates the use of frequencies?
2. List the FCC categories and give an example of a user for each category.
3. The _____ is a layer of the earth's atmosphere.
4. Name two advantages that microwave signals have over UHF and VHF.
5. All television broadcasts can be found in frequency bands ranging from _____ through _____.
6. Explain how images are produced on the television screen.
7. _____ route telephone calls from the source to the destination.
8. Explain online services.
9. What do each of the following acronyms stand for?

   A. CRT.

   B. FCC.

   C. DBS.

   D. ILS.
10. What is a geosynchronous orbit?

ACTIVITIES

1. Send messages to friends using a variety of radios: citizen band, walkie-talkie, and ham radio. List the advantages and disadvantages of each system that you experience while using these systems. Report your findings to the class.
2. Determine the frequency of your favorite radio station. Dial this frequency into an oscilloscope to actually "see" the wave. Explain to your instructor how the radio station is sending the broadcast.
3. Develop a technical illustration of how geosynchronous satellites provide worldwide service. Use this as an aid for a short oral presentation to the class explaining geosynchronous orbits.
4. Design a telephone system for use in your classroom. Have students represent electronic devices such as relays, switches, and telephone equipment. Have other students represent telephone messages. Use this model to explain how a telephone call gets from the source to the destination.

CHAPTER 22
LIGHT COMMUNICATION

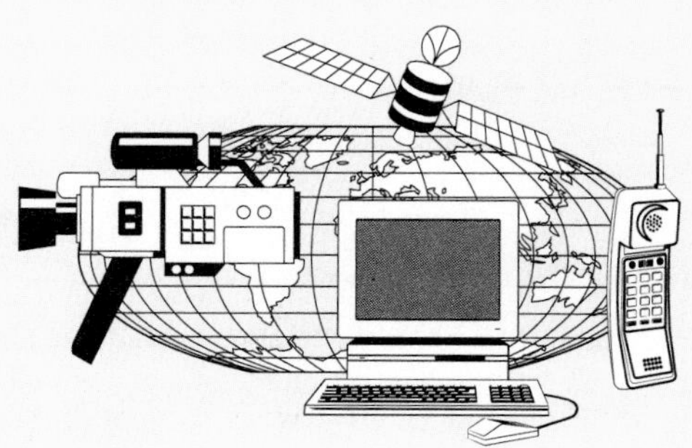

After studying this chapter, you will be able to:

- *Describe the purposes and uses of light in modern communication systems.*
- *Explain how light signals are created and received by humans and machines.*
- *List the uses of laser and fiber optic technologies.*

Although it may seem strange, light is a very common communication medium. Can you think of some typical examples? Lighthouses warn ships of dangerous shorelines or shallow waters. Traffic lights control the flow of cars and trucks on roadways. Neon signs and lighted displays are effective for advertising in stores. The projectors used in theaters and in your school classroom are a form of light communication. Compact disc players and video disc players rely on laser light for producing clear sounds and pictures.

PURPOSES AND USES

The purpose of communication technology is to help transmit information. Light communication is no exception, Figure 22-1. It is useful in many control and information systems. Many examples of light communication should already be familiar to you.

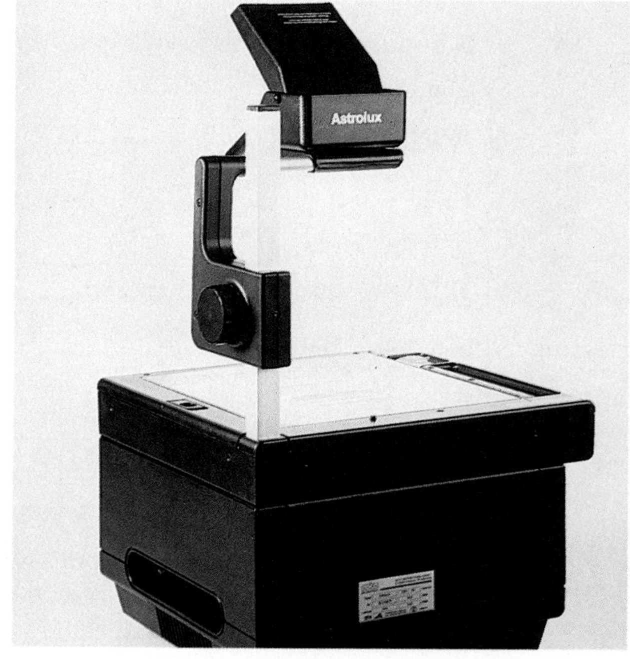

Figure 22-1. Many presentations and oral reports are aided by showing vital information on a screen. Have any of your instructors ever used an overhead projector in class? Projected imagery is a form of light communication. (Staedtler, Inc.)

TRAFFIC CONTROL

Many forms of transportation rely on signs and signals to direct their flow, Figure 22-2. You can probably give several examples of how light is used to direct cars, trucks, and trains. However, the control of sea and air traffic is also critical. Light is used in controlling these types of transportation as well.

Light signals are very important in ground travel. Lights at busy intersections direct cars and trucks. Flashing lights along roadways inform you of hazardous areas. In addition, various signals inform railroad engineers if any trains are on the tracks ahead. This is known as the ***block signaling system,*** Figure 22-3.

Figure 22-2. There are many different ways that light is used to direct traffic. (Jack Klasey)

Figure 22-3. Railroads use lights called "block signalling systems" to communicate with trains. (Jack Klasey)

Many forms of light are used in directing air traffic as well. Have you ever seen a rotating airport beacon at night? The green, red, or white signals guide airplanes as they fly overhead. Other lights along the runways assist approaching aircraft in landing. Flashing strobe lights also "point" the direction for planes headed toward runways, Figure 22-4. Light communication is very important to the safe operation of any airport system.

Water, or ***marine,*** vehicles also rely on light signals for direction and safety. Perhaps the best example of this type of signal is a lighthouse, Figure 22-5. The earliest lighthouses were simply fires built on high places. Today lighthouses operate electrically and have strong signal beacons (lights). During the day, most lighthouses can be recognized by their shape or distinctive stripes.

Many other forms of light communication are used to guide boats and ships. ***Buoys*** mark channels (deeper water) and harbors. Buoys are stationary floating devices with lights on top. Light

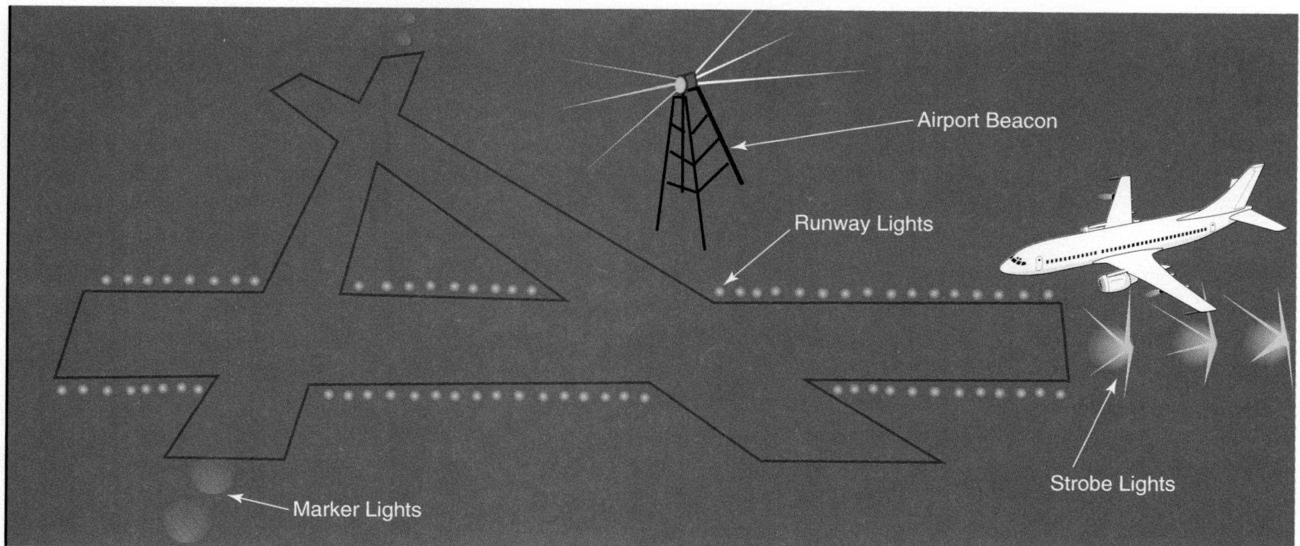

Figure 22-4. Light communication systems at airports are critical to the safe landing and takeoff of aircraft.

Figure 22-5. Lighthouses use strong lights to warn ships of dangerous waters and to lead them to port. This type of signaling is one of the earliest examples of light communication. (Kathy Kopf)

towers have also been built in the water miles off of coastlines, Figure 22-6. These large structures serve as points of reference for mariners (sailors). Their bright lights mark the entrance to local ports.

Figure 22-6. Modern light towers are positioned miles offshore to mark the entrance to ports and harbors.

ADVERTISING

Another important use of light communication is in advertising. Signs, banners, and other visual displays can be seen everywhere in your community. Most are lighted to attract a customer's attention, Figure 22-7. These lighted displays identify shops and create interest.

Figure 22-7. Lighted advertising displays can "grab" your attention.

Can you think of ways signs are lighted? Many signs are merely boxes with fluorescent lights inside. ***Fluorescent*** lights are the long, white tubes that can be found in most schools and offices. The plastic or glass coverings of these signs create an appearance of shape or color. Other advertising displays have flashing border lights. Colored lightbulbs draw attention to the message on a sign. A common type of colored light is produced using neon gas. These are called ***neon lights.***

Neon lights are made by glass blowers. Glass tubing is heated and bent into the shape of letters and designs, Figure 22-8. The tubing is then filled with neon or other gas. The gas acts as a conductor of electrical current. As electricity flows through the tube, the gas glows brightly. Different colors are produced by mixing various types of gas with the neon.

Figure 22-8. Neon lights are popular for commercial signs and advertising displays. These lights add bright colors to signs and make the signs more visible.

Flashing lights are another technique used to create interest in advertisements or other displays. Flashing lights attract more attention than light displays that do not flash. Flashing lights create movement and repetition. The human eye is naturally drawn to movement. Examples of flashing lights include portable roadway signs and signs for movie theaters. Warning signs usually have flashing lights, too. Red or yellow flashing lights signal dangerous areas. Police and other emergency vehicles have flashing lights to warn the public, Figure 22-9.

Flashing lights can work in two ways. In one method, all the lights go on and off at the same time. This creates the flashing effect but no movement. The second way is to have an electric current turn each bulb on in sequence. When one light goes off, the next one comes on. This procedure repeats itself and movement is created. This is often seen on theater marquees (signs). Marquees often have lights that form an arrow. With the lights being turned on and off in sequence, the arrow appears to move.

Figure 22-9. Emergency vehicles have many flashing lights to warn people. The lights are usually a combination of red, blue, white, and yellow lights. (Jack Klasey)

An additional use of light in communication is evening ***illumination.*** Lighted signs and displays line your city's streets and roads. Billboards are often equipped with bright lights to help travelers read them at night. Public buildings and monuments are also illuminated at night for appearance and safety.

As these examples have shown, light is very important to advertisers and related businesses. It brings life to many visual displays. What would your community be like without lighted signs and billboards?

INFORMATION TRANSMISSION

Light has always been important in the transmission of information. One of the earliest means of transmitting light signals was by ***reflection.*** Mirrors and other shiny objects were used to reflect the sun's rays. Pioneers heading west in frontier days signaled other travelers by this same method. The U.S. Navy still sends messages between ships using a series of light signals.

These examples of light communication involve the use of very basic technical principles. You are also informed by modern light systems. In airports, lighted signs mark gates and exits, Figure 22-10. Radio and TV stations use lighted signs to tell others of "live" shows being broadcasted. Different types of lights in elevators show you which floor you are on while in a highrise.

Indicator lights are found on most technological "gadgets." Lights show you if the oven, freezer, and microwave are working. Display lights on the dashboard of a car indicate trouble. The same is true of industrial machinery. Various lights tell if each machine is functioning properly, Figure 22-11.

Figure 22-10. Airports use lighted panels to inform passengers where various parts of the airport are located. Video monitors also tell passengers of departure and arrival times of flights. (Chicago Department of Aviation)

Figure 22-11. Production workers can monitor the functions of a machine by watching indicator lights. If trouble develops along the line, warning lights will flash on a panel. (Rockwell International Corp.)

Many machines exchange messages or "read" information by light signals. One example is a computer. A light pen is often used to enter information into a computer system, Figure. 22-12. Grocery stores use bar code readers to "scan" the item you are purchasing. In the construction and automobile industries, laser light is useful in determining distances. Laser light acts

Figure 22-12. Light pens can be used to enter items into a hand-held computer for inventory purposes. The "bar code" is scanned much like a cashier at the grocery store does. (Radio Shack, A Division of the Tandy Corporation)

as a surveying tool in measuring land areas. In the design of new cars, laser light helps determine sizes and shapes, Figure 22-13.

Figure 22-13. Laser light is often used to measure and record data in industry. (Chrysler Corp.)

Modern information systems also use light as a transmission medium. In Chapter 19 you learned that fiber optics use coded messages transmitted as pulses of light. Light, in the form of lasers, is also used to record vast amounts of data on computer disks, Figure 22-14. Computer CD-ROM and floptical drives can hold much

Figure 22-14. Floptical drives use light to read and write information. Floptical computer disks can hold much more information than conventional magnetic storage disks. (Hewlett-Packard Co.)

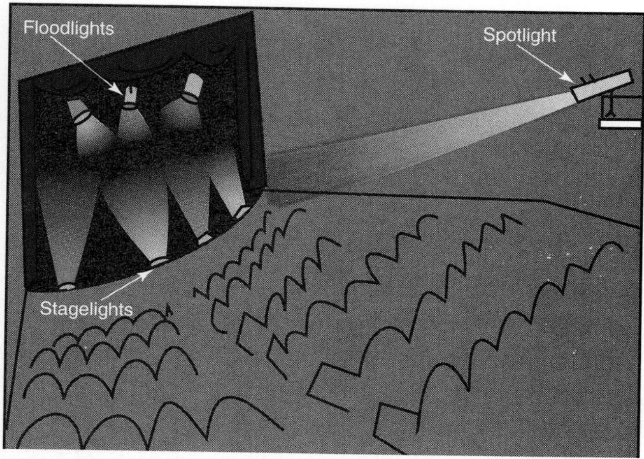

Figure 22-15. Theater lights illuminate the stage area from many angles.

more information than conventional, magnetic hard drives. At home, compact disc players and laser disc players are popular. Information in the form of audio sounds and video images is "read" from the disc by a laser.

ENTERTAINMENT

Light is also used for entertainment purposes. Both slide and movie projectors use light to project images onto a screen. Perhaps the most common example of ***projected imagery*** is a movie shown at a theater.

Another exciting use for light is found in concerts and stage shows. Large spotlights are used to illuminate the stage area, Figure 22-15. Brightly colored lights add much to the musical entertainment. In fact, light displays are often just as "exciting" as the music at many concerts and shows.

Three dimensional (3-D) images can be created with light. These displays are known as ***holograms.*** Most holograms are developed by beams of light intersecting in space. The light is usually projected through a fog or mist. A lifelike image is produced at the point where the light waves meet. Holograms also have important commercial value far beyond recreational. Credit cards are imprinted with holograms to help deter counterfeiting. Holograms are impossible to produce without special equipment and knowledge. Without these things, it is impossible to counterfeit a credit card.

Clearly, light is used in many ways. As a communication tool, visible light has become quite popular. Another form of light, the laser, is presented in the next section of this chapter. You will look at how lasers are used in communication.

LASERS IN COMMUNICATION SYSTEM

The term ***laser*** is an acronym. (An acronym is a word made up of letters that stand for something.) The acronym "laser" comes from the words **L**ight **A**mplification by **S**timulated **E**mission of **R**adiation. Therefore, laser light is a form of radiation that is amplified (boosted) to a high energy level. Laser light produces a strong, narrow beam of light. It does not disperse (spread out) and become lost energy when used. Laser light can be focused on a very tiny point, a long distance away. Laser light is coherent light. ***Coherent light*** means that the wavelengths of the light are all the same frequency. In other words, laser light is all the same "color." Laser light wavelengths are usually quite short. Short wavelengths are ideal for communication systems. With short wavelengths, messages can be sent faster and in large groups. A single pulse of light can contain thousands of messages. In addition, these signals can travel along a single medium at the same time. Laser light signals can be sent through the atmosphere or through transparent materials, like glass.

Sending light waves through the atmosphere has major drawbacks. For example, beams of light only travel in straight lines. This is often called ***line of sight transmission.*** Light energy cannot travel around corners of buildings or over hilly terrain. Another drawback is that these signals are easily interrupted. Light signals are affected by poor weather conditions, such as fog, rain, or clouds. Interference among different light signals also creates problems.

However, a system of transmitting light signals through "wires" has been developed. This method of communication is called ***fiber optics.*** The "wires" in fiber optics are called ***fiber-optic cables.*** Fiber-optic cables are made up of many smaller "wires" called ***optic fibers,*** Figure 22-16. Fiber optics avoids the drawbacks of sending signals through the atmosphere. Also, there is very little energy lost with fiber optics.

Fiber-optic cables can be made of glass, plastic, or a mixture of silica and other compounds. It is important that fiber-optic cables be free of impurities (defects and flaws). Flaws and defects interfere with the light signals being sent. Less impurities mean better transmissions.

Fiber-optic components are quickly replacing traditional electrical wires and circuits in many applications. Most long distance telephone calls travel on fiber-optic networks. Computer circuitry is now being made with fiber optics as well. The applications for fiber optics is virtually limitless. The following sections explain how fiber optic communication systems function.

Figure 22-16. In fiber optics, messages and data are transmitted as pulses of light that travel along optic fibers. Several optic fibers makeup a fiber-optic cable. A fiber-optic cable can relay millions of telephone calls at the same time. (Courtesy of Sprint)

TRANSMISSION OF FIBER OPTIC SIGNALS

Many telephone and cable TV companies use fiber-optic cables for sending messages, Figure 22-17. At the source of the transmission, signals (sound or video images) must be changed into pulses of light. This light source can be one of two forms: light emitting diodes (LEDs) or lasers.

An ***LED*** gives off visible light. A common use of LEDs is on calculator displays. LEDs can also be used in fiber optics. They are less costly and longer lasting than lasers.

A laser emits (gives off) coherent light. There are several different types of lasers available. Some produce red light. Other lasers may produce green or blue light. Despite costs, lasers are used more often than LEDs in fiber optics because they are more powerful. Lasers have the power to send a very strong signal.

Optic fibers have a number of advantages over standard copper wires. For example, optic fibers can carry many more signals than a copper wire. This is because light travels faster than electrical current.

Another advantage is that optic fibers are much smaller and lighter than copper wires, Figure 22-18. Optic fibers are about the thickness of a human hair. They can be used in places where there is little space. Optic fibers are free from most of the noise that occurs with copper wires.

A third advantage of fiber optics is that light signals do not fade as quickly as electrical signals. Copper wires need repeaters about every

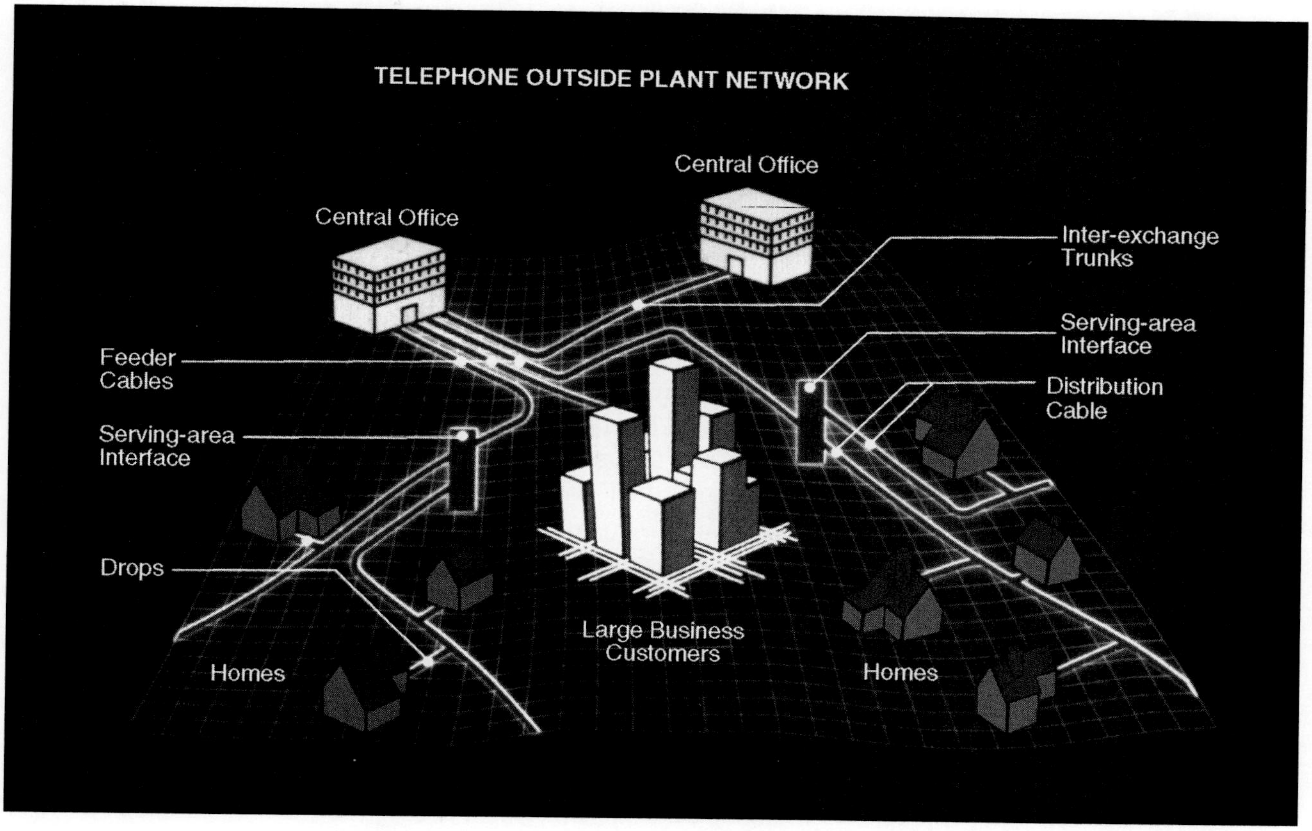

Figure 22-17. A typical fiber optic transmission system connects a telephone "central office" to businesses and homes. (Corning Glass Works)

Figure 22-18. A typical optic fiber (right) is actually the thickness of a human hair. A much larger copper cable (left) that is made up of many copper wires is needed to carry the same amount of information as a single optic fiber. (Courtesy of Sprint)

mile to boost signals. However, fiber-optic cables need repeaters only about every 14 miles.

When a signal reaches its destination, it must be decoded. In fiber optics, the light signal must be changed into an electronic signal. For example, if the destination is a computer, the light signals must be decoded into an electronic signal that the computer will understand.

CHAPTER 22 REVIEW

SUMMARY

Light is a very common communication medium. It can be as simple as a traffic light or as complex as a fiber-optic transmission. Light communication is used often in traffic control, advertising, information transmission, and the entertainment industry.

The laser is a very important tool used in light communication. Lasers can be used to communicate with spacecraft and satellites. Lasers are also used in fiber optics. Lasers and LEDs are used as a light source for sending thousands of messages over fiber-optic cables. These cables are made up of many small "wires" called optic fibers.

Light communication is a growing technology. Advances in light communication often allow advances in other technologies as well. Computers that use light for their circuits instead of electrical currents are one example.

KEY WORDS

All of the following words have been used in this chapter. Do you know their meanings?

Block signaling system
Buoys
Coherent light
Fiber optics
Fiber-optic cables
Fluorescent
Hologramsl
llumination
Laser
LED
Line of sight transmission
Marine
Neon lights
Optic fibers
Projected imagery
Reflection

TEST YOUR KNOWLEDGE

Place your answers on a separate sheet of paper. Please do not write in this book.

1. List three examples of light communication used in traffic control, entertainment, and advertising.
2. Today, _____ warn ships of dangerous waters. These devices are one of the earliest forms of light communication.

MATCHING QUESTIONS: Match the definition in the left-hand column with the correct term in the right-hand column.

3. Used in the evening to make signs and streets more visible.
4. Three-dimensional image created with light.
5. Used to mark channels of deep water and harbors.
6. An early method used for transmitting light signals.
7. Colored light made by glass blowers.

A. Buoys.
B. Holograms.
C. Neon lights.
D. Illumination.
E. Reflection.

8. What does the acronym "laser" mean?
9. Name two disadvantages to sending laser transmissions through the atmosphere.
10. In fiber optics, signals are sent as ______ of light along optic fibers.

ACTIVITIES

1. Waves of light from the sun are not coherent (they are incoherent). This means the waves of light are of different lengths (frequencies). Split a beam of sunlight with a prism to see these different lengths. Each color is a different frequency. Identify which colors have the highest frequencies. Write a short report on the differences between coherent light (lasers) and incoherent light (sunlight).
2. Make a list of light communication devices located in your home and in your school. Create a display board showing each of these devices. Give a short oral presentation explaining how these devices work.
3. Invite a representative from a telephone company to talk to your class about the latest uses for fiber optics. Ask the representative to explain how the systems they use work, what size load they can handle, and what costs are involved to install and maintain these systems.

CHAPTER 23 ACOUSTICAL COMMUNICATION

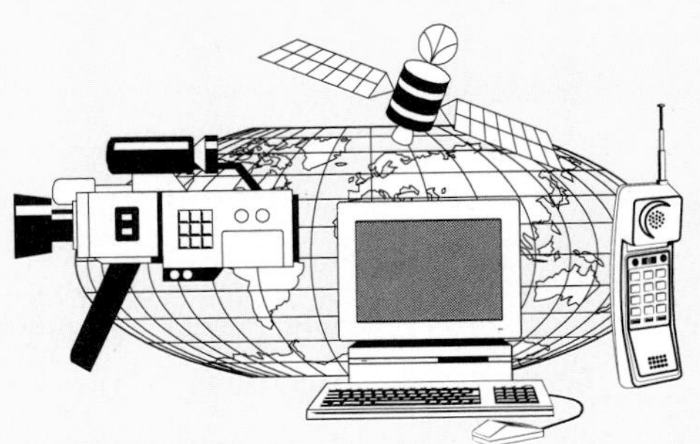

After studying this chapter, you will be able to:

- ❖ *Describe how audible signals are transmitted.*
- ❖ *List several acoustical communication systems.*
- ❖ *Identify the components of a stereo system.*
- ❖ *Explain the processes for making CDs and tapes.*
- ❖ *Illustrate sonar operation.*

Acoustical communication involves transmitting information with sound, Figure 23-1. The sounds in acoustical communication may be audible or inaudible to humans. You will recall that ***audible*** sounds are those that can be heard by humans. ***Inaudible*** sounds are also sounds, even though they cannot be heard by humans. A dog whistle, for example, is acoustical communication even though humans cannot detect the sound.

Figure 23-1. Musicians use their voices and instruments to create sounds. This is a form of acoustical information. This guitar is called an "acoustical guitar" because it can produce sounds without electronic amplification.

HOW SOUND WAVES TRAVEL

Like radio signals, sound also travels in waves. However, sound waves are created when there is a disturbance in a medium that has mass and is elastic.

Think of the medium as water in a swimming pool. Movement by your hand creates a disturbance which starts the wave. The ***mass*** of this first wave is the quantity (amount) of matter (water) that forms the wave. As this wave travels through the water, it builds up strength and speed. This is called ***momentum.*** The mass of the first wave has, therefore, built up momentum. The wave will continue until it hits the side of the pool or fades due to lack of momentum.

The wave also has elasticity. ***Elasticity*** is the ability of a mass to return to its original shape after an outside force has been removed. This means that after one wave travels through the water at a given spot, the water returns to its original shape. Then another wave can travel through the water. This motion will continue until the source of the motion (your hand) stops.

It is very important to note then that sound waves do not cause the medium to move. They are carried *through* the medium. Think of a boat that you may have seen in rough seas. The waves do not carry the boat along. Rather, the boat appears to just go "up" and "down" as the waves pass by it.

Now look at an example to put all this information together, Figure 23-2. Suppose someone standing next to you claps his or her hands. The pressure of two hands (mass) coming together (disturbance) creates a wave in the air (medium) surrounding you. The elasticity of the air allows the wave to ripple through the air. The wave then passes through your ear canal and strikes your eardrum. The eardrum also is elastic. It vibrates from the pressure of the wave. The frequency and pressure of the sound wave is duplicated (copied exactly) by the eardrum. The eardrum in turn sends a signal to your brain. This is how you hear.

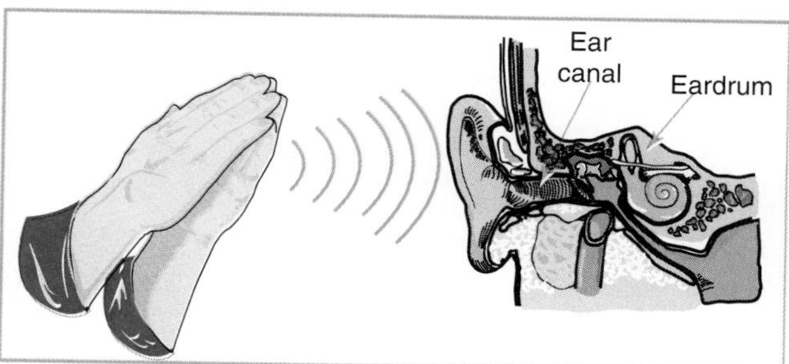

Figure 23-2. Can you identify the source, medium, and destination in this drawing?

In acoustical communication, messages are transmitted by sound waves (acoustical energy). The distance the message will travel depends on its pitch and intensity. Pitch and intensity make up the "power" of sound.

Pitch is determined by the frequency of the wave. A high-frequency wave will create a high-pitched sound. ***Intensity*** is determined by the power, or amplitude, of the wave. ***Loudness*** is how "strong" a sound seems to human ears. Loudness is a relative measurement. That means that how "loud" a sound is may vary from person to person. Therefore, a high-pitched, intense sound (that might seem "loud") will likely travel farther than a low-pitched, less intense sound (that might not seem "loud"). In addition, all sound waves are affected by interference from objects or natural occurrences (rain, snow, wind). Interference will also affect the distance a message will travel.

Acoustical information can also be transmitted with the aid of electrical energy. Electricity can help the acoustical signal to cover long distances. Radios and telephones are just two examples of acoustical information being helped by electrical energy. An acoustical sound is converted into electrical pulses. A receiver or speaker then converts the electrical signal back to a sound you understand.

A telephone uses a diaphragm to create a disturbance in the air (which is elastic). A ***diaphragm*** is a flexible membrane (similar to a rubber disk) attached to a solid frame, Figure 23-3. Electricity is used to "excite" the diaphragm. This makes the diaphragm vibrate. When the diaphragm vibrates, a sound wave is produced. This sound wave is identical to the original sound wave.

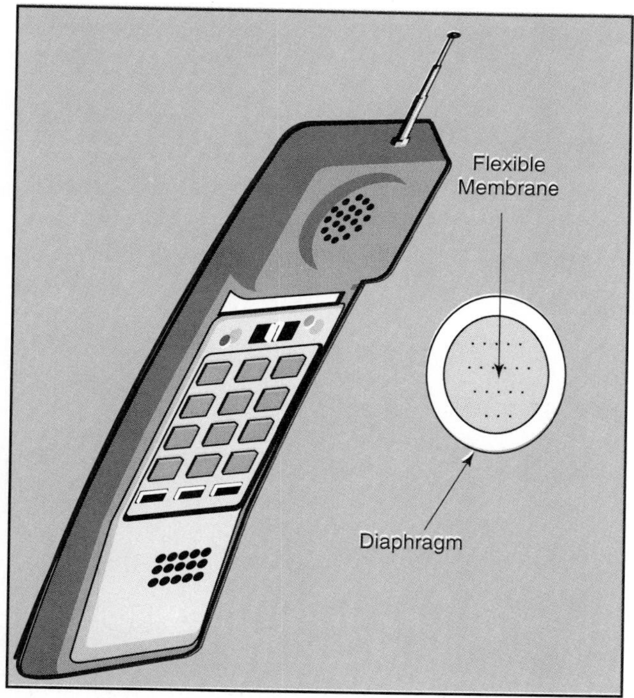

Figure 23-3. Telephone diaphragms are located in the receiver and in the transmitter of the handset. These diaphragms vibrate either creating an electrical signal or because of an electrical signal.

USES AND PURPOSES

Acoustical communication is used in many ways and for many purposes. Perhaps the most common use is for entertainment. Digital audio tapes (DATs), compact discs (CDs), and cassette tapes are all examples of entertainment. A sonar unit uses acoustical waves for measuring and locating purposes. Acoustical communication is also used to aid the handicapped. For example, to aid the blind, books are often read aloud and recorded on CDs or tapes, Figure 23-4.

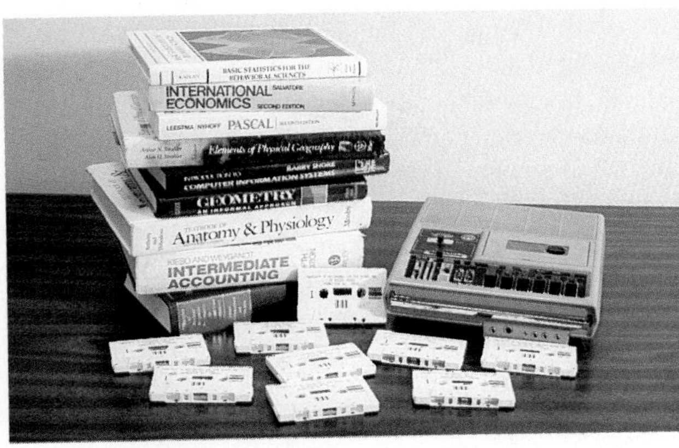

Figure 23-4. Audio tapes of books enable blind people to enjoy written works. (Courtesy of Recording for the Blind)

Acoustical Systems

Bells and horns can communicate many different messages. An alarm in the morning informs you when it is time to wake up. A fire engine siren warns of a dangerous situation. The sound of a car horn might also send a message.

Public address (PA) systems and loudspeakers can be found in many places. Nearly all schools and offices have PA systems. At school, a PA system might be used to make general announcements. In an office setting, it might be used to page (call) employees.

Another acoustical communication system you may know is a stereo system. A stereo system can be used for entertainment or information purposes. A typical stereo system may have a CD player, a receiver, and a tape deck.

You may not be very familiar with sonar systems, Figure 23-5. In sonar, sound waves are used to send signals through water. Sonar is rarely used for communication between two points. Rather, it is used for such things as measuring water depth and detecting the presence of solid objects. These objects may be either on top or underneath the water.

Figure 23-5. Sonar systems are used largely by industry and the military. Sonar systems are also used to identify the location of fish. (GE Aerospace)

STEREO SYSTEMS

Do you have a large collection of CDs and tapes? Do you know someone else who does? The recording industry is large and profitable. Every year, millions of music enthusiasts (those who enjoy music) buy millions of recordings. In order for them to enjoy their CDs or tapes, stereo systems are required.

The stereo system is designed to give a full, lifelike transmission of a recording. Stereo systems come in many forms. They can be small and portable, like a personal cassette player. Others can be large and complex. Power can range from weak to strong.

No matter what the size or power of a stereo system, however, they usually contain the following equipment: receiver, amplifier, playback unit (tape deck/CD player), and speakers, Figure 23-6. These components contribute to the overall sound quality produced by the system. One bad piece of equipment will cause the entire system to sound bad.

Figure 23-6. A variety of stereo systems are available to consumers. Some are large and others can be very small. (Sony Corp.)

Receiver

The ***receiver*** in a stereo system "tunes in" FM and AM radio signals. A receiver is the component that contains the buttons for selecting the bands (AM, FM) and for selecting the radio station. The receiver is also known as the ***tuner,*** Figure 23-7. In very simple systems, the receiver is called a radio.

Figure 23-7. A receiver, or tuner, is the part of the stereo system that receives and amplifies radio signals. Receivers usually are the "control center" of the stereo system and many of the other components operate through this component. (Sony Corp.)

Amplifier

The amplifier is the most important part of a stereo system, Figure 23-8. The ***amplifier*** accepts electrical signals from the CD player, tape deck, or receiver. The amplifier then powers (boosts) the signals enough to activate the speakers.

A good amplifier will closely reproduce the sound. That is, the final sounds are nearly identical to the transmitted signal. In addition, it will boost the signals without introducing interference of any kind.

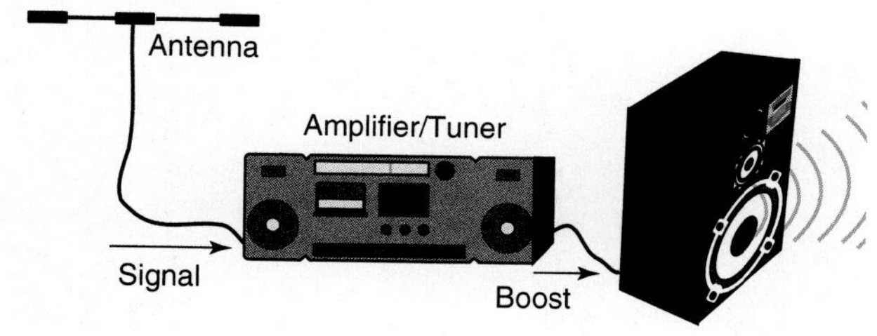

Figure 23-8. Amplifiers are often housed along with the tuner in modern stereo systems.

Speakers

Speakers change electrical energy back into acoustical energy. They should reproduce a broad range of sounds. Just how good or bad a speaker "sounds," however, depends largely on personal taste.

Speakers come in several types. Crystal speakers and electrostatic speakers are often used along with other speakers for quality reproduction. A dynamic speaker is perhaps the most common speaker for home stereo systems.

A dynamic speaker works using a wire wrapped around a permanent magnet. The magnet is mounted next to a diaphragm. When the electric current comes through the wire, a magnetic field is created between the magnet and the diaphragm. As the magnetic field changes, the diaphragm vibrates. This vibration produces sound waves.

A speaker produces sound by making sound waves in a cone-shaped area. Each speaker has two of these areas. They are called the woofer and the tweeter, Figure 23-9. Low-frequency sounds are sent out through the ***woofer.*** This is because low-frequency waves move slowly back and forth over a large area. The woofer is large enough to send out a low-frequency wave with good sound. The ***tweeter*** is used to send out high-frequency sound. High-frequency waves move rapidly over a small area. Therefore, the smaller tweeter is used to produce high-frequency tones.

Figure 23-9. Stereo speakers are an important part of a stereo system. A stereo only sounds as good as the speakers connected to it. (Fisher)

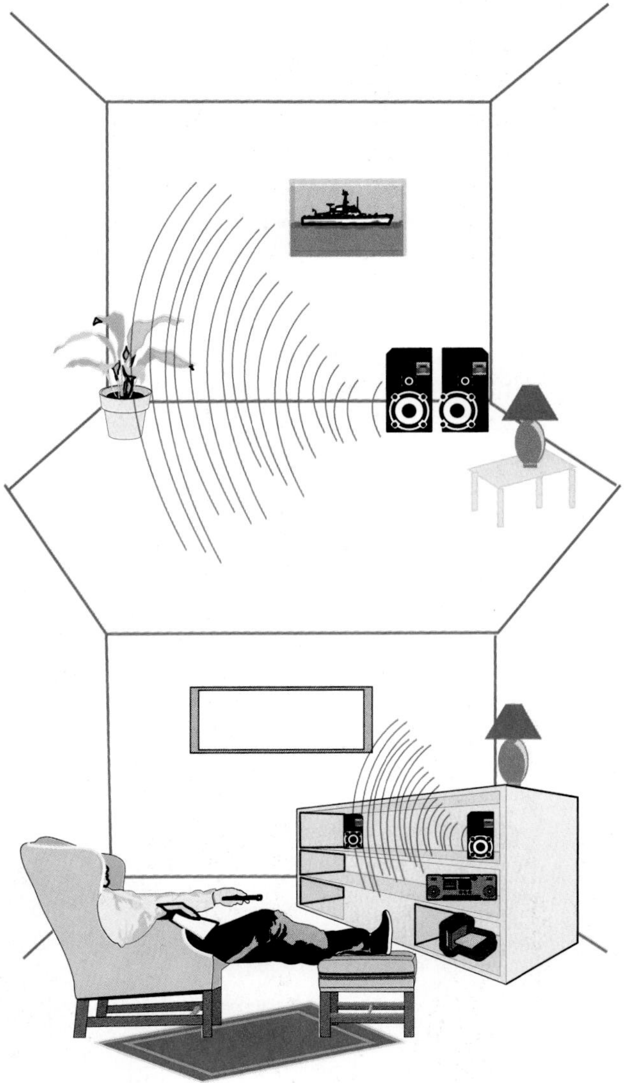

Figure 23-10. Sound can travel much farther in a room with a few pieces of furniture and a high ceiling (top). Furniture, plants, and carpet can all absorb a great deal of sound (bottom).

The sound reproduced by speakers depends a great deal on where they are placed. For example, in a room with a low ceiling that contains a great deal of furniture, volume may need to be turned up. This is because the sound is absorbed by all the furniture. Just the opposite is true for a room with high ceilings and a few pieces of furniture, Figure 23-10.

Compact disc player

A ***compact disc player*** uses a laser to "read" a compact disc. The disc is usually made of polycarbonate (a type of plastic) with a thin metal plate inside. The metal plate is what gives a CD the silver color. The metal plate is etched with high and low spots, or "pits," that represent a binary code. This binary code represents the music that was recorded on that disc.

CD players come in many styles and varieties, Figure 23-11. Some can only play one disc at a time. Others can have five, six, or more discs loaded into them. These ***multidisc CD players*** can be programmed to play at random, in a certain order, or from the first track on the first CD to the last track on the last CD. Some of these players even allow you to change the discs while one of the discs is playing.

Figure 23-11. Compact disc players come in a variety of sizes with many different features. All use a laser to "read" a compact disc. (Sony Corp.)

Tape Deck

The ***tape deck*** is used to record and/or play audio tapes. The recording or playing of a tape is done by stationary heads. Stationary means they do not move. Good machines have three heads. One head is for erasing, one is for recording, and one is for playback.

There are three types of tape decks: cassette, reel-to-reel, and cartridge. You are probably most familiar with cassette decks. They use cassette tapes and are the most common. A cassette tape is a plastic "case" that contains two spools. The tape inside will wind on one spool as it unwinds from the other. Cassette tapes have two "sides."

A reel-to-reel tape deck uses reel-to-reel tape. The tape starts out entirely on one reel. It is threaded past the heads to the take-up reel, Figure 23-12. When all the tape is used, it will all be on the take-up reel. This is the same way that a cassette tape works, but the reels are much larger and not enclosed in a case. A reel-to-reel tape usually has only one "side."

A cartridge tape deck also uses a tape that is contained inside a plastic case (like cassettes are). However, a cartridge tape contains one continuous loop of tape. Rewinding is not needed with cartridge tapes. Radio stations use this type of tape deck for advertisements and sound bites (short samples of voices or sounds). This type of tape usually has four "sides."

Compact Discs and Tapes

How useful would a stereo system or tape deck be if there was nothing available to play on it? CDs and tapes are used to store acoustical information for playback.

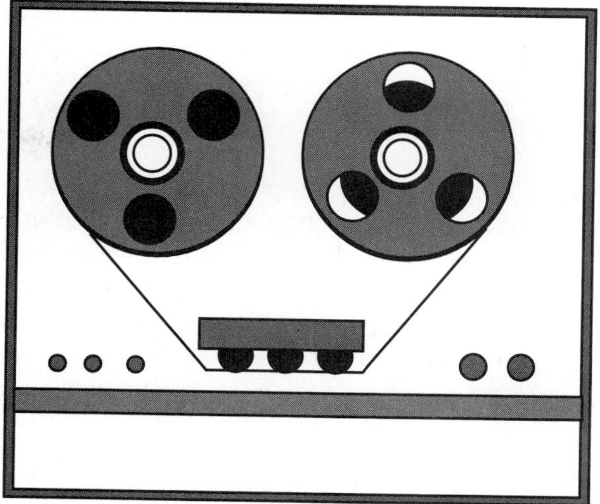

Figure 23-12. A reel-to-reel recorder is often used in audio production work.

Almost all music recorded today is recorded in ***stereophonic,*** or "***stereo.***" Stereophonic recordings are made using several microphones. They are placed in different areas of the recording studio. During the recording process, the recording levels of these microphones are adjusted between the left and right "channels." The result of this is that during playback the sounds seem to be "split apart" because each ear hears different sounds. Microphones are used to change human voices and musical instruments into electrical signals. As electrical signals, they can be recorded.

Compact discs are a very popular storage device for recorded sounds. A laser beam "reads" the sound information from the disc. The sound is recorded as a series of high and low spots on the surface of the disc. These "pits" represent a binary code. When the disc is played, it rotates past the laser. Change in the surface of the disc causes the laser signal to fluctuate (change). The fluctuations are interpreted as a binary code. The binary code is then changed into electric signals. These signals make the cones in the speakers vibrate, which in turn produce acoustical waves.

One of the most important advantages of CDs is the quality of the sound produced. Dust and wear on a tape can be picked up by the tape head. This becomes noise in the sound transmission. With compact discs, the laser does not read dust. In addition, there is no physical contact with the CD. Therefore, compact discs avoid the problem of sounding "old" and "worn out." Compact discs and compact disc players are inexpensive and readily available. This technology has almost completely replaced records just as cassette tapes replaced 8-track tapes.

Tapes are plastic strips coated with a magnetic material. When a recording is made on tape, sound waves from the microphone or instrument are changed into electrical signals. These signals are sent into an electric coil. This coil is known as a ***recording head.*** As the tape passes by the head, the electrical signals change the coating of magnetic material on the tape. Refer to Figure 23-13.

STEREO SYSTEM OPERATIONS

Playing back, or retrieving, sound recordings is a simple process. Very generally stated, playback is the reverse of recording. When a machine is reproducing the sound on a tape or CD, it is "reading" the code on the tape or CD. The technical systems used for playback are usually very similar to the systems used to record the sounds.

Analog Stereo Systems

Tape recordings are played back by running the tape past a ***playback head.*** The tape must pass the playback head at the same speed that the recording was made. The magnetic signals on the tape create an electrical current in the coil on the head. This current will reproduce (copy) the sound recorded. The signal is amplified and projected through a speaker system, Figure 23-14.

This is analog recording because the code, or electrical impulses, on the tape tend to vary constantly (or "smoothly"). You will recall from Chapter 19 that digital signals represent discreet numbers while analog signals tend to vary constantly.

Digital Stereo Systems

Have you listened lately to a compact disc recording? Did you notice the quality of the sound? Did the music sound "live?" Compact disc players can be components of digital stereo systems. Digital Audio Tape (DAT) players can also be components of digital stereo systems.

Digital recordings change the analog signals from microphones and conventional musical instruments to digital, or ***binary,*** code. (Some musical instruments called MIDI instruments produce digital signals.) The binary code is then imprinted on a CD or DAT. When a CD or DAT is played, the binary code is changed back to analog waves. These electrical analog signals are sent to the speakers which reproduce the original sound waves. This process works much the same way telephone signals are converted in digital phone systems.

The sound quality of digital stereo systems is much greater than that of analog systems. In addition, the storage devices (CDs and DATs) last much longer than conventional tapes. These and other advantages are making digital stereo systems more popular every year.

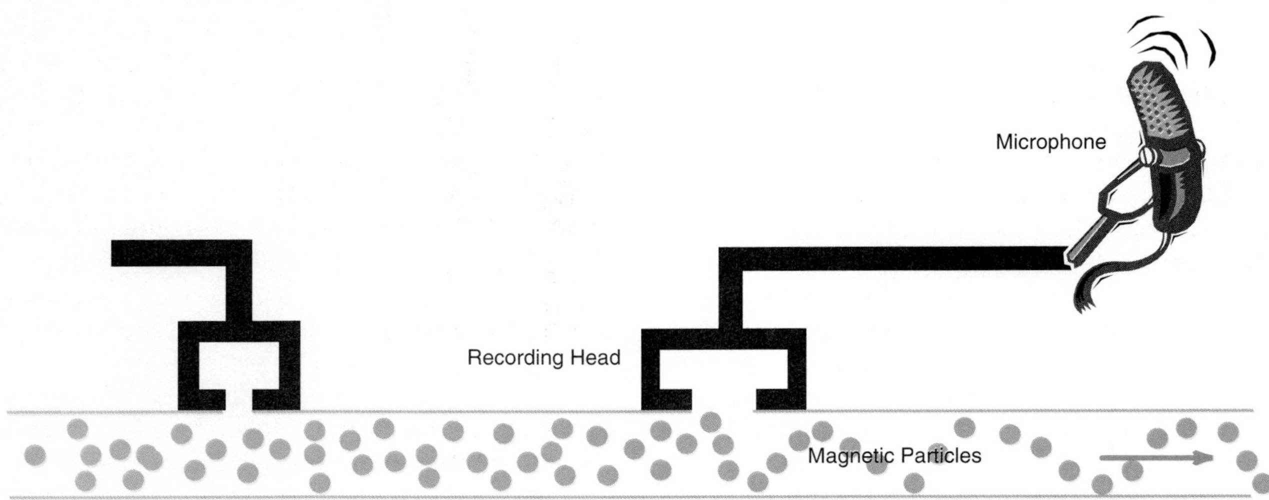

Figure 23-13. When recording on tape, the recording head "aligns" the magnetic particles on the tape. This creates a pattern that represents the sound being recorded.

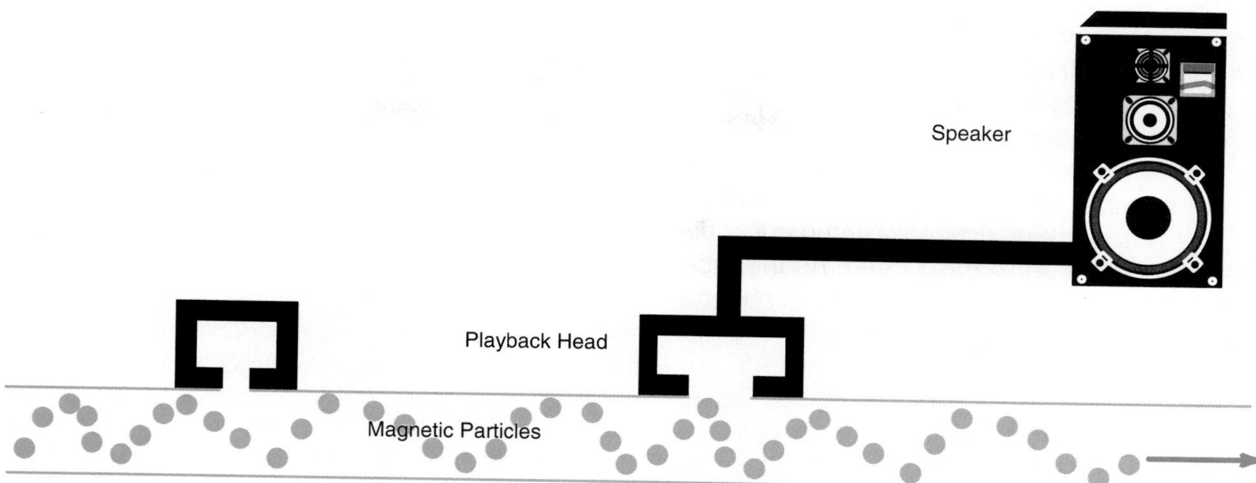

Figure 23-14. When a recorded tape is played, the playback head detects the aligned magnetic particles of the tape. The head then converts this into an electrical signal.

SONAR SYSTEMS

Sonar is a system that uses sound to locate objects underwater or on the water's surface. Sonar can detect old sunken ships, schools of fish, submarines, or distant surface ships. Sonar stands for **So**und **Na**vigation and **R**anging.

Sonar Operation

Sonar works using sound waves, Figure 23-15. Since sound is actually a wave of pressure, a sound wave moves easily through water. Sonar is often used to determine the depth of water. Sonar can "find" the ocean floor and determine its surface features. It is also used by ships to detect submarines and by submarines to detect ships. Sonar is not very useful for sending messages. It is primarily used as a source of information. This would be a form of machine-to-human communication.

Sonar uses "echoes" to determine the location of objects. You probably have seen a movie where sonar has been used. The "pings" or "echoes" that are heard when a submarine is tracking a ship is the sonar being used. A pulse of acoustical energy is transmitted through the water. This sound wave travels until it strikes an object large enough to reflect the original wave. The reflection of the original wave travels back toward the source of the sound. This reflection is detected as an ***echo*** at the source. The size and distance of the reflected object can be learned by studying the echo. The amount of original wave that was reflected will give the shape. The time that passed between the original transmission and the receiving of the echo determines the distance.

Figure 23-15. The U.S. Navy uses sonar in search and recovery work. The sonar creates a visual image of the sea floor. The image appears on the ship's monitor. (U.S. Navy)

Sound waves in sonar are made by a transducer. The ***transducer*** is a device that acts like an underwater microphone and loudspeaker. It picks up and sends out sound waves. Two types of sonar are used commonly: passive and active.

Passive sonar is used to listen for sounds. It does not transmit sound waves. With the use of passive sonar, position, distance, and depth cannot be learned. The only thing that can be determined with passive sonar is whether or not an object, like a ship, is in the water.

Active sonar sends out and listens for sound waves. It is used when distance, depth, and location must be known. Active sonar will not only determine that there is an object in the water, it will also give the exact location of that object.

Basically, there are three ways to use active sonar. First, active sonar can be used by ships by dropping a transducer, much like an anchor, Figure 23-16. Any echoes sent back reach a receiver on the bottom of the ship.

A second method for using active sonar is the ***sonubuoy,*** Figure 23-17. This is a transducer with a collar to keep it afloat. Sonubuoys are dropped by aircraft and float in the water, with the transducer lowered on a line, several hundred feet below the surface. Any sounds picked up by the transducer are sent back to the aircraft. This is done through a transmitter located in the buoy.

Fixed sonar is another method for using active sonar, Figure 23-18. In this way, the transducer is attached to the vessel, usually a submarine or fishing boat. The sound waves are sent out from the ship and the echoes are received in the same location.

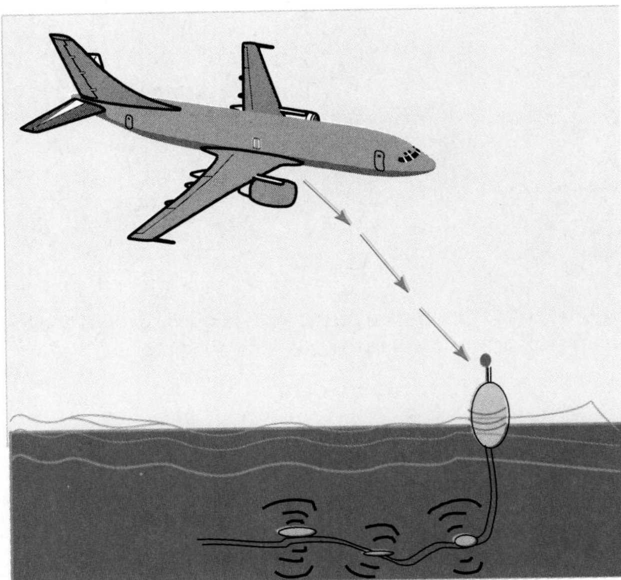

Figure 23-17. Sonubuoys float in the water. A transducer is suspended below the water that sends and receives sonar signals. These signals are transmitted by radio waves to planes flying overhead.

Figure 23-16. Ships use sonar to detect sea depth. When the signal detects bottom, an echo is reflected back to the ship.

Figure 23-18. Submarines use fixed sonar to detect underwater objects and ships on the surface.

CHAPTER 23 REVIEW

SUMMARY

Acoustical communication involves communicating with sound. Sound travels in waves. The waves are created by a disturbance in a medium that has mass and elasticity. The distance a message travels depends on pitch and intensity. However, several electrical devices will aid acoustical communication in traveling farther.

Many types of acoustical communication systems exist in the world today. One of the most popular is the stereo system. A stereo system consists of a receiver, amplifier, playback unit, and speakers. Each component has a specific function to do. CDs and tapes are also part of the stereo communication system.

Sonar is another acoustical communication system. Sonar uses sound to detect underwater objects. Sonar has many applications in the exploration of the ocean, in military and rescue situations, in archaeology to find sunken ships, and to locate schools of fish.

KEY WORDS

All of the following words have been used in this chapter. Do you know their meanings?

Active sonar
Audible
Amplifier
Binary
Compact discs
Compact disc player
Diaphragm
Echo
Elasticity
Fixed sonar
Inaudible
Intensity
Loudness
Mass
Momentum
Multidisc CD player
Passive sonar
Pitch
Playback head
Receiver
Recording head
Sonar
Sonubuoy
Speakers
Stereo
Stereophonic
Tape deck
Tapes
Transducer
Tuner
Tweeter
Woofer

TEST YOUR KNOWLEDGE

Place your answer on a separate sheet of paper. Please do not write in this book.

MATCHING QUESTIONS: Match the definition in the left-hand column with the correct term in the right-hand column.

1. The ability of a body to return to its original shape.	A. Pitch.
2. Sounds that cannot be heard by humans.	B. Mass.
3. The amount of matter that forms an object.	C. Momentum
4. Building of strength and speed.	D. Elasticity.
5. Frequency of a sound.	E. Inaudible.
6. Strength of a sound.	F. Intensity.

7. List three common uses of acoustic communication.
8. List four applications for sonar and explain how sonar is used in each application.
9. In speakers, low-frequency sounds are sent out through the _____ and high-frequency sounds are sent out through the _____.
10. Explain the difference between analog stereo systems and digital stereo systems.
11. Define "stereophonic."

ACTIVITIES

1. Research sound and different properties of sound. Write a short report on your research.
2. Bring in articles from magazines and newspapers on trends in acoustical communication. Use these articles for a class discussion on acoustical communication.
3. Collect examples (or photos of examples) of the uses of sonar. Get examples of commercial, industrial, and personal uses. Prepare a short oral report on your research.
4. Ask a stereo store sales representative to explain the latest in stereo components. Ask how these devices operate, which devices are the most popular, and the differences between the new devices and older devices.

Though intense, realistic graphics may be what interest you in new video games, sound remains an important part of the game. Different sounds may alert you to "danger" nearby, or may tell you that you have reached a bonus level. Next time you play your favorite video game, turn the sound off. How is the game different? (Nintendo of America)

CHAPTER 24

BROADCASTING

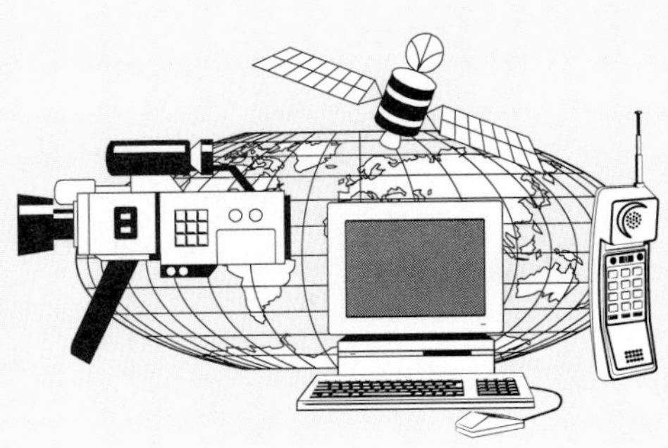

After studying this chapter, you will be able to:

- ❖ *Explain the daily operations of a typical broadcasting station.*
- ❖ *Identify the types of equipment used to broadcast TV and radio programs.*
- ❖ *Describe the purpose and duties of various personnel at a broadcasting station.*

Broadcasting has become a major part of everyday life for people around the world, Figure 24-1. Yet, broadcasting is a very young industry. Radio has only been around since the 1920s. Network television has only existed since the 1950s. Cable TV stations only became popular as recently as the 1970s.

Figure 24-1. Many different types of TV shows can be seen everyday. These programs inform, educate, and entertain. (Columbia College Chicago)

TV and radio programming provide hours of information and enjoyment each day. You stay informed of local and world events by watching or listening to news broadcasts. Weather warnings allow you to plan for bad weather. Sports programs provide entertainment. Game shows amuse you and challenge your knowledge. You hear current "hits" by listening to the radio or watching music videos, Figure 24-2.

Figure 24-2. DJs play the music that you hear on the radio. How often do you listen to you favorite songs on the radio? (Columbia College Chicago)

Commercial broadcasting often seems fairly simple to the common viewer or listener. However, the technical side of modern broadcasting is very complex.

INTRODUCTION TO BROADCASTING

You have learned that broadcasting includes the transmission of television and radio signals. These broadcasts take many forms. Some of the basic types of broadcasts include commercial, private, recreational, and federal/military broadcasts.

Network stations (ABC, CBS, NBC, and Fox) send out ***commercial broadcasts. Private*** and ***recreational broadcasts*** are sent and received by certain interested groups. CBs, ham radios, and walkie-talkies are used for private and recreational purposes. ***Federal/military broadcasts*** are conducted by the government and the Armed Forces. In this chapter, you will look at commercial broadcasting. Commercial broadcasting is perhaps the most common type of broadcasting.

Basic Equipment and Facilities

Commercial TV and radio broadcasts use much of the same equipment. Also, they both are created in a ***studio.*** This is the center of activity and attention. Most broadcast programming is recorded in the enclosed studio area. A radio studio is often smaller than a television studio, Figure 24-3. Both radio and TV studios are designed for the electronic equipment they must contain. Soundproof glass and padded walls prevent noise from entering the sound studio. Support equipment is kept out of the way of announcers and newscasters. In TV studios, an attractive "set" hides ugly walls and fixtures. Cameras are always positioned to show only the set and not the other parts of the studio, Figure 24-4.

Figure 24-4. Cameras in a TV studio must always be placed so that the bare walls and floors are not shown on TV. Here, this individual is making sure that all of the cameras are in the correct places. (Columbia College Chicago)

Next to most studios is the control room, Figure 24-5. From this area, the producer can monitor programming as it happens. From here, shows can be edited, special effects added, or commercials inserted into the broadcast. The radio or TV signals leaving the control center go directly to the transmitter facilities.

Many types of electronic equipment are used inside TV and radio studios. Perhaps the most common is a ***microphone*** (or "mike").

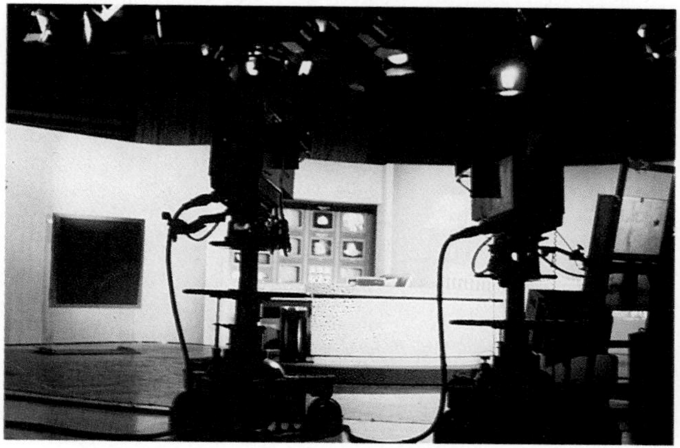

Figure 24-3. Television and radio studios can be quite different. A television studio must be large enough for a set, cameras, and workers (left). A radio studio often has the controls, disc and tape players, and microphone in one small room (right). (NBC, Columbia College Chicago)

Figure 24-5. Control rooms are used to monitor television and radio programs. From the control room, the producer can direct the actions of the crew. (Columbia College Chicago)

Figure 24-7. In the radio studio, boom microphones keep the control area clear. (Ball State University)

Microphones come in many forms. ***Directional microphones*** are placed in various positions around the studio. When only one voice is to be heard, a ***unidirectional microphone*** is used, Figure 24-6. "Unidirectional" means in one direction only. Therefore, a unidirectional microphone will pick up sounds in only one direction. Announcers often use unidirectional mikes to quiet background noise. ***Boom microphones*** can be suspended (hung) above the speaker or actors. This is done to keep the microphone out of the way of the workers, Figure 24-7. Boom microphones are used very often in TV to keep the microphone out of the picture. Other microphones include ***shotgun*** and ***cardioid*** models.

Some types of equipment are used only in TV or only in radio broadcasting. For example, cameras, lights, and videotape recorders are found only in television stations. Devices found most often in radio studios include audio recorders and reel-to-reel tape equipment.

Broadcasting Personnel

Personnel are workers at a business. Broadcasting firms employ many people. The most recognized job is that of the "on-air" personality, Figure 24-8. These people work as actors, newscasters, and disc jockeys.

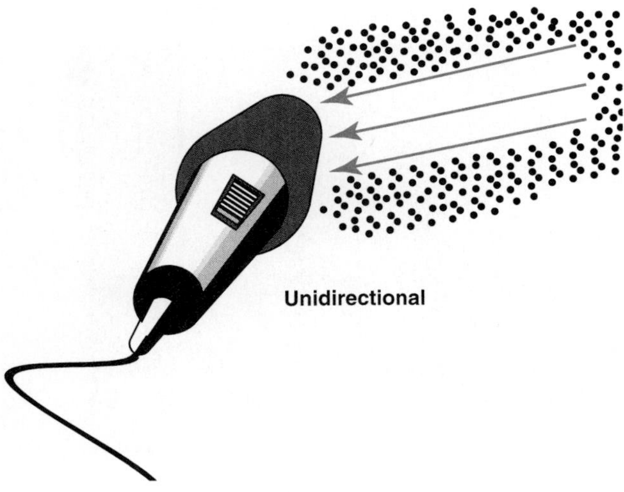

Figure 24-6. Unidirectional microphones pick up sound coming from one area in a room.

Figure 24-8. The most recognized people in the broadcast industry are those that can be seen or heard on air. (WGN Television)

While on-air positions may seem glamorous, the workload is heavy. These people work even when they are not on the air. For example, television newscasters often research their own stories. At a small radio station, a disc jockey might also sell advertising time to local businesses. Many on-air personalities have advanced degrees. Training in speech and journalism is common for all on-air staff.

In broadcasting, many people work "behind-the-scenes." The jobs done by these people are as important as the work of the on-air personality. The ***chief engineer*** is responsible for the equipment at the station. The chief engineer must make sure all equipment works correctly. Without a chief engineer, the station would not be able to broadcast.

Radio and TV shows require a ***producer*** to keep the show running. For example, when a radio talk show takes calls from listeners, the producer picks those calls that will get on the air. The producer also alerts the host when commercial breaks are coming. Talk shows often have additional personnel giving news and sports updates.

Other personnel prepare the script (or copy) for a broadcast. These people are known as ***script writers.*** The script is the text that will be read over the air. Some people write the news stories for announcers. Others create advertising slogans and feature items. These employees usually have a college education in a field like journalism, English, or communication. Other behind-the-scenes personnel include sales staff and camera operators, Figure 24-9. The ***sales staff*** is responsible for selling "air-time" for commercials. The ***camera operators*** "shoot" the action as it is happening.

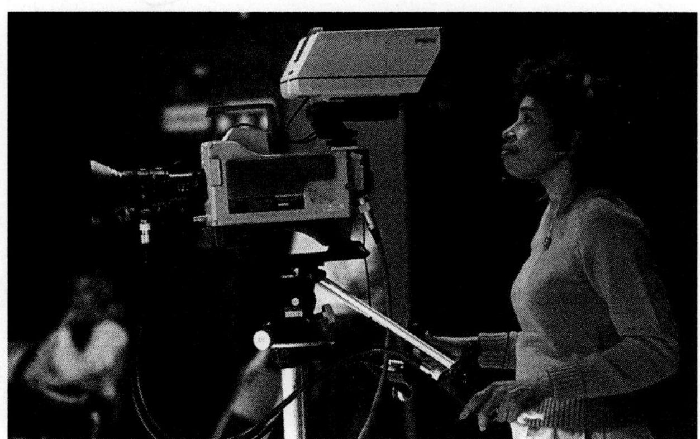

Figure 24-9. Camera operators have specialized training to effectively do their jobs. (Columbia College Chicago)

COMMERCIAL RADIO BROADCASTING

Being organized is the key to success in broadcasting. This means all employees are working as a unit to reach a common goal. The common goal is often to have the best (most listened to) station. To reach this goal, the station must be organized. Some people must be in charge. Others must be willing to listen. Most commercial radio stations are organized in the same way: ownership, management, and staff, Figure 24-10.

Figure 24-10. The organization of a radio station begins with the owners and is carried down to the staff.

Ownership

Many people own things. Some people own cars. Some own houses. Radio stations are also owned by someone. Often it is not just one person that owns a radio station, but a group of people. This form of ownership is called a ***corporation.*** Many stations are owned by other companies. The owner holds the broadcasting license to the station.

Owners have the final word concerning the radio station. They set policies for the station. For example, the owner decides what type of advertising and programming will be used. Owners also make key decisions concerning money. This may include buying a new transmitter or increasing the salary of a disc jockey.

Management

Radio station owners normally are not present at the station itself. They are not involved in the day-to-day work. Instead, owners rely on the management group to run the station. A ***station manager,*** or ***general manager,*** heads the team. Other managers (or supervisors) direct each area of the station, Figure 24-11.

The most important job of station managers is deciding which market they want as listeners. A ***market*** is a certain group of people that the station wants to attract. For example, stations that are aimed at the adult market usually have more talk and not as much popular music by current groups. Stations that are aimed at a teen-age market usually play "top 40" music or "album-oriented radio (AOR)." Foreign language stations specialize in delivering news to certain ethnic groups.

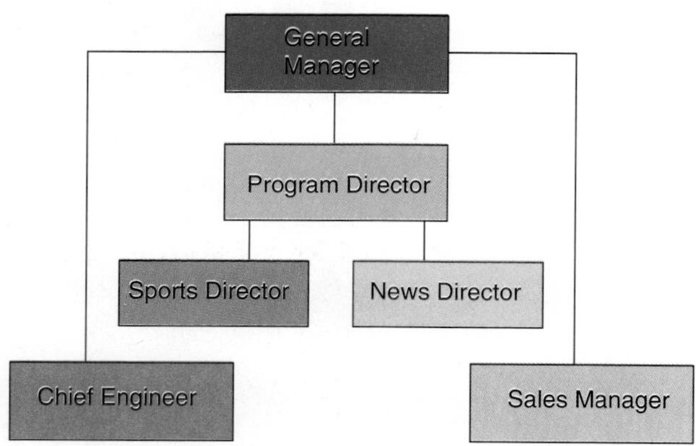

Figure 24-11. The management team in a radio station is quite complex.

Once managers decide which market they want to appeal to, many more decisions are made. The biggest is whether to go all music, all talk, all news, or a combination. This is called the format. ***Format*** is the type of programs the stations will provide. After the decision is made on the format, managers then decide what type of on-air personalities to hire. They also plan the broadcast day. The daily schedule is often shown as a ***program clock,*** or ***wheel,*** Figure 24-12.

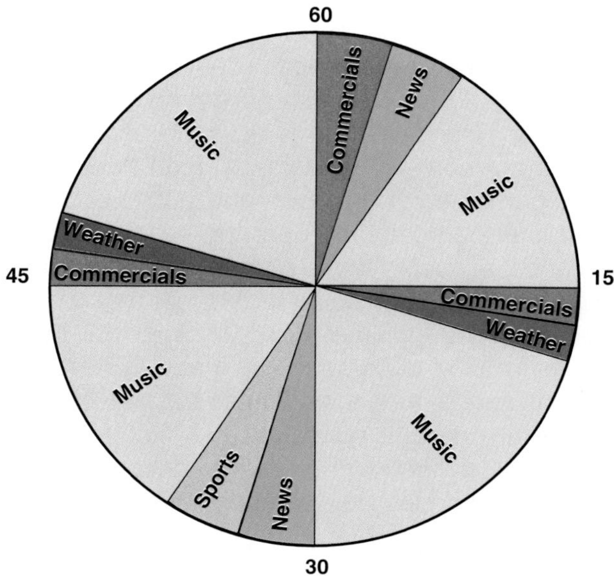

Figure 24-12. A program clock (or wheel) shows the programming for a station. What format do you think is used at this station?

Staff

The staff actually performs the day-to-day tasks of the station. Staff includes disc jockeys, newscasters, engineers, office assistants, and receptionists. The combined efforts of these people make the station successful. Depending upon the size of the station, staff jobs vary. Larger stations have different people for almost every task. Staff at smaller stations often perform more than one job.

Programming and Script Writing

Programming involves deciding what kind of features will be broadcast. It also includes the time of day that the features will be broadcast. Refer back to Figure 24-12. Programming is an important part of any successful radio station. Good programming will match the "wants" of the intended market to the broadcast. This will attract the desired listeners.

The programming format varies with the station. Music stations can play rock-and-roll, alternative, jazz, classical, or other types of music. An all-news format would have different items featured throughout the day. Interviews and talk shows might be aired late in the day. Sports programs are many times broadcast "live" (as it happens). Live broadcasts may interrupt the normal schedule of the station.

Script writing is not used as much in radio as it was in the 1930s and 1940s. At that time, before television, radio stations broadcast popular shows such as *The Shadow, The Lone Ranger,* and *Little Orphan Annie.* These were similar to television shows of today, except that everything was done through the use of sound only. There was no visual image. These shows required a script that was well developed to communicate scenes and action without a "picture" to aid the listener. Some shows such as *Days of Our Lives, Gunsmoke,* and *The Lone Ranger* carried over to TV when that medium became popular. For the most part, TV meant the end of these types of shows on radio. However, there are still some of these radio shows being broadcast. Nation Public Radio (NPR) airs several programs of this type nationally.

Script writing is now used most often for commercials and public service announcements (PSAs). Many businesses ask the station on which they advertise to write their commercials. The business supplies information for the commercial. The ***continuity writer*** works this into a script. Music and/or sound effects are often included in the commercial. This same process occurs for PSAs, Figure 24-13.

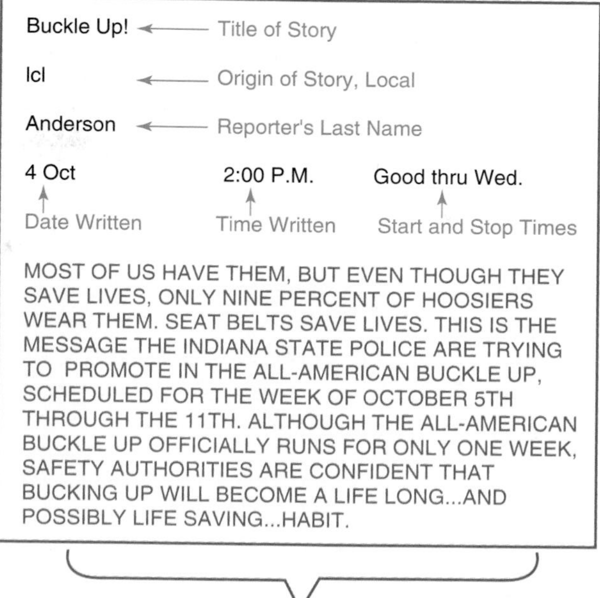

Figure 24-13. A script is used by radio announcers so that they do not have to memorize everything that needs to be said. (WBST, Muncie, Indiana)

Production Techniques

Production means getting all the needed items together in order to put a show on the air. Different formats need different production techniques.

Good sound quality is important for a music format. Therefore, the best playback equipment must be used. Tapes or compact discs (CDs) are used to broadcast music. The sound quality of these media is much improved from records.

Music shows also require a large music library. Usually a music show can be run by the disc jockey (DJ). DJs can play commercials, read the news, and play music without the help of others. With the use of digital electronics and computers, even DJs can be replaced with machines. A complete, around-the-clock radio broadcast can be run from a computer sitting on a desk connected to a multidisc CD player. (In this case, the entire staff of the radio station can be effectively reduced to one part-time employee.)

Standard radio work involves mixing audio sounds for transmission. Speech, music, and other sounds are picked up by microphones. These different signals are mixed, or combined, in a console. All audible sounds should be recorded as close to the same level as possible. On the control panel, a meter that shows volume units (VUs) shows the signal strength. (A VU meter is similar to the "recording levels" on your home stereo system.)

From the production area, the radio signal goes to the transmitter. The transmitter boosts the signal to the assigned frequency of the station. Radio transmitting antennas are often hundreds of feet tall. Transmission antennas are the devices which beam the signals to your home and car radios.

A great deal of work goes into a commercial radio broadcast. You have looked at the basic work that is done. This work is exciting and important. Many people rely on radio broadcasts to stay informed. Radio broadcasting is an important part of the communications family.

COMMERCIAL TELEVISION BROADCASTING

Over 97 percent of homes in the country have television sets. This means television has some impact on almost everyone's life. You have looked at how television works and how the signals are transmitted. Do you know how a commercial TV station operates?

Like commercial radio, television stations have three levels of personnel: owners, managers, and staff. However, the purpose of these areas and the work done can differ.

Ownership

Many television stations are owned by the four major networks: ABC, CBS, NBC, and Fox. These large corporations are responsible for their local stations. Local stations are called ***affiliates.*** Some commercial stations are owned by smaller companies, not by a major network. These stations are called ***independent stations.*** Owners of independent stations often become more involved in the station operation than network owners.

Management

As in radio, the station manager, or general manager, is the top official in the station, Figure 24-14. The station manager is concerned with the entire station. They see that operating policies and FCC rules are followed. They also make major programming decisions. Often, these decisions are based upon years of broadcasting experience.

Figure 24-14. Station managers must make many decisions.

Working beneath the general manager are the ***department managers,*** Figure 24-15. A typical station will have sales, production, news, administration, and engineering departments. This is also similar to the setup of a radio station.

However, the operation of a television station does differ from that of a radio station. Each show on a TV station usually has its own organizational structure. A producer is normally in charge of the production of a single program. It is the producer who brings the entire television show together. The producer makes up the budget, supervises the project, markets the program, and manages the talent (actors). Each show in a TV broadcast requires its own organization structure because of the additional preparation involved that is not found in a radio broadcast.

Staff

A TV station typically has five different areas. These areas are administration, sales, news, programming, and engineering, Figure 24-16. Each of these areas has its own staff. These personnel must work together to make the TV station run smoothly.

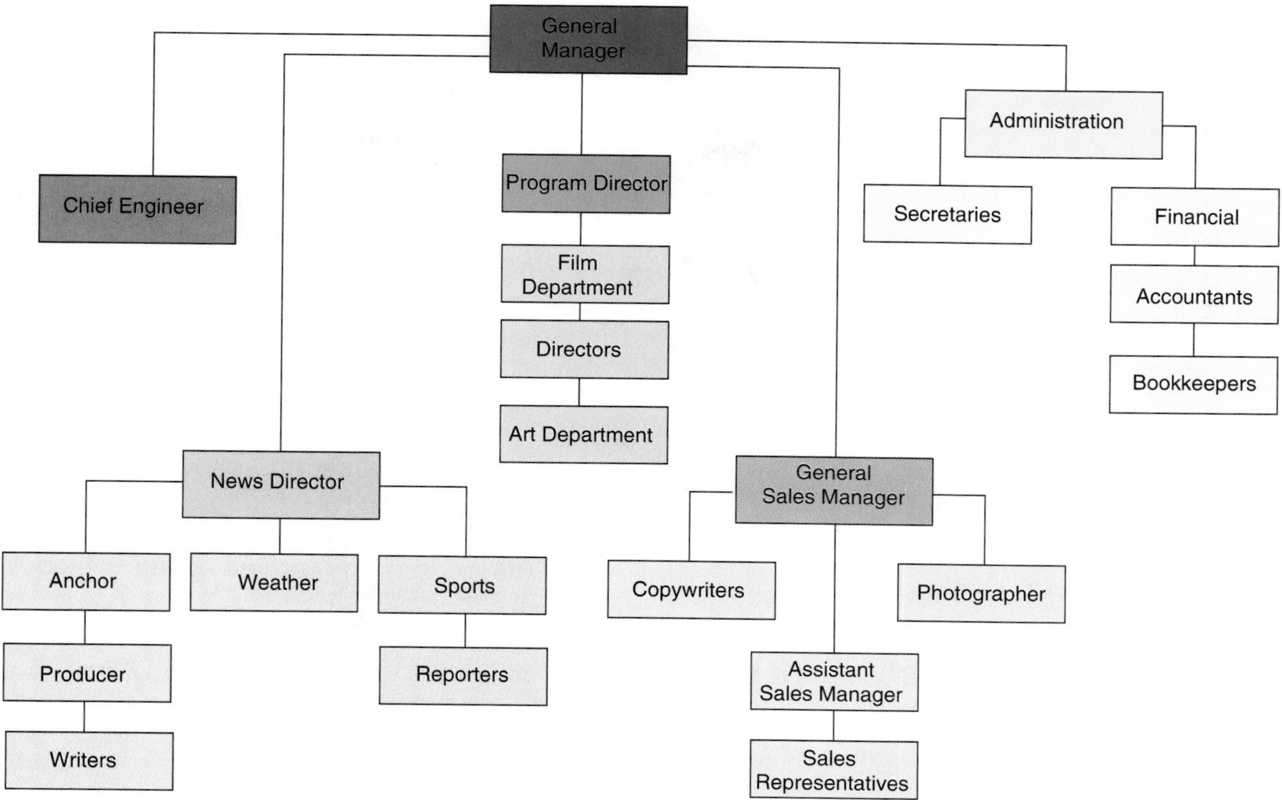

Figure 24-15. Many people and many different levels are involved in the successful operation of a radio station.

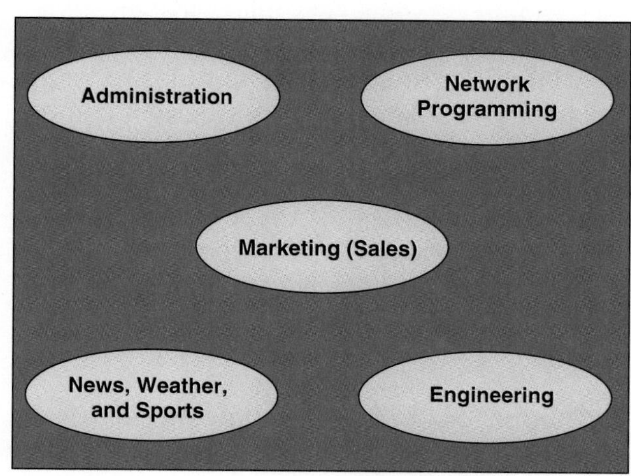

Figure 24-16. There are typically five staff areas that work in a television station.

Administrative staff may include office assistants, receptionists, and personnel directors. The administrative staff is responsible for the "front office" of the station. The administrative staff also includes the financial area. Accountants and bookkeepers keep track of the company money.

The sales staff is part of the marketing effort. These people sell commercial time to businesses. Other salespeople work with distributors of shows. Money raised by the sales staff is the major source of income for the station. The sales staff is also interested in getting more viewers to "tune in" to the station.

Most television stations feature news programs and specials. The station staff must research and write stories for broadcast. A news department handles this task. Reporters and camera crews attend local events to record important news stories, Figure 24-17. Film and audio tracks are then combined. The result is a "location" broadcast often seen on news programs.

The programming department produces the programs shown on the station. Writers and set designers plan the show. Make-up artists and wardrobe assistants help with costumes and other details. Camera and sound personnel record the action on the stage. Then post-production staff finish the program for broadcast. Film editors and individuals who add "voice overs" to the program are also part of the pro-

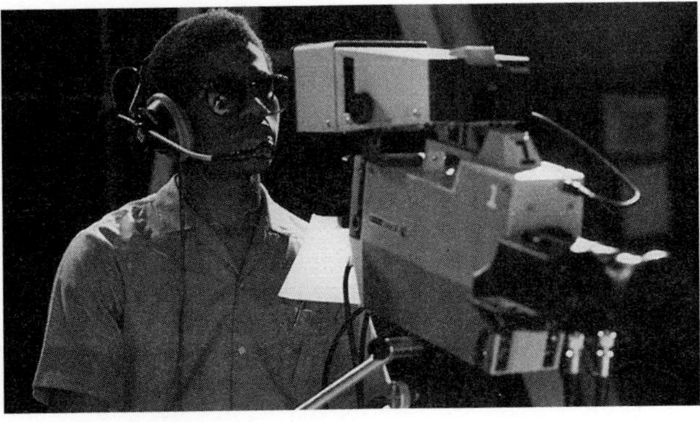

Figure 24-17. Camera operators film live action and reporters as they cover local news events for local stations. If the stories have nation-wide impact, the stations might sell the stories to the major networks. (Columbia College Chicago)

gramming department. (A voice over is adding a voice "track" over an existing video taped segment. This is often used to correct errors in the original taping.)

Engineers are responsible for transmitting the signal to viewers. There are a number of positions in this area. Maintenance engineers set-up, maintain, and repair equipment, Figure 24-18. Remote broadcasts are handled by field engineers. Electrical engineers test and install new equipment at the station. If any of these people fails to perform their job, the signal transmission may be interrupted.

Figure 24-18. Maintenance engineers need to test equipment to make certain it is working correctly. (Zenith Electronics Corp.)

Programming and Script Writing

In television work, ***programming*** involves planning and producing shows. These shows can come from three sources. The show can be produced locally. The show can come from the network. Some shows are obtained from an independent production group.

When shows are obtained from the network or an independent group, they are complete and ready for broadcast. Many times, as in the case of "prime time," the station simply receives a satellite "feed" from the network and then sends the signal directly out from their own transmitter. Other times the show may be sent on video tape, or transferred to video tape from a satellite transmission. The station can fit a taped show into the programming schedule where it is best suited.

Locally produced shows are done with the local audience in mind. Programming may include news features, children's shows, and local sporting events. Also, many educational shows are produced locally. Many larger cities even offer high school and college classes through TV broadcasts.

For programs produced locally in the station studio, planning is done on a ***storyboard.*** A storyboard serves as an outline for any audiovisual presentation. A storyboard may appear like a large comic book. It is a series of rough sketches. Each sketch shows a certain camera shot. Video and audio directions are also given underneath each sketch. A storyboard form is shown in Figure 24-19. When the "camera work" is being done, the storyboard will serve as instructions for the production staff.

Production Techniques

Production involves obtaining all items needed for putting a show on the air. The production techniques used in television are not the same as those used in radio. Most television programs are created in studios. In these studios are lights, cameras, microphones, and sets. During production, personnel trained in various phases of production operate the cameras, lights, and microphones.

Lights and microphones are important production equipment. Lights illuminate the scene so that the proper image will be recorded. Microphones are used to pick up the proper

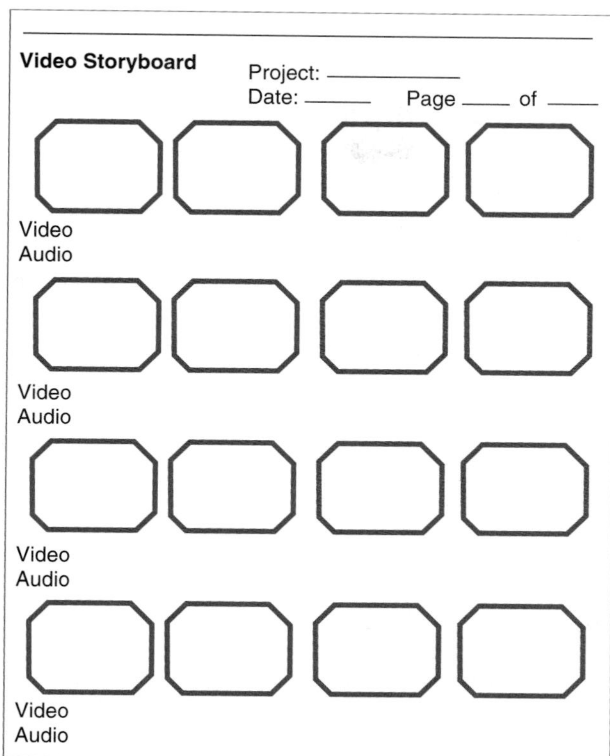
Video Storyboard
Project: ______
Date: ______ Page ____ of ____
Video
Audio
Video
Audio
Video
Audio
Video
Audio

Figure 24-19. Storyboards help organize all of the camera shots that are needed.

sounds. Lights and microphones are kept out of the way of personnel during production. Therefore, these pieces of equipment are not seen "on screen." Lights are often hung from permanent supports. Microphones are also put on the end of booms. Booms are long metal rods that can be extended over the action. Boom microphones can be kept out the camera's view. They also can be moved as the performers move.

Two types of lighting are used in television production. One type is the basic light needed by cameras to pick up a picture. This is called ***spot lighting.*** Spot lights are usually intense, white lights that illuminate part of a scene. The can also be used to illuminate the entire set.

The other type of lighting used is ***creative lighting.*** These types of lights are usually colored. Creative lighting is used to create a certain effect. For example, beaming a number of colors onto the stage provides an interesting visual effect. Spot lights can be used in creative lighting as well. For example, if the entire set is dark, a spot light can be focussed on an actor to give a dramatic effect.

Perhaps the most important piece of equipment in the television studio is the camera. Cameras capture the video information in television broadcasts. This information can be recorded on video tape or it can be sent directly to the production staff. Large floor units are used in major television studios. Hand-held models are useful for remote broadcasts, Figure 24-20.

Figure 24-20. Lightweight, hand-held video cameras can be used for on-location broadcasts. (Sony Corp.)

Most productions require several cameras to record different angles. Different camera angles allows the audience a number of views of any one scene. For example, on the evening news, you may notice the anchorperson turn their head to look into another camera. Switching camera angles is done to keep the audience interested. Imagine how bored you would become if only one camera angle was used for a full thirty minutes!

Like lighting, cameras are used in several ways. One type of camera viewpoint is used a great deal in newscasts. It is called ***reportorial.*** The newscaster speaking directly to the camera is an example of a reportorial viewpoint. With a reportorial viewpoint, the person on the TV screen appears to be talking directly to you.

In ***objective*** viewpoint, the camera watches the action. This is the viewpoint used most often in television. Sports broadcasting is a common example of an objective viewpoint. This is also used quite often in TV shows. This type of view point is as if you could "look into" a scene without anybody knowing you were there.

A third camera viewpoint is called ***subjective.*** In this instance, the camera takes the view of the actor or actress. Subjective viewpoint is used well in many dramas. Perhaps you recall seeing this used in a made-for-TV movie. In this type of viewpoint, an actor seems to be talking to you as if you were another character that is in the show. This is often used when two characters are close together. When one character speaks, the camera will show that character's face. When the other character responds, the camera will then "switch" and show the second character's face. This is different from a reportorial view because the actors are talking to other characters, while in a reportorial view the actor appears to be talking to a real person who is not in the studio (you).

Special effects are used to show an unusual event. Often these are natural occurrences, such as fire, rain, or fog. While some effects require costly equipment, many are simple to produce. For instance, dry ice (solid, or "frozen," carbon dioxide) or smoke is used to depict fog. Other effects can be quite complex. Representing a natural disaster requires much time, effort, and money.

Audio special effects are easy to produce. Adding crowd noises or laugh-tracks is a common practice. Laugh-tracks are the laughter that can be heard in the background of many comedies. Strange music or tones help create excitement in horror films. Any sound can be added during post-production work.

Set Design

A ***set*** is the area used as the location of the show. It includes all the equipment, scenery, and props needed for airing a show. ***Set design*** is the organization of all these items. Set design creates an area for the production of the show. Cameras are placed where they will best record the action. Lights are placed in the proper location. Backdrops are constructed behind the stage. ***Backdrops*** represent walls or scenery. Backdrops can be simply painted onto large sheets of plywood.

Staging

If you were asked to build an area to look like your classroom, how would you do it? What kind of furniture would you pick? What kind of lighting would you use? Would the lighting be bright or dim? Would you use plants, posters, or bulletin boards? Making these decisions and selecting the items is called ***staging.*** Staging creates a feeling of a certain place. The idea is to make the set look as authentic (real) as possible.

Scenery helps a great deal to make an area seem real. There are three types of scenery: settings, set dressings, and props. ***Settings*** are the large pieces that make up the areas of the set. For example, a setting for one show might include a kitchen wall, a porch, and a stairway, Figure 24-21. Settings are made with a particular show in mind.

Furniture is the major part of ***set dressings.*** However, also included are other items such as trees, books, lamps, and carpets. Set dressings

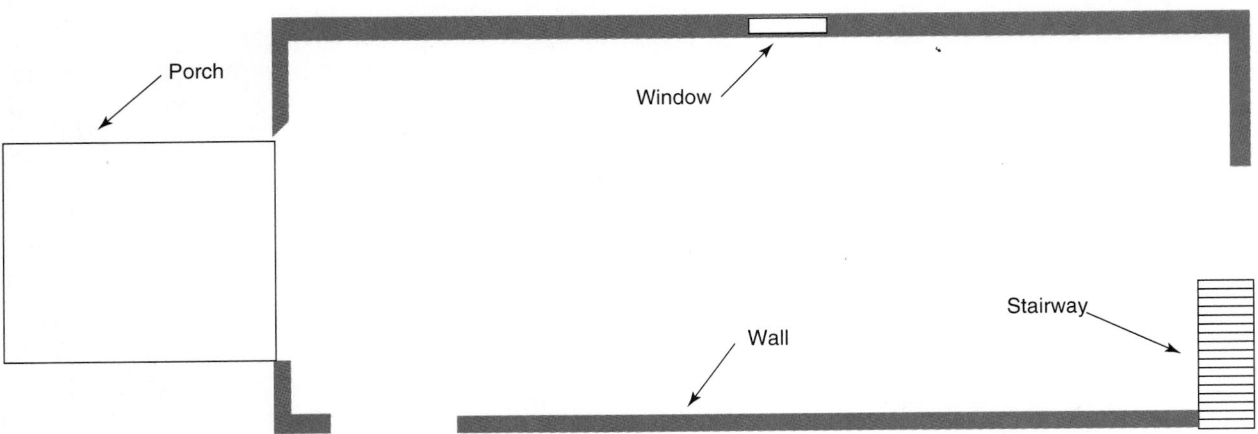

Figure 24-21. The setting for a kitchen includes the walls, windows, and a stairway.

include items that might be found in the location being shown, Figure 24-22.

Props are those items actually used during the acting portion of the show. Telephones, tissues, purses, and food cartons are all props, Figure 24-23. Props are different from set dressings because they are used by the actors and actresses while they perform on the set. Set dressings are merely on the set and add to the look and feel of the set.

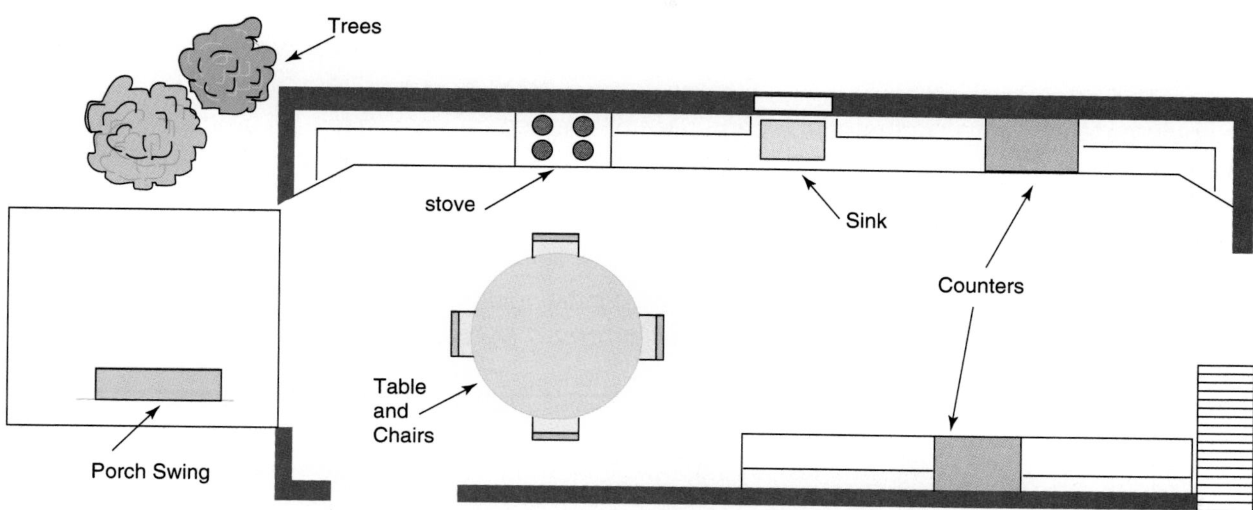

Figure 24-22. Set dressings for a kitchen include a stove, a table, a sink, and chairs.

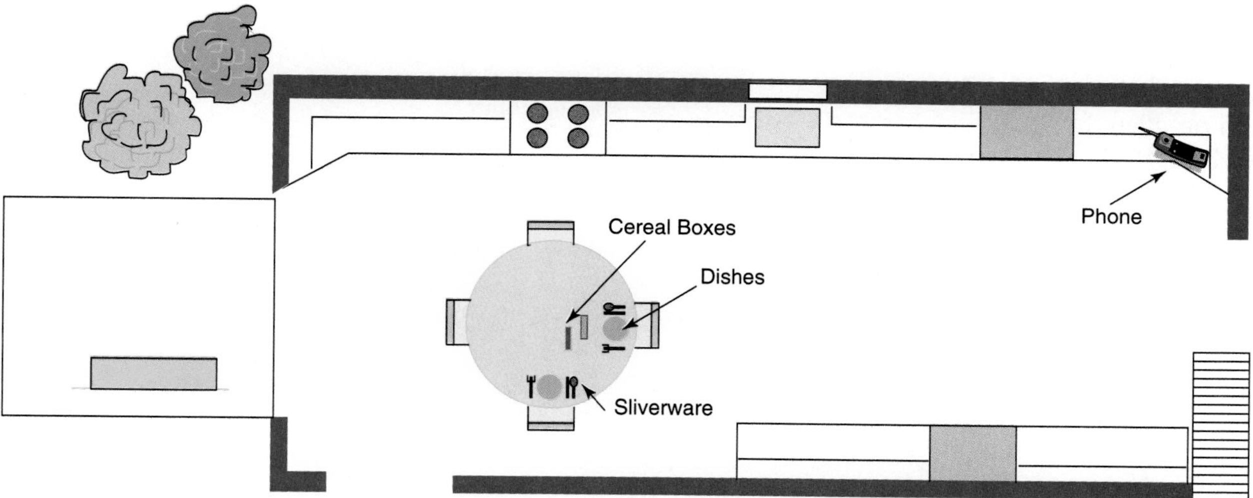

Figure 24-23. Cereal boxes, silverware, and dishes are added to a kitchen setting to be used as props.

CHAPTER 24 REVIEW

SUMMARY

In this chapter, you have looked at the basics of modern broadcasting. This is an exciting industry. Radio and television entertainment is a part of your everyday life.

The production of a program is a complex task. Many resources are needed. People, equipment, and creative material (scripts) are all needed for the successful production of a broadcast. Radio and TV programs are created in studios. Announcers or actors create the program for broadcast. Microphones and cameras "capture" the action on tape or film. The programs are then prepared for transmission by the station personnel.

It takes many talented individuals to operate a broadcasting station. Managers bring together the work of many staff members. Most individuals work "behind-the-scenes" developing programs. They support the familiar "on air" personalities.

KEY WORDS

All of the following words have been used in this chapter. Do you know their meanings?

Affiliates
Backdrop
Boom microphones
Camera operator
Cardioid microphone
Chief engineer
Commercial broadcast
Continuity writers
Corporation
Creative lighting
Department managers
Directional microphones
Federal/military broadcast
Format
General manager
Independent stations
Market
Microphone
Objective
Personnel
Producer
Private broadcast
Production
Program clock
Programming
Props
Recreational broadcast
Reportorial
Sales staff
Script writers
Set
Set design
Set dressings
Settings
Shotgun microphone
Spot lighting
Staging
Station manager
Storyboard
Studio
Subjective
Unidirectional microphones
Wheel

TEST YOUR KNOWLEDGE

Place your answers on a separate sheet of paper. Please do not write in this book.

1. Both TV and radio broadcasts are created in a _____.

Matching questions: Match the definition in the left-hand column with the correct term in the right-hand column.

2. Types of programs a station broadcasts.
3. Group of listeners a station wishes to attract.
4. People who create the script for a broadcast.
5. Person who directs an entire radio or TV station.
6. A local station owned by a major network.

A. General manager.
B. Script writer.
C. Format.
D. Affiliate.
E. Market.

7. What is involved in programming?
8. Name three sources from which television shows can be obtained.
9. What is AOR?
10. Explain the differences between settings, set dressings, and props.

ACTIVITIES

1. Watch a TV comedy show. List the props used by individuals on the program. Write a short report explaining how each item was used in the show.
2. Plan, write, and record a 10-minute news/weather/sports program for your school. Present this video to the class.
3. Develop a program clock for your favorite radio station. Prepare a short oral report explaining what the station format is, how the station operates, and what the market is for the station.
4. Build a model of a broadcasting set for a news program, game show, and comedy program. Prepare a short oral report using this model to explain how these three types of programs differ.
5. Take a portable video camera to a local sporting event. Record the action on videotape. Compare your tape to a sportscast on TV. How does your tape differ from the one on TV? What, if anything, can you do to make your tape better? Record another sporting event using what you have learned. Show the two tapes to your class explaining what you did differently.
6. Visit a local broadcasting station to watch a show being taped and produced. Write a short report on what you saw.
7. Storyboard a video presentation describing your favorite hobby or game. Present this to the class as a short oral report.

CHAPTER 25
COMPUTERS AND DATA PROCESSING

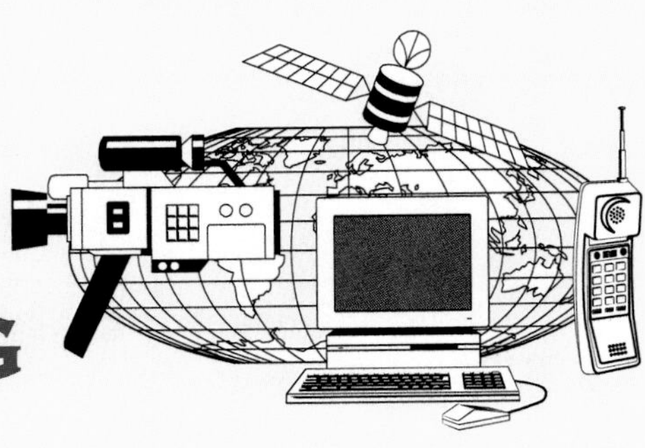

After studying this chapter, you will be able to:

- ❖ *Explain the uses and purposes of computers and data processing.*
- ❖ *Identify and explain the differences between hardware and software.*
- ❖ *List the parts of computer hardware and how they work.*
- ❖ *Cite different input and output devices.*

Computers are a part of daily life. They are used in grocery stores, classrooms, and hospitals. In fact, nearly every business uses computers in some way. Computers also come in many forms. A hand-held calculator is a computer. The machines that keep satellites in their orbit are also computers. Many of you may come in contact with computers every day at school. Some may be found in the library for student use. Others may be used in the office to prepare reports or budgets, Figure 25-1.

Figure 25-1. A computer has many types of outputs. A computer output could be a pie chart, a letter, or even a technical drawing. (IBM)

COMPUTER BASICS

A computer is a machine that accepts, stores, alters, and transfers information. The information is often called ***data.*** Data is typically information that is not organized. Data is input to a computer and processed into usable form. The "processed" data is then released as output data. This is how data processing got its name. ***Data processing*** is changing, organizing, or refining information using a computer.

USES AND PURPOSES

Computers serve many purposes in processing data, Figure 25-2. In an office, they can do word processing. ***Word processors*** organize, store, and print words, Figure 25-3. A word processor can be a machine that does nothing but word-processing. More often, computer word-processing software is used. This eliminates the need for a special machine that does nothing but word-processing.

Word processors are often used to type simple letters that are sent to many people. These letters are called form letters. The letter is typed once. The text (words) of the letter is displayed on the monitor (screen). Typing errors (typos) can be corrected. Entire paragraphs can even be switched around. Once the letter is completed, it is stored in the memory of the processor. Then

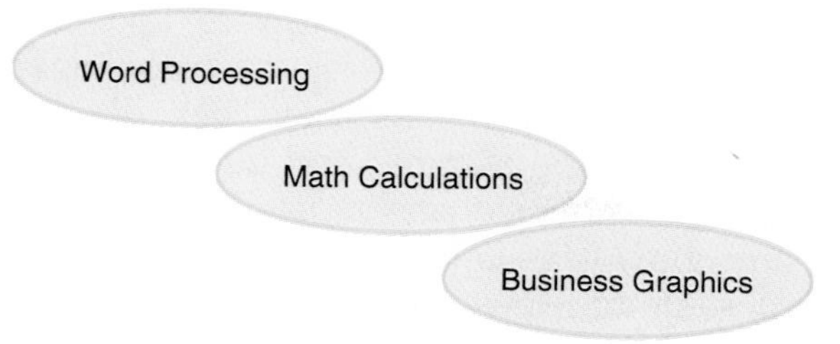

Figure 25-2. A computer has many uses in the office.

Figure 25-3. Word processors can be used to type, print, and copy text. (IBM)

the letter can be retrieved from the computer memory. Only the name and address must be changed, not the whole letter. This saves a lot of time.

Computers are also used to do math calculations. A business might calculate the total dollars of sales for a month. In an engineering company, complex math problems might be done on a computer. In a factory, boxes being sent out might be counted by a computer. A computer can be used to print out a graphic representation (chart) of the company's earnings.

Computers are also used to process numerical data (numbers). This might take the form of a spreadsheet. A ***spreadsheet*** is a grid made up of rows (going across) and columns (going down) on a page, Figure 25-4. A spreadsheet is used to keep information organized.

Many computer systems are designed to operate spreadsheet programs. Accountants use spreadsheets to keep the finances of their clients in order. Inventory control workers use spreadsheets to maintain a current count of products on hand. Spreadsheets can also be used to track a family's budget.

Computers are also used for desktop publishing. ***Desktop publishing*** is creating a document in a computer. The computer is usually a desktop computer, hence this is how the term "desktop publishing" came about. Much of this book was completed using desktop publishing techniques.

There are other uses for computers as well. For example, computers are used to detect mechanical problems in a car, Figure 25-5. After the technician examines the car, data is input

	A	B	C	D	E	F
1		Total Sales by Region				
2	Region	June	July	August	Summer Total	Percent
3						
4	Africa	$80	$88	$97	$265	10.7 %
5	Asia/Pacific	$100	$110	$121	$331	13.4 %
6	Central Europe	$200	$220	$242	$662	26.7 %
7	Northern Europe	$99	$109	$120	$328	13.2 %
8	Southern Europe	$70	$77	$85	$232	9.3 %
9	South America	$105	$116	$127	$348	14.0 %
10	North America	$95	$104	$115	$314	12.75%
11	**Total**	**$749**	**$824**	**$906**	**$2,479**	**100.0%**

Figure 25-4. Spreadsheets are very helpful in organizing finances. Computers make it very easy to create spreadsheets.

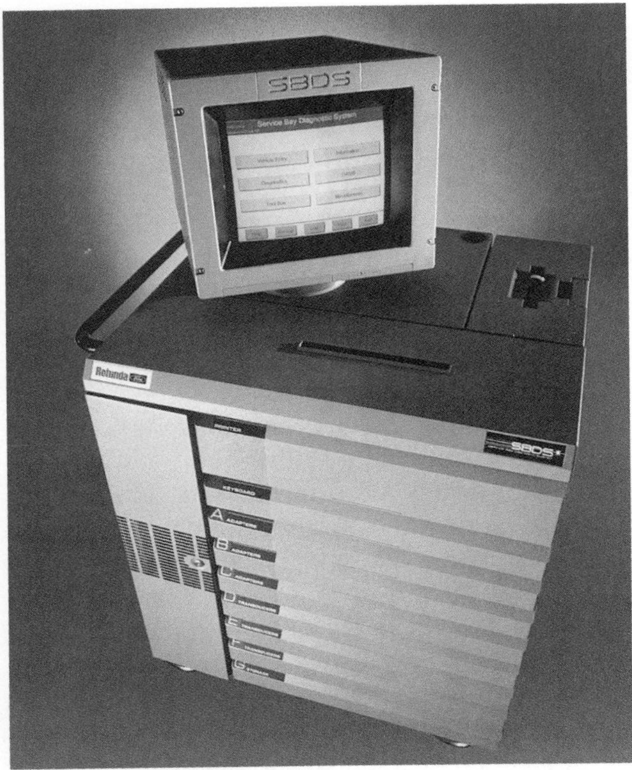

Figure 25-5. Computers are used to assist service technicians in diagnosing problems on cars. (Ford)

into the computer. This data is processed. The output informs the technician where the problem is located. Most cars have computers in them as well. Computers can be used to control steering, braking, suspension, climate, and many other things.

Computing and data processing are exciting areas of technology. Through their use, people, businesses, and schools are able to better communicate.

HARDWARE AND SOFTWARE

The terms hardware and software are often used in data processing. ***Hardware*** is the physical equipment that makes up an entire system. Hardware refers to monitors, keyboards, hard drives, CD-ROM drives, and printers. ***Software*** is a set of instructions used to run the computer. These instructions are used for doing various processing. Software is also known as ***programs.*** Software is stored on floppy disks, CDs, hard drives, and flopticals.

Computers need both hardware and software in order to work. The hardware is combined with the software to process data. Think of hardware and software as a car and driver. The car (tire, seats, engine, etc.) is the solid equipment—the hardware. All the items are needed for driving down the street. However, the car cannot drive itself. A driver is needed to do the driving. The driver is like computer software. The driver directs and controls the car. In the same way, software directs, or controls, the hardware. In this way, you can make the computer do what you want.

MAINFRAME AND PERSONAL COMPUTERS

Two types of computers are often used today. They are the mainframe and the personal computer. Personal computers include desktop computers, laptop computers, and notebook computers.

A ***mainframe computer*** is a large-scale machine, Figure 25-6. It has a very large memory and is used when a large number of calculations are required. Complex engineering problems are a common use for mainframe computers. Also, large companies may have a mainframe computer system so that all of their computers have access to the same files. Supercomputers are a type of mainframe computer. These computers have very large memories and perform high-speed calculations. Mainframe computers have many uses in business and industry.

Figure 25-6. Mainframe computers have powerful memories. Mainframes are capable of completing a variety of tasks. (IBM)

Microcomputers, or ***personal computers (PCs),*** are small, self-contained units, Figure 25-7. This type of system often fits on top of a desk, thus the name "desktop" computers. Other PCs are so small that they can fit on your lap. These are called "laptop" or "notebook" computers. PCs were first used for personal purposes. That is why they are called "personal computers." However, PCs are now used by businesses as well as in the home. PCs have the same features as a mainframe, but on a smaller scale. To increase the computer's resources, PCs can be connected to other PCs. This is called ***networking.***

Figure 25-7. Personal computers are used often in businesses and homes. (Apple Computers, Inc.)

Computers have a countless number of uses in the Information Age. There are very few tasks that cannot be done using computers. Therefore, it is important to know the basic workings of computers.

COMPUTER HARDWARE

As you have learned, computer hardware is the physical equipment that makes up a computer system. Hardware includes both the computer and any attachments. These attachments are called ***peripherals.*** Examples of peripherals include printers, keyboards, monitors, disk drives, and joysticks.

All systems have four basic pieces of equipment. They are the central processing unit (CPU), memory, storage, and the input/output devices.

Central Processing Unit

The ***central processing unit (CPU)*** is the "brain" of the computer. This is where all data is processed. In addition, all basic computer functions are performed in the CPU. One example of a basic function is "booting" the computer. ***Booting*** is when the computer starts the operating system.

The CPU contains the microprocessor. The ***microprocessor*** is a computer chip, Figure 25-8. A ***computer chip*** is a small piece of material, typically silicon, Figure 25-9. The chip contains thousands of transistors, resistors, and other electronic devices. This chip is then enclosed in a protective plastic coating. This unit is called the microprocessor. A microprocessor performs all of the calculations in a computer.

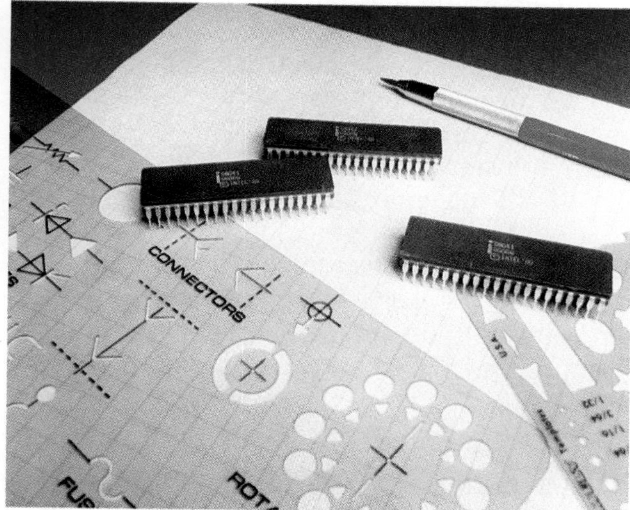

Figure 25-8. The microprocessor performs all of the calculations in a computer. (Intel Corp.)

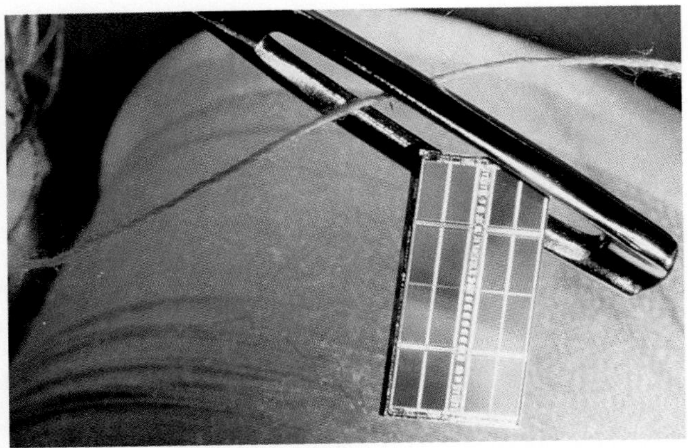

Figure 25-9. A computer chip can contain thousands of transistors and can be as small as a needle's eye. (IBM)

Memory

The ***memory*** of a computer holds information for use by the CPU. Computers have two types of memory: random-access and read-only. Memory is not the same as available disk space. If you notice computer advertisements, a computer may have a 270 megabyte hard drive and 4 megabyte of memory. The memory that the computer has is 4 megabytes, not 270 megabytes. A megabyte is a unit of measure used for disk storage space.

Random-access memory (RAM) contains information for use by the CPU. Software loaded into a computer goes to the RAM. This information is stored only while the computer is turned on. When the computer is shut off, the program is erased from the memory. Any input data is also erased unless it has been "saved." Data is often saved on disks, hard drives, or computer tapes.

Read-only memory (ROM) is installed at the factory. It cannot be erased and is difficult to change. Instructions in ROM can only be "read" by the CPU. Programs or data cannot be stored in it.

ROM contains the commands that allow a computer to function properly. For instance, when you press the letter "T" on a keyboard, a "T" appears on the screen. This happens because instructions in ROM send the proper signal to the monitor.

Storage

Often, data needs to be stored for a length of time. In these cases, the data is placed on a storage device. There are many kinds of storage devices now in use. Disks are used most often with personal computers, Figure 25-10. Tapes and CDs are used for long-term storage.

Figure 25-10. Computer disks are common storage devices. Information can be stored on disks and then retrieved at a later date.

Input/Output Devices

You learned devices hooked onto a computer system are called peripherals. Many peripherals allow data to be put into the computer. Others are used to get information out of the system. Therefore, peripherals are referred to as ***input/output (I/O) devices.***

An ***input device*** is any piece of hardware used to input data into a computer. The most common example of an input device is a computer keyboard, Figure 25-11. Other examples include bar code readers, joysticks, and light pens. A mouse is also an input device. Many computers get data over telephone lines, through an input device called a ***modem.*** Disk and tape storage systems are also examples of input devices.

An ***output device*** allows the user to get information out of a computer. This is done when data needs to be studied or recorded. A video monitor is a common output device. Other examples include computer printers, storage units, and audio speakers. Have you ever heard a computer "talk?" The output is an audible sound, rather than text on a screen or printer.

I/O devices are necessary for working with computers. They allow human-to-machine (computer) communication. The computer would be useless without the ability to input and output data.

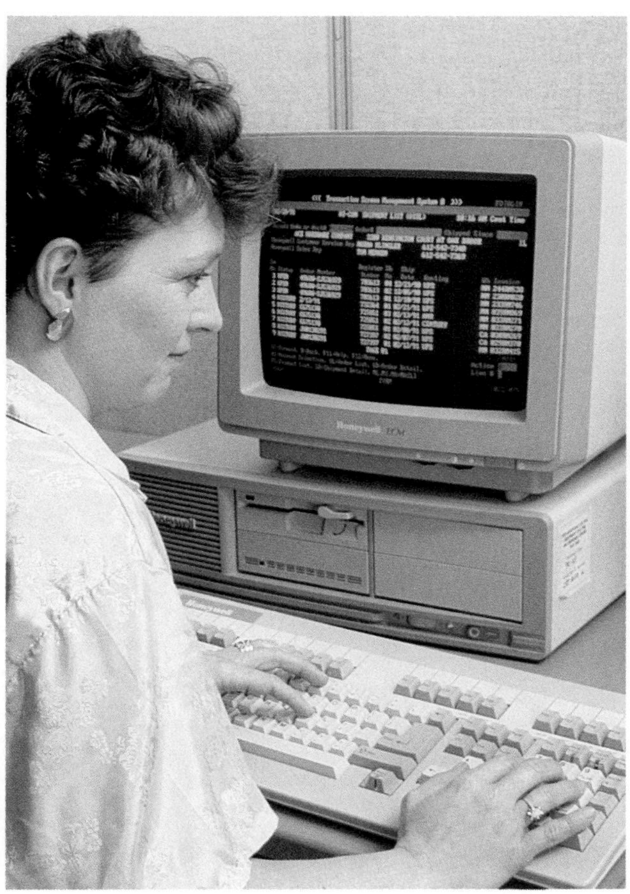

Figure 25-11. The most common input device is the computer keyboard. (Honeywell Inc.)

Figure 25-12. An interpreter acts as a "go between" for people who speak different languages.

COMPUTER SOFTWARE

Computer software is a set of instructions used to run a computer. There are several different computer "languages." There are also different types of programs.

Languages

A ***computer language*** is a set of commands that the computer can use to work with data. When these commands are put together as a related set, a program is made. When the computer reads the commands, it changes them into a language it can use. This process is similar to the work done by an interpreter.

An interpreter translates information between people who do not speak the same language, Figure 25-12. The interpreter must understand the languages being spoken. They can then act as the "go between," allowing these persons to communicate. A CPU works in the same way. The CPU "translates" inputted software into instructions it can understand.

Like spoken languages, computer languages have a vocabulary (words) and grammar rules, Figure 25-13. Some common computer languages include:

- ***BASIC*** (**B**eginner's **A**ll-purpose **S**ymbolic **I**nstruction **C**ode). It can be used in most personal computers.
- ***COBOL*** (**Co**mmon **B**usiness **O**riented **L**anguage). As the name states, COBOL is used a great deal in business.
- ***C.*** C is used widely for scientific and engineering programs.
- ***Pascal.*** Pascal is used as a training language.

Types of Software

In a computer system there are usually two types of software. These two types are system and application, Figure 25-14.

System software consists of the operating system, language translators, and some utility programs. The ***operating system*** software is used to control the computer and its I/O and storage devices. It operates the hardware using a set

```
#include <iostream.h>
float tax (float);

int main()
{
    float purchase, tax_amt, total;
    cout << "\nAmount of purchase: ";
    cin >> purchase;

    tax_amt = tax (purchase);
    total = purchases + tax_amt;
    cout.precision(2);
    cout << "\nPurchase is: "<< purchase;
    cout << "\nTax: " << tax_amt;
    cout << "\ntotal: " << total;

    return 0;
}
float tax (float amount)
{
    float rate = 0.065;
    return (amount * rate);
}
```

Figure 25-13. BASIC is a very simple computer language.

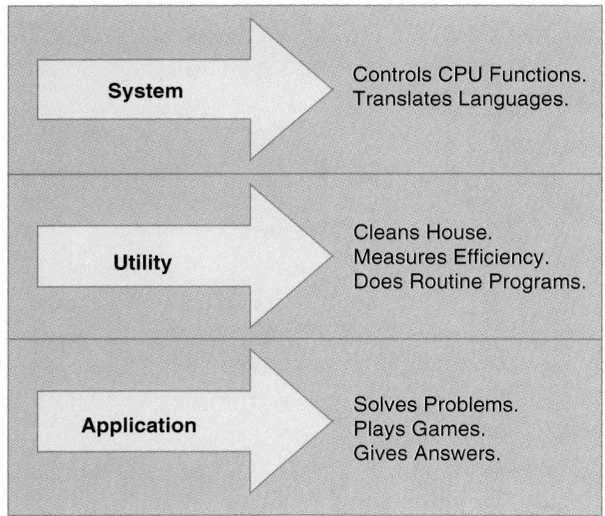

Figure 25-14. There are three basic types of software.

of computer programs. These programs control all the other programs used on the computer. The operating system decides which program the CPU will work on at any time.

Application software does the data processing rather than control functions. These programs do the actual "work," Figure 25-15. They allow you to solve problems, play games, and

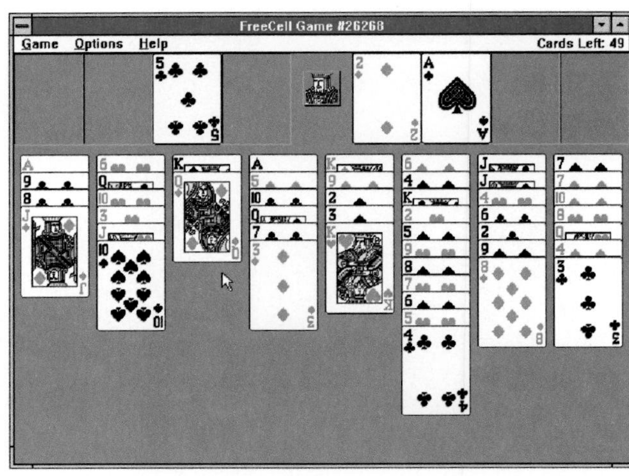

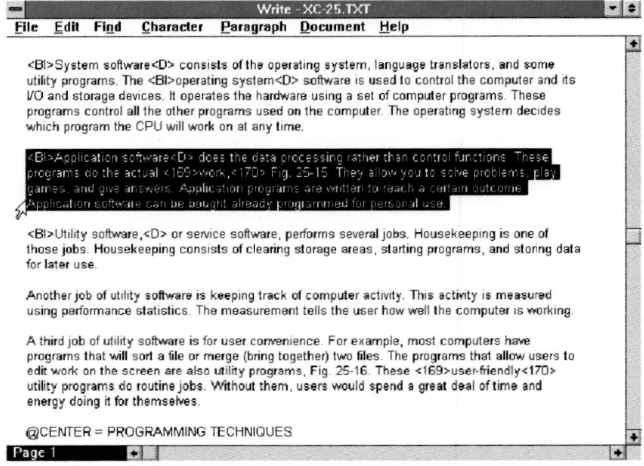

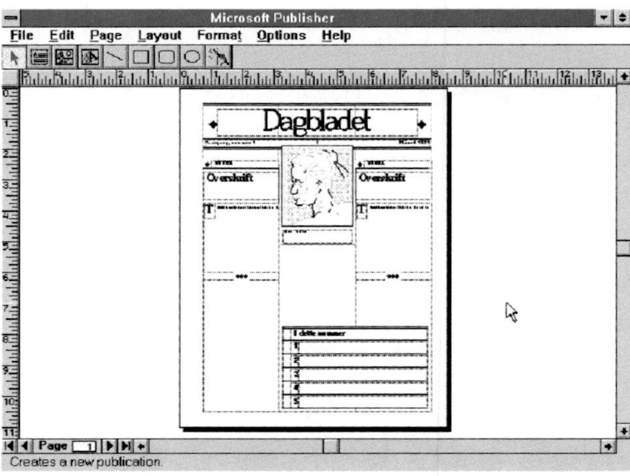

Figure 25-15. Application software allows a computer user to play games, do word processing, and complete desktop publishing projects. Many other types of application software are also available.

give answers. Application programs are written to reach a certain outcome. Application software can be bought already programmed for personal use, Figure 25-16.

Figure 25-16. Editing functions allow the user to replace, reorganize, or reword existing copy. If this function was not available, users would have to retype any changes. (IBM)

PROGRAMMING TECHNIQUES

To be a good programmer, good program design is needed. ***Program design*** is the path a program follows to reach the desired outcome. There is usually more than one way to design a program. However, one design is usually better than any of the others. A good programmer will decide which method is best and use it. This process is called the ***design phase.*** Programmers use various tools, or ***programming techniques,*** to help them in designing software.

Flow Chart

One common technique to help design a program is the ***flow chart,*** Figure 25-17. A flow chart can be used to aid in coding (writing in a certain language) the program. Flow charts can be done at two levels: general and detailed.

A ***general flow chart*** gives major functions and logic needed in a program. Often this is too simple to aid in coding. A ***detailed flow chart,*** however, is used to give specific points of a program. This type of flow chart will match the actual logic used to complete the program. Figure 25-18 gives the America National Standards Institute (ANSI) meanings of the symbols used in Figure 25-17.

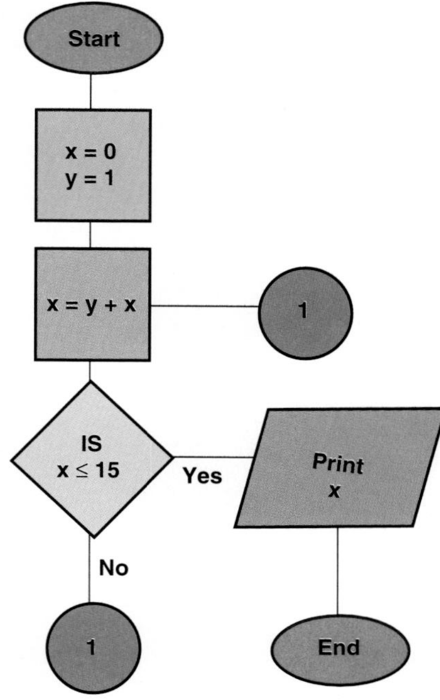

Figure 25-17. A general program flow chart shows the basic ideas for a program.

Symbol	Symbol Name	Meaning
	Terminal	Start or end of an operation.
	Input/Output	Input/Output operations.
	Process	A kind of processing function.
	Decision	A logical decision to be made.
	Connector	Connection between parts of a flow chart.

Figure 25-18. ANSI has set up specific meanings for symbols used in flow charts.

Basic Instructions

BASIC instructions are another type of programming technique. Like a utility program, they save time for the programmer. By using a certain word, an entire function is done.

BASIC instructions are either ***executable*** or ***non-executable.*** Executable instructions are program instructions. They tell BASIC what to do while a program is running. Non-executable instructions cause no change in program flow or in the running of the program. Figure 25-19 shows some examples of BASIC instructions.

DATA	Stores string or numerical data that are accessed by a ***READ*** instruction.
DELETE	Deletes program lines.
END	***ENDS*** program execution.
FOR-NEXT	Executes a series of instructions in a loop, a given number of times.
GO TO	Branches to a specified line number.
IF	Tests a condition and changes program.

Figure 25-19. Some BASIC instructions are executable.

Reserved Words

Certain words have special meanings in certain languages. These words are known as ***reserved words,*** Figure 25-20. They include all commands, statements, function names, and operator names. Reserved words often send the program in a certain direction. If they were used in any other way, the program would most likely fail to work. This is because, except as reserved words, they have no meaning.

LET	Assigns a value to a variable.
LIST	Lists the program that is currently stored in memory.
PRINT	Displays program data on the screen.
PRINT USING	Displays data according to a specified format.
READ	Reads a value from a data instruction and assigns it to a variable.
REM	Inserts comments into a program.
RENUM	Renumbers program lines.
RUN	Begins program execution.
SAVE	Saves a ***BASIC*** program on a diskette.
SQR	Returns the square root of a number.
TAB	***Tabs*** the cursor to a position on the screen.

Figure 25-20. Some words in computer programming are reserved words.

WRITING A COMPUTER PROGRAM

Computer programs can be written in any number of languages. No matter what language a program is written in, there are certain steps to follow when writing the program. These steps provide the programmer with an outline to follow.

Often, the first step in writing a program is to write a general flow chart. This flow chart provides the basic requirements of the program. It is used to outline the logic.

After the flow chart is written, it is reviewed by system analysts and management. At this point, the general flow chart is broken down into modules (or sections). A detailed flow chart is developed for each module.

The detailed flow chart is used by applications programmers as an outline for the actual coding (instructions) of the program. A detailed flow chart has the same logical structure as the finished program.

The next step is to start coding the program. A program consists of a number of instructions that the computer understands. When these instructions are put in a certain sequence (order), the computer will do what you want. A program may consist of only one line or it may consist of 10,000 lines. Length is determined by the complexity (degree of difficulty) of the problem to be solved by the program.

The final portion of programming is typing in the code. Each line of code is given a number. These line numbers tell the computer the sequence to follow when working the program. It is important to remember that the computer "knows" how to count. So, even if you number lines out of sequence, the computer will process them in order, Figure 25-21.

```
10 Print "Computers";
30 Print "Fun";
20 Print "Are";
40 End
```

Figure 25-21. The words in quotation marks are printed to construct a sentence.

A common programming technique is to number lines in multiples of 10. In this way, if a line must be added at a later time, it is not necessary to renumber lines, Figure 25-22.

```
10 Print "Computers";
20 Print "Are";
25 Print "Great";
30 Print "Fun";
40 End
```

Figure 25-22. This program is the same as in Fig. 25-21, except one line has been added. What happens in this program now?

"End" and "run" are two important commands in a program. "End" tells the computer that it has reached the end of the program. "Run" tells the computer to begin processing the program. This command is usually typed in separately from the code.

If a program is "clean," it will run correctly and you will receive the output you expect. Often, however, there are problems on the first few runs. These problems are called ***bugs.*** The process of correcting these problems is known as ***debugging.***

"Syntax error" is a common bug. This means that, at some point in the program, language rules were not followed. If a statement does not make sense to the computer, it can not be processed. This stops processing on the entire program.

A flow chart outlining the basic steps in writing a program is shown in Figure 25-23.

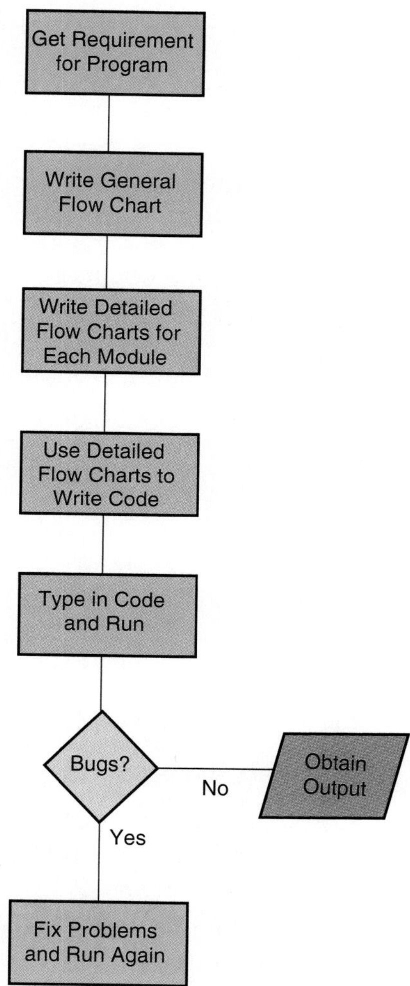

Figure 25-23. Flow charts help develop a program.

CHAPTER 25 REVIEW

SUMMARY

Computers serve many purposes. They can be used in the office, school, or home. In the office, computers can be used to type letters or control inventories. At school or home they can be used to type reports or to design a budget. There are two basic types of computers. They are the mainframe and the personal computer.

Mainframes are large machines with large memories. PCs are used for personal or for business use. Some PCs are called desktop computers. Others are small enough to be carried around and are called laptop or notebook computers.

Computers operate using hardware and software. Hardware is the physical elements of a system. Hardware includes central processing units, storage devices, and input/output devices. Software is the programs that are run on the system. Programs are written in a language. Some common languages are BASIC, COBOL, Pascal, and C. There are two types of software used with computers: system and application. Programs are written using techniques such as flow charts and reserved words.

When writing a program, certain steps are followed. These steps are used as an outline by management, systems analysts, and applications programmers.

Writing a general flow chart is the first step. From there, detailed flow charts are written for specific modules. Using the detailed flow charts, the program is coded and typed into the computer.

Once the program is completely input, the computer is instructed to run the program. If the program is clean, the expected output is obtained. However, if the program has bugs, it will need additional work to run properly.

KEY WORDS

All of the following words have been used in this chapter. Do you know their meanings?

Applications software
BASIC
Booting
Bugs
C
Central processing unit (CPU)
COBOL
Computer chip
Computer language
Computer software
Data
Data processing
Debugging
Desktop publishing
Design phase
Detailed flow chart
Executable
Flow chart
General flow chart
Hardware
Input devices
Input/Output (I/O)
Mainframe computer
Memory
Microprocessor
Modem
Networking
Non-executable
Operating system
Output device
Pascal
Peripherals
Personal computers (PCs)
Programs
Program design
Program techniques
Random-access memory (RAM)
Read-only memory (ROM)
Reserved words
Software
Spreadsheet
System software
Word processors

TEST YOUR KNOWLEDGE

Place your answers on a separate sheet of paper. Please do not write in this book.

1. ______ are used for primarily text only.
2. Explain the difference between hardware and software.
3. What do the following stand for?

   A. RAM.

   B. CPU.

   C. ROM.

   D. I/O.

   E. CD-ROM.
4. Name three types of storage devices used with computers.

Matching questions: Match the definitions in the left-hand column with the terms in the right-hand column.

5. Programs that do the data processing.	A. Application software.
6. Words that have special meanings.	B. Language translators.
7. Changes information for the CPU.	C. Utility software.
8. Programming technique that shows the logic of a program.	D. Operating system.
9. Software used to operate the computer and input/output devices.	E. Flow chart.
10. Software capable of housekeeping.	F. Reserved words.

11. What are "bugs?"

ACTIVITIES

1. Visit a computer store to learn more about personal computers. Collect literature on various models made by a number of manufacturers. Learn about the different uses for the computer. Prepare a short oral report on your research.
2. Visit your school's (or a nearby company's) data processing center to see a working mainframe computer. Write a short report on what you saw. Include topics such as what the computer was being used for, how many terminals it had, and what kind of I/O devices were being used.
3. Design a class newsletter using a microcomputer and a software package. Print it on an output device. Distribute copies to your classmates.
4. Develop a flow chart showing how to change a tire on a car. Be sure to use ANSI flow chart symbols. Present this as an oral report to the class.

Section 4 Review

This section introduced the applications of the electromagnetic spectrum. All electronic communication media include devices and systems that transmit signals as waves. These waves of energy are part of the electromagnetic spectrum. Common examples of electronic communication technology include acoustical, telecommunication, and fiber optic systems. This area also includes computers and data processing.

Many electronic communication systems involve the transmission of invisible radio waves through the air. For instance, you can't see the radio signals that arrive at a home stereo or TV set. Yet, the signals are there. These electronic devices convert the signal into sound and pictures that you enjoy. The transmission of programs is called broadcasting. Both radio and television programs are broadcast through the atmosphere. Often, the signal enters a home or business through a coaxial cable. Cable TV is an example of this.

Telecommunication systems generally involve sending messages over long distances. These systems include telephone, data, and satellite links. Some signals run along wires and cables. Other signals are transmitted through the Earth's atmosphere or outer space. Microwave towers and satellite dishes are two examples of telecommunication devices.

Computers have been greatly improved over the past decades. Modern systems are smaller, faster, and less expensive. Today, computers are often linked to laser printers, CD-ROM drives, and color monitors. By connecting telephone lines to a computer modem, you can access large databases and electronic mail services. Getting on the Internet is just one way of connecting to the information superhighway.

Section 4 Activities

1. Television and radio programs are created for large audiences. That's why TV and radio are often called mass media. Survey your classmates. What are the most popular TV and radio shows among the students in your class? How does this compare to the rest of the nation? What is the average amount of time spent watching TV per week? How does this compare to the amount of time spent in school or asleep? Create a graph or chart that illustrates the most popular programs for your class and the nation. Follow the design principle given in Section 3.

2. Computers provide numerous examples of input/output systems. Create a poster that illustrates this common hardware. Don't limit yourself to just computers. For example, your chart might show printers, monitors, and speakers as output devices. What would you include as an input system? What are other output devices? How

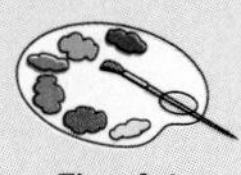

do these devices work together? How is society affected by these devices? Prepare a short report and present it to the class.

3. The media department in your school should have a variety of microphones. Some microphones (or "mikes") collect sound from large areas. Other mikes just gather music or voices from in front of the source. Ask your media specialist to demonstrate the microphones available in your school. Prepare a poster that illustrates how the various microphones operate. Include how and where each type of microphone is used.

4. Compact discs (CDs) represent a large improvement in audio systems. The sound reproduction is cleaner and tones are more like the original sounds. Obtain a record player, cassette deck, and CD player. Then, get a recording of the same tune or a similar song for each device. Play the record first, then the cassette tape, and finally the compact disc. Which range of tones are better? Which are worse? How has the development of these different types of recording media affected society? Conduct a class discussion on these topics.

5. Certain properties of electromagnetic waves can be demonstrated with waves in water. Set up a wave tank. One may be available in your school's physics lab. If not, a large, shallow container will work. Demonstrate the different properties of waves. Vary the amplitude and frequency of the waves. Place different objects in the water to represent buildings or mountains. How do the waves move around the objects (or don't move around them)? How does this affect your TV or radio reception? Can you think of any ways to help control or change the waves? Conduct a class discussion. Prepare a short report on the demonstration.

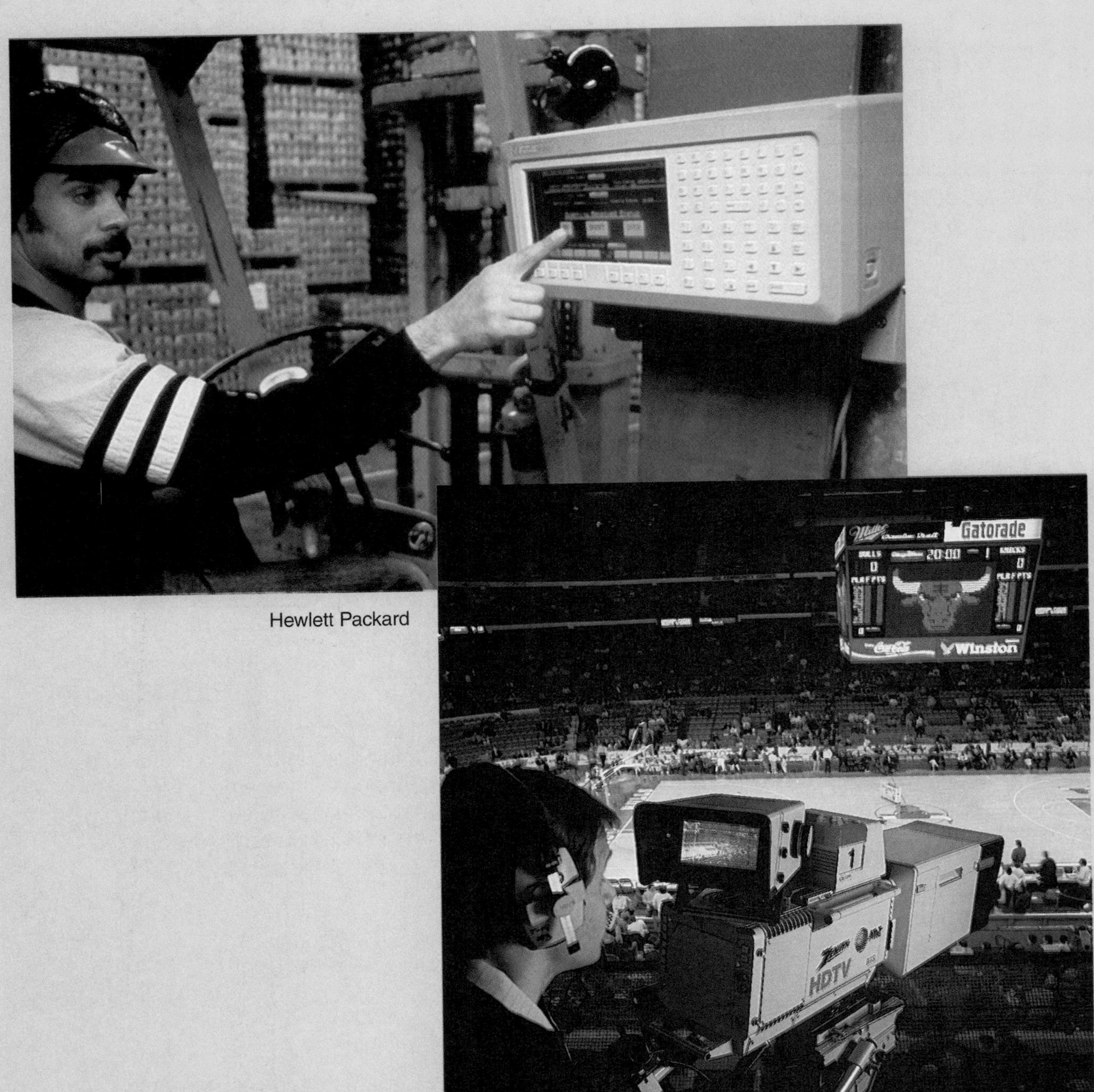

Hewlett Packard

Zenith

Section 5 Communication and Society

Motorola

CHAPTER 26
COMMUNICATION ENTERPRISES

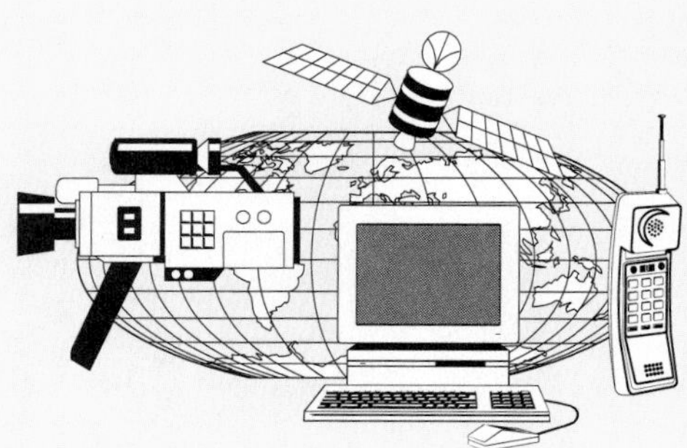

After studying this chapter, you will be able to:

- *Explain how to form a communication enterprise.*
- *Discuss the steps followed in establishing a corporation.*
- *Diagram the structure of a corporation.*
- *Describe the function of each department found within a corporation.*
- *Summarize the closing of an enterprise.*

Are you familiar with the term enterprise? An ***enterprise*** is a business organization or company. The purpose of an enterprise is to make a profit from the sale of a product or service, Figure 26-1. If the amount of money made from sales is greater than the expenses to the company, the company will be successful.

Figure 26-1. The success of an enterprise is measured by the profit made.

There are many types of business enterprises. Farms, shipping companies, and banks are all business enterprises. In the communication industry, publishing and broadcasting businesses are quite common. Many types of enterprises profit from the exchange of information in today's society. Communication industries are also called ***information industries.***

FORMING A COMMUNICATION ENTERPRISE

Modern communication enterprises come in a large number of shapes and sizes. From the smallest printing firm to the largest computer company, most are formed in the same way.

First, the owners decide what to market (sell). Perhaps they have noticed a particular consumer (buyer) need or want. Maybe they have an idea for a product or service people may buy. In either case, the owners must decide how to produce the goods or service. Therefore, a goal is set for the company. All successful enterprises start with a goal.

The next step is to decide what form of ownership will be used. The three most common types of ownership are proprietorship, partnership, and corporation, Figure 26-2.

TYPES OF OWNERSHIP

One type of business is called an ***entrepreneurship.*** An entrepreneurship is a business started by a person or group of people who take on the financial risks. The business that an entrepreneur starts may be totally unique, or it

Figure 26-2. There are three common forms of ownership.

may be similar to existing businesses. An entrepreneurship can be a proprietorship, a partnership, or a corporation. These are the three types of ownership.

A business owned by just one person is called ***proprietorship.*** The owner is known as a ***proprietor.*** Proprietorships are formed when a business will be small and the capital needs are small. ***Capital*** is the money needed to start and run a business.

A ***partnership*** is formed when two or more people own a business. A partnership has several advantages over a proprietorship. With several owners, a larger amount of capital is available. Also, more management and problem-solving skills are available.

The third form of ownership is the corporation. A ***corporation*** is a business that is set up following specific legal guidelines. (The corporation setup is discussed later in this chapter.) After setting up a corporation, the business is seen as a corporation by the law and must follow special rules and regulations. However, there are benefits to a corporation.

Many communication businesses choose to form corporations because large amounts of capital are needed to reach company goals. Corporations are often owned by a large group of people, called stockholders. ***Stockholders*** buy "shares" of the corporation. Their shares give them part ownership of the company. Many corporations have thousands of stockholders. Therefore, when one owner buys or sells shares, management is not usually affected. The selling of stock allows the corporation to get the capital it needs. Larger communication companies in the United States are corporations, Figure 26-3.

Figure 26-3. Many large corporations produce several different products and services. Some corporations may be associated with a certain product, such as electrostatic copiers, although the corporation may provide many other products and services. (Xerox Corp.)

OBTAINING RESOURCES

One of the first challenges of the owners is to learn what resources are needed. The typical resources of an enterprise are money, people, materials, and knowledge, Figure 26-4. These resources are needed for the company to work. In small companies, the owner (or owners) may be responsible for finding the necessary resources. However, in large businesses, the owners hire people to locate what is needed. For example, one activity includes hiring a management team to lead the company. The management team plans for and secures the company's resources.

The result of the wise use of resources is the production of goods or services. If you think of resources as "inputs," then the final products are "outputs," Figure 26-5.

Can you think of items which may be considered "outputs" of communication enterprises? You are reading one! This book was produced by a type of communication firm: a publishing company. Other outputs include TV programs, computer software, billboards, school portraits, and telephone calls.

LICENSING A COMMUNICATION ENTERPRISE

In the United States, communication industries are highly regulated. To form and operate an enterprise, there are several legal steps that must be followed. One of the first steps is that the owners must learn what agencies control their particular industry. For example, small printing firms may only require a vendor's license from the local government. However, telephone and broadcasting businesses are regulated by the Federal Communications Commission (FCC). The FCC grants a commercial license to broadcasting companies.

An FCC license is required in the radio and television industry. This organization assigns broadcast frequencies and governs transmitter power and location. The FCC also grants operating permits (licenses) to station personnel. These permits are granted through various testing procedures.

Once a station is "on-the-air," the FCC constantly reviews it. A broadcasting log (record) must be kept. This details what went on the air

Figure 26-4. There are four typical resources needed in a successful communication enterprise—money, people, materials, and knowledge.

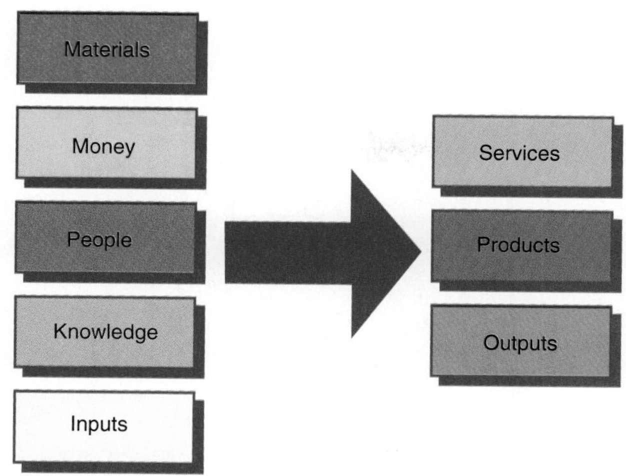

Figure 26-5. The products or services resulting from communication enterprises are called outputs.

and when. In order to be granted a renewal of its operating license, a station must meet certain standards.

ESTABLISHING A CORPORATION

There are two main legal documents used when forming a corporation. They are the Articles of Incorporation and the corporate bylaws. Every corporation has to prepare and file these items with governmental authorities.

The ***Articles of Incorporation*** are an outline of the structure and purpose of the business. Among the important items listed on this charter are:

- Name and address of the proposed company.
- Purpose of the proposed corporation.
- Names and addresses of the persons forming the corporation.
- Location of the corporation office within the state.
- Amount and kind of stock to be offered.
- Names of principal officers of the company.

This information is supplied to the state government where the corporation is to be located. If approved, a charter will be granted to the enterprise. This allows the new organization to conduct business as a corporate body.

In addition, the ***bylaws*** of the enterprise must be drawn up. This document provides rules about the operation of the company. For example, bylaws outline the number and duties of company directors. Bylaws also describe the business practices of the firm. A list of those items that need stockholder approval is also included in the bylaws. Finally, important details related to the stockholders are covered. Voting procedures and stockholders' rights are guaranteed by this document.

Upon completion and approval of all legal requirements, the enterprise begins operation. A company organization (structure) is developed. The major groups of the business include personnel, finance, marketing, and production, Figure 26-6.

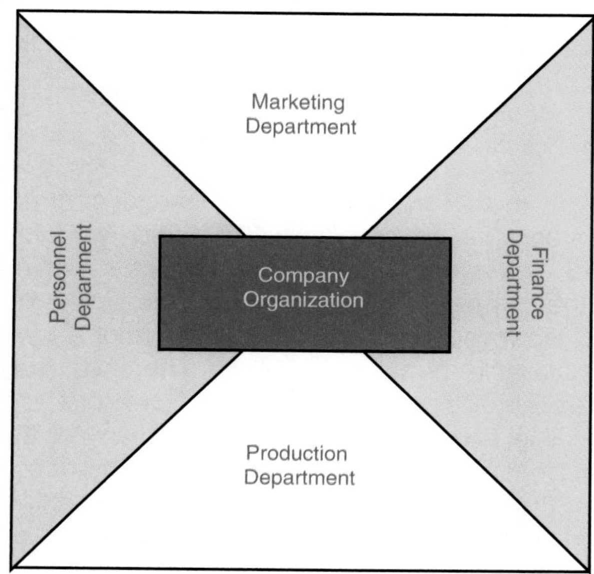

Figure 26-6. There are four major departments in a communication firm.

STRUCTURE OF A CORPORATION

Many communication enterprises have a small staff that performs many tasks. Larger companies may have an entire department just to pay debtors and bill creditors. (Debtors are people that you owe money to and creditors are people who owe you money.) However, all enterprises usually have at least four activities in common. These include the finance, personnel, marketing, and production functions. In most corporations, each activity is done by a certain department. A management team directs their activities, Figure 26-7.

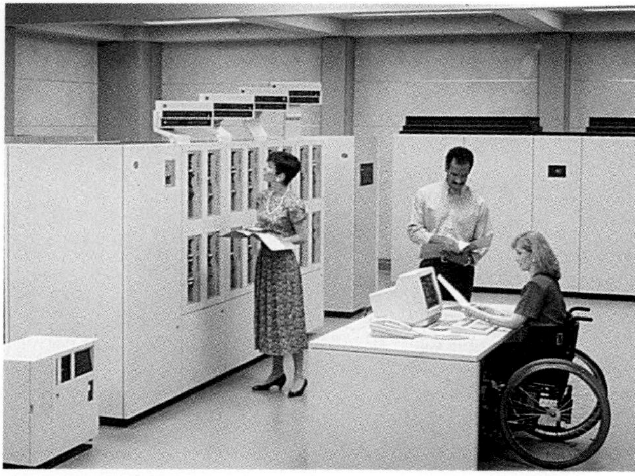

Figure 26-7. Managers are in charge of different operations in large corporations. Large computer systems must be managed by a person called a systems operator, or sysop. Here, data processors consult with the sysop. (IBM)

Corporate Management

In most corporations, the managerial structure contains several "levels" of authority, Figure 26-8. The owners have the final say in the running of the company. These people are the stockholders. However, all the stockholders cannot always be available to make key rulings. Therefore, their interests are covered by a board of directors.

The ***board of directors*** make many of the decisions for the stockholders. They make decisions and establish policies as they feel stockholders would. They also advise management on important issues.

The top person in the executive staff is called the ***president*** or ***chief executive officer (CEO).*** This person directs the company's day-to-day work schedule. The president is responsible for all work of the business. Since this is a large task, a vice-president is usually in charge of each department. ***Vice-presidents*** watch over the work done in their departments. Each vice-president reports to the president of the company.

Below each vice-president are managers. ***Managers*** have many functions in communication firms. First, they set goals for the enterprise. This includes planning and organizing the company's resources. Managers then direct the daily functions of the company through a staff.

The ***staff*** is made up of people hired to do specific jobs. For example, the staff at your school consists of secretaries, teachers, guidance counselors, and cafeteria workers. These people are hired because of their talents for a specific job. Corporations hire staff workers based on the needs of the company.

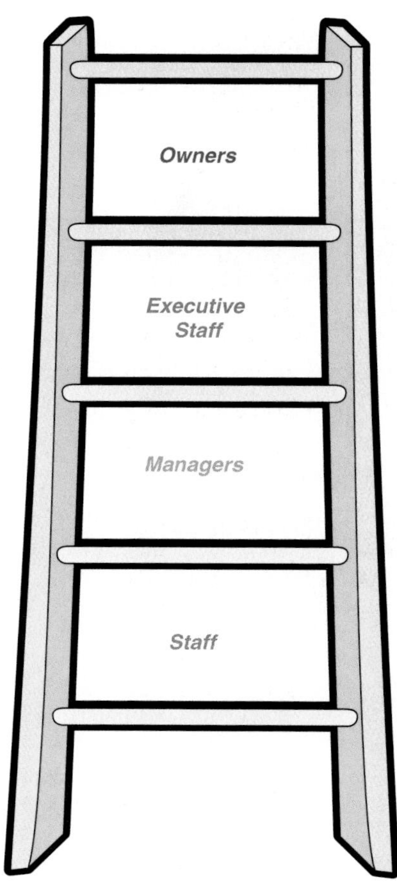

Figure 26-8. There are four common levels of authority in a business.

Finance

The ***finance department*** controls a corporation's legal and monetary affairs, Figure 26-9. This includes raising capital (money) for the enterprise. Finance employees also keep track of money through record keeping activities, like budgeting and accounting. Paying taxes is another important task for this department. The finance group is also responsible for purchasing supplies. Supplies include items like typing paper, glue, pens, and stationery.

The finance department often handles the legal matters of the company as well. This department may work with many government agencies. Obtaining an operator's license or charter is an important task. Maintaining legal paperwork is

Figure 26-9. There are two primary functions of a finance department—legal affairs and monetary affairs.

also vital to the company's affairs. These tasks are often conducted by the finance department.

The finance department also prepares many reports concerning the status of the company. These details are available to the public, in written reports. One kind of written report is the ***annual report,*** Figure 26-10. The report includes information such as stock price ranges, summaries of operation costs, and a note to the stockholders (owners).

Figure 26-10. Annual reports are prepared by the finance department and made available to all interested persons.

Personnel

The ***personnel department*** hires and cares for the company's workers. The personnel department is also the company's link to the local community. Therefore, the personnel department is also in charge of public relations (PR). If a labor union represents workers in the company, the personnel department deals with the labor leaders.

The primary function of the personnel department is to bring together a workforce for the company. Personnel hires and maintains a good workforce. After all, people are the most important resource in any company, Figure 26-11. All businesses need a variety of skilled workers and managers, Figure 26-12. Each employee will add their own skills, knowledge, and experience to the business.

Figure 26-11. People are any company's most important resource. This person uses his skill and training to perform many useful tasks for the company.

The steps taken when hiring employees follow a fairly common path, Figure 26-13. However, there are several ways to recruit employees. For example, many firms make jobs known in local newspapers. You may see these "help wanted" ads in your local newspaper every day. Other enterprises announce auditions or tryouts. This is common in the entertainment industry. Many businesses let local or state employment agencies find employees for the firm. Once ads have been answered, interviews completed, or auditions held, the best person for the position is hired.

Television Station	
General Manager	Sports Reporters
Engineers	Camera Operators
News Director	Stagehands
Photographers	Sales Representatives
Producer	Audio Technician
Anchors/Announcers	Video Technician
Writers	Special Effects Director
News Reporters	Makeup Artist
Weather Reporters	Hairdresser

Newspaper	
Publisher	Composing Staff
Editor-In-Chief	Librarians
General Manager	Classified Staff
Managing Editor	Press Operators
Advertising Manager	Photographers
Production Manager	Reporters
Circulation Manager	Copy Editors
Sports Editor	Secretarial Staff
News Editor	Sales Staff

Radio Station	
General Manager	Music Director
Sales Manager	Newscasters
News Reporter	Disc Jockeys (DJs)
Program Director	Audio Technician
Sports Director	Engineers
News Director	Sound Mixer
Script Writers	Sales Staff
Researchers	Music Librarian
Copy Editors	Secretarial Staff

Figure 26-12. Different communications enterprises have different positions in the company.

Figure 26-13. The basic steps in hiring workers are the same no matter what the business.

Managers hire people they believe will give the most to the enterprise. For example, advanced training from a college or technical school may make one applicant more desirable than another applicant. Having a cheerful, pleasant personality is also desirable. Employers look for responsible, safe, and loyal persons when filling available positions.

Production and Service

Communication enterprises are formed to sell an item or a service. This includes activities like publishing books, developing film, and transporting mail through computers (known as ***e-mail***).

Businesses that sell ***products*** give buyers an item they can actually hold. For example, printing firms produce books, magazines, and newspapers. Larger companies assemble items like radios and television sets. Other communication firms produce and market compact discs, tapes, and computer disks.

Providing a service is quite different than providing a product. A ***service*** is a function that fulfills a need or desire. There is no physical "object" with a service. Telephone companies provide a service. Through the use of a telephone company's equipment, you are able to call friends. There is no physical product. They provide you with the materials necessary for making a phone call. This is a service. You pay for this service with your telephone bill. Many communication firms are "service-related," Figure 26-14.

Service-Related Communication Industries	
Cable Systems	Television
Radio	Videotext
Telephone	Satellites

Figure 26-14. Several communication industries are "service-related" industries.

The television industry is also service-related. Actors and actresses perform on various shows. Anchors on the local station report the day's important news. While you never hold any physical object, you are being entertained. This is a service. Like the telephone, you pay for this service. With cable TV, you pay a monthly bill. With "free" TV there are ***indirect costs.*** For example, advertising time on a popular show is very costly. Despite the high cost, however, many companies will advertise during that show. In order to pay the advertising fee, companies often raise the price of their goods or services. This is an example of "indirect" costs.

Marketing

Marketing involves getting consumers to buy a company's products or services. Advertisers inform the public what new items are available. A sales force will complete the task of selling the goods or services to potential buyers. Then the distribution unit delivers the items to customers. This area may also include a marketing research division to access customer needs and desires. The major functions of a marketing area are listed in Figure 26-15.

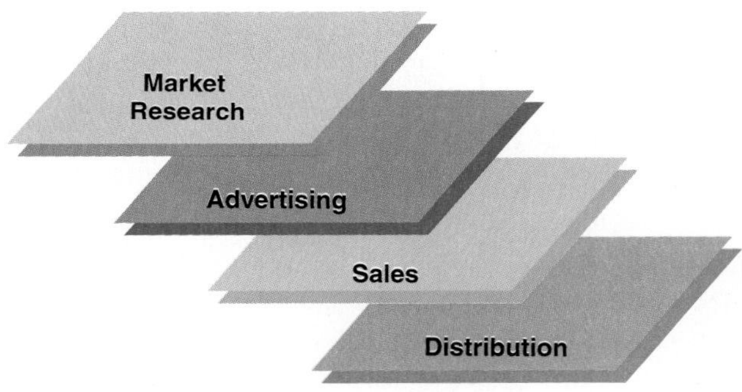

Figure 26-15. There are four basic functions of a marketing department.

Marketing research is vital to any enterprise. For the company to succeed, it must understand consumer wants and needs. By surveying many people, firms find out the desires of their audience. For example, researchers determine what TV programs are highly viewed. They also follow trends in entertainment and business. If they see, for example, that videos are very "big," they may style their ads in a video format. Marketing departments also measure the success of sales efforts.

All companies promote their products or services in some manner, Figure 26-16. Common means of advertising include TV commercials, newspaper ads, and billboard displays. In Chapter 3 you learned that messages can inform, persuade, instruct, and entertain.

Figure 26-16. Advertisements appear in various forms, in different places. Do you recognize any of these common ads?

Advertisements are messages. Therefore, advertisements can serve any of the purposes of a message. For example, persuasive advertisements include providing coupons or promoting sales.

Sellers and buyers in communication firms vary by industry, Figure 26-17. For example, sales representatives (reps) for a cable company sell their TV service to local customers. Publishers sell books and magazines to individuals, stores, or schools. Large TV networks sell advertising time to clients. The marketing staff at a recording company sells CDs and tapes to stores. Other companies sell movie or concert tickets to consumers.

Examples Of Product/Services Offered To Customers	
Company	***Purchaser Buys***
Stage Production Firm	Tickets to Concerts/Plays
Television or Radio Station	Advertising Time "On The Air"
Computer Software Firm	Complex Computer Programs
Publishing Firm	Books and Magazines Available to General Public
Film Production Business	Movies (Films) for Theater Showings
Recording Company	Popular Records and Tapes

Figure 26-17. Communication products and services are purchased by a variety of customers.

A marketing department is made up mostly of a sales force. These people contact potential buyers of the company's goods or services. A sales manager directs the company's sales force. The manager assigns areas (sales territory) to staff members. This area may include a geographic region or certain accounts. Experienced salespeople work with the larger customers.

Members of a sales force often have years of selling experience. Many salespeople spend large amounts of time traveling to clients (customers) and potential clients. Most salespeople are paid a salary for their work. In addition, they might also receive a share of each sale. This share is known as a ***sales commission.***

The marketing function also includes a distribution group. Distribution involves sending products to buyers. This function varies by industry. Small companies often deliver their products or services directly to consumers. Large firms let other distributors sell their products. Businesses in the recording and entertainment industry can have a complex distribution system.

MANAGING THE CORPORATION

Communication enterprises must be managed in an efficient manner. Managers direct the operation of the business. They serve as supervisors, directors, or administrators. Their knowledge and experience is vital to the success of the company.

Among the activities to be managed are the design, production, and transmission of messages. Hiring and training personnel is important. Also, financial affairs must be closely watched.

Designing Products and Services

Products and services are designed by creative persons. Reporters write their news reports. Artists and graphic designers lay out magazines, flyers, and posters, Figure 26-18. Stage crews produce the set designs for TV shows. Authors write the manuscripts for books. Photographers compose visual images for TV shows and motion pictures. Drafters develop complex drawings with the aid of computers, Figure 26-19. However, design activities in communication industries are not limited to these few examples.

Figure 26-18. Graphic artists and designers create exciting visual displays.

Figure 26-19. Industrial designers often develop working drawings with the aid of computer systems. (Hewlett-Packard Co.)

Transmission of Media Messages

Management is important in mass media. A large number of messages are constantly sent. Messages are transmitted by audio, visual, and audiovisual means. There must be people in charge of organizing and reviewing this information.

Among the most familiar audio messages is the radio program. Popular music and talk shows are transmitted to homes and workplaces. Radio station managers decide what type of shows will be broadcast. The visual media include photographs and printed materials. Television and motion pictures are types of audiovisual communication, Figure 26-21. Managers of theaters decide what films will be shown.

Production of Messages

Production tasks include recording, filming, and printing messages. Managers direct workers who do these jobs. For example, supervisors direct the operators of various production equipment, Figure 26-20. The technical director at a radio station engineers a radio broadcast.

Figure 26-20. Supervisors make sure that the necessary work is completed correctly and on time. (IBM)

During production, managers check the progress of all work. They decide if changes are needed. This may include shifting resources or schedules. Also, managers decide if quality standards are being maintained.

Figure 26-21. In a theater, employees who work in the projection booth are known as projectionists. Projectionists are responsible for loading the film and operating the projector. (Andy Johnston)

MAINTAINING FINANCIAL RECORDS

Financial records of businesses are often kept in computers, Figure 26-22. These records include money earned and spent. The official record of all financial matters is a ***general ledger.*** Company income is derived from the sale of products or services. This money is used to pay the expenses of the company, Figure 26-23. For example, managers receive a salary for their efforts. Workers are paid for their productive time. Equipment and facilities are a major expense in most companies. Materials and supplies are often the most costly expenses. Utilities and other operating expenses must be paid, too.

Figure 26-22. Many companies use computers to keep financial records of the business. (NCR)

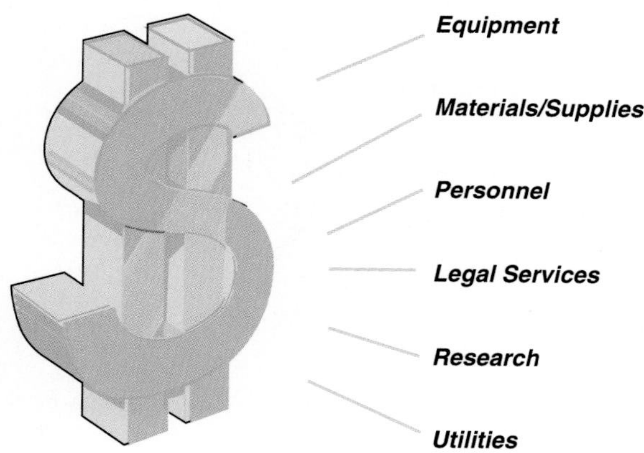

Figure 26-23. A communication enterprise has many different types of expenses.

After paying all the bills, the remaining money is called ***profit,*** Figure 26-24. A successful firm will return a profit to investors in the business. The profits are normally split among the owners of the firm. In a corporation, stockholders receive a ***dividend*** for each share of stock they own. The dividend is their share of the company's profits.

Figure 26-24. The major goal of every enterprise is to make a profit.

CLOSING THE ENTERPRISE

Many new corporations are formed each year. Others are terminated (they stop conducting business). Companies that fail to make a profit are often closed down by stockholders. Owners may then invest their money elsewhere. Due to financial or legal problems, the courts may order a firm to halt operation.

Closing a corporation requires several legal steps. First, owners are informed of plans to close the company. Then a vote is taken at a meeting of stockholders. If the vote is approved, the corporation is dissolved.

Company officials then fill out the paperwork required to terminate the firm. The ***Articles of Dissolution*** are filed with the federal government. The Articles of Dissolution legally stop the corporation from operating. Company assets are sold. ***Assets*** include equipment, buildings, and property. Extra materials are sold to other firms who use those materials. Employees are laid off from their jobs. Then all bills are paid in full.

Any remaining funds are distributed to the original owners. However, if the corporation has been in debt, there will probably not be any leftover money.

CHAPTER 26 REVIEW

SUMMARY

An enterprise is a business organization or company. Communication enterprises profit from the exchange of information or ideas. They produce materials or provide services to customers. Businesses in the communications area are known as information industries. Information enterprises are often formed as corporations. These corporations include many owners, called stockholders.

Forming a communication enterprise involves many legal steps. Approval is obtained from governmental agencies. A charter and/or license is granted to the firm. Then managers gather the needed resources to start the enterprise. Corporations have many levels of authority. Managers direct employees who design, produce, and transmit messages. The company profits from selling products or services to customers.

KEY WORDS

All of the following words have been used in this chapter. Do you know their meanings?

Annual report
Articles of Dissolution
Articles of Incorporation
Assets
Board of directors
Bylaws
Capital
Chief executive officer (CEO)
Corporation
Dividend
E-mail
Enterprise
Entrepreneurship
Finance department
General ledger
Information industries
Indirect costs
Managers
Marketing
Partnership
Personnel department
President
Products
Profit
Proprietor
Proprietorship
Sales commission
Services
Staff
Stockholder
Vice-president

TEST YOUR KNOWLEDGE

Place your answers on a separate sheet of paper. Please do not write in this book.

1. What is the first step in forming a communication enterprise?

   A. Decide on the form of ownership.

   B. Determine what to market.

   C. File Articles of Incorporation.

   D. Choose a managerial structure.

2. A(n) _____ is the only owner of a business.

3. Give two advantages of a partnership over a proprietorship.
4. Owners of a corporation are called _____.
5. Name four resources needed by most businesses.
6. Explain the process of establishing a corporation.
7. Most corporations have:

   A. Finance departments.

   B. Personnel departments.

   C. Marketing departments.

   D. Production departments.

   E. All of the above.
8. The term CEO stands for _____.
9. Job openings are typically made known in one of three ways. What are these three methods?
10. Explain how products and services differ.
11. What is the name of the legal document filed when closing an enterprise?

ACTIVITIES

1. Have your class start a communication corporation. Choose a name. Determine what you will "sell." (Remember, what you "sell" can be a product or a service.) Take every step, from filing the proper papers and documents, to closing the enterprise. Have your instructor represent the FCC.
2. Tour several local service-related and product-related information industries. Compare their operations. List the products or services they offer to customers. Explain the differences in a short report.
3. Interview the president of a communication enterprise. List the daily activities of this person. Record your interview on paper and turn it in as a short report.
4. Choose a major communication corporation. Follow the stock values for that company. Use companies listed on the New York Stock Exchange (NYSE). Keep a written record of your company. How did it do over five days? Compare how you did with how the rest of the class did. Conduct a discussion with the class concerning why some companies made more money than others.
5. Collect the annual reports of major information firms. Have a class discussion about the various charts. What do they mean? How are these companies doing financially? What does the company sell?

Many people are now working in home offices. Graphic designers, writers, editors, and sales people are finding new freedom with the advances in computer technology. Electronic communication allows somebody who works out of a home office to quickly and effectively communicate with nearly anybody else in the world. As computers continue to advance communication technology, these home-based communication enterprises will continue to grow. (Xerox)

CHAPTER 27
COMMUNICATION—TODAY AND TOMORROW

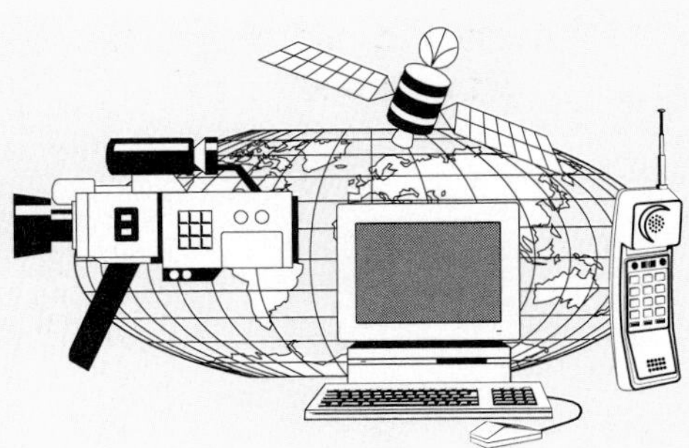

After studying this chapter, you will be able to:

- ❖ *Explain trends in communication technology.*
- ❖ *Identify possible developments in the future of communication systems.*

Technological growth has occurred rapidly in the last few years. Mathematicians describe this development as an exponential increase. Instead of a gradual (slow) increase in technology, growth has skyrocketed, Figure 27-1. This steady growth pattern is called ***exponential growth.*** This growth results from inventors building upon the knowledge and improvements of other inventors.

CURRENT TRENDS IN COMMUNICATION TECHNOLOGY

The area of communication has progressed rapidly. For example, traditional billboards have been replaced with electronic display boards. These painted and lighted signs are quite lifelike. They are also very effective in attracting the attention of potential buyers. As another example, colorful T-shirts are easy to make with the help of computer scanners that separate colors automatically. Automatic screen process presses allow the printing of four or more color prints.

In lithography, modern presses can print several colors at one time. A laser process can receive information through microwaves and produce a plate from the signals alone. This replaces negative filming and stripping procedures. Offset presses have platemakers connected to them that automatically develop and load the plate.

Desktop publishing is constantly growing. Very realistic computer illustrations can now be created. This is called ***photorealism.*** Text and graphics are created and merged into documents that were traditionally completed by manual methods. Computer technologies have improved communication systems more than any other single factor.

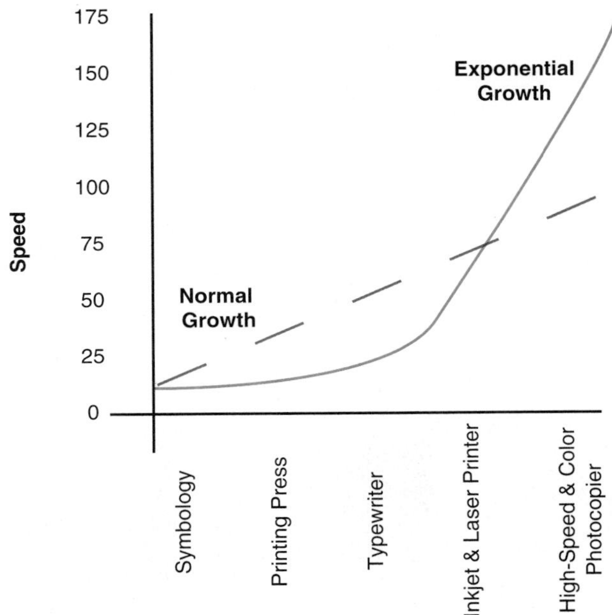

Figure 27-1. Advances in communication technology happen at a rapid rate. The improvement in printing is shown as a solid line. The dashed line shows a normal rate of progress. Growth that occurs faster than normal is said to be "exponential."

Photographic films are now available for unusual light or speed conditions. Very "fast" films (ISO 1600 or faster) are used to photograph sporting events or dark indoor events. "Slower" films are used for portraits or bright outdoor events. A range from ISO 64 to ISO 3200 is available at most photography shops.

Cameras are becoming very easy to operate. Fully automatic cameras adjust the focus and set the f-stop electronically. Some cameras "tell" the user if the light is sufficient to take a particular shot. Photography is advancing so much that film may even become a thing of the past. Photos are now recorded on CDs that can be played on players connected to a TV or on computer CD-ROM drives. If "read" from a CD-ROM drive, photo images can be directly placed in electronic publishing.

Photocopying machines now reduce and enlarge prints easily. They can also print on both sides, collate (sort), and pull data from computers. Color copiers are becoming common in business. Color laser printers are very popular in many industries.

Satellites are capable of keeping track of weather conditions. This is helpful for meteorologists (people that study the atmosphere and weather) who need to follow the path of a storm. Satellites also are used to complete long distance telephone calls and to transmit TV programs directly to homes. Satellites also aid in ship navigation and surveillance, Figure 27-2.

Figure 27-2. Communication satellites allow messages to be sent around the globe at the speed of light. They are the basis of worldwide telecommunication networks. (AT&T)

Home and office telephone service has changed a great deal over the past few years. Household telephones can now handle multiparty calls, call waiting, and multiple lines. Automatic dialing is another popular feature on many phones. Most business phones have ***voice mail.*** Voice mail is similar to an answering machine, but the message is recorded digitally in the phone system. Some business systems permit the transfer of pictures or financial data over normal telephone lines, Figure 27-3. Cordless phones and answering machines are very popular, Figure 27-4. The cellular phone is also a very popular means of communicating both in the home and office.

Figure 27-3. Telephones are not used just for voice communication anymore. Many companies transmit business data directly over phone lines. Special receivers display the data and allow voice communication to be maintained simultaneously.

Videocassette recorders (VCRs) are found in more homes than ever before. They come in a variety of models. Home movie rental is now a multi-billion dollar business. When was the last time you rented a video cassette to watch at home?

Perhaps the greatest progress in communication technology has been with personal computers. Lower costs and improved technology have made computers available to nearly everyone. Individuals and businesses alike use computers for day-to-day operations. Computer-aided design (CAD) is popular with designers

Figure 27-4. Cordless phones and answering machines help you communicate. These devices are found in most homes and offices. (AT&T, AT&T/Michael Gaffney)

Figure 27-6. A computer monitors a car's performance and keeps the driver informed. Computers are being used to control more functions of a car including environmental controls, performance, and entertainment systems. (Buick)

and engineers. CAD is used to quickly and accurately design, draw, and produce house plans and mechanical drawings, Figure 27-5.

Computers appear in many forms. In cash registers, computers total grocery bills. Computers in wristwatches keep time for a number of years. Computers also control several functions of cars. Electronic sensors inform the driver how the car is operating. Many cars have digital instrument panels that are controlled by a computer, Figure 27-6.

Figure 27-5. Computer-aided drafting can save a great deal of time. Revisions and changes are much easier with CAD systems.

COMMUNICATION TECHNOLOGY OF THE FUTURE

Researchers make educated forecasts about the future by reviewing past trends and reviewing "cutting edge" technological developments. Many researchers believe that the future in communication/information technology is only limited by the imagination. If an idea or product is important enough, or if a profit can be made, the technology will be developed to make it a reality. Many of the new communications devices that can be found on the market are improvements of existing products. The cellular telephone and picture phone are improvements to the traditional phone. The compact disc is an improvement to the cassette tape and vinyl record. Microelectronics and computer technology have led to many of today's innovative products. (An ***innovation*** is something that is new, either a new product or a new approach to an existing product.)

Television

Large screen projection TVs have been refined with clearer pictures. However, the video imagery is still fairly crude when compared to photographs. In the near future, high-definition televisions (HDTVs) will be available, Figure 27-7. Many HDTVs will feature 3D pictures. Many will have flat screens that will not require much space.

Figure 27-7. High-definitions televisions (HDTVs) have a very clear picture. Many of these TVs will have three-dimensional screens. Others will have flat screens that take up little space. As this technology emerges, many possibilities are present. (Thomson Consumer Electronics)

Cable TV continues to grow. Cable companies now charge for some special events like boxing matches or music concerts. These are called ***pay-for-view*** programs. Eventually, all special programming may be "pay-for-view."

Printing

Digital offset presses will soon be in common use. These presses eliminate the need for a plate. A laser scans the image directly onto the blanket cylinder, Figure 27-8. This allows text and artwork that has been assembled in a computer using desktop publishing software to be sent directly to the press. By doing this, much time and effort is eliminated. Also, by eliminating several steps, the chances for error are reduced.

Smart Cards

Credit cards have been available from major banks since the 1950s. Today, a type of credit cards called ***smart cards*** is emerging. These cards are based on a ***debit system.*** In a debit system, the card holder must have money in the account to use the card (similar to a checking account). As the card is used, money is automatically transferred from the user's account.

What makes smart cards different from normal credit cards is that they have a computer chip placed in the material of the card (the plastic). This chip stores personal information about the

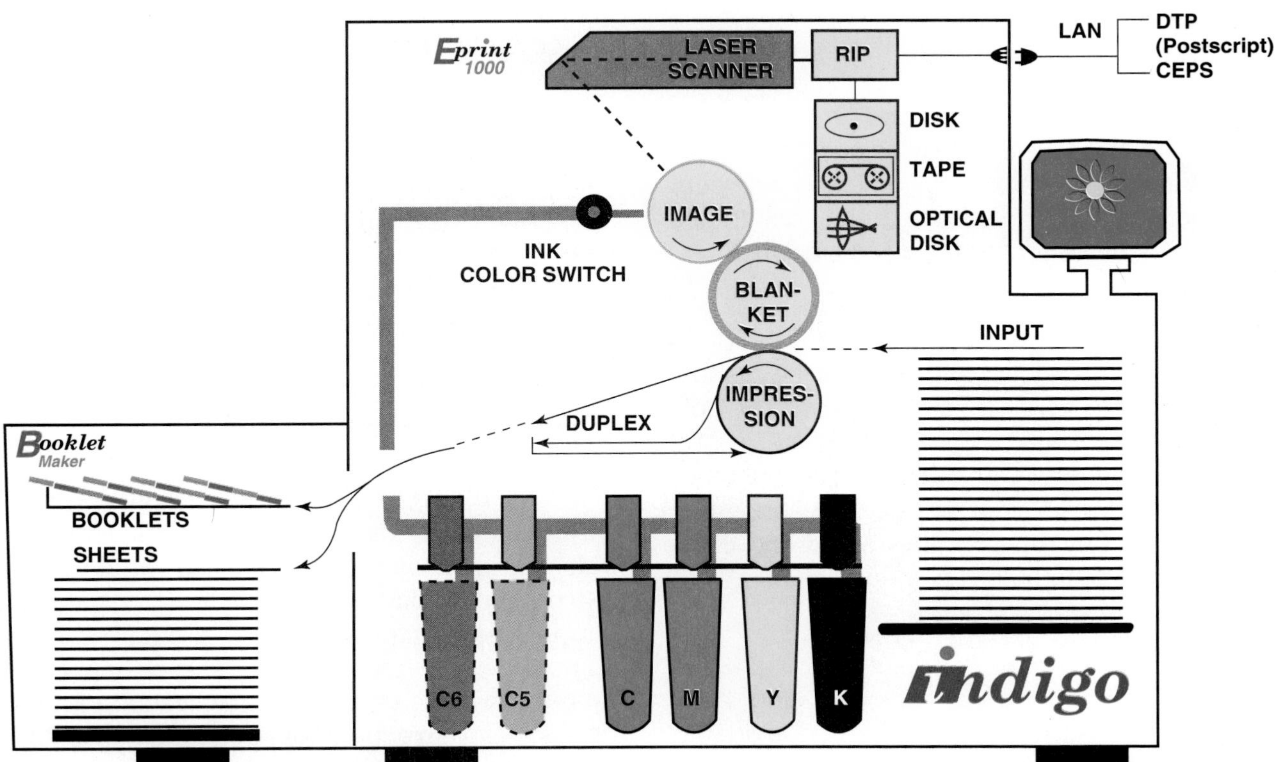

Figure 27-8. Digital offset presses have no plates. A laser scans the image directly onto the blanket cylinder. (Indigo America, Inc.)

card holder. Smart cards eliminate the need to carry cash. This reduces the chances of theft. Smart cards can be used in telephones, parking meters, vending machines, and at grocery stores, Figure 27-9. These types of machines operated mechanically in the past. Now that they operate electronically, maintenance costs are reduced.

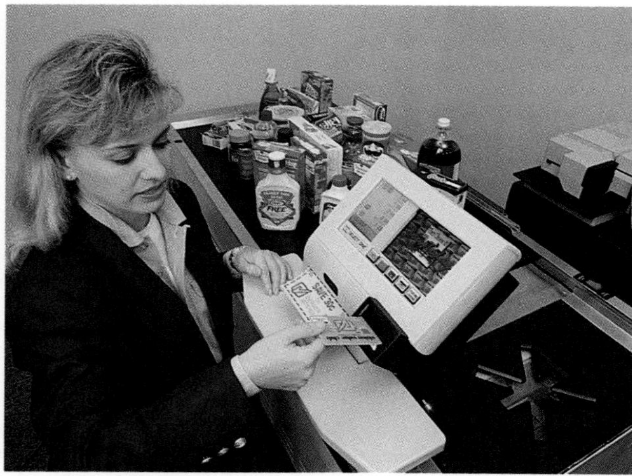

Figure 27-9. Smart cards operate on the debit system. In order for the card holder to use the card, they must have money in the account. Smart cards will be used in supermarkets, at vending machines, and at parking garages. (Advanced Promotion Technology)

Smart cards are now used in Japan and Europe. Trial uses are currently being conducted in North America. The next time you are in a grocery store, parking facility, or sports arena, look to see if there are any smart card facilities available.

Satellites

Many homes now have satellite TV dishes. However, in the future these dishes will not only be able to receive TV signals, but receive and *send* many types of signals, including computer signals. This means that you can be connected with almost anybody in the world by voice (phone), data (computer), or video.

Computers

Computers are constantly changing business, entertainment, and the home. Coupled with other technologies, computers are making human activities more efficient and increasing human potential. Online services are a good example. ***Online services*** provide routine access to virtually any information a person could want, anywhere in the world. These services continue to improve their quality and what information is offered. Magazines, newspapers, and encyclopedias are available "online," as is access to the Library of Congress. Even some museums can be accessed online, Figure 27-10. As these services are improved, more shopping, banking, research, and entertainment will be completed at home or in the office through the use of online services.

Multimedia will be used more in both education and business. ***Multimedia*** refers to the use of a computer to combine sound, graphics, animation, and information into a presentation. The presentation can be for learning, business, or entertainment. Multimedia systems typically allow the user to redirect their focus at any point in the presentation to learn more about a specific area of the presentation. This will become a very powerful tool in education and business in the future.

Virtual reality is the creation of a simulated environment through the use of computer, light, and sound technologies. Virtual reality is similar to multimedia. Virtual reality "transports" the user into a make-believe world. Visual and audio information is provided to the user in response to the user's actions. The computer receives information on the users movements from sensors in gloves or a helmet, Figure 27-11. The computer then reacts to the movement of the sensors and provides the appropriate information back to the user. Eventually, the sensors will not need to be worn by the user. The sensors will be located inside walls of special rooms. These rooms will in effect "become" different places or worlds. In addition, the sensation of touch will be created. Virtual reality has many applications in the design and entertainment industries.

Voice activation will become readily available in the future. ***Voice activation*** allows the user to control a device with voice commands. The computer (or other device) "recognizes" what you tell it to do and responds accordingly. For instance, if you tell the computer to "print" a document, the computer will understand your voice input and prepare the document. Voice activation will also become available for other uses as well. Lights in your home may be controlled by voice activation. The remote control for your stereo and TV may also be replaced by voice activation.

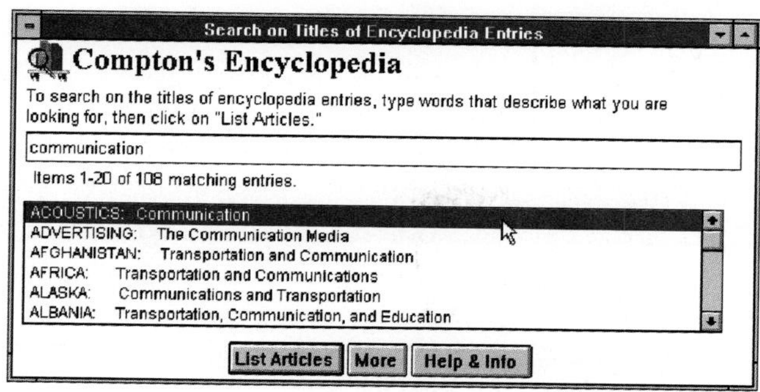

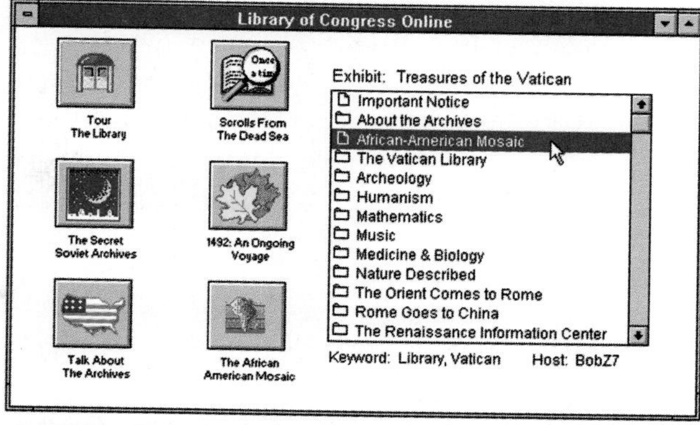

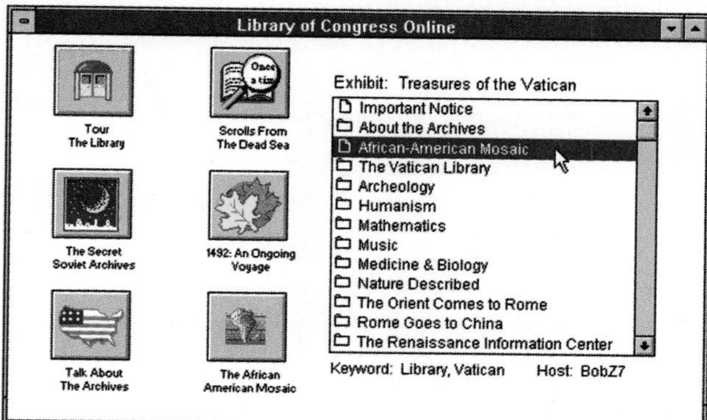

Figure 27-10. Magazines, newspapers, encyclopedias, library access, and museum access are all available "online." As online services continue to improve the quality and quantity of information available, much of your shopping, banking, and research will be done at home in the future. (America Online©, Inc.)

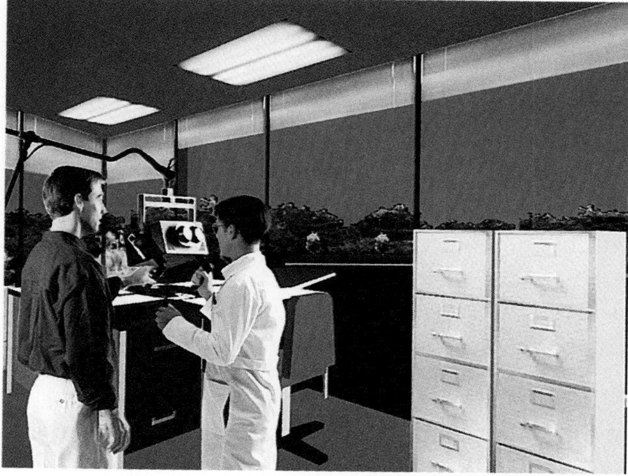

Figure 27-11. Virtual reality (VR) has many applications in the design area. VR allows the designer to "step into" the area being designed. VR has many other applications in the design and entertainment fields. (Courtesy of Fakespace and the Army Research Institute)

CHAPTER 27 REVIEW

SUMMARY

Technological advancements and innovations continue to occur rapidly. This rapid development is known as exponential growth. Rapid development in communication technology is expected to continue.

Current trends that are associated with this growth are in color printing and copying, automatic and filmless cameras, cellular telephones, FAX transmission, and computer-aided design (CAD).

Researchers have quite a lengthy list of what you might expect in the future. Included on this list are flat screen TVs, electronic newspapers and magazines available in every home, and home satellite communication. Continued improvements in online services will allow almost everybody to shop and bank at home. Multimedia and virtual reality will soon become an important part of business and education.

KEY WORDS

All of the following words have been used in this chapter. Do you know their meanings?

Debit system
Exponential growth
Innovation
Multimedia
Online services
Pay-for-view
Photorealism
Smart cards
Virtual reality
Voice activation
Voice mail

TEST YOUR KNOWLEDGE

Place you answers on a separate sheet of paper. Please do not write in this book.

1. What is exponential growth?
2. What is an innovation?
3. List current trends in printing, photography, satellite communication, telephone, television, and computer technology.
4. Researchers make accurate forecasts of the future by reviewing _____ _____ and cutting edge _____ _____.

5. What can be expected in television in the future?
6. What is an electronic newspaper?

Matching questions: Match the definition in the left-hand column with the term in the right-hand column.

7. Network that allows a computer user to do banking, "chatting," and shopping.
8. Combining audio, video, and animation to create a presentation that conveys information.
9. Software servants.
10. Using computers to create an environment and "transport" the user into that environment.

A. Online services.
B. Multimedia.
C. Smart cards.
D. Virtual reality.

ACTIVITIES

1. Interview several people over the age of 55. Ask them to describe the changes in communication they have witnessed during their lifetimes. Tape record the interviews and play them back to the class. Conduct a discussion on what these people had to say about changes in communication.
2. Talk to an office worker at your school or your parents' offices. Ask about new communication devices being used in the office today. Write a short report on you research.
3. Read a science fiction book from about ten years ago. Make a list of communication devices mentioned in the book. Are any of these devices actually in use? Read a new science fiction book (less than five years old). Which of these devices do you think will be in use in the future? Write a short report comparing the two books and the technological devices in each book.
4. With your classmates, develop a list of communication devices you would like to see invented. Make illustrations of what these new devices might look like. Discuss the possibility of these devices actually being invented. What technology would be needed for your "new" devices to be a reality?

Section 5 Review

Today, we live in an "information age." That's because creating and exchanging information is the major task of so many individuals and companies. People who work at the telephone company are information workers. So are publishers and the staff at copy centers. News reporters, advertisers, radio DJs, and photographers are other examples of information workers. Movie producers and recording artists are also a part of the information age.

The basis for modern society is individuals and companies that deal with information. When discussing companies, these groups are called enterprises. An enterprise might be owned by a single proprietor, a partnership of two or more people, or a corporation. Large firms like AT&T, CNN, IBM, or HBO are corporations. Many individuals own stock in these enterprises.

Information enterprises, like all companies, exist to make a profit. Television and radio stations make money by selling advertising time. Film production companies make their profits from the sale of movie tickets and video rentals. Recording companies make millions of dollars selling audio cassettes and CDs. Instant printing firms charge individuals to make photocopies of documents.

The influence of communication devices and systems in everyday life will continue to increase rapidly. This rapid rate of change is called exponential growth. Examples of this growth can be seen every day. For instance, digital technology allows you to enjoy better sound and graphics programs. Direct broadcast satellite dishes can provide hundreds of television channels to each household. These things were not around just a few years ago. For the near future, advanced navigational systems may soon guide vehicles as you travel. Your home computer may soon fit into a box the size of a cassette tape. The advancement of technology seems almost limitless.

Section 5 Activities

1. Many enterprises in your neighborhood are classified as information industries. List the companies that fit this description. Note the primary service or products they offer the public. How does this affect everyday life? What would happen if that type of business no longer existed? Prepare a short report about each company. Sketch a view of each company to include with the description. If a CAD system is available, use it to sketch the company. Present your report to the class.

  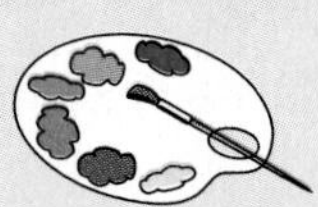

2. Write to several Fortune 500 companies with services and products related to communication technologies. Request a copy of their annual report. Note what new products and services are being offered to consumers. Prepare a short report

summarizing each company. Create a poster showing the firm's location. Include a chart showing the company's basic operations and products. What do these companies have in common? How are they different? How do they affect your personal life and the lives of your family? How do the new products or services they offer fill a need in society? How do you think they went about designing that product or service?

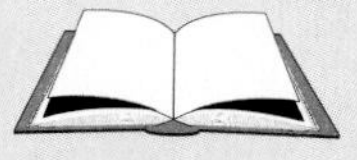   

3. Enterprises, like the companies identified above, attempt to profit from their products and services. Create a bar graph comparing the amount of profit each firm made last year from each of their top five products. What percentage of the firm's total profits were from each product? Explain your findings to the class. How are these products used by society? Are they benefiting society?

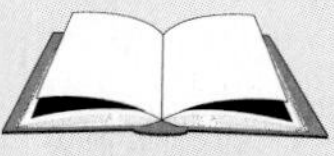  

4. Information enterprises need many skilled workers and managers. Ask a social science and a technology teacher what traits employers are looking for. Identify universities and community colleges in your state that offer communication courses. Are classes offered that will help develop these traits? Make a chart showing the abilities required to excel in the information age. Include the universities and community colleges that you feel will help develop these abilities.

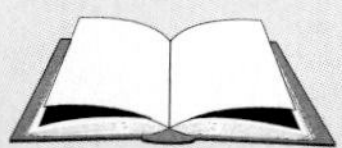  

5. If you could invent any new communication device, what type of device or system would you create? Develop a sketch of your new invention. Use a CAD system if possible. Prepare a short description of the device or system. Explain your invention to the class. Explain how it will help society. Explain the different technologies and sciences needed to create your invention.

  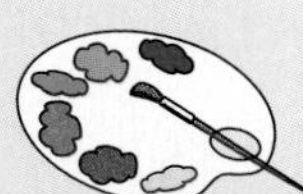 

GLOSSARY

A

Accuracy: Free from mistakes or errors.

Active sonar: Sends out and listens for sound waves. It is used when distance, depth, and location must be known. Active sonar will not only determine that there is an object in the water, it will also give the exact location of that object.

Advertising agency: A large organization that specializes in the task of creating advertisements for other companies

Affiliates: Stations that carry the programs of one of the major networks.

Aftermarket fonts: Fonts that are not included with the original DTP or word processing software.

Amateur bands: Frequencies used for long-distance personal communication. These frequencies allow more options than CB bands. For example, amateur bands allow the user to send transmissions around the world. This can be helpful during emergency situations. Other people use these frequencies to communicate as a hobby. These people are called "ham" radio operators.

Amperage: A measure of electric current.

Amplification: The process of making light, sound, or feelings more intense.

Amplifier: Increases the power, or amplitude, of the signal. An amplifier is used on weak signals. By amplifying the signal, the signal becomes powerful enough to be used.

Amplitude: One half of the distance (height) between the crest and trough of a wave.

Amplitude modulation (AM): A form of radio communication where the amplitude of the radio wave is changed to transmit the message.

Analog signals: These signals tend to vary constantly. They are smooth and continuous. Voices are analog signals. Voices change constantly over a wide range.

Annual report: The report produced every year (annually) by a corporation or other company to report on financial matters. An annual report typically includes information such as stock price ranges, summaries of operation costs, and a note to the stockholders (owners).

Antennas: Aid in receiving signals sent through the atmosphere.

Aperture: The physical size of the shutter opening of a camera.

Applications software: The programs that complete certain tasks. Application software can be a word processor, a spreadsheet program, a CAD program, or a game. Each program tells the computer to work in a different way and allows the user to complete many different types of work.

Apprenticeship: The time spent observing and working with a person who has achieved the classification of "master" (master printer, for example).

Architectural drawings: Plans for homes and buildings.

Architectural illustrations: Finely detailed drawings that represent what the final building will look like.

Artificial intelligence (AI): A term used to describe machines that can "think." Computers that have AI are capable of making decisions and ethical judgments.

ASCII: (pronounced as-ski) The most common standard code for software. ASCII stands for American Standard Code for Information Interchange.

Assembly drawings: These drawings show how several items or parts of an object are assembled. These drawings are also called exploded view drawings.

Assets: The things a company owns that can be sold. Assets include equipment, buildings, property, and inventory.

Asynchronous transmission: Data transmission where each bit is sent by itself. Serial transmissions can be synchronous or asynchronous.

Atom: The building block of all substances. Land, water, and people are all made up of atoms.

An atom is made up of protons, neutrons, and electrons.

Audible: Sounds that can be heard by humans.

Audio communication: Involves the sense of hearing.

Audiovisual communication: Involves both the sense of hearing and the sense of sight.

B

Backdrops: These represent walls or scenery on a set. Backdrops can be simply painted onto large sheets of plywood.

Bakelite®: A material that can be molded while it is hot. Once this material is cooled, it becomes permanently solid.

Balance: Deals with the location of parts or objects within a layout. If the parts are centered, the layout is referred to as having "formal balance." In this case, each item is orderly and evenly weighted. If the arrangement of objects is random, the layout has "informal balance."

Balanced: When the number of protons equals the number of electrons in an atom.

Binary code: A code of digital data that is used in computers.

Block printing: Printing that uses an image (picture) or text cut into a wooden block. These blocks were used to print images on plaster, textiles, and parchment or paper. This was a big improvement over handwriting. However, the process was still very slow since each page had to be carved in a single wooden block and the block had to be placed on each page by hand.

Block signaling system: A signaling system that uses light signals to inform railroad engineers if any trains are on the tracks ahead.

Bounded transmission channels: Containing a transmission in a controlled medium. Examples include wire pairs, coaxial cables, waveguides, and fiber-optic cables.

Braille: A code of raised, printed "dots." These dots represent letters, words, and numbers. By moving their fingers across a page a blind person can "feel" the words.

Brayer: A small roller used to help apply pressure. It has many applications in graphic communication including film work.

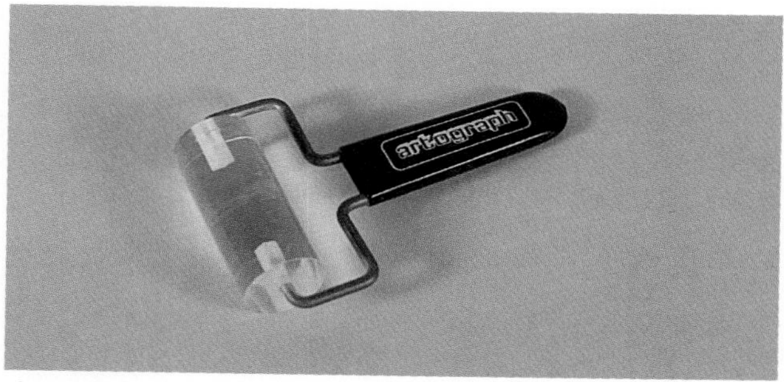

A brayer.

Break line: Shows a break in the total distance of very long objects when those objects are drawn. A section of the object is "removed." The removed section will have no features on it that are not already explained and indicated in the drawing. Examples of objects that may have break lines used to draw them include pipes, steel beams, and walls.

Bugs: Problems with a program that prevent it from running properly.

Buoys: Devices that float in rivers, lakes, and other bodies of water to mark important areas, such as channels, or to warn of potential dangers.

Burn out: Describes what happens when too much pressure or adhering fluid is used to apply a stencil to a screen for screen process printing. When burn out occurs, part of the stencil that forms the image will be removed. This is not desired.

Burning: The process of transferring an image from film to a printing plate.

C

C: A programming language used in computers. The most commonly used language today.

Cables: Allow the transmission of electromagnetic signals to be controlled. This is because the signals are sent along wires enclosed in a protective covering. These cables can be buried underground, run aboveground between poles, or laid underwater. The signals inside of the cable are almost totally free from weather interference.

California job case: A container that is used to store foundry type. The type is not arranged in alphabetical order but rather in the order of use.

Camera: A "box" that controls the transfer of light to film. Most cameras consist of two major parts: the body and the lens.

Camera ready: Refers to a layout being ready to make exposures on film. The film is then used to make the plates that will be used to print the images.

Capital: The money needed to start and run a business.

Carrier wave: The wave that "carries" the information (message).

Cartographers: The drafters who draw maps from the information provided by surveyors.

Cartography: Simply stated, cartography is map making. Many areas of land are measured for distance and elevation (height). Maps of the terrain (land) are then prepared from the measurements taken.

Cathode-ray tube (CRT): A type of display device used for computers and TVs. The CRT contains an electron gun that shoots electrons out onto the television screen.

CD-ROM: A computer storage device that uses compact disc technology. A CD-ROM drive reads information from a CD that contains computer information.

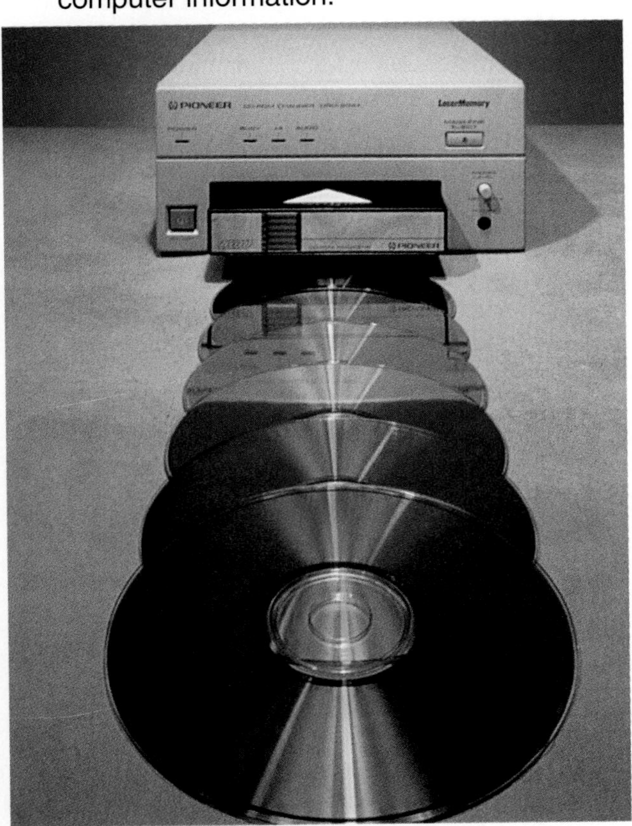

Multi-disc CD-ROM drive. (Pioneer)

Centerlines: Used to show the centers of objects. They are made up of a series of alternating long and short dashes with short spaces in between.

Central processing unit (CPU): The internal memory or "brain" of a computer. This electronic device can calculate and manipulate information at great speeds. Early CPUs often filled entire rooms and required large amounts of energy. With the invention of the silicon chip, computers have become smaller. Microprocessing CPUs are small enough to fit into wristwatches and small toys.

Citizens band: Frequencies used for short distance communication and remote control products. For example, CB radios, garage door openers, and television remote controls all use frequencies that are citizens band.

Clip art: Drawn by professional artists, clip art is available in book form with several drawings on each page. Clip art is also available on CDs for use with computers that have a CD-ROM drive.

Codes: Signals and symbols used to transmit messages.

Coherent light: Light that is made up of all the same wavelength. Laser light is an example of coherent light.

Color: Used to add emphasis to graphic work. Red and yellow attract attention. Blue and green are calming (or mild) colors. Changing the color of text draws attention to the printed material.

Communication: The process of exchanging information.

Communication industry: The creating and transferring of information.

Communication technology: The process of transmitting information from a source to a destination using codes and storage systems.

Compact disc player: A piece of stereo equipment that uses a laser to "read" a compact disc.

Compact discs: A very popular storage device for recorded sounds. A laser beam "reads" the sound information from the disc. The sound is recorded as a series of high and low spots on the surface of the disc. These "pits" represent a binary code.

Companies: Business enterprises that conduct economic activities.

Comprehensive layout: Used by the layout person as a guide during the reproduction work. However, the actual type (typeset text) and illustrations are not used at this point. Therefore, final corrections of the layout can still be made.

Computers: Devices that perform calculations and process data.

Computer graphics: The use of computers to develop drawings. Also known as computer-aided drafting or computer-aided design (CAD).

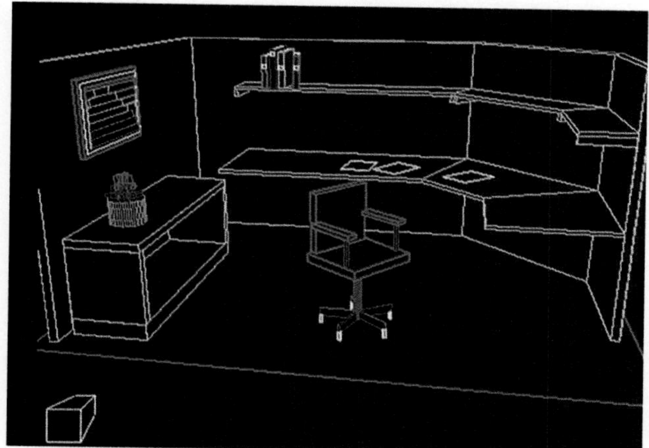

Computer-aided design.

Computer language: A set of commands that the computer can use to work with data. When these commands are put together as a related set, a program is made.

Computer software: A set of instructions used to run a computer. There are several different computer "languages." There are also different types of programs.

Computer-aided drafting (CAD): Using computer systems and software to help create technical drawings.

Conductor: A material, such as copper or silver, that allows easy movement of free electrons.

Construction lines: Used to give a drawing its basic shape. These lines are drawn very lightly.

Contact print: A one-sheet print of all the negatives from a single roll of film. This allows the photographer to examine all of the pictures and print only the ones desired.

Continuous tone photography: The term used to describe making images with a camera and chemically treated film. When you take pictures at home with your camera, you are using continuous tone photography.

Contrast: Important in providing a point of emphasis in a layout. Contrast can be achieved with colors, text, or lines. Bold styles of lettering often provide contrast. Color or shading of artwork can also provide contrast. Attempts to "catch" your eye usually are examples of contrast.

Convention: A universal (worldwide) system for communicating ideas. A convention is also an accepted way of doing things. In drafting, a convention is followed when using symbols so that any drafter can look at a drawing and know what is being communicated.

Converter: A converter in an AM radio changes the incoming signal frequencies to a single, specific frequency. The signal can then be amplified and converted back to audio.

Copy board: Holds the original artwork in place for photographing. Typically a copy board is used with a process camera.

Corporation: A business that is owned by shareholders and set up following specific legal guidelines. A corporation is run by a board of directors that makes business decisions for the company. Some corporations are very large. Other corporations can be small.

Creation: The assembling and recording of ideas.

Creative lighting: These types of lights are usually colored. Creative lighting is used to create a certain effect on a scene.

Crest: The highest point of a wave.

Cropping: A common way of removing unwanted sections of a negative from the print. It is similar to "cutting" the unwanted parts out of the photograph, but done during the exposure. Cropping can only be used to change the outside dimensions of the photograph. Cropping cannot be used to take out features in the middle of the photograph.

Cutaway views: Show features (usually internal features) you would not be able to see without "cutting away" the part.

Cybernetics: The study of automatic control systems (that may be electro-mechanical), or one machine controlling another.

D

Daguerreotype: The first practical photograph. Named after Louis Daguerre of France who invented the process.

Daisy wheel printers: Primarily capable of producing text only. These printers are used in schools and businesses where only text is printed. Examples include printing invoices, letters, and package labels.

Data communication: The process of transmitting information in binary form between two points.

Data processing: Using a computer to store and perform functions on information (such as reports, accounts receivable information, and client addresses).

Database: Information kept in electronic files for future use.

Debit system: A system of using a credit card where the user must have money in their account to use the card. This is similar to how a checking account works.

Debugging: The process of correcting bugs, or problems, in a computer program.

Demodulator: Sends out only the original audio signal. The amplifier in the demodulator boosts the signal to the power levels needed by the speakers. The speakers then deliver the original sound.

Design elements: Includes shape, mass, texture, lines, and color.

Design firms: Also called design agencies. Design firms are companies that specialize in the creative design of commercial items.

Design principles: Includes balance, contrast, rhythm, proportion, and unity.

Designing process: Includes ideation, purpose, and creation.

Desktop publishing (DTP): Involves using a personal, or "desktop," computer to perform compositions that were previously done by hand. Today a variety of word processing and graphic programs can be combined using a personal computer, publishing software, and a high-resolution printer.

Developer: The chemical that reveals the image on exposed film.

Developing: The process of making a latent image on film visible and permanent. This procedure is also called processing.

Diaphragm: A flexible membrane (similar to a rubber disk) attached to a solid frame.

Diazo printing: Transfers an image by passing the original image through a diazo machine along with a special light-sensitive copy paper. The image is copied by exposing the paper to light. The copied image is developed by exposing it to ammonia gases.

Digital signals: These signals can represent only discrete numbers. The most common example is 0 or 1. There is nothing that represents 1.5 or .25, only a 1 or a 0.

Digitizers: Devices that take information from drawings or objects and translates that information into data a computer can use. This data can then be used to create a drawing on the computer.

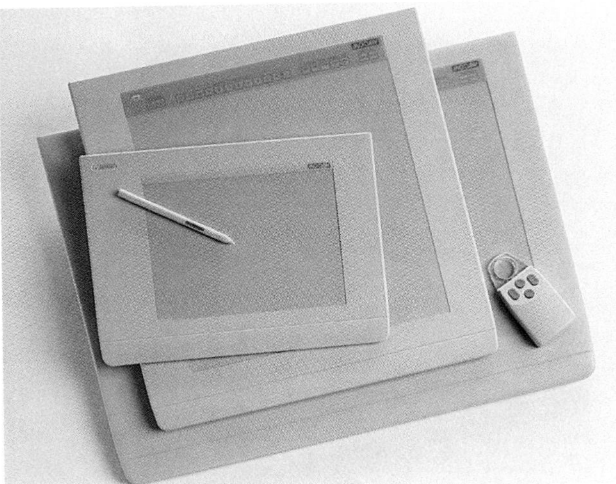

Digitizing tablets. (WACOM)

Digitizing: Converting drawings, text, photographs, or other "hard copy" images into computer images by electronically tracing over them.

Dimension lines: Used to show the dimensions of an object. They usually have arrowheads at the ends of the lines. Dimension lines are light and thin.

Direct broadcast satellites (DBS): These particular satellites broadcast directly to the home. (This is a technology currently under development.) Current satellite broadcasts are supplied by communication companies who own the satellites. DBS systems would have enough power to transmit signals to a smaller (and less costly) antenna than is currently needed.

Direct feedback: Information is returned to the sender by direct observation of the receiver.

Direct-image plates: Uses plates made of paper (most are purchased commercially). Various methods are used for creating images and text on the plate. Images can be hand drawn with special reproducing pencils and pens. These instruments leave a deposit on the plate that will absorb ink. Typewriters with carbon-based ribbons are also used.

Disc: A compact disc. May be for audio or CD-ROM.

Disk: A computer disk. May be called a floppy disk. May also be used in reference to a computer hard drive.

Distributed networks: Contain a central computer attached to other computers. Resources in this network are spread among all the computers. One computer does not contain all the information.

Ditto printing process: Works by typing or drawing onto a special master. This leaves a carbon deposit on the carrier sheet. A spirit fluid softens the carbon during the printing process. This allows the images to be deposited on paper.

Dot matrix printers: These printers form text and images with tiny "dots" transferred from a ribbon. A set of "pins" mechanically drives the ribbon into the paper. These printers are referred to by the number of "pins" they have (9 pin, 24 pin). These printers are also known as "pin printers."

Downlink: Transmitting information from a satellite to earth.

Drafting: The presentation of ideas through line drawings. Drafting can also be defined as the sketching and drawing of plans.

Drafting board: The surface that drafters and designers use to make drawings on. The board is large enough to hold a drawing without crowding the drafter. Drafting boards are often part of a drawing table.

Parallel-rule drafting board.

Drafting machine: A mechanical device that attaches to the drafting board or table. It can move both horizontally and vertically. Many have a "head" that can be rotated to draw angled lines. A drafting machine makes certain that all lines are drawn at the proper and same angles.

E

Elasticity: The ability of a mass to return to its original shape.

Electric current: The actual "flow" of electrons.

Electricity: The movement of electrons.

Electromagnetic energy: Energy in the form of waves. Radio waves, microwaves, visible light, infrared light, and X-rays are all examples of electromagnetic energy.

Electromagnetic field: A field of magnetic energy produced by electric current.

Electromagnetic spectrum: The range of electromagnetic energy.

Electromagnetic waves: Created by the oscillation of an electromagnetic field.

Electronic communication: Involves the use of electrical energy to transmit information between individuals or systems.

Electronic scanners: Allow line artwork and photographs to be digitized and used with computer programs.

Electrons: Revolve around the nucleus of an atom in "rings," much like planets revolve around the sun. Electrons are smaller than protons and neutrons. Electrons have a negative (-) electrical charge.

Electrostatic copiers: Uses powdered inks for copying. The powdered ink, called toner, is electrically charged. The paper is then given the same charge. The image is given the opposite charge. Since science has demonstrated that opposite charges attract, the toner is attracted to the image area but repelled from the rest of the paper.

Ellipse: How circles appear in isometric projections. Ellipses are an oval. If you were to "squeeze" a circle from the top and the bottom, the result would be an ellipse.

E-mail: Stands for electronic mail. This is a form of communication where messages, or "letters," are sent using a computer and a modem connected to a computer network.

Engineering drawings: Plans for manufactured products.

Enterprise: A business organization or company. The purpose of an enterprise is to make a profit from the sale of a product or service.

Exploded view drawings: Show how all the parts of an object fit together. These drawings are also called assembly drawings.

Exponential growth: A growth that does not follow a straight line, but rather starts off slow and then increases quickly.

Exposure time: The amount of time that the film receives light.

Extrasensory perception (ESP): Thought to exist outside of normal human senses. (Extrasensory means "outside of the senses.") People with ESP claim to have mind-reading abilities. Some scientists believe in this form of communication. Others doubt it can be proved.

Extraterrestrial: Means outside the earth. Anything that is extraterrestrial comes from space.

Eye level: The viewing plane that is positioned horizontally in front of your eyes. All objects that are on this plane appear to be directly in front of you. Objects above or below this viewing plane appear slightly different than they would if they were at "eye level."

F

f-stop: A number indicating the aperture size. The higher the f-stop number, the smaller the aperture. A smaller aperture means less light will strike the film.

Federal Communications Commission (FCC): A government agency that regulates radio, TV, and telephone communication.

Feedback: Information returned to the sender to show that a message has been received.

Fiber optics: The technology of using glass "wires" (optic fibers) to send signals in the form of light pulses.

Fiber-optic cables. (GE Plastics)

Fiber-optic cables: Similar to copper wire cables but fiber-optic cables are made up of many optic fibers. Used to carry data in fiber optics.

Fixed sonar: A method for using active sonar. In this way, the transducer is attached to a vessel, usually a submarine. The sound waves are sent out from the ship and the echoes are received in the same location.

Fixer: A chemical that makes the developed image on film permanent.

Flat: A ruled (lined) goldenrod sheet used when preparing artwork for making a printing plate. A hole, or "window," is cut in the sheet. Developed film that has the desired image on it is placed in the window. The flat is then used to make the plate.

Floppy disk: A computer disk that is removable. Commonly referred to as a floppy or a disk.

Floptical: A computer disk that has information stored on it by using light. Information is read from the disk using light as well.

Fluorescent lights: Long, white tubes that can be found in most schools and offices.

Font: The way a particular typeface "looks." For example, type can be generated as Courier, Helvetica, Schoolbook, Times Roman, or other fonts.

Foreshortening: A term used to describe how items appear smaller when observed from farther away. Foreshortening is the reason a mountain appears only inches high from a distance.

Formal balance: Describes the arrangement of a layout if the objects are placed in an orderly and even manner on the page.

Format: The type of programs a station will provide.

Foundry type: A form of relief printing. Foundry type was developed by Johannes Gutenberg. (Gutenberg invented the "type mold" that made certain that each piece of type was exactly the same. This made movable type practical.) This system of movable type is still useful in the production of certain items, such as rubber stamps.

Freelance photographers: People who take photographs but are not employed with a company. These people are hired to do a single job.

French curves: Also called irregular curves. French curves are tools used for drawing curved lines. These tools have multiple curved edges. Any two points on a French curve will have different radii (plural form of radius). French curves are useful when drawing objects that have curved surfaces with many different radii.

Frequency: The number of waves passing a given point in one second. Frequency is a timed measurement. Frequency and wavelength are inversely proportional. This means that the higher the frequency, the shorter the wavelength.

Frequency modulation (FM): A form of radio communication where the frequency of the radio wave is changed to transmit the message.

G

Gamma rays: The shortest waves in the electromagnetic spectrum. Gamma rays also have the highest frequency.

Geosynchronous orbit: A satellite orbit that is in a fixed position above the earth.

Graph paper: Paper that has a grid (lines) printed on it. This grid guides the drafter in keeping lines straight, parallel, or of equal length.

Graphic communication: Consists of two subareas: technical graphics and printed graphics.

Graphic frames: Temporary guidelines used when laying out a page in desktop publishing.These guidelines "define" where graphics will be placed on the page. These "frames" can be moved around on the page until everything is in the precise locations that the graphic designer wants.

Gravure printing: The industry term for "intaglio printing."

Gray scale: A strip of film with a range of grays from clear to totally black. It aids in developing the film the proper amount of time.

Grid system: A system of lines that are used to aid in drawing proportional items. This grid system is much like graph paper, except that the second grid will be as large or as small as the proportion that you are trying to achieve. For example, if you want to make a drawing twice the original size (proportionally double) then the second grid will be twice the size as well.

Guides: Indicators on a printing base to make certain that the transfer medium is placed at the exact same spot for every printing. These are different from registration marks because they are used to locate the transfer medium, not the screen or stencil.

H

Halftone negative: A photograph that is converted into a series of dots. The dots then make up the image. A halftone image is required for most printing processes.

Hand composition: Assembling text and graphic images manually.

Hardware: The "equipment" or actual physical components of a computer.

Computer hardware—the actual physical components. (Hewlett-Packard Co.)

Hard-wired systems: Systems or equipment permanently connected by wire. The telephone is a good example.

Heat transfer printing: Bonds images that were created by screen process printing to the final surface. Usually this process is used with textile (cloth).

Hidden lines: Used to show edges or parts of an object that are not visible. They are drawn using a series of short dashes and spaces.

Hieroglyphics: A ancient form of writing that used pictures to communicate ideas.

Hieroglyphs: The drawings used in hieroglyphics. Hieroglyphs are similar to the letters used in our alphabet.

Holograms: Holograms can be developed by beams of light intersecting in space. A lifelike image is produced at the point where the light waves meet. Holograms also have important commercial value far beyond recreational. Credit cards are imprinted with holograms to help deter counterfeiting.

Horizontal line: A line that is parallel to the top and bottom of the paper.

Human-to-human communication: Information moving between humans using only basic forms of technology. No complex machines assist the sensory system in receiving messages.

Human-to-machine communication: Information moving from a person to a machine.

I

Ideation: Getting and working on ideas.

Illumination: Using lights to "light up" darkness.

Image focus: How sharp an image appears to the eye.

Imagesetters: Machines that take the artwork and layout from a computer and electronically print those images on film. The machine will then develop the film. The resulting image (usually a negative) can then be used to "burn" the plate.

Importing: Taking text (or an image) from a different computer application (program) and moving it into the program that you are using (a DTP program). This is a major advantage of desktop publishing software.

Impressions: The transferred images that result from type being pressed into a transfer medium (paper).

Inaudible: Sounds that cannot be heard by humans.

Inclined lines: Straight lines that are not parallel or perpendicular to either the top or side edges of the paper.

Incoherent light: Light that has a variety of frequencies (wavelengths). Different "colors" of light are caused by these varying wavelengths. Light from the sun is incoherent light.

Independent stations: Stations that are not affiliates of the major networks. These stations may be special interest stations, such as religious stations, or they may carry syndicated shows.

Indirect feedback: Information returned to the sender by observing the results of a receiver's actions.

Individual communication: Communicating with other individuals.

Induction: The process of producing an electrical current by moving a wire through a magnetic field.

Industry: A group of related businesses.

Informal balance: Describes the arrangement of a layout if the objects are randomly placed on the page.

Information: Knowledge that can be conveyed between two people.

Information industries: A term used to refer to communication industries.

Information overload: Exposure to an excessive amount of information.

Ink jet printers: These printers use droplets of ink "shot" onto the paper to form text and images. These printers are controlled by computers.

An ink jet printer. A form of input/output device. (Courtesy of Epson)

Innovation: Something that is new, either a new product or a new approach to an existing product.

Input devices: A means for putting data into the computer. The keyboard on a microcomputer is the most common input device.

Input/Output (I/O) devices: Computer peripherals.

Insider trading: The illegal exchange of information on the stock market.

Instrument Landing System (ILS): Uses coded waves to guide the direction of aircraft. All major airports are equipped with this system.

Insulator: A material, such as plastic or glass, that does not allow easy movement of electrons. In other words, an insulator resists or prevents the flow of electricity.

Intaglio printing: (pronounced in-'tal-yo) This printing transfers ink from an image engraved into (below) a surface. In industry, this engraving is done on a metal plate or cylinder. Ink is applied to the engraved surface. A blade is used to wipe off excess ink from the surface of the plate. The ink will stay below the surface in the engraved areas. When paper is pressed onto the surface, ink lifts out of the engraved image area and is transferred to the paper. The plate must be created wrong-reading, or backwards. In industry, this is better known as "gravure printing."

Integrated circuits (ICs): Devices that combine distinct functions into a single unit. ICs are complete electronic systems manufactured on a single silicon chip. The integrated circuit was first patented in 1959.

Intensity: Determined by the power, or amplitude, of a wave.

Interference: A distortion of the signals intended for the receiver.

Ionosphere: The part of the Earth's atmosphere that reflects electromagnetic waves back down to the earth.

ISO rating: Indicates the amount of light needed to expose the film. (ISO stands for International Standards Organization.) Low ISO ratings (like ISO 100) are slow films and will produce sharp images. Faster film (like ISO 400) are useful for photographing in limited lighting and for photographing moving objects. A "slow" film requires more light to reproduce the exact same image as a "fast" film.

Isometric drawings: Show all of the object lines at the true proportions (same "size"), like orthographic drawings. However, all of the object lines can be seen in a single view, not in three views like orthographic drawings. In other words, they are three-dimensional representations. Height lines are parallel to the side borders of the drawing. The width and depth lines angle upwards at (typically) a 30° angle.

Isometric paper: Graph paper that has horizontal, vertical, and angled lines. The angled lines are typically at 30° to the horizontal lines. This type of paper is useful in sketching isometric drawings.

Isometric projections: Three-dimensional drawings that show objects very similar to how they appear to the eye. Vertical edges are shown as vertical lines. Depth is usually shown with lines extending back to the right at a 30 degree angle. Width is usually shown with lines extending back to the left at a 30 degree angle. Isometric projections are similar to oblique projections. Isometric projections are more realistic than oblique projections, however, they are more difficult to lay out.

Isometric template: A template that permits the construction of clean, neat ellipses. Several different sizes of ellipses appear on the template. Typically, these templates are made for isometric projections where both the width and depth lines extend at 30° angles.

K

Kinetoscope: The first commercial "moving picture machine." Introduced in 1893 by Thomas Edison's company.

L

Landscape: A printing setup where the text and graphics are oriented on the "height" dimension of a page. If you were to write in your notebook "sideways," you would be writing in landscape orientation.

Laser: Stands for the words **L**ight **A**mplification by **S**timulated **E**mission of **R**adiation. Laser light is a form of radiation that is amplified (boosted) to a high energy level. Laser light produces a strong, narrow beam of light. It does not disperse (spread out) and become lost energy when used.

Latent image: The invisible image that is created on film during exposure.

Layout: The assembly of copy (text) and artwork (illustrations).

Light emitting diodes (LEDs): Diodes that give off visible light. A common use of LEDs is on calculator displays. LEDs can also be used in fiber optics. They are less costly and longer lasting than lasers.

Line of sight transmission: Refers to light communication using unbounded transmission channels (the air, for example). Beams of light only travel in straight lines. Light energy cannot travel around corners of buildings or over hilly terrain.

Lines: Strokes made with pens or pencils, or they can be formed using tape or computers.

Lithography: Printing based on the scientific principle that grease and water do not mix. An image is placed on the printing surface (limestone in early times) using a greasy ink. The printing surface is then covered with a thin coating of water. The water will not stick to the greasy image area but will adhere to the non-image area. The printing ink is then spread on the printing surface. Since this ink is also greasy, it will only stick to the image area. The water will repel the ink from the non-image area. This type of printing is sometimes known as offset printing.

Loudness: How "strong" a sound seems to human ears. Loudness is a relative measurement. That means that how "loud" a sound is may vary from person to person.

M

Machine-to-human communication: Information moving from a machine to a human.

Machine-to-machine communication: One machine providing information to another machine.

Mainframe computer: A large-scale computer. A mainframe has a very large memory and is used when a large number of calculations are required. Many large corporations and universities use mainframe computers.

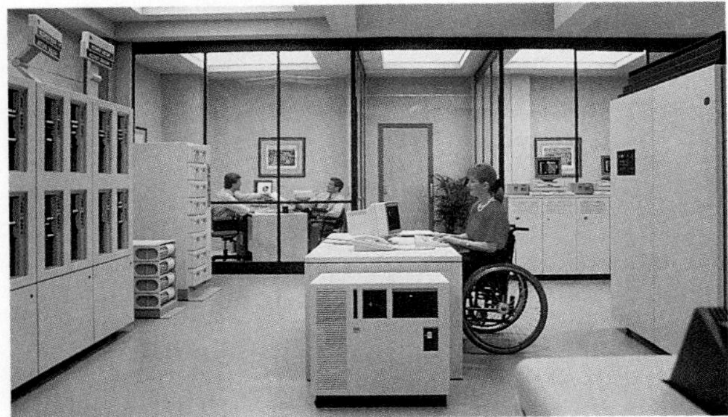

A mainframe computer system. (IBM)

Marine: Means having to do with water.

Market: A certain group of people that is the target of an action. A TV station might want to attract teen viewers. Therefore, the TV station's market is teens.

Masking off: Using masking tape or heavy paper to block the area of a screen that the stencil does not cover, but that you don't want ink to pass through.

Mass: Refers to the amount of space taken up on the page. Larger objects, those with more mass, are noticed before smaller objects. Dark (or bold) objects give the appearance of mass (appear larger).

Mass communication: Communicating with large numbers of people.

Master plate: The plate that will be used to do the actual printing in offset lithography.

Master printers: People with many years of printing experience.

Mechanical layout: A neatly prepared layout that is placed on a clean, white sheet of paper or cardstock. Tracing paper or special layout sheets can also be used. Artwork and type must be located and positioned. Blue pencils are used in marking the pasteup sheets. Mechanical layouts are done after pasteups.

Mechanical lead holder: A form of mechanical pencil used in drafting and artwork. Lead holders are more convenient than standard pencils because the lead is replaceable and the pencil never needs sharpening. (The lead needs a "point" put on it. This is easily done with the use of a small, hand-held "lead pointer.") Several standard widths and hardness of lead are available.

Media: What is used to "carry" messages. Common media include air, fluid, and solid materials such as wire or gears. (Media is the plural form of medium.)

Medium: What is used to "carry" a message. Paper is an example of a medium. (Medium is the singular form of media.)

Memory: Holds information for use by the CPU. Computers have two types of memory: random access and read-only. Memory is not the same as disk space.

Microelectronics: The reducing of circuits to miniature (very small) size.

Microphone: Also called a "mike." This is a device that detects sounds and converts the sound into an electrical signal that can be recorded.

Microprocessors: Very small components that are the "brain" of a computer.

Mimeograph printing process: Similar to screen process printing. The master acts like a stencil. This stencil is attached to a cylinder on a mimeograph machine. Ink is forced through the openings of the master. As paper passes the master, a deposit of ink is transferred. Black ink is most commonly used.

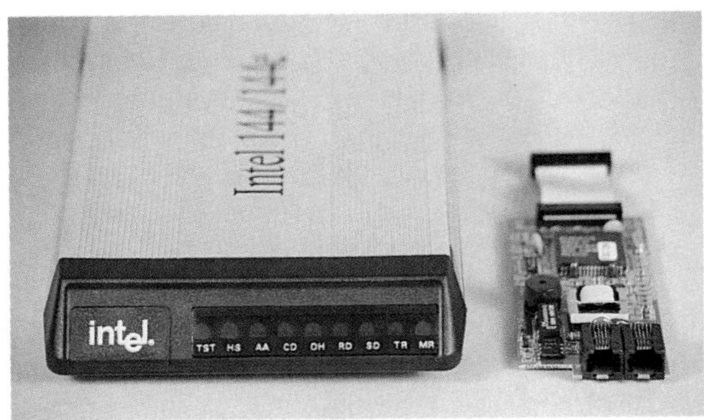

Left—External modem. Right—Internal modem.

Modem: A device that allows a computer to communicate with other computers over telephone lines.

Modulation: The process of controlling a carrier wave.

Momentum: Momentum is when something, such as an object or a wave, picks up speed and force as it moves.

Movable type: A system of printing that uses "blocks" with a letter or number carved on them that can be assembled in different arrangements. Movable type was perfected in the West around the year 1450 by Johannes Gutenberg. The type was a block of metal made to a uniform size with a raised letter on one end. The letter was cut reverse reading, or backward. The pieces of type could be assembled, used to print with, and then taken apart to be used again in other applications.

Moving pictures: Images that reproduce the action recorded on film. In 1893, Thomas Edison's company introduced the first commercial "moving picture machine," called a kinetoscope.

Multimedia: Refers to the use of a computer to combine sound, graphics, animation, and information into a presentation. The presentation can be for learning, business, or entertainment.

Multiview drawing: Refers to the procedure of projecting images from an object. In order to project a view, a viewing plane is established. This plane will be perpendicular (at a right angle) to the object. All features of the object are then projected onto the perpendicular viewing plane. This is also known as orthographic projection.

N

Negative: Developed film where the image appears the exact opposite of the original. For example, white appears as black and black appears as white (actually clear since the negative is transparent).

Neon lights: Glass tubes filled with neon gas. These lights can be very colorful and are used in many types of signs.

Network: A network is a system of interconnected subsystems that work together. Telephones are one example. Computers can also be "networked." The telephone network is worldwide and provides a common "link."

Neutrons: Neutrons have neither a positive or negative charge. Neutrons are "neutral." Protons and neutrons are the same size.

Noise: Any signal not present in the source message.

Nucleus: The center of an atom. Inside the nucleus are protons and neutrons.

O

Object lines: Used to show the visible edges of an object. These lines are heavy and thick.

Objective viewpoint: A type of camera viewpoint where the camera watches the action. This is the viewpoint used most often in television. Sports broadcasting is a common example of an objective viewpoint. This is also used quite often in TV shows. This type of view point is as if you could "look into" a scene without anybody knowing you were there.

Oblique drawings: Show all of the object lines at the true proportions (same "size"), like orthographic drawings. (An exception is a type of oblique drawing called a *cabinet oblique* that has depth lines not true length.) However, all of the object lines can be seen in a single view, not in three views like orthographic drawings. In other words, they are three-dimensional representations. Height and width lines are perpendicular to each other. The depth lines angle upwards at (typically) a 30° angle.

Oblique projections: Three-dimensional drawings that contain a front view that is parallel to the picture plane. Depth is added by extending lines back at any angle. However, a 30 degree angle is used most often. Oblique projections are similar to isometric projections. Oblique projections are easier to construct, but may not always appear realistic.

Offset printing: Based on the scientific principle that grease (oil) and water do not mix. A greasy ink is used to create the image area. Water is then placed on the printing area. The greasy ink will repel the water. The printing ink is then placed on the printing surface. Since this ink is also grease-based, it will adhere to the image area only. The term "offset" comes from the process of transferring the image to a "blanket" cylinder before being printed on the transfer medium (paper). By "offsetting" the image, a right-reading master can be created. This type of printing is also known as lithography.

One-way radios: Only send messages or receive messages between a source and a destination. There is no feedback involved. AM and FM broadcasts are one-way.

Online services: Computer networks that provide routine access to virtually any information a person could want, anywhere in the world. Most of these services are available to anybody who has a computer and a modem.

Operating system: A set of instructions that "tells" the computer how to function.

Orthochromatic film: Reproduces images in black and white.

Orthographic drawing: The system of organizing the different views of an item. Most items require more than one view to fully describe their features. Orthographic drawings allow several views of an object to be created so that all of the features can be fully explained.

Orthographic projection: Refers to the procedure of projecting images from an object. In order to project a view, a viewing plane is established. This plane will be perpendicular (at a right angle) to the object. All features of the object will then be projected onto the perpendicular viewing plane. Also called multiview drawing.

Orthographic view: The view that results from projecting the features of an object onto a perpendicular viewing plane. There are typically three orthographic views in a multiview or orthographic drawing.

Oscillate: To rapidly change direction back and forth.

Oscillator: This device produces repeating signals. These signals are of a certain frequency and amplitude. An oscillator is a special type of amplifier.

Output devices: Devices that allow the user to obtain information stored in a computer in a usable form. A computer monitor (screen) is the most common type of output device. Words, numbers, and pictures appear on the screen for quick reference.

Overlapping: Occurs when objects are observed from a distance. At a distance, certain things may get in the way or "block" the view of parts of the object. This causes one object to appear "on top of" another object.

P

Page composition: Refers to assembling text and graphic images in an appropriate order, or layout.

Paint programs: Also called draw programs. These programs allow people to create graphic images on a computer.

Parallel transmissions: Several pieces (bits) of information are sent on several wires at the same time.

Partnership: Formed when two or more people own a business.

Pascal: A programming language used in computers. Commonly used for teaching programming.

Passive sonar: Used to listen for sounds. It does not transmit sound waves.

Pasteup: An assembly of the complete message. In this process, the copy (text) is set in type and the necessary artwork is located, or "pasted," on the page.

Pay-for-view: Also called pay-per-view. This is a way of receiving movies, shows, or sporting events on your home TV. The user pays only for the shows that are watched.

Peripherals: The devices that are attached to a computer. Printers, modems, plotters, trackballs, and external drives are all examples of peripherals.

A trackball is a computer peripheral device.

Perpendicular viewing plane: The viewing plane that is used in orthographic drawing. The lines that are projected from the object onto the viewing plane are perpendicular to the major surface of the object. All surfaces are seen as flat, even if the surface is actually curved. Viewing a drawing from a perpendicular viewing plane means the drawing has the proper height and width but no depth. Another view (top or right-side) is required to show the depth or thickness.

Personal computers (PCs): Small computers that typically can fit on a desktop.

Personnel: The workers at a business.

Perspective drawings: Three-dimensional drawings that show objects as they appear to the eye. The object lines are not necessarily shown at true proportions. Perspective drawings are the most accurate and most realistic views for showing objects. This is due to the use of vanishing points. Items in these types of drawings are drawn as they appear to the eye. Lines extend to the horizon rather than at 30 degree angles as in oblique and isometric projections.

Persuasion: Somebody or something influencing your decisions.

Photo-direct plates: Designed for runs of under 100 copies. A platemaker is required to expose these plates. The platemaker projects an image of the original design onto a light-sensitive paper. This paper becomes the printing plate. Paper used for plates comes in rolls or sheets.

Photocopying: The common term for "electrostatic printing."

Photographic composition: Arranging or selecting scenes so that the final picture has a nice appearance. Photographic composition is the design stage in the communication process when the transmission medium is a photograph.

Photography: Producing images by capturing light on a film or by electronic means. The invention of photography occurred in the early 1800s. The first practical photograph was called a daguerreotype.

Photorealism: A term used to describe computer images that appear as a photograph would appear (in other words, very realistic). Many photorealistic images are very difficult to tell from an actual photo or from a real scene.

Phototypesetting: Making type (text) photographically on light-sensitive film.

Pictorial drawings: Three-dimensional representations of an object. The term "pictorial" comes from the fact that the drawings resemble a "picture" (photograph).

Pictorial sketches: Shows all three dimensions: height, width, and depth.

Pin printers: Also known as "dot matrix printers."

Pitch: Determined by the frequency of a wave. A high-frequency wave will create a high-pitched sound.

Platemaker: A machine that is used to "burn" a plate used for printing. This machine has an intense light source that will expose the plate once the light is passed through the "positive" image.

Platen: A smooth, flat plate used in early printing presses. The platen forced the type into the paper or other transfer medium.

Plotters: Devices used to make hard copies (images on paper) of drawings. Although these devices can be used for text, the text quality is low. Plotters are used typically for drawings only.

Point size: Refers to the size of the type. The size of the type is measured in points.

Portrait: A printing setup where the text and graphics are oriented on the "width" dimension of a page. When you write in your notebook, you are writing in portrait orientation.

Positive: A right-reading image on film. The image appears in the proper colors, which may be black and white or full color. This is the exact opposite of a "negative."

Presensitized plates: These plates allow a very high-quality reproduction. Presensitized plates are usually made of aluminum. Many have both sides prepared for printing purposes. This permits images to be developed on either side. All copy and artwork for presensitized plates must be created with opaque (black) markings on a white background. A line and/or halftone negative is produced from this original. The halftone is then used to expose the plate in a platemaker.

Press: A machine that prints an image onto a transfer medium (such as paper). The invention of the press made printing much cheaper than previous methods.

Press make-ready: The process of preparing the printing press for a printing run.

Printed circuit boards: Thin, wafer-like boards that contain electronic circuits. Metal foil printed directly on the board replaces the metal wires of older circuits.

Printed graphics: The work of design and printing professionals. Printed graphics include items printed on printing presses, screen printed products, and images created and printed using a computer. Examples include billboards, posters, cereal boxes, newspapers, magazines, and books.

Printers: Devices connected to a computer that allow the user to make hard copies (images on paper) of text, drawings, and graphics.

Printing: Refers to enlarging a negative and making a photograph. Also a general term used to describe the process of transferring an image to a medium (for instance, printing a newspaper).

Printing base: Used in screen process printing. It is the surface that the transfer medium will rest on during the screening process.

Process camera: A camera that is typically stationary (mounted on the floor or wall). The film is loaded in flat sheets. Many adjustments are possible on these cameras.

Processing: Also known as developing.

Production: Means getting all the needed items together in order to put a show on the air.

Profit: The remaining money that is left over after a company pays all of its bills and expenses.

Programmers: The people that write software.

Programming: Writing code, or software, to be used by a computer.

Programs: Also called software.

Projected imagery: Using light to project an image. Both slide and movie projectors use light to project images onto a screen.

Proof: A rough copy of page composition.

Propaganda: The use of false or misleading information to harm someone or something.

Proportion: How two objects that look similar are described. If *all* features of the smaller object are one-half the size of the same features on the larger object, the objects are said to be proportional (one-half proportional in this example).

Proprietor: The owner of a proprietorship.

Proprietorship: A business owned by just one person.

Props: Items actually used during the acting portion of the show. Telephones, tissues, purses, and food cartons are all props.

Protons: The part of the atom that has a positive (+) electrical charge. Protons and neutrons are the same size.

Publishing houses: Companies that get newspapers, magazines, and many forms of books printed and sold. Publishing houses do not typically perform the actual printing.

Purpose: A reason for an action.

Q

Quick printers: Provide "while you wait" printing service for simple items.

R

Radio: Uses radio waves to carry signals through the atmosphere to radio receivers. Modern radio is based on the wireless telegraph invented by Guglielmo Marconi.

A radio receiver.

Radio waves: A form of electromagnetic energy. Radio waves are used for radio broadcasts and radar.

Random-access memory (RAM): Contains information for use by the CPU. Software loaded into a computer goes to the RAM. This information is stored only while the computer is turned on. When the computer is shut off, the program is erased from the memory.

Read-only memory (ROM): Contains permanent information for use by the CPU. It cannot be erased and is difficult to change. Instructions in ROM can only be "read" by the CPU. Programs or data cannot be stored in it.

Receiver: The final electrical stop for a message. Here, the signal is detected and converted back to the source message.

Receiving: The process of acquiring and decoding a message.

Recorder: A device that can store sounds or visual images for later reproduction. The phonograph was the first audio recorder.

Recording head: An electric coil used to "write on" magnetic tapes. As the tape passes by the head, the electrical signals change the coating of the magnetic material on the tape. This is how sounds are recorded.

Refined sketches: Have more lines and details than a thumbnail sketch. The sketch begins to look more like the finished product, but the lines are typically not clean or refined. Proportions and line length may not be accurately represented.

Reflection: An image or light that is "bounced off" of a surface.

Register: The alignment of the printing. You have seen color photos in the newspaper that appear "blurry." This is because they are "out of registration."

Registration marks: Indicators, usually "X's," placed on a stencil so that overlays will be in the same place every time. Registration marks are used quite often in screen process printing to make certain that the screen is placed on the transfer medium exactly the same for every print. This is especially useful when several different colors are being placed on one medium.

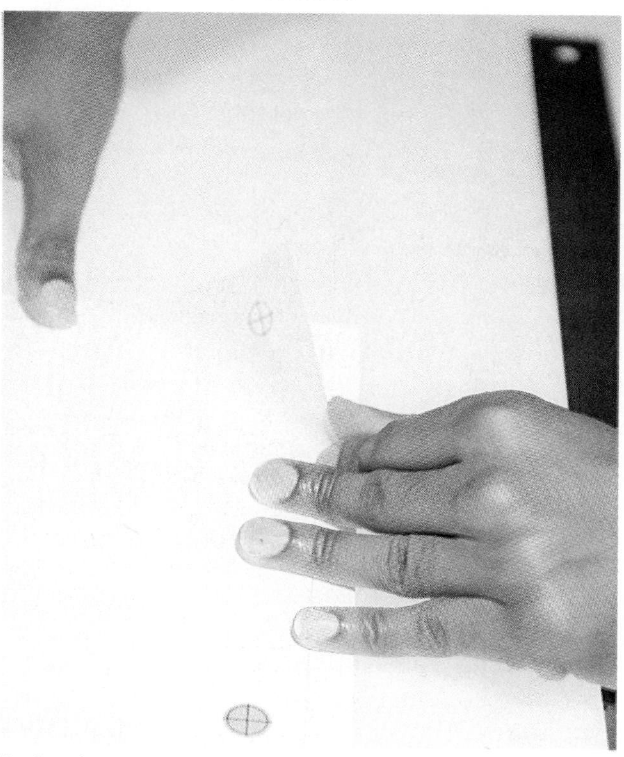

Registration marks.

Relief printing: The transfer of images from a raised surface. Typically, this surface is type (letters and numbers) contained on engraved blocks. All relief work is prepared in reverse. When pressed into paper, the image becomes readable, or "right-reading."

Rendering: The process of shading and/or adding color to a three-dimensional drawing to make the drawing appear more realistic. Rendering can be done by hand or with the aid of a computer. A *rendering* is a drawing that has been rendered. When done properly, a rendering can look quite real. Some computer renderings are impossible to tell from actual photographs.

Reportorial viewpoint: A type of camera viewpoint typically used in news reporting. With a reportorial viewpoint, the person on the TV screen appears to be talking directly to you.

Resistance: The opposition to electric current. Resistance can be caused by a material, substance, component, or device. Resistance is found in every part of an electric circuit. Even the wires in a circuit provides resistance.

Resistors: Devices placed in electric circuits that divide voltage and/or limit current.

Resolution: Determined by the number of "dots" that can be drawn per inch. More dots per inch means a higher resolution resulting in a smoother image.

Rhythm: Deals with the way a message is constructed. Certain designs seem to guide your eye through the message.

Right-reading: Refers to an image or text being printed so that you can read it. In other words, the image or text is *not* printed backwards.

Rough layout: More accurate and detailed than a thumbnail sketch. A rough layout is produced to scale. This means text and artwork will be shown in their proper proportions. A rough layout is used to show how the text and art will fit together. In other words, a rough layout will appear very similar to the final product, only less refined.

S

Satellite: A device that orbits the earth for communication or other purposes.

Scanning: A term used to describe using a computer to transfer an image. The image can be text or art, or it can be a photograph. The computer "looks at" every line of the image and then converts that information into digital information. The computer can then be used to enhance or change the image.

Schematic drawings: Technical drawings that show the parts of a system, how the parts are connected, and how the parts work together. Schematic drawings can be used to describe electrical, hydraulic, or pneumatic systems. The actual physical locations of the parts are *not* shown, only how the parts are connected together.

Screen process printing: Works by forcing ink through prepared screens. The image area is the only area on the screen that will allow the ink to pass through. The rest on the screen is "blocked out" so that ink will only go through the image area. This process is also called silk screening because the early screens were made of silk.

Serial transmissions: Bits of information are sent one at a time over a single wire. Computer modems are usually connected to a computer's serial port.

Set: The area used as the location of the show. It includes all the equipment, scenery, and props needed for airing a show.

Set design: The organization of all the items on a set. Set design creates an area for the production of the show.

Set dressings: Items such as furniture, trees, books, lamps, and carpets are all set dressings. Set dressings include items that might be found in the location being shown.

Settings: The large pieces that make up the areas of a set.

Shading: The process of placing lines on a drawing to represent a shadow. Shading is typically only done on three-dimensional drawings.

Shadow: A darkened area either on or behind an object. A shadow results from light being projected onto an object. Some areas of the object will block the light from other areas of the object. The object in general will block light from the surface that the object is resting on. Next time you are standing in bright sunlight, look at the ground. See how you cast a dark spot on the ground? This is your shadow.

Shape: The result of the combination of lines and mass. Examples include rectangles, circles, and other geometric designs.

Signal: A sound or image that is transmitted.

Signing: A language that uses the hands and fingers to represent different signals. Each signal represents a letter or a number. In this way, words can be spelled out and people who are deaf can communicate.

Silicon chips: ICs that are so small they are printed on silicon or germanium chips. Many ICs can be placed on a silicon chip not much bigger than the eye of a needle.

Sketching: Creating simple pictures with no formal rules or guidelines. Usually drawn with nothing more than a pencil and paper, but can also be drawn on a computer.

Smart cards: These are credit cards, but are based on a debit system. With a debit system, the card holder must have money in their account to use the card. This is similar to how a checking account works, however, the card holder does not need to write out a check for every purchase.

Smart card transaction. (InterBold)

Software: The instructions that "tells" a computer what to do. There are several different types of software that can do everything from word processing to allowing you to play a game. Also called a program. This is the information contained *on* a computer disk, not the disk itself.

Sonar: Stands for Sound Navigation and Ranging. Sonar system use reflected sound waves to determine location and distance of underwater objects.

Sonubuoy: This is a transducer with a collar to keep it afloat.

Sounder: The part of a telegraph that reproduces the coded message. The sounder creates the familiar "clicking" sound of a telegraph.

Source: The starting point of messages to be sent.

Speakers: Devices that change electrical energy into acoustical energy.

Special-purpose printers: Produce materials for specific uses. These materials typically require procedures not available at most printers.

Spot-lighting: Spotlights are usually intense, white lights that illuminate part of a scene.

Spreadsheet: A grid made up of rows (going across) and columns (going down) on a page. A spreadsheet is used to keep information organized.

Squeegee: A rubber device used to spread ink in screen process printing. Can also be used to wipe water off film in photography.

Staging: Making the decisions and selecting items for the design of a set. Staging creates a feeling of a certain place. The idea is to make the set look as authentic (real) as possible.

Standard stock: Paper that is made to a standard size set by the printing industry. This means that the paper will always be the same size. There are several standard sizes available.

Stereophonic: Describes recordings made using several microphones. They are placed in different areas of the recording studio. During the recording process, the recording levels of these microphones are adjusted between the left and right "channels." The result of this is that during playback the sounds seem to be "split apart" because each ear hears different sounds.

Stop bath: The chemical solution that "stops" the developer from developing the film any further.

Storage: The recording of a message for long-term use.

Studio: Most broadcast programming is recorded in an enclosed studio area.

Style: Refers to how a typeface appears on the page. Style can be normal, **bold,** *italics,* ~~strikethru~~, or reverse.

Subjective viewpoint: A type of camera viewpoint where the camera takes the view of the actor or actress. Subjective viewpoint is used in many dramas. In this type of viewpoint, an actor seems to be talking to you as if you were another character that is in the show.

Subscriber: A household that rents a service (such as cable TV).

Supplemental systems: Forms of communication that cannot be put into the four larger categories. (Those categories are human-to-human, human-to-machine, machine-to-human, and machine-to-machine.) Supplemental systems include extrasensory perception (ESP), extraterrestrial, animal, plant, and mineral systems.

Surveyors: The people who take measurements of land features. These measurements can be used to plan building sites, develop plot plans, or create maps.

Switches: Direct the flow of electricity. They are very basic to electronic communication. Switches allow electricity to flow along the correct path.

Switching systems: Telephone switching systems route calls from the source to the destination.

Symmetry: A term that describes an object that is the same on both sides or both ends. If an object is symmetrical, you should be able to "fold" the object in half on a centerline and each side will match.

Synchronous transmission: Bits are sent in groups, or "blocks."

System software: The operating system, language translators, and some utility programs used by the computer to "run."

T

Tape deck: A piece of stereo equipment that is used to record and/or play audio tapes.

Tapes: Plastic strips coated with a magnetic material.

Targeting: Directing messages to particular groups.

Technical graphics: The work of drafters. Technical drawings are prepared with instruments and machines or computers. Technical graphics show assembly details, pictorial views, schematics, building plans, and topographical features (features of the land).

Technical illustration: Typically a perspective drawing that describes technical devices or systems.

Telecommunication: Refers to any exchange of messages over long distances using light or electricity. It is much more than a local telephone call to a neighbor. Modern telecommunication systems operate around the globe.

Telegraph: A machine used to transmit coded messages in the form of electrical pulses.

Cellular phones are telecommunication devices. (Siemens)

The telegraph uses electrical current in a coil to attract an iron lever called a sounder.

Telemarketing: Selling or soliciting a product or service over the phone.

Telephone: A device that can transmit sounds over a distance through wires or fiber-optic cables. Invented by Alexander Graham Bell, the telephone uses a diaphragm (flexible disk) to vary the current in a circuit. The variations in the current move another diaphragm. Thus, the sound is reproduced at the receiving end.

Telephony: Means that transmitted sounds (for example, music or talking) are easily understood by the listener.

Templates: Typically made out of plastic and have holes in them that can be traced. Templates are used to create curves, circles, boxes, lines, and several other shapes.

Test sheet: Usually produced to determine exposure time. A test sheet is a sample of the image with different exposure times. This allows the best exposure time to be determined.

Text frames: Temporary guidelines used when laying out a page in desktop publishing. These guidelines "define" where text will be placed on the page. These "frames" can be moved around on the page until everything is in the precise locations that the graphic designer wants.

Texture: Describes the surface of an object. In other words, texture tells whether the surface of an object is smooth or rough. The texture of a surface affects what you see or feel. Shading on drawings creates a feeling of texture.

Thermofax® machine: Has an intense light that "burns" the image onto a ditto master. Also used to produce overhead transparencies.

Thumbnail sketch: Gives simple shapes with only a few lines. Only a general appearance is communicated. Typically, no specific details are given.

Time-sharing network: Any number of terminals are connected to one large central computer. Users rent part of the computer for as long as they need it.

Tolerance: A range that a manufactured part can vary from the actual dimension on the drawing and still be acceptable. The tolerance range listed on drawings gives the maximum and/or minimum sizes permitted.

Transducer: A device that acts like an underwater microphone and loudspeaker. It picks up and sends out sound waves.

Transistors: Transistors are powerful amplifiers. They also perform the same switching function as vacuum tubes. Modern transistors are made of germanium or silicon. Most are very small and inexpensive.

Transmission link: The transmission link relays the signals from the transmitter to the receiver (destination).

Transmitter: Used to start a message on its journey in radio communication. The transmitter changes the message into electrical signals. The signals may be analog or digital.

Transmitting: Sending a message.

Trough: The lowest point of a wave.

T-square: A device that is used to draw either horizontal or vertical lines. It has a straight edge that is used to draw lines. At 90° to the straight edge is a "lip" that is held tight against the edge of the drafting board (which is straight).

Tuner: A term for the receiver in a stereo system.

Tweeter: The part of the speaker that is used to send out high-frequency sounds.

Two-dimensional sketches: Show only *two* dimensions of an object, such as the height and width. Most engineering drawings are two-dimensional.

Two-way radios: With two-way radios, it is possible to have feedback. You can respond directly to messages on two-way devices. Taxi radios and CB radios are examples of two-way radios.

Type mold: Invented by Johannes Gutenberg around the year 1450. This mold allowed several identical pieces of type to be made. This uniformity (all the same) made movable type practical. (Movable type had been invented by the Chinese about four hundred years earlier, but because of their complex language, it was never used.) Movable type allowed pages of text to be easily assembled into large racks. This development led to an increase in the amount of printed material. Books became available to many people, both for education and entertainment.

U

Ultraviolet light waves: These waves are slightly shorter than visible light waves.

Unbounded transmission channels: A transmission is not contained in a controlled medium such as wires. The atmosphere and outer space are two examples of unbounded transmission channels used in data communications. These channels are affected by noise.

Unity: Used to "pull" the total design together. Designs that lack unity rarely communicate a message well. The exchange of ideas or feelings becomes confusing.

Universal Product Code (UPC): A standard code that is used to identify many items for sale. The UPC symbol is the black lines that can be found on many packages. The lines are a coded message describing that product. The UPC symbol is "read" with a laser.

PD072193 MAGN 0.90 BWR 2.0 07/21/93 336524-19

EXPLORING COMMUNICATIONS

GGX ASSOCIATES, INC. SPEC. # C121 NEG/UP

The UPC code for this text.

Uplink: Transmitting information to a satellite.

Utility software: Also called service software. This software performs several jobs. Housekeeping is one of those jobs. Housekeeping consists of clearing storage areas, starting programs, and storing data for later use.

V

Vanishing points: Points located along the horizon (either on a perspective drawing or in real life) where all lines of an object will meet if extended.

Vertical line: A line that is perpendicular to the bottom edge of the paper.

Viewfinder: The part of the camera that you look through to see what image will be exposed on the film.

Viewing plane: The imaginary plane that the features of an object are projected onto. This allows the features of a three-dimensional object to be described in a two-dimensional (flat) drawing. All surfaces are seen as flat, even if the surface is actually curved.

Virtual reality: The creation of a simulated environment through the use of computer, light, and sound technologies. Virtual reality is similar to multimedia. Virtual reality "transports" the user into a make-believe world. Visual and audio information is provided to the user in response to the user's actions. The computer receives information on the users movements from sensors in gloves and a helmet. The computer then reacts to the movement of the sensors and provides the appropriate information back to the user.

Visible light: The human eye can see only a small portion of the electromagnetic spectrum. You cannot see above violet or below red in the spectrum. Other visible colors in the spectrum include orange, yellow, green, blue, and indigo.

Visual communication: Involves the sense of sight.

Visualization: Creating an idea of a final project in your mind or on paper.

Voice activation: Allows the user to control a device with voice commands. The computer (or other device) "recognizes" what you tell it to do and responds accordingly. For instance, if you tell the computer to "print" a document, the computer will understand your voice input and prepare the document.

Voice mail: Voice mail is similar to an answering machine, but the message is recorded digitally in the phone system.

Voltage: The potential for electron flow. The higher the voltage, the greater the potential.

W

Wavelength: The distance (length) between two sequential (in order) waves. Wavelength is a physical measurement. Frequency and wavelength are inversely proportional. This means that the higher the frequency, the shorter the wavelength.

Whiteprints: Prints where the background is white and all lines are blue, although these drawings are sometimes referred to as "blueprints." These prints are made using a diazo machine.

Woofer: The part of a speaker that transmits low-frequency sounds.

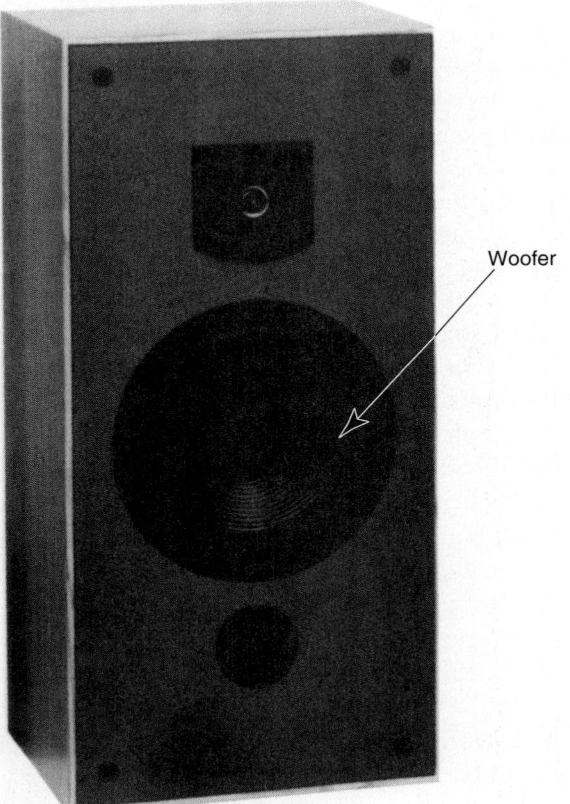

The woofer of a speaker. (Fisher®)

Word processing: Creating the text (body) of a document using computer software.

Wrong-reading: When an image or text is printed backwards.

X

X-rays: These wavelengths are slightly longer than gamma ray wavelengths.

Z

Zoom in: In desktop publishing programs, you can magnify, or zoom in, the page that you are working on. Paint programs also allow you to zoom in.

Zoom out: In desktop publishing programs, you can "step back" from the page, or zoom out. Paint programs also allow you to zoom out.

Virtual reality has many applications, including games. (Evans and Southerland)

INDEX

A

B

C

D

E

H

I

K

L

M

N

O

P

Q

R

S

T

U

V

W

X

Z